P9-DBN-271

# OUR "REGULAR" READERS RAVE!

"I love the *Bathroom Readers*... I take them everywhere I go. Before I found the BRI, I was unpopular with the ladies; now that I'm a walking font of knowledge, they can't keep their hands off me. Thanks!"

***—Dwayne R.***

"I've constructed a special shrine for my *Bathroom Readers*. I heard that people spend about ten months in the throne room during their lifetime. I'm sure, thanks to you, I'll spend a couple of years."

***—William F.***

"Thank you for the *Bathroom Readers*. I no longer have to read the backs of my shampoo bottles. My husband and I read so much in the bathroom that we refer to it as 'the study'."

***—Charissa A.***

"It's perfect for any occasion. When we needed a house warming gift, we got an *Uncle John's*. When we needed Christmas presents, we gave *Uncle John's*. We were invited to a birthday party for three men and needed gifts for all three. Not knowing what they liked or needed, we bought three *Bathroom Readers*! The response?... They can't stop talking about it. Thank you."

***—John J.***

"Thank you for helping me get an 'A' in my college speech class. We had to do an impromptu tribute speech and I chose *Uncle John's Bathroom Reader* for my subject. I actually made my professor laugh all through the speech."

***—CeCe R.***

"You're the best thing to happen to the reading room since indoor plumbing and store-bought tissue (them cornhusks can get mighty rough you know!) Keep up the good work and Go with the Flow!"

***—Rick B.***

"Your books are the greatest I have ever read. The eternal struggle for reading material has finally been quenched!"

***—Tucker J.***

"I found your website very commodious—quite easy to get a handle on. Frankly, I was bowled over, flushed actually, and almost fell off my stool when I discovered that Vol. 6 was not the end of your roll. I could barely keep the lid down! And the new books seem to have twice as many sheets as the prior ones—a seemingly endless supply of two-ply reading if ever there was one! Thank God there's Uncle John to float us through tough times."

***—Uncle Harry Jr.***

"Thank you for making something that makes me want to read. I have a short attention span, but the *Bathroom Readers* keep me reading. I'm on my third book! They're the only books I've been able to read start to finish. I just want to say thank you, and please, don't stop making books."

***—Michelle F.***

"Several years ago, for Father's Day, we sent my Dad a gift certificate to a book store. He purchased a *Bathroom Reader*. We continued to send gift certificates; he continued to buy *Bathroom Readers*. When he passed away last year, my mom gave me his collection. He had 7. Since then, I've started buying more volumes. My son, Mitchell, even bought *Uncle John's Bathroom Reader For Kids Only* with his own money. Now three generations of my family enjoy your books."

***—Mark A.***

"Your books are such a CLASSY collection of information. I have become one of your bigger fans. You folks are GREAT!"

***—John D.***

"I love your material. I now have three of your books. Guests coming to my place can't wait to use the facilities because of your books. In fact, I'm thinking that I might change the color scheme of my bathroom so it doesn't clash with your books."

***—Darren McK.***

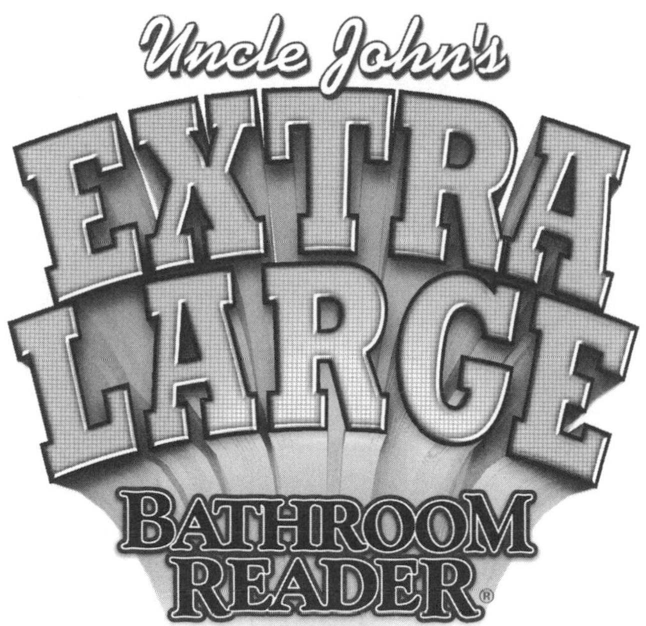


By the
Bathroom Readers'
Institute

Bathroom Readers' Press
Ashland, Oregon

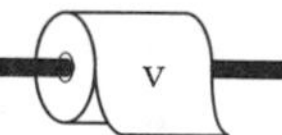



**Uncle John's Extra Large Bathroom Reader**
is a compilation of the following previously published
Bathroom Reader titles:
*Uncle John's Ahh-Inspiring Bathroom Reader*
ISBN-13: 978-1-57145-873-5 (first printing: 2002)
*Uncle John's Unstoppable Bathroom Reader*
ISBN-13: 978-1-59223-116-4 (first printing: 2003)



For information, write…
The Bathroom Readers' Institute
P.O. Box 1117, Ashland, OR 97520
*www.bathroomreader.com*

Cover design by Michael Brunsfeld, San Rafael, CA
(Brunsfeldo@comcast.net)
BRI "technician" on the back cover: Larry Kelp

ISBN-13: 978-1-60710-893-1 / ISBN-10: 1-60710-893-3

Library of Congress Cataloging-in-Publication Data
Uncle John's extra large bathroom reader.
pages cm
ISBN 978-1-60710-893-1 (pbk.)
1. American wit and humor. 2. Curiosities and wonders.
I. Bathroom Readers' Institute (Ashland, Or.)
PN6165.U5339 2013
081.02'07--dc23

2012049143

Printed in the United States of America
Second printing: August 2013
2 3 4 5 6 17 16 15 14 13

# THANK YOU!

*The Bathroom Readers' Institute sincerely thanks the people whose advice and assistance made this book possible.*

Gordon Javna
Jay Newman
Trina Janssen
John Dollison
Thom Little
Jeff Altemus
Jennifer Hart
Julia Papps
Sharilyn Hovind
Michael Brunsfeld
Angela Kern
Janet Spencer
Alan Reder
Sam Javna
Gideon Javna
Jim McCluskey
Jolly Jeff Cheek
Malcolm Hillgartner
Jahnna Beecham
Maggie McLaughlin
Amanda Wilson
Terry Budden
Raingirl Thering
Brian Henry
Jesse Clark
Melinda Allman
JoAnn Padgett
Aaron Guzman
Jennifer Frederick
Ginger Winters
Mana Monzavi
Monica Maestas
Lilian Nordland
Sydney Stanley
Sharon Freed
Jess Brallier
Joyce Slayton
Steve Pitt
Lyne Brennanski
Bruce Carlson
David Harp
Nate Hendley
Claudia Bauer
Hazel Daniels
Teri Morin
William Coleman
Pat Perrin
Felix the Dog
John Javna
Thomas Crapper

**Hiya Sophie! Hiya Jessie!**

# CONTENTS

Because the BRI understands your reading needs, we've divided the contents by length as well as subject.

**Short**—a quick read

**Medium**—2 to 3 pages

**Long**—for those extended visits, when something a little more involved is required

***Extended**—for those leg-numbing experiences

*   *   *

## UNDERWEAR IN THE NEWS

Malaysian police arrested Doomsday cult leader Petrus Ratu Doren, self-described "holiest of them all," after he predicted that the end of the world would come in October 1995—and that the only way that his followers could protect themselves was to "wear their underpants on their heads." In custody, Doren admitted that he'd made the whole thing up because he wanted "fame and power."

Police rounded up more than 200 of Doren's followers, who fled into the jungle with their weapons (and their underpants) to await the end of the world. "We want to get to the root of the matter about this guy who has used the name of God in vain," police told reporters. "Especially that bit on the underwear."

# INTRODUCTION

Here we go again! Welcome one and all to this extra-large helping of two vintage, hard-to-find editions—*Uncle John's Ahh-Inspiring Bathroom Reader* and *Uncle John's Unstoppable Bathroom Reader.* We've included the very best articles from these two books, which, if it's not immodest of me to say, are two of our finest. I asked around the Bathroom Readers' Institute, and everyone agrees—it is immodest of me.

If this is your first *Bathroom Reader*, welcome to our family. If you're one of our loyal readers, it's good to have you back. You're the reason we keep writing these books. Of course, we love researching and writing—it gives us an excuse to keep learning about, say, shrunken heads (page 209)—but knowing you're out there, loving what we do, is the real payoff for us. How do we know you're out there? We get enthusiastic letters of support every day. The most common question we're asked—along with the lavish praise (aw, shucks)—is this one: How do you guys keep churning out amazing bathroom reading year after year?

I answered that in the original *Unstoppable* introduction by explaining that a "mad inventor" named Dr. Flipseater had built us a contraption called the Information Grinder. Here's how it works: We shovel mountains of books, newspapers, and magazines into one end of the Information Grinder, flip the switch, and after a few minutes of buzzing and whirring, it spits out a book. For *Extra Large*, we've upgraded to the Information Grinder 2000! It basically does the same thing, but there's a "2000" added to its name, which means it cost more.

But for you, dear reader, the value is better than ever. Awaiting you are more than 750 pages full of incredible articles—many of which have become BRI classics. You'll find Jay's multi-part story about *Saturday Night Live*. Also included is Thom's classic piece about the amazing opossum. And then there's John D's exposé about what takes place after you flush—"Number Two's Wild Ride" (which, I must say, is not only one of our all-time best articles, but maybe the best title we've ever come up with).

What else will you find in *Extra Large*? There are way too many great topics to list, but here are some of our personal favorites:

• **Blunders:** The newspaper that lasted a day, the dumbest crooks of the Old West, and the worst business decision in U.S. history

• **Sports and Games:** The rise of video games, how professional wrestling went mainstream, who Stanley was and why hockey players want his Cup, and how to play Toilet Golf

• **Origins:** The helicopter, superglue, reality TV, windshield wipers, the bagel, dynamite, and the Democrats and Republicans

• **Canada:** The Rhinoceros Party, the King of Canada, and how the folks in Gander, Newfoundland, helped out after nine-eleven

• **Pop Culture:** Alternate endings to Hollywood movies, the lasting impact of the Beatles' *Sgt. Peppers Lonely Hearts Club Band*, and truths and untruths about Mr. Rogers

• **The Strange and the Macabre:** Celebrities you didn't know had missing body parts, how to read tombstones, why a crowd gathered near Colorado's Pikes Peak in 1923...to whale-watch, and one of our favorite *Bathroom Reader* articles of all time: Mike the Headless Chicken, who lost his head and became a star

So don't be a saprostomous liripoop and get reading! (To find out what a saprostomous liripoop is, see page 522.) In the meantime, we're already hard at work on the next humongous *Bathroom Reader*! (Hmm..."Humongous" might be a fun title.)

As always...

*Go with the Flow!*

**Uncle John, Felix the Dog, and the BRI Staff**

P.S. We're having lots of fun on our blog (*www.bathroomreader.com*) and on our Facebook and Twitter pages, too. We also have an iPhone app that's full of surprises. So follow Uncle John online for fun contests, sales, news, and exclusive bathroom reading!

# YOU'RE MY INSPIRATION

*It's always fascinating to find out where the architects of pop culture get their ideas from. These may surprise you.*

**VULCAN HAND SALUTE.** Leonard Nimoy invented this for Mr. Spock during the filming of a *Star Trek* episode. The gesture was borrowed from the Jewish High Holiday services. The Kohanim (priests) bless the congregation by extending "the palms of both hands... with thumbs outstretched and the middle and ring fingers parted." Nimoy used the same gesture for Spock, only with one hand.

**SNOOPY.** Based on the black-and-white dog that Peanuts creator Charles Schulz owned when he was 13 years old. The real dog's name was Spike, which Schulz used as the name of Snoopy's brother.

**SAVING PRIVATE RYAN.** Steven Spielberg's WWII drama was inspired by a real-life story: A few weeks after D-Day, Sergeant Fritz Niland learned that his three older brothers had been killed in action. Army policy states that no family should suffer the loss of more than two sons, so, over Niland's protests, he was sent home.

**ANIMAL (the Muppets' drummer).** Apparently Jim Henson was a rock 'n' roll fan. He based the out-of-control drummer on another out-of-control drummer: The Who's Keith Moon.

**COSMO KRAMER.** While Larry David and Jerry Seinfeld were laying the groundwork for *Seinfeld*, David's eccentric neighbor, Kenny Kramer, would often pop in and bug them. Just like his TV counterpart, Kramer had no real job but dabbled in schemes and inventions (he patented glow-in-the-dark jewelry). "Unlike the TV Kramer," says Kenny, "my hairbrained schemes work."

**DR. EVIL.** Mike Myers's inspiration for Austin Powers's archenemy comes from the James Bond villain, Blofeld, in *You Only Live Twice*. But Dr. Evil's famous mannerism comes from a 1979 photograph of Rolling Stones guitarist Keith Richards. It shows the rocker "in the exact pinky-biting pose favored by Dr. Evil."

**Monday is the only day of the week that has an anagram: dynamo.**

# COURT TRANSQUIPS

*The verdict is in! Court transcripts make some of the best bathroom reading there is. These were actually said, word for word, in a court of law.*

**Judge:** I know you, don't I?
**Defendant:** Uh, yes.
**Judge:** Alright, how do I know you?
**Defendant:** Judge, do I have to tell you?
**Judge:** Of course, you might be obstructing justice not to tell me.
**Defendant:** Okay. I was your bookie.

**Lawyer:** How do you feel about defense attorneys?
**Juror:** I think they should all be drowned at birth.
**Lawyer:** Well, then, you are obviously biased for the prosecution.
**Juror:** That's not true. I think prosecutors should be drowned at birth, too.

**Judge:** Please identify yourself for the record.
**Defendant:** Colonel Ebenezer Jackson.
**Judge:** What does the "Colonel" stand for?
**Defendant:** Well, it's kinda like the "Honorable" in front of your name—not a damn thing.

**Judge:** You are charged with habitual drunkenness. Have you anything to say in your defense?
**Defendant:** Habitual thirstiness?

**Plaintiff's Lawyer:** What doctor treated you for the injuries you sustained while at work?
**Plaintiff:** Dr. J.
**Plaintiff's Lawyer:** And what kind of physician is Dr. J?
**Plaintiff:** Well, I'm not sure, but I remember that you said he was a good plaintiff's doctor.

**Q:** Do you have any children or anything of that kind?

**Q:** Do you have any suggestions as to what prevented this from being a murder trial instead of an attempted-murder trial?
**A:** The victim lived.

**Q:** You don't know what it was, and you didn't know what it looked like, but can you describe it?

**Defendant:** If I called you a son of a bitch, what would you do?
**Judge:** I'd hold you in contempt and assess an additional five days in jail.
**Defendant:** What if I thought you were a son of a bitch?
**Judge:** I can't do anything about that. There's no law against thinking.
**Defendant:** In that case, I think you're a son of a bitch.

**It takes 4,000 grains of sugar to fill a teaspoon.**

# HUMAN HAILSTONES

*Hailstones are formed when ice crystals in a thunderhead are tossed around, gathering successive coats of ice. But people can get caught in thunderheads, too.*

## THE PILOT

In 1959 Lt. Col. William Rankin bailed out of his single-engine plane when the engine failed at 47,000 feet above Virginia. A storm was in progress, and he fell right through the middle of it. It would normally take a man 13 minutes to fall 47,000 feet, but Rankin got caught in the updrafts and remained aloft for 45 minutes. He tumbled about in –70° temperatures, covered with ice and sleet, his body bruised by hailstones. Fortunately, his parachute opened at 10,000 feet and he landed intact in a tree in North Carolina, 65 miles from where he'd bailed out. He made a complete recovery.

## THE GLIDERS

In 1930 a German glider society held an exhibition. Five glider pilots flew into a towering thunderhead hoping to set new altitude records by using the updrafts. But the updrafts were more than they had counted on—the gliders were torn to pieces by the violent winds. The pilots bailed out but were carried to the upper regions of the cloud, where they were coated by ice. All but one froze to death before finally falling to the ground.

## THE PARACHUTIST

In 1975 Mike Mount jumped from a plane 4,500 feet over Maryland, expecting a two-minute fall to Earth. Although thunderstorms were building, Mount had over 400 jumps under his belt and thought he could steer himself through the clouds. He couldn't. He was sucked into the storm and pulled up to 10,000 feet. The storm swept him up and dropped him again and again. He debated whether to cut himself free of his main chute and freefall through the storm, relying on his reserve chute to save him. But he wasn't sure he'd be able to see the ground approaching. Finally the storm released its grip and he landed, cold but unharmed, nine miles from his intended drop zone. His wild ride had lasted 30 minutes.

**Mars attacks: In 1911 a meteor from Mars fell to Earth in Nakhla, Egypt, killing a dog.**

# PENNY WISE

*Some people collect coins; Uncle John collects trivia about coins.*

Abraham Lincoln was the first president to be depicted on a U.S. coin, a penny issued in 1909. The penny is the only U.S. coin where the person faces right instead of left.

Why was the Lincoln penny issued beginning in 1909? To commemorate the 100th anniversary of Abraham Lincoln's birth.

When the Citizens Bank of Tenino, Washington, closed on December 5, 1931, the town was without ready cash to do business, so denominations of 25 cents, 50 cents, and $1 were printed on three-ply Sitka spruce wood, the first wooden money issued as legal tender in the U.S.

Spanish doubloons were legal tender in the United States until 1857.

Until 1965, pennies were legal tender only up to 25 cents. A creditor couldn't be forced to accept more than 25 pennies in payment of a debt. Silver coins were legal tender for amounts not exceeding $10 in any one payment.

The 1921 Alabama Centennial half-dollar was the first U.S. coin designed by a woman, Laura Gardin Fraser.

During World War II, the United States minted pennies made of steel to conserve copper for making artillery shells.

Booker T. Washington was the first African American to be depicted on a U.S. coin, a half-dollar issued in 1946.

Codfish were depicted on many of the early coins of the infant United States from 1776 to 1778.

The first U.S. cent, which was the size of today's 50-cent piece, was coined in 1793. In 1856 the Mint produced the first penny of today's size.

In 1932 Congress issued a commemorative coin—the Washington quarter—to celebrate the 200th birthday of George Washington. The quarter was intended to be used for only one year, but it was so popular that it was continued as a regular-issue coin from 1934 on.

# OOPS!

*Everyone enjoys reading about someone else's blunders. So go ahead and feel superior for a few minutes.*

## CUT IT OUT!

"Lyn Thomas was working on a home-improvement project when he cut through a gas main, requiring the entire street to be evacuated. Moments after the gas engineers left, he went back to work...and promptly broke a water main, flooding his and his neighbor's properties."

—*U.K. Mirror*

## GETS RID OF PLAQUE

"A plaque intended to honor deep-voiced actor James Earl Jones at Lauderhill, Florida's 2002 celebration of Martin Luther King Day, caused city officials incredible embarrassment. Somehow the plaque's maker inscribed this extremely incorrect message:

'Thank you James Earl Ray for keeping the dream alive.'

"Ray was the man convicted of assassinating King in Memphis, Tennessee, in 1968."

—*ABCNews.com*

## WHAT A TANGLED WEB WE WEAVE

"A married couple in Beijing, China, ended up brawling after realizing they had unwittingly courted each other over the Internet. After a month of secret online flirting, the man arranged to meet up with his mystery girlfriend, only to discover it was actually his wife. He had known only her user name, I Want You.

"They each agreed to carry a certain newspaper to identify themselves, but were shocked when they came face to face and started fighting in the street. Passersby eventually alerted security guards, who had to separate the two."

—*Ananova.com*

## TRAVELIN' LIGHT

"In 1986 an Orion Airways chartered jetliner took off from Birmingham, England, carrying 100 passengers to the Greek island of Crete. A few minutes into the flight the captain announced the

**Fat City: Each employee at Ben & Jerry's headquarters gets three pints of free ice cream a day.**

plane had to return to the Birmingham Airport. Technical difficulties? No, they forgot the luggage."

***—Kickers: All the News That Didn't Fit***

## DON'T ASK, DON'T TELL

"It was the law in the ancient Greek city of Amyclae to hold one's tongue. The Amyclaeans had often panicked when they heard rumors that the powerful Spartan army was coming, so to put an end to defeatism, a law was passed forbidding rumors. Violators were to be executed.

"When the Spartans actually did appear, no one had the courage to report it, and the city was overcome without a fight."

***—Amazing Lost History***

## A TAXING EXPERIENCE

"Eager to spread the word of the Bush administration's $1.3 trillion tax cut in 2001, the IRS sent more than half a million notices to taxpayers informing them they were going to receive the maximum possible tax cut refund check...when in fact they weren't.

"Officials placed the blame on a computer program. 'What we're doing now,' the IRS announced when the goof was discovered, 'is working to get a corrected notice out to the taxpayers—all 523,000 of them.'"

***—The Denver Post***

## GOIN' BATTY

"A man trying to warn sleeping relatives about a fire in their garage at 4:00 in the morning was mistaken for a burglar and beaten with an aluminum baseball bat. Police said Joe Leavitt of Florence, Alabama, who was visiting his parents, suffered bruises to the back and a gash to the head that required stitches."

**—MSNBC**

## CAN'T PULL THE WOOL OVER THEIR EYES

"According to British researchers, five years of studying sheep brains to determine if mad cow disease may have jumped species must now be thrown out because someone mislabeled the brains. They were studying cow brains the whole time."

**—"The Edge," *The Oregonian***

**Smallest, shallowest ocean on Earth: The Arctic Ocean.**

# "HERE SPEECHING AMERICAN"

*Let's face it: English can be pretty tough to grasp, especially if it's not your first language. Uncle John gives the authors of these signs and labels an "A" for affort.*

***In an Austrian ski lodge:***
Not to perambulate the corridors in the house of repose in the boots of ascension.

***In a Japanese hotel room:***
Please to Bathe inside the tub.

***From a chopstick wrapper in a Chinese restaurant:***
Can you eat with chopsticks Doctor told us / Be intell / eat by using chopsticks / Lots of people use chopsticks / So try eat your chopsticks / Right Now!

***Air conditioner directions in a Japanese hotel room:***
Cooles and Heates: If you want just condition of warm in your room, please control yourself.

***Outside a Russian monastery:***
You are welcome to visit the cemetery where famous Russian and Soviet composers, artists, and writers are buried daily except Thursday.

***In a Finland hostel:***
If you cannot reach a fire exit, close the door and expose yourself at the window.

***In a Copenhagen airport*:**
We take your bags and send them in all directions.

***From a Majorcan (Spain) shop entrance*:**
Here speeching American.

***Warning label on Chinese lint-cleaning roller:***
**1.** Do not use this roller to the floorings that made of wood and plastic.
**2.** Do not use this roller to clean the stuffs that dangerous to your hands such as glass and chinaware.
**3.** Do not use the roller to people's head, it is dangerous that hair could be sticked up to cause unexpected suffering.

***In a Nairobi restaurant*:**
Customers who find our waitresses rude ought to see the manager.

**But can it shoot a basket? A bison can jump as high as six feet off the ground.**

# FAMILIAR PHRASES

*We're back with one of our regular features. Here are the origins of some common phrases.*

**TO TRIP THE LIGHT FANTASTIC**

**Meaning:** To dance

**Origin:** "Coined by English author John Milton, best known for his 1667 masterpiece, *Paradise Lost*. Milton's poem 'L'Allegro'—which means the cheerful or merry one—was written in 1631. He writes: '*come, and trip it as ye go / On the light fantastic toe*.'" (From *Inventing English*, by Dale Corey)

**TO FEEL GROGGY**

**Meaning:** To feel dazed

**Origin:** "This phrase originally referred to drunkenness, and got its name from the ration of rum, known as 'grog,' which was issued to sailors in the Royal Navy until 1971." (From *Everyday Phrases*, by Neil Ewart)

**IN LIKE FLYNN**

**Meaning:** Assured success

**Origin:** "This is often assumed to refer to Errol Flynn's notorious sexual exploits. The earliest example of the phrase, however, in a glossary of air force terms from WWII, claims that the allusion is to the ease with which Flynn accomplished his swashbuckling cinematic feats." (From *Jesse's Word of the Day*, by Jesse Sheidlower)

**TO BE WELL-HEELED**

**Meaning:** To have plenty of money or be well-to-do

**Origin:** "It might be assumed that *well-heeled* originally alluded to the condition of a rich person's shoes. But that is not the case. In the 18th century, it was a fighting cock that was 'well-heeled,' that is, fitted with an artificial spur before facing an opponent in the pit. From that, men began to 'heel' themselves, to carry a gun, before entering a trouble zone. Perhaps because most troubles can be alleviated by money, the expression took on its present financial aspect." (From *Heavens to Betsy!*, by Charles Earle Funk)

**Odds that a grain of rice grown in the U.S. will end up being brewed into beer: 1 in 10.**

# PROMOTIONS THAT BACKFIRED

*When a company wants to drum up new business, they sometimes sponsor special promotions... but things don't always work out as planned. Here are two promos that these companies wish they could take back.*

**Promotion:** Disco Demolition Night

**What Happened:** In 1979, Chicago DJ Steve Dahl came up with this idea to get fans to a Chicago White Sox doubleheader, and the team's promotional director, Mike Veeck, thought it was great: any fan who brought a disco record to the stadium would get in for 98¢. Then, between games the disco records would be blown up. Veeck announced it for the July 12 games against Detroit and told the security crew to be ready for about 35,000 fans.

**The Backfire:** *Sixty thousand* fans showed up... ready for destruction. They were drinking, burning effigies of John Travolta, and throwing disco records at opposing players throughout the first game. When Dahl dynamited over 1,000 disco records after the first game, the crowd went crazy. Thousands of fans mobbed the diamond. They ripped up the pitcher's mound, tore down fences, and started a bonfire in center field, causing thousands of dollars in damage. Riot police were finally called in and they got the crowd off the field, but it was too late. The White Sox had to forfeit the second game—only the fourth time that's happened in Major League history.

What happened to Mike Veeck? He was forced to resign. He developed a drinking problem and didn't work in baseball again for 10 years. "I went down the sewer," he said.

**Promotion:** "Monday Night Winning Lineup" scratch-off game

**What Happened:** Chicago-based food giant Beatrice Inc. came up with this campaign in 1985. The cards were given away at grocery stores around the country and players had to scratch off tiny footballs on the cards to pick the correct number of touchdowns in eight NFL games. Prizes ranged from food coupons and TV sets to the Grand Prize: a trip to the Super Bowl or the cash equivalent—$5,500.

*Linonophobia* is a fear of string.

Frank Maggio of Atlanta got 50 of the cards off a store display rack and played them. And he noticed a pattern. Turns out there were only 320 different cards. He kept getting more cards until he had a complete set. That meant he could scratch off the top row of numbers on a new card, match it up to a master, and know what the rest of the numbers would be. "It was like picking off sitting ducks," he said.

He and a friend, Jim Curl, started grabbing all the cards they could get their hands on, in stores, from sales representatives, and even in the mail directly from the company. They started scratching.

**The Backfire:** Three weeks later, Maggio and Curl turned in their tickets—worth several million dollars. Beatrice immediately canceled the contest and refused to pay, even though the men had offered to show them their mistake and take a measly $1 million for their trouble.

The two men went home…and *really* started scratching. "That weekend cost Beatrice about $10 million," said Maggio. In 1988 the legal battle was finally over, and Beatrice paid out $2 million in a class-action settlement to 2,400 other winners and settled separately with Maggio and Curl for an undisclosed sum (estimated to be about $12 million). Maggio's friends reported that the 25-year-old salesman left town and retired.

* * *

## CONTROVERSY AND *SATURDAY NIGHT LIVE*

• *Saturday Night Live* always airs live…almost. Twice the show was broadcast on a seven-second delay. NBC demanded it so that censors would have a chance to bleep out swearing. Who was too risky for live TV? Richard Pryor (December 13, 1975) and Andrew Dice Clay (May 12, 1990). Nora Dunn boycotted Clay's show; so did scheduled music guest Sinead O'Connor.

• Two years later, O'Connor stirred up controversy when she ripped up a picture of Pope John Paul II after her second song. NBC received 4,484 complaints. But the most severe complaint came from the Vatican, which used its clout to force NBC to edit out the ripping in reruns. O'Connor has since been ordained as a minister.

**Democrats are more likely than Republicans to own a cat.**

# FAMOUS FOR 15 MINUTES

*Here's proof that Andy Warhol was right when he said that "in the future, everyone will be famous for 15 minutes."*

**THE STAR:** Dennis Tito, a millionaire businessman

**THE HEADLINE:** *Money Talks; Man Become's World's First Space Tourist*

**WHAT HAPPENED:** Tito, a former NASA aerospace engineer, had always wanted to be an astronaut, but engineer was about as far as he got...until he switched careers. He became a financial consultant, made millions of dollars, and then decided to buy his way into space. He found a willing seller: the cash-strapped Russian Space Agency agreed to blast him into space for $20 million, which covered nearly the entire cost of the launch.

NASA and its counterparts in Europe, Canada, and Japan all opposed Tito's trip, but Tito started his training in Russia anyway. Everything went smoothly until about a week before the launch, when he and his crew went to the Johnson Space Center in Houston for a week of preflight training and NASA refused to admit him to the facility. When the Russian astronauts announced that they wouldn't train either, NASA blinked—and let them in.

In April 2001, Tito rocketed into orbit aboard a Russian spacecraft. He spent six days aboard the International Space Station and then returned to Earth. "They might not know it," Tito told reporters after the trip, "but this is the best thing that's happened to NASA."

**THE AFTERMATH:** Tito must have been right, because in February 2002, NASA adopted a set of guidelines for selecting future "guests" to the Space Station. Since then, a South African Internet tycoon named Mark Shuttleworth became space tourist #2, and 'N Sync star Lance Bass nearly became #3, but his trip was canceled when sponsors couldn't come up with the cash.

**THE STAR:** Kate Shermak, a fifth-grader at Jamestown Elementary School in Jamestown, Michigan

**THE HEADLINE:** *Ask and Ye Shall Receive...Forever, for Free*

**WHAT HAPPENED:** In 2002 Kate's fifth-grade teacher John Pyper gave the class an unusual assignment, designed to teach kids that letter-writing can be fun: he told them to write to a local business and make an "outrageous request." Kate wrote to the Arby's franchise in nearby Hudsonville. "My outrageous request is to get a lifetime supply of curly fries for free," she wrote. "They're my favorite fries. If you can't meet my outrageous request, I understand."

To Kate's surprise, Arby's said yes, and presented her with a certificate good for a lifetime supply of free curly fries.

**THE AFTERMATH:** The *Grand Rapids Press* printed the story a few days later; it was picked up by the Associated Press and soon appeared in newspapers all over the world. Not everyone in Kate's class was as lucky with their requests—one student wrote to his future sixth-grade teacher asking to be excused from a year's worth of homework. (Request denied.)

**THE STAR:** An unknown *Star Wars* fan

**THE HEADLINE:** *Phantom Phan Phixes Philm*

**WHAT HAPPENED:** In 1999 the fan, whose identity has never been revealed, went to see *Star Wars Episode 1: The Phantom Menace*. Like a lot of people, he was disappointed by what he saw; unlike anyone else, he decided to do something about it. When the movie came out on VHS, he used his computer to re-edit it, as he (or she) put it, "into what I believe is a much stronger film by relieving the viewer of as much story redundancy, pointless Anakin action and dialog, and Jar Jar Binks as possible." He called his new, 20-minute-shorter version of the film *The Phantom Edit*.

The Phantom Editor never tried to sell his version of the film, but he did give it to friends...and they gave copies to their friends...and soon thousands of copies of the re-edit were circulating all over the Internet, making it arguably the most successful bootleg in Hollywood history. Many who saw it thought *The Phantom Edit* better than the original.

**THE AFTERMATH:** The popularity of the first re-edit prompted scores of wannabes to do their own versions with names like *Episode 1.2* and *The Phantom Re-Edit*. The phenomenon began to get covered by the mainstream press; newspapers as prestigious as the

*Chicago Tribune* even began printing movie reviews of the bootleg versions.

Lucasfilm had initially chalked the re-edits up to fans having fun, but as the craze continued to grow, the studio threatened legal action against bootleggers. Ultimately the Phantom Editor—or someone claiming to be him (or her)—e-mailed an apology to Lucas via a website called *Zap2it.com*, calling his film "a well-intentioned editing demonstration that escalated out of my control." If you look hard enough, you can probably still find the film online.

**THE STAR:** Randee Craig Johnson

**THE HEADLINE:** *Can-do: Candidate for Sheriff Brings Unique Qualifications to the Race*

**WHAT HAPPENED:** When Crawford County Sheriff Dave Lovely took early retirement in February 2002, the panel of three county officials invited applications from the public to fill the position of interim sheriff until the next election. One person who wrote in to apply was Randee Craig Johnson, 41, who cited his military experience and his "familiarity with the law" as things that made him a good candidate for the job.

What did Johnson mean, exactly, by his "familiarity with the law"? Johnson wrote his letter from a cell inside the Crawford County Jail, where he'd been held since July 2001 while awaiting trial for murder. In his letter, Johnson predicted that he would be acquitted and asked the panel to look past his current circumstances when they made their choice. "I believe everyone deserves a chance to prove themselves," he wrote.

The Traverse City *Record-Eagle* ran a story on Johnson's candidacy; it was picked up by the national wire services. The contest for Crawford County Sheriff wasn't actually a real election, it was just three panel members appointing a temporary sheriff; but even so, when Johnson entered the race, newspapers all over the country ran the story, making it the most widely covered sheriff's race in the United States.

**THE AFTERMATH:** Johnson lost his bid for sheriff—the panel promoted Undersheriff Kirk Wakefield without even considering Johnson's application. But he did prove himself in the end: On May 24, 2002, a jury unanimously acquitted him of murder and after 307 days in jail he walked out a free man.

**SUV drivers are twice as likely to talk on a cellphone as drivers of other kinds of cars.**

# HOLY PUNCTUATION

*Isn't it funny how the funniest things in life are usually not meant to be funny? These church bulletins from BRI stalwart Jim deGraff are a great example.*

Due to the rector's illness, Monday's healing service will be discontinued until further notice.

The eighth graders will be presenting Shakespeare's *Hamlet* on Friday. The congregation is invited to attend this tragedy.

The audience is asked to remain seated until the end of the recession.

Low Self-Esteem Support Group will meet Thursday at 7:00 p.m. Please use the back door.

Remember in prayer the many who are sick of our church and community.

A songfest was hell at the Methodist church Tuesday.

Don't let worry kill you. Let the church help.

Thursday night potluck supper. Prayer and medication to follow.

Pastor is on vacation. Massages can be given to church secretary.

Ushers will eat latecomers.

The Rev. Adams spoke briefly, much to the delight of his audience.

The Senior Choir invites any member of the congregation who enjoys sinning to join the choir.

Today—Christian Youth Fellowship House Sexuality Course, 1 p.m.–8 p.m. Please use the rear parking lot for this activity.

Smile at someone who is hard to love. Say "hell" to someone who doesn't care much about you.

The Outreach Committee has enlisted 25 visitors to make calls on people who are not afflicted with any church.

Scouts are saving aluminum cans, bottles, and other items to be recycled. Proceeds will be used to cripple children.

Weight Watchers will meet at 7 p.m. Please use large double door at the side entrance.

Will the last person to leave please make sure that the perpetual light is extinguished.

**Makes sense: The horsefly can pierce horse hide with its mouth.**

# OVER MY DEAD CHICKEN!

*Are you an activist? How far would you be willing to go for a cause you believed in? Here are some folks who went pretty far.*

**PROTESTOR:** Larry Eaton of Wilsonville, Oregon
**BURNING ISSUE:** Six months after Eaton finished building his $300,000 dream house, the state announced it was going to build a minimum security prison across the street. The 40-year-old Eaton and several of his neighbors demanded that the zoning be changed from residential to commercial, so they could sell their houses for a reasonable price, but state officials refused.
**WHAT HE DID:** In October 2001, after four years of attending city council meetings and begging for help, Eaton finally had had enough. He got a backhoe, dug some huge holes in his front yard and started planting school buses, nose down. He said they represented the family values the state buried when they put the prison in. He also said he'd plant a new one every month until the zoning was changed. "I promise you," he said, "these buses won't move until I do."
**OUTCOME:** He was up to five front-yard buses at last count. But even though it made national news, the state still won't change the zoning. "It looks like Easter Island," said one reporter.

**PROTESTOR:** Chuay Kotchasit of Thamuang, Thailand
**BURNING ISSUE:** In the early 1990s, Kotchasit invested his life savings of 580,000 bahts—about $13,000—in a mutual fund at the Government Savings Bank. The 65-year-old had hoped to use the interest from his nest egg for his retirement. But by 2001, the fund had lost two-thirds of its value. Kotchasit blamed the bank.
**WHAT HE DID:** On August 14, 2001, Kotchasit walked into the local branch of his bank with a bag, tore it open, and drenched himself with human excrement. "It is more bearable than the stink of mismanagement," he said. He told reporters that he had spent five days planning the protest.
**OUTCOME:** Account closed.

**PROTESTORS:** Six hundred women in Escravos, Nigeria

**BURNING ISSUE:** The exploitative practices of oil giant ChevronTexaco, whose multibillion-dollar refinery operations took place next to their impoverished villages.

**WHAT THEY DID:** In July 2002, the women—unarmed—stormed Nigeria's main oil export terminal and threatened to strip naked. They took 1,000 workers hostage and completely halted all traffic in and out of the terminal and said that if any of the workers tried to leave the plant, they would take off their clothes—a powerful shaming gesture in Nigeria. Furthermore, they vowed to stay until negotiations with oil officials began.

**OUTCOME:** Talks began immediately, and after 10 days the women agreed to end the siege. They won a written contract from the company to hire local workers, build schools and hospitals, and provide electricity and water to their villages.

**AFTERSHOCK:** The success of the Escravos protest spurred copycat protests at five more refineries over the next month. Those protests also ended with deals from ChevronTexaco to improve the areas they did business in.

**PROTESTORS:** Chicken supporters in Sonoma, California

**BURNING ISSUE:** In early 2002, city officials in Sonoma started "removing" flocks of wild chickens that had lived freely and roamed the city for decades. Officials claimed the chickens were a danger to children, were a health hazard, and generally stunk up the town. The protestors argued that the birds were part of the town's old-country charm and that the officials and real-estate developers were "ruining it in the name of progress."

**WHAT THEY DID:** "Chicken drops." As soon as officials began removing the birds, other birds would mysteriously appear in the middle of the night—at the library, in the plaza, and at the Chicken Carwash, where a flock of more than 100 had once lived. Officials would take them away, but more would appear to take their place.

**OUTCOME:** The conflict continues. Officials keep taking the chickens away, and protestors keep dropping off new ones. Says one chicken-hating resident, "It's a comedy and it seems funny—until it's happening to you."

**Is it a pine? Is it an apple? It's neither—the pineapple is actually a very big berry.**

# FICTIONARY

*The* Washington Post *runs an annual contest asking readers to come up with alternate meanings for various words. Here are some of the best (plus a few by the BRI).*

**Carcinoma** (n.), a valley in California, notable for its heavy smog.

**Abdicate** (v.), to give up all hope of ever having a flat stomach.

**Esplanade** (v.), to attempt an explanation while drunk.

**Unroll** (n.), a breadstick.

**Mortar** (n.), what tobacco companies add to cigarettes.

**Flabbergasted** (adj.), appalled over how much weight you've gained.

**Balderdash** (n.), a rapidly receding hairline.

**Innuendo** (n.), an Italian suppository.

**Semantics** (n.), pranks conducted by young men studying for the priesthood.

**Lymph** (v.), to walk with a lisp.

**Gargoyle** (n.), an olive-flavored mouthwash.

**Instigator** (n.), do-it-yourself reptile kit. Just add water.

**Laughingstock** (n.), an amused herd of cattle.

**Coffee** (n.), one who is coughed upon.

**Hexagon** (n.), how a mathematician removes a curse.

**Reincarnation** (n.), the belief that you'll come back as a flower.

**Paradox** (n.), two physicians.

**Prefix** (n.), the act of completely breaking a partially broken object before calling a professional.

**Atheism** (n.), a non-prophet organization.

**Rectitude** (n.), the dignified demeanor assumed by a proctologist immediately before he examines you.

**Flatulence** (n.), emergency vehicle that transports the victims of steamroller accidents.

**Eyedropper** (n.), a clumsy optometrist.

**Zebra** (n.), ze garment which covers ze bosom.

**Think (Boston) tea is Massachusetts's state beverage? Try again—it's cranberry juice.**

# THE COST OF WAR (MOVIES)

*Here's a behind-the-scenes look at the role the Pentagon plays in shaping how Hollywood depicts the military.*

## PROFITEERS

If you're going to make a war movie, chances are you're going to need army tanks, fighter planes, ships, and maybe even submarines to film some of your scenes.

There are two ways to get them: One is to pay top dollar to rent them on the open market from private owners or the militaries of foreign countries like Israel and the Philippines. That can add tens of millions of dollars to the budget. The other is to "borrow" them from the U.S. military, which makes such items available to filmmakers at a much lower cost.

Critics charge that Pentagon cooperation with the film industry is a waste of taxpayer money, but the all-volunteer U.S. military sees it differently: Supporting a movie like *Top Gun*, for example, doesn't cost all that much, and the resulting film is a two-hour-long Armed Forces infomercial starring Tom Cruise.

## NO FREE LUNCH

The catch is that the military will only support films that cast the Armed Forces in a positive light. If a movie producer submits an unflattering script, the Pentagon will withhold its support until the script is changed. If the producer refuses to make the recommended changes, the Pentagon withholds its support, and the cost of making the film goes through the roof.

The original script for *Top Gun*, for example, called for Tom Cruise's character to fall in love with an enlisted woman played by Kelly McGillis. Fraternization between officers and enlisted personnel is against Navy rules, so the Navy "suggested" that producer Jerry Bruckheimer rework the McGillis character. "We changed her to an outside contractor," Bruckheimer told *Brill's Content* magazine. The resulting movie was such an effective recruiting tool that the Navy set up booths in theater lobbies, to sign up enthusiastic recruits after they saw it.

## THE PENTAGON SEAL OF APPROVAL

*Here's a look at a few films that have been through the Pentagon's screening process:*

***Independence Day* (1996),** starring Will Smith and Jeff Goldblum

**Story Line:** Evil aliens try to destroy the world.

**Status:** Cooperation denied. "The military appears impotent and/or inept," one Pentagon official complained in a memo. "All advances in stopping aliens are the result of civilians."

***G.I. Jane* (1997),** starring Demi Moore

**Story Line:** A female Navy recruit tries out for the Navy SEALs.

**Status:** Cooperation denied. The title was bad, for one thing, because "G.I." is an Army term and there are no G.I.s in the Navy. The military also objected to a bathroom scene in which a male SEAL who shares a foxhole with Moore has difficulty urinating in front of her. As one naval commander put it, "the urination scene in the foxhole carries no benefit to the U.S. Navy."

***Goldeneye* (1995),** starring Pierce Brosnan as James Bond

**Story Line:** Russian mobsters and military men are out to rule the world using the GoldenEye—a device that can cut off electricity in London to control world financial markets.

**Status:** Cooperation approved. The military did, however, object to one character in early drafts of the script, a U.S. Navy admiral who betrays America by revealing state secrets. "We said, 'Make him another Navy,'" the Pentagon's Hollywood liaison, Philip Strub says. "They made him a French admiral. The Navy cooperated."

***Forrest Gump* (1994),** starring Tom Hanks

**Story Line:** The life story of a developmentally-disabled man named Forrest Gump, who spends part of the movie fighting in Vietnam.

**Status:** Cooperation denied. The Army felt the film created a "generalized impression that the Army of the 1960s was staffed by the guileless, or soldiers of minimal intelligence," as one memo

**The Great Salt Lake is six times saltier than seawater.**

put it, arguing that such a depiction is "neither accurate nor beneficial to the Army." Separately, the Navy objected to the scene where Gump shows President Lyndon Johnson the battle scar on his buttock, complaining that "the 'mooning' of a president by a uniformed soldier is not acceptable cinematic license."

***Windtalkers* (2002),** starring Nicolas Cage and Christian Slater
**Story Line:** Based on true events, the film is about Navajo Indians who served as "code-talkers" during World War II. Their Navajo-based code so confused the Japanese military that they were never able to crack it. The top-secret code-talkers were so valuable that each was protected by a bodyguard who also had instructions to kill him rather than let him be captured by the Japanese.
**Status:** Cooperation approved...but only after the producers agreed to tone down the "kill order." The characters *imply* that there's an order to kill, but they never get to say it because the military "would not let them say the words 'order' or 'kill.'"

***Courage Under Fire* (1997),** starring Denzel Washington and Meg Ryan
**Story Line:** A military investigator (Washington) tries to solve the mystery of how a helicopter pilot (Ryan) died in combat.
**Status:** Cooperation denied. "There were no good soldiers except Denzel and [Meg]," says the Pentagon's Strub. "The general was corrupt. The staff officer was a weenie."

***Apocalypse Now* (1979),** starring Marlon Brando and Martin Sheen
**Story Line:** An Army officer (Sheen) is sent to Vietnam to "terminate" a colonel who has gone insane (Brando).
**Status:** Cooperation denied. *Apocalypse Now* ran into the same problem with semantics that *Windtalkers* did: the military balked at supporting a film that portrays it ordering one officer to kill another. Director Francis Ford Coppola refused to change the word "terminate" to "arrest" or "detain," so the Pentagon withdrew their support. Coppola ended up having to rent helicopters from the Philippine Air Force. That cost a fortune and helped put the film months behind schedule...because the helicopters kept getting called away to battle Communist insurgents.

**40% of U.S. Army personnel are members of an ethnic minority.**

# HEADLINES

*These are 100% honest-to-goodness headlines. Can you figure out what they were trying to say?*

*Factory Orders Dip*

SUN OR RAIN EXPECTED TODAY, DARK TONIGHT

PSYCHICS PREDICT WORLD DIDN'T END YESTERDAY

CAPITAL PUNISHMENT BILL CALLED "DEATH ORIENTED"

CHICAGO CHECKING ON ELDERLY IN HEAT

TIPS TO AVOID ALLIGATORS: DON'T SWIM IN WATERS INHABITED BY LARGE ALLIGATORS

**Here's How You Can Lick Doberman's Leg Sores**

*Coroner Reports on Woman's Death While Riding Horse*

CHEF THROWS HIS HEART INTO HELPING FEED NEEDY

CINCINNATI DRY CLEANER SENTENCED IN SUIT

*High-Speed Train Could Reach Valley in Five Years*

***FISH LURK IN STREAMS***

***KEY WITNESS TAKES FIFTH IN LIQUOR PROBE***

JAPANESE SCIENTISTS GROW FROG EYES AND EARS

SUICIDE BOMBER STRIKES AGAIN

**DONUT HOLE, NUDE DANCING ON COUNCIL TABLE**

POLICE NAB STUDENT WITH PAIR OF PLIERS

**MARIJUANA ISSUE SENT TO JOINT COMMITTEE**

***Girl Kicked by Horse Upgraded to Stable***

KILLER SENTENCED TO DIE FOR SECOND TIME IN TEN YEARS

COURT RULES BOXER SHORTS ARE INDEED UNDERWEAR

**Nuns Forgive Break-in, Assault Suspect**

*ELIMINATION OF TREES COULD SOLVE CITY'S LEAF-BURNING PROBLEM*

**No wonder they're skinny: lobsters can crawl as far as a mile a day looking for food.**

# UNCLE JOHN'S STALL OF FAME

*We're always amazed by the creative way people get involved with bathrooms, toilets, toilet paper, etc. That's why we've created Uncle John's "Stall of Fame."*

**Honoree:** Henry Pifer, a truck driver from Arkansas

**Notable Achievement:** Standing up for the rights of workers who are sitting down...you know where

**True Story:** In June of 1999 Pifer was hit by a coworker's truck while he was at work. His injuries were serious enough that he had to take time off from his job, so he applied to the state Workers' Compensation Commission for benefits...and was turned down. Reason: At the time of the accident, Pifer was returning from a bathroom break. "Doing your business" at your place of business doesn't count as work, the commission concluded, because it is not an "employment service." Your boss isn't paying you to poop.

Rather than take the decision sitting down, Pifer fought it all the way to the Arkansas Supreme Court...and won. In March 2002 the court ruled that Pifer's bathroom break "was a necessary function and directly or indirectly advanced the interests of his employer."

Little Rock attorney Philip Wilson called the ruling "a landmark decision, because it's the first time the Supreme Court has defined employment services with respect to going to the bathroom."

**Honoree:** The Toto Company of Japan, the world's largest manufacturer of toilets and plumbing fixtures

**Notable Achievement:** Creating the "Miracle Magic Pavilion"

**True Story:** In 2002 Toto wanted to make a big impression at Japan's Kitakyusyu Expo trade show, so they spent a lot of money making a promotional movie touting the company's plumbing fixtures. Rather than just project it onto an ordinary boring movie screen, the company commissioned the "Miracle Magic Pavilion," also known as the "Toilet Theater." It's just what it sounds like it is: a toilet so big that it can be used as a movie theater. Viewers enter through a door built into the side of the huge toilet bowl, then sit on genuine life-sized toilets to watch the film.

Have you ever been at a movie and had to use the bathroom really bad, but you didn't want to leave your seat for fear of missing an important scene? Even in the Toilet Theater, you'd still be out of luck—none of the toilet-seat theater seats are actually hooked up to plumbing. More bad news: Toto has no plans to screen feature films in its enormous toilet, either. You get to watch Toto infomercials. That's it.

**Honoree:** Max Reger, a turn-of-the-century German composer
**Notable Achievement:** Being best remembered for something he composed…in the bathroom
**True Story:** Have you ever heard of Max Reger? Probably not; his name isn't even that familiar to music buffs. In fact, Reger is remembered less for his music than for his response to a scathing review of his work written by a critic named Rudolph Louis in 1906.

"Dear sir," Reger wrote in reply, "I am sitting in the smallest room of my house. I have your review before me. In a moment it will be behind me."

**Honoree:** The Rowanlea Grove Entertainment Co. of Canada
**Notable Achievement:** Putting Osama Bin Laden in his place
**True Story:** It wasn't long after 9/11 that the folks at Rowanlea decided to sit down and be counted: they downloaded a picture of Osama Bin Laden from the Internet and printed it on a roll of toilet paper; now anybody that wants to pay him back with a little "face time" can do it. Rowanlea also prints Osama's face on tissue paper, garbage bags, air-cushion insoles for your smelliest pair of shoes, and even sponges for use on those really disgusting cleaning jobs. Bonus: printing Osama's face on toilet paper without his permission violates his "right to publicity."

Osama "Ex-Terrorist-Commando X-Wipe" rolls aren't cheap—they sell for $19.95 for one or $49.95 for a pack of four, plus shipping and handling. The inkjet ink runs and may irritate sensitive skin, which is why Rowanlea recommends an alternative to wiping: "placing a sheet in the toilet bowl before doing your business. Then bombs away!"

**Construction of the Great Wall of China was financed—in part—by lotteries.**

# OLD HISTORY, NEW THEORY

*We tend to believe what science tells us about history—until science tells us something else. Here is a new finding that may change the history books…for now.*

**The Event:** The sinking of the *Titanic*. The luxury liner sank on its maiden voyage in 1912, killing more than 1,500 passengers and crew members.

**What the History Books Say:** Just before midnight on April 14, 1912, the *Titanic* struck an iceberg in the North Atlantic. The impact gouged a hole in the hull so large that the "unsinkable" ship went down in just two hours and 40 minutes. What remains in question is exactly how the hull was breached…and why.

One popular theory is that the steel used to make the hull was defective, and that when chilled by the icy cold waters of the North Atlantic, it became so brittle that the steel plates fractured on impact when the ship hit the iceberg.

The theory fails on two points. The steel used by the Harland and Wolff shipyards was "battleship quality," strong enough to be used in warships, not just ocean liners. And at the time of impact, the water in the *Titanic*'s ballast tanks was unfrozen, indicating that the North Atlantic wasn't nearly cold enough that night to turn steel brittle, even if it were defective. The theory also fails to explain a strange sound that passengers heard during the impact. One witness described it sounding "as though we went over about a thousand marbles."

**New Theory:** The discovery of the wreck of the *Titanic* in 1985 has helped to shed light on the mystery. Submersibles recovered some of the iron rivets that were used to secure the steel plates together, and one of the rivets ended up in the hands of Dr. Tim Foecke, a metallurgist with the National Institute of Standards and Technology. Foecke cut the rivet in half…and found a flaw: pieces of "slag," or glass added to the wrought iron to give it strength, were not evenly distributed in the iron as they should have been. Instead, they were concentrated in clumps, which weakens the iron instead of strengthening it.

A properly formed rivet would stretch but remain intact during a collision with an iceberg, but if it were defective the head of the rivet could pop off, leaving a hole in the steel plate about an inch in diameter. Pop enough rivets in a line along the hull—something that might sound "as though we went over about a thousand marbles"—and the plates would separate, letting in enough seawater to sink a ship. And even if the steel plates remained in place, there would be enough one-inch holes in the hull to take on water and send the *Titanic* to her watery grave.

Still, one defective rivet does not sink a ship. So when Foecke learned the submersible was making another trip down to the *Titanic*, he asked them to bring him back some more to study. The submersible brought back 48 rivets. Nineteen of them were defective.

*    *    *

## K...FOR KILLER

In 1917 the British Admiralty decided to build a fleet of "K-boats"—325-foot-long steam-powered submarines. Bad idea:

• K2 caught fire on its maiden dive.

• K3 sank for no apparent reason (with the Prince of Wales aboard) and then mysteriously surfaced again. Later it was rammed by K6 and sank for good.

• K4 ran aground.

• K5 sank and all on board were killed.

• K6 got stuck on the sea bottom.

• K7 rammed K17 and went to the junk heap.

• K14 started leaking before ever leaving the dock, and was later rammed by K22 and sank.

• K17 went out of control and sank.

• K22 was rammed by an escorting cruiser.

• In 1918 (after the deaths of some 250 British sailors) the K project was abandoned.

**The first health food store opened in Boston in 1830.**

# HE SLUD INTO THIRD

*These were actually uttered on the air by sports announcers.*

"He dribbles a lot and the opposition don't like it—you can see it all over their faces."

**—Ron Atkinson,**
***soccer announcer***

"This is really a lovely horse, I once rode her mother."

**—Ted Walsh,**
***horse racing announcer***

"And here's Moses Kiptanui, the 19-year-old Kenyan, who turned 20 a few weeks ago."

**—David Coleman,**
***track and field announcer***

"We now have exactly the same situation as we had at the start of the race, only exactly the opposite."

**—Murray Walker,**
***motor sports announcer***

"It's a partial sellout."

**—Chip Caray,**
***baseball announcer***

"The Phillies beat the Cubs today in a doubleheader. That puts another keg in the Cubs' coffin."

**—Jerry Coleman,**
***baseball announcer***

"Anytime Detroit scores more than 100 points and holds the other team below 100 points, they almost always win."

**—Doug Collins,**
***basketball analyst***

"There are no opportune times for a penalty, and this is not one of those times."

**—Jack Youngblood,**
***soccer announcer***

"Coming on to pitch is Mike Moore, who is six-foot-one and 212 years old."

**—Herb Score,**
***baseball announcer***

"That was a complicated play, folks. So let's have a replay for all of you scoring in bed."

**—Bob Kelly,**
***hockey announcer***

"He slud into third."

**—Dizzy Dean,**
***baseball announcer***

"We'll be back with the recrap after this message."

**—Ralph Kiner,**
***baseball announcer***

**First animated characters on TV commercials: the Ajax pixies. They sold cleanser.**

# WHEN THE BIG ONE HIT

*The Great San Francisco Earthquake was one of the costliest—in both lives and money—natural disasters to hit the United States in the 20th century. Here's the story.*

## A TUESDAY LIKE NO OTHER

Most of San Francisco's 450,000 people were asleep at 5:13 a.m. on Tuesday, April 18, 1906. Firefighters lay exhausted in their beds after fighting a fire at the California Cannery Company the night before. *The Daily News* was about to go to press with an article noting that San Franciscans had collected $10,000 for the victims of the recent earthquake in Formosa. It mentioned that committees had been meeting in town to discuss how to handle such a disaster should it ever happen in San Francisco.

Then it happened. The jolt from the earthquake was felt from Los Angeles to Coos Bay, Oregon, a distance of 730 miles. San Francisco stood at the epicenter. It's not known how high on the Richter scale the quake was—some estimates say more than 8.5—but when the earth shook, electric lines came down, trolley tracks twisted, water pipes shattered, bridges collapsed, and buildings crumpled. In some areas, the ground moved 20 feet. It was over in 48 seconds.

All services—including communication, transportation, and medical—were either completely gone or heavily damaged. The city lay in ruins, and the casualties mounted. The situation was bad...and it was about to get worse.

## IGNITION

Smaller earthquakes had hit the town in 1857, 1865, 1868, and 1890. As the city was reconstructed over the years, people built their homes out of wood, knowing it withstood shaking better than brick. But there was a problem with wood: it burned. So anywhere a gas line was ruptured, a stove was upset, or a lantern was overturned, there was enough ready fuel to start a serious fire...and that's exactly what happened.

People reported more than 50 fires within the first half hour following the quake, but because the city's alarm system was out, San Francisco's 585 firefighters had no way of pinpointing the locations. And even if they could, there was little they could do because most of the water mains were broken. Worse yet, Fire Chief Dennis Sullivan lay dying of injuries suffered in the quake. The fires quickly began to consume San Francisco.

## HERE COMES FUNSTON

Brigadier General Frederick Funston, stationed at the Presidio, an army outpost on the northern edge of San Francisco, was flung from his bed by the quake. He immediately sprang into action. Funston knew that army troops were needed to help with the disaster, but he also knew that federal law prevented soldiers from entering the city without first being invited by local authorities. So he headed to City Hall to find Mayor Eugene Schmitz. What he found instead was the building in ruins, fires in the distance, and no sign of the mayor. He decided that troops were needed—whether or not the proper channels were followed. He sent messengers to the Presidio and to Fort Mason, which was also at the north end of the city, and less than two hours after the quake the first of 500 soldiers were on their way into the stricken city. Later they would be joined by sailors, marines, and the National Guard.

Funston organized survivors, ordering some people to gather and distribute all the food that they could find. Others were sent to find wagons and go to neighboring towns for food and supplies. More were sent in search of any bakeries still standing with orders to help get them back in business. And still others were ordered to begin collecting and burying the dead. At 10:15 a.m., Funston sent a telegram to Washington, D.C., asking Secretary of War William Howard Taft for emergency assistance and tents for 20,000 people. It wasn't long before he revised the request to 100,000. Even that wouldn't be enough.

## MAYOR'S ORDERS

Mayor Schmitz finally arrived at City Hall at 7 a.m., as bodies were being pulled from the rubble. He immediately moved into the Hall of Justice and later moved his headquarters four more times as the fires grew and spread. His first order of business was to send out messengers—one to find a telegraph office that was still operating, one to Oakland to ask for fire engines, hoses, and dynamite, and one to the governor requesting that food and water be sent with all possible haste.

**There are about as many nerve cells in your brain as there are stars in our galaxy.**

Schmitz also ordered troops to shoot looters on sight, a rule that was so strictly enforced, it was claimed that people were shot while searching through the rubble of their own homes. Others claimed the troops did most of the looting.

## NOWHERE TO RUN

Fires continued to pop up, grow, and join with other blazes to become huge walls of flame. By 9:00 a.m., a fire was moving across the city, devouring entire blocks at a time. In some areas, the flames advanced as fast as a human can run. By noon, 11 blocks had burned and Market Street had turned into a flaming tunnel.

Meanwhile, the streets became clogged with refugees, soldiers, firefighters, and police. Sightseers coming from outlaying areas to view the damage soon found themselves trapped by the crowds and confusion. And before long they were all trapped by the flames. The entire city of San Francisco and many of its citizens were in danger of being reduced to ashes.

***Turn to page 176 to find out how the city was saved.***

* * *

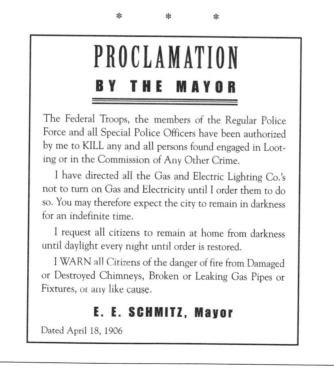

# PROCLAMATION

## BY THE MAYOR

The Federal Troops, the members of the Regular Police Force and all Special Police Officers have been authorized by me to KILL any and all persons found engaged in Looting or in the Commission of Any Other Crime.

I have directed all the Gas and Electric Lighting Co.'s not to turn on Gas and Electricity until I order them to do so. You may therefore expect the city to remain in darkness for an indefinite time.

I request all citizens to remain at home from darkness until daylight every night until order is restored.

I WARN all Citizens of the danger of fire from Damaged or Destroyed Chimneys, Broken or Leaking Gas Pipes or Fixtures, or any like cause.

**E. E. SCHMITZ, Mayor**

Dated April 18, 1906

**Call me Rock: The odds that a stage or screen actor has changed their name is about 75%.**

# QUEEN OF THE JAIL

*From our Dustbin of History files: Here's a true story of danger, seduction, betrayal, and a deadly escape.*

**THE SETTING**

Allegheny County Jail, Pittsburgh, Pennsylvania, 1901

**THE CAST**

| **Katherine Soffel** | **Ed Biddle** | **Jack Biddle** | **Peter Soffel** |
|---|---|---|---|
| The warden's beautiful wife | Famous outlaw | Ed's accomplice and younger brother | The prison warden |

## PROLOGUE

Jack and Ed were "the Biddle Boys," leaders of a gang of small-time outlaws who relied more on brains than brawn to carry out their nefarious crimes. Sometimes they used chloroform to render their potential victims unconscious; sometimes they used beautiful women as distractions. They carried guns, too...just in case.

On April 12, 1901, the gang was robbing a house next to a small grocery store in Mt. Washington, Pennsylvania. A female accomplice kept the grocer occupied while the boys searched the adjoining house, looking for a pile of cash. The distraction didn't work, though—the grocer heard a noise and went to investigate. A struggle ensued, shots were fired, and the grocer ended up dead on his living-room floor. The Biddle brothers fled the scene and holed up in a safehouse, but the police soon caught up with them. After a violent shootout, the outlaws were arrested, but not before a policeman was killed. The trial was quick and the sentence severe: the Biddle Boys were to be hanged for their crimes on February 25, 1902.

## SECRET LOVE AFFAIR

Peter and Katherine Soffel were in the midst of a divorce when the Biddles arrived at the Allegheny County Jail. Katherine, who had previously spent time in an asylum, showed no interest in her husband. Instead, she spent most of her time visiting the prisoners, offering them spiritual advice and bringing them Bibles. For the

**President Lyndon Johnson had an aunt named Frank. (Her parents wanted a son.)**

inmates, Katherine Soffel was a welcome sight. They called her "Queen of the Jail."

She first went to see the Biddles out of curiosity; their exploits throughout the Midwest had made them somewhat notorious. Ed's charm and good looks soon won her over, though. She became infatuated and visited him more and more often, at least 25 times over the next few months, sneaking him food and books. The warden knew his wife had taken an interest in the outlaw but must not have realized just how keen an interest. He allowed her to keep visiting.

After a few months, Ed and Jack convinced Katherine that they were innocent and asked her to help them escape so they could live honest lives as coal miners in Canada. She agreed.

## DARING ESCAPE

As luck would have it, Ed's cell could be seen from Katherine's bedroom window. The two designed a secret alphabet code with which Katherine could point to various body parts, representing different letters, and spell out messages about the warden's movements. This allowed the Biddles to devise a plan. Then they had Katherine—at great risk to herself—smuggle in two saws and a revolver.

On Wednesday night, January 29, 1902, the boys cut through their cell bars. They apprehended three guards and locked them in a cell. As they were leaving the prison, they were met by a waiting Katherine, which was *not* a part of the plan. She was supposed to lay low and meet them in Canada a month later. But Katherine, mad with love, took a page out of the Biddles' book and chloroformed her husband, then snuck away in the night. She didn't want to be away from Ed Biddle.

The warden awoke to a nasty headache and an empty house. When he was told the Biddle Boys had escaped, he knew Katherine was involved and immediately put out an all-points-bulletin on the three of them.

## ON THE RUN

Meanwhile, Ed agreed to let Katherine come along, much to the dismay of Jack, who thought she'd slow them down. But Ed was the boss. They stole a horse and a sleigh from a nearby farm and made it to Cooperstown, 38 miles north of Pittsburgh. They

**There are enough calories in a Big Mac to run a vacuum cleaner for 98 minutes.**

planned to have a quiet breakfast there and slip away unnoticed, but news of the breakout had beat them to the town. The Pennsylvania winter was harsh, and the three fugitives didn't have any warm clothes. They were easily identified and the police were now hot on their trail. They stopped for lunch in Mount Chestnut, 54 miles from Pittsburgh, and Ed and Katherine consummated their relationship. Time, however, was running out.

## FINAL SHOWDOWN

With their horse and sleigh, the Biddle Boys and Katherine Soffel left Mount Chestnut on the snowy afternoon of January 31, 1902. They had only traveled a few miles when a posse met them head-on at the crest of a hill. Ed stopped the sleigh, handed the reins to Katherine, and he and Jack jumped off, each with gun in hand. The sherriff told them to surrender. Ed told them to go to hell and opened fire. The lawmen responded with a hail of bullets.

When the shootout was over, Ed was shot twice, Jack 15 times, and Katherine—who had grabbed a gun and joined in the fray—was shot once by Ed after pleading for him to take her life. She didn't want to live without him.

The three were taken to nearby Butler Hospital. Katherine's wound was treatable; Ed and Jack were not so lucky. As they lay on their deathbeds, they told police varying accounts of what had happened. Ed claimed he'd never loved Katherine, that he just used her to help him escape. Katherine claimed that Ed was just saying that to protect her. Love letters he wrote her while still in prison backed her up, but only Ed knew for sure. He and Jack both died on the night of February 1, 1902.

## POSTMORTEM

The Biddle Boys' bodies were put on display at the Allegheny County Jail for two hours. More than 4,000 people came to see the famous bandits. Katherine served 20 months in prison and lived out the rest of her life in shame. She died a brokenhearted woman on August 30, 1909.

* * *

"We wouldn't have been captured if we hadn't stuck to the woman."

**—Jack Biddle**

**Q: How many toothpicks can you make from one cord of wood? A: 75 million.**

# Q&A: ASK THE EXPERTS

*Everyone's got a question or two they'd like answered—basic stuff, like "Why is the sky blue?" Here are a few of those questions, with answers from some of the nation's top trivia experts.*

## THEY'RE NO CHICKENS

**Q:** *Do ostriches bury their heads in the sand?*

**A:** "No, they do not. This ancient belief may have come about because baby ostriches often fall on the ground and stretch out their long necks when they are frightened. This largest of all birds cannot fly and therefore does need protection, but burying its head is not the answer. The ostrich's protection from danger lies in its very powerful legs and its ability to run at speeds of about 40 miles an hour." (From *The Question and Answer Book of Nature*, by John R. Saunders)

## HOT STUFF

**Q:** *What makes food sizzle?*

**A:** "There is water inside food. When you put it in a hot pan, the water comes out in tiny drops. As soon as they hit the hot pan, the drops dance around, exploding into little puffs of steam. Dancing and exploding, they make little waves in the air that travel to your ears as a sizzling sound." (From *Why Does Popcorn Pop?*, by Catherine Ripley)

## THAT'S SWELL

**Q:** *Why do your feet swell up in an airplane?*

**A:** "It is a common myth that feet swell up when you ride in an airplane because of changes in atmospheric pressure due to high elevation. Feet swell up on planes, especially during long flights, for the same reason they swell up on the ground—inactivity.

"And it does not matter if you leave your shoes on or off; they will swell either way. If left on, they will provide external support, but will inhibit circulation a bit more and probably feel tighter

**More Americans claim German ancestry (46.5%) than any other. Irish ancestry is #2 at 33%.**

during the latter part of the flight. If taken off, comfort may be increased, but the shoes are likely to be more difficult to put on once the flight is over.

"Podiatrists normally recommend 'airplane aerobics' to help circulation—including help for swelling feet." (From *The Odd Body: Mysteries of Our Weird and Wonderful Bodies Explained*, by Dr. Stephen Juan)

## STORM'S A-BREWIN'

**Q:** *Why do clouds darken to a very deep gray just before it's about to rain or prior to a heavy thunderstorm?*

**A:** "Clouds normally appear white when the light which strikes them is scattered by the small ice or water particles from which they are composed. However, as the size of these ice and water particles increases—as it does just before clouds begin to deposit rain—this scattering of light is increasingly replaced by absorption. As a result, much less light reaches the observer on the ground below and the clouds look darker." (From *The Last Word 2*, edited by Mick O'Hare)

## MY HEART GOES BOOM!

**Q:** *If nitroglycerin is an explosive, why don't people who take nitroglycerin for heart conditions explode?*

**A:** "We all know that nitroglycerin is a highly explosive compound. It's a volatile chemical cocktail combining carbon, hydrogen, nitrogen, and oxygen. 'Nitro' taken in pill form helps heart patients by acting directly on the wall of the blood vessels. It dilates the vessels, which both increases the blood supply to the heart and reduces the work of the heart by reducing blood pressure.

"But according to Dr. Thomas Robertson, chief of the cardiac diseases branch of the U.S. National Institutes of Health, the amount of 'nitro' in heart medications is too small to cause any possible danger of a patient exploding—even if the patient overdosed a little and jumped up and down." (From *The Odd Body: Mysteries of Our Weird and Wonderful Bodies Explained*, by Dr. Stephen Juan)

* * *

Youth is a malady of which one becomes cured a little every day.

***—Italian proverb***

**What did they use before that? The first chalkboard was used in a school in 1714.**

# FREE PORK WITH HOUSE

*Have you ever been stuck in the bathroom with nothing to read? (Our greatest fear.) Try flipping through the classifieds to look for ones like these.*

FREE

**Beautiful 6-month-old kitten,** playful, friendly, very affectionate **OR...** Handsome 32-year-old husband—personable, funny, good job, but hates cats. Says he goes or cat goes. Come see both and decide which you'd like.

***Free!*** 1 can of pork & beans with purchase of 3-Bedroom, 2-bath home

**German Shepherd** 85 lbs. Neutered. Speaks German.

FOR SALE

**1-man, 7-woman hot tub,** $850

**Amana Washer** Owned by clean bachelor who seldom washed.

**Cows, Calves** never bred... also 1 gay bull for sale.

**Tickle Me Elmo**, still in box, comes with its own 1988 Mustang, 5l, Auto, Excellent Condition $6800

**Georgia Peaches** California Grown—89¢ lb.

**Fully cooked** boneless smoked man—$2.09 lb.

**Kellogg's Pot Tarts**: $1.99 Box

**Exercise equipment:** Queen Size Mattress & Box Springs—$175

**Used tombstone**, perfect for someone named Homer Hendelbergenheinzel. One only.

**For Sale:** Lee Majors (6 Million Dollar Man)—$50

**Turkey for sale**: Partially eaten, eight days old, drumsticks still intact. $23 obo

MISCELLANEOUS

**Have Viagra**. Need woman, any woman between 18 & 80.

**Shakespeare's Pizza**—Free Chopsticks

**Hummels**—Largest selection. "If it's in stock, we have it!"

**Wanted:** Somebody to go back in time with me. This is not a joke. You'll get paid after we get back. Must bring your own weapons. Safety not guaranteed. I have only done this once before.

**Hairobért**: If we can't make you look good...You ugly!

**Tired** of cleaning yourself? Let me do it.

**The word "cranberry" comes from *crane berry*—the stalk it grows on looks like a crane's neck.**

# LUCKY FINDS

*Ever found something really valuable? It's one of the best feelings in the world. Here's an installment of a regular* Bathroom Reader *feature.*

HONEST STAN

**The Find:** $20,000

**Where It Was Found:** In a drawer

**The Story:** On January 29, 2002, home inspector Stan Edmunds was checking out a house in Hinsdale, New Hampshire, for a prospective buyer. To get to the attic, he had to go through a closet, and an odd wooden shelf support kept catching his eye. The third time through, he pulled on it—and out slid a hidden drawer. Inside it: $20,000 in $100 bills.

Edmunds could have put it in his pocket and walked away, but he didn't—he called the real-estate agent. The agent contacted the heirs of the homeowner, who divided the money up. And one of them sent Edmunds a check for his honesty…for $50. He said he would be donating it to charity.

CHICAGO HOPE

**The Find:** Superbowl Championship ring

**Where It Was Found:** In a couch

**The Story:** In 1996 retired Hall of Fame running back Walter Payton was coaching a high school basketball team outside of Chicago. As an exercise in trust, he gave one of the boys, Nick Abruzzo, his 1986 Superbowl ring—complete with his name and 41 diamonds—to hold for a few days. Nick and his friends passed it around in awe…and then lost it.

Five years later, college student Phil Hong bought an old couch for his dorm room from his friend Joe Abruzzo—Nick's younger brother. One day, while looking in the couch for a lost dog toy, he found the ring. The longtime Chicago fan knew what it was immediately. "Growing up, Walter Payton was my idol," he said. Unfortunately, Payton died of cancer in 1999, but Hong returned the ring to his widow, Connie Payton. "This ring was what he worked for his whole life," he said. "It needs to be back in the family."

## HANGING IN PLAIN SIGHT

**The Find:** Masterpiece painting

**Where It Was Found:** Hanging on a wall

**The Story:** In July 2001, an elderly couple in Cheltenham, England, decided to sell an old painting that had been hanging on a wall in their house for decades. They figured it was worth a few thousand dollars. They wrapped it in a blanket and took it to Christie's auction house. "They arrived in their van and I came outside to look at what they had," said appraiser Alexander Pope. "It was a classic valuation moment." It turned out to be a masterpiece by 17th-century French artist Nicolas Poussin. Sale price at auction: $600,000.

## GIVE ME A RING SOMETIME

**The Find:** Diamond ring

**Where It Was Found:** In a bar in Vancouver, British Columbia

**The Story:** In 1998 a man selling costume jewelry approached 21-year-old Tanya Tokevich while she was sitting in a Vancouver bar. She ended up buying a ring for $20. "It didn't look like much," she said. "It was dull, but I just thought it was nice." She decided to have it appraised to find out whether she'd gotten a good deal. She had. It wasn't costume jewelry—it was an antique engagement ring with a 2.05-carat diamond worth $11,000.

## THE CASE OF THE MISSING LIST

**The Find:** Famous list

**Where It Was Found:** In a suitcase in Germany

**The Story:** When a Stuttgart couple found an old suitcase in their parent's loft after they died in 1999, they didn't think much of it—until they saw the name on the handle: O. Schindler. Inside were hundreds of documents—including a list of the names of the Jewish slave-laborers and their fake jobs that factory owner Oskar Schindler gave to the Nazis during WWII. The bold move saved 1,200 Jews from extermination and inspired the movie *Schindler's List.* Apparently, friends of Schindler's had used the loft as a storage space decades earlier and then forgot about it. The couple gave the suitcase and all the documents to a newspaper, but asked for no money in return. It now resides in Yad Vashem Holocaust Museum, in Jerusalem.

**Makes sense: *Radish* comes from the Latin *radix,* meaning "root."**

# WEDDING SUPERSTITIONS

*If you're planning a wedding, there's a lot to remember. And if you're superstitious, you may have even more to juggle.*

## THE BIG DAY

**Good Luck:** Pick a date when the moon is waxing (increasing in size) and an hour when the tide is rising. Also be sure to time the wedding ceremony so that it ends in the second half of the hour, when the minute hand is rising on the face of the clock. Don't stop there: Everything associated with the wedding should be moving up, up, up! Anything that rises or grows promises rising fortunes for you and your spouse.

**Bad Luck:** *Don't* schedule the wedding for early in the morning. That will bring bad luck—and it's not just a superstition: in the old days the groom, and sometimes even the bride, needed ample time to clean themselves up after morning farm chores, lest they risk showing up at church smelling of animals and manure. (Nowadays it gives the groom a chance to recover from his bachelor party or whatever antics went on the night before.)

## THE DRESS

**Good Luck:** White has been a lucky color for formal weddings in the West for more than a century; for informal ceremonies, any color will do...except for black or red.

**Bad Luck:** Black symbolizes death—only widows can wear it—and red, the color of the devil, is unlucky too. If a woman wears a red wedding dress, 1) she and her husband will fight before their first anniversary or 2) her husband "will soon die."

## THE VEIL

**Good Luck:** The woman who puts the veil on the bride should be happily married. If possible, the bride should wear the veil her grandmother wore, to ensure "that she will always have wealth."

**Bad Luck:** No one other than members of the bride's family should see her veil before the ceremony, and once she is fully dressed, she shouldn't look in the mirror again until after the ceremony is over. She should leave one small article of dress, perhaps a ribbon or a pin, undone so that she can add it at the last minute without having to look in a mirror.

## JEWELRY

**Good Luck:** Wearing earrings will bring the bride good luck.

**Bad Luck:** Don't wear pearls—not in the earrings or the necklace, on the dress, or anyplace else. Pearls symbolize tears. "For every pearl a bride wears, her husband will give her a reason to cry."

## OMENS

**Good Luck:** The animals you see on the way to church are full of omens. Lambs, doves, wolves, spiders, and toads are all good luck. If birds fly directly over your car, that's also good luck—it means you're going to have a lot of kids. (Okay, maybe that's *bad* luck…)

**Bad Luck:** If a pig crosses your path on your way to the wedding, that's bad luck. If a bat flies into the church, that's bad luck too.

## DON'T BE SHY—GO AHEAD AND CRY

**Good Luck:** Tears are such good luck that if the bride can't cry on her own, she should create tears "by virtue of mustard and onions" if necessary. Tears symbolically wash the bride's old problems away, giving her a fresh start.

**Bad Luck:** *Not* crying is *very* bad luck. This is a throwback to the days when people believed that witches can only shed three tears, and these only from her left eye. By crying, a bride demonstrated to the assembled guests that she was not a witch, thereby avoiding being burned at the stake (also bad luck).

## MISCELLANY

**Good Luck:** When she enters and leaves the church, the bride should step across the threshold with her right foot first.

**Bad Luck:** The bride shouldn't have anything to do with making either her wedding cake or her wedding dress. Don't eat anything while you're getting dressed, either—that's bad luck too.

**Hands off: On average, kids aged 2 to 5 put their hands in their mouths 10 times an hour.**

# STRANGE LAWSUITS

*These days, it seems that people will sue each other over practically anything. Here are some real-life examples of unusual legal battles.*

**THE PLAINTIFF:** Wawa, a food store chain
**THE DEFENDANTS:** Tamilee Haaf and George Haaf, Jr., owners of the HAHA market
**THE LAWSUIT:** In late 1996, Wawa, which controls 500 convenience store outlets in eastern Pennsylvania, filed a suit claiming that HAHA is too similar in sound and could confuse people into believing that HAHA is affiliated with Wawa. The Haafs claim they have a right to use the name since it is simply an abbreviation of their last name.
**THE VERDICT:** It may sound funny, but HAHA lost. The judge ruled that "HAHA" sounds so close to "Wawa" that it dilutes Wawa's trademark. HAHA boo-hoo, Wawa yee-ha.

**THE PLAINTIFF:** Associate Humane Societies
**THE DEFENDANT:** Frank Balun
**THE LAWSUIT:** Balun went into his Hillside, New Jersey, garden in July 1993 to check on his tomato vines and discovered that some of the plants had been eaten by rats. So he set a squirrel trap, hoping to catch one. He did. Then he called the Humane Society to pick it up. But before they could respond, the rat tried to escape and Balun hit it on the head with a broom handle, killing it. The Humane Society in Newark then filed charges against Balun for "needlessly abusing a rodent." Complaining that Balun should have dealt with it more humanely, the Humane Society said, "It may only be a rat, but it's a living creature, and there is no reason to abuse a living creature."
**THE VERDICT:** A municipal judge dismissed the charges, citing a statute that allows people to kill vermin that attack their "crops."

**THE PLAINTIFF:** State of Colorado
**THE DEFENDANT:** Eugene Baylis

Makes sense: *Sahara* comes from the Arabic word *sahra* meaning "desert."

**THE LAWSUIT:** Forty-two-year-old Baylis walked into a biker bar in Colorado Springs, armed with an AK-47 rifle, four hand grenades, and a pistol. Seeing the heavily armed man, several of the bar's regular patrons advanced on him—allegedly to keep him from doing any harm. But Baylis got scared and opened fire, killing two people and injuring five.

In court, Baylis argued that he'd gone to the bar to look for a man who'd shot him with a pellet gun earlier in the day. He claimed he merely wanted to hold his attacker until the police arrived, but when he was accosted by the men in the bar, he felt he had no choice but to shoot them...in "self-defense."

**THE VERDICT:** Incredibly, a jury found Baylis not guilty on all counts. One of the jurors said the prosecution never proved Baylis had had any real intentions of killing anyone when he entered the bar and "didn't disprove that Baylis acted in self-defense."

**THE PLAINTIFF:** Peter Maxwell

**THE DEFENDANT:** Peter Maxwell

**THE LAWSUIT:** Maxwell owned a urethane-manufacturing company in Chino, California. He was also on the payroll as a worker, taking a salary of $10,000 a year. One day while he was operating a mixing machine, his sweater got caught on an exposed bolt. He was pulled into the device and severely injured. Maxwell, the employee, hired an attorney and sued Maxwell, the owner, for negligence. Maxwell, the owner, hired another lawyer to defend the company against the lawsuit.

**THE VERDICT:** Both Maxwells decided they could settle their dispute out of court and negotiated that Maxwell, the owner, should pay Maxwell, the employee, $122,500 for his injuries.

**AFTERMATH:** When the IRS caught wind of the deal, they demanded that Maxwell, the employee, pay $64,185 of the settlement in income tax. They also wanted Maxwell, the owner, to cough up $58,500 because he tried to write off the payment as a business expense. Maxwell was outraged—and so was Maxwell. Maxwell, the owner, side by side with Maxwell, the employee, appealed the IRS's judgment to the U.S. Tax Court. In 1990 Judge Robert Ruwe ruled that Maxwell, the employee, could have the settlement income tax-free and that Maxwell, the owner, could deduct the entire amount as a business expense.

**During 33 seasons on the air, Mr. Rogers's trolley traveled more than 100 miles on its track.**

# UNCLE JOHN'S "CREATIVE TEACHING" AWARDS

*Another round of the BRI's Creative Teaching Awards, because we're just so proud of teachers who continue to make education an exciting and creative experience.*

**SUBJECT:** Animal care

**WINNER:** Leslie Davis, of Savannah, Georgia

**APPROACH:** In May 2002, Davis assembled her elementary school students and took them to a nearby park—where they stole a duck from the pond. Then they went back to the school, where they planned to release the duck as a prank.

**REACTION:** The 23-year-old teacher was charged with public drunkenness, obstruction, and contributing to the delinquency of minors.

**SUBJECT:** Fashion

**WINNER:** Vice Principal Rita Wilson, Rancho Bernardo High School, Poway, California

**APPROACH:** During the 2002 April Dance, Ms. Wilson wanted to make sure that female students were following the dress code. So, as they were entering the building, she lifted up the girls' skirts to see if they were wearing thong underwear, which was prohibited. According to a source, she even did so in front of male students.

**REACTION:** The Poway Unified School District investigated and concluded that the vice principal "used poor judgment"...then demoted her to a classroom teaching job.

**SUBJECT:** Civics

**WINNER:** School administrators at Hamilton High School, in Chandler, Arizona

**APPROACH:** As part of a law-enforcement training class, four students took part in a "gun drill," storming school hallways with fake guns, shouting "Don't make me do it!" But apparently someone had failed to warn the faculty about the drill.

**First African American to win the Nobel Peace Prize: Ralph Bunche, in 1950.**

**REACTION:** Panicked students and teachers locked down the classrooms until they were sure they were safe. The instructor who planned the drill—Police Officer Andy McIlveen—was asked not to return to the school district. Said Assistant Principal Dave Constance, "This is not an appropriate way to teach school safety."

**SUBJECT:** Humanities

**WINNER:** Ronald Cummings, of Santa Ana, California

**APPROACH:** For some reason, Cummings drove a group of students—a 14-year-old boy and two 18-year-olds—to a gang fight and then gave them a cigarette lighter that looked exactly like a pistol.

**REACTION:** Immediately put on leave from the school, he was charged by police with contributing to the delinquency of minors, making terrorist threats, and using a fake firearm in a threatening manner. He faces eight years in prison.

**SUBJECT:** History

**WINNER:** School officials in West Palm Beach, Florida

**APPROACH:** To make sure students would fulfill state requirements in history, the officials developed a 100-question test—and then required that students answer only 23 of them correctly to pass.

**REACTION:** Not much. Some teachers complained, but the school board defended the low grade scale...and the test went on anyway. Bottom line: The students can get three-quarters of the answers wrong and still pass.

**SUBJECT:** Ethics

**WINNER:** Third-grade teacher Betty Bettis and gym teacher Thomas L. Sims, of Kansas City, Missouri

**APPROACH:** When a lunch money collection in Bettis's class came up $5 short, the teacher strip searched the students. She took the girls into a restroom, had them strip to their underwear, and then had them check each others' panties. Sims took the boys into a gym and had them strip and then shake their underwear.

**REACTION:** Outraged parents made the story international news. One student even went on a talk show to describe the incident. By the way, they found the missing money in a rest room...but not as a result of the strip search.

**The traditional gift for a 44th wedding anniversary is...groceries.**

# THE WORLD'S FIRST VIDEO GAME

*Ever heard of William Higinbotham? He's the guy who invented the world's first video game. But he never made a cent off his invention and hardly anyone has heard of him. Uncle John thinks it's time he got the credit he deserves.*

## HOWDY, NEIGHBOR

How would you feel if a nuclear reactor came online just down the street from your house? Would knowing that it was just a "small" research reactor, dedicated to finding "peaceful uses" for atomic energy, make you feel any better? That's what happened in 1950 at the Brookhaven National Laboratory in Long Island, New York.

Despite all of its public assurances, local residents were visibly concerned about the potential dangers of the new plant. One way the facility tried to ease public fears was by hosting an annual "Visitor's Day," so that members of the community could look around and see for themselves what kinds of projects the scientists were working on. There were cardboard displays with blinking lights to look at, geiger counters and electronic circuits to fiddle with, and dozens of black-and-white photos that explained the different research projects underway at the lab.

In other words, Visitor's Day was pretty boring.

## SOMETHING TO DO

In 1958 a Brookhaven physicist named William Higinbotham decided to do something about it. Years earlier, Higinbotham had designed the timing device used to detonate the first atomic bomb; now he set his mind to coming up with something interesting for Visitor's Day. "I knew from past visitor's days that people were not much interested in static exhibits," he remembered. "So that year, I came up with an idea for a hands-on display."

## FOLLOW THE BOUNCING BALL

Looking around the labs, Higinbotham found an electronic testing device called an oscilloscope, which has a cathode ray tube display similar to a TV picture tube. He also found an old analog computer (modern computers are digital, not analog) that he could hook up to the oscilloscope in such a way that a "ball" of light would bounce randomly around the screen.

"We found," Higinbotham remembered, "that we could make a game which would have a ball bouncing back and forth, sort of like a tennis game viewed from the side." The game he came up with looked kind of like this:

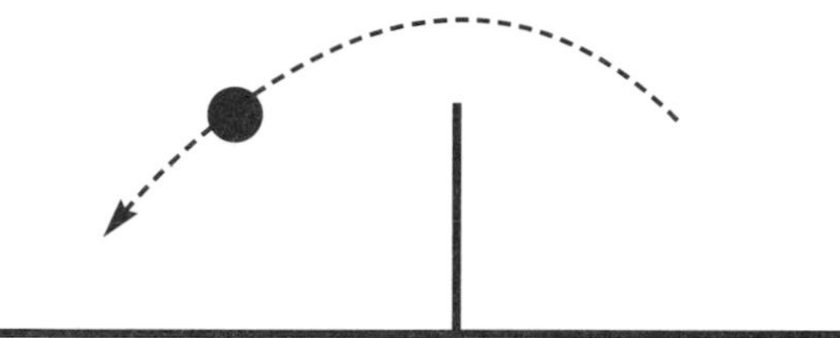

Two people played against one another using control boxes that had a "serve" button that hit the ball over the net, and a control knob that adjusted how high the ball was hit. And just as in real tennis, if you hit the ball into the net, it bounced back at you.

## BEST OF SHOW

It took Higinbotham two hours to draw up the schematic diagram for "Tennis for Two," as he called it, and two weeks of tinkering to get it to work. When Visitor's Day came around and Higinbotham put it on a table with a bunch of other electrical equipment, it only took the visitors about five minutes to find it. Soon hundreds of people were crowding around it, some standing in line for more than an hour for a chance to play the game for a minute or two. They didn't learn much about the peaceful applications of nuclear energy that Visitor's Day in 1958. But they sure had fun playing that game.

Higinbotham didn't have an inkling as to the significance of what he'd done. "It never occurred to me that I was doing anything very exciting," he remembered. "The long line of people I thought wasn't because this was so great, but because all the rest of the things were so dull."

**Seeing is believing: Frogs use their eyeballs to push food down their throat.**

## GAME OVER

So what happened to Higinbotham's video tennis game? He improved it for Visitor's Day 1959, letting people play Tennis for Two in Earth gravity, or low gravity like on the moon, or very high gravity like that found on Jupiter.

Then, when Visitor's Day was over, he took the video game apart and put the pieces away. He never brought them out again, never built another video game, and never patented his idea.

Willy Higinbotham would probably be completely forgotten today were it not for a lawsuit. When video games began taking off in the early 1970s, Magnavox and some other early manufacturers began fighting in court over which one of *them* had invented the games. A patent lawyer for one of Magnavox's competitors eventually learned of Higinbotham's story and brought the Great Man into court to prove that he, not Magnavox, was the true father of the video game.

## OUCH!

In 2001 Americans spent more on video game systems and software—$9.4 billion—than they did going to the movies—$8.35 billion. What did Higinbotham, who died in 1994, have to show for it? Nothing. He never made a penny off his invention. Not that he could have—he worked for a government laboratory when he invented the game, so even if he had patented the idea, the U.S. government would have owned the patent.

"My kids complained about this," he joked, "And I keep saying, 'Kids, no matter what, I wouldn't have made any money.'"

***For more about the history of video games, follow the bouncing ball to page 124 for "Let's Play Spacewar!"***

* * *

## SEA-ING THINGS

Dolphins sometimes play chase in long lines, like people doing a snake dance or snap-the-whip. Sailors, seeing this long line of something moving in the water, have sometimes reported seeing huge sea serpents.

**It's easy to spot someone with *hexadectylism*: six fingers on one hand or six toes on one foot.**

# "I SPY"...AT THE MOVIES

*You probably remember the kids' game "I spy, with my little eye..." Moviemakers have been playing it for years. Want to play? Here are some in-jokes and gags you can look for the next time you see these films.*

**SPIDER-MAN (2002)**

**I Spy...** Lucy Lawless, star of *Xena: Warrior Princess*

**Where to Find Her:** She appears as the red-haired punker who makes the astute observation: "A man with eight arms? Sounds like a good time to me!" (*Spider-man* director Sam Raimi worked as a producer on *Xena*.)

**AMERICAN PIE (1999)**

**I Spy...** Blink 182

**Where to Find Them:** During the Internet scene, the popular band can be seen watching the Webcast. Their song "Mutt" is playing in the background.

**HOW THE GRINCH STOLE CHRISTMAS (2000)**

**I Spy...** Director Ron Howard's favorite hat

**Where to Find It:** On the Grinch's head—when he is "directing" his dog Max to become a reindeer. Legend has it that Jim Carrey stole the hat and ad-libbed an imitation of Howard. Howard thought the bit was funny and left it in the movie, hat and all.

**ERIN BROCKOVICH (2000)**

**I Spy...** The real Erin Brockovich

**Where to Find Her:** When the fake Erin (Julia Roberts) is in a restaurant with her kids, their waitress is the real Erin. Her name tag reads "Julia."

**SPIES LIKE US (1985)**

**I Spy...** Blues legend B.B. King

**Where to Find Him:** He's one of the CIA agents at the drive-in theater/missile silo. In the credits, he's listed as "Ace Tomato Agent."

**FERRIS BUELLER'S DAY OFF (1986)**

**I Spy...** References to several of director John Hughes's movies

**Where to Find Them:** On the license plates of various cars. VCTN (*National Lampoon's Vacation*), TBC (*The Breakfast Club*), MMOM (*Mr. Mom*), and 4FBDO (*Ferris Bueller's Day Off*).

**MONSTERS, INC. (2001)**

**I Spy...** Pixar's phone number

**Where to Find It:** At the end of the simulation that begins the film, a monster reaches for a knob on the control panel. Just below it and to the left is a series of 10 numbers. Dial them and you'll reach Pixar, the studio that made the movie.

**THE MATRIX (1999)**

**I Spy...** Andy and Larry Wachowski, the film's directors

**Where to Find Them:** They're the two window washers outside the office where Neo is being chastised for arriving late to work.

**THE SHAWSHANK REDEMPTION (1994)**

**I Spy...** A photograph of Morgan Freeman's son

**Where to Find It:** The parole papers that repeatedly receive a rejected stamp show a picture of Red (Morgan Freeman) when he was a young man. Morgan's son Alfonzo was used for the shot.

**GEORGE LUCAS MOVIES**

**I Spy...** THX-1138

**Where to Find It:** *THX-1138* was the name of Lucas's first feature film, and he has paid homage to it throughout his career. A license plate in *American Graffiti* reads "1T1H3X8." Luke Skywalker rescued Princess Leia from Cell Block 1138 in *Star Wars*. In *Raiders of the Lost Ark*, a loudspeaker in the submarine dock states, "*Ein, Ein, Drei, Acht*" ("One, one, three, eight" in German). A battle droid in *The Phantom Menace* has the designation—you guessed it—1138. (Note: We don't know if there are any references to it in *Howard the Duck*—we couldn't make it through a complete viewing.)

* * *

One falsehood spoils a thousand truths.

**—Ashanti wisdom**

**Cowabunga! As many as 17 million people around the world surf.**

# THE FINAL DAYS OF KING CHARLES II

*Next time you feel yourself coming down with a cold, thank your lucky stars for 21st-century medicine.*

**MONDAY**

On the morning of February 2, 1685, King Charles II of England was preparing to shave when he suddenly cried out in pain, fell to the floor, and started having fits. Six royal physicians rushed in and administered emergency "aid."

• They let (drained) 16 ounces of blood.

• Then they applied heated cups to the skin, which formed large round blisters, in order to "stimulate the system."

• They let 8 more ounces of blood.

• They induced vomiting to purify his stomach, gave an enema to purify his bowels, and made him swallow a purgative to clean out his intestines.

• Then they force-fed him syrup of blackthorn and rock salt.

• They shaved his hair and put blistering plasters on his scalp. The king regained consciousness. The treatment seemed to be working, so they kept at it.

• They gave him another enema.

• Then they applied hellebore root to the nostrils, more blistering plasters to the skin, and powdered cowslip flowers to the stomach.

• Special plasters made from pigeon droppings were attached to his feet. After 12 hours of care, they put the ailing king to bed.

**TUESDAY**

• Charles awoke and seemed much improved. The attending physicians congratulated themselves and continued the treatment.

• They let 10 more ounces of blood.

• They gave him a potion of black cherry, peony, lavender, crushed pearls, and sugar. Charles slept for the rest of the day and throughout the night.

### WEDNESDAY

- He awoke, had another fit, and was bled again.
- They gave him senna pods in spring water, and white wine with nutmeg.
- They force-fed him a drink made from "40 drops of extract of human skull" of a man who had met a violent death.
- They made him eat a gallstone from an East Indian goat.
- Then they proudly announced that King Charles was definitely on the road to recovery.

### THURSDAY

- The king was near death.
- He was blistered again, re-bled, repurged, and given another enema.
- He was given Jesuits' powder—a controversial malaria remedy—laced with opium and wine. His doctors were mystified by the king's weakening condition.

### FRIDAY

- Showing no improvement, the king was bled almost bloodless.
- They scoured the palace grounds and created a last-ditch antidote containing "extracts of all the herbs and animals of the kingdom."

### SATURDAY

The king was dead.

**Postmortem:** It was rumored at the time that King Charles II had been poisoned, but no proof was ever found. Modern doctors offer three theories as to cause of death:

**1.** He *was* poisoned—but not by an enemy—by himself. He often played with chemicals in an unventilated palace laboratory, where he contracted acute mercury poisoning.

**2.** He suffered from kidney failure.

**3.** He had a brain hemorrhage.

Would the king have survived without treatment? Probably not. But at least his death wouldn't have been so excruciating.

**There are 10,800 feet of film in a two-hour movie.**

# AMAZING ANIMALS: THE OPOSSUM

*When we saw the opossum on a list of wildlife that thrives in cities, it made us curious about how it manages to survive in such a hostile environment. Turns out that this tough little critter is quite an amazing animal.*

## OLD-TIMER

Of all the mammals on Earth, opossums are among the oldest. Fossil records show it going back more than 100 million years. Remarkably, the gray-and-white, pink-nosed, rat-tailed opossums we see in our backyards today are almost identical to the ones that walked around with the dinosaurs. They have survived that long with very few evolutionary changes.

The opossum is a *marsupial*, a primitive type of mammal distinguished by its unique reproductive system. It gives birth to embryos that develop into viable "pups" in an external pouch—like a kangaroo. There used to be thousands of species of marsupials in North America, but over tens of millions of years they migrated south, into what is now South America.

Continental drift prevented them from returning until fairly recently (less than eight million years ago) and by that time another type of mammal had evolved: *placental* mammals, which develop their young *inside* their bodies. Placental mammals dominated. Of all the South American marsupial species that could have survived in North America, only one did: the opossum.

## SURVIVOR

The evolutionary cards are stacked against the opossum.

It's not fast: it has a top speed of 1.7 mph.

It's not large: adults range from 6 to 12 pounds.

It's not exceedingly smart: it has almost the smallest brain-to-body ratio of any land mammal.

It's not aggressive, nor well-suited for fighting to defend itself. So why is the primitive opossum the only marsupial that made it in

**How long have mammals been on Earth? 200 million years. Homo sapiens? 150,000 years.**

North America? Here are some features that helped opossums beat the odds:

• They'll eat anything. They can survive on worms, snails, insects, snakes, toads, birds, fruits, vegetables, or garbage. (They'll also eat cat food and dog food.)

• Opossums are unusually resistant to diseases, including rabies. They're also very resistant to snake venom—a dose of rattlesnake venom that would kill a horse barely affects an opossum.

• They have a prehensile (grasping) tail that they can use to gather branches and grass for nesting, climb trees, and escape predators.

• Opossums are the only animals besides primates that have an opposable thumb. It's on their hind feet, and they use it to grasp with, like humans do.

• Male opossums have another unique appendage: a forked penis. Females have a two-channel vagina, so everything has to line up correctly for successful mating. This means that the opossum can't crossbreed with other species, which is another reason it has changed so little over the eons.

## PLAYING 'POSSUM

Another unique trait that plays a big part in the opossum's survival is its ability to "play dead." Is it playing? Not exactly.

When an opossum is threatened by an enemy, it doesn't have a lot to work with. It doesn't want to fight and avoids it at all costs. It hisses and growls, baring its mouthful of teeth—it has 50, the most of any land mammal. It will even emit a foul odor, vomit, or defecate to repel the enemy. Sometimes these strategies work.

But if the predator is really hungry and still a threat, the opossum has one more weapon. It passes out. It's not an act, it's an involuntary reaction to overwhelming danger. It goes into a coma or shocklike state: the heart rate drops drastically, the body temperature goes down, the tongue hangs out, and it drools. It is, for all appearances, dead. Why is that good? Most predators won't eat dead animals. They'll usually sniff around, then leave it alone.

After a while, as short as a minute or as long as six hours, the opossum will "wake up" and waddle on its way to survive another day, another week, and who knows, maybe another 100 million years.

**In 2000 Italian pastry chefs built an edible Ferrari out of 40,000 cream pies.**

# LIVE FROM NEW YORK, IT'S SATURDAY NIGHT!

*In our* Third Bathroom Reader, *we covered the origin of* Saturday Night Live. *Why write about it again? Because it's one of the most influential TV shows of all time. Over the years, it has had its ups and downs, but it remains essentially the same show Lorne Michaels devised back in 1975.*

## A CONSERVATIVE MEDIUM

In the late 1960s, America's youth spoke out against the war in Vietnam, against racism, and against a government they saw as a growing threat to the freedom of speech. How did the big three TV networks react to this dissent? They mostly ignored it.

Take the popular variety show *Laugh-In*, which was marketed to younger people. It featured a head writer who also happened to be a Nixon speechwriter. The result: More fluff than substance. And *The Smothers Brothers Comedy Hour* coasted along fine until Tommy Smothers began speaking out openly against the war. CBS swooped in and quickly canceled the show in 1969. By the end of the decade, the message was clear: "The revolution will not be televised."

## UNDERGROUND COMEDY

In the early 1970s, the revolution took an unexpected turn: it showed up in underground comedy. *MAD* magazine and *National Lampoon* spread the anti-establishment message on their pages; comedy troupes such as Second City in Chicago and Toronto and The Groundlings in Los Angeles performed cutting-edge satire with no rules, no limits, and no censorship—all things that TV network executives stayed well away from. To them, comedy was Johnny Carson and Dick Cavett for adults, and *The Brady Bunch* and *Gilligan's Island* for kids.

There was, however, one word that the network brass has always pricked up its ears for: ratings. And NBC's late-night Saturday ratings were so low in 1975 that they were giving away advertising spots in the time slot as a free bonus to attract primetime advertising deals. They blamed the low ratings on the time of night rather than on what they were broadcasting: *Tonight Show* reruns. But everyone was growing tired of having Johnny on six, and sometimes seven, nights a week. NBC was ready to replace the reruns with something else. They were considering a weekly variety show hosted by impressionist Rich Little and singer Linda Rondstadt.

They gave the task of creating the new show to a young executive named Dick Ebersol, who didn't even bother pursuing Little; he wanted to do something new and fresh that younger viewers could identify with. A fellow executive told him, "Dick, there's only one guy you should talk to."

## LORNE MICHAELS

By the time he was 30 years old, Canadian Lorne Michaels (born Lorne Lipowitz) had graduated with an English degree from the University of Toronto, sold cars in England, starred as one-half of a comedy team on Canadian television, been a writer for *Laugh-In* (all of his jokes about Nixon were rejected), produced a TV special for Lily Tomlin, and submitted an idea for a late-night variety show to NBC—twice.

But the timing for his show wasn't right until 1975, when Ebersol sought him out. At their first meeting, Michaels told Ebersol: "I want to do a show for the generation that grew up on television." His concept was already mapped out: an anything-goes comedy show featuring edgy satire, commercial parodies, fake news, rock music, and a celebrity host. It had to be live—a practice network television had abandoned in the 1970s—otherwise it wouldn't have the spontaneity it needed. Ebersol agreed and pitched the idea to the network, selling it as a "youth" show and pointing to the dismal ratings NBC was getting in the 18 to 34-year-old market. To Ebersol's and Michaels's amazement, the network was convinced... mostly.

## HEEERE'S JOHNNY

By the 1970s, Johnny Carson had as much clout as anybody at NBC. The *Tonight Show* had done so much for the network that what Johnny wanted, Johnny got. And one thing Johnny *didn't* want was competition. Worried that a new comedy show would compete with his "King of Late Night" status, Carson summoned Michaels and Ebersol.

**Odds that a Minnesota driver has steered with their legs at least once: 20%**

But one of Michaels's strengths was his diplomatic skill—he calmly reassured the "Great One" that his show would be very different than Carson's: no interviews, a bunch of unknowns, a completely different format aimed at a completely different audience. Carson was duly impressed with the two young men and gave them—and the network—his approval. He would come to regret that decision.

## PUTTING IT TOGETHER

Michaels signed a deal with NBC, fittingly, on April 1, 1975. He and Ebersol were given Studio 8H on the 17th floor of New York's Rockefeller Center. Michaels wanted to call the new show *Saturday Night Live*, but ABC was putting together a show by the same name—hosted by Howard Cosell and featuring the "Primetime Players." So they called it *NBC's Saturday Night*, then just *Saturday Night*. (The show wasn't called *Saturday Night Live* until the March 26, 1977, episode.)

Michaels began a search for "enlightened amateurs"—comedians who, according to Doug Hill and Jeff Weingrad in their book *Saturday Night*, spouted "drug references, casual profanity, a permissive attitude toward sex, a deep disdain for show business convention, and bitter distrust for corporate power." Michaels wanted to combine that rawness with the style of his all-time favorite comedians: Monty Python's Flying Circus.

Michaels approached one of the hottest comedians of the mid-1970s, Albert Brooks, with the idea of hiring him as the permanent celebrity host. Brooks declined, saying that he wanted to focus on a movie career. He did, however, offer an alternative idea. "You don't want a permanent host anyway," he told Michaels. "Every show does that. Why don't you get a different host every week?" So they did. But they still needed a cast.

## STAR SEARCH

That summer, word of the new show quickly spread through the show biz world. Ads for auditions went into trade papers all over the country. In New York, comedy clubs put their best acts on when the *Saturday Night* people arrived. But Michaels wanted more than stand-up comedians, he wanted socially conscious performers who could act, improvise, do impressions, sing, and dance. He scoured the ranks of *National Lampoon*, comedy troupes, even serious repertory theaters. Michaels could only pay his performers $750 per episode, but he was offering something most couldn't refuse: exposure on national television. One more rule: none of *Saturday Night*'s talent would be over 30 years old.

## THE NOT READY FOR PRIMETIME PLAYERS

First hired was Gilda Radner, whom Michaels had performed improv with in the 1960s. In 1975 Radner was with Second City in Chicago, along with Dan Aykroyd, Bill Murray, and John Belushi. Michaels was reluctant about Belushi—who was known as much for being uncontrollable as he was for being a brilliant comedian. But Belushi did so well as a samurai pool hustler in his audition that he was hired over Murray, who had already signed a tentative deal with ABC's *Saturday Night Live*.

From the improvisational group The Proposition he found Jane Curtin, who fit the bill as the "white bread" woman, and from The Groundlings in Los Angeles, Laraine Newman. She was chosen partly for her audition performance and partly for her red hair, which would offset Curtin's sandy blonde and Radner's brunette locks. To round out the appearance of the cast, Michaels wanted a black man. He'd originally hired Garrett Morris as a writer. But even though Morris had no comedic experience, Michaels was impressed with his acting ability in the 1972 film *Cooley High*, so Morris was made a cast member instead. Now that the cast was set, they needed a name. Michaels mocked ABC's Saturday-night show by calling NBC's performers the "Not Ready For Primetime Players."

In addition to performers, Michaels also sought out talented young writers, including the team of Al Franken and Tom Davis, a cynical *Lampoon* writer named Michael O'Donoghue (who was responsible for a lot of *SNL*'s darker material), and a former *Smothers Brothers Comedy Hour* writer named Chevy Chase. Chase wanted to act, but there was no more money in the budget for cast members, so Michaels signed him as head writer (which actually paid more money than the players were getting). Michaels and Chase immediately became buddies, and Chase got preferential treatment, including the "Weekend Update" job, much to the dismay of the cast. It was a sign of things to come.

***The cast and crew were set. Now all Michaels and Ebersol had to do was make a show.*** ***Turn to page 141 for Part II of the story.***

**Official state dance of Utah: square dance.**

# WEIRD CANADA

*Canada: land of beautiful mountains, clear lakes, bustling cities...and some really weird news reports. Here are some of the oddest entries from the BRI newsfile.*

## SNOW DAY

In January 2002, a 30-year-old Ontario man named Nona Thusky was charged with public drunkenness and violation of probation. He was kept in custody awaiting sentencing on a previous conviction for assaulting a police officer when, two weeks later, he was suddenly released. Why? Because it snowed.

Mr. Thusky is a member of the Algonquin tribe from the Barriere Lake reservation, and he's the only community member who knows how to operate the snowplow. After a severe February snowstorm, judge Jean-Francois Gosselin decreed that "community service"—i.e., clearing snow from the streets—made more sense than jail time.

## I THOUGHT THEY WERE A HOCKEY TEAM

Toronto Mayor Mel Lastman found himself in a storm of criticism in January 2002. He had staged a photo session shaking hands with and receiving a T-shirt from a member of the Hell's Angels. Members of the notorious motorcycle gang had been involved in a vicious six-year drug war with rival gangs in Quebec in which more than 150 people were killed. Police organizations, city officials, and citizens blasted the mayor for the move, calling it grossly insensitive. Mayor Lastman threw the T-shirt away and apologized, saying he didn't know that the Hell's Angels...dealt drugs. Afterwards, the gang demanded an apology from the mayor—for throwing away the present they gave him.

## BEYOND THE CALL OF DOOTY

In 1943, 17-year-old Hugh Trainor enlisted in the army and passed a preliminary test in his hometown on Prince Edward Island. He then traveled by ferry to an army barracks in Halifax, Nova Scotia. Once there, he failed his medical test and never officially became a member of the armed forces. But Trainor claimed that his time on

**The first crash test dummy, created in 1949, was nicknamed Sierra Sam.**

the ferry—about a 10-mile ride—qualified as "war service," because German submarines had previously attacked ships in Canadian waters. In 2002 the Federal Court of Canada ruled that 75-year-old Trainor was entitled to veteran's benefits for his service and awarded him $1,000 a month for the rest of his life.

### THE PLOP THICKENS

The state provincial fair in Calgary, Alberta, offered a new thrill to attendees in 2002: Cow Patty Bingo. They divided a field up into squares, painted numbers on them, and let people bet on the numbers. Then they let the cows into the field. The person whose square got the first "lucky patty" won a prize. Organizers denied claims that the cows had been given laxatives to speed the game up.

*   *   *

## HOOT OFF THE PRESS

### WANTED

"Salespeople needed. If you are now employed but wish to improve your position, or in a dead-end job, call now for opportunity in cemetery sales."

—***Toronto Star***

"Career opportunity for a firefighter position: 'We offer a smoke-free work environment.'"

—***Calgary Herald***

### ANNOUNCEMENTS

"All residents will now be collected on Thursday."

**—Ontario waste-systems company notice**

"At a meeting of the cemetery commission, the burial rates were increased slightly to reflect the higher cost of living."

**—Nova Scotia church bulletin**

### CLASSIFIEDS

"Visitors are needed for a man having trouble with blindness and a German-speaking woman."

—***The Ottawa Citizen***

"Lots of stuff! All ex-hubby's remains."

—***South Delta Today*, B.C.**

"Wedding gown worn once by mistake. Size 9–10. Asking $20."

—***Oshawa Times***

### NEWS FLASH

"A third grain-elevator fire in east-central Alberta has investigators wondering if there's a cereal arsonist at work."

—***Calgary Herald***

# INTERNATIONAL ELVIS

*Decades after his death, Elvis is more popular than ever. He sells more records, generates more revenue, and has more fans worldwide than he did when he was alive. If you need proof, look to these Elvis impersonators.*

**LATINO ELVIS** (Robert Lopez, a.k.a. "El Vez," Mexico)
**Claim to Fame:** First Mexican Elvis to think he was the *second* Mexican Elvis
**Taking Care of Business:** Lopez, who is famous all over Mexico and has appeared on MTV and *The Tonight Show,* grew up absolutely convinced that Elvis Presley was Mexican. "When I was a kid in the '60s, I had uncles with continental slacks and pompadours in that Elvis style," he says. "I thought Elvis looked like my uncles."

Lopez got a rude awakening when he realized that the King wasn't in Mexico even when he was *supposed* to be: "The first movie I ever saw him in was *Fun in Acapulco.* I found out later that it wasn't even filmed in Mexico, but on a sound stage." No matter—El Vez is still dedicated to emulating the King. "I don't think that you can do this unless you love and admire Elvis," he says. "This isn't just some fat-man-on-pills parody."

**REFUSNIK ELVIS** (Vassil Angelov, Bulgaria)
**Claim to Fame:** Put his life on the line by impersonating the King
**Taking Care of Business:** When he was a young man in the 1960s, Angelov had to hide his admiration of Elvis because sideburns and rock music were illegal in communist Bulgaria. But the communist era ended in 1990 and today Angelov runs Bulgaria's only Elvis fan club and openly tours the country imitating his idol. Someday he hopes to travel the world. "I want to look for people and places," he says, "where I can show off my God-given talent."

**TOKYO ELVIS** (Mori Yasumasa, Japan)
**Claim to Fame:** Became the first non-American to win an Elvis impersonator contest in Memphis, Tennessee, the Elvis capital of the world

**It's worth it: After a three-week vacation, your IQ can drop by as much as 20%.**

**Taking Care of Business:** Yasumasa didn't even hear his first Elvis song until he was 18, but quickly made up for lost time. It wasn't long before he had perfected an Elvis imitation and was performing on U.S. Army bases all over Japan. In 1992 he made the trip of a lifetime when he traveled to Memphis, entered the International Elvis Impersonator Contest…and won. The victory has only deepened his appreciation of the King. "Although he didn't compose or write his songs and leave any deep messages, I believe that he himself is the message," Yasumasa says. "He was using his own body and soul to convey the message of freedom to the world. This to me is really incredible."

**KIWI ELVIS** (Brian Childs, New Zealand)

**Claim to Fame:** He's living the life of Elvis…in reverse

**Taking Care of Business:** Elvis was a singer who collected police badges and always wanted to be in law enforcement—and Brian Childs was a New Zealand police constable who always wanted to be the King. He started out impersonating Elvis in his spare time, but his chief didn't like it and in January 2002, told him he'd have to quit his hobby. Constable Childs quit his job instead. Today he is the reigning champion Elvis Presley impersonator in neighboring Australia and is considering suing the force for wrongful dismissal.

**FILIPINO ELVIS** (Rene Escharcha, a.k.a. "Renelvis", Philippines)

**Claim to Fame:** He takes care of business—by telephone

**Taking Care of Business:** It's not easy to stand out from the crowd when you're an Elvis impersonator—even if you're a Filipino Elvis living in North Carolina. One of the ways Escharcha makes his mark is by whipping out his long-distance phone card in the middle of a performance and calling his cousin in the Philippines (also an Elvis impersonator) so that they can belt out Elvis tunes together, a cappella, over a speakerphone. Escharcha also keeps the King's legacy fresh by writing his own songs. In "Elvis on Terrorism," Escharcha sings, "I wonder if Elvis were here today, what would he do? I can assure you, he would do something."

Why is he so dedicated to being the King? "If you want to be somebody, you have to work at it," Renelvis explains.

**43% of single American men say they didn't go on a date in 2001.**

# POLITALKS

*Politicians aren't getting much respect these days—but then, it sounds like they don't deserve much, either.*

"Wherever I have gone in this country, I have found Americans."

**—Alf Landon (R-KS)**

"We shall reach greater and greater platitudes of achievement."

**—Richard J. Daley (D), *mayor of Chicago***

"I hope I stand for anti-bigotry, anti-Semitism, anti-racism."

**—George H. W. Bush**

"This is the worst disaster in California since I was elected."

**—Gov. Pat Brown (D-CA), *discussing a flood***

"Mr. Nixon was the thirty-seventh president of the United States. He had been preceded by thirty-six others."

**—Gerald Ford**

"If God had wanted us to use the metric system, Jesus would have had ten apostles."

**—Jesse Helms (R-NC)**

"This legislation has far-reaching ramifistations."

**—Gib Lewis (D-TX)**

"I didn't intend for this to take on a political tone. I'm just here for the drugs."

**—Nancy Reagan, *asked a political question during a "Just Say No" rally***

"I am not a chauvinist, obviously....I believe in women's rights for every woman but my own."

**—Harold Washington (D), *mayor of Chicago, 1984–87***

"Those who survived the San Francisco earthquake said, 'Thank God, I'm still alive.' But, of course, those who died—their lives will never be the same again."

**—Barbara Boxer (D-CA)**

"The state of California has no business subsidizing intellectual curiosity."

**—Gov. Ronald Reagan, (R-CA), *responding to student protests on college campuses***

"Politics would be a helluva good business if it weren't for the goddamned people."

**—Richard Nixon**

# THE KING OF COTTON

*When you hear the name Eli Whitney, you probably think of his invention, the cotton gin. But you may not realize how profoundly it (and his other inventions) changed the world. Here's the history they never taught you in school.*

## LOOKING FOR WORK

In 1792 a 27-year-old Massachusetts Yankee named Eli Whitney graduated from Yale University and landed a tutoring job in South Carolina. He was glad to get it—he needed the money to pay off his school debts. But when he arrived there he discovered that the job paid half of what he'd been promised, which meant he'd never be able to save any money. He turned the job down.

Suddenly he was jobless, penniless, and stranded in the South, hundreds of miles from home. But he'd made the trip from New York with a friend named Phineas Miller, who was escorting *his* employer, a widow named Mrs. Greene, back to Georgia. When Greene invited Whitney to spend a week at her plantation outside of Savannah, he gladly accepted. He had no place else to go.

Whitney repaid Mrs. Greene's generosity by designing an embroidery frame for her. Greene was impressed by the cleverness of the design, and it got her thinking. If Whitney was this clever, maybe he could solve a problem that plagued her and other planters—how to "gin," or remove the seeds from, cotton...without doing it by hand.

Upland cotton, the only kind that grew in the interior regions of the South, had seeds that were "covered with a kind of green coat resembling velvet," as Whitney put it. These fuzzy seeds stuck to the cotton fibers like Velcro. Removing them by hand required so much labor—one person could clean only about a pound of cotton per day—that upland cotton was essentially worthless.

## MASS PRODUCTION

If a way could be found to remove the seeds more easily, upland cotton had the potential to become a very valuable export crop. Why? The Industrial Revolution had transformed the English tex-

**The word *ecology* comes from the Greek word for "household."**

tile industry (which turned the cotton into thread and the thread into cloth) into a monster and caused demand for cotton to soar.

As late as the 1730s, spinners and weavers made cloth just as they had for centuries: slowly and by hand. One person, sitting at a spinning wheel, could spin raw cotton into only one string of yarn at a time. It took 14 days to make a pound of yarn, which one or two weavers could then weave into a single piece of cloth.

In the mid-1700s, English inventions with colorful names like the flying shuttle (1733), the spinning jenny (1764), the water frame (1769), and the mule (1779), changed all that; so did the introduction of steam power in 1785. Now a single unskilled laborer—even a child or someone formerly thought too old to work—could tend machines that made hundreds and eventually thousands of strands of yarn at once, or that wove it into yards and yards of cloth, faster than the eye could see.

## THE BIG BANG

Because of these inventions, the English textile industry's appetite for cotton became enormous and grew exponentially from year to year. In 1765 spinners and weavers in England had turned half a million pounds of cotton into cloth; by 1790 the new machines were consuming 28 million pounds of cotton per year, nearly all of it imported from other countries. As demand for raw cotton soared, it got harder and harder to find enough of it to feed all of the new machines.

How much of the imported raw cotton came from the American South? Almost none. As late as 1791, the year before Whitney arrived in Georgia, exports for the entire South totaled a few hundred bags at most. But not for long.

## NO PROBLEM

So how long did it take Whitney to solve the problem that had vexed Southern planters for years? Ten days. It took several months to perfect the design, but after just 10 days, this Yankee, who'd landed at Greene's plantation purely by chance, managed to invent this revolutionary machine.

The design was so simple that it was a wonder nobody else had thought of it before. It consisted of a wooden roller with wire "teeth" that grabbed the cotton fibers and pulled them through a slotted iron screen. The slots in the screen were wide enough to let the teeth and the cotton fibers through, but they were too narrow for the seeds, which separated out and fell into a box.

A rapidly rotating brush then removed the cotton fibers from the teeth and flung them into a bin. This allowed the user to feed raw cotton into the machine indefinitely, without having to stop every few minutes to clean the teeth.

Using Whitney's cotton gin, in one day a laborer could clean as much as 10 pounds of upland cotton, which before would have taken 10 days to clean by hand. If a larger gin powered by water or a horse was used, a laborer could clean as much cotton in one day as would have taken more than *seven weeks* to clean by hand.

## BRAVE NEW WORLD

Over the next several decades, Whitney's cotton gin transformed the South. Tens of thousands and eventually millions of acres of wilderness were cleared to make way for enormous cotton plantations. By 1810 U.S. exports of cotton to England had grown from almost nothing to 38 million pounds, making the South the largest supplier of cotton to that country.

And that was only the beginning. By the start of the Civil War, the Southern "cotton belt," as it came to be known, was exporting *920 million* pounds of cotton to England each year, more than 90% of its cotton imports. Cotton had become, as one historian described it, "the largest single source of America's growing wealth." Cotton was king.

## THE CLOTHES ON YOUR BACK

But Whitney's invention had more far-reaching effects than increasing U.S. exports. The industrialization of cotton production vastly increased the supply of cotton cloth. That changed cotton from one of the most expensive fabrics on Earth to one of the cheapest—and in the process, it clothed the world.

Between 1785, the year that steam power was introduced to the textile industry, and the early 1860s, the price of cotton cloth fell by more than 99%. That's the equivalent of a price of Tommy Hilfiger jeans falling from $5,000 to $50.

In the past almost no one had been able to afford cotton, (how many $5,000 pairs of jeans could you afford?), and things like

**Odds that someone caught shoplifting is a teenager: 50%.**

leather and wool made poor substitutes. (Don't believe it? Treat yourself to a pair of wool underpants and you'll see what we mean.) "Most of humanity," historian Paul Johnson writes in *A History of the American People*, "were unsuitably clothed in garments which were difficult to wash and therefore filthy."

Cheap, abundant cotton cloth changed that, too. "There is no instance in world history where the price of a product in potentially universal demand came down so fast," Johnson writes. "As a result, hundreds of millions of people, all over the world, were able to dress comfortably and cleanly at last."

## CHAINS OF COTTON

There is yet another aspect to Eli Whitney's cotton gin—an ugly, inhuman side, that cast a shadow over all of the good it did. Many Americans think of Whitney's invention as an emancipator, a machine that freed the slaves from having to do the hand ginning of cotton. On the contrary, the rise of cotton cultivation in the South actually helped to entrench the institution of slavery, condemning millions of black Americans to its horrors just when many opponents of slavery thought it might finally be dying out.

Between 1775 and 1800 the price of slaves had fallen from about $100 per slave to $50, and abolitionists predicted that if the institution were left alone, it would die on its own. Or at the very least, as slavery weakened, it would become easier to abolish.

But the invention of the cotton gin changed everything. As the amount of acreage brought under cultivation in the South soared, so did the demand for slaves to work the plantations. Between 1800 and 1850, the price of a slave rose from $50 to as much as $1,000. Slavery, formerly thought to be in decline, quickly became integral to the new Southern economy.

As such, the leaders of the Southern states became increasingly militant in their determination to defend it and even expand it beyond the South. For a new generation of Southern leaders, the institution of slavery—because of the prosperity that came with it—was something to be defended, even to the death.

The cotton gin had made it happen... and made the Civil War inevitable.

***Part II of the story of Eli Whitney starts on page 167.***

**Dolphins can hear underwater sounds from as far as 15 miles away.**

# IS THIS BRAIN LOADED?

*Before they allow some people to buy guns, maybe police should skip the background check and give the applicants an IQ test. Here's why.*

• A Washington man became frustrated trying to untangle Christmas lights in his driveway and became even more frustrated when his daughter came home and drove over them. So he went inside, got his .45-caliber pistol, took it into his backyard, and fired several shots into the ground, after which he was arrested.

• A man at Dallas–Fort Worth Airport damaged a window and caused panic among passengers when he accidentally fired his hunting rifle at a security checkpoint. The gun went off while he was demonstrating to guards that it wasn't loaded.

• A 32-year-old man was treated for a gunshot wound in his thigh in a Kentucky hospital. He had accidentally shot himself, he explained, while practicing his quick draw...with a snowman.

• Daniel Carson Lewis was charged with criminal mischief, driving while intoxicated, weapons misconduct, and assault after shooting a hole in the Alaskan Pipeline north of Fairbanks. Result: 280,000 gallons of crude oil were spilled over two acres of tundra before crews could stop the leak, the worst in about 20 years. Cleanup costs were estimated at $7 million. He did it, said his brother, "just to see if he could." He faces up to 10 years in prison.

• Chaddrick Dickson, 25, was treated for wounds received while trying to get the gunpowder out of a .22-caliber bullet by holding it with pliers and smashing it on the floor. The bullet exploded, hitting him in the leg. Dickson needed the gunpowder, he said, to put in his dog's food "to make him meaner."

• To get the attention of officers in a passing police car after getting a flat tire, a man in Pretoria, South Africa, shot his gun at it. The officers didn't help him with the flat, but they did charge him with attempted murder.

**Most popular seafood in America: tuna. The average American eats 3.6 pounds a year.**

# INVASION OF THE FRANKENFISH

*We don't want to scare you, but some strange creatures have been showing up on our doorsteps lately. They weren't invited... and they won't go away.*

**INVADING SPECIES:** Golden Apple Snail

**BACKGROUND:** A native of South America, the golden apple snail became a popular addition to aquariums around the world because it is considered "pretty." In the early 1980s, some private snail farms found a new use for the easy-to-raise, protein-rich snails. They were shipped to snail farmers in Taiwan and the Philippines in the hopes of starting escargot industries.

**LOCK THE DOORS, HERE THEY COME:** Unfortunately, the escargot business never took off and prices plummeted, so farmers simply dumped the snails. Bad idea. Golden apple snails are voracious eaters, munching continuously for up to 24 hours a day, and their preferred food is rice seedlings. And what's the primary source of food and employment in Asia? Rice.

Laying as many as 500 eggs a week, the renegade snails quickly multiplied. By the mid-1990s they had destroyed an estimated two million acres of rice fields in the Philippines alone, and had spread to nearly every Asian nation, causing billions of dollars in damage.

And they're not done yet. The snails were discovered in U.S. waters in the 1990s, probably escapees or throwaways from aquariums. Several states have made owning a golden apple snail a crime.

**INVADING SPECIES:** Zebra Mussel

**BACKGROUND:** Originally from the Caspian Sea in Russia, by the 1800s, this freshwater mollusk had spread into other waterways in western Europe. In 1988 the zebra mussel showed up on this side of the Atlantic. How? Transatlantic ships probably brought the mussels over in their ballast tanks and unknowingly dumped them into North American ports.

**LOCK THE DOORS, HERE THEY COME:** Female zebra

mussels produce as many as a million eggs per year, with a very high survival rate. Once they appear, they take over, depleting rivers and lakes of oxygen and killing off native clams, snails, and fish. Not only that, they get into water pipes that feed to power plants and public waterworks, causing massive clogs. It's estimated that they cause $5 billion of damage every year. By 2002 they had spread to the Mississippi, Arkansas, Illinois, Ohio, and Tennessee Rivers . . . and they're still on the move.

**MORE BAD NEWS:** The zebra mussel brought a friend. The small (10-inch) but superaggressive round goby fish tagged along in the ballast tanks and has found a new home in the Great Lakes. Its long breeding period and ability to feed in complete darkness give it a competitive edge over native fish species . . . which it eats. The fact that it eats baby mussels too—though not enough to control them—means that the goby has an unlimited food source and will likely follow the zebra mussel, wreaking havoc throughout the Mississippi River system and beyond.

**INVADING SPECIES:** Northern Snakehead Fish

**BACKGROUND:** This Chinese fish is considered a delicacy in Asia. You can find them in some Asian markets in the United States. In June 2002, a man was fishing a pond in Crofton, Maryland, when he caught a fish he didn't recognize. Biologists later identified the 26-inch specimen as a snakehead. How'd it get there? An unnamed man admitted to dumping his two pet snakeheads after he got tired of feeding them. A subsequent search of the pond turned up more than 100 babies.

**LOCK THE DOORS, HERE THEY COME:** The snakehead, dubbed "Frankenfish" by the press, can get up to three feet long and an adult can eat prey as large as itself . . . including birds and small mammals. Worse: With no natural predators, it can devour everything in sight. Then, if conditions are just right, it can use its long fins as legs to *crawl across land to find a new pond or river*. It can actually survive on land for up to four days.

Officials are hoping that hasn't happened yet and said they'll use a pesticide to kill the snakeheads—and everything else in the pond—just so the Frankenfish doesn't spread. "It's not a dead or alive thing," biologist Bob Lunsford told the *Washington Post*, "we just want it dead."

**. . . Western astronomers did. (And then many Westerners mistook them for planets.)**

# I WANT TO RIDE MY BICYCLE!

*It took dozens of tries and more than a century—not to mention a lot of scraped knees and broken bones—to develop the bicycle. Here's the story.*

## ROLL CALL

Humanity has had the wheel for thousands of years, but not until about 200 years ago were people able to use the wheel to get around without the aid of a horse or some other animal.

Exactly when and where the idea for the bicycle originated is unknown. Some historians claim that images of crude machines resembling bikes appeared on the walls of Egyptian tombs. Others argue that the ancient Romans had them in the city of Pompeii. There is even a drawing of a machine that resembles a modern bicycle in *Codex Atlanticus*, a collection of Leonardo da Vinci's mechanical drawings from 1493, but whether or not Da Vinci drew it is heavily disputed (many argue it was forged by the monks who were restoring the drawings in the 1970s). So for all intents and purposes, the history of the bicycle doesn't begin until very recently: the turn of the 19th century.

## STOP HORSING AROUND

The first known bike was based on a toy. In 1790 in Versailles, France, the Comte Mede de Sivrac built an adult-sized version of a child's hobbyhorse. He called it the *velocifere*, Latin for "fast" and "carry." Judith Crown and Glenn Coleman describe it in their book *No Hands*:

> It must have been a delightfully silly sight: two wood wheels joined by a stub of beam, saddled and shaped to resemble a horse, with de Sivrac running wildly astride it until the thing rolled fast enough to coast a few yards. Fashionable aristocrats soon were huffing across the royal gardens on their own velociferes—some machines outfitted as horses, others as lions or serpents—lifting their legs gleefully as they spun past amused pedestrians.

As much fun as the velocifere may have been, it was equally danger-

**On the very first traffic light (London, 1868), red meant "stop" and green meant "caution."**

ous. It lacked two important features—steering and brakes. Riders and unsuspecting pedestrians were injured so often that the craze soon fizzled out and wouldn't be tried again for almost 30 years.

## YABBA DABBA DO

A German man named Baron Karl von Drais de Saverbrun wasn't fond of horses, finding them stubborn and moody, difficult to groom and saddle, and constantly leaving piles in their wake. Unfortunately, his job required that he ride one. He was the "master of forests," a land surveyor for the wealthy duke of Baden's very large estate. Von Drais needed some way to travel short distances without a horse.

In 1817, using the velocifere for inspiration, von Drais invented a new machine. It looked sort of like a modern bike but operated more like something out of the *Flintstones*: it had no pedals, so it required "foot power" to move it along. Von Drais's machine was constructed entirely out of wood, weighed about 50 pounds, and was steered by handlebars connected to the front wheel. The rider leaned forward on a belly brace—a cushioned piece of wood that rested beneath the handlebars—and pushed off with his feet. By leaning forward, the rider could coast along at speeds of up to 10 mph. Von Drais called it the *Laufsmachine*, or "walking machine," but most people referred to it as the *draisienne*.

Von Drais sold several of his machines to the French postal service. They were praised at first, but complaints of injuries soon started coming in. Although draisiennes rode well on the smooth fields that surrounded Duke of Baden's property, they were no match for the potholes, hills, and harsh weather that the postal carriers often encountered—not to mention the fact that the rider's feet were the closest thing the draisienne had to brakes. But despite its shortcomings, the draisienne got people excited about the possibilities of self-propelled machine travel.

## IRONING OUT THE ERRORS

Working around the same time as von Drais, an English coach maker named Denis Johnson came up with a better solution. He created the "hobby horse," a version of the draisienne made out of wrought iron instead of wood. Like the draisienne, his machine lacked pedals, but the durable iron body was a vast improvement

**More ships have been sunk by hurricanes than by warfare.**

over wood and made for a much smoother ride. Johnson sold some "hobby horses" to wealthy Londoners, but creating them was so expensive, time consuming, and unprofitable that he soon stopped production.

## PUT THE PEDAL TO THE METAL

Sometimes necessity is the mother of invention; at other times, boredom is. In 1839 a Scottish blacksmith named Kirkpatrick MacMillan changed transportation forever when he decided to pass the hours of a slow day away by tinkering with an old "hobby horse." He pondered the idea of attaching iron rods and foot pedals to the rear wheel. That way, he figured, riders could move the machine without having to push their feet against the ground. Rather, the rods and the pedals would crank the rear wheel and create motion, much like the locomotive, another recent invention. MacMillan built a prototype, gave it a ride, and lo and behold, it worked!

Being a natural showman, MacMillan amazed townspeople by riding his contraption at top speeds through the streets. But instead of being revered as a great invention, his new "hobby horse" was viewed as a dangerous menace. MacMillan could often be seen crashing into trees and flying over the handlebars. His escapades were put to an abrupt end when he was arrested for knocking down a small child in 1842 (the first known cyclist-related offense).

Although he never really marketed his invention and died before it caught on with the masses, many regard MacMillan as the father of the modern bicycle. A plaque is displayed at the site of his blacksmith shop which reads: "Kirkpatrick MacMillan: He builded better than he knew."

***Round and round and round she goes. For Part II of the story, just follow your nose...to page 205.***

# SHARK ATTACK!

*Ever since Uncle John saw* Jaws, *he's been afraid of the ocean. This list of shark facts didn't help.*

• Sharks can detect the heartbeats of other fish.

• Mako sharks have been known to jump into the very fishing boats that are pursuing them.

• Bull sharks have been known to kill hippopotamuses in African rivers.

• Approximately 10 times more men than women are attacked by sharks.

• While in a feeding frenzy, some sharks bite their own bodies as they twist and turn.

• A 730-pound mako shark caught off Bimini in the Bahamas contained in its stomach a 120-pound swordfish—with the sword still intact.

• Lemon sharks grow a whole new set of teeth every two weeks.

• Sharks have a sixth sense. They can navigate by sensing changes in the Earth's magnetic field.

• Sharks will continue to attack even when disemboweled.

• Greenland sharks have been observed eating reindeer when they fall through ice.

• Three men who spent five days adrift in the Atlantic in 1980 had a shark to thank for their rescue. They fell asleep, but when the attacking shark nudged their raft, they woke up...in time to flag down a passing freighter.

• Some sharks can detect one part of blood in 100 million parts of water.

• Bull sharks have been known to pursue their victims onto land.

• The jaws of an eight-foot shark exert a force of 20 tons per square inch.

• The average shark can swallow anything half its size in one gulp.

• The original idea for steak knives derived from shark teeth.

• Approximately 100 shark attacks on humans occur worldwide each year.

# WRITING ON THE WALL

*Why do writers write? These quotes from famous authors may provide some answers.*

"I write for the same reason I breathe—because if I didn't, I would die."

**—Isaac Asimov**

"The good writing of any age has always been the product of *someone's* neurosis, and we'd have mighty dull literature if all the writers that came along were a bunch of happy chuckleheads."

**—William Styron**

"My first rule is, if it sounds like writing, rewrite it. Another rule is to try to leave out the parts people skip. Oh, and never start with the weather. With those rules you can go all the way."

**—Elmore Leonard**

"Contrary to what you might think, a career in letters is not without its drawbacks—chief among them the unpleasant fact that one is frequently called upon to sit down and write."

**—Fran Lebowitz**

"I'm so sick of Nancy Drew I could vomit."

**—Mildred Benson, *author of 23 Nancy Drew novels***

"You don't write because you want to say something; you write because you've got something to say."

**—F. Scott Fitzgerald**

"The best time for planning a book is when you're doing the dishes."

**—Agatha Christie**

"People want to know why I do this, why I write such gross stuff. I like to tell them that I have the heart of a small boy…and I keep it in a jar on my desk."

**—Stephen King**

"I don't want to sound commercial, but I'm in it for the money, not the awards. This is my job; it's how I feed my family. What do I care if someone reads my books a hundred years from now? I'll be dead."

**—Tom Clancy**

"We write to taste life twice."

**—Anais Nin**

"There are three rules for writing a novel. Unfortunately, no one knows what they are."

**—W. Somerset Maugham**

# GREAT STORY... JUST CHANGE THE ENDING

*It might surprise you to learn that some of your favorite movies were changed from the originals to "improve" them. Did it work? Here are a few examples. You be the judge.*

### *A FISH CALLED WANDA* (1988)

**Original Ending:** More in line with the dark and deceitful nature of the characters, Otto (Kevin Kline) gets killed by the steamroller. And Wanda (Jamie Lee Curtis) ditches Archie (John Cleese) at the airport, keeping all of the stolen jewels for herself.

**But Wait:** Test audiences didn't approve. Two more endings were filmed before viewers were satisfied—Otto lives, and Wanda and Archie go to South America together. The result: *A Fish Called Wanda* was a box-office smash, bringing in nearly $200 million.

### *BLADE RUNNER* (1982)

**Original Ending:** Director Ridley Scott's original existential ending confused test audiences, leaving many questions unanswered, most notably Deckard's (Harrison Ford) identity. Was he a replicant or not?

**But Wait:** Warner Bros. had invested a lot in the film and ordered Scott to "fix it." Reluctantly, he added narration by Ford and filmed a more typically violent Hollywood ending in which Deckard is indeed a replicant. Ten years later, in one of the first "director's cut" videos, Scott restored the film to his original vision. Which one is better? Both are available, so you can decide for yourself.

### *THE SCARLET LETTER* (1995)

**Original Ending:** Hollywood is notorious for altering novels but it outdid itself with this one. In Nathaniel Hawthorne's classic tale, Hester Prynne is judged an adulteress and sentenced to wear the letter "A" for the remainder of her days. After her secret lover confesses to the people, he dies in Hester's arms—an ending that echoed the sentiment of the times.

**The Cliffs Notes edition of *The Scarlet Letter* outsells Nathaniel Hawthorne's edition by 3 to 1.**

**But Wait:** Demi Moore's Hester is a bit more "modern"—she gets revenge on her oppressors and the reunited family lives happily ever after. Defending the new ending, Moore attested that "not many people have read the book anyway." Even fewer people saw the movie.

### *FATAL ATTRACTION* (1987)

**Original Ending:** Dan (Michael Douglas) is charged with murder as we hear a voice-over of Alex's (Glenn Close) suicidal confession. Test audiences yawned their disapproval.

**But Wait:** Months after filming was completed, the cast was called back to film the more climactic ending in which Dan's wife (Anne Archer) murders Alex in the bathtub.

### *BUTCH CASSIDY AND THE SUNDANCE KID* (1969)

**Original Ending:** Paul Newman's and Robert Redford's characters are shot by soldiers in a gruesome death scene.

**But Wait:** The version released to the public ends with a freeze-frame of the two stars making their final charge, thereby immortalizing them instead of killing them.

### *THELMA AND LOUISE* (1991)

**Original Ending:** Similar to *Butch Cassidy and the Sundance Kid*, Geena Davis and Susan Sarandon's car falls all the way to the canyon floor, presumably smashing them to bits.

**But Wait:** Fearing a negative reaction to killing off the film's stars, the theatrical release shows their car sailing off the cliff, but leaves their fates up in the air, so to speak. The DVD includes the alternate ending.

### *THE PRINCESS DIARIES* (2001)

**Original Ending:** The original finale had Mia (Anne Hathaway) simply agreeing to fly off to the fabled European kingdom of Genovia to become a princess.

**But Wait:** Director Garry Marshall's five-year-old granddaughter felt shortchanged; she wanted to see the castle. Marshall acquiesced and had Disney buy stock footage of a European castle and digitally add the flag of Genovia to it. "It cost us a penny or two," explained Marshall, "but it made my granddaughter happy."

**Charge! First year Americans used credit cards more than cash: 1995.**

# MOTHERS OF INVENTION

*There have always been women inventors...even if they've been overlooked by the history books. Here are a few you may not have heard of.*

**MARY ANDERSON**

**Invention:** Windshield wipers

**Background:** In 1903 Anderson, an Alabaman, took a trip to New York City. One snowy afternoon she decided to tour the city by streetcar, but instead of sightseeing found herself staring at the streetcar conductor, who had to keep stopping to wipe the snow off his windshield.

On the spot, Anderson made a drawing in her sketchbook of a device consisting of a lever that "activated a swinging arm that mechanically swept off the ice and snow" from the windshield. She got her patent the following year; ten years later windshield wipers were standard equipment on automobiles.

**DONNA SHIRLEY**

**Invention:** Sojourner Mars Rover

**Background:** In 1991 Shirley, an aerospace engineer, was appointed manager of NASA's Mars Explorer Program. Her team was charged with developing the rover vehicle that would go to Mars aboard the unmanned Pathfinder spacecraft. The rover was to be about the size of a pickup truck, with rockets to blast it off the surface of Mars and back to the Pathfinder for its return to Earth. They'd already built a one-eighth-scale prototype; now they were using it to design the full-scale rover.

There was just one problem: sending a truck-sized rover to Mars and then returning it to Earth was too expensive. The craft only had a budget of $25 million. That may seem like a lot but, says Shirley, "for a planetary spacecraft it's incredibly cheap; $25 million would pay for a few commercials for the Super Bowl."

That's when Shirley got the idea that saved the mission. "While her male colleagues were ready to scrap the whole project,

**A man once lost his car in parking garage for two years. The tab: $3,400.**

Shirley suggested that perhaps size was not that important," Ethlie Vare writes in *Patently Female*. "Could not the prototype of the rover become the vehicle itself?"

It could and it did: On July 4, 1997, the Sojourner Rover landed on Mars and began exploring the surface. It's going to be there a while, too—the rockets that were supposed to send it home got cut from the budget.

## LAURA SCUDDER

**Invention:** Potato chip bag

**Background:** Before a Southern California businesswoman named Laura Scudder came along in the mid-1920s, potato chips were sold in bulk in large barrels. When you bought chips at the store, the grocer scooped them out of the barrel and into an ordinary paper bag. If you got your chips from the bottom of the barrel, they were usually broken and stale.

It was Laura Scudder who hit on the idea of taking wax paper and ironing it on three sides to make a bag, then filling it with potato chips and ironing the fourth side to make an airtight pouch that would keep the chips fresh until they were eaten. Scudder's self-serve, stay-fresh bags were instrumental in turning potato chips from an occasional treat into a snack food staple.

## MARTHA COSTON

**Invention:** Signal flare

**Background:** Martha Hunt was only 14 when she eloped with a Philadelphia engineer named Benjamin Coston...and only 21 when he died bankrupt in 1848, leaving her destitute with four small children. Not long after his death she found something interesting among his possessions: a prototype for a signal flare. She hoped that if it worked, she could patent it and use it to restore her family's fortunes.

But it didn't—so Martha started over from scratch, and spent nearly 10 years perfecting a system of red, white, and green "Pyrotechnic Night Signals" that would enable naval ships to communicate by color codes over great distances at night. (Remember, this was before the invention of two-way radio.) The U.S. Navy bought hundreds of sets of flares and used them extensively during the Civil War. They are credited with helping main-

**Amount Tiger Woods's caddie made in 2000: $1 million.**

tain the Union blockade of Confederate ports, and also with saving the lives of countless shipwreck victims after the war.

### ROMMY REVSON

**Invention:** Scünci

**Background:** In 1987 Revson was divorced from Revlon cosmetics heir John Revson, and the divorce settlement was so bad that she had to find a job to support herself. Appearances count, so she had her hair bleached before she started applying for jobs. Big mistake—the chemicals damaged her hair to the point that "it was coming off in handfuls," Revson remembers. She decided the only thing to do was pull her hair back into a ponytail, but it was so brittle that she couldn't use rubber bands. She came up with something better: an elastic band covered with soft fabric.

So did Revson ever get around to applying for a job? Who knows—she decided to patent her ponytail holder instead, naming it the Scünci after her Lhasa Apso puppy. Today they're better known as "scrunchies," and at last count Revson has sold more than two billion of them.

*  *  *

## SPEEDY JUSTICE

**Defendant:** John Cracken, a Texas personal injury lawyer

**The Crime:** Flaunting his wealth in public

**Background:** In 1991 Cracken represented a disabled widow in a lawsuit against her husband's employer, the Rock-Tenn Company. Rock-Tenn was a recycling company, and the man was killed in a bailing machine. Cracken sued for $25 million, but Rock-Tenn's case was so weak that there was talk that the jury might award as much as $60 million. Shortly before deliberations were to begin, however, some of the jurors happened to spot Cracken in the courthouse parking garage, driving a brand-new red Porsche 911.

**The Sentence:** The jury awarded Cracken's client only $5 million. Why so little? One juror explained, "There was no way I'm going to buy that lawyer another fancy car."

# UNCLE JOHN'S PAGE OF LISTS

*Some random bits from the BRI files.*

**5 Most Germ-ridden Places at Work**

1. Phone
2. Desktop
3. Water fountain handle
4. Microwave door handle
5. Keyboard

**5 Movies That Feature a One-Armed Man**

1. *Bad Day at Black Rock* (1955)
2. *The One-Armed Swordsman* (1967)
3. *The Fugitive* (1993)
4. *The Blade* (1995)
5. *Twin Peaks: Fire Walk with Me* (1992)

**7 States with Lowest Life Expectancy**

1. South Carolina
2. Mississippi
3. Georgia
4. Louisiana
5. Nevada
6. Alabama
7. North Carolina

**4 Forest Service Tips on What to Do if You Encounter a Cougar**

1. Don't "play dead"
2. Be aggressive Don't act like prey
3. Don't run
4. Blow an air horn (if one's handy)

**3 Most Dangerous Foods to Eat in a Car**

1. Coffee
2. Tacos
3. Chili

**2 Topics at the 2002 Taiwan Toilet Seminar**

1. Practical Means to Eliminate Bad Smells in Toilets
2. Citizen's Satisfaction of Public Toilets in Korea

**2 Famous Number Threes**

1. Dale Earnhardt
2. Babe Ruth

**7 Places You Can Legally Carry a Concealed Weapon in Utah**

1. A car
2. A city bus
3. A train
4. A mall
5. A bar
6. A church
7. A school

**3 Things Rats Can Do**

1. Wriggle through a hole the size of a quarter
2. Survive being flushed down a toilet
3. Multiply so fast a single pair could have 15,000 descendants in a year

**5 Things That Have Been Sold in Vending Machines**

1. Emu jerky
2. Poached eggs
3. Holy water
4. Beetles
5. Live shrimp

# YOU AIN'T GOT IT, KID

*It's hard to imagine anyone rejecting the opportunity to hire Harrison Ford, but people make mistakes. Here are a few examples of a few unbelievable rejections.*

**What They Said:** "With your voice, nobody is going to let you broadcast."
**Who Said It:** CBS producer Don Hewitt, 1958
**Rejected!** Barbara Walters (she signed with NBC)

**What They Said:** "Stiff, unappealing. You ain't got it, kid."
**Who Said It:** Columbia producer Jerry Tokovsky, 1965
**Rejected!** Harrison Ford

**What They Said:** "You have a chip on your tooth, your Adam's apple sticks out too far, and you talk too slow."
**Who Said It:** Universal Pictures executive, 1959
**Rejected!** Clint Eastwood

**What They Said:** "The girl doesn't have a special perception or feeling which will lift that book above the curiosity level."
**Who Said It:** Anonymous publisher, 1952
**Rejected!** *The Diary of Anne Frank*

**What They Said:** "Go learn to cook. Your book will never sell."
**Who Said It:** A literary agent in the early 1970s
**Rejected!** Danielle Steel, who got a new agent, and has since sold over 350 million books.

**What They Said:** "The band's okay but, if I were you, I'd get rid of the singer with the tire-tread lips."
**Who Said It:** BBC radio producer at a 1963 audition
**Rejected!** The Rolling Stones—and their lead singer, Mick Jagger

**What They Said:** "His ears are too big. He looks like an ape."
**Who Said It:** Talent scout Darryl F. Zanuck
**Rejected!** Clark Gable

***Companion* is from the Latin *com*, "with," and *panis*, "bread"—one you break bread with.**

# NEW VIETNAM

*Most families vacation in Florida because of the warm weather and abundance of theme parks. You can shake hands with Mickey Mouse at Disney World, feed the dolphins at SeaWorld... and duck and cover in New Vietnam. Well, at least that was the idea.*

## BACKGROUND

In 1975 Reverend Carl McIntire, a New Jersey fundamentalist preacher and pro-Vietnam War activist, began construction on what was to be "New Vietnam." Spread out over 300 acres of land in Cape Canaveral, Florida, McIntire and his partner, former Green Beret Giles Pace, envisioned a theme park where people could get a glimpse of the Vietnam War.

What would the theme park look like? Here are a few of the attractions McIntire planned:

• ***Sampan* ride.** A *sampan* is an Asian sailboat. Tourists would take a sampan ride around a moat that encircled a recreated Vietnamese village with a neighboring Special Forces camp.

• **Special Forces camp.** The camp would be made up of simple concrete barracks displaying weapons "used by the Commies in Vietnam." Around the barracks would be trenches and mortar bunkers complete with sandbag walls and sham machine guns.

• **The perimeter.** The camp would be surrounded with row upon row of barbed wire, *punji* stakes, and fake Claymore mines to add to the atmosphere. "We'll have a recording, broadcasting a firefight, mortars exploding, bullets flying, Vietnamese screaming," McIntire explained, while hired GIs shoot blanks at the enemy. Visitors would be encouraged to take cover in the barracks or station themselves behind a machine gun and get in on the action.

• **A Vietnamese village.** The village would be made up of 16 thatched huts and four concrete upper-class Vietnamese homes that would double as retail shops and snack bars serving traditional Vietnamese cuisine. So after working up an appetite manning the machine guns, park visitors could stop in for a bowl of rice and noodles. The village was to be completely authentic, with irrigated

**That little statue on the grill of every Rolls Royce car has a name: "Spirit of Ecstasy."**

paddies, water buffalo, cows, chickens, ducks, and palm trees.

• **Vietnamese people.** Vietnamese people—real refugees from the real war—would travel through the village in traditional outfits and make New Vietnam come to life. McIntire planned this as a make-work program for Vietnamese refugees arriving in Florida at the end of the war. "Every penny will go back to the Vietnamese. The Bible says love your neighbor."

"They'll work anywhere for a paycheck," Pace commented. "And this will be work that won't be in competition with anyone else. There's nothing offensive about it."

## INTO THE MORASS

The idea bombed and the park was never completed. Vietnamese refugees, having just experienced the horrors of a real war, weren't about to participate in a fake one. "My wife won't walk around that village in a costume like Mickey Mouse," refugee Cong Nguyen Binh told reporters. "We want to forget. We want to live here like you. We don't want any more war."

*  *  *

## MISNOMERS

• The rare **red** coral of the Mediterranean is actually **blue**.

• The **gray** whale is actually **black**.

• Whale**bone** is actually made of **baleen**, a material from the whales' upper jaws.

• The Atlantic **salmon** is actually a member of the **trout** family.

• **Heart**burn is actually pyrosis, caused by the presence of gastric secretions, called reflux, in the lower **esophagus**.

• The Caspian **Sea** and the Dead **Sea** are both actually **lakes**.

• The horseshoe **crab** is more closely related to **spiders** and **scorpions** than crabs.

• The Douglas **fir** is actually a **pine** tree.

• A **steel**-jacketed bullet is actually made of **brass**.

• Rip**tides** are actually **currents**.

# HAPPY HOLIDAYS

*Here's some holiday trivia you may not have come across before.*

## LABOR DAY

In 1893 amid growing labor unrest, President Grover Cleveland sent 12,000 federal troops to stop a strike at the Pullman train car company in Chicago. The strike was broken, but two men were killed and many more were beaten. For Cleveland and the Democrats, the move backfired—the pro-business brutality only served to bolster the growing union movement.

To win back constituents, Congress passed legislation the following year making the first Monday in September a national holiday honoring labor. It was a presidential election year, so President Cleveland promptly signed the bill into law, hoping it would appease American workers. It didn't. Cleveland was defeated...but Labor Day was established for good.

## GROUNDHOG DAY

February 2, the midpoint between winter solstice and spring equinox, has been celebrated for eons. The Celts called it *Imbolc* ("in the belly"—for sheep pregnant with lambs); Romans had *Lupercalia*, a fertility celebration. For other cultures, too, the day was marked by rituals of "rebirth" and hope for a bountiful new growing season.

According to Irish tradition, a snake emerges from "the womb of Earth" and tests the weather to see if spring has arrived. The Germans had a similar tradition, except that they watched for badgers waking from hibernation. If the day was a sunny, shadow-casting day, more winter weather was to come. No shadow meant an early spring.

When German settlers came to Pennsylvania in the 1700s, they brought the custom with them...but there were no badgers, so they substituted another hibernating animal: the groundhog.

## ~~COLUMBUS~~ AMERICAN INDIAN DAY

Attempts to designate a national day honoring Native Americans have been made—unsuccessfully—for nearly a century. In 1914 Red Fox James, a Blackfoot Indian, rode 4,000 miles on horseback

**The carnation's name means "fleshlike." (Their pink color reminded people of meat.)**

in support of a national day of recognition for Native Americans. He ended the journey in Washington, D.C., where his proposal for the holiday was adopted by 24 state governments. The state of New York became the first to officially designate an American Indian Day, in May 1916.

While it has yet to be recognized as a national holiday, several states, South Dakota being the first, have officially changed another time-honored holiday to American Indian Day: the second Monday in October—Columbus Day.

## MERRY MITHRAS

The Bible doesn't say when Jesus was born, but many historians think it was in April. So why is Christmas celebrated on December 25? One possible reason: *Mithras*. Mithras was a Persian diety known as The Conquering Sun, and his birthday was traditionally celebrated at the winter solstice in late December. Mithraism and Christianity were both becoming popular in the Mediterranean region at about the same time. But early Christians were determined to prevail, so they adopted December 25 as the date of the Nativity. By the third or fourth century A.D., the already popular day was firmly entrenched as Christmas.

*　　*　　*

## THIS AIN'T NO PARTY

In April 2002, a Veterans of Foreign Wars group in Utah issued a resolution demanding that the date of Earth Day be changed. Why? April 22 is former Soviet leader Vladimir Lenin's birthdate. The group refused to celebrate on the birthday of "the godless master of manipulation, misinformation, and murder."

Not only that, members claim the day was chosen intentionally and that former Wisconsin senator Gaylord Nelson, founder of Earth Day, is a communist sympathizer. "He voted against funding the Vietnam War," said one post commander.

The 86-year-old Nelson says it was a coincidence. "Several million people were born on any day of the year. Does the VFW want to change it to another day on which, undoubtedly, some really evil person was born? Hitler? Mussolini? Genghis Khan?"

Another April 22 birthday: St. Francis of Assisi.

**Q: What do you get when you add zinc to copper? A: Brass.**

# AMAZING COINCIDENCES

*We're constantly finding stories about amazing coincidences, so in this* Bathroom Reader, *Uncle John listed a few of his favorites.*

## NEEDS WORK

While eating dinner at Notting Hill Gate restaurant in 1992, a London publisher had her car broken into. One of the things taken from the car was a manuscript she had been reading and found extremely promising. Apparently the thieves weren't interested in literature, though—they threw the manuscript over a fence while driving away. On Monday morning she was desperately trying to come up with a way to explain how she lost the manuscript when the author called. Before she got a chance to apologize, the author asked, "Why did you have my manuscript thrown over my front fence?"

## STROKE OF LUCK

During the 1988 Olympic games in Seoul, South Korea, Karen Lord of Australia and Manuella Carosi of Italy swam in different heats of the women's 100-meter backstroke. Both finished with times of exactly one minute 4.69 seconds, tying them for 16th place. Only one swimmer could hold a lane in the consolation final, so Lord and Carosi were forced to swim again. Amazingly, after the swim-off the officials reported the times were exactly the same, one minute 5.05 seconds. Officials decided that the two had to swim yet one more time. At the end of the unprecedented third consecutive race Carosi was declared the winner. Her time: one minute 4.62 seconds. Lord's time: one minute 4.75 seconds—13 hundredths of a second behind.

## LONG SHOT

In 1893 Henry Ziegland of Texas jilted his fiancé, and she killed herself over it. Her brother swore revenge. He took his gun and went after Ziegland, shot him in the face and then turned the gun on himself. But the bullet only grazed Ziegland and then got lodged in a tree. Twenty years later, Ziegland was removing the tree that had the bullet buried in it, using dynamite to make the job easier. The explosion blasted the bullet out of the tree…striking Ziegland in the head and killing him.

## BANK ON IT

In 1977 Vincent Johnson and Frazier Black broke into the Austin, Texas, home of Mr. and Mrs. David Conner and stole two TVs and a checkbook. A few hours later, the two men showed up at a local bank with a check made out to themselves for $200. When they asked the teller to cash it for them, she asked them to wait a minute, and then called security. Why? The bank teller was Mrs. David Conner.

## OTHERWISE ENGAGED

Brenda Rawson became engaged to Christopher Firth in 1961. He gave her a diamond ring, but she lost it while they were on vacation in Lancashire, England. In 1979 she was talking to her husband's cousin, John. For some reason the conversation turned to metal detectors and John mentioned that 18 years earlier, one of his kids had discovered a diamond ring near Lancashire. It was her ring.

## SPARE ME

In 1971 Mrs. Willard Lovell of Berkeley, California, accidentally locked herself out of the house. She had spent 10 minutes trying to find a way in again when the postman arrived with a letter for her from her brother, who'd been staying with her a few weeks earlier. The letter contained a spare key to the house, which he had borrowed and forgotten to return.

*    *    *

## EAT YOUR WORDS

• *Zucchini* comes from an Italian word meaning "sweetest."

• The Sanskrit word *naranga*, meaning "fragrant," gives us our *orange*.

• *Tangerines* were named after the city of Tangier, Morocco, which was well known for the fruit.

# SMELLS LIKE...MURDER

*Premature death seems almost like an occupational hazard among rock stars. But that doesn't make fans—or conspiracy theorists—any less suspicious, particularly in the case of suicide. And this one seems more suspicious than most.*

**The Deceased:** Kurt Cobain, leader of Seattle grunge band Nirvana. Gained notoriety with the 1991 angst-filled anthem "Smells Like Teen Spirit."

**How He Died:** On April 8, 1994, an electrician spotted Cobain's dead body lying on the floor of a greenhouse room above the detached garage at the musician's Seattle residence. Police determined that Cobain had injected himself with heroin, then stuck a shotgun into his mouth and pulled the trigger. Near the body they found a "suicide note." According to media reports, Cobain's wallet, open to his driver's license, was next to the body, ostensibly to make identification easier after the blast to the head.

To the police (and most of the media), it looked like a clear case of another rock star destroyed by his demons. But did the police overlook evidence that might point to a different conclusion?

## SUSPICIOUS FACTS

• At the time Cobain was shot, he had three times the lethal dose of heroin in his blood. According to experts, even an addict like Cobain would be comatose with that level of the drug in his body, incapable of positioning a gun and pulling the trigger. Cobain had two fresh needle marks, one on each arm. Did he inject himself twice? If he was intent on committing suicide, why didn't he just let the overdose do its work? Or were the second injection and the shotgun blast the work of someone else?

• There were no legible fingerprints on the shotgun that killed Cobain. (The gun wasn't even tested for fingerprints until nearly a month after his death.) Fingerprints can be wiped off a gun, but is that what happened here? If so, who wiped the gun clean, and why?

• Only part of the "suicide note" found by Cobain's body sounds like he planned to kill himself—the last four lines—and some experts

**So *that's* why we bail water: The handle of a bucket or a kettle is called the *bail*.**

question whether those lines are in his handwriting.

Most of the note is an anguished apology to his fans for his lack of enthusiasm and seems more about his resignation from the music industry than suicide. (Shortly before his death he decided not to headline the Lollapalooza tour.) Only the last four lines are addressed to his wife and daughter. Was suicide an afterthought, or did he actually have no intention of killing himself?

• The driver's license by the body wasn't left there by Cobain—the first police officer on the scene found Cobain's wallet nearby and displayed the license by the body for photographs.

• Someone attempted to use Cobain's credit card until just hours before the body was discovered, even though, according to the coroner's report, Cobain had died four days earlier. Cobain himself had last used the card to buy a plane ticket from Los Angeles to Seattle on April 1. The card was not found in his wallet.

## WHAT REALLY HAPPENED?

If suicide seems unlikely, accidental death looks next to impossible. How could Cobain, a hardened addict, so seriously misjudge his heroin dose? After such a dose, could he have accidentally positioned the shotgun on his chest and pulled the trigger? And if suicide and accident are ruled out, that leaves only... murder. But who would have wanted to kill Cobain and make it appear a suicide?

## THE LOVE CONNECTION

Cobain's wife, rock star Courtney Love, was in the L.A. area at the time Cobain's body was discovered. But according to Tom Grant, an L.A. private investigator, Love may have been involved in a conspiracy to kill her husband, possibly with the aid of Michael Dewitt, the male nanny who lived at the Cobain residence. Possible motives according to Grant:

✔ Cobain may have told Love he was leaving her; if the pair divorced, Love would get half of Cobain's estate. With a suicide she would get it all.

✔ Cobain's record sales would increase after a suicide, giving Love even more money.

✔ Her own career would benefit. (Love's band, Hole, headlined the Lollapalooza tour in place of Cobain and Nirvana.)

**Gossip: Why did young Courtney Love do time in juvenile hall? For shoplifting a Kiss T-shirt.**

## IS THIS LOVE?

Grant has a unique perspective—Love hired him to find Cobain after Cobain escaped from a drug rehab center just a few days before he died. Grant continued his investigation after the body was found and was disturbed by the inconsistencies and contradictions in Love's behavior:

✔ Love phoned in a missing persons report on April 4, the day Cobain died, according to the coroner's report. Claiming she was Cobain's mother, Love told Seattle police he had bought a shotgun and was suicidal. But a receipt found on Cobain's body showed that his best friend Dylan Carlson bought the gun for him almost a week earlier, *before* Cobain entered rehab. According to Carlson, Cobain wanted the gun for protection, not suicide. By phoning in the report, was Love trying to plant the idea that Cobain was suicidal?

✔ Love directed Grant to look for Cobain in a number of Seattle hotels and to check out his drug dealers. Even though Dewitt, the nanny, had told Love he'd talked with Cobain at their residence on April 2, Love did not tell Grant he'd been seen there. Was Love trying to keep Grant from finding Cobain too soon?

✔ When Grant visited the Cobain residence with Carlson the day before Cobain's body was found, there was evidence that Dewitt had been there recently. (Neither Grant nor Carlson looked in the greenhouse.) Later that day Dewitt told friends he was leaving for Los Angeles. Grant says he had the feeling Dewitt was avoiding him.

✔ The electrician who found Cobain's body was hired by Love to check the security system at the residence and, according to Rosemary Carroll, Love's entertainment lawyer, she specifically told him to check the greenhouse. Was she setting him up to find the body?

## FADE AWAY

In the note found beside Kurt Cobain's body, his last words, before the disputed last four lines, were "…it's better to burn out than to fade away." Did he think shooting himself was the only way out of his apathetic malaise, or did he simply plan to leave the music scene near the peak of his popularity to avoid becoming just another mass-marketed rock star, ultimately drifting into irrelevance? The police investigation is closed…so we'll probably never know.

# VIDEO TREASURES

*Here's our latest installment of great movies you may have never seen. Take this with you the next time you go to the video store with no idea what to rent.*

**SAY ANYTHING** (1989) *Comedy*
**Review:** "Satisfying teenage comedy-drama about a self-assured loner (John Cusack) who goes after the class brain (Ione Sky), and finds her surprisingly human. Amusing, endearing, and refreshingly original; written by first-time director Cameron Crowe." (*Leonard Maltin's 2001 Movie & Video Guide*)

**RAISE THE RED LANTERN** (1991) *Foreign/Drama*
**Review:** "Director Zhang Yimou spins an intimate, intense tale of an oppressed woman's descent into madness. Set entirely within the claustrophobic compound where a Chinese nobleman lives with his four wives, the film is always engrossing, enlivened by the director's stunning use of color." (Stephen Farber, "Movieline")

**SIX DEGREES OF SEPARATION** (1993) *Drama*
**Review:** "A young man (Will Smith) arrives on the doorstep of a sophisticated New York couple (Stockard Channing and Donald Sutherland) claiming to be a friend of their children... and the son of Sidney Poitier. Witty, complex, always engaging study of identity and more." (*Halliwell's Film and Video Guide 2001*)

**THINGS CHANGE** (1988) *Comedy*
**Review:** "Director David Mamet and co-writer Shel Silverstein have fashioned a marvelously subtle and witty comedy about an inept, low-level gangster (Joe Mantegna). He goes against orders to take an old shoe-shine 'boy' (Don Ameche) on one last fling before the latter goes to prison for a crime he didn't commit." (*Video Movie Guide 2001*)

**SILENT RUNNING** (1971) *Science Fiction*
**Review:** "The future: Plants do not exist on Earth anymore. Greenhouses in orbit contain the last samples of Earth's dying forests. But one day the government decides that the program has

**Poll result: 50% of Americans believe humans lived at the same time as dinosaurs.**

to be stopped. Directed by Douglas Trumbull, master of special effects who worked on *2001: A Space Odyssey*. A cult movie for SF fans." (Scifi.com)

**THE KILLER** (1989) *Foreign/Action*

**Review:** "John Woo's best film features Chow Yun-Fat as an honorable assassin trying to get out of the business. Impeccable pacing and incredible action choreography create an operatic intensity that leaves you feeling giddy. Available both dubbed and in Cantonese with English subtitles." (*Video Movie Guide 2001*)

**THE TAKING OF PELHAM ONE TWO THREE** (1974) *Suspense*

**Review:** "Ruthless Robert Shaw and three cohorts hijack NYC subway train, hold passengers for one million in cash—to be delivered *in one hour!* Outstanding thriller, laced with cynical comedy, bursts with heart-stopping excitement, terrific performances, and first-rate editing." (*Leonard Maltin's 2001 Movie & Video Guide*)

**MONSOON WEDDING** (2001) *Drama*

**Review:** "Rarely do films come along that are as intelligent and moving as *Monsoon Wedding*. Director Mira Nair's kaleidoscopic portrait of an Indian family preparing for their daughter's marriage succeeds in creating a vivid panoply of characters and telling a variety of stories." (Reel.com)

**SLAP SHOT** (1977) *Comedy*

**Review:** "A profane satire of the world of professional hockey. Over-the-hill player-coach Paul Newman gathers an oddball mixture of has-beens and young players and initiates them, using violence on the ice to make his team win. Charming in its own bone-crunching way." (*VideoHound's Golden Movie Retriever 2001*)

**TWENTY BUCKS** (1993) *Drama*

**Review:** "Whimsical film follows a $20 bill from its 'birth' in a cash machine to its 'death' as it is returned to the bank, tattered and torn, for shredding. The bill is passed from owner to owner, sometimes simply and briefly, sometimes altering fate." (*VideoHound's Golden Movie Retriever 2001*)

**Tomatoes have more flavor at room temperature than they do when chilled.**

# AN A-PEEL-ING HISTORY

*According to one legend, the fruit that Eve found irresistible in the Garden of Eden was not an apple, but a banana. Is it true? Who knows? But for thousands of years, the banana has been a source of pleasure... and sometimes trouble.*

## HOW THEY SPREAD

• Bananas are believed to have originated in the rainforests of Southeast Asia, where a wide variety of species still grow.

• Arab traders brought the banana to the Middle East and Africa in the seventh century. But these weren't the large fruit we know today—they were just a few inches in length. In fact, some historians believe "banana" comes from *banan*, the Arabic word meaning "finger."

• By the late 1400s, bananas were a staple food along the western coast of Africa where Portuguese sailors collected plants and brought them to the Canary Islands, between Africa and Spain.

• In 1516 Tomás de Berlanga, a Spanish priest, brought banana stalks to the New World, to the island of Hispañiola (now Haiti and the Dominican Republic). And he took plants with him to the mainland when he was made bishop of Panama in 1534.

• Another priest, Vasco de Quiroga, brought banana plants from Hispañiola to Mexico in the mid-16th century. From there, bananas spread and flourished throughout the Caribbean basin, leading many to believe—erroneously—that they were native to the region.

## COMING TO AMERICA

Despite the banana's popularity in the tropics, it remained virtually unknown in the United States until the late 1800s. It was formally introduced to the American public at the 1876 Centennial Exposition in Philadelphia, which included a 40-acre display of tropical plants. A local grocer sold individual bananas, wrapped neatly in tinfoil, for 10¢—an hour's wage at the time. The fruit would remain an expensive luxury for years.

But bananas never would have become a popular snack food if

**On-the-job injury: Pool shark Minnesota Fats was once hospitalized for "cue-tip-chalk lung."**

it hadn't been for a few enterprising entrepreneurs. Cape Cod sea captain Lorenzo Baker was the first merchant to successfully capitalize on the banana when he discovered the curious fruit in Jamaica and brought a load of them to New Jersey in 1870. He sold 160 bunches for a substantial profit and soon began shipping them back to the East Coast on a regular basis. In 1885 he and Boston businessman Andrew Preston formed the Boston Fruit Company.

## GETTING ON TRACK

At about the same time, an ambitious 19-year-old from Brooklyn discovered bananas too. In 1871 Minor Keith and two of his brothers went to Costa Rica to work for their uncle, who had won a government contract to build a railroad line from the capital, San José, to the port city of Limón. It was a treacherous project over miles of dense mountainous jungle and ultimately claimed the lives of some 5,000 workers, including Keith's brothers and uncle.

In spite of the hardship, however, Keith persisted. And as the railroad construction proceeded, he planted banana plants on any and all nearby land. Why? The quick-growing fruit was a cheap way to feed the workers.

The railroad was completed in 1890, but Keith was in financial trouble. The Costa Rican government refused to pay him, and there weren't enough passengers to support the line. What could he do? Forced to find another source of revenue, Keith decided to experiment with the bananas he'd planted: his railroad could cheaply transport them to Limón, where they could be shipped to markets in the United States. The experiment was so successful that the banana business quickly overshadowed his meager passenger service.

## MERGER

Despite a decade of success, in 1899 Keith once again found himself in trouble. His financial partner went bankrupt, leaving him without enough money to run the railroad. So, as a way to preserve his business, he went to Boston and arranged with Lorenzo Baker and Andrew Preston to merge their two companies. (The company they formed, the United Fruit Company, still exists as part of United Brands.)

By the end of the century, advances in refrigerated steamship

**Slow down! One hundred cups of coffee consumed in 4 hours can cause a heart attack.**

and rail transportation made it possible to ship bananas to all parts of North America. As improved production led to lower prices, the United Fruit Company was poised for a banana boom. Now affordable, the banana quickly became a popular snack, and production shifted into high gear. But there was a dark side to the business that the American public knew little about.

## BANANA REPUBLICS

Behind the scenes, the banana business played a huge part in the economy and politics of Central America. The United Fruit Company, as well as other banana companies such as Standard Fruit (today part of Dole), made sweetheart deals with Central American dictators, buying or leasing vast tracts of land at bargain prices and paying little, if any, taxes.

While bananas created wealth in Central America, it mostly enriched government officials—without benefitting the common people. In 1910 American author O. Henry coined the term *banana republic*, and by the 1930s, it was commonly used to describe the corrupt Central American countries controlled largely by banana companies.

## GUNBOAT DIPLOMACY

U.S. foreign policy stood firmly behind the banana companies too. Under President William Howard Taft (1909–1913), the goal of diplomacy was to support (or create) stable governments favorable to U.S. interests. And later, when "dollar diplomacy" failed, the U.S. government resorted to "gunboat diplomacy." American troops were sent in to ensure the pro-U.S. outcome of elections in Honduras, Nicaragua, and other Latin American countries.

In the 1950s, for example, Jacobo Arbenz, a progressive Guatemalan president, proposed reclaiming lands owned by the United Fruit Company and other large landowners and distributing them to landless peasants. It never happened—in 1954, citing the threat of communism, the United States backed a military coup that ousted Arbenz and ended the immediate threat of land reform.

But times were changing for the banana companies. Worker strikes led to labor reforms. The monopoly of United Fruit Company was broken by an antitrust suit in 1958 that forced it to sell parts of the company to competitors and Guatemalan entrepreneurs.

**Makes sense: Baby seahorses are called "colts."**

Today, imperialist politics have taken a backseat to more modern business practices. But bananas are still big business, and remain America's most popular fruit.

## BANANARAMA

• Americans eat an average of 75 bananas a year per person.

• The banana split was invented in 1904 by Dr. David Strickler, a drugstore pharmacist in Latrobe, Pennsylvania.

• Technically the banana is a berry.

• Ever wonder why bananas have no seeds? Because of natural mutations, the kind we eat don't have any. The dark dots in the center are all that's left. (They reproduce by underground stems, or rhizomes.)

• There are several hundred varieties of bananas worldwide, but the one that most of us slice on our cereal is the Cavendish. The Cavendish is favored by commercial producers for its size, flavor, and, most importantly, resistance to diseases.

• A banana has about 110 calories and is high in fiber, potassium, and vitamin C.

• The banana has never been a Fruit-of-the-Month selection.

• A few forgotten banana products: banana wine, banana flour (cheaper than wheat flour), banana ketchup, banana pickles, banana vinegar, and Melzo, a powdered-banana drink mix.

• To let the public know that bananas should be allowed to ripen at room temperature, not in the refrigerator, in 1944 United Fruit commissioned a song and a character: Chiquita Banana. The song was so popular it was once played on the radio 376 times in one day. And Chiquita herself was named "the girl we'd most like to share our foxhole with" by American servicemen.

• The song "Yes, We Have No Bananas" was an enormous hit in 1923—selling at the rate of 25,000 copies of sheet music per day. The popularity of the song spurred a new craze: dancing the Charleston on banana peel–covered floors.

***And speaking of peels—they have a story, too. Turn to page 197 to find out how the banana peel altered the urban landscape.***

**Surf's up: The level of the world's oceans is 500 feet higher than it was 25,000 years ago.**

# FLUNKING THE PEPSI CHALLENGE

*Lots of companies have ad campaigns that flop, but Pepsi seems to have more than its share. Here are a few classic bombs.*

## KEEP ON TRUCKIN'

For its "Pepsi 400" contest in the summer of 2001, Pepsi offered to send the holders of five winning tickets on an all-expenses-paid trip to Florida's Daytona 400 auto race. One of the five would get to drive home in the grand prize, a brand-new Dodge truck; the other four would each get $375 worth of free gas. There was just one problem: contest organizers accidentally printed 55 winning tickets instead of five. Rather than risk alienating the winners—not to mention millions of Pepsi drinkers—Pepsi sent all 55 winners to Daytona, gave away five trucks instead of one, and spent $20,625 on free gas instead of $1,825. Estimated cost of the error: about $400,000.

## OVER-STUFFED

In April 1996, Pepsi canceled its "Pepsi Stuff" merchandise giveaway campaign months ahead of schedule. Reason: Too many winners. The company underestimated how many people would redeem the points by 50%, forcing it to spend $60 million more than expected on free merchandise. "We're outpacing our goals on awareness," a company spokesperson explained.

## JET LAG

Another disaster from the "Pepsi Stuff" campaign: 21-year-old John Leonard tried to redeem seven million award points for the Harrier fighter jet he saw offered in a Pepsi Stuff TV ad. The rules stipulated that contestants could buy points for 10¢ apiece, so that's what he did. Leonard (who studied flawed promotions in business school) raised $700,000 to buy the required points and then sent the money to Pepsi, along with a letter demanding they hand over the $50 million jet. When Pepsi refused, claiming the offer was made "in jest," Leonard filed suit in federal court. Three years later, a judge ruled that "no objective person could reasonably have concluded that the commercial actually offered consumers a Harrier jet." Pepsi lucked out...case dismissed.

## THE KING OF (SODA) POP

Even Pepsi's biggest successes can become colossal flops. In 1983 they signed the largest individual sponsorship deal in history with pop singer Michael Jackson. It was a multi-year deal and Pepsi made millions from it...only to find itself linked to one of the most lurid scandals of the 1990s when Jackson abruptly cancelled his Pepsi-sponsored "Dangerous" tour in 1993. Jackson's reasons for quitting: (1) stress generated by allegations that he had sexually molested a young boy, and (2) addiction to painkillers he took "to control pain from burns suffered while filming a Pepsi ad."

## THE NAME GAME

In 1983 another Pepsi contest ran into budget trouble when the company offered $5 per letter to any customer who could spell their own last name using letters printed on Pepsi bottle caps and flip tops. Pepsi hoped to control the number of cash prizes by releasing only a limited number of vowels...but it failed to take into account people like Richard "no vowels" Vlk, who turned in 1,393 three-letter sets and pocketed $20,985 for his efforts. Vlk, a diabetic who does not drink Pepsi, collected the letters by taking out classified ads offering to split the winnings with anyone who sent him a matching set. "I don't even remember making one whole set myself," he says. "I didn't buy any Pepsi." (The company got even by mailing him his winnings in $15 increments, one check for each winning set.)

## THEY CAN SEE CLEARLY NOW

In 1992 Pepsi introduced Crystal Pepsi, an attempt to cash in on the booming popularity of see-through soft drinks like Clearly Canadian. Sales were less than half of what Pepsi projected, even after the company reformulated the product. Marketing experts point to two critical flaws that they say doomed Crystal Pepsi from the start: (1) customers balked at paying extra for a product that, because it was clear, was perceived to have fewer ingredients than regular Pepsi, and (2) after more than a century of conditioning, consumers *want* colas to be dark brown in color. "Clear colas are about as appetizing as brown water," an industry analyst explains.

**A single mushroom can produce as many as 40 million spores in a single hour.**

# TRUST ME...

*Call it doublespeak, call it spin, call it "a different version of the facts." The truth is—it's still a lie.*

**TRUST ME...** "I wouldn't call it an accident. I'd call it a malfunction."

**SAID BY:** Dr. Edward Teller, "father of the hydrogen bomb," referring to Three Mile Island, 1979

**THE FACT:** It was a real accident—250,000 gallons of radioactive waste leaked out.

**TRUST ME...** "Our one desire is that...the people of Southeast Asia be left in peace to work out their own destinies in their way."

**SAID BY:** President Lyndon B. Johnson, 1964

**THE FACT:** Maybe he meant "left in pieces"—the war in Vietnam was well underway and escalating.

**TRUST ME...** "I have no more territorial ambitions in Europe."

**SAID BY:** Adolf Hitler, 1938

**THE FACT:** Within two years of saying this, Germany invaded Czechoslovakia, Denmark, Norway, Holland, Belgium, and France.

**TRUST ME...** "I would have never owned those ugly-ass shoes."

**SAID BY:** O. J. Simpson, in a 1996 civil lawsuit, denying he owned a pair of Bruno Magli "Lorenzos"

**THE FACT:** A month later, 30 photographs were discovered that showed Simpson wearing the shoes at a 1993 Buffalo Bills game.

**TRUST ME...** "The army is the Indian's best friend."

**SAID BY:** General George Armstrong Custer, 1870

**THE FACT:** He then wiped out most of the Sioux nation before being killed at Little Big Horn.

**TRUST ME...** "As long as I own the Cleveland Browns, they will remain in Cleveland."

**SAID BY:** Brown's owner Art Modell, 1993

**THE FACT:** He moved the franchise to Baltimore in 1996.

**97 out of 100 Americans who buy engagement rings this year will buy one with a diamond.**

# FADS

*Here's a look at the origins of some of the most popular obsessions from days gone by.*

**THE SMURFS**

Created by Belgian storybook illustrator Pierre "Peyo" Culliford in 1957, the Smurfs developed followings in Germany, Italy, Spain, and Scandanavia (where the blue creatures were known as Schlumpfe, Puffo, Pitufo, and Smolf, respectively), but they remained more or less unknown in the rest of the world.

Then in 1978, British Petroleum launched an advertising campaign featuring the creatures, which it renamed the Smurfs for the English audience. The ads sparked a Smurf craze in England, prompting an American importer to bring them to America... where they caught the eye of the daughter of the president of NBC. Her enthusiasm prompted dad to order up a Saturday morning Smurf cartoon show for the network. The show became an enormous hit, turning NBC into a Saturday morning juggernaut and launching a Smurf craze in the United States. By 1982 the Smurfs were the biggest-selling toy merchandising line in the country, outselling even *E.T.* and *Star Wars*.

**"BABY ON BOARD" SIGNS**

In 1984 an executive recruiter named Michael Lerner decided to start his own consumer products business. The only problem: he couldn't think of any products to sell. Lucky for him, an old college friend told him about a couple who'd just come back from a vacation in Germany, where they'd seen small signs suction-cupped to automobile windows warning motorists to drive carefully because a baby was on board. The couple wanted to start selling the signs in the United States.

Lerner offered them a deal: If they would agree to let *him* market the signs, he would give them a royalty. Deal! Lerner founded a company called Safety 1st; by the end of 1985 he was selling 500,000 of the little diamond-shaped yellow signs a month. The couple made more than $100,000 for doing absolutely nothing.

Soon imitators stole his idea and swamped the market with

**Lead melts at 620°F; tin at 446°F. Mix them together and they melt at 356°F.**

humorous signs like "Beam Me Up Scotty" and "Ex-Husband in Trunk." Lerner couldn't sue—he didn't have a patent, but that wasn't a problem: He just used his Baby On Board profits to branch out into other child-safety products. He eventually took Safety 1st public, and in April 2000 it sold to a Canadian company for $195 million.

## PAINT BY NUMBERS

In 1952, a Detroit paint-company owner named Max Klein got together with an artist named Dan Robbins and formed Craft Master, a company that sold the world's first paint-by-numbers kits. The kits consisted of numbered jars of paint and a rolled-up canvas (later cardboard) stamped with the outline of a painting; each section of the painting had a number that corresponded to a particular color of paint. Price, including paints and brush: $1.79

So who did Klein and Robbins get the idea from? Leonardo da Vinci. "I recalled reading about da Vinci, and when he got large and complicated commissions, he would give numbered patterns to his apprentices to block in areas for him that he'd go back and finish himself," Robbins explains. "It took two years to get off the ground; then they took off like a rocket." By 1954 more paint-by-numbers paintings were hanging in American homes than were original works of art.

At the peak of the fad, Craft Master was producing 50,000 kits a day. Their slogan was "Every man a Rembrandt." Among the Rembrandts: Nelson Rockefeller, Ethel Merman, Andy Warhol, J. Edgar Hoover...and even President Dwight D. Eisenhower.

## SLOT CARS

The world's first toy slot cars were introduced by the Aurora Plastics Company in 1960. Aurora's cars came with special slotted tracks that kept the cars on the road, thanks to a small projection under the car's nose that inserted into the slot. Cost: $3.00 to $8.00 per car, or $20–40 for an entire racing set, which made them affordable for just about everyone. The cars went up to 600 mph in scale, and since the "drivers" were in continuous control of their vehicles' speeds, the cars were more challenging—and more fun—to operate than toy cars had ever been.

Because of all of this, the cars became hugely popular. Entre-

**Standard English: During his lifetime, Shakespeare's last name was spelled 83 different ways.**

preneurs built huge multilevel slot-car racing centers that competed with pinball arcades for America's pocket change, and home enthusiasts spent $1,500 or more building their own elaborate speedways at home. In all, Americans spent $100 million on slot cars and tracks in 1963—more than they spent on model railroads—and by 1965 more than 3.5 million Americans were racing slot cars on a regular basis. For a time it seemed that slot cars might even become more popular than bowling, but the fad didn't last long—sales dropped off sharply in 1967 and never recovered.

## INSTANT TANS

*Dihydroxyacetone* is a drug that's used as an antidote for cyanide poisoning. It has a side effect: It stains human skin brown on contact. A sun worshipper named John Andre noticed this in the late 1950s and decided to mix the medicine with alcohol and fragrances and sell it as a self-tanning aftershave called Man-Tan. Andre sold $3 million worth of the stuff in 1960, giving both aftershave and suntan lotion companies quite a scare. They needn't have worried: paint-on tans were just a flash in the pan, and sales "virtually disappeared" the following year. (Update: Man-tan is still gone, but thanks to the established link between sunlight and skin cancer, paint-on tans are more popular than ever.)

## SHMOOS

In 1948 cartoonist Al Capp added a new character to his L'il Abner comic strip: the *shmoo*, a strange creature, described as "a cross between Casper the Ghost and a misshapen dinosaur." In Capp's comic-strip world, the shmoos were as much a part of the food supply as they were a part of the story line: they laid eggs, produced butter, and gave milk in glass bottles. If you broiled them, they turned into steak; if you boiled them, they turned into chicken.

And if you made a toy out of them, manufacturers learned in the late 1940s, they sold by the millions. Companies made fortunes selling shmoo ashtrays, clocks, piggy banks, pencil sharpeners, clothing, candy, and even shmoo meat products. By 1950 more than $25 million worth of shmoo items had been sold, yet for some reason, Capp decided to write the characters out of the story line. He created a "shmooicide squad" that gunned down every single shmoo in the strip, and the fad died out soon after that.

**The skin of a tiger shark is 10 times as strong as ox hide.**

# A FAMOUS PHONY

*Most people have fantasized about being someone else, but few of us have actually done it. Here's an amazing story of a man who pretended to be someone he wasn't... and pulled it off.*

**BACKGROUND:** Ferdinand Waldo Demara, Jr. was one of the most prolific imposters in history. Born in Lawrence, Massachusetts, in 1921, the high school dropout had successfully passed himself off as a doctor of philosophy, a zoologist, a Trappist monk, a prison counselor, a biologist doing cancer research, a sheriff, a soldier, and a sailor by the time he was in his 30s.

**MOMENT OF "TRUTH":** His greatest ruse came during the Korean War when he used the identity of Dr. Joseph Cyr, and enlisted in the Royal Canadian Navy in 1951. He served aboard a destroyer off the Korean coast. Under intense battle conditions, Demara *was* the ship's surgeon: he pulled teeth, removed tonsils, administered anesthesia, and even amputated limbs. But most incredibly, after studying the procedure in a book, he successfully removed a bullet from a wounded soldier that was less than an inch from his heart. Onlookers let out a cheer as he completed the impeccable operation and saved the man's life. In all his time as a doctor in Korea, he never lost a single patient.

**UNMASKED:** His success turned out to be his undoing—photographs of the heroic doctor made it into Canadian newspapers. The real Dr. Cyr's mother saw them and alerted authorities. Amazingly, no charges were filed; Demara had saved too many lives. A naval board of inquiry released him—with back pay. Demara was later arrested for posing as a teacher in the United States and served a six-month sentence. When asked why he did it, noting that he didn't get rich from his escapades, he answered, "Rascality, pure rascality."

**IMMORTALITY ACHIEVED:** In 1961 Hollywood made a movie based on the Demara story, *The Great Imposter*, starring Tony Curtis and Karl Malden. Director Robert Mulligan was a finalist for the Director's Guild Award for the film. And Demara himself got a minor part in another movie: In 1960 he appeared in the melodrama *The Hypnotic Eye*. He played... the doctor.

**Number of documented deaths-by-piranha in human history: One.**

# THE MAN IN THE MASK

*Classical "Greco-Roman" wrestling can trace its roots all the way back to the ancient Greeks and Romans. But what about "professional" wrestling—the kind where costumed buffoons hit each other with folding chairs? How old is that? Older than you might think.*

## WORLD-CLASS WRESTLING

In 1915 some fight promoters organized an international wrestling tournament at the Opera House in New York. A rising American star named Ed "Strangler" Lewis headlined a roster of other top grapplers from Russia, Germany, Italy, Greece, and other countries. These were some of the biggest matches to be fought in New York City that year.

There was just one problem: almost nobody went to see them.

## HO-HUM

Wrestling, at least as it was fought back then, could be pretty boring for the average person to watch. As soon as the bell rang or the whistle was blown, the two wrestlers grabbed onto each other and then might circle round... and round... and round for hours on end, until one wrestler finally gained an advantage and defeated his opponent. Some bouts dragged on for nine hours or more.

Wrestling could also be hard to understand, which made it even more boring. In baseball, an outfielder either caught a fly ball or they didn't. In football, the person with the ball either got tackled or they didn't. Wrestling was different—when two grapplers circled for hours, who could tell at any point in the match who was winning? Did anyone even care?

Even by wrestling standards, 1915 was a particularly boring year because the world's youngest and best wrestlers were all off fighting in World War I. Those that were left were often past their prime and not very entertaining. Not surprisingly, the organizers of the tournament at the Opera House were having trouble filling seats. For the first day or two it looked like they were going to lose a lot of money.

For the first day or two.

**38% of American companies say they monitor their employees' e-mails.**

## MYSTERY MAN

Things were about to change, thanks to one spectator. He was huge, but he didn't stand out just because of his size—he stood out because he was wearing a black mask that covered his entire head. There was no explanation for what the man was doing there or why he was wearing the mask. He just sat there watching the matches each day, and when they ended he left as silently as he came.

Then, a few days into the tournament, the masked man and a companion suddenly stood up and loudly accused the promotors of banning the masked man from the tournament. He was the best wrestler of all and the promoters knew it, they claimed. That was why he was being kept out of the tournament, and they demanded that he be let back in. Security guards quickly hustled the pair out of the building, but they came back each day and repeated their demands, generating newspaper headlines in the process. By the end of the week, much of New York City was demanding that the masked man be allowed into the tournament.

## OH, ALL RIGHT

Finally, on Saturday, the promotors gave in to the pressure and agreed to let him compete. Just days earlier, some of the world's most famous wrestlers had battled one another in a nearly empty Opera House. No one cared. Now throngs of New Yorkers ponied up the price of admission to watch the mysterious masked man fight, even though—or more likely *because*—they had no idea who he was or whether he even knew how to fight.

Sure enough, the Masked Marvel delivered—although not quite as much as he promised, because he lost one match and only wrestled "Strangler" Lewis to a draw. But he whipped everyone else he wrestled, bringing the packed tournament to a thrilling end. Considering the amount of excitement that led up to those final bouts, it's a good bet that the people who saw the masked man fight remembered the experience for the rest of their lives.

## MYSTERY REVEALED

The following year, the Masked Marvel was officially *un*masked after losing a match with a wrestler named Joe Stecher. He turned out to be…Mort Henderson, a railroad detective from Altoona,

**When kids were asked to name "the most important person in the world"…**

Pennsylvania, who made his living throwing hobos off trains when he wasn't in the ring. Henderson had wrestled for years under his own name, but he lost many of his matches and had gone nowhere in the sport. Even when he *wasn't* wearing a mask, nobody knew who he was.

So how did Henderson do so well at the Opera House? The whole thing was a setup—the promoters planted him in the audience hoping that he would generate publicity and sell tickets. The other wrestlers were in on the scam, too; that was how he won so many fights.

Many New Yorkers realized that they'd been had, but nobody seemed to mind. The Masked Marvel was *fun*.

## FROM SPECTACLE...TO SPORT...TO SPECTACLE

Wrestling had long been full of colorful characters. After all, legitimate professional wrestling traced its roots back to the days when carnival strongmen traveled the country offering cash prizes to any locals who could pin them to the mat.

By 1915 wrestling had matured into a legitimate sport, a test of strength and skill, not quite as exciting as boxing but still a sport that took itself seriously. Mort Henderson could not have realized it at the time, but on the day he donned his mask the first time in 1915, he changed professional wrestling forever. It was "at this point," Keith Greenberg writes in *Pro Wrestling: From Carnivals to Cable TV*, "promoters began copying techniques from vaudeville to keep spectators interested."

## PUTTING ON A SHOW

A lot of the credit for changing pro wrestling into what it is today goes to a former vaudeville promoter named Joseph "Toots" Mondt. Mondt saw wrestlers as little different from theatrical performers, and their matches as just another act to be managed so that profits were maximized.

Rather than let a match run on for hours, he set time limits, which allowed him to book more fights back to back. His traveling troupe of wrestlers fought the same fights—with the same rigged outcomes—in every town they visited. Since the wrestlers didn't have to focus on winning, they were free to thrill audiences with moves like flying drop kicks, airplane spins, and leaps across

**...God came in 19th place, just after *Harry Potter* author J. K. Rowling.**

the ring feet first to kick opponents in the chest.

Landing fake body blows like these—ones that appeared devastating without actually causing serious physical harm—was elevated to a fine art. "When a grappler threw a punch, he tried to connect using a forearm instead of a fist, softening the blow," Greenberg writes. "A man diving on a foe from the ropes actually grazed the man with a knee or elbow, rather than landing on him directly and causing injury."

## ONE-RING CIRCUS

The next big wave of innovation came during the Great Depression of the 1930s, when dwindling ticket sales forced promoters to resort to even greater gimmickry to draw crowds. Wrestlers assumed false ethnic identities so that blue-collar immigrants could root for someone of their own ethnic group, and also to capitalize on whatever geopolitical goings-on might make for an interesting villain. Evil German counts and Japanese generals were popular during World War II; in peacetime, crazy hillbillies and snooty English lords filled the bill, grappling with the noble Indian chiefs and scrappy Irish brawlers that the audiences loved.

Wrestlers fought tag-team matches. They battled it out in cages. They wrestled while chained together. They fought in rings filled with mud (of course) as well as ice cream, berries, molasses, and other gooey substances. Women wrestled. Midgets wrestled. Giants wrestled. Morbidly obese people wrestled, and so did people with disfiguring diseases. Maurice Tillet, the French Angel, suffered from a glandular disease called *acromegaly* that gave him enlarged, distorted facial features. He was such a successful villain that he spawned a host of imitators, including the Swedish Angel, the Golden Angel, the Polish Angel, and the Czech Angel, a number of whom suffered from the same disease.

## OLD SCHOOL

What happened to the "genuine" professional wrestlers, the guys who refused to showboat and took their sport seriously? They continued to wrestle one another in honest matches for legitimate championship titles. In 1920, for example, Ed "Strangler" Lewis won a world championship match against Joe Stecher in a three-hour-long bout; he held the title off and on for the next 13 years.

**90% of all insects live in the soil for at least part of their lives.**

After that the title turned over several times before it passed to a wrestler named Lou Thesz, who would win and lose it several times into the 1950s.

Not that anyone cared. Thesz wasn't above a little showmanship—his specialty holds were the Kangaroo and the Airplane Spin—but "there was little interest in the championship among the public," Graeme Kent writes in *A Pictorial History of Wrestling*. "This was mainly because Thesz scorned gimmicks, relying on his wrestling ability to carry him through."

## STAY TUNED...

Yet it was a gimmick at the end of World War II that would provide the biggest boost to professional wrestling. The emerging medium of TV—and a wrestling innovator called Gorgeous George—helped bring wrestling into American living rooms.

***The Masked Marvel was responsible for turning wrestling from a sport into a spectacle, but Gorgeous George deserves the credit for bringing professional wrestling into full bloom.*** ***That story is on page 246.***

* * *

## IT'S A WEIRD, WEIRD WORLD

"Alain Robert, the French 'spider-man' famous for climbing the Eiffel Tower and Empire State Building, walked away from China's 88-story Jinmao Tower—too risky. In February 2001, Han Qizhi, a 31-year-old shoe salesman, just happened to be passing the popular landmark and was 'struck by a rash impulse.' When security guards weren't looking, Han, who had never climbed before, launched himself upon the skyscraper and began to climb. 'He walked around Jinmao a couple of times, told his colleague he was going up, dropped his jacket, and started climbing,' said a police spokesman. Han, bare-handed and dressed in ordinary street clothes, was grabbed by policemen just short of the summit."

**—Reuters**

**What are a *carapace* and a *plastron*? The top and bottom parts of a turtle shell.**

# KNOW YOUR OLOGIES

*You may have heard of psychology, biology, and ecology, but chances are you've never heard of any of these "ologies."*

**Rhinology:** The study of noses

**Nosology:** The study of the classification of diseases

**Hippology:** The study of horses

**Dactylology:** Communication using fingers (sign language)

**Ichthyology:** The study of fish

**Myrmecology:** The study of ants

**Potamology:** The study of rivers

**Anemology:** The study of wind

**Sinology:** The study of Chinese culture

**Mycology:** The study of fungi

**Glottochronology:** The study of when two languages diverge from one common source

**Neology:** The study of new words

**Oenology:** The study of wines

**Conchology**: The study of shells

**Otology:** The study of ears

**Oneirology:** The study of dreams

**Semiology:** The study of signs and signaling

**Cetology:** The study of whales and dolphins

**Vexillology:** The study of flags

**Deontology:** The study of moral responsibilities

**Axiology:** The study of principles, ethics, and values

**Phantomology:** The study of supernatural beings

**Histology:** The study of tissues

**Trichology:** The study of hair

**Malacology:** The study of mollusks

**Dendrochronology:** The study of trees' ages by counting their rings

**Morphology:** The study of the structure of organisms

**Oology:** The study of eggs

**Eschatology:** The study of final events as spoken of in the Bible

**Don't let the name fool you: Mississippi Bay is off the coast of Yokohama, Japan.**

# HOMER VS. HOMER

*On the left we have the wisdom of Homer, Greek poet and philosopher, who lived 3,000 years ago. And on the right we have the other Homer.*

| ***Homer the Greek*** | ***Homer the Simpson*** |
|---|---|
| "It is the bold man who every time does his best." | "I don't know, Marge. Trying is the first step toward failure." |
| "The charity that is a trifle to us can be precious to others." | "You gave both dogs away? You know how I feel about giving!" |
| "The fates have given mankind a patient soul." | "Give me some peace of mind or I'll mop the floor with you!" |
| "Nothing in the world is so incontinent as a man's accursed appetite." | "Ahh, beer...I would kill everyone in this room for a drop of sweet beer." |
| "I detest he who hides one thing in his heart and means another." | "But, Marge, it takes two people to lie: one to lie, and one to listen." |
| "The man who acts the least, disrupts the most." | "It is better to watch things than to do them." |
| "A sympathetic friend can be quite as dear as a brother." | "Television—teacher, mother, secret lover!" |
| "A multitude of rulers is not a good thing. Let there be one ruler, one king." | "I'd blow smoke in the president's stupid monkey face and all he'd do is groooove on it!" |
| "Never, never was a wicked man wise." | "I am so smart! S-M-R-T, I mean S-M-A-R-T." |
| "How mortals take the gods to task! Yet their afflictions come from us." | "I'm not normally a religious man, but if you're up there, save me, Superman!" |

**Bad luck? The Confederate flag had 13 stars...but there were only 11 Confederate states.**

# NUMBER TWO'S WILD RIDE

*Uncle John feels a responsibility to "eliminate bathroom ignorance." So for this edition of the* Bathroom Reader *we're going to answer the basic question: What happens after you flush? (It's more complicated than you think.)*

**READY, SET, GO!**

For you, the trip has ended. You've "done your business," (hopefully you've also had a few minutes of quality reading time), you've flushed the toilet, and you've moved onto the next thing.

But for your "business," a.k.a. organic solid waste, a.k.a. "Number Two," the trip is just beginning. Here's a general idea of what happens next.

**CONNECTIONS**

If you live in a rural area, your house is probably hooked up to a septic tank. We'll get to that later.

Before the 20th century, "sanitary systems" typically dumped raw sewage directly into rivers, streams, and oceans. Today, if you live in an urban area or a suburb, chances are your toilet and all of the water fixtures in your house—the sinks, showers, bathtubs, dishwasher, washing machine, etc.—are all hooked into a sewer system that feeds into a wastewater treatment plant. So the journey begins when Number Two mixes with all of the rest of the wastewater leaving your house. Then it enters the *sewer main* that runs down the center of your street (usually about six feet beneath the road surface), and mixes with the wastewater coming from your neighbors' homes.

From there the sewer main probably joins with other sewer mains to form an even bigger sewer main. Depending on how far you are from the wastewater treatment plant, the sewer mains may repeatedly join together to form ever larger pipes. By the time you start getting close to the plant, the pipe could be large enough in diameter to drive a truck through it.

**In 1876 an English cricket player hit the ball 37 miles. (It landed on a moving railroad car.)**

## PRIMARY TREATMENT

By now Number Two has a lot of company, especially if any storm drains feed into your community's system. Anything that can be swept into the storm drains—old shoes, tree branches, cardboard boxes, dead animals, rusty shopping carts—is now heading through the giant pipes toward the treatment plant.

This floating garbage would destroy the equipment in the plant, so the first step is to remove it from the wastewater. This is accomplished by letting the water flow through a series of screens and vertical bars that trap the really large objects but let everything else—including Number Two—float through. The big stuff is then removed and disposed of, often in landfills.

## THE NITTY GRITTY

Now the trip starts to get a little rough:

• The wastewater flows into a grinder called a *communitor*. The communitor is like a huge garbage disposal: It takes everything that's still in the water, Number Two included, and grinds it down into a sort of liquified mulch that's easier to treat chemically and easier to remove. Number Two has now "become one," so to speak, with all the other solid matter still in the wastewater.

• Next this slurry flows into a *grit chamber*, where inorganic materials—stuff that can't rot, like sand, gravel, and silt—settle to the bottom of the chamber. Later, they're disposed of in a landfill.

• The wastewater then flows from the grit chamber into a closed *sedimentation tank*, where it is allowed to sit for a while so that the organic matter still in the water has a chance to settle to the bottom of the tank, where it can be removed.

• Have you ever dropped a raisin into a glass of 7-Up and watched the bubbles carry it to the top of the glass? So have the folks that design treatment plants. Some plants use a *flotation tank* instead of a sedimentation tank: They force pressurized air into the wastewater, then pump this mixture into an open tank, where the bubbles can rise to the surface. As they float up, the bubbles carry a lot of the organic matter to the surface with them (including what's left of poor Number Two), making it easier to skim from the surface and remove.

By the time the wastewater has been processed through the

sedimentation tank or the flotation tank, as much as 75–80% of solid matter has been removed.

## THE SLUDGE REPORT

So what happens to all of the organic solid matter (i.e., Number Two and all his friends) that has just been removed from the sedimentation tank? It gets turned into fertilizer.

• It goes into a *thickener*, where it's—you guessed it—thickened.

• Then it's fed into a closed anaerobic tank called a *digester*, where it's—right again—digested. Enzymes break down the solid matter into a *soluble* (dissolvable) form. Then acid-producing bacteria ferment it, breaking it down even further, into simple organic acids. Bacteria then turns these organic acids into methane and carbon dioxide gasses. The entire process of decomposition can take anywhere from 10 to 30 days, during which time it will reduce the mass of the organic matter by 45–60%.

• What's left of the digested sludge is pumped out onto sand beds, where it's allowed to dry. Some of the liquid in the sludge percolates down into the sand; the rest evaporates into the air. The dried organic material that's left can then be used as a soil conditioner or a fertilizer. (Moral of the story: wash your vegetables before you eat them.)

## SECONDARY TREATMENT

That takes care of the organic matter—the part of the process known as *primary treatment*. Number Two's trip is now at an end. But what about the liquid in the sedimentation and flotation tanks? Taking care of that is known as *secondary treatment*:

• Some treatment plants pump the water through a *trickling filter*, where the water flows over a bed of porous material that's coated with a slimy film of microorganisms. The microorganisms break the organic matter down into carbon dioxide and water.

• Another process utilizes *activated sludge*—living sludge that is made up millions upon millions of bacteria cells. The wastewater is pumped into a tank containing the sludge, and the bacteria absorb any remaining organic matter.

• Finally, the wastewater is processed in something called a *secondary clarifier*, which removes the bacteria before they are discharged back into the environment.

**Is your Adam's apple larger than normal? That means you're "cock-throppled."**

• Some water treatment facilities don't use trickling filters or activated sludge, they just pump the water into a lagoon or a *stabilization pond*, where the water is allowed to sit while naturally occurring bacteria and other microorganisms do the same job on their own, only a little slower.

## ADVANCED TREATMENT

Most wastewater that has received both primary and secondary treatment is considered safe enough to go back into the environment. But some water does require further treatment, especially if it is going to be reused by humans.

• Processes with such names as *reverse osmosis* and *electrodialysis* can remove "dissolved" solids—solids that can pass easily through other kinds of filters. Then the water is filtered and treated chemically to remove phosphorous, ammonia, nitrogen, and phosphates.

• If the water is going to be made safe for drinking, it is also treated with chlorine or disinfected by ozone.

That's it! The water is clean. (Uncle John wouldn't want to drink it, but that doesn't mean it isn't clean.)

## DOWN-HOME FLUSHING

Not everyone is hooked up to a water treatment facility. If you live out in the country, you may be hooked up to a septic tank, which performs the same wastewater treatment functions, only more simply and naturally:

• The water from your toilets, bathtubs, showers, and sinks feed into a simple tank, usually made of concrete, cinder blocks, or metal.

• Solid matter settles to the bottom and the liquid remains on top.

• The liquid overflows into a system of underground trenches, often filled with rocks or gravel, where it can safely dissipate into the surrounding soil and biodegrade naturally.

• The solids settle at the bottom of the tank and break down organically. You can help the process along by adding special yeast and other treatments to the septic tank; if this isn't enough, it may have to be pumped out.

* * *

"Power corrupts. Absolute power is kind of neat."

***—John Lehman, US secretary of the Navy***

**Fastest way to wake up a penguin, according to French scientists: Touch their feet.**

# BRI BRAINTEASERS

*BRI stalwart David Zapp collected these puzzles...and dared us to solve them. Naturally, Uncle John immediately took them to our "research lab" and pronounced them bona fide bathroom reading. Now, we "pass" them on to you. (Answers are on page 747.)*

**1.** A murderer is condemned to death. He has to choose between three rooms. The first is full of raging fires, the second is full of assassins with loaded guns, and the third is full of lions that haven't eaten in three years.

Which room is safest?

**2.** Can you name three consecutive days without using the words Monday, Tuesday, Wednesday, Thursday, Friday, Saturday, or Sunday?

**3.** A man is found dead in the Arctic with a pack on his back.

What happened?

**4.** A man pushes a car up to a hotel and tells the owner he's bankrupt.

What's going on?

**5.** You have two plastic jugs filled with water. How can you put all the water into a barrel, without using the jugs or any dividers, and still tell which water came from which jug?

**6.** This is an unusual paragraph. I'm curious how quickly you can find out what is so unusual about it? It looks so plain you would think nothing was wrong with it. In fact, nothing is wrong with it. It is unusual, though. Study it, think about it...but you still may not find anything odd.

**7.** A carrot, two lumps of coal, and a pipe lie together in the middle of a field.

What happened?

**8.** A woman shoots her husband. Then she holds him under water for over five minutes. Finally, she hangs him. But five minutes later, they both go out and enjoy a wonderful dinner together.

How can this be?

**9.** What's black when you buy it, red when you use it, and gray when you throw it away?

**10.** A man is born in 1972 and dies in 1952 at age 25.

What's the deal?

**Longest name in the Bible: Mahershalalhashbaz (Isaiah 8:1).**

# UNDERWEAR IN THE NEWS

*A cosmic question: when is underwear newsworthy? The answer: it's newsworthy when it's...*

## HEAD-WARMING UNDERWEAR

In March 2002, Reuters reported that maternity wards in Sweden were using underpants as caps for newborns. Why? Because when they use real baby caps, people steal them. "We got tired of buying new caps all the time," said one nurse; so they started using adult hospital-issue underwear instead. She said if you roll up the underpants nicely on the baby's tiny head, it doesn't look that bad.

## MODERN ART UNDERWEAR

In April 2001, San Francisco conceptual artist Nicolino unveiled his latest sculpture: a 1,000-pound "Bra Ball" made up of bras donated by 20,000 women, including supermodel Naomi Campbell. That wasn't Nicolino's first brassiere-inspired work. He once tried to fly a 40,000-bra tapestry over the White House using 10 breast-shaped helium balloons to support it.

## PRISONERS' UNDERWEAR

Officials in Linn County, Oregon, have banned underwear for jail inmates, saying it's too expensive to wash and replace. It's also dangerous: an inmate recently tried to hang himself with the elastic on his briefs, said a sheriff. When a prisoner protested the new policy, claiming that it's his "constitutional right" to wear underpants, Sheriff Dave Burright noted, "I don't remember Thomas Jefferson putting anything about underwear in the Constitution."

## "SHOW-ME" UNDERWEAR

Every July, people from all over the world travel to Berlin, Germany, to celebrate "freedom and sensuality" at the city's annual "Love Parade." In 2002 city officials came up with an odd promotion for the event: they decided to sell pairs of thong underwear as tickets to the subway. Available in black or white, the unisex garments cost 12 euros (about $8) and were good for travel all day. To get on the train, all riders had to do was show their thongs. Ticket inspectors said that people wouldn't have to remove the underwear to get on the train...but they would need to be "flashed."

## DUTY-FREE UNDERWEAR

Customs officers in the Czech Republic stopped a car at the border and promptly arrested the driver for smuggling. To avoid paying import duties, the man had hidden contraband inside every door and seat of the car and even behind the dashboard. The contraband: 1,400 pairs of ladies' panties.

## EDIBLE COSMIC UNDERWEAR

In 1999 Russian scientists reported that they were working to solve a problem as old as the space program: what to do with the dirty underwear? Storage space is precious on the ever-longer trips, and engineers have increasing difficulty finding room for used undies. Cosmonauts complain when they're ordered to wear their underwear too long, so the scientists came up with a solution: develop a bacteria that can eat underwear. They hope to have it perfected by 2017. Bonus: The bacteria will also release methane gas, which could then be used as fuel.

## HAVOC-WREAKING UNDERWEAR

In June 2001, after two sewer breakdowns that caused massive "solid-waste" flooding, officials in Kannapolis, North Carolina, issued this plea to residents: Stop flushing your underwear down the toilet. According to Jeff Rogers, operations manager with the Sewer Department, workers pulled wadded rags from the lift station pump...and they looked a lot like underwear. "People flush all kinds of different things that they shouldn't be flushing," he said. "We definitely don't want them flushing any underpants."

## SANCTIFIED UNDERWEAR

Two women have opened a store in Raleigh, North Carolina, hoping to create a new market: lingerie for religious women. The Seek Ye First Lingerie shop appeals to women who want to be "alluring, but not sleazy," said the two Baptist owners. Apparently customers like the idea of it's-no-sin underwear—the owners report brisk sales at the "thong rack."

# MY BODY LIES OVER THE OCEAN

*When someone passes away and their remains are buried or cremated, it's said that they are being "laid to rest." Unfortunately, that's not always the case. For some people, the journey is just beginning.*

## DOROTHY PARKER

**Claim to Fame:** Writer, critic, and member of New York's famous Algonquin Round Table in the 1920s and 1930s

**Final Resting Place:** Her ashes were interred in 1988, after spending more than 15 years in a filing cabinet.

**Details:** Parker died in June 1967. She left instructions that her body be cremated, but didn't specify what she wanted done after that. When nobody showed up to claim the ashes, the funeral home stored them (for a few years), then mailed them to her lawyers. The lawyers put the box containing her ashes on top of a filing cabinet, apparently waiting for Parker's friend and executor, Lillian Hellman, to collect them. Hellman never did, so when she died in 1984, the law firm began meeting with Parker's surviving friends to figure out what to do.

Parker had left her entire estate to Martin Luther King, Jr. (whom she had never met), and when he was assassinated, everything went to the NAACP. When both the Algonquin Hotel (her legendary hangout) and the *New Yorker* magazine (her publisher) turned down Parker's ashes, the NAACP volunteered to create a memorial garden for her at their headquarters in Baltimore. Finally, in 1988, Parker's ashes were placed in an urn next to a marker inscribed with Parker's self-penned epitaph: "Excuse My Dust."

## THOMAS PAINE

**Claim to Fame:** Founding Father and author of "Common Sense," a political pamphlet that helped spark the American Revolution

**Final Resting Place:** Unknown

**Details:** Paine didn't mince his words; he offended just about everyone he knew in the United States, England, and France.

**There are over 15,000 miles of neon lights in the signs along the Las Vegas strip.**

When he died in 1809 at the age of 72, he had few friends left among the Founding Fathers. He was buried on his farm in New Rochelle, New York; only six people attended his funeral.

Ten years later, an English admirer named William Cobbett decided to return Paine to England, where he could be given a proper funeral and burial. Rather than getting permission from Paine's relatives or the new owners of his farm, Cobbett just dug the body up and snuck it to England in a shipping crate. But since he didn't have money for a funeral or a decent grave, Cobbett had to stage a series of "bone rallies" across England, raising money by charging for a peek at Paine's corpse.

No luck—the public wasn't interested. When Cobbett couldn't even interest people in buying locks of the dead man's hair, he finally gave up and stored the bones under his bed.

When Cobbett died penniless in 1835, the bones were seized as part of his estate and scheduled to be auctioned off to pay his creditors. Even that plan failed—the auctioneer balked at the idea of selling human remains to satisfy a debt. Paine's skeleton was turned over to Cobbett's son, and what he did with it remains a mystery.

## THE HEART OF LOUIS XIV

**Claim to Fame:** King of France from 1643 to 1715

**Final Resting Place:** An English dinner plate

**Details:** During the French Revolution, as the country collapsed into anarchy, Louis XIV's tomb was raided and his embalmed heart was stolen. It was eventually purchased by an English nobleman named Lord Harcourt. Harcourt sold it to the Reverend William Buckland, dean of Westminster Cathedral; when Buckland died in 1856, the heart was passed on to his son Francis.

Francis Buckland was a peculiar man with some peculiar theories. He believed that the way to assure national security was to make England completely food self-sufficient and that the best way to do that was to raise—and eat—exotic animals. How exotic? Over time Buckland graduated from eating ostrich and buffalo to more unusual fare, including moles, flies, slugs, and porpoise heads. He eventually decided that even the king of France himself was fair game as a protein source, so one night he cooked up the royal heart and ate it. "Never before," he told his astonished dinner guests, "have I eaten the heart of a king."

**Bad omen? If you add up all the numbers of the roulette wheel (1 to 36), the sum is 666.**

# AMAZING LUCK

*Sometimes we're blessed with it, sometimes we're cursed with it—dumb luck. Here are some examples of people who lucked out…for better or worse.*

## DOMO ARIGATO

Jason Powell worked on a grass farm in Corvallis, Oregon. In early 2002, he lost his wallet somewhere in the fields and figured it was gone for good. But it wasn't. Apparently it was picked up by a combine, then baled up with the straw and exported to Japan. Six months later, Powell received the wallet in the mail—returned to him by the Japanese farmer who found it—with his driver's license, credit cards, and $6 still inside.

## GOOD THING THEY DIDN'T CLEAN UP

While visiting their sons in Nebraska, Larry and Leita Hatch stopped at a local Burger King. Larry bought a soft drink and when he peeled off the "Cash Is King" game sticker, he became the only $1 million winner in the entire country. (Wait, it gets better.) He stopped at a grocery store to make a copy of the ticket, but when he got to his son's house, he found he'd lost the original. So he went back to the grocery store—three hours later—and calmly picked up the ticket where it was lying…on the floor in the checkout line.

## GOOD THING THEY DIDN'T CLEAN UP, PART II

Even if you have a winning lottery ticket, you have to turn it in before the deadline in order to claim your prize. In 1994 Duane and Nancy Black of Bullhead City, Arizona, read about an unclaimed lottery ticket. Value: $1.8 million. So just for the heck of it they decided to look through their stash of old tickets—and they found the winner. They immediately got on a plane to Phoenix and claimed their prize…two hours before the six-month ticket expired.

## HEEEERE, LITTLE FISHY

In October 1999, 56-year-old Bev Marshall-Smith was surf-fishing off New Zealand's North Island when a large fish chased her lure into the shallows. Thrilled, she grabbed a piece of driftwood and charged into the water to get it. She must not have been able to see what she'd caught because when the fish refused to go quietly, she started clubbing it. "Every time he wrestled, I hit him," she said. Ultimately, she beat it to death... but the wrestling match could have ended differently. When she went in to collect her prize, she discovered she'd been wrestling with a six-foot blue shark.

## THE LUCKIEST-UNLUCKIEST AWARD

On April 3, 1996, Mohamed Samir Ferrat, an Algerian business associate of U.S. Commerce Secretary Ron Brown, was scheduled to fly with Brown from Bosnia to Croatia. In a bizarre twist of fate, Ferrat backed out of the trip at the last minute. Brown's plane crashed, killing all 35 passengers. Ferrat probably felt like a lucky man, but only three months later, on July 17, he boarded TWA flight 800, which exploded over Long Island Sound, killing all 230 passengers and crewmembers... including Ferrat.

## PICK *ME* A WINNER

Every year the Dearborn Heights Police Supervisors Association holds a raffle in Taylor, Michigan, and because it's a fundraiser for the police, they're careful to be sure everything is aboveboard. The prize for the 2001 raffle was a $20,000 Harley-Davidson Road King Classic; the winning ticket was to be picked by the 2000 winner, an autoworker named Tom Grochoki. There were 7,800 tickets in the barrel. Grochoki picked one, handed it to Lt. Karl Kapelczak, and went back to the crowd to hear the winner's name announced. The winner: Tom Grochoki.

## THE UNLUCKIEST-LUCKIEST AWARD

It was bad luck when a 20-year-old Greek man accidentally shot himself in the head with his speargun while fishing off the island of Crete. A lifeguard found him floating in the water six hours later, the spear entering his jaw, going through his brain, and protruding from the top of his skull. But it was incredibly good luck when surgeons discovered that the spear had passed through one of the spaces in the brain that are nonfunctional—if it was just millimeters to the left or right he would have suffered serious brain injury or died. They removed it in a three-hour operation that left the man with no brain damage and no health problems.

# CAUGHT IN THE ACT

*Things aren't always as they seem, and savvy marketers can turn lying into an art form. But sometimes they get caught.*

**THE PRODUCT:** Heinz Ketchup

**YOU ASSUME:** When you buy a bottle of ketchup that says "20 oz." on it, you get 20 ounces of ketchup.

**WOULD THEY LIE TO US?** Bill Baker of Redding, California, bought a 20-ounce bottle of ketchup for his wife's meatloaf. The recipe called for 20 ounces exactly, but when they poured it in the measuring cup, it was an ounce and a half short.

**EXPOSED:** Bill got ticked off. "If it says 20 ounces, it should be 20 ounces," he said. He called the state's Division of Measurement, setting off a five-year statewide investigation of H. J. Heinz Co. What did they find? Heinz's bottled products, from the 20-ounce to the 64-ounce size, were regularly 0.5% to 2% short. That may not seem like much, but officials estimated that Californians had been cheated out of 10 million ounces—78,124 gallons—of the red stuff. That's $650,000 worth of ketchup. Heinz was ordered to pay $180,000 in civil penalties, and agreed to overfill their bottles for one year—by about 10 million ounces.

**THE PRODUCT:** Used cars

**YOU ASSUME:** When you buy a used car from big-name automaker's dealership, you're getting a safe, reliable car.

**WOULD THEY LIE TO US?** Auto manufacturers buy back about 100,000 cars every year because of defects. Under federal "lemon laws," if they can't fix a car's problem, they have to buy it back. Where does it go from there? For years automakers claimed they would never resell a defective car; it would either be destroyed or studied by their engineers.

**EXPOSED:** In March 2001, in a lawsuit over a "laundered lemon" sold to a North Carolina couple, DaimlerChrysler was forced to reveal some incriminating facts: Between 1993 and 2000, the auto giant had paid $1.3 billion to buy back more than 50,000 vehicles—and resold nearly all of them, recouping two-thirds of the buyback cost. They had been sold to Chrysler dealers who then resold them to the public. And, most damaging to the company, many of the legally required disclosure forms were unsigned, meaning buyers were told nothing about the cars' histories.

In July 2001, Chrysler settled with the couple for an undisclosed amount, but the company was still facing a class-action suit inspired by the case. In December 2001, another couple in California won a similar case against Ford Motor Co., who, the jury ruled, had knowingly resold them a lemon. Amount the jury ordered Ford to pay: $10 million.

**THE PRODUCT:** Movie reviews

**YOU ASSUME:** The movie reviews you read in newspapers and magazines are from authentic, unbiased movie critics.

**WOULD THEY LIE TO US?** In 2001 several advertisements for Sony-made films featured quotes from reviews by "David Manning" of "*The Ridgefield Press*," a small paper in Connecticut. Manning always seemed to give Sony's movies high praise. His take on *A Knight's Tale* star Heath Ledger: "This year's hottest new star!"

**EXPOSED:** After *Newsweek* reporter John Horn questioned the authenticity of the ads in June 2001, and the state of Connecticut investigated, Sony admitted they'd written the reviews themselves. David Manning didn't exist, and the real *Ridgefield Press* knew nothing about it. The investigation also revealed that people appearing in Sony's TV commercials—who seemed to be genuine moviegoers—were actually Sony employees. "These deceptive ads deserve two thumbs down," said state Attorney General Richard Blumenthal. In February 2002, Sony was fined $325,000 and agreed to stop the practice. After the case, Universal Pictures, 20th Century Fox, and Artisan Entertainment all admitted that they, too, had used employees and actors posing as moviegoers in their TV ads.

**OVEREXPOSED:** Shortly after the fake reviewer was revealed, two men in California filed a class-action lawsuit against Sony for "deliberately deceiving consumers." By July, 10 more had been filed against all of Hollywood's major movie studios over deceptive advertising practices. The verdict? Coming soon to a courthouse near you.

**Face facts: In a standard deck of cards, the king of hearts is the only king with no moustache.**

# WARNING LABELS

*Some things in life should go without saying, but there's always the occasional moron who needs to be told not to use a blowtorch while sleeping.*

**On a Duraflame fireplace log:** "Caution—Risk of Fire."

**On a compact disc player:** "Do not use the Ultradisc 2000 as a projectile in a catapult."

**On a propane blowtorch:** "Never use while sleeping."

**On a box of rat poison:** "Warning: Has been found to cause cancer in laboratory mice."

**On an air conditioner:** "Avoid dropping air conditioners out of windows."

**On a vacuum cleaner:** "Do not use to pick up anything that is currently burning."

**On a Batman costume:** "Warning: Cape does not enable user to fly."

**On a bottle of hair coloring:** "Do not use as an ice cream topping."

**On a curling iron:** "Warning: This product can burn eyes."

**On a cardboard sunshield for a car:** "Do not drive with sunshield in place."

**On a toner cartridge:** "Do not eat toner."

**On a toilet bowl cleaning brush:** "Do not use orally."

**On a pair of shin guards:** "Shin pads cannot protect any part of the body they do not cover."

**On a portable stroller:** "Caution: Remove infant before folding for storage."

**On a plastic, 13-inch wheelbarrow wheel:** "Not intended for highway use."

**On a laser pointer:** "Do not look into laser with remaining eye."

**In a microwave oven manual:** "Do not use for drying pets."

**In the instructions for a digital thermometer:** "Do not use orally after using rectally."

# LET'S PLAY SPACEWAR!

*Three years after a government physicist named William Higinbotham created the first video game, Tennis for Two (see page 44), some students at MIT invented a game called Spacewar! Here's their story.*

## NOT EXACTLY A LAPTOP

If you ever get a chance to see a picture of the Electronic Numerical Integrator and Computer (ENIAC for short), you probably won't recognize it for what it is. Completed in 1945, the ENIAC is considered to be the first practical digital computer ever made.

ENIAC was *the* supercomputer of its day. It was as big as a three-bedroom house and weighed more than 60,000 pounds. It contained more than 18,000 vacuum tubes, each one the size of a lightbulb. And because the tubes burned out so frequently (2,000 a month on average), ENIAC was out of order about a third of the time.

Even when it was working, ENIAC couldn't do very much: Its operators programmed it manually, spending hours or even days flipping switches and rewiring circuits. And ENIAC couldn't store these "programs," so each time the operators finished one computational task (calculating the path of an artillery shell, for example) and wanted to start another (nuclear weapons research), they had to flip the switches and rewire the whole computer all over again. ENIAC didn't have a keyboard or video screen, and it was more than 10,000 times slower than a modern personal computer.

## COLLEGE SCREENING

Computers evolved slowly. Computers with video monitors, for example, were extremely rare through the 1960s. Only three universities in the entire United States—Stanford, the University of Utah, and MIT—had one.

So if it took 15 years for computer technology to progress to the point where exactly three American universities could own computers with video screens, how long do you think it took students at these universities to program the first video games into these supercomputers? A couple of months, at most.

## SOMETHING TO SEE

MIT's legendary Whirlwind computer, for example, had a demonstration program called Bouncing Ball. Technically, it wasn't a video game because the viewer didn't do anything. You could only watch as a ball appeared at the top of the screen, then fell to the bottom and bounced around the screen, with a *thwok!* sound coming from the computer's speaker at each bounce. Eventually the ball lost its momentum and settled on the floor, finally rolling off to one side and out of the picture, at which point another ball would drop from the top of the screen.

But Bouncing Ball and the computer "games" that followed weren't supposed to be taken seriously. They were just things the early programmers dreamed up to amuse themselves and to demonstrate the number-crunching power of the Whirlwind computer. The best games were designed to tax the abilities of the computers to the limit. But other than that, they were "hacks," as they were called even then—programs with no constructive purpose whatsoever. The people who made them called themselves "hackers."

Mouse in the Maze was one of the earliest hacks. Designed for a supercomputer called the TX-O, it consisted of a mouse (the animal), a maze, and a piece of cheese. Using a special light pen, the player drew a maze right on the screen and then placed the cheese in the maze. Then the mouse searched through the maze and ate the cheese, leaving crumbs wherever it ate. An "improved" version had the mouse searching for martinis and after drinking the first one, staggering around the maze looking for the rest. There were other games—Tic-Tac-Toe, and a pattern-generating program called HAX—but nothing that would hold the interest of players for more than a few minutes.

## COMPUTER TRAINING

Then in the fall of 1961, the Digital Equipment Corporation donated a state-of-the-art computer called the Programmable Data Processor (PDP-1) to MIT. The PDP-1 was smaller than the TX-O, much faster, and a lot easier to use.

Even before it arrived at MIT, the PDP-1 had captured the imagination of the university's Tech Model Railroad Club (TMRC). Club members had already spent several years "requisitioning" computer equipment from around campus and using it to automate their huge model railroad. They'd also spent a lot of time learning how to program the TX-O, so when the PDP-1 finally arrived on campus, they were already the best computer programmers around. And they were ready to hack.

The PDP-1 came with no software at all; almost everything had to be programmed from scratch. MIT students were doing much of the programming for little or no pay, so the professors who controlled access to the computer agreed to give them plenty of hack time in return. And what did they do with the hack time? They invented games.

## LOST IN SPACE

Many TMRC members were science-fiction buffs; so it didn't take them long to decide what kind of game they wanted to create for the PDP-1: a space game—one that would push the computer's processing power to its limits. "The basic rules developed quickly," MIT alumnus J. M. Graetz remembers. "There would be at least two spaceships, each controlled by a set of console switches.... The ships would have a supply of rocket fuel and some sort of a weapon—a ray or a beam, or possibly a missile."

## SPACEWAR!

TMRC member Steve "Slug" Russell wrote the first version of the game, taking about six months and 200 hours of computer time to do it. The game he came up with consisted of two spaceships, one wedge shaped, the other long and thin, which flew around the screen and battled one another by shooting "torpedoes"—dots of light—at each other. Each ship was controlled by a different set of four toggle switches on the PDP-1 console. One toggle switch made the ship rotate clockwise; a second made it rotate counterclockwise; a third switch provided thrust; and a fourth fired the torpedoes. (Ever play Asteroids? The controls were pretty much the same.)

Both ships were controlled by human players. There was no way to play the computer as your opponent, because once everything else had been programmed into it, "there wasn't enough computing power available to do a decent opponent," Russell remembered. He named his game Spacewar!

**The "average" American CEO's pay has increased more than 600% since 1990.**

## A THOUSAND POINTS OF LIGHT

As soon as Russell got the game up and running, other TMRC members began making improvements:

• At first the game had no stars in the background, but the blank screen made it difficult to tell whether slow-moving ships were drifting closer to each other or farther apart. So Russell added a series of random dots… but they didn't last long. Using an astronomical reference book, another club member, Pete Samson, programmed in an accurate map of the night sky, including the relative brightness of each star.

• Another TMRC member named Dan Edwards inserted a sun—complete with accurate gravitational field—into the center of the screen. Now instead of sitting still in empty space, the ships were constantly being pulled toward the sun, and if they crashed into it they were destroyed. That helped to make the game more interesting, because it inserted an element that was beyond the players' control. It also made strategy more important, because skilled players could figure out ways to use gravity to their advantage.

• Graetz added a feature called "hyperspace." If a player got into trouble and was about to get killed, flipping the hyperspace toggle caused the ship to disappear for a few seconds and then reappear somewhere else on the screen, hopefully someplace less dangerous and not close to the sun. Graetz also inserted an element of risk—if a player hit hyperspace one too many times, their ship would be destroyed.

## TOO MUCH OF A GOOD THING

The improvements made the game more interesting… which created a new set of problems. Spacewar! addicts played for hours on end, frantically flipping the toggle switches on the $120,000 computer until their elbows hurt. Needless to say, the computer wasn't designed with that kind of use (or abuse) in mind.

Rather than risk breaking the $120,000 computer, a couple of TMRC members scrounged wire, switches, and other parts from the model railroad and made another innovation—individual game controllers that they connected to the PDP-1 with lengths of electrical wire. Now the players could stand back from the computer and play as furiously as they wanted to, without damaging the computer or getting sore elbows.

## BIRDS OF A FEATHER

So what do Steve Russell and the developers of Spacewar! have in common with Willy Higinbotham, creator of Tennis for Two? Two things—they never patented their invention; and they never made any money from it. Digital Equipment ended up giving Spacewar! away as a diagnostic program and it became popular with computer engineers and programmers all over the country… including a University of Utah student named Nolan Bushnell, who later founded Atari.

It turns out there was a way to make money off of Spacewar!… it just involved waiting for the price of computer technology to come down. In the mid-1970s, well after the video arcade craze was underway, an MIT graduate student named Larry Rosenthal decided to build an arcade version of Spacewar! as his master's thesis project. The game he created—sold as Space War and then as Space Wars—happened to hit the arcades in 1977, the same year that *Star Wars* hit the big screen.

Space War(s) had nothing to do with *Star Wars*, of course, but nobody cared. It quickly became the most popular arcade game ever… until a game called Space Invaders came along in 1978.

## MEETING OF THE MINDS

As for Steve Russell, he not only never made a penny off the game he was largely responsible for creating, he never even graduated from MIT. He relocated to Seattle and got a job with a computer time-share company. One of his responsibilities was hiring local high school kids to come into the office and see if they could get the computers to crash. Lots of kids tried, but, according to Russell, only one kid had enough computer savvy to make the computers crash every time, no matter how hard Russell and his colleagues tried to thwart him.

The kid's name was Bill Gates. He never graduated from college, either.

***The next phase of the history of video games will take us to the video arcade, so turn to page 225 and let's play Pong.***

# LOST INVENTIONS

*True or false: Ever since some caveman got the bright idea of making tools, it's been a steady advance of ideas and innovation, from the wheel to the automobile and beyond. False. History is much messier than that. Many inventions have been made, lost, and reinvented later. Here are a few examples.*

## THE ELECTRIC BATTERY

The National Museum of Iraq has a collection of clay jars made by the Parthians, who once ruled the Middle East. One jar, however, dating from about 200 B.C., is not your ordinary container.

It's just over five inches high by three inches across. The opening was once sealed with asphalt, with a narrow iron rod sticking through it. Inside the jar was a copper sheet rolled into a tube and closed at the bottom with a copper disc. The iron rod hung down in the center of the tube.

The odd jar didn't attract much attention until around 1960, when researchers discovered that if the jar was filled with an acidic liquid (vinegar or fermented grape juice), it generated a small current, between 1.5 and 2 volts. Their conclusion: the jar was an electric battery. In the acidic liquid, electrons flowed from the copper tube to the iron rod—much like the batteries invented by Italian physicist Alessandro Volta around 1800.

But what would anyone in ancient Baghdad use a battery for? The most likely explanation is that they linked a series of batteries that were used to electroplate gold onto silver. Electroplating is a way of covering the surface of one metal with another metal, creating the false appearance of a solid gold object. It involves passing an electric current through a solution, forcing positively charged metal particles onto a negatively charged surface. Experiments have shown that electroplating can indeed be done with modern batteries just like that ancient jar.

## THE COMPUTER

In 1900 sponge divers found the wreck of an ancient ship 140 feet under water, near the Greek island of Antikythera. Many of the items retrieved from it were taken to the National Archaeological Museum in Athens, among them lumps of corroded bronze that looked like parts of a statue. But an archaeologist noticed some words inscribed on the metal and then found gears—and then realized it wasn't a statue, it was a machine.

Originally held together by a wooden box that fell apart when taken out of the water, the mechanism had dials on the outside and a complicated arrangement of wheels and differential gears inside. The inscription dated it between 100 B.C. and 30 A.D. and indicated that the contraption had something to do with astronomy.

A 1959 *Scientific American* article compared the object to "a well-made 18th-century clock." The "Antikythera mechanism," it said, was a model of the solar system which, like a modern computer, "used mechanical parts to save tedious calculation." Turned by hand, or perhaps by water power, the machine would calculate and display the position of the sun, moon, planets, and stars.

The find meant that historians had to rethink their whole concept of the ancient Greek world—and their concept of when computing machines were first invented.

## THE SEISMOGRAPH

Domemico Salsano, an Italian clockmaker, is usually credited with inventing the seismograph in 1783. His "geo-sismometro" used an inked brush attached to a pendulum. The brush recorded earth-shaking vibrations on an ivory slab. It was sensitive enough to register quakes from 200 miles away.

But 1,500 years before that, a Chinese philosopher named Chang Hêng had already invented a device for detecting distant earthquakes. It was shaped like a big wine jar, about six feet across. On the outside were eight dragon heads with an open-mouthed toad beneath each one. Each dragon held a ball in its mouth. When a distant earthquake occurred, the dragon pointing in the direction of the quake dropped the ball into the mouth of the toad.

Nobody is sure exactly what mechanism was inside the jar, but modern seismologists assume that a pendulum was connected to the dragons. And, according to ancient records, the dragon jar worked.

# SPACE BATHROOM ALPHA

*We're always interested in how astronauts "take care of business" in the weightlessness of space. Now that the International Space Station is up and running, we figured that it's time to revisit the subject.*

## BRAVE NEW WORLD

As we told you on page 25, millionaire American businessman Dennis Tito made history in April 2001 when he bought his way onto the International Space Station, also known as Space Station Alpha, by paying the Russian Space Agency a cool $20 million for the privilege of becoming the world's first space tourist.

Since then, NASA has agreed to allow more such trips. So in case you're planning to take a Space Station vacation, you might like to know what to expect if you get up there and have to... use the facilities.

The toilet on Space Station Alpha has a toilet seat and a bowl, but that's where any similarity to Earth toilets ends. Since there's no gravity in the space station, they can't use water to flush the toilet—there's no way to keep it in the bowl. The toilet flushes with "air currents." What does that mean? That's NASA's polite way of saying that you're pooping into a toilet bowl hooked up to a vacuum cleaner.

## LOOKING OUT FOR NUMBER ONE

As for peeing, there's a special vacuum hose in the bathroom designed for that purpose. Everyone has to use the same hose, but each astronaut is issued their own custom-fitted "personal urine funnel" (yes, the male funnels are shaped differently from the female funnels). These special attachments help to prevent leakage into the Space Station's atmosphere and also helps to minimize the "yuck" factor associated with everyone having to pee into the same hose.

What happens next? Unlike the Space Shuttle, where the urine is collected into a storage tank and periodically vented into outer space, Space Station Alpha doesn't have that luxury. The Space Shuttle makes short trips and returns to Earth on a regular basis, so

**The city of Chicago tows 55,000 junked cars to wrecking yards per year.**

its water tanks are refilled before each new mission. But Space Station Alpha (hopefully) is never coming back down, and the astronauts who live and work there will be in space for weeks or even months on end. Sending up fresh supplies of water every couple of months would cost a fortune, so NASA developed a different strategy: the station is designed to recycle every single drop of water possible, including sweat, including the moisture the astronauts exhale when they breathe, *and* their urine.

## WASTE NOT, WANT NOT

The Space Station toilet pumps the astro-urine into a machine called a Urine Processor, or UP (pronounced "you pee") for short. It works kind of like the spin cycle on a washing machine: the urine enters a cylindrical drum that rotates more than 300 times a minute; this causes the liquid to spread out in a thin layer across the surface of the drum. Most of the air has already been sucked out of the drum, creating a low-pressure environment that allows the water in the urine to boil off into steam at close to room temperature. The steam is then condensed back into liquid form. Everything else in the pee—minerals and salts—is collected in a filter, and the filters are changed at least once a month.

## RIGHT BACK AT YOU

After the UP is finished, the "water" is pumped into a "Potable Water Processor," where it is mixed with all the other reclaimed water in the Space Station: shower water, water used when the astronauts wash their hands or brush their teeth, and moisture that's removed from the air by dehumidifiers. This waste water is pumped through a filter that removes any particles or debris. Then it's pumped through several other filters to remove any chemicals, and finally it's oxidized, or treated with oxygen, to remove any remaining chemicals and kill off any living organisms.

End result: Purified, drinkable water that is actually much cleaner than the water that comes out of your faucet at home. Really. It has almost no taste, because the water doesn't contain any dissolved minerals like tap water does on Earth. There's no smell, either. "That's easy to get rid of," says Alan Mortimer, head of Space Life Sciences at the Canadian Space Agency. "The things that smell are easy to take out."

**Wasps kill more people in the U.S. every year than snakes, spiders, and scorpions combined.**

## HOUSTON, WE HAVE A PROBLEM

In all, the system is able to recycle about 95% of the space station's water. But what about the "solids"? The poop that's collected in Space Bathroom Alpha can't be recycled. Instead, it will be stored in sealed "toilet canisters" until one of the unmanned Russian *Progress* supply ships docks at the Space Station. After the fresh supplies are unloaded, the *Progress* is filled with the poop cans (and other garbage) and then jettisoned away from the station. Gravity pulls it back into the Earth's atmosphere, where it burns up on reentry.

These flaming fireballs of space poop are a huge improvement over the original Space Shuttle toilets. Those toilets had a 14-day holding capacity and could not be emptied during a mission. As soon as they filled up, the astronauts had to either return to Earth…or improvise. And even back on Earth, the toilets were not easily emptied. They had to be removed from the shuttle and flown to Houston to be cleaned by highly trained technicians.

## WASHING UP

The International Space Station also has a shower, something the shuttle astronauts had to do without. (They had to make do with sponge baths and shampoo, originally designed for hospital patients, that didn't need to be rinsed out.)

Taking a shower in space is similar to taking one on Earth, except that in the absence of gravity, the water doesn't fall to the floor. It just floats around inside the shower stall, which is sealed to prevent the water from escaping into the rest of the Space Station. One advantage: Since the water floats around instead of going down the drain, you don't need as much to take your shower as you would on Earth. You only use about a gallon of water, and instead of moving in and out from under the showerhead, you just grab the floating globs of water and rub them on yourself. When you're finished, there's a vacuum hose attached to one wall that you use to suck up all the drops before leaving the shower.

*　*　*

According to surveys, 57% of Americans shower daily, 17% sing in the shower, 4% shower with the lights off, and 3% clean their pets by showering with them.

# THE WORLD'S WORST...

*We were going to do a page of "bests"—but worsts are funnier. So put on a happy face and read about the worst...*

**...TRAFFIC CONGESTION** A 2002 study found that traffic moved through central London at an average speed of 2.9 mph—slower than walking.

**...VIEW** The Grand Banks of Newfoundland, Canada, are blanketed by heavy fog for an average of one out of every three days—often for weeks at a time.

**...CROSSWORD PUZZLE ANSWER** In 1971, the *London Times* included this word in one of its daily puzzles: *honorificabilitudinitatibus*.

**...REJECTION** When King Harald Grenske of Norway proposed marriage to Queen Sigrid Storrada of Denmark in 996, she had him executed.

**...MOVIE** According to a nationwide poll conducted by the Hastings Bad Cinema Society, the worst movie of the 20th century was John Travolta's *Battlefield Earth*.

**...VOTING "ERROR"** In the 1928 Nigerian presidential election, Charles King beat Thomas Faulkner by 600,000 votes. One problem: Nigeria only had 15,000 registered voters.

**...CONSTRUCTION PROJECT** Workers spent 90 years building the Church of Corcuetos in Spain. The day after it was finally completed in 1625, it collapsed.

**...TOURISTS** According to a survey by the online travel service *expedia.com*, "Britons are the rudest, meanest, and worst-behaved holidaymakers in the world."

**...HANDS IN FOOTBALL** Quarterback Warren Moon fumbled the ball 161 times during his 17-year career.

**...CAR** Click and Clack, the *Car Talk* guys, polled listeners to find the lousiest make of car ever produced. The winner...er, we mean, loser: the Yugo.

# LOVE AT FIRST SIGHT?

*Uncle John actually fell in love at first sight. So smooth and shiny. Those perfect proportions. That beautiful white…porcelain. You thought we were talking about* Mrs. Uncle John? *Oh, yeah. Her too.*

## HERE'S LOOKING AT YOU

You're looking around a crowded room, and your eyes meet the eyes of another. Pow! A shock runs through your whole body! Are you in love? Maybe. Read on to find out. That jolt isn't imaginary. Scientists say that part of your brain actually perks up when you exchange looks with a person you consider attractive.

And just how did they discover that? British researchers used a special helmet to scan the brains of 16 volunteers (8 men and 8 women). Wearing an fMRI (functional magnetic resonance imaging) helmet, each volunteer looked at 160 photos of 40 complete strangers.

In some photos, the strangers were looking directly at the camera—which made them appear to be looking directly at the volunteer. In others, the stranger's eyes were turned away.

As the photos went flashing by—one every 3.5 seconds—the helmets recorded which part of the volunteer's brain was active. After the brain scan was finished, the volunteers went back to the pictures and rated each one for attractiveness. The results of the experiment were published in 2001 in *Nature* magazine.

## REAL SPARKS

Every time a volunteer saw an attractive person looking right at them, the volunteer's ventral striatum lit up—that part of the brain is linked to the anticipation of a reward. But when the stranger in the photo was looking away, the magic didn't happen; there was much less brain activity, no matter how attractive the person in the photo. The researchers attributed that to disappointment—the volunteer had failed to make eye contact with an attractive face.

The brain response happened fast—in just nanoseconds.

Researchers think this means that it's automatic, that we're all wired for that kind of reaction.

## EYES OF THE BEHOLDER

Does this mean that everybody responds to certain kinds of looks? The leading researcher, Dr. Knut Kampe of the Institute of Cognitive Neuroscience in London, commented that we all might naturally respond to people who look strong and healthy. That could be connected with survival. But Kampe said that each of the volunteers defined attractiveness in different ways, and conventional beauty wasn't the only important thing. Some looked for cheerfulness, others for a face that seemed to show empathy. Some even looked for motherliness.

## IS IT LOVE?

So does it mean that love at first sight is real? Can we expect to instantly recognize our perfect mate? Probably not. Consider the following:

• Seeing a certain someone can get your brain buzzing—but so can seeing food when you're hungry. The ventral striatum that responded to the photos is the same area that lights up in hungry lab animals who think they're about to get fed. Gamblers and drug addicts have the same kind of reaction to the objects of their desire. That part of your brain gets excited when it expects *any* kind of reward.

• The brain's quick response helps explain why we make snap judgments about people we meet. But first impressions can be wrong.

• The same brain area lit up for any attractive face—no matter whether it was the opposite sex or the same sex as the volunteer. Researchers think that's because attractiveness often gets associated with social status. So maybe your brain assumes that hanging out with attractive people could improve your position. (In the case of monkeys, bonding with an animal higher up in the pecking order brings increased social status.)

So if you're expecting a future with someone based on the jolt you got when your eyes met—slow down. You'll have to engage some other part of your brain to find out whether the two of you actually get along.

**The name "Ann" is used as a middle name 10 times more often than as a first name.**

# ROLL THE DICE

*Tired of reading palms? Sick of tea leaves? Ouija bored? Uncle John predicted that you would be. If you have a pair of dice lying around, here's another way to tell your fortune.*

## ASTRAGALOMANCY

Have you ever played Yahtzee or rolled dice in a bar? In Victorian England, people known as "dicers" told fortunes by tossing dice from a small cup held in their left hands. Telling fortunes with two dice is known as *astragalomancy*. (Using three dice is *cleromancy*.)

Give it a try! Tossing a pair of dice around is good for a few minutes of fun even if you aren't a true believer.

## HOW TO DO IT

- Draw a circle about 12 inches in diameter on a piece of paper.
- Decide on a question that you want answered and ask it either silently or aloud as you shake the dice in your hand or in a cup. Then throw the dice into the circle, either one at a time or both at the same time.
- Add up the numbers on both dice to get the answer to your question. Sometimes the answer is precise, sometimes it's vague. (What did you expect? This *is* fortune telling, after all.)

## ANSWERS

2—The answer is no.

3—If you act cautiously in the coming days, you can expect a pleasant surprise.

4—You will have good luck when you expect it least.

5—Your question will be answered in a surprising way.

6—Some form of divine intervention will provide you with an answer.

7—You will win.

8—You already know the answer to your question (so stop playing with dice and find something better to do).

9—If the answer is yes, it's only because of a twist of fate.

10—Count on success!

11—Stay calm, be prepared, know that fate is on your side.

12—Regardless of what happens, you will feel content about it.

## CIRCULAR LOGIC

How many of your dice fell within the circle? That's part of your fortune, too:

• One die outside the circle means that you're likely to get the answer you want *eventually* but only "after your own thoughts set your wishes into motion."

• Two dice outside the circle: You'll get the answer you want, sooner than you think.

## YES AND NO

Now here's where using dice to tell your fortune can get confusing:

• Let's say you ask the question, "Will I make a million dollars?" You want the answer to be "yes," but your roll adds up to two, so the answer is "no."

• But both dice land outside the circle, which means you'll get the answer you want—"*yes*" (instead of the "no" you just rolled), and you'll get that "yes" sooner than you think. But wait a minute—you just rolled a "yes" *and* a "no." What's that supposed to mean? Does it mean maybe? Do you roll the dice again?

• Uncle John solved the problem by asking the question, "Does fortune telling with dice really work?"

He rolled a two. You're on your own.

* * *

## MORE WAYS TO TELL A FORTUNE

**Ailuromancy:** Observe how a cat jumps.

**Sycomancy:** Write a question on a leaf, leave the leaf in the sun. "If the leaf shrivels quickly, the answer is no." Otherwise the answer is yes.

**Keriomancy:** Study the flickering flame of a candle.

**Aleuromancy:** Read messages in baked balls of dough.

**Oomancy:** Crack an egg into a glass of water and study the shapes the egg white forms in the water.

**Scrying:** Study "crystals, mirrors, bowls of water, ink, blood, flames, or other shiny objects."

**Ceromancy:** Drop some melted wax into water and study the shapes that are formed.

**The 13th step of the state capitol in Denver, Colorado, is exactly one mile above sea level.**

# D.C. FOLLIES

*Some people say the best comedy is on TV.
We say it's in Washington, D.C.*

## DON'T QUIT YOUR DAY JOB

"Concerned that 'the pickup owners of this nation might get screwed in all this gas-guzzler talk about SUVs and vans,' **Zell Miller (D-Ga.)** introduced an amendment to keep pickup fuel economy requirements at 20.7 mpg. He also co-wrote, sang, and recorded 'The Talking Pickup Truck Blues.'

"A sample of the lyrics: 'Sure, an SUV is classy travel, / But it ain't much good for haulin' gravel, / Or hay or seed or bovine feces. / So please, don't make my pickup truck an endangered species.'"

—***Fox News***

## SHAMELESS EXPLOITATION

"A controversy started September 11 when **Brian Kerns (R-Ind.)** gave the *Indianapolis Star* a harrowing account of watching a hijacked plane slam into the Pentagon during his commute on George Washington Memorial Parkway. 'I'm in shock,' he said. 'I still can't believe it. I drove into the office and told my staff to go home.'

"The *Indianapolis Star* reported, however, that the plane in question never flew over that parkway. And an American Legion official said he remembers being in Kerns's office with the congressman when networks reported the Pentagon attack. Kerns's response when pressed on whether he was mistaken about what he saw: 'Who knows?'"

**—Associated Press**

## TOOT-TOOT

**"Patrick Kennedy (D-R.I.)** was accused of causing $28,000 in damage to a rented yacht on a Y2K booze cruise. He later appeared at a political roast dressed in a sailor suit and capped off the evening by singing 'Patrick the Sailor Man.' At the same roast, the admitted former cokehead joked about Senator Lincoln Chafee (R-R.I.), another admitted former cokehead: 'Now when I hear

**Bess Truman is the only First Lady to have a hurricane named after her.**

someone talking about a Rhode Island politician whose father was a senator and who got to Washington on his family name, used cocaine, and wasn't very smart, I know there is only a 50-50 chance it's me.'"

***—Mother Jones***

## TAKE YOUR CHILD TO WORK DAY?

"Answering questions about whether his recent election was helped by nepotism (after receiving $1 million from the Republican Party's coffers), **Bill Shuster (R-Pa.)**, son of Pennsylvania representative Bud Shuster, insisted 'This is about Bill Shuster… and Bill Shuster standing on his own two feet.' Maybe. We wonder if Solicitor of the Labor Department Eugene Scalia, son of Antonin; Health and Human Services Inspector General Janet Rehnquist, daughter of William; FCC chair Michael Powell, son of Colin; and President George W. Bush feel the same way."

***—Roll Call***

## ROCKET MAN

"In September 1996, **Mickey Kalinay (D)** was defeated in the Democratic primary for the U.S. Senate in Wyoming… despite his tantalizing proposal to make the space program more efficient by constructing a 22,000-mile-high tower so that space stations can be accessed by electromagnetic rail cars."

***—News of the Weird***

## SOME THINGS NEVER CHANGE

"The last time **former Vice-President Dan Quayle (R)** lived in Washington, his words were parsed almost as closely as the current president's. He still lets off the occasional zinger; during an appearance on MSNBC's *Hardball*, as he tried to 'set aside the Middle East peace situation' from the war on terrorism, he asked: 'How many Palestinians were on those airplanes on September 9? None.'"

***—Salon.com***

## WHAT!?!

"In 1988, **Tom DeLay (R-Tx.)** explained to reporters his lack of service in the Vietnam War, despite being eligible and healthy. 'So many minority youths had volunteered,' he claimed, 'that there was literally no room for patriotic folks like myself.'"

**—online columnist, Ted Barlow**

# *SNL* PART II: ON THE AIR

*Lorne Michaels had all of the ingredients for* Saturday Night, *now he had to figure out how to mix them together. (Part I is on page 53.)*

## BARELY CONTROLLED CHAOS

The scheduled air date for the first episode of *NBC's Saturday Night* was October 11, 1975. Just about everyone—from the executives to the crew—didn't see the show lasting an entire season... except for Lorne Michaels. He reassured his worried cast and writers on the 17th floor that their grandchildren would be watching reruns of the first episode in history class. But no one was convinced. And the chaos of the final week leading up to the premiere didn't help matters.

By the time Saturday rolled around, Michaels had no lighting director (he had fired two already); the antiquated sound system had broken down; and instead of the brick wall they were promised for a backdrop, they had a ton of uncut bricks piled in the middle of the floor.

While Michaels was busy ordering script changes and settling various arguments, Ebersol brought news that the network had ordered the show's celebrity host, George Carlin, to wear a suit and tie—the embodiment of everything *Saturday Night* was against. (Carlin compromised by wearing a sport coat with a T-shirt underneath.)

## THE FIRST SKETCH

A lot of thought went into the best way to begin the show. Michaels wanted people to know from the get-go that they were seeing something different. His solution: Begin with a "cold opening." When the clock struck 11:30 p.m., viewers were pulled immediately into a sketch featuring Michael O'Donoghue and John Belushi as, respectively, professor and student.

**O'Donoghue:** "Let us begin. Repeat after me. I would like..."

**Belushi** (*in a thick foreign accent*)**:** "I would like..."

**O'Donoghue:** "... to feed your fingertips..."

**Belushi:** "... to feed your feengerteeps..."

**O'Donoghue:** "... to the wolverines."

**Belushi:** "... to thee wolvereeenes."

*This goes on for a few minutes until O'Donoghue clutches his heart and keels over. Belushi sits there, shrugs, then grabs* his *heart and keels over. The puzzled audience is left hanging for a moment, and then* **Chevy Chase** *enters wearing a stage manager's headset. He looks at the two figures lying on the floor, then breaks out into a big grin and says to the camera:* "Live from New York, it's Saturday Night!"

The show didn't go off without a hitch, but despite a few miscues, they had pulled it off—within the allotted budget—a feat that impressed the skeptical NBC brass.

## SHOCKING COMEDY

The ratings for the first few episodes were considerably better than those for *Tonight Show* reruns (although still not enough to pull in major advertising dollars), while the initial reviews were a bit mixed. But a big boost came from the highly touted TV critic Tom Shales:

> *NBC's Saturday Night* can boast the freshest satire on commercial TV, but it is more than that, it is probably the first network series produced by and for the television generation.... It is a live, lively, raucously disdainful view of a world that television has largely shaped. Or misshaped.

Younger viewers agreed. Here was a show that actually *made fun* of television. Dick Ebersol referred to it as "the post-Watergate victory party for the Woodstock generation."

As much as kids loved the show, grown-ups hated it. Johnny Carson echoed a lot of aging comedians' views when he described the Not Ready For Primetime Players as a bunch of amateurs who couldn't "ad-lib a fart at a bean-eating contest." It was a completely different brand of comedy than they were used to. Comedians like Bob Hope and Milton Berle made their audience comfortable, then made them laugh. By mocking the establishment, *Saturday Night* made some viewers uncomfortable. Just to make fun of politicians in general wasn't enough, this new show singled out specific politicians, particularly presidents, and ridiculed them. All of a sudden, the revolution was being televised.

## "I'M CHEVY CHASE AND YOU'RE NOT"

The first season belonged to Chase. Because he anchored "Weekend

**The Bayer Aspirin Company trademarked the brand name Heroin in 1898.**

Update," he got to say his name every week, and he was the only one who did. The show opened without naming any of the cast, so Chase's tagline, along with his clumsy portrayal of President Ford, thrust him into the spotlight. He alone was nominated for an Emmy Award and then was named "heir apparent to Johnny Carson" by *New York* magazine. The other cast members were jealous—especially Belushi—creating an intense air of discord backstage.

But it didn't matter. Chase left shortly into the second season to pursue a woman (he married her) and a movie career in Hollywood. He later called his departure one of the biggest mistakes of his career. Michaels, on the other hand, realized that the show had an amazing potential to make stars, so he added the cast members' names and pictures to the opening credits. Meanwhile, ABC's *Saturday Night Live* was canceled, so Bill Murray was available to replace Chase in 1976.

## SECOND SEASON SUCCESS

The ensuing season saw the cast, writers, and crew start to really come together. Recurring characters like the Coneheads and the Bees (which Belushi always hated) were quickly becoming household names. Catchphrases like "Jane, you ignorant slut" and "No Coke, Pepsi!" were becoming part of the national lexicon.

In the first season, Lorne Michaels had to search long and hard for willing hosts and musical guests; in the second season, they were calling him. When stand-up comedian Steve Martin first watched the show in a hotel room, he was blown away. "They did it," he said to himself. "They did the show everyone should have been doing." And then he made it his goal to be a part of it, which he did in the second season. He has since gone on to host *SNL* more times than anyone else.

## HIGH TIMES

Another part of the show's success: drugs. "From the beginning," say Hill and Weingrad, "grass was a staple of the show, used regularly and openly." Cocaine was also used, although by fewer people and behind closed doors. One of *SNL*'s early masterpieces, a sketch called "The Final Days" that chronicles Nixon's downfall, was written by Tom Davis and future U.S. Senator Al Franken while they were on LSD. Drugs found their way into the sketches,

**Percentage of (dead) people who were cremated in 1975: 7%. In 2000: 26%.**

too, something that some cast members, most notably Chase—who once demonstrated the proper way to "shoot up"—would later regret. But it was just this kind of humor that made *Saturday Night* so popular with the youth culture.

## THE BLUES BROTHERS RULE

By 1977 Belushi and Aykroyd were the show's big stars, and they often flexed their muscles by threatening to quit if they didn't get their way. Meanwhile the women—Radner, Newman, and Curtin—were feeling alienated by the drugged-out and sexist behavior of the men. Michaels was running himself ragged trying (unsuccessfully) to keep everyone happy, while Ebersol was under constant pressure from the network to curb the controversial subject matter.

In 1978 Chase hit it big with his movie *Foul Play*. Aykroyd and Belushi knew that movie careers were waiting for them as well and left after the fourth season to make *The Blues Brothers*. Instead of replacing them, Michaels hired only one new cast member, comedian Harry Shearer (who, years later, would add his vocal talents to *The Simpsons*).

## FEATURED PLAYERS

In his quest to find the next big star, Michaels devised a billing called "featured player." Because they didn't have full cast-member status, he didn't have to pay them as much. He tried out band member Paul Shaffer (of David Letterman fame), writers Al Franken, Tom Davis, and Don Novello (Father Guido Sarducci), as well as Brian Doyle-Murray (brother of Bill), and Peter Aykroyd (brother of Dan). The result: A disastrous 1979 season.

Bill Murray and Gilda Radner, who dated on and off during *SNL*'s previous years, now couldn't stand each other. In fact, Murray couldn't stand anything about the show—the writers, the cast, his parts—and spent most of his time launching tirades. Laraine Newman and Garrett Morris were both battling depression, drug addictions, and the realization that Hollywood didn't want them. Lorne Michaels was also exhausted, and when contract negotiations broke down for a sixth season, he quit.

***Things looked bad for* Saturday Night Live. *Could it get worse? Yes.*** ***Turn to page 220 for Part III of the story.***

# DID THE PUNISHMENT FIT THE CRIME?

*They don't give judges awards for creativity—but maybe they should. Do these guys deserve a prize? You be the judge.*

**THE DEFENDANT:** Edward Bello, 60, a vending machine repairman and small-time crook

**THE CRIME:** Conspiracy to use stolen credit cards, with which he racked up more than $26,000 in charges

**THE PUNISHMENT:** Federal District Court Judge Alvin K. Hellerstein sentenced Bello to 10 months of home detention... *with no TV*. The tube-free environment would "create a condition of silent introspection that I consider necessary to induce the defendant to change his behavior." Despite a 30-year history of committing petty crimes, Bello has never spent a day in prison and says he's grateful to the judge for sparing him from the slammer one more time. But he's appealing the no-TV sentence anyway, claiming that it's a form of censorship and violates his First Amendment rights. "Let's face it," he says, "a television is sort of like your umbilical cord to life."

**THE DEFENDANT:** Albert Brown, a repeat drug offender in San Francisco, California

**THE CRIME:** Selling drugs to an undercover cop

**A NOVEL APPROACH:** Rather than decide the sentence himself, Judge James Warren of San Francisco handed Brown one of his judicial robes and told him to put it on. "This is your life," he told Brown. "You are your own judge. Sentence yourself."

**THE PUNISHMENT:** Brown, in tears, gave himself six months in jail. Then, according to news reports, he tacked on a "string of self-imposed conditions such as cleaning himself up for his kids, and steering clear of the neighborhood where he got busted."

"The Probation Department recommended six months and a good lecturing," Judge Warren told reporters. "But I figured, I'm not that good at lecturing. He, on the other hand, was very good at lecturing himself. And maybe this time it will stick. I had the transcript typed up and sent over to him. Just in case he forgets."

**THE DEFENDANT:** Alan Law, 19, of Derwent, Ohio
**THE CRIME:** Disturbing the peace by driving through town with his truck windows rolled down and the stereo blasting
**THE PUNISHMENT:** Municipal Court Judge John Nicholson gave Law a choice: pay a $100 fine or sit and listen to polka music for four hours. Law chose facing the music. A few days later, he reported to the police station and was locked in an interview room, where he listened to the "Blue Skirt Waltz," "Who Stole the Kishka," "Too Fat Polka," and other hits by Cleveland polka artist Frankie Yankovic. Law managed to sit through it and has since abandoned his plans to buy an even louder stereo for his truck.

**THE DEFENDANT:** A youth in the Wake County, North Carolina, Juvenile Court (names of juvenile offenders are sealed)
**THE CRIME:** Burglary and theft
**THE PUNISHMENT:** Judge Don Overby sent the miscreant home to get his most-prized possession. The kid returned with a remote-controlled car, which he handed over to the court. The judge then took a hammer and smashed it to smithereens. Judge Overby has done this with other first time offenders as well. He says he got the idea after someone broke into his house and stole his CD player, his VCR, and $300 in cash. "I remember wishing these folks could feel the same sense of loss as I did," he says.

* * *

## A BRAINTEASER

**Question:** You are competing in a race and overtake the runner in second place. Which position are you in now?

**Answer:** If you answered that you're now in first place, you're wrong. You overtook the second runner and took their place, therefore you're in second.

**The cheetah is the only member of the cat family that cannot retract its claws.**

# THE REST OF THE UNITED STATES

*America is more than just 50 states. You may be interested to learn that the United States owns some interesting real estate.*

## STATES OF THE UNION

All told, the United States owns a dozen "territories" and two "commonwealths." The definitions of both terms are a little vague but they have a few things in common: All of them are under the jurisdiction of the United States, which means the U.S. government controls their trade, foreign relations, immigration, citizenship, currency, maritime laws, declarations of war, legal procedures, treaties, radio and television regulations, and other such areas. Residents have fundamental rights under the U.S. Constitution, and U.S. citizens don't need a passport to go to there.

Residents of the commonwealths (Puerto Rico and the Northern Mariana Islands) and the inhabited territories (Guam, the U.S. Virgin Islands, and American Samoa) have a bit more in common:

• They have elected local governments, similar to those of states, but commonwealths are semi-autonomous, with a constitution and more control of their internal affairs than territories.

• They don't vote in federal elections.

• They elect non-voting delegates to Congress.

• They don't pay federal income tax (no taxation without representation).

• They do pay Social Security taxes.

• They are eligible for welfare and other federal aid programs.

• They are served by the U.S. Postal Service and have their own zip codes.

• Residents of Puerto Rico, the Northern Mariana Islands, Guam, and the U.S. Virgin Islands are U.S. citizens. Residents of American Samoa are considered U.S. nationals, not citizens.

• English is the official language (although some have a second or even third official language as well).

**Twenty-four U.S. states do not allow first cousins to marry each other.**

• The official currency is the U.S. dollar.

With that simplified explanation in mind, here is a list of America's island outposts.

## COMMONWEALTHS

### *Puerto Rico*

**Location:** Between the Caribbean Sea and the North Atlantic Ocean, east of the Dominican Republic

**Size:** 3,500 square miles

**Population:** Four million

**Background:** Columbus "found" this island in 1493, on his second voyage to the New World, and claimed it for Spain. He named it San Juan Bautista. When Ponce de Leon conquered it in 1509, it was inhabited by the Taino, descendents of Amazonian Indians who had migrated into the Caribbean. Most of the Taino were decimated by European diseases and mistreatment; the rest were enslaved and forced to work on sugar plantations. A recent genetic study showed that a surprising number of Puerto Ricans carry Taino blood, suggesting that many natives were assimilated.

Spain gave Puerto Rico to the United States in 1898 following its defeat in the Spanish-American War. (In the same deal, the U.S. got Guam, bought the Philippines, and won independence for Cuba.) The island became a territory of the United States in 1917. Seeking more autonomy, Puerto Ricans voted in 1951 to become a commonwealth.

### *Northern Mariana Islands*

**Location:** North Pacific Ocean, between Hawaii and the Philippines

**Size:** 180 square miles

**Population:** 75,000

**Background:** The Northern Marianas are 14 islands in a 500-mile chain. Only the three southernmost islands of Saipan, Tinian, and Rota are developed. (There's a Wal-Mart, a McDonald's, and a Pizza Hut on Saipan.)

The native Chamorros, probably descendants of migrants from Malaysia, first encountered Europeans in 1521 when explorer Ferdinand Magellan stopped by on his round-the-world voyage. Spanish missionaries and merchants showed up in the 1600s and dominated the Chamorros for the next three centuries.

In the early 20th century, control of the islands went from Spain to Germany and then to Japan. The Americans took the islands from the Japanese in one of the bloodiest battles of World War II. It remained a U.S. territory until 1975, when the people of the Northern Marianas voted to become a commonwealth.

Today the Chamorros are about 30% of the population. About half the population—Filipinos mostly—are nonresident aliens connected to the huge garment-making industry. And the Japanese are back—as tourists spending nearly half a billion dollars a year.

## INHABITED U.S. TERRITORIES

### *Guam*

**Location:** North Pacific Ocean, between Hawaii and the Philippines

**Size:** 212 square miles

**Population:** 158,000

**Background:** Guam is the 15th island in the chain that includes the Northern Marianas.

Guam was also discovered by Magellan in 1521 and formally annexed by Spain in 1565. It was ceded to the United States by Spain in 1898, at the end of the Spanish-American War. The Japanese occupied it in 1941; the U.S. retook it three years later. A U.S. military installation dominates the island, with more than 23,000 military personnel and dependents. About half the population are Chamorros; 35% of the population are under the age of 15. Guam is currently seeking commonwealth status.

### *U.S. Virgin Islands*

**Location:** Caribbean Sea and the North Atlantic Ocean, east of Puerto Rico

**Size:** 136 square miles

**Population:** 122,000

**Background:** This island paradise comprises three islands—St. Thomas, St. John, and St. Croix—as well as numerous smaller islets.

Columbus came across the larger archipelago in 1493 on his second voyage to the New World and named it the Virgin Islands, in honor of the 11,000 virgin followers of St. Ursula. During the 17th century, the islands were divided into two territorial units, one British and the other Danish. The British possessions were called the Virgin Islands; the Danish part was called the Danish West Indies.

The largest slave auctions in the world took place on St. Thomas. Sugarcane, produced by slave labor, drove the islands' economy in the 18th and early 19th centuries. And it was a shopper's paradise, as the Danes allowed Blackbeard and other pirates to openly sell their stolen treasures on the streets of St. Thomas.

Because of its strategic importance for control of the Caribbean basin and protection of the Panama Canal, the United States purchased the Danish portion in 1917 for $25 million in gold and renamed it the U.S. Virgin Islands. For clarity, the U.K. appended "British" to its territory (BVI for short).

Today tourism accounts for 70% of the islands' economy and employment, with two million visitors a year.

***American Samoa***

**Location:** South Pacific Ocean, between Hawaii and New Zealand

**Size:** 76 square miles

**Population:** 67,000

**Background:** Settled around 1000 B.C. by Polynesians. The first European to visit the islands of Samoa was Dutch sea captain Jacob Roggeveen, in 1722. The islands became a strategic stopover for whalers and South Sea spice traders.

Germany and the United States divided the islands between themselves in 1899. Germany was driven out by New Zealand during World War I. Western Samoa gained independence in 1962.

The U.S. part, American Samoa, is composed of five islands and two coral atolls, including the deep-water harbor of Pago Pago.

Although the Samoans embraced Christianity when the first missionaries showed up in the 1830s, in many ways they have maintained their traditions better than other Pacific islanders. Nearly all land is owned communally, and there is a social hierarchy that stresses one's responsibility to the extended family. However, Samoans have become heavily dependent on U.S. aid and imports. They spend about 40% of their income on imported food.

***But wait, there's more. Go to page 319 for the uninhabited U.S. territories (just in case you ever want to get away from it all).***

**Strawberries got their name because the plant "strews" its runners across the ground.**

# THE LEGEND OF LINCOLN'S GHOST

*Here's a trivia question you can use to win a bet: Who was the first president to claim he saw Lincoln's ghost? Answer: Lincoln himself.*

## BACKGROUND

Take America's "royal residence," the White House; examine tales of hauntings that have surrounded it for nearly two centuries; and add Abraham Lincoln, an odd president who believed in the occult and was murdered while in office, and you have the recipe for America's most famous ghost story.

• According to legend, shortly after Lincoln was elected to his first term in 1860, he saw a double image of himself while gazing in a mirror at his Illinois home. One was his normal reflection, the other a pale double. Mrs. Lincoln didn't see the second image but was convinced that it was a sign. The sharper image, she said, represented Lincoln completing his first term; the other was a sign that he would be reelected, but would die before completing his second term.

• As Lincoln began his first term, the nation was on the verge of the Civil War. In the midst of trying to reunify the divided country, Lincoln faced a terrible personal tragedy—his 11-year-old son, Willie, died from a fever in 1862. A grief-stricken Mrs. Lincoln conducted séances in the hopes of contacting the boy. Although the skeptical president never participated in the séances, historians say his wife's belief in the supernatural may eventually have rubbed off on him.

• Lincoln suffered restless nights filled with nightmares and premonitions of his own death. He once told his wife about a dream where he was asleep, then was woken by the sounds of someone crying. He went to the East Room and found the source of the sobs: mourners and a casket. He asked a woman, "Who died?" "The assassinated president," she told him. Lincoln walked over to the casket and saw himself inside.

• Several months later, on the morning of April 14, 1865, Lincoln called an emergency meeting of the Cabinet and delivered a cryptic message: "Expect important news soon. I have had a dream," he told them, "I am on a boat, alone in the ocean. I have no oars, no rudder. I am helpless." That evening, while attending a play at Ford's Theater, Lincoln was shot from behind by John Wilkes Booth; he died the next morning at 7:22 a.m.

## RESTLESS SOUL?

Parapsychologists define ghosts as "people who died with unfinished business"—and Lincoln certainly fits the bill. The Confederacy had surrendered only five days before Lincoln's assassination, but the United States was in disarray. The economy of the South had been decimated by the war; hatred and animosity were rampant. Lincoln's plans for repairing the nation were cut short by his murder. As a result, does Lincoln's ghost still roam the halls of 1600 Pennsylvania Avenue? Many subsequent residents and visitors have been convinced it does.

## REPORTED SIGHTINGS

### The Teddy Roosevelt White House (1901–1909)

"I think of Lincoln, shambling, homely, with his strong, sad, deeply furrowed face, all the time. I see him in the different rooms and in the halls." Skeptics maintain that this quote by President Roosevelt was taken out of context. But believers in the spirit world say that Roosevelt was speaking literally—that he actually saw Lincoln's ghost.

### The Coolidge White House (1923–1929)

Calvin Coolidge's wife, Grace, claimed she saw the tall figure of Lincoln "at the window in the Oval Office, hands clasped behind his back, gazing out over the Potomac River, perhaps still seeing the bloody battlefields beyond."

### The FDR White House (1933–1945)

• While sleeping in the White House, Queen Wilhelmina of the Netherlands was awakened one night by knocks at her bedroom door. When she answered it, the former president was standing before her. The queen fainted. When she came to, the ghost was gone.

• For a time, the Lincoln Bedroom was Eleanor Roosevelt's study, and the First Lady claimed she could feel the presence of the former president. "Sometimes when I worked at my desk late at night I'd get a feeling that someone was standing behind me. I'd have to turn around and look."

• A few years later in the same room, a seamstress was working on the drapes and kept hearing the sound of someone approaching the bedroom door, but no one ever came. She found a White House butler and asked him why he kept pacing back and forth. "I don't know what you're talking about," he said. "I haven't been on that floor. That was Abe."

• Winston Churchill, a frequent guest during World War II, had an "eventful" night in the Lincoln Bedroom. He was found the next morning sleeping on the floor of the room across the hall. He told no one what had happened that night and vowed never to set foot in the Lincoln Bedroom again.

**The Ford White House (1974–1977)**

Gerald Ford's daughter Susan was so sure she felt Lincoln's ghost in the White House that she wouldn't set foot in the Lincoln Bedroom, either.

**The Reagan White House (1981–1989)**

• The most prominent modern sighting comes from yet another presidential daughter, Maureen Reagan, along with her husband, Dennis Revell. One night while in the Lincoln Bedroom, they both saw "an aura, sometimes red, sometimes orange." According to Reagan, it was the ghost of Lincoln.

• Just as mysterious is the fact that the Reagan's dog Lucky would never enter the Lincoln Bedroom. She would, however, stand in the hallway and bark at something inside.

**The Clinton White House (1993–2001)**

"A high percentage of people who work here won't go in the Lincoln Bedroom," said President Clinton's social secretary, Capricia Marshall. According to Marshall, many White House maids and butlers swear they've seen Lincoln's ghost.

**Need time off? Move to Italy. On average, Italians get 42 vacation days every year.**

# BEHIND THE HITS

*Ever wonder what inspired some of your favorite songs? The answers may surprise you.*

**The Artist:** The Beatles

**The Song:** "Come Together" (1969)

**The Story:** In 1969 Timothy Leary intended to run for governor of California against a B-movie actor named Ronald Reagan. One of Leary's battle cries was "Come together," and he asked his friend John Lennon to write a song based on it for the campaign. By the time Lennon got around to it, Leary's campaign was dead (he had to drop out when he was convicted of marijuana possession).

Lennon liked the phrase, though, and decided to build a song around it anyway. He loosely based it on the old Chuck Berry tune, "You Can't Catch Me." He even left in the line, "Here come old flat-top." Other than that, it's nothing like the Berry song, but because Lennon admitted to borrowing the line, Berry's publisher sued him. The settlement: Lennon agreed to record two Chuck Berry songs on his 1975 solo album, *Rock N Roll.* Written and recorded in a single session at the studio, "Come Together" was one of Lennon's favorites: "It's funky, it's bluesy. You can dance to it. I'll buy it!"

**The Artist:** Sheryl Crow

**The Song:** "All I Wanna Do" (1993)

**The Story:** After years of trying to break into the Los Angeles music scene—including singing backup on Michael Jackson's "Bad" tour—Crow finally got a record deal in 1991.

During a recording session, Crow wrote what she thought was a pretty good song... musically, anyway; she hated the words. She was stuck, so her producer ran across the street to a bookstore and bought 10 books of poetry, selected at random. He gave them to Crow, locked her in the bathroom, and told her to come out when she had something. Crow picked a poem entitled "Fun" and started singing the words, taking out some of the poet's lines and adding her own. "'All I Wanna Do' was the throwaway track of the album. It was one that wasn't going to go on the record," she recalled. Good thing it did—after A&M released it, the song won a Grammy and propelled Crow to superstardom. Meanwhile, an English teacher in Vermont named Wyn Cooper began receiving royalty checks for a poem he'd written 10 years earlier.

**The Artist:** Led Zeppelin

**The Song:** "Whole Lotta Love" (1969)

**The Story:** While recording their second album, guitarist Jimmy Page came up with a bluesy riff and the rest of the band started jamming around it. Singer Robert Plant "improvised" some words, but they weren't really his. He borrowed them from a song called "You Need Love" written by blues legend Willie Dixon. And although Led Zeppelin had credited Dixon for two songs on their first album, they kept the writing credit on "Whole Lotta Love" for themselves. Why? "We decided that it was so far away in time," explained Plant. (Actually, it had only been seven years since Dixon wrote it.) "Whole Lotta Love" became the only Zeppelin song ever to reach the top 10 in the United States.

Fifteen years later, Dixon heard the song for the first time and noticed the resemblance. Dixon sued the band and settled out of court in 1987. He used the proceeds to set up the Blues Heaven Foundation to promote awareness of the blues.

**The Artist:** Little Richard

**The Song:** "Tutti Frutti" (1955)

**The Story:** After a long, unproductive recording session in 1955, Little Richard couldn't get the sound his producer, "Bumps" Blackwell, wanted. Exasperated, they took a lunch break and went to the local dive, the Dew Drop Inn. The place had a piano, so Richard started banging on it and wailing out some nonsense words: "Awop-Bop-a-Loo-Mop a-Good Goddam... Tutti Frutti, Good Booty!" It was the sound Blackwell was looking for.

Richard had actually written the song while he was washing dishes at a bus station in Macon, Georgia. "I couldn't talk back to the boss," he said. "So instead of saying bad words, I'd say, 'Wop-Bop-a-Loo-Bop-a-Lop-Bam-Boom,' so he wouldn't know what I was thinking." Blackwell cleaned up the lyrics ("good booty" became "aw rootie"), and they recorded it that day. The single reached #17 on the pop charts. (Believe it or not, Pat Boone covered the song and it outdid Richard's version on the hit parade.)

**Old news: By the year 2050, the world's elderly will outnumber the young for the first time.**

# HOUDINI'S HEADLINES

*Uncle John is no Houdini. When he was a little kid, he accidentally locked himself in the bathroom and couldn't get out. But it didn't matter—by the time someone answered his calls for help, he'd decided to stay.*

Harry Houdini was a genius at performing death-defying feats of magic. But he was more than that—he was also a genius at getting free publicity. Everywhere he went, he staged stunts specifically designed to get newspaper headlines.

## *CHEEKY CHALLENGER COPS COPPERS' CUFFS!*

• When Houdini first went to London, he had no bookings. He boasted about his talents to a stage manager, but the man was skeptical, and told Houdini, "I'll hire you—but only if you can get out of handcuffs at Scotland Yard." Houdini rounded up some reporters, then challenged police at Scotland Yard to cuff him.

• Wrapping Houdini's arms around a pillar, the police superintendent snapped on the cuffs, and turned to leave, saying, "We'll be back in an hour to release you."

• As they headed for the door, Houdini called out, "You better take your cuffs with you!" He had undone the handcuffs in less time than it took the cops to walk across the room.

• The reporters were impressed, and made sure Houdini got a lot of free publicity from the stunt. The result: a six-month run in London.

## *SNEAKY SERGEANT CAN'T STUMP HOUDINI*

• From then on, challenging local police departments became one of his regular gimmicks. It always worked—even when he failed.

• In 1899 Sergeant Waldron of the Chicago police challenged Houdini to escape from his special handcuffs.

• Houdini agreed, then struggled to release himself for over an hour as the audience laughed and jeered.

• The cuffs had to be cut off—and only after the theater had emptied did Waldron admit that he had tampered with the cuffs, dropping molten lead in the lock so it would be jammed.

**73% of Americans in their twenties say playing hooky from work "would improve their...**

• When the trick was revealed, the local newspaper ran the story and Houdini garnered even more free publicity.

### *EXAMINER EXPOSÉ: HOUDINI A FRAUD!*

• The *San Francisco Examiner* ran an story claiming that Houdini's secret was extra hidden keys.

• In response, Houdini announced he would pit himself against any restraint the San Francisco police could throw at him. A reporter was assigned to cover the event.

• Houdini was stripped, searched, and shackled. His hands were cuffed behind his back; his ankles were locked in irons; and 10 pairs of manacles were placed on him. He was then locked in a closet.

• Ten minutes later, he was free. The newspaper retracted their exposé and ran another story…applauding his talents.

### *HOUDINI JOLTS JUDGE AND JURY!*

• In Germany, Houdini wanted to stage a stunt where he would jump—roped and chained—off a boat into a river. The police refused to give permission—but he did it anyway. As he pulled himself out of the river and walked up the riverbank, he was arrested.

• The only thing the cops could charge him with, though, was walking on the grass. The story made the papers all over the country.

• To get even, in 1902 the head of the Cologne police, Schutzmann Werner Graff, denounced Houdini as a fraud and a swindler.

• Houdini demanded an apology. When none was forthcoming he sued for slander. Graff told the judge and jury he could prove what he said was true just by chaining Houdini up.

•Houdini consented to be chained, then demonstrated to the judge and jury (but he refused to show Graff) exactly how he was able to release himself. He won the case, the police were fined, and Graff was ordered to apologize.

• But Graff had other plans: he appealed to a higher court. There, he produced a specially made lock that was supposed to be impossible to open. Houdini escaped in four minutes.

• This time, Graff was ordered to pay court costs and run an apology in all German newspapers. He refused again and instead took the case to Germany's highest court. Graff argued that Houdini's

**…mental health and productivity." Only 50% of Americans over 65 agrees.**

claim that he could escape from safes was false—yet Houdini successfully escaped from a safe right in front of the judge.

• For the third time, Graff lost his case. Thanks to the stubborn policeman, the publicity for Houdini was enormous.

## *HOUDINI COMMITS RANDOM ACTS OF PUBLICITY...*

• Houdini became famous for escaping from straitjackets while hanging upside down from his feet over public streets. He sought out the newspapers in each town he traveled to and offered to perform the stunt while hanging from their roof. It made the front page in every town he played.

• On his first trip to Europe, Houdini hired seven bald men to sit in a row on the pavement next to a popular café. At regular intervals, the seven men would simultaneously remove their hats and nod their heads forward. Each man had one letter written on his bald head, and together they spelled "Houdini."

• In 1901 Houdini escaped from the manacles that had been worn by a sadistic murderer named Glowisky when he had been beheaded just three days earlier. It made great newspaper copy.

• A rival magician once interrupted one of Houdini's performances with loud protests that he, The Great Cirnoc, was the true handcuff king. Houdini invited him onstage to prove himself by escaping from some special cuffs. Cirnoc first insisted that Houdini demonstrate that it was possible to do (which he did, in the privacy of his cabinet, using a secret key). The Great Cirnoc then struggled to release himself from the same cuffs but couldn't. He was hooted offstage, and the papers were full of the story the next day.

## *...AND KINDNESS!*

Popular singer Sarah Bernhardt was honored at a reception at the Met in New York. There, she was presented with a bronze bust of herself. However, no one had paid the bill for the bust. When the $350 bill was sent to her, she returned the bust to the maker. Houdini immediately stepped in and paid the bill. Within a few days, his gesture had been covered in no less than 3,756 newspapers. A reporter estimated that if Houdini had bought that much newspaper space outright, it would have cost him $56,340.

***How'd he do all this stuff? Turn to page 207 to find out.***

**Doggone: Houdini trained his dog to escape from a pair of miniature handcuffs.**

# NO CITY DUST HERE

*We're back with another installment of anagrams...words or phrases whose letters are rearranged to form new words or phrases. Here's an extra bonus: the new phrase has more or less the same meaning as the old one.*

A TELEPHONE GIRL *becomes*...**REPEATING "HELLO"**

THE COUNTRYSIDE *becomes*...**NO CITY DUST HERE**

THE PUBLIC ART GALLERIES *becomes*... **LARGE PICTURE HALLS, I BET**

THE GREAT NEW YORK RAPID TRANSIT TUNNEL *becomes*... **GIANT WORK IN STREET, PARTLY UNDERNEATH**

THE HOSPITAL AMBULANCE *becomes*... **A CAB, I HUSTLE TO HELP MAN**

HEAVY RAIN *becomes*... **HIRE A NAVY**

VACATION TIMES *becomes*...**I'M NOT AS ACTIVE**

A DOMESTICATED ANIMAL *becomes*... **DOCILE, AS A MAN TAMED IT**

CONVERSATION *becomes*... **VOICES RANT ON**

THE UNITED STATES BUREAU OF FISHERIES *becomes*...**I RAISE THE BASS TO FEED US IN THE FUTURE**

SOFTWARE *becomes*... **SWEAR OFT**

LISTEN *becomes*...**SILENT**

"THAT'S ONE SMALL STEP FOR A MAN, ONE GIANT LEAP FOR MANKIND."—NEIL A. ARMSTRONG *becomes*... **A THIN MAN RAN, MAKES A LARGE STRIDE, LEFT PLANET, PINS FLAG ON MOON! ON TO MARS!**

**Christmas lite: Only 10% of U.S. households put cookies out for Santa on Christmas Eve.**

# AROUND THE HOUSE

*The next time you're doing some home improvement, chances are you'll use one at least one of these three products.*

## TAKES THE CAKE

In 1894 Theodore Witte was applying putty around a window frame with a butter knife—and it was a messy job. Sometime later, while waiting in line at a bakery shop, he noticed a baker squeezing icing onto a cake from a tube attached to a nozzle...with complete precision. Witte went straight home and designed a "puttying tool." He patented his idea of "using a ratcheted piston to force window putty through a nozzle to effect a smooth, weatherproof seal." Witte never made much money for his invention, but to his credit, he got it right the first time; very little about the caulking gun has changed since then.

## SOMETHING'S FISHY

After someone spilled raw fish oil on his metal deck, a Scottish fishing boat captain named Robert Fergusson noticed that—over time—the deck stopped rusting. So after he landed in New Orleans, Fergusson spent many years trying to formulate a fish-oil based paint that would inhibit rust and corrosion. His biggest problem wasn't getting it to work, but getting it to work without smelling fishy. Finally in 1921, after working with more fish oil than any person should ever have to, Fergusson unveiled a new paint that stopped rust, dried overnight, and left no lingering aroma: Rust-Oleum.

## ROCKET SCIENCE

Norm Larsen, a chemist at the Rocket Chemical Company, had unsuccessfully tested 39 compounds that would prevent corrosion and eliminate water from electrical circuitry. He finally got it right in 1953 and labeled the compound Water Displacement Formula 40. Other workers snuck the stuff home and discovered that in addition to preventing corrosion, it also stopped squeaks and unstuck locks. So the Rocket Chemical Company marketed it for home use. The product, now called WD-40, hit store shelves in 1958. Today more than a million cans are sold every week.

# PARLIAMENTARY MANNERS

*Canadians have a well-deserved reputation for being polite. Turns out it's all an act—at least for politicians. This excerpt from the "Dear Miss Parliamentary Manners" column in the Canadian* National Post *shows us that American politicians have a lot to learn.*

**DEAR MISS PARLIAMENTARY MANNERS,**
**A recent news story contended that decorum is taking a bruising in Canadian legislatures. The article quoted a Cabinet minister as saying, "There is a certain level of civil discourse to be expected in the house even during heckling." How can you be civil and heckle at the same time?**

**ANSWER:** Actually, it's very easy to hector with ferocity and yet remain civil and mannerly—once you've mastered the subtle nuances of the parliamentary vernacular.

**Expression:** "My learned colleague."
**Translation:** "You cheese-eating throwback."

**Expression:** "If the honorable member will forward his request to my department, we will provide the relevant documents."
**Translation:** "Talk to the hand."

**Expression:** "I would be happy to address the member's question."
**Translation:** "I yearn to bleach your skull and use it on my desk as a novelty pencil holder."

**Expression:** "If the member had concerns, he should have made them known at the proper time."
**Translation:** "Your mother didn't have any complaints last night."

**Expression:** "Mr. Speaker, the people of Canada deserve an answer."
**Translation:** "Leave my mother out of this—I swear, I'll cut you!"

**Expression:** "I am outraged by your craven duplicity!"
**Translation:** "I'm not really upset; I just wanted to get on the news. Want to have dinner tonight?"

**No way: According to one expert, the most frequently used English noun is "way."**

# THE MIRACLE WORKER

*Observations about life from Helen Keller.*

"Security is mostly a superstition. It does not exist in nature.…Life is either a daring adventure or nothing."

"When one door of happiness closes, another opens; but often we look so long at the closed door that we do not see the one which has been opened for us."

"Keep your face to the sunshine and you cannot see the shadow."

"Instead of comparing our lot with that of those who are more fortunate than we are, we should compare it with the lot of the great majority of our fellow men. It then appears that we are among the privileged."

"I am only one, but still I am one. I cannot do everything, but still I can do something."

"Science may have found a cure for most evils, but it has found no remedy for the worst of them all—the apathy of human beings."

"No pessimist ever discovered the secrets of the stars, or sailed to an uncharted land."

"It is wonderful how much time good people spend fighting the devil. If they would only expend the same amount of energy loving their fellow men, the devil would die in his own tracks of ennui."

"There is no king who has not had a slave among his ancestors, and no slave who has not had a king among his."

"As selfishness and complaint pervert and cloud the mind, so love clears and sharpens the vision."

"The heresy of one age becomes the orthodoxy of the next."

"Life is a succession of lessons which must be lived to be understood."

"The most pathetic person in the world is someone who has sight, but no vision."

**First song ever sung in space: "Happy Birthday," to the Apollo astronauts on March 8, 1969.**

# RAINFOREST CRUNCH

*We've heard about "saving the rainforests" for years, but why are they so important? Here are some facts about some of nature's most amazing phenomena.*

## RAINFORESTS ARE DIVERSE

**The Facts:** Rainforests—forests with an average year-round temperature of 70°F and annual rainfall of more than 60 inches—are home to 50% of life on Earth... even though they make up only 6% of the landmass.

• More types of woody plant species grow on the slopes of a single forested volcano in the Philippines than grow in the entire United States from coast to coast. Forests in the tiny country of Panama contain as many plant species as all of Europe.

• More species of fish live in the Amazon River than in the entire Atlantic Ocean. One study found more species of ants living on a single tropical stump than are found in all of the British Isles.

• Yet scientists estimate that they have discovered and identified only one-sixth of the species living in rainforests.

## RAINFORESTS ARE UNIQUE ECOSYSTEMS

**The Facts:** The ecosystem of a rainforest is upside down compared to other forests: nutrients are stored not in the soil, but in the canopy of plants above it.

• In forests with temperate climates, the deciduous trees all drop their leaves at roughly the same time, triggered by the change of seasons. Dead leaves gradually decompose and turn into rich soil.

• That doesn't happen in the rainforest—there is no change of season; tropical trees drop their leaves gradually over the entire year.

• The constant heat and moisture of the climate spur the continuous growth of bacteria, insects, and fungi, which feed on the dead leaves—causing the forest floor to act as a huge living stomach.

• Result: Decomposition (which can take one to seven years in a temperate forest) takes only six weeks in a rainforest. Downside: The rich loamy soil that accumulates in temperate forests never gets a chance to build up on a rainforest's floor.

**Most destructive disease in human history, according to health experts: malaria.**

## RAINFORESTS ARE FRAGILE

**The Facts:** The forest canopy protects the ground. Some areas of the Amazon receive up to 400 inches of rain annually. But without leaves and branches to shield the ground from pounding rain, water would run off immediately, taking any topsoil with it.

• Millions of years of daily rainfall combined with constant heat have drained nutrients from rainforests' subsoil, leaving it high in toxic aluminum and iron oxides. This makes it unable to support much plant life.

• If exposed to the sun, the ground would become unproductive, hard-packed, and cement-like. The small amounts of nutrients left in the soil would be quickly leached away.

• The balance is fragile. It's estimated that the Amazon produces 20% of all the oxygen generated by land plants on Earth. Without the climate moderation of the forest, the greenhouse effect—rising temperatures and plummeting rainfall—may be greatly accelerated.

## RAINFORESTS ARE IN DANGER

**The Facts:** Over half of the world's rainforests are gone forever—most have disappeared since 1960.

• Loggers, ranchers, miners, and farmers cut or burn the Amazon jungle down at the rate of 40 to 50 million acres annually.

• A 2.5-acre tract of healthy, growing rainforest loses about three pounds of soil through erosion annually. Cut the trees, and the same forest can lose up to 34 tons in a year.

• As settlers clear the forest to make room for agriculture or livestock, they discover the land supports them for only a few years.

• Once the forest is cleared, the only nutrients left are in the ashes. When the soil disappears, the rainfall diminishes, and the forest is gone for good. The damage is irreversible.

• Today, an area the size of the state of Washington is bulldozed every year. At that rate, it will take less than 50 years to destroy the remaining jungle. Some ecologists estimate that the Amazon will be completely gone by the year 2040.

• Scientists fear species are becoming extinct before they are even discovered—a scary prospect since roughly 25% of all prescription drugs contain ingredients originating in the rainforest.

**In Japan, the James Bond film *Dr. No* was originally translated as *We Don't Want a Doctor*.**

## LARGEST RAINFOREST ON EARTH: THE AMAZON

**The Facts:** The Amazon contains half the world's tropical forests, spread over an area the size of the continental United States.

• While North American forests rarely have more than 15 species of trees in their entire ecosystem, the Amazon can contain between 100 and 250 different species in a five-acre plot. You can sometimes travel a mile or more before finding two trees of the same species in the Amazon.

• More than 100 types of plants and 1,700 kinds of insects can be found in the branches of a single mature tropical tree.

• The Amazon has more than a million interdependent—and exotic—species of plant and animal life. A few examples:

trees with 6-foot-long leaves

flowers with 3-foot-long petals

plants that can cradle 10 gallons of water in reservoirs formed by their leaves

rodents that weigh up to 100 lbs.

slugs the size of small snakes

butterflies the size of dinner plates

bees the size of birds

tarantulas so big they eat birds

catfish so big they've been known to eat children

* * *

## MORE ON THE AMAZON

**Why is the Amazon so diverse?**

Thirty million years ago, the area that is now the Amazon jungle entered a dry period lasting thousands of years. The drought wiped out most of the region's tropical forests—only isolated pockets of jungle survived. Over time, each jungle followed its own evolutionary course.

Then, following the last ice age (10,000 years ago), the climate became warm and wet again, and the different types of jungle grew together, each contributing many different plant and animal species.

# MYTH-CONCEPTIONS

*"Common knowledge" is frequently wrong. Here are some examples of things that many people believe... but that according to our sources, just aren't true.*

**Myth:** Dry cleaning is *dry* cleaning.

**Fact:** Dry cleaning isn't really dry. The clothes are put in a large washing machine and treated with a variety of chemical solutions, such as perchloroethylene, after which a drier removes the solvents. Cleaned, yes. Dry, no. It's called "dry" cleaning because no water is used.

**Myth:** If you stop exercising, your muscle will turn into fat.

**Fact:** Muscle and fat are different tissues; one can't turn into the other. If you used to be muscular, but are getting fat, it's probably either because you're exercising less...or eating more.

**Myth:** Snake charmers "charm" snakes with their hypnotic music.

**Fact:** This art form dates back to the third century B.C. But the charmers don't work their magic with music...because snakes can't hear it. It's the wind from the charmer's flute—as well as various hand and head gestures—that capture the snake's attention.

**Myth:** New York is the largest city in the United States.

**Fact:** The largest city isn't New York or even Los Angeles. It's Juneau, Alaska. The city covers 3,108 square miles, making it nearly *seven* times larger than Los Angeles. The largest city in the contiguous 48 states is Jacksonville, Florida, which is 841 square miles—nearly twice the size of Los Angeles.

**Myth:** Jockey shorts (men's briefs) make men sterile.

**Fact:** This idea has haunted Jockey shorts since they were introduced in the 1930s. They don't.

**Myth:** The word *dinosaur* means "terrible lizard" in Latin.

**Fact:** Richard Owen coined the term in 1842. He used the word *deinos*, which is Greek—not Latin. It means ("fearfully great.")

# THE "AMERICAN SYSTEM"

*In Part 1 of our story (page 62), we told you how Eli Whitney's invention of the cotton gin in 1792 built the pre-Civil War* Gone-with-the-Wind *South. Here's the story of Whitney's other invention—the one that destroyed it.*

## LIKE MONEY IN THE BANK

Even before Eli Whitney ginned his first handful of upland cotton, he believed that he was on his way to becoming a wealthy man. "Tis generally said by those who know anything about [the cotton gin], that I shall make a Fortune by it," Whitney wrote in a letter to his father. His friend Phineas Miller certainly agreed—Miller became Whitney's business partner, providing money that Whitney would use to build the machines. They would both grow rich together... or so they thought.

## COPYCATS

Things didn't work out quite as planned. There were two problems with Whitney and Miller's dreams of grandeur:

First, just as Whitney had intended, his cotton gin was so simple and so easy to make that just about anyone who was good with tools could make one. So a lot of planters did, even though doing so violated Whitney's patent.

Second, Whitney and Miller were too greedy for their own good. They knew that even if they had enough cash to build a cotton gin for every planter who wanted one (they didn't), the planters didn't have enough cash to buy them. So rather than build gins for sale, Whitney and Miller planned to set up a network of gins around the South where *they* would do the ginning in exchange for a share of the cotton they ginned. A *big* share—40%, to be exact. That was more than the planters were willing to part with, least of all to a Yankee. The planters fought back by ginning their cotton in machines they made themselves or by buying illegal copycat machines made by competitors.

And there were rumors: that Whitney himself had stolen the idea for the cotton gin from a Southern inventor; that the copycat gins were actually "improved" models that didn't infringe on

Whitney's patents; and, worst of all, that Whitney's machines damaged cotton fibers during the ginning process. That last rumor stuck: By the end of 1795, the English were refusing to buy cotton ginned on Whitney & Miller machines; only cotton ginned on illegal (and usually inferior) machines would do. "Everyone is afraid of the cotton," Miller wrote in the fall of 1795. "Not a purchaser in Savannah will pay full price for it."

## COURT BATTLES

Whitney and Miller spent years battling the copycats in court and convincing the English textile mills that their cotton was still the best. The stress may have contributed to Miller's death from fever in 1803, when he was only 39. Whitney carried on, and finally won his last court fight in 1806. But the victory came too late to do any good, because the patent on the cotton gin expired the following year. Now copying Whitney's cotton gin wasn't just easy, it was also perfectly legal.

So how much money did Whitney make on the invention that created huge fortunes for Southern plantation owners? Almost none. In fact, some historians estimate that after his several years of legal expenses are taken into account, he actually *lost* money.

The cotton gin would clothe humanity, but in the process of inventing it, Whitney had lost his shirt. "An invention can be so valuable as to be worthless to the inventor," he groused.

## THIS MEANS WAR

But Whitney was already working on another invention—one that would establish his fortune and transform the world again... even more than the cotton gin had.

In March of 1798, relations between France and the United States had deteriorated to the point that it seemed a war might be just around the corner. This presented a problem, because France was the primary supplier of arms to the United States. Where would the country get muskets now?

Congress had established two national armories beginning in 1794, but they had produced only 1,000 muskets in four years, and the government estimated that 50,000 would be needed if a war with France did come. Private contractors would have to supply the rest. Whitney, facing bankruptcy, was determined to be one of them.

**Who needs a Stairmaster? There are 898 steps in the Washington Monument.**

## ONE THING AT A TIME

Until then, all firearms were made by highly skilled artisans who made the entire weapon, crafting each part from scratch and filing and fitting them by hand. Each part, and by extension each musket, was one of a kind—the trigger made for one gun wouldn't work on any other because it fit only that musket. Broken muskets could only be repaired by expert craftsmen. If the weapon broke in the middle of a military campaign, you were out of luck. Armorers capable of such skill were scarce, and new ones took forever to train, which was why the U.S. arsenals were having such a hard time making muskets.

## IF YOU'VE SEEN ONE, YOU'VE SEEN THEM ALL

Whitney proposed a new method of making muskets, one he'd been thinking about since trying to speed up production of his cotton gins:

• Instead of using one expert craftsman to make an entire gun, he would divide the tasks among several workers of average skill. They'd be easier to train, and easier to replace if they quit.

• Each worker would be taught how to make one part. They would use special, high-precision machine tools, designed by Whitney.

• The tools would be so precise that the parts would be virtually identical to each other. Each part would fit interchangeably in any of the muskets made in Whitney's factory.

• Once the pieces for a musket had been made, assembling them into the finished weapon would be—literally—a snap.

• Ready-made interchangeable spare parts would make it possible for any soldier to fix his musket himself.

## BETTER LATE THAN NEVER

On June 14, 1798, Whitney signed a contract with the U.S. government to deliver 10,000 muskets within two years. But the war with France never came. Good thing, too, because Whitney missed his deadline by eight years. Supply shortages and yellow fever epidemics disrupted the schedule, so it took him longer to make his machine tools than he originally thought.

Whitney's reputation as a genius helped him to get extensions and advances against his government contract. But more than anything, what gave Whitney freedom to take the time necessary to perfect his new system was a demonstration he gave to President-elect Thomas Jefferson and other high officials in 1801. Dumping a huge pile of interchangeable musket parts onto a table, Whitney invited them to pick pieces from the pile at random and assemble them into complete muskets. For the first time in history, they could.

## THE AMERICAN SYSTEM

It may not sound like a big deal, but it was. Whitney had devised a method of manufacturing more muskets of higher quality, in less time and for less money, than had ever been possible before. And he did it without the use of highly skilled labor. Once again, Whitney had invented something that would change the world.

What worked with muskets would also work with clothing, farm equipment, furniture, tools, bicycles, and just about anything else people could manufacture. Whitney called his process "the American system." Today it's known as *mass production*. In time it would overshadow even the cotton gin itself in the way it would transform the American economy.

Only this time, the transformation would be felt most in the North…and it would bring the South to its knees.

***For Part III of the Eli Whitney story, turn to page 316.***

* * *

## Q&A: ASK THE EXPERTS

**Q:** *How do those luminous light sticks work?*

**A:** "You mean those plastic rods full of liquid chemicals that are sold at festivals and concerts, and that start glowing with green, yellow, or blue light when you bend them, and that gradually lose their light after an hour or so? When you bend the stick, you break a thin glass capsule containing a chemical, usually hydrogen peroxide, that reacts with another chemical in the tube. The reaction gives off energy, which is absorbed by a fluorescent dye and reemitted as light. As the chemical reaction gradually plays itself out because the chemicals are used up, the light fades." (From *What Einstein Told His Barber*, by Robert L. Wolke)

**Not b-a-a-d: According to scientists, sheep can remember 50 faces for two years.**

# WONTON? NOT NOW

*Palindromes are words or phrases that are spelled the same way backward and forward. Here are some of the best we've found.*

Oozy rat in a sanitary zoo.

Rats paraded a rap star.

Too hot to hoot.

No. It is opposition.

Won't I panic in a pit now?

Panic in a *Titanic*? I nap.

Damn! I, Agassi, miss again! Mad!

O, Geronimo—no minor ego!

Boston ode: Do not sob.

Gateman sees name, garageman sees name tag.

Wonton? Not now.

"Red?" "No." "Who is it?" "'Tis I." "Oh, wonder!"

Todd erases a red dot.

I saw a Santa—at NASA was I.

Mad, a detail of Eden: one defoliated Adam.

Amy, must I jujitsu my ma?

Trapeze part.

No, sir! Away! A papaya war is on!

Men, I'm Eminem.

Satan, oscillate my metallic sonatas!

Snot or protons?

On a clover, if alive, erupts a vast, pure evil: a fire volcano.

Nurses run.

A six is a six is a six is a...

No lava on Avalon; no lava, no Avalon.

Egad! A base tone denotes a bad age.

Lapses? Order red roses, pal.

*And finally, there is a town called Yreka near the Bathroom Readers' Institute. You can buy bread at the*... Yreka Bakery.

**Daily salary of a U.S. senator in 1789: $6. Daily salary in 2001: $580.**

# PET ME!

*Some people have pet peeves.*
*Uncle John has pet trivia.*

• Sir Isaac Newton invented the swinging door…for the convenience of his cats.

• Most dogs run an average of 19 mph.

• Ancient Egyptians could be put to death for mistreating a cat.

• Does your dog seem wary of going out in the rain? It's not because it's afraid to get wet. Rain amplifies sound…it hurts dogs' ears.

• Total Dog is an L.A. health club…for dogs. It has treadmills, masseuses, and an aerobics course. Cost: $800/year.

• Toy-breed dogs live an average of 7 years longer than large breeds. (Tibetan Terriers live up to 20 years.)

• In ancient Rome, it wasn't officially dark until you could no longer tell the difference between a dog and a wolf howling in the distance.

• Average cat bill at the veterinarian: $80/year for life.

• Most popular dog names in Russia: Ugoljok (Blackie) and Veterok (Breezy).

• In Japan, you can rent a dog as a companion for $20/hour.

• John Candy once paid $19,000 for a German Shepherd. (He didn't know the average price for a Shepherd was $1,500.)

• In 1997 a member of Australia's parliament proposed that all cats be eradicated from the country by 2002.

• Why do dogs try to mate with human legs? It's nothing personal. In an excited state, a dog will mount almost anything.

• A schoolteacher in Kansas was ordered not to feed his pet python in class. Why? He wanted to feed it puppies.

• A Persian cat named Precious survived 18 days without food. She was found when rescue crews heard her cries—across the street from the site of the World Trade Center.

• The heaviest (and longest) dog ever recorded was an Old English Mastiff named Zorba: 343 lbs (and 8 feet 3 inches from nose to tail).

• Julius Caesar hated cats.

**Frogs drink through their skin.**

# OLD HISTORY, NEW THEORY

*Here's another example of new findings that may change history books.*

**The Event:** On May 6, 1937, the German blimp *Hindenburg* exploded over a New Jersey airfield, killing 36 people, and effectively ending the age of passenger airships.

**What the History Books Say:** The explosion was caused when the highly volatile hydrogen gas that kept the airship afloat was ignited, most likely by a static electric charge.

**New Theory:** Two boards of inquiry couldn't explain how the hydrogen escaped from sealed gas cells, which it had to do before it could explode. Yet investigators still determined that hydrogen was the cause of the explosion. According to Dr. William Van Vorst, a chemical engineer at UCLA, they were wrong.

A frame-by-frame analysis of film footage suggests that whatever it was that first ignited, it wasn't the hydrogen. "The picture indicates a downward burning. Hydrogen would burn only upward," Van Vorst says, "with a colorless flame." Eyewitnesses described the explosion as more like "a fireworks display."

So what caused the explosion? Van Vorst says it was the *Hindenburg*'s skin. The ship's cotton shell was treated with chemicals so volatile that they "might well serve as rocket propellant," he says. And the way it was attached to the frame allowed for the buildup of large amounts of static electricity, which, when discharged, were enough to ignite the fabric.

**Smoking Gun:** It turns out that the Zeppelin Company quietly conducted its own investigation after the disaster...and concluded the same thing. The *Hindenburg*'s sister ship, *Graf Zeppelin*, was reconstructed using new methods and materials, and went on to fly more than a million miles without incident.

Publicly, however, the company blamed hydrogen. Why? Politics. The United States controlled the world supply of helium, which is nonflammable, but refused to sell any to Nazi Germany. So Zeppelin had to use explosive hydrogen gas...which made the United States look bad when the *Hindenburg* went down in flames.

**Ohio had 161 horse-and-buggy crashes in 1999, the last year that statistics were kept.**

# PATENTLY ABSURD

*Here's proof that the urge to invent something—anything—is more powerful than the urge to make sure the invention is something that people will actually want to use.*

**THE INVENTION:** Musical Baby Diaper Alarm
**WHAT IT DOES:** Three women from France marketed this alarm to mothers in 1985. It's a padded electronic napkin that goes inside a baby's diaper. When it gets wet, it plays "When the Saints Go Marching In."

**THE INVENTION:** The Thinking Cap
**WHAT IT DOES:** Improves artistic ability by mimicking the effects of autism. The cap uses magnetic pulses to inhibit the front-temporal, or "left brain" functions. This, say the two Australian scientists behind the project, creates better access to extraordinary "savant" abilities. They reported improved drawing skills in 5 of 17 volunteers in a 2002 experiment.

**THE INVENTION:** Pantyhose x3
**WHAT IT DOES:** Patented in 1997, they are three-legged panty hose. No, they're not for three-legged people, they're for women who know what it's like to get a run in their stockings. Instead of having to carry spares, you just rotate the legs. The extra leg is hidden in a pocket in the crotch; the damaged leg rolls up to take its place.

**THE INVENTION:** The Breath Alert
**WHAT IT DOES:** This pocket-sized electronic device detects and measures bad breath. You simply breathe into the sensor for three seconds, then the LCD readout indicates—on a scale of 1 to 4—how safe (or offensive) your breath is.

**THE INVENTION:** Weather-Reporting Toaster
**WHAT IT DOES:** Robin Southgate, an industrial design student at Brunel University in London, hooked up his specially made toaster to the Internet. Reading the day's meteorological stats, the toaster burns the day's predictions into a slice of bread: a sun for

**During Prohibition, half of all federal prison inmates were in jail for violating liquor laws.**

sunny days, a cloud with raindrops for rainy days, and so on. "It works best with white bread," says Southgate.

**THE INVENTION:** Separable Pants
**WHAT IT DOES:** You don't take them off, you take them apart. The zipper goes all the way around the crotch, from the front to the back. That way, you can mix and match the legs with other colors and styles, making your own artistic, customized pants.

**THE INVENTION:** Vibrating Toilet Seat
**WHAT IT DOES:** Thomas Bayard invented the seat in 1966. He believed that "buttocks stimulation" helps prevent constipation.

**THE INVENTION:** Automatic-Response Nuclear Deterrent System
**WHAT IT DOES:** A relic from the Cold War era, this idea was patented by British inventor Arthur Paul Pedrick in 1974. He claimed it would deter the United States, the USSR, and China from ever starting a nuclear war. How? Put three nuclear warheads on three orbiting satellites. If sensors on the satellites detected that nuclear missiles had been launched, they would automatically drop bombs: one each on Washington, Moscow, and Peking.

**THE INVENTION:** Lavakan
**WHAT IT DOES:** It's a washing machine…for cats and dogs. This industrial-strength machine soaps, rinses, and dries your pet in less than 30 minutes. One of the inventors, Andres Díaz, claims that the 5-by-5-foot, $20,000 machines can actually reduce pet stress. "One of the dogs actually fell asleep during the wash," he said. Cats weren't quite as happy about being Lavakanned. "But it's better than having a cat attach itself to your face, which is what can happen when you try to wash one by hand."

* * *

## MILITARY INDUSTRIAL SIMPLEX

Andorra is a small country between Spain and France. In the 1970s it reported an annual defense budget of $4.90. The money was used to buy blanks to fire on national holidays.

**Teacher's pet fact: 39% of teachers say their favorite kind of apple is Red Delicious.**

# AFTER THE QUAKE: THE FIRE WAR

*In Part I of the story of the Great San Francisco Earthquake of 1906 (page 27), we told you how the quake set off massive fires around the city. Here's how the flames were fought.*

## BLASTING THE BLAZE

Within hours after the San Francisco earthquake, fires had broken out all over the city. The fires had many allies: the San Francisco hills, a steady breeze, the slow-burning redwood that composed 75% of the city's structures, numerous aftershocks, and insufficient water to fight them. So as a last resort, Mayor Schmitz decided to fight fire with fire.

What San Franciscans *did* have a lot of was dynamite—so they used it to build firebreaks, the theory being that disintegrating a building before the flames could reach it would cut off the fire's fuel supply. But this plan only partly worked; new fires sprouted up from the explosions. By noon much of downtown was engulfed in flame.

The destruction continued: The Army Medical Supply Depot went up in flames, taking with it material that could have been used in the disaster. One of the city's highest skyscrapers, the Call Building—which had withstood the quake—was reduced to ashes. Also leveled were the St. Ignatius Church (which housed a priceless pipe organ), the Examiner building, the Emporium department store, the Hall of Justice, Chinatown, the Columbia Theater, the California Academy of Sciences, and the Opera House, where world-famous Italian tenor Enrico Caruso had sung the previous night. One by one, San Francisco's most beloved buildings, including more than 30 schools, were destroyed. By midnight on Wednesday, most of the downtown district was in ruins, and there was more destruction to come.

## ONE STEP FORWARD...

Wherever firefighters stopped the path of the fires, other avenues of fire opened up. The city streets were so narrow and the buildings so close together that there was more than enough fuel for the flames. One place where firefighters almost got the upper hand was Powell Street. Because it was very wide, the flames couldn't reach both sides and couldn't create the dangerous tunnels of fire that were spreading elsewhere in the city. And the massive St. Francis Hotel formed a huge firebreak. Surrounded by vacant lots, it gave the firefighters room to work and the flames no place to go. It looked like the fire might run out of real estate.

It would have, too, if it hadn't been for a few tired and hungry soldiers on the other side of the firebreak. They went into the empty Delmonico Restaurant to rest and find something to eat. They decided they wanted hot food, so they built a small fire to cook with. Bad idea. The "Ham and Eggs Fire," as it was later called, got out of hand and quickly spread. Soon the entire restaurant was in flames, followed by the Alcazar Theater next door, followed by every building on Geary Avenue. Then it headed toward Powell Street, scattering enraged firefighters and forcing them to regroup elsewhere.

## TWO STEPS BACK

At this point, Mayor Schmitz decided the next fire line would be drawn at Van Ness Avenue. He ordered troops to start dynamiting homes to form another firebreak—an unpopular decision because many of the town's wealthiest and most influential people lived there. While one Army officer was sent to begin evacuation procedures, another was sent to take the fastest boat to the nearest city to replenish the town's exhausted stock of dynamite.

But somehow the message was misconstrued and the boat never left. With Van Ness Avenue completely evacuated and firefighters forming a line, they waited for the arrival of the dynamite...and waited...and waited. In disgust, Brigadier General Funston finally commandeered another boat and sent it on its way—but by then it was too late. In desperation, some firemen tried to set a backfire, but it failed to stop the advance of the flames, and Van Ness was on fire before the boat returned.

Next, the firefighters fell back to Franklin Street. It was narrow, but it was their only hope. Once again, residents were evacuated and firefighting forces were gathered. Demolition teams detonated home after home. Then the wind changed and it appeared that the fire was stopped. Bystanders rejoiced—until

**What a drag: Each puff of smoke inhaled from a cigarette contains 4 billion particles of dust.**

they realized the flames were just being pushed in a new direction. The exhausted firefighters had to drum up the energy to make yet another stand.

On the other side of the city, 20th Street was chosen as a firebreak. It was a fairly wide street with some open ground downhill from a large cistern that still had some water in it. Buildings on the north side of the street were quickly dynamited, and the engines pulled by horses were taken up the hill to the cistern. When the horses gave out, dozens of citizens pushed the engines up the hill themselves to get the water. Their efforts worked. The fire was stopped at 20th street.

After four days of battling the blazes, the firemen slowly began to get the upper hand. By Saturday, only remnants of the great fire were left smoldering in pockets around the city. Late that night a much-needed rain began to fall, and the smoke finally began to clear.

## AFTERMATH

About 700 people died as the result of the quake and the fires, but countless more were saved by General Funston, Mayor Schmitz, and all of the brave men and women who stayed to fight the fires and help others. Property losses topped $500 million. Some 497 city blocks covering 2,831 acres lay in ruins. Twenty-eight thousand buildings were gone. Half of the city's population, amounting to a quarter of a million people, were homeless. But San Franciscans were determined to save their city; rebuilding began almost immediately.

Secretary of War Taft rushed a bill through Congress requesting half a million dollars in relief funds for the city. It was passed the same day. He ordered 200,000 rations sent from the Vancouver, Washington, Army Base, and ordered every military post in the nation to send all tents without delay. Then he sent another bill through Congress increasing his request for financial aid to $1 million. It was approved. In addition, $10 million more poured in from 14 nations.

Fundraisers for San Francisco were held all over the nation. Songwriter George M. Cohen sold souvenir newspapers for $1,000 per copy, and boxing champion Jim Jeffries sold oranges for $20 each. Relief distribution centers provided aid—the Red Cross served over 313,000 meals on April 30 alone.

**China has a longer border than any other country on Earth (13,700 miles).**

## GETTING BACK TO NORMAL

Ten days later, water service was restored. Soon after came the lights along the main streets and the trolley cars. And the rebuilding continued nonstop. Within three years, 20,000 of the 28,000 ruined buildings had been replaced, and this time most of the buildings were made of brick and steel—not wood.

In 1915 San Francisco hosted the World's Fair, and by then there was barely any evidence left of the Great San Francisco Earthquake and fires.

## A TRAGIC LEGACY

San Franciscans got a rude reminder of the big quake on October 17, 1989. An earthquake hit the area, and although it was much smaller, it was still big enough to cause extensive damage.

Way back in 1915 when they were still rebuilding, many new structures were built in the Marina District. Engineers used rubble, mud, and sand to fill in the shallow bay. But the new land wasn't properly compacted before the buildings went up. After the Exposition ended, homes and other buildings were constructed on top of this unstable base. Without solid ground to stand on, the Marina District was severly damaged in the 1989 quake.

***Schmitz and Funston weren't the only heroes. Turn to page 255 for some of the other stories.***

* * *

## FUZZY MATH

*Here's a U.S. Postal Service ad from 1996, defending its policy to raise the price of stamps:*

"In 1940, a one-pound loaf of bread cost 8 cents, and in 1995 cost 79 cents; a half-gallon of milk went from 25 cents to $1.43 in the same period; and a first-class postage stamp went from 3 cents to 32 cents. Which, bottom line, means that first-class postage stamps remained well below the rate of inflation."

***Do the math:*** Actually, those figures prove that the price of stamps rose 9% faster than the price of bread and 105% faster than the price of milk.

**Raised-bump reflectors on U.S. roads are called "Botts dots." (Elbert Botts invented them.)**

# MY END IS NEAR

*Uncle John predicts that his death will come…on the last day of his life. As creepy as it sounds, some people have actually been able to predict their deaths much more accurately than that. Take these folks…*

## ARNOLD SCHOENBERG

**Claim to Fame:** Austrian composer…and a man obsessed with the number 13

**Prediction:** Schoenberg was born on September 13, 1874 and believed he would probably die on the 13th as well. Which month and year? Probably, he decided, on a Friday the 13th, and most likely in 1951, when he was 76 (7 + 6 = 13).

**What Happened:** That year, July 13 fell on a Friday, and Schoenberg stayed in bed all day, awaiting death. Late that night, his wife went to his room to check on him and scold him for wasting the day so foolishly. When she opened the door, Schoenberg looked up at her, uttered the single word "harmony," and dropped dead. Time of death: 11:47 p.m.…13 minutes before midnight.

## FRANK BARANOWSKI

**Claim to Fame:** Host of "Mysteries Around Us," a radio show that dealt with issues of the paranormal

**Prediction:** Early in January 2002, Baranowski announced to his listeners that he expected to die on January 19.

**What Happened:** As advertised, Baranowski became an eerily suitable topic for his own show by dying on January 19—exactly as he said he would. Cause of death: congestive heart failure. "It's like he just produced his last show," a co-worker told reporters.

## DAVID FABRICIUS

**Claim to Fame:** German astronomer and Protestant minister

**Prediction:** For some reason, Fabricius became fixated on the idea that he would die on May 7, 1617. Rather than tempt fate, when the day came, Fabricius decided to play it safe and stay home.

**What Happened:** About two hours before midnight, he decided

**Tablecloths originally served as big napkins: people wiped their hands and faces on them.**

that the danger had passed. He stepped outside to get some air…and was promptly murdered by a man from his own church.

**THE REVEREND FREDDIE ISAACS**

**Claim to Fame:** Founder of the Reformed Apostolic Church in Cradock, South Africa

**Prediction:** In January 2002, Reverend Freddie told his followers that he would soon be "going home." He had received a message from the Lord to join Him in Heaven, he said, and God had set the date for Saturday, February 2. He had his grave dug in advance and even booked the town hall for the funeral, busing in hundreds of "mourners" from all over South Africa. He also went on a shopping spree of Biblical proportions, sure that the Creator would take care of the bills after he was gone. "We will miss his earthly body," one church member told reporters, "but we know that he will be sitting at the right hand of the Father."

**What Happened:** February 2 came and went…and Freddie didn't die. A spokesperson explained to his enraged and humiliated followers that there had been a misunderstanding, saying, "His actual announcement was, 'I am going home.' That is why it is important for us to sit down and clarify certain words and terms, such as the difference between death and going home."

**FELIPE GARZA, JR.**

**Claim to Fame:** A 15-year-old high school student living in Patterson, California, in 1985

**Prediction:** Felipe had a crush on a classmate named Donna Ashlock, who had a degenerative heart disease and was only weeks away from death when Felipe's mother saw a newspaper article about her condition and read it to Felipe. "I remember his voice in the next room," Mrs. Garza remembered. "He said, 'I'm going to die, and I'm going to give my heart to Donna.'"

**What Happened:** Although Felipe seemed to be in perfect health, he died a few days later when a blood vessel in his brain suddenly burst. His family donated his heart to Donna the following day.

**Final Chapter:** Unfortunately, the ending was not a happy one. Donna's body rejected Felipe's heart a few years later, and she died in March 1989 before another suitable donor could be found. She and Felipe are buried in the same cemetery.

**63% of U.S. presidents have been members of a fraternity of some kind.**

# TOM SWIFTIES

*This classic style of pun was originally invented in the 1920s. Here's a modern collection that was sent to us by BRI member Bryan Henry. They're atrocious, but we couldn't resist including them.*

"Welcome to Grant's Tomb," Tom said cryptically.

"Smoking is not permitted in here," Tom fumed.

"Your boat is leaking," Tom said balefully.

"I prefer to press my own clothes," Tom said ironically.

"It's the maid's night off," Tom said helplessly.

"You're burning the candle at both ends," Tom said wickedly.

"I hope I can still play the guitar," Tom fretted.

"They pulled the wool over my eyes," Tom said sheepishly.

"Someone removed the twos from this deck," Tom deduced.

"Like my new refrigerator?" asked Tom coolly.

"I'll have to send that telegram again," Tom said remorsefully.

"The criminals were escorted downstairs," said Tom condescendingly.

"I haven't caught a fish all day!" Tom said, without debate.

"A thousand thanks, Monsieur," said Tom mercifully.

"I'd love some Chinese soup," said Tom wantonly.

"I forgot what to buy," Tom said listlessly.

"I need a pencil sharpener," said Tom bluntly.

"I punched him in the stomach three times," said Tom triumphantly.

"...and you lose a few," concluded Tom winsomely.

"I was removed from office," said Tom disappointedly.

"I wonder what it was like being one of Zeus's daughters," Tom mused.

"He only likes whole grain bread," Tom said wryly.

"I'm definitely going camping again," said Tom with intent.

"Oh no! I dropped my toothpaste," said Tom, crestfallen.

# LORD STANLEY'S CUP

*The Stanley Cup, awarded annually to the best team in the National Hockey League, is the oldest trophy in professional sports. And whether you like hockey or not, we bet you'll find the cup's history fascinating.*

## THE FATHER AND SONS OF HOCKEY

Lord Arthur Frederick Stanley of Preston, England, son of the 14th Earl of Derby, was appointed Governor-General of the Dominion of Canada in 1888. When he arrived in the country he brought his seven ice-skating sons with him. They fell in love with the rough-and-tumble game of hockey and went on to become some of the best players of their time.

Nineteen-year-old Arthur Stanley and his brother Algy nagged their father for support in organizing the game into teams and leagues, and for a trophy to show as "an outward and visible sign of the ice hockey championship." Dad finally came through. At a dinner for the Ottawa Amateur Athletic Association on March 18, 1892, a member of the Governor-General's staff, Lord Kilcoursie (also a hockey player), made this announcement on behalf of Lord Stanley:

> I have for some time been thinking that it would be a good thing if there were a challenge cup which should be held from year to year by the champion hockey team in the Dominion. There does not appear to be any such outward sign of a championship at present, and considering the general interest which matches now elicit, and the importance of having the game played fairly and under rules generally recognized, I am willing to give a cup which shall be held from year to year by the winning team.

## THE TROPHY

Lord Stanley instructed an aide in England to order a gold-lined silver bowl to be used as the trophy. The bowl measured 7½ inches high and 11½ inches in diameter, and cost about $50. Original name: Dominion Hockey Challenge Cup. But everyone called it the Lord Stanley Cup.

Stanley appointed two trustees and outlined some conditions:

- The winners are to return the Cup promptly when required by the trustees in order that it may be handed over to any other team which may win it.

• Each winning team is to have the club name and year engraved on a silver ring fitted on the Cup.

• The Cup is to remain a challenge competition and not the property of any one team, even if won more than once.

• The trustees are to maintain absolute authority in all disputes over the winner of the Cup.

• A substitute trustee will be named in the event that one of the existing trustees drops out.

## GOING HOME

The boys got their trophy, and the game of hockey grew in popularity. But, ironically, they never got to play for it, and Lord Stanley, the father of organized hockey, never saw a Stanley Cup game. In July 1893, Stanley's brother died and Stanley was called back to England to become the 16th Earl of Derby. He never returned to watch a game for the trophy that bore his name.

Lord Stanley had the trustees present the trophy the first year, 1893, to the Montreal Amateur Athletic Association, which had won an amateur tournament. Then they arranged for an actual championship game between his hometown Ottawa team and Toronto. But the game never took place.

Ottawa was considered the best team, but the trustees insisted they play a "challenge game" since it was a "challenge cup." They also insisted that the game be played in Toronto. Ottawa refused to do it. So the trustees declared the Montreal AAA the first Stanley Cup champions in 1893 without a playoff.

## PLAYOFFS BEGIN

The first official Stanley Cup playoff game took place on March 22, 1894, when Ottawa challenged Montreal in the Montreal Victoria Arena before 5,000 fans. Montreal got to keep the Cup, winning the game 3–1.

Lord Stanley's announcement and his order of a small silver cup would mark the beginning of what would become Canada's national sport... and a game still played internationally more than a century later.

# THE STRANGE TRAIL OF THE STANLEY CUP

*Okay, you just read about the origin of the Stanley Cup... but that's only the beginning. The Cup itself has an unusual history.*

**STANLEY CUP FACTS**

• In 1919 the Spanish flu struck the Montreal Canadiens. They offered to play the last scheduled game with substitutes, but their opponents, the Seattle Metropolitans, declined, and for the only time in history, nobody won the Cup.

• In 1924 the trustees started putting more than just the team names on the cup. Today it is the only trophy in professional sports that has the names of winning players, coaches, management and club staff engraved on it.

• In 1927, after decades of being a multi league championship, the cup came under the exclusive control of the NHL.

• It got bigger: With each winner, a new ring was added to the lower portion of the cup. By the 1940s, it was a long, tubular trophy nearly three feet high. In 1948 it was reworked into a two-piece trophy with a wider base. In 1958 it was reworked again and got the five-ring, barrel-like shape it has today. It now weighs 35 pounds.

• In 1969 the original bowl was retired to the Hockey Hall of Fame in Toronto because of its fragile state. A silversmith in Montreal made an exact replica—down to scratches, dents—and bite marks—which is awarded today.

• There's one name crossed out. Peter Pocklington, the owner of the 1984 champion Edmonton Oilers, put his dad's name on it. The NHL wasn't amused, and covered it with "XXXXXXX."

• There were 2,116 names on the Stanley Cup as of May 2002.

• Seven women have their names engraved on the Stanley Cup.

• The cup is actually out of compliance with Lord Stanley's wishes—he wanted it to be a trophy for amateur athletes only.

## ROWDY GAME, ROWDY TROPHY

Since each winning player and even the management gets to take the Stanley Cup home for a day, it has seen its share of wild times. Here are a few of the more notorious escapades:

• After the Ottawa Silver Seven won the Stanley Cup in 1905, one of the partying players boasted he could kick it across the Rideau Canal. The drunken group went home and groggily remembered the incident the next day. Luckily, the canal was frozen over. When they went back, the cup was sitting on the ice.

• In 1907 the Montreal Wanderers wanted their team picture taken with the Cup. After the photo session, the team left the studio—and forgot the Cup. It stayed there for months until the photographer's housekeeper took it home and grew geraniums in it.

• In 1924 the cup-winning Montreal Canadiens went to Coach Leo Dandurand's house for a late-night party. The car carrying the Cup got a flat, and the players put the Cup on the side of the road while they changed the tire. Then they drove off... without it. When they got to Dandurand's house, Mrs. Dandurand asked, "Where's the Cup?" They realized what they'd done and went back. Incredibly, the Cup was right where they'd left it.

• Muzz and Lynn Patrick found the Cup in their basement in Victoria, B.C., in 1925. (Their father was the coach of the championship Victoria Cougars.) The boys etched their initials onto the Cup with a nail. Fifteen years later, they got their names on it for real—as members of the 1940 champion New York Rangers.

• When the New York Rangers won the Cup in 1940, the players celebrated by urinating in it.

• The Cup was stolen from the Hockey Hall of Fame twice in the late 1960s. One of the thieves threatened to throw it into Lake Ontario unless the charges against him were dropped.

• In 1962 the Montreal Canadiens were playing the defending champions, the Chicago Blackhawks. During one of the games, a Montreal fan went to the Chicago Stadium lobby display case where the Cup was kept, took the Cup out of the case, and walked away. He almost made it to the door when he was stopped by a security guard. Later, he said he "was taking the Cup back to Montreal, where it belongs."

• Chris Nilan of the 1986 champion Montreal Canadiens photographed the Cup with his infant son in it. He said, "His butt fit right in."

• A player on the 1987 champion Edmonton Oilers (purported to be Mark Messier) took it to a strip joint across the street from the rink and let everybody drink out of it. (It happened again in 1994 when the New York Rangers won. Mark Messier was also on that team.)

• In 1991 the Cup turned up at the bottom of Pittsburgh Penguin Mario Lemieux's swimming pool.

• In 1994 Mark Messier and Brian Leetch took the cup on *The Late Show with David Letterman.* There it was used in a sketch called "Stupid Cup Tricks."

• In 1996 Sylvain Lefebvre of the Colorado Avalanche had his daughter baptized in it.

• Rangers Brian Noonan and Nick Kypreos brought the Cup on *MTV Prime Time Beach House*, where it was stuffed with raw clams and oysters.

• The Rangers took the Cup to fan Brian Bluver, a 13-year-old patient awaiting a heart transplant at Columbia-Presbyterian Medical Center. According to his father, Brian "smiled for the first time in seven weeks."

• The Cup was once used as a feed bag for a Kentucky Derby–winning racehorse.

* * *

## UNCLE JOHN'S DUBIOUS ACHIEVEMENT AWARD

**Winner:** Dr. Jukka Ammondt, professor of literature at Finland's University of Jyväskylä

**Achievement:** Not content with translating several of the King's greatest songs into Latin ("It's Now or Never" became "Nunc Hic Aut Numquam") Dr. Ammondt recorded an album of Elvis Presley songs in ancient Sumerian—a language spoken in Mesopotamia around 4000 B.C. ("Layoff of my blue suede shoes" translated as "My sandals of sky-blue, do not touch.")

# FOR SALE BUY OWNER

*We're back with one of our favorite features. More proof that some of the funniest things in life aren't necessarily meant to be funny.*

**In an office:** "Would the person who took the step ladder yesterday please bring it back or further steps will be taken."

**On the door of a photographer's studio:** "Out to lunch: If not back by five, out for dinner also."

**Outside a new town hall:** "The town hall is closed until opening. It will remain closed after being opened. Open tomorrow."

**Outside a London disco:** "Smarts is the most exclusive disco in town. Everyone welcome."

**In a safari park:** "Elephants Please stay in your car"

**Outside a photographer's studio:** "Have the kids shot for Dad from $24.95."

**At a railroad station:** "Beware! To touch these wires is instant death. Anyone found doing so will be prosecuted."

**In a department store:** "Bargain Basement Upstairs"

**In an office building:** "Toilet out of order. Please use floor below."

**Outside a Burger King:** "Now Hiring Losers"

**In Cape Cod:** "Caution Water on Road During Rain"

**In Pennsylvania:** "Auction Sunday—New and Used Food"

**Next to a red traffic light:** "This light never turns green"

**Outside a house:** "For Sale Buy Owner"

**At a McDonald's:** "Parking for Drive-Thru Service Only"

**In Massachusetts:** "Entrance Only Do Not Enter"

**Also in Massachusetts:** "Lake Chargoggagoggmanchauggagoggchaubunagungamaugg"

**Seven thousand U.S. troops invaded Grenada in 1983. They...**

# AN EXPLOSIVE IDEA

*The Nobel Prizes are perhaps the most respected awards on Earth. They're awarded every December 10, the anniversary of the death of their creator and namesake, Alfred Nobel. Here's a look at the man and his medals.*

## STRONG STUFF

In 1846 an Italian chemist named Ascanio Sobrero stumbled onto the formula for a powerful liquid explosive that he called *pyroglycerine*. Soon to become known as *nitroglycerine*, the substance was several times more powerful than black powder or any other explosive known to scientists at the time.

But nitroglycerine was also terribly unstable. It was difficult to make the stuff without blowing yourself up in the process, and it was just about impossible to transport it safely. A bump in the road, a change in air temperature, even prolonged exposure to sunlight was enough to trigger an explosion. Yet there was no easy way to detonate nitroglycerine in a controlled, predictable fashion. As far as Sobrero was concerned, nitroglycerine was more trouble than it was worth, a laboratory curiosity with no practical value.

## WORTH A TRY

But nitroglycerine was *powerful*—and there was a lot of money to be made if someone could work the bugs out. So, in the late 1850s, a bankrupt Swedish munitions manufacturer named Immanuel Nobel decided to try in the hope that nitroglycerine would restore his family fortune.

Success would come at a terrible price: In 1864 Nobel's 20-year-old son, Emil, died in an explosion while experimenting with nitroglycerine. In spite of setbacks, though, Nobel's older son, Alfred, kept plugging away, moving his workshop to a barge in the middle of a lake after the Swedish government forbade him from rebuilding the one that had blown up. In 1865 the 32-year-old Alfred made a breakthrough—he invented the detonating cap. Instead of trying to set off the nitroglycerine directly, he got the idea of detonating a small amount of explosives—usually gunpow-

...received 8,612 medals for their efforts.

der or fulminate of mercury—and using the shock waves from that explosion to set off the nitroglycerine.

## DOWN TO EARTH

That took care of the detonation problem, but nitroglycerine was still very unstable and dangerous to work with. Nobel solved that problem in 1866, when he came upon the idea of mixing nitroglycerine with an inert, porous type of earth called *kieselguhr*. The kieselguhr soaks up the nitroglycerine and forms a malleable, puttylike "plastic" explosive that can be molded into any shape—sticks, for example—and dried into solid form, which is much stabler than liquid nitroglycerine. Nobel named his new explosive *dynamite*, after *dynamis*, the Greek word for "power."

## BACK IN BUSINESS

Nobel's timing could not have been better. The mid to late 1800s was an era of unprecedented public works projects, as countries all over the world constructed bridges, tunnels, dams, roads, railroads, mines, harbors, and canals. Dynamite was up to eight times more powerful than black powder, so wherever there was solid rock to be blasted through, it became the explosive of choice.

The military applications of dynamite were obvious, and although Nobel had pacifist tendencies, where profits were concerned, he was decidedly apolitical; he gladly sold explosives to just about any combatant who asked for it. During the Franco-Prussian War (1870–1871), for example, he made a killing—both figuratively and literally—selling explosives to both sides.

## NOBEL'S SUR-PRIZE

Nobel became one of the wealthiest men in Europe, and his name became a household word. But if he assumed that wealth and fame would also bring him respect, he received what must have been a rude awakening when his brother Ludwig died in 1888. As we told you in *Uncle John's Absolutely Absorbing Bathroom Reader*, many newspapers mistakenly assumed that *Alfred* was the one who had died and wrote scathing obituaries attacking him as a merchant of death and "bellicose monster" whose contributions to science "had boosted the bloody art of war from bullets and bayonets to long-range explosives in less than 24 years."

**Makes sense: Jersey cows come from Jersey, an island in the English Channel.**

When Alfred Nobel died—this time for real—from a cerebral hemorrhage on December 10, 1896, the world was shocked to learn the details of his will: With the exception of a few small personal bequests, all of his assets were to be liquidated and the resulting cash invested in interest-bearing securities. Each year, the interest earned would be divided into five equal amounts and "awarded in prizes to those persons who shall have contributed most materially to benefit mankind during the year immediately preceding." The awards would be presented in five categories: Physics, Chemistry, Medicine, Literature, and Peace.

So, why did Alfred Nobel, "merchant of death," instruct that his estate be used to fund a Peace Prize? "Most of Nobel's biographers," writes Burton Feldman in *The Nobel Prize*, "feel that he was greatly influenced by his brother Ludwig's death—or rather, the inaccurate obituaries that followed it."

## PRIZE FIGHTERS

Today the annual award of the Nobel Prize is taken for granted, but in 1896 the picture was far less clear. For one thing, Nobel's relatives were determined to fight his will so that they could claim a share of the estate. Not only that, the French government wanted to claim Nobel as a legal resident so that it could tax the estate. Either contest to Nobel's bequest would have left little money remaining for prizes. Both the Nobel family and the French government were eventually beaten back, but other questions remained.

The will stipulated that the prize winners would be chosen by the Swedish Academy of Sciences (Physics and Chemistry); the Karolinska Medical Institute (Medicine); and the Swedish Academy (Literature). The Peace Prize winner would be chosen by a committee of five persons appointed by the Norwegian Parliament. Would these organizations even agree to take up the tasks Nobel assigned them? The will said that all of the money would go toward prizes, but made no mention of how the organizations would be compensated, if at all, for their work. If even one of the parties balked, the entire will would be voided and the Nobel Prizes would never come to pass.

In 1897 it was finally decided that 20% of the interest income would go toward expenses; the remaining 80% would be awarded as prizes. That did the trick—on June 11, 1898, the last holdout,

**No wonder the lines are so long: 14 of the world's 20 busiest airports are located in the U.S.**

the Swedish Academy of Sciences, approved Nobel's will. The first Nobel Prizes were awarded in 1901, on the fifth anniversary of Nobel's death.

### BAD PRESS IS GOOD PRESS

So how did the Nobel Prizes become so famous? They were the most valuable prizes of the day, but that alone isn't responsible for their fame. The credit goes to Marie Curie.

Marie Curie and her husband, Pierre, shared the 1903 Nobel Prize for Physics for their pioneering work in the discovery and study of radioactivity. When Pierre died in an accident in 1906, Marie carried on their work. A few years later, in 1911, she was being considered for a second Nobel Prize, this time in Chemistry, for discovering the radioactive elements radium and polonium.

At the same time, Curie was caught up in a public scandal involving her affair with French physicist Paul Langevin, who was married and had four children. All of the tawdry details of the romance—including death threats, duels, and steamy passages from the couple's stolen love letters—were published in newspapers across Europe for the world to see. And then she won her second Nobel Prize.

"Because of Curie," Feldman writes, "newspapers around the globe changed their way of reporting the Nobel Prize, generating endless publicity, and thereby finally changing the meaning of the awards."

It was tabloids as much as talent, that made the Nobel Prizes as popular as they are today.

***Want to win a Nobel Prize? Turn to page 223 to find out how.***

*   *   *

## MONKEY BUSINESS

The Swedish newspaper *Expressen* gave 10,000 kronor ($1,250) each to five stock-market analysts and one chimp named Ola. They were free to play the market as they wished, the goal being to make the biggest profit. The humans used their expertise; Ola picked his stocks by throwing darts at the financial page. A month later, Ola was 1,541 kronor ($190) richer and the winner of the competition.

**Poll: 68% of teenage girls said if they could change one body part, it would be their stomach.**

# THE SAGA OF SILLY PUTTY

*What's stretchy and bouncy and comes in an egg? Silly question. Here's one of Uncle John's favorite toy stories: the origin of Silly Putty.*

## THE WRIGHT STUFF

During World War II, Japanese invasions of rubber-producing countries in the Far East vastly reduced the availability of rubber in the U.S. In the early 1940's, the U.S. War Production Board asked General Electric for help in developing a cheap substitute that could be used in the production of boots and tires. G.E. hired an engineer named James Wright to head the project.

In 1943 Wright accidentally dropped some boric acid into silicone oil. Result: he created an unusual compound that stretched further and bounced higher than rubber. Not only that, it was impervious to mold, didn't decay the way rubber did, and stayed stretchy and bouncy in extreme temperatures. The only problem was that neither scientists nor the military could find a good use for the stuff. In 1945, G.E. mailed samples to scientists all over the world, to see if they could figure out what to do with it.

## GETTING SILLY

An advertising copyrighter named Paul Hodgson was at a party where one of the samples was being passed around. No one was coming up with any scientific uses for it, but they sure were having fun playing with it. To Hodgson it was clear: This was a toy.

It just happened that Hodgson was in the process of creating a catalog for a local toy store. He convinced the owner of the shop to feature what he dubbed "Bouncing Putty." It outsold everything else in the catalog (except a 50-cent box of crayons). Still, the store owner wasn't interested in manufacturing or marketing it, so Hodgson bought the rights and went into business himself. He renamed the product Silly Putty.

In 1950 Hodgson bought 21 pounds of the putty for $147 and hired a Yale college student to cut it up into one-ounce balls and put it into plastic eggs. Sales were slow at first, but Silly Putty's big break came several months later when it was mentioned in *The New Yorker* magazine. Hodgson's phone started ringing off the hook. He received 250,000 orders in only four days. A few years later, Silly Putty was racking up sales of over six million dollars annually—Hodgson was a millionaire.

Today, Binney & Smith, makers of Crayola, own the rights to Silly Putty and produce about 500 pounds of it every day. Over 300 million eggs have been sold since its inception—enough to form a ball of Silly Putty the size of the Goodyear Blimp. It now comes in 16 different colors including glow-in-the-dark, glitter, and hot fluorescent colors. In 2000 Metallic Gold Silly Putty was introduced to celebrate the toy's 50th anniversary. There's even Silly Putty that changes color depending on the temperature of your hands. In 2001 Silly Putty was inducted into the National Toy Hall of Fame, taking its place beside such classics as G.I. Joe, Lincoln Logs, and Monopoly.

## SILLY PUTTY FACTS

• In 2000 Binney & Smith sponsored a "Silliest Uses for Silly Putty Contest." The winner: replace your stockbroker by throwing a ball of Silly Putty at the stock page in the newspaper and investing in whatever stock it lifts from the newsprint. (Second place went to the woman who suggested it could be used to form a fake swollen gland to get out of an unwanted date.)

• One of the original Silly Putty eggs is on display at the Smithsonian Institution's National Museum of American History.

• Silly Putty cost a dollar in 1950 when it was first introduced, and still cost a dollar in 1976 when Hodgson died. Price in 2002: still under $2.

• Why did Hodgson pack Silly Putty in eggs? It was Easter.

• In 1968 *Apollo* 8 astronauts used a new adhesive to fasten down tools during their voyage into weightlessness: Silly Putty.

• In 1989 a grad student at Alfred University wanted to find out what would happen to a ball of Silly Putty dropped from a roof. He dropped a 100-lb. ball from the top of a three-story building. The ball first bounced about eight feet into the air, but it shattered into pieces on the second bounce.

**In 2001 Indian railroads cited 14 million people for riding without a ticket.**

# UNCLE JOHN'S MEDICINE CABINET

*There's a story behind every item in your medicine cabinet. Here are a few.*

• Before World War I, "Aspirin" was a registered trademark of the German company, Bayer. When Germany lost the war, Bayer gave the trademark to the Allies as a reparation in the Treaty of Versailles.

• Why do men wear fragrances? Isn't that a little "girly?" It used to be. But thanks to some clever marketing during World War II, Old Spice aftershave became part of the soldier's standard-issue toiletry kit and changed the smell of things.

• Hate taking care of your contact lenses? It could be worse. Early contacts were made from wax molds (wax was poured over the eyes). The lenses, made of glass, cut off tear flow and severely irritated the eyes. In fact, the whole ordeal was so painful that scientists recommended an anesthetic solution of cocaine.

• On average, each person uses 54 feet of dental floss every year. That may sound like a lot, but dentists recommend the use of a foot and a half of dental floss each day. That's equal to 548 feet a year.

• In the late 1940s, aerosol hair spray was a growing fad among American women. The only problem was that it was water insoluble, which made it hard to wash out. Why? The earliest fixative was shellac, more commonly used to preserve wood.

• Women ingest about 50% of the lipstick they apply.

• Ancient Chinese, Roman, and German societies frequently used urine as mouthwash. Surprisingly, the ammonia in urine is actually a good cleanser. (Ancient cultures had no way of knowing that.)

• Almost half of all men who have dyed their hair were talked into it the first time by a woman.

# SORRY, CHARLIE

*A whole page of gossip about famous people named Charles.*

**Charlie Sheen.** When he was engaged to actress Kelly Preston, he accidentally shot her in the arm. She left him and married John Travolta.

**Prince Charles.** As a child, he was teased so much about the size of his ears that his great-uncle Lord Mountbatten told the queen to surgically fix the "problem." The queen declined. The prince's ears remain big to this day.

**Charles Lindbergh.** His father was a U.S. congressman. During a visit to the Capitol as a boy, he locked the doors of the bathroom and threw lightbulbs onto the street below.

**Charlie Brown.** If he were a real person, he'd be four and a half feet tall: his head would take up two of those feet, his body another two feet, and his legs six inches. Also, his head would be two feet wide.

**Charles Barkley.** After Tonya Harding called herself the "Charles Barkley of figure skating," Barkley said this: "My initial response was to sue her for defamation of character, but then I realized that I had no character."

**Charles Darwin.** Born on the same day as Abraham Lincoln, Darwin originally wanted to be a doctor, but had to give it up because he "wasn't smart enough."

**Charlie Chaplin.** His mansion was next door to notorious Hollywood rake John Barrymore's. Chaplin installed a telescope to spy on his neighbor's nightly exploits.

**Charlie Chan.** From 1925 to 1949, there were 47 movies made about the fictional Chinese detective. Six actors played Chan—not one was Chinese.

# BANANA PEELS

*To most people, the banana peel is little more than a convenient wrapper around the fruit. We told you the history of the banana on page 92...but it turns out the peel has a story too.*

## SLIPPERY SUBJECT

Early 20th-century cities had a huge garbage problem. In those days, litter was a part of urban life—it was everywhere. In the wealthier areas of town, streets were cleaned on a regular basis, but in the poorer neighborhoods, they weren't. The result: the streets were polluted with rotting food, horse manure, and trash.

And then came the banana. By the late 1890s, better transportation methods made the banana so cheap that it became a common snack food, particularly popular among the working class. What happened to the peel after the banana was eaten? It ended up on the street.

Magazines, such as *Harper's Weekly* warned that "whosoever throws banana skins on the sidewalk does a great unkindness to the public, and is quite likely to be responsible for a broken limb." The *Sunday School Advocate* told the story of a man who slipped and broke his leg, which had to be amputated. Unable to work, he saw his family end up in a poorhouse. "All this sorrow," the *Advocate* said, "was caused by the bit of banana peel which Miss Sweet-tooth dropped on the sidewalk."

Banana peels were certainly no worse than all the other refuse on the street. But they were bright yellow, which made them highly visible, so they quickly became a symbol of a trash problem that was already out of control...and getting worse.

## THE BIG APPLE

New York was the first city to seriously address the trash problem. The police department had been responsible for keeping the streets clean, but the men appointed by the police often did little more than just collect their paychecks. In 1895 Col. George E. Waring, Jr. was appointed the new Commissioner of Streets, assigned to overhaul the ineffective street-cleaning system. A military man, he required his sanitation workers to wear white uniforms and instilled a sense of pride in them. Parades of the uniformed street cleaners impressed city residents and slowly raised public awareness about the importance of clean streets.

It would be years before anti-littering and "Beautify America" campaigns permanently changed the national landscape. But the banana was the turning point. The new science of city sanitation spread to other cities, and within a few years the banana peel, once a symbol of filth and ignorance, became synonymous with the movement for clean city streets.

## FIVE THINGS TO DO WITH BANANA PEELS

Is the banana peel just trash? Some people claim it has beneficial uses:

• To get rid of a wart, tape a one-inch square of banana peel over the wart, inside part against your skin. Change the dressing every day or so until the wart is gone—probably within a month or two.

• Use the same treatment to get rid of a splinter. Tape a piece of peel over the splinter. By morning the enzymes (or something) in the peel should bring the splinter to the surface.

• To draw the color from a bruise, hold a banana peel over it for 10 to 30 minutes.

• In the late 1960s, a rumor spread that the inner part of the peel contained an hallucinogenic substance called *banadine*. Supposedly one could smoke it and get legally high. It didn't work (trust Uncle John), but *for historical purposes only*, here's the recipe:

> 1. Take 15 pounds of ripe yellow bananas. 2. Peel them. 3. Scrape off the insides of the skins with a knife. 4. Put all scraped material into a large pot and add water. Boil for three to four hours until it gets a pastelike consistency. 5. Spread this paste on cookie sheets and dry it in an oven for about 20 minutes. This will result in a fine black powder (banadine), which you roll into a cigarette and smoke. Supposedly you'll feel something after smoking three or four. (Unfortunately, it's a really bad headache.)

• To relieve the headache you just got from smoking a banana peel, tape or hold the inner side of a banana peel to the forehead and the nape of the neck. Supposedly the peels increase the electrical conductivity between the two spots.

**In the 3 weeks that baby sparrows are in the nest, Mom and Dad make 5,000 trips for food.**

# URBAN LEGENDS

*We're back with one of our most popular features. Remember the rule of thumb for an urban legend: if a wild story sounds a bit too "perfect" to be true, then it probably isn't.*

**THE LEGEND:** A young woman who lives near a beach becomes pregnant but swears it's a mistake. It turns out that she accidentally swallowed microscopic octopus eggs while swimming and has a baby octopus growing inside her, spreading its tentacles to various parts of her body.

**HOW IT SPREAD:** The story was first published in the *Boston Traveler* in the 1940s and is kept alive mainly in coastal towns.

**THE TRUTH:** No medical records have ever been found to verify this story, but the universal fear of foreign bodies growing inside us keeps it afloat. Similar legends exist about eating pregnant cockroaches in fast food.

**THE LEGEND:** The Chevy Nova had dismal sales in Latin American countries because in Spanish the word *Nova* sounds like *no va,* which translates to "doesn't go."

**HOW IT SPREAD:** It began circulating in business manuals and seminars in the 1980s warning of the follies of failing to do adequate market research before releasing products in foreign markets. It spread from there to newspaper columnists. (Even Uncle John was duped—we included it in *The Best of Uncle John's Bathroom Reader.*)

**THE TRUTH:** When Chevrolet first released the Nova in Mexico, Venezuela, and other Spanish-speaking countries in 1972, the car sold just fine, even better than expected in Venezuela. According to *www.snopes.com*'s Urban Legends page, the very nature of the tale is absurd:

> Assuming that Spanish speakers would naturally see the word "Nova" as equivalent to the phrase "no va" and think, "Hey, this car doesn't go!" is akin to assuming that English speakers would spurn a dinette set sold under the name "Notable" because nobody wants a dinette set that doesn't include a table.

**Even "clean" air may contain as many as 1,500 specks of dust per cubic inch.**

**THE LEGEND:** Teenagers drive around looking for open car windows at red traffic lights, yell, "Spunkball!" and throw a gasoline-soaked rag with a lit firecracker connected to it, hoping to start a fire inside the vehicle.

**HOW IT SPREAD:** Via e-mail, beginning in February 2000.

**THE TRUTH:** This is another variation on a common urban legend—the "gang initiation" legend. (Like the one about someone who flashed a friendly warning at an oncoming car without lights, only to be shot dead by recently-initiated gang members.) No police reports or news items exist to substantiate either legend. The "spunkball" e-mail looked even more credible when the name Bea Maggio, FCLS, Allstate Insurance Co., began appearing underneath it. After reading it, she supposedly passed it along to some friends—not in a company capacity—but just as a regular concerned (and duped) citizen. Her name stuck with the e-mail, giving it an "official" look, but have no fear, there's nothing official about it.

**THE LEGEND:** Walt Disney's body was cryogenically stored after he died in 1966, with instructions to reanimate him when the technology is available. He's supposedly stored underneath "The Pirates of the Caribbean" ride at Disneyland.

**HOW IT SPREAD:** The story began in the early 1970s, but who started it remains unknown. Disney's slow decline in health, his family-only funeral, and the fact that the public was not notified of his death until *after* he was buried all added fuel to the legend. It was given new life when it was reported in two unauthorized—and widely discredited—Disney biographies that were published in the late 1980s.

**THE TRUTH:** No documented evidence exists anywhere claiming this to be true. Disney's daughter Diane said in 1972, "There is absolutely no truth to the rumor that my father, Walt Disney, wished to be frozen. I doubt that my father had ever heard of cryonics." He wasn't frozen; in fact, he was cremated and buried in the Forest Hills cemetery in Glendale, a suburb of Los Angeles. Disney's very private life, along with his cult status, has put him in the same league with Elvis and Marilyn as a target for urban legends.

# HUMANS OF THE SEA

*Ever since he first saw* Flipper *in the 1960s, Uncle John has been fascinated by dolphins. He's not alone—some scientists think dolphins are humans' closest relatives. Whether they are or not, we've still got a lot in common.*

**ANIMAL MAGNETISM**

Few other animals evoke such mystery and curiosity as the dolphin. The more we study them, the more we want to know about them. We know that dolphins live 30 to 40 years. They have a distinct social structure, traveling in flexible groups of between 6 and 12 called *pods*. Young dolphins stay with their mothers for three years or longer before moving on to a new pod. Yet, remarkably, a daughter will often return to her mother's group to have her first calf.

A dolphin's cerebral cortex—the portion of the brain that plans, thinks, and imagines—is larger than a human's and, indeed, dolphins are adept at planning, thinking, and imagining. According to professional trainers, there is no limit to what a dolphin can learn.

Here are some amazing examples of dolphin intelligence:

• **Dolphins learn quickly.** Two dolphins at Sea Life Park in Hawaii knew entirely different routines. One day the trainer accidentally switched the two dolphins and didn't know why they seemed so nervous about performing the stunts. One dolphin, trained to jump through a hoop 12 feet in the air, refused to jump at all until she lowered it to 6 feet. The other seemed shaky about navigating through an underwater maze while blindfolded. Not until the show was over did the trainer discover the error. The dolphin who had jumped through the 6-foot-high hoop had not been trained to go through a hoop at all. The other dolphin was familiar with the blindfold but had never navigated the underwater maze. Yet, somehow, each one had figured out how to perform the other's tricks before the end of the routine.

• **Dolphins can learn sign language.** They can understand syntax and sentence structure, knowing the difference between "Pipe fetch

**Every two hours, somebody somewhere files a lawsuit against Wal-Mart.**

surfboard" ("Fetch the pipe and take it to the surfboard") and "Surfboard fetch pipe" ("Fetch the surfboard and take it to the pipe"). When asked, "Is there a ball in the pool?" the dolphin is able to indicate yes or no—meaning it has understood the language, formed a mental image of the object referred to, and deduced whether the object is or is not there. This is called *referential reporting* and is otherwise documented only in apes and humans.

• **Dolphins consistently demonstrate imagination and creativity.** At the Kewalo Basin Marine Mammal Lab in Hawaii, two young trainers were working with a pair of bottlenose dolphins named Akeakemai and Phoenix. The trainers got the dolphins' attention and then, together, they tapped two fingers of each hand together, making a symbol for "in tandem." They both threw their arms in the air, the sign language gesture that means "creative."

The instruction was "Do something creative together." The two dolphins broke away and began swimming around the tank together. Then in perfect choreography they leapt high into the air while simultaneously spitting water out of their mouths. Because dolphins don't normally carry water in their mouths, the move had to be planned and synchronized before they left the water, proving that this was not a matter of two dolphins playing follow-the-leader. When other games of "Tandem Creative" were played, the dolphins did such things as backpedaling and then waving their tail flukes, or doing simultaneous back flips. The trainers were always surprised.

• **Dolphins have a sophisticated language of their own.** Dr. Jarvis Bastian, a University of California psychologist, taught a game to two dolphins named Doris and Buzz. They were instructed to press one lever (on the left) when they saw a flashing light and another lever (on the right) when they saw a steady light. Then he taught them a new twist: when the light came on, Doris had to wait until Buzz pressed his lever, then she could press her lever. When they had this down pat, Dr. Bastian placed a barrier between the two dolphins so they couldn't see each other and only Doris could see the light. When the light flashed, Doris waited for Buzz to press his lever. Buzz, not knowing the light was on, did nothing. Doris then gave off a burst of whistles and clicks, and Buzz immediately pulled the correct lever. And he pulled the cor-

**Like parrots, captive dolphins can imitate human voices.**

rect lever every time the test was repeated.

• **Dolphins play jokes.** Dolphins in a San Francisco oceanarium were taught to "clean house," receiving a reward of fish for each piece of trash they brought to their trainer. A dolphin named Mr. Spock kept bringing in soggy bits of paper, getting reward after reward. The trainer finally discovered that the dolphin had hidden a big brown paper bag in a corner of the pool and was earning dividends by tearing off tiny pieces, one at a time.

At Busch Gardens in Florida, scuba diving "janitors" periodically entered the dolphin tank with large underwater vacuum cleaners to pick up debris from the bottom of the pool. On one occasion, the divers were puzzled because they were unable to find any garbage. Only the observers above the tank could see that a dolphin named Zippy was going in front of the divers, just out of their sight, picking up pieces of trash and transferring them to the area behind the divers, which had already been swept.

• **Dolphins enjoy playing games.** They have been observed playing catch, tag, and keep-away. They've been known to sneak up on birds resting on the surface of the ocean and grab them by the feet, pulling them under before releasing them. They intercept swimming turtles, turning them over and over. Once, two dolphins in an aquarium wanted to play with a moray eel, but the eel was hiding in a crevice under a rock where they couldn't reach it. One dolphin picked up a dead scorpionfish and poked at the eel with the spines. The eel swam into the open, where it was caught by the dolphins and teased until being released.

• **Dolphins are affectionate.** Researchers observing them in the wild have noted that a large part of a dolphin's day is spent in physical contact with other dolphins. They swim belly to belly or side by side, sometimes looking like they're holding "hands." They rub their bodies together, pet each other with their fins and flukes, and enjoy sex for the pleasure of it.

• **Dolphins echo the worst of human nature.** The world of dolphins is not all sweetness and light. Just as with humans, there seems to be a wide variation in dolphins' behavior toward members of their own species. Some dolphins exhibit violent aggression and fight with others by ramming and biting them, sometimes

**Four most common names for popes: John, Gregory, Benedict, and Clement, in that order.**

to the point of death. Male dolphins occasionally build harems, and one researcher even documented a case of a male kidnapping a female and holding her captive. Groups of strong males may gang up on young, smaller dolphins, harassing them. Adult males will sometimes kill infants fathered by another male. They are also consummate predators, ruthless in their kills, and have been known to kill for reasons other than hunger.

• **Dolphins also echo the best of human nature.** There are documented instances of dolphins coming to the aid of other dolphins. Healthy dolphins will support a sick or injured dolphin to the surface, helping it breathe. If one member of a pod becomes entangled in a fishing net, others will come to its assistance, often becoming entangled themselves. Female dolphins will guard another female who's giving birth. There are also many instances on record of dolphins coming to the aid of humans in trouble.

In November 1999, twelve Cubans boarded a small boat in an attempt to escape to the United States. Rough seas sank the boat, drowning most of the people on board. The mother of five-year-old Elian Gonzales stuck him inside an inner tube. When rescuers found him, he was surrounded by dolphins who had broken waves for him and driven away sharks for the two terrible days he had floated alone on the ocean.

* * *

## SPARE CHANGE

• Coin collecting was so popular in the late 19th century that the U.S. government issued two coins just for collectors: the Columbian half-dollar of 1892 and the Isabella quarter of 1893. Both coins marked the 400th anniversary of the discovery of America by Columbus. The portrait of Queen Isabella of Spain was the first foreign monarch on an American coin.

• According to experts, only one country in modern times never issued coinage: the Republic of Texas. In 1836 Texas broke away from Mexico and became an independent nation. From 1836 to 1845, when it became the 28th state in the U.S., Texas issued paper money, but no coins. For small change it used U.S. cents and Mexican reals.

# I WANT TO RIDE MY BICYCLE! PART II

*In Part I (page 69), we saw the bike go from a modified toy to a useful mode of transportation. But even with all of the improvements, by the middle of the 19th century, bikes were still thought of by most as curious—and dangerous—monstrosities. Here's Part II.*

## MOVING ON UP

The pedals on Kirkpatrick MacMillan's improved "hobby horse" gave the rider a lot more control, but pedaling required brute strength. In 1862 a French carriage maker named Pierre Lallement improved on MacMillan's design by switching the iron rods and pedals from the rear wheel to the front wheel (technology that's still used in children's tricycles). The result: the *veloce.* Now the rider could crank the wheel and create motion with much less effort. As Lallement rode his veloce through the streets of Paris, creating a stir among townsfolk, he knew had something special, so he moved to the land of opportunity: America.

## LOOK OUT BELOW!

Lallement arrived in Ansonia, Connecticut, in 1865. With little money to his name, he got a job in a carriage shop and in his spare time built what historians consider to be the first American bicycle.

He arranged to exhibit his new machine by staging a four-mile ride from Ansonia to the neighboring town of Derby and back. The first leg was mostly uphill, which was difficult. The ride back, however, was disastrous. At first, spectators were amazed to see Lallement speeding down the hill, but their excitement turned to horror when they realized he had no control over his machine—the veloce hit a rut, stopped, and the Frenchman went flying over the handlebars.

Undeterred, Lallement earned an American patent in 1866, but the rough New England roads and even rougher winters made the veloce a tough sell. So Lallement finally gave up and returned to France. When he got to Paris, what he saw amazed him: Parisians were riding around on veloces!

Lallement's former employer, carriage maker Pierre Michaux, had copied Lallement's design and renamed it the *velocipede* (rough translation: "speed through feet"). With the help of his son, Ernest, Michaux built the first velocipede in 1863. In 1867 they displayed it at the Paris World's Fair and it attracted so much attention that Michaux decided to dedicate all of his resources to producing them. Soon velocipedes—"boneshakers" as they were nicknamed because of their lack of suspension and adequate brakes—became popular all over Europe.

## THE PENNY-FARTHING

English mechanics came up with the next big innovation in bicycles—they increased the size of the front wheel. Because the pedals were attached directly to the axle, the larger the wheel, the farther a person could go with one rotation of the pedals. In some instances, the front wheel was four or five feet in diameter. At the same time, the rear wheel shrunk in size to give the bicycle better balance. The new machine became known as the "penny-farthing" because of the drastic disparity between the size of the front and rear wheels (it resembled two British coins, the penny and the farthing, placed next to each other). Now the rider had to carefully climb up the bike to get it going—not an easy task. But thankfully, penny-farthings were the first bikes with brakes.

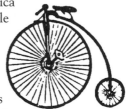

The penny-farthing was introduced to America at the 1876 Philadelphia World's Fair, and people loved it. To cash in on the public interest, a Boston architect named Frank W. Weston founded a company to import penny-farthings from England. They were a big hit, but because they cost well over $100 each ($1,670 in today's dollars), they were only available to the rich. Aristocrats formed exclusive "riding clubs" in upscale neighborhoods with indoor tracks and private riding instructors. Middle-class people wanted to join in on the fun, but few could afford the expensive import.

Colonel Albert Pope, however, was about to change all that.

***For Part III of the story, turn to page 264.***

**In some parts of India, girls get names with an odd number of syllables; boys get even.**

# HOUDINI'S SECRETS

*From 1896 to 1926, Harry Houdini was the world's most famous escape artist. He could get out of anything. There was no lock or latch that could hold him. How'd he do it? We'll never tell. Okay, you talked us into it.*

**THE TRICK:** Escaping from a locked container

**THE SECRET:** Hidden tools

**EXPLANATION #1:** Houdini often hid tools by swallowing them. He learned the trick while working for a circus, when an acrobat showed him how to swallow objects, then bring them up again by working the throat muscles. Houdini practiced with a potato tied to a string...so he could be pull it back up if needed.

**EXPLANATION #2:** Houdini would ask several men from the audience come up onstage, first to search him to for hidden tools, and second, to examine whatever he was about to be locked up in: a safe or a coffin or a packing crate. He would then solemnly shake hands with each man. But the last man was a shill—someone who had been planted in the audience. And during the handshake, a pick or a key would be passed from hand to hand.

**EXPLANATION #3:** Houdini sometimes hid a slim lockpick—like a thin piece of wire—in the thick skin of the sole of his foot.

**THE TRICK:** One of his greatest—escaping from a water-filled milk can...without disturbing the six padlocks that secured the lid

**THE SECRET:** A fake can

**EXPLANATION:** Houdini folded himself into the cylinder (or body) of an old-fashioned milk can. But the neck of the can wasn't really attached to the body. It appeared to be held together by rivets, but the rivets were fake. The two sections actually came apart. Houdini could easily break the neck from the cylinder, step out of the milk can, and then reattached it. And because the can was placed inside a box, the audience never knew how it was done.

**THE TRICK:** Escaping from handcuffs

**THE SECRET:** Sleight of hand

**EXPLANATION:** If he couldn't pick the lock, Houdini had

another trick: he'd insist the handcuffs be locked a little higher on his forearm, then simply slip them over his wrists.

**THE TRICK:** Mind reading

**THE SECRET:** Secret stage code (and a clever assistant)

**EXPLANATION:** Houdini's wife, Bess, often participated in the show. For mind-reading tricks, they worked out a secret code where one could tip off the other using words that stood for numbers: pray = 1, answer = 2, say = 3, now = 4, tell = 5, please = 6, speak = 7, quickly = 8, look = 9, and be quick = 0.

If Houdini was divining the number from a dollar bill, Bess would say, "Tell me, look into your heart. Say, can you answer me, pray? Quickly, quickly! Now! Speak to us! Speak quickly!" Then Houdini the "mind reader" would correctly reply: 59321884778.

**THE TRICK:** Escaping from a straitjacket

**THE SECRET:** There was no trick—he did it in plain sight using a combination of technical skill and brute strength

**EXPLANATION:** From his 1910 book *Handcuff Escapes*:

> The first step is to place the elbow, which has the continuous hand under the opposite elbow, on some solid foundation and by sheer strength exert sufficient force at this elbow so as to force it gradually up towards the head, and by further persistent straining you can eventually force the head under the lower arm, which results in bringing both of the encased arms in front of the body.
>
> Once having freed your arms to such an extent as to get them in front of your body, you can now undo the buckles of the straps of the cuffs with your teeth, after which you open the buckles at the back with your hands, which are still encased in the canvas sleeves, and then you remove the straitjacket from your body.

**ONE LAST SECRET:** Often Houdini would escape quickly from his entrapment, then sit quietly out of sight of the audience, calmly playing cards or reading the paper while waiting for the tension to grow: "Is he dead yet?" "He's never going to get out alive!" Then, when the audience's murmurings and accompanying music had grown to a fever pitch, he would drench himself in water to make himself look sweaty before stepping triumphantly out in front of the curtain to humbly accept the raucous cheers.

**Three words pulled from Microsoft Word's thesaurus in 2000: idiot, fool, and nitwit.**

# THE INCREDIBLE SHRINKING HEADS

*There have been many head-hunting cultures in the world—even the French had the guillotine—but only one made shrunken heads. Here's the story.*

## THE JIVARO

The Jivaro (pronounced "hee-var-o") tribes live deep in the jungles of Ecuador and Peru. They don't do it anymore as far as anyone knows but as recently as 100 years ago they were ardent head shrinkers. The Jivaro tribes were constantly at war with other neighboring tribes (and with each other), and they collected the heads of their fallen enemies as war trophies. The head, once shrunk, was called *tsantsa* (pronounced "san-sah"). For the Jivaro the creation of tsantsa insured good luck and prevented the soul of the fallen enemy from seeking revenge.

As Western explorers came in increasing contact with the Jivaro tribes in the late 19th century, shrunken heads became a popular souvenir. Traders would barter guns, ammo, and other useful items for shrunken heads; this "arms-for-heads" trade caused the killing to climb rapidly, prompting the Peruvian and Ecuadorian governments to outlaw head shrinking in the early 1900s. If you buy a head today, it's guaranteed a fake.

## THE JOY OF COOKING...HEADS

Here's the Jivaro recipe for a genuine shrunken head (Kids, don't try this at home): Peel skin and hair from skull; discard skull. Sew eye and mouth openings closed (trapping the soul inside, so that it won't haunt you). Turn inside out and scrape fat away using sharp knife. Add jungle herbs to a pot of water and bring to a boil; add head and simmer for one to two hours. Remove from water. Fill with hot stones, rolling constantly to prevent scorching. Repeat with successively smaller pebbles as the head shrinks. Mold facial features between each step. Hang over fire to dry. Polish with ashes. Moisturize with berries (prevents cracking). Sew neck hole closed. Trim hair to taste.

**Second grossest fact in this entire book: You inhale about 700,000 of your own skin flakes daily.**

# GOOD DOG

*Can a dog be a hero? These people sure think so.*

**GOOD DOG:** Blue, a two-year-old Australian Blue Heeler
**WHAT HE DID:** One evening in 2001, Ruth Gay of Fort Myers, Florida, was out walking her dog when she accidentally slipped on some wet grass and fell. The 84-year-old woman couldn't get up, and no one heard her cries for help—except a 12-foot alligator that crawled out of a nearby canal. Gay probably would have been gator food if Blue hadn't been there to protect her. The 35-pound dog fought with the gator, snarling and snapping until the reptile finally turned tail. Then Blue ran home barking, alerting Gay's family that she was in trouble. Gay was saved. And Blue? He was treated for 30 puncture wounds. "It's amazing what an animal will do in a time of need," said the vet. "He's a pretty brave dog."

**GOOD DOG:** Trixie, a six-year-old mixed breed
**WHAT SHE DID:** In 1991, 75-year-old Jack Fyfe of Sydney, Australia, was home alone when he suffered a paralyzing stroke. Unable to move, he lay helpless, waiting for someone to discover him as the temperature outside climbed to 90 degrees. Fyfe was crying for water—and that's just what Trixie brought him. She found a towel, soaked it in her water dish, then laid it across Fyfe's face so he could suck out the moisture. She repeated this every day until her water dish ran dry, then she dipped the towel in the toilet. After nine days, Fyfe's daughter stopped by and found him—still alive...thanks to Trixie.

**GOOD DOG:** Sadie, an English Setter
**WHAT SHE DID:** Michael Miller was walking Sadie when he had a massive heart attack. He was unconscious, but his hand was still wrapped around Sadie's leash. Sadie tried to revive him by licking his face. When that failed, the 45-pound dog began pulling the 180-pound man toward home. For an hour and a half the dog labored to pull his body homeward, a third of a mile away. Finally reaching the back door, the dog howled until Miller's wife came out. Because of the dog's heroism, Miller recovered.

# BAD DOG

*Can a dog be a pain? These people sure think so.*

**BAD DOG:** Bear, a Newfoundland

**WHAT HE DID:** Glen Shaw, a trash collector in New Hampshire occasionally brought Bear along on his route. On December 20, 2001, Shaw got out of his 10-wheeled compactor truck to load some garbage into the back and Bear somehow released the hand brake. As the truck began to roll downhill, Shaw ran after it but it was no use. The runaway truck plunged into the Souhegan River, and Shaw plunged in behind it to rescue the dog. Good news: the dog survived. Bad news: it took a hazardous waste crew more than two hours to clean up the mess.

**BAD DOG:** Jake, a three-month-old Rottweilier

**WHAT HE DID:** The Dodson family of Norman, Oklahoma, went out and left Jake in the same place they always left him: the utility room. They returned hours later to find Jake…and a smoking pile of rubble where their home used to be. Evidently Jake had flipped the gas line switch, filling the room with natural gas and when the hot water heater kicked on, the gas exploded. Jake was hurled clear of the explosion…and escaped unharmed.

**BAD DOG:** a boxer

**WHAT HE DID:** Muammer Guney, 46, of Denizli, Turkey, had a heart attack while he was walking his dog in the park. The animal stood guard over his fallen master, barking and keeping would-be helpers at bay. By the time relatives arrived on the scene to pull the dog away, it was too late; doctors pronounced Guney dead.

**BAD DOG:** Stinky, a six-year-old mongrel

**WHAT HE DID:** In December of 2000 Stinky and his master, Kelly Russell, were out hunting near their New Zealand home. Russell set down his rifle for a moment and Stinky jumped on it. The gun went off, hitting Russell in the foot. At the Waikato hospital, doctors were unable to save his foot. Russell was also fined $500 for hunting illegally in an exotic forest.

**No ump-dump rule: In pro baseball, you can't replace an umpire unless he's injured or sick.**

# BATHROOM NEWS

*Here are a few choice bits of bathroom trivia we've flushed out over the years.*

## ARTSY FARTSY

In 2001 a new work of art by Alphonse Gradant appeared in the Museum of European Art in Paris. Praised as "art in its rawest form... an expression of 21st-century angst, comparable to the best work of Picasso and Salvador Dali," the work later sold for $45,000.

Who is Alphonse Gradant? The museum janitor.

Someone swiped one of his diagrams, had it framed, and hung it in the museum as a joke. Is it art? "No," says Gradant. "It's the layout of the men's toilet," which he colored in with red and black pens to make it easier to understand. "I needed a simple diagram that the contractor could follow," he explains. "All I was trying to do was make his work easier, not create a work of art." Museum officials refunded the $45,000. "If it was meant as a joke," says a spokesperson, "It wasn't a very funny one."

## SANITATION ACROSS THE NATION

In March 2002, Parrot Products introduced the Enable Kit, designed for drivers who are grossed out by bathrooms in highway truck stops and rest areas. Each $3.79 kit comes complete with hand wipes, "area and fixture wipes," rubber gloves, toilet paper, a paper seat cover, and even a face mask to protect against "any particulates floating around." Company founder Joe Gawzner says he invented the kit after years of experiencing "negative restroom conditions." "Why suffer when nature calls?" he asks.

## WIPE AWAY THE CRACKS

In 2000 the city of St. Louis, Missouri, started using a new material to seal freshly tarred cracks in its roads: toilet paper. The paper reduces the tackiness of the tar so that it doesn't stick to people's shoes or to the tires of cars. T.P. offers advantages over traditional materials like sand and leaf mulch: it's cheap, it doesn't clog sewers, it doesn't stink like leaf mulch, and it's easy to apply—just slap

**Wide load: Americans ate 15,000 tons of snack food during Super Bowl XXXVI (2002).**

some onto a paint roller, attach a broom handle, and unroll it right over the tar. Bonus: As the toilet paper degrades, it adds an optical illusion. "Stoop down and look at it," says Nigel Martin, a city worker assigned to T.P. duty. "It looks like snow, doesn't it?"

## TASTES LIKE...SWITZERLAND

In February 2001, a Swiss man named Roger Weisskopf won a lifetime supply of toilet paper after he went on the German television show *Wetten Dass?* and demonstrated his unusual talent: being able to identify the name and country of origin of any brand of toilet paper...by tasting it. More precisely, by "licking, sucking, and chewing" wads of the stuff until it gives up its secrets.

No word on whether Weisskopf ate his prize. It took him a year of practice to develop his skill, which friends and loved ones encouraged by bringing home foreign toilet paper whenever they traveled abroad. According to Weisskopf (and he would know), Swiss paper tastes the best, while Japanese paper tastes the worst. "It tastes like moth balls," he says. "It nearly turned my stomach when I was practicing." Weisskopf is now developing a singing toilet lid to cash in on his fame.

## LIKE MONEY IN THE TANK

In the 1960s, the exchange rate for Indonesian currency was 325 *rupiah* to one U.S. dollar. Distressed by the high cost and low quality of Indonesian toilet paper, some western tourists started buying *sen* notes—worth 1/100 of a *rupiah*, or 32,500 to the dollar—and using them for toilet paper.

## WHAT GOES DOWN...

Japanese engineers had a problem in 1993 with some of their new high-speed bullet trains. Everything in the trains was high-tech—except the toilets, which were the old, hole-in-the-floor style. The problem: when the train went through a tunnel, it created "compressed atmospheric pressure." In other words, whatever went down the hole came back up, splattering whoever was there. So were the toilets recalled? Not a chance—railroad officials just posted signs warning passengers not to use the toilets while the trains were going through a tunnel. (They also set up a fund to pay for hot baths and laundry service...just in case.)

**How does an orangutan warn other orangutans that danger is near? He belches—*loudly.***

# IF THEY MARRIED

*We finally found a use for celebrities... well, not the whole celebrity, just the name. Somebody actually took the time to invent these celebrity marriages, and we salute them.*

• If Bo Derek married Don Ho, she'd be **Bo Ho**.

• If Yoko Ono had married Sonny Bono, she would have been **Yoko Ono Bono**.

• If Dolly Parton had married Salvador Dali, she would have been **Dolly Dali**.

• If Oprah Winfrey married Depak Chopra, she'd be **Oprah Chopra**.

• If Olivia Newton-John married Wayne Newton, then divorced him to marry Elton John, she'd be **Olivia Newton-John Newton John**.

• If Sondra Locke married Eliot Ness, then divorced him to marry Herman Munster, she'd become **Sondra Locke Ness Munster**.

• If Bea Arthur married Sting, she'd be **Bea Sting**.

• If Liv Ullman married Judge Lance Ito, then divorced him and married Billy Beaver (game show host), she'd be **Liv Ito Beaver**.

• If Shirley Jones married Tom Ewell, then Johnny Rotten, then Nathan Hale, she'd be **Shirley Ewell Rotten Hale**.

• If Ivana Trump married, in succession, actor Orson Bean, King Oscar of Norway, Louis B. Mayer (of MGM fame), and Norbert Wiener (mathematician), she would then be **Ivana Bean Oscar Mayer Wiener**.

• If Javier Lopez married Keiko the whale, and Edith Piaf married Rose Tu the elephant, they would be **Javier Keiko and Edith Tu**.

• If Tuesday Weld married Hal March III, she'd be **Tuesday March 3**.

• If Snoop Doggy Dogg married Winnie the Pooh, he'd be **Snoop Doggy Dogg Pooh**.

# WORD ORIGINS

*Ever wonder where these words came from?*
*Here are the interesting stories behind them.*

**DOOZIE**

**Meaning:** Something wonderful, superior, or classy

**Origin:** "The word comes from Duesenberg, an eminently desirable motor car of the 1920s and '30s. The Duesenberg featured a chromed radiator shell, gold-plated emblem, hinged louvered hood, stainless-steel running boards, beveled crystal lenses on the instrument panel, Wilton wool carpet, and twin bugle horns. Magazine ads for the luxury car carried the slogan: 'It's a Duesie.'" (From *The Secret Lives of Words*, by Paul West)

**TO KOWTOW**

**Meaning:** To show servile deference

**Origin:** "The word is Chinese and literally means 'knock the head.' It was an ancient Chinese custom to touch the ground with the forehead when worshiping or paying one's respects to an illustrious personage." (From *Why Do We Say It?*, by Frank Oppel)

**TO NAG**

**Meaning:** To annoy by constant urging or fault-finding

**Origin:** "European households of the early Middle Ages had a problem—rats infested every nook and corner; squirrels nested in the roofs. Between the rats and squirrels, the noise of gnawing was very disturbing. The Germans developed the word *nagen*, from an old Scandinavian term meaning 'to gnaw.' Eventually a person who gnawed at another by constant fault-finding was said to *nag*, and the word soon lost its earlier meaning." (From *I've Got Goose Pimples*, by Marvin Vanoni)

**MANURE**

**Meaning:** Animal excrement used to fertilize plants

**Origin:** "From the Latin *manu operati*, 'to work by hand.' Farming was constant manual labor, especially the fertilizing, which required mixing by hand. Genteel folks who objected to the word *dung*, the excrement of animals, were responsible for its euphemistic displacement with the more 'refined' *manure*.

"Even *manure* became objectionable to the squeamish; they preferred *fertilizer*. According to a famous story about Harry S Truman, the president was explaining that farming meant manure, manure, and more manure. At which point a lady said to the president's wife: 'You should teach Harry to say "fertilizer," not "manure."' Mrs. Truman replied, 'You don't know how long it took me to get him to say "manure."'" (From *The Story Behind the Words*, by Morton S. Freeman)

## ADMIRAL

**Meaning:** High-ranking commissioned officer in a navy or coast guard

**Origin:** "This is an artificial spelling of the French *amiral*. The Arabian word *amir*, commander, is commonly followed by *al*, as in *amir-al bahr*, 'commander of the sea,' from which *amiral* resulted." (From *More About Words*, by Margaret S. Ernst)

## BUCCANEER

**Meaning:** Pirate or adventurer

**Origin:** "The literal sense of the word was based on a native West Indian word meaning 'one who cures flesh on a barbecue.' Thus the name was initially applied to woodsmen in the West Indies in the 17th century. The word was transferred to pirates of the 'Spanish Main' whose culinary habits were similar." (From *Dunces, Gourmands & Petticoats*, by Adrian Room)

## TEMPURA

**Meaning:** A Japanese dish of deep-fried vegetables or seafood

**Origin:** "Neither a native Japanese dish, nor a Japanese name. When the Portuguese arrived in the 17th century, the Japanese noticed that at certain 'times' (Portuguese, *tempora*), notably Lent, they switched from meat to fish. With typical subtlety the Japanese concluded that the word meant a variety of seafood." (From *Remarkable Words with Astonishing Origins*, by John Train)

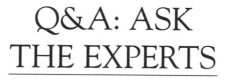

# Q&A: ASK THE EXPERTS

*More random questions, with answers from the nation's top trivia experts.*

## FEELIN' GROOVY

**Q:** *Who first faded out the music at the end of a record, rather than having a proper ending?*

**A:** "Fade-outs became widespread in the United States as the result of a trade survey in the early fifties. This showed that when records were played on jukeboxes, people felt more inclined to replay a record that faded out because it left a subconscious feeling that you hadn't completely heard it. The only other innovation to stimulate jukebox plays was pioneered by the Chess Record Company. They developed a groove-cutting technique which ensured that when played on jukeboxes, their records were one-third louder than all other records in the machine." (From *The Best Ever Notes & Queries*, edited by Joseph Harker)

## COUNTER CULTURE

**Q:** *When spilled coffee dries on my kitchen counter, it forms a brown ring, with almost nothing inside. Why does all the coffee go to the edges to dry?*

**A:** "When a coffee puddle finds itself on a flat, level surface, it tends to spread out in all directions. The liquid will stop spreading when it hits a barrier, any slight irregularity in the surface that it can't cross, such as a microscopic ditch. Depending on where the barriers happen to be, the puddle will take on a certain shape: longer in this direction, shorter in that, like an amoeba.

"As evaporation takes place, the puddle will start to dry first where it's thinnest: at the edges. That has the effect of making the puddle shrink, pulling its edges back, but it can't do that because they're stuck in the ditches. So as water evaporates from the edges, it has to be replenished from somewhere, and the only place it can come from is the interior of the puddle.

"Thus, there's movement of water from the interior of the puddle to the edges, where it evaporates. That water carries along with it the microscopic brown coffee particles which then find themselves stranded at the edges when the puddle finally runs out of water." (From *What Einstein Told His Barber*, by Robert Wolke)

## A HAIR OF A DIFFERENT COLOR

**Q:** *Why does hair turn gray?*

**A:** "Gray (or white) is the base color of hair. Pigment cells located at the base of each hair follicle produce the natural dominant color of our youth. However, as a person grows older, more and more of these pigment cells die and color is lost from individual hairs. The result is that a person's hair gradually begins to show more and more gray.

"The whole process may take between 10 and 20 years—rarely does a person's entire collection of individual hairs (which can number in the hundreds of thousands) go gray overnight." (From *How Things Work*, by Louis Bloomfield)

## CHALK IT UP TO EXPERIENCE

**Q:** *There is a common scene on TV and in the movies where there has been a murder. The body has been removed, but its outline is preserved on the floor in white tape or chalk. Do the police really do this?*

**A:** "At one time, maybe, but according to investigators we surveyed, it's really not done anymore. Why? While chalk or tape might make for dramatic TV, they also contaminate the crime scene, and contamination is a major headache for crime scene investigators." (From *The Straight Dope*, by Cecil Adams)

## W-A-A-A-H!

**Q:** *Besides humans, do any other animals cry?*

**A:** "Only one other land animal cries: the elephant. Marine animals that cry include seals, sea otters, and saltwater crocodiles (the so-called 'crocodile tears'). All of these animals cry only to get rid of salt. However, one scientist, Dr. G. W. Steller, a zoologist at Harvard University, thinks that sea otters are capable of crying emotional tears. According to Dr. Steller, 'I have sometimes deprived females of their young on purpose, sparing the lives of their mothers, and they would weep over their affliction just like human beings.'" (From *The Odd Body*, by Dr. Stephen Juan)

# HARD-BOILED

*Here's our tribute to some classic (and not so classic) Hollywood movies.*

**Burt Lancaster:** "Why did you bolt your cabin door last night?"

**Eva Bartok:** "If you knew it was bolted you must have tried it. If you tried it, you know why it was bolted."

**—*The Crimson Pirate***

"My first wife was the second cook at a third-rate joint on Fourth Street."

**—Eddie Marr, *The Glass Key* (1942)**

"When I have nothing to do at night and can't think, I always iron my money."

**—Robert Mitchum, *His Kind of Woman* (1951)**

**Guy Pearce:** "All I ever wanted was to measure up to my father."

**Russell Crowe:** "Now's your chance. He died in the line of duty, didn't he?"

**—*L.A. Confidential* (1997)**

"I used to live in a sewer. Now I live in a swamp. I've come up in the world."

**—Linda Darnell, *No Way Out***

"He was so crooked he could eat soup with a corkscrew."

**—Annette Bening, *The Grifters* (1990)**

"It looks like I'll spend the rest of my life dead."

**—Humphrey Bogart, *The Petrified Forest* (1936)**

**Rhonda Fleming:** "You drinkin' that stuff so early?"

**Bill Conrad:** "Listen, doll girl, when you drink as much as I do, you gotta start early."

**—*Cry Danger* (1951)**

"You're like a leaf that the wind blows from one gutter to another."

**—Robert Mitchum, *Out of the Past* (1947)**

"I've got an honest man's conscience… in a murderer's body."

**—DeForest Kelley, *Fear in the Night* (1947)**

"I'd hate to take a bite out of you. You're a cookie full of arsenic."

**—Burt Lancaster, *Sweet Smell of Success* (1957)**

**Peaches used to be known as "Persian apples."**

# *SNL* PART III: EDDIE

*When its tumultuous first era finally ended,* Saturday Night Live *had no big stars and no producer, but NBC wasn't about to give up on it. (Part II is on page 141.)*

## SATURDAY NIGHT DEAD

In the summer of 1980, only a few months before the fall season started, associate producer Jean Doumanian was promoted—against Lorne Michaels's departing advice—to executive producer. The remaining cast and writers, who agreed with Michaels that Doumanian wasn't up to producing the show, also left. Could *Saturday Night Live* survive without any of its original talent?

Hundreds of wannabes tried to get on the revamped show. Doumanian's plan, basically, was to "do what Lorne did" and find seven unknowns—three women and four men. She ended up with Gail Matthius, Denny Dillon, Ann Risley, Gilbert Gottfried, Joe Piscopo, and Charles Rocket, whom Doumanian envisioned as the new star. She still wanted an "ethnic"—so dozens of black and Hispanic comics were brought in to audition. One standout was a foul-mouthed, 19-year-old kid named Eddie Murphy. Doumanian had someone else in mind, but talent coordinator Neil Levy talked her into hiring him. Still, she only made him a featured player and limited his on-air time.

The ensuing season was bad, probably *SNL*'s worst. After the first new episode, Tom Shales echoed the public's sentiments when he wrote, "From the 7 new performers and 13 new writers hired for the show, viewers got virtually no good news." As the ratings began to sag for "Saturday Night Dead"—as it was being called—morale at Studio 8H hit an all-time low. No one could stand Doumanian or the show's arrogant star, Charles Rocket, who sealed his fate by saying the F-word on live television. Both were fired in the spring of 1981.

## MR. MURPHY'S NEIGHBORHOOD

Few other shows could have rebounded from such a debacle, but NBC still had faith in *Saturday Night Live*. Dick Ebersol replaced Doumanian. Knowing that recurring characters and biting commentary had propelled the show in the 1970s, he set out to recapture that early magic. He fired the entire cast—save Murphy and Piscopo—and brought in new faces. Mary Gross and Tim Kazurinsky were recommended by their friend John Belushi. Young comedians Brad Hall, Julia-Louis Dreyfus (later of *Seinfeld* fame), and Gary Kroeger were brought in. John's younger brother Jim Belushi, also a veteran comedy troupe performer, joined the cast reluctantly in 1983 (he hated being compared to John).

## OTAY!

Ebersol's first move: let Eddie loose. Murphy's characters, such as Gumby, Buckwheat, and Mr. Robinson (an urban parody of Mr. Rogers), became as popular as Belushi's samurai warrior and Radner's Roseanne Roseannadanna from the original cast. Ebersol later admitted that "it would have been very difficult to keep the show on the air without Eddie."

But Murphy's growing stardom soon alienated the other performers, especially his friend Joe Piscopo, the show's second-most-famous cast member. After starring in the hit film *48 Hours*, Murphy became too big for the show, even television in general. He left after the 1983 season to make *Trading Places* with fellow *SNL* alum Dan Aykroyd. To this day, Murphy—not Dan Aykroyd or Bill Murray or Mike Myers—holds the record as the highest-earning former *SNL* cast member.

## STAR POWER

In 1984, trying to fill the huge void left by Murphy's absence, Ebersol did something new for *SNL*: he hired established names, hoping they would attract viewers. Billy Crystal's Fernando ("You look mahvelous!") and Martin Short's Ed Grimley ("I must say!") were funny, but they weren't Murphy. And viewers wanted Eddie Murphy. In fact, the highest rated episode of the entire 1984–85 season was on December 15, when he returned to host the show. At the end of a difficult season, Ebersol had had enough. He quit.

***Here we go again: no producer, low ratings. Would* Saturday Night Live *rebound? Of course it would!***
***Turn to page 300 to find out how.***

**A $100,000 computer 20 years ago computed about as much as a $10 chip can today.**

# FREEDOM'S VOICE

*Born a slave in 1817, Frederick Douglass secretly learned to read and write. He escaped slavery in 1838 and went on to become an acclaimed orator, newspaper publisher, abolitionist, and advisor to presidents Lincoln and Grant.*

"Find out just what any people will quietly submit to and you have the exact measure of the injustice and wrong which will be imposed on them."

"There is not a man beneath the canopy of heaven that does not know that slavery is wrong."

"A little learning, indeed, may be a dangerous thing, but the want of learning is a calamity to any people."

"Power concedes nothing without a demand. It never did and it never will."

"The soul that is within me no man can degrade."

"I prefer to be true to myself, even at the hazard of incurring the ridicule of others, rather than to be false, and to incur my own abhorrence."

"Men are whipped oftenest who are whipped easiest."

"I know of no rights of race superior to the rights of humanity."

"You are not judged on the height you have risen but on the depth from which you have climbed."

"Liberty is meaningless where the right to utter one's thoughts and opinions has ceased to exist. That, of all rights, is the dread of tyrants."

"Men may not get all they pay for in this world, but they certainly pay for all they get."

"They who study mankind with a whip in their hands will always go wrong."

"The simplest truths often meet the sternest resistance."

"No man can put a chain about the ankle of his fellow man without at last finding the other end fastened about his own neck."

**The droplets in a sneeze can travel 12 feet and remain in the air for as long as three hours.**

# SO YOU WANT TO WIN A NOBEL PRIZE...

*We told you about the history of the Nobel Prize on page 189. Now, how do you win one? Well, it turns out it's not as simple as "make a major contribution to humanity"—THERE ARE RULES! Here are a few of them.*

**You can't nominate yourself.** Anyone who does is automatically disqualified. No exceptions.

• **You must be alive**. Nominating dead people has never been allowed, but until 1974 if you died *after* you were nominated—but *before* the winner was chosen—you could still win, even though you were dead. (Dag Hammarskjöld, for example, won the 1961 Peace Prize after he died in a plane crash.) In 1974 the rules were tightened up—people who die after they are nominated can no longer win, even if they're the only person nominated.

• **There are no runners-up.** People who are alive when they are selected as the winner (usually in October or November) but die before the awards are handed out on December 10, are still considered winners, even though they're dead. So if you come in second behind someone who drops dead before they pick up their medal, you still lose.

• **You can't win by default.** What happens if you come in second behind someone who refuses to accept their Nobel Prize? Do you win…or at least get their prize money? Answer: No and no. When a person declines a Nobel Prize, they are still entered into the official list of Nobel laureates; the only difference is that they just get the annotation "declined the prize," next to their name. The forfeited prize money goes back in the bank. Who says "no" to a Nobel Prize? Vietnamese politician Le Duc Tho declined it in 1973.

• **There's no such thing as a team effort.** With the exception of the Nobel Peace Prize, which can be awarded to entire organizations, such as the International Red Cross (1917) or Doctors Without Borders (1999), no single prize can be awarded to more than three people. That's true no matter how many people contribute to the endeavor. So if you and three of your friends find a cure for cancer next year, one of you is going to be out of luck. Of all the Nobel rules, this one is "probably the most damaging on a personal level," says Dr. Paul Greengard, winner of the 2000 Nobel Prize for Medicine. "The scientific world is full of embittered team members who were left out."

• **Nobel Prize in Economics? What Nobel Prize in Economics?** Alfred Nobel's will stipulated five prizes: Physics, Chemistry, Medicine, Literature, and Peace. In 1968 the Nobel Foundation approved the addition of a prize for Economics, but it is awarded by the Central Bank of Sweden. Its official name is the "Central Bank of Sweden Prize in Economic Sciences in Memory of Alfred Nobel." So even if you win it, Nobel purists will tell you that it's not *really* a Nobel Prize. Only the five original categories are considered true Nobel Prizes. Adding insult to injury: If you do win the Economics Prize, they don't engrave your name on the face of the medal like they do with other prizes—they just inscribe it on the outer rim.

• **Prizes don't necessarily have to be awarded every year.** If war or some other problem makes it impossible for the prize committees to meet (as in World War I and World War II), or if the foundation just decides that nobody deserves an award that year, they don't give them out. The Peace Prize has been withheld 19 times—more often than any other Nobel Prize.

• **You don't get a laurel.** The term "Nobel Laureate" is just an expression. If you win a Nobel Prize, you get a gold medal, a diploma with your name on it, and a cash prize. If you want to wear a crown of leaves, you've got to make it yourself.

• **Good news: If you do win, you will get more prize money now.** Over the years, taxes, inflation, overly cautious investment strategies, two world wars, and the Great Depression ate into the Nobel Foundation's assets. It wasn't until 1991 that the prizes finally recovered their full value and were worth more than they were in 1901. Since then, their value has continued to rise; in 2000 the payout for each prize was about $1 million.

• **More good news (and some bad news):** If your government orders you to decline the Nobel Prize (as Hitler did to German winners after 1936), the Nobel Foundation will hold the award until you're able to accept it—but you won't get the cash prize; that goes back to the Foundation.

**Did you hear the one about the guy who invented the door knocker? He won the "No Bell" prize.**

# LET'S PLAY PONG!

*If you know anything about the pop culture of the 1970s, the name Atari is synonymous with video games. So what happened? Where did Atari go? Here's the story.*

## THE GAMBLER

In the early 1960s, a University of Utah engineering student named Nolan Bushnell lost his tuition money in a poker game. He immediately took a job at a pinball arcade near Salt Lake City to make back the money and support himself while he was at school.

In school, Bushnell majored in engineering and, like everyone else who had access to the university's supercomputers, was a Spacewar! addict. But he was different. To his fellow students, Spacewar! was just a game; to Bushnell, it seemed like a way to make money. If he could put a game like Spacewar! into a pinball arcade, he figured that people would line up to play it.

## FALSE START

Bushnell graduated from college in 1968 and moved to California. He wanted to work for Disney but they turned him down, so he took a day job with an engineering company called Ampex. At night he worked on building his arcade video game.

He converted his daughter's bedroom into a workshop (she had to sleep on the couch) and scrounged free parts from Ampex and from friends at other electronics companies. The monitor for his prototype was a black-and-white TV he got at Goodwill; an old paint thinner can was the coin box.

When he finished building the prototype for the game he called Computer Space, he looked around for a partner to help him manufacture and sell it. On the advice of his dentist, he made a deal with a manufacturer of arcade games, Nutting Associates. Nutting agreed to build and sell the games in exchange for a share of the profits, and in return Bushnell signed on as an engineer for the firm.

If you've never heard of Computer Space, you aren't alone. The game was a dud. It *sounded* simple—the player's rocket has to destroy two alien flying saucers powered by the computer—but it

**The Caribbean island of St. Barts is named for Bartolomeo Columbus, Christopher's brother.**

came with several pages of difficult-to-understand instructions.

The fact that it was the world's first arcade video game only made things worse. Neither players nor arcade owners knew what to think of the strange machine sitting next to the pinball machines. "People would look at you like you had three heads," Bushnell remembered. "'You mean you're going to put the TV set in a box with a coin slot and play games on it?'"

## NUTTING IN COMMON

Still, Bushnell was convinced that Nutting Associates, not the game, was to blame for the failure. And he was convinced that he could do a better job running his own company. So he and a friend chipped in $250 apiece to start a company called Syzygy (the name given to the configuration of the sun, the earth, and the moon when they're in a straight line in space).

That's what Bushnell *wanted* to name it... but when he filed with the state of California, they told him the name was already taken. Bushnell liked to play Go, a Japanese game of strategy similar to chess. He thought some of the words used in the game would make a good name for a business, and company legend has it that he asked the clerk at the California Secretary of State's office to choose between *Sente*, *Hane*, and *Atari*.

She picked Atari.

## FAKING IT

Bushnell hired an engineer named Al Alcorn to develop games. Meanwhile, Bushnell installed pinball machines in several local businesses, including a bar called Andy Capp's Tavern. The cash generated by the pinball machines would help fund the company until the video games were ready for market.

Alcorn's first assignment was to build a simple Ping-Pong-style video game. Bushnell told him that Atari had signed a contract to deliver such a game to General Electric and now it needed to get built.

According to the official version of events, Bushnell was fibbing—he wanted Alcorn to get used to designing games and wanted to start him out with something simple. Ping-Pong, with one ball and two paddles, was about as simple as a video game can be. In reality, there was no contract with G.E. and Bushnell had no intention of bringing a table tennis game to market. He was convinced that the biggest moneymakers would be complicated games like Computer Space. "He was just going to throw the Ping-Pong game away," Alcorn remembers. But then Alcorn gave him a reason not to.

## OUT OF ORDER

Instead of a simple game, Alcorn's Ping-Pong had a touch of realism: if you hit the ball with the center of the paddle, the ball bounced straight ahead, but if you hit it with the edge of a paddle, it bounced off at an angle. With Alcorn's enhancements, video Ping-Pong was a lot more fun to play than Bushnell had expected.

As long as the game was fun, Bushnell decided to test it commercially by installing Pong, as he decided to call it, at Andy Capp's Tavern.

Two weeks later, the owner of Andy Capp's called to complain that the game was already broken. Alcorn went out to fix it, and as soon as he opened the machine he realized what was wrong—the game was so full of quarters that they had overflowed the coin tray and jammed the machine.

That was only half of the story. The bar's owner also told Alcorn that on some mornings when he arrived to open the bar, people were already waiting outside. But they weren't waiting for beer. They'd come in, play Pong for a while, and then leave without even ordering a drink. He'd never seen anything like it.

That was their first indication that Pong was going to be a hit.

## JUST A COINCIDENCE?

But did Nolan Bushnell really come up with the idea for Pong… or did he lift it from another video game company? Video history buffs still debate the issue today.

Here's what we do know: In the late 1960s, a defense industry engineer named Ralph Baer invented a video game system that could be played at home on a regular television. The system featured 12 different games, including Table Tennis.

Magnavox licensed Baer's system in 1971 and prepared to market it as Odyssey, the world's first home video game system. The company planned to sell the system through its own network of dealers and distributors. In May 1972, the company quietly began demonstrating the product around the country…and on May 24 it demonstrated it at a trade show in Burlingame, California.

"In later litigation," Steven Kent writes in *The Ultimate History of Video Games*, "it was revealed that Bushnell not only attended the Burlingame show but also played the tennis game on Odyssey."

## UNANSWERED QUESTIONS

Did Bushnell have a revelation when he played the Odyssey game? Did it convince him that simple games like Pong would be more popular than complicated games like Computer Space?

Or was it just as he claimed—that he instructed Alcorn to invent a ping-pong game, perhaps inspired by the Magnavox Odyssey, only because it was the simplest one he could think of? We'll probably never know for sure.

As far as the law is concerned, the only thing that really mattered was that, unlike Willy Higinbotham (Tennis for Two) and Steve Russell (Spacewar!), Ralph Baer actually *had* patented his idea for playing video games on a TV screen and had even won a second patent for video Ping-Pong. His patents predated the founding of Atari by a couple of years.

Bushnell never applied for a patent for Pong, and didn't have a case for proving that he'd invented it. And even if he did, he didn't have a chance fighting a big corporation like Magnavox in court.

## SMART MOVE

So why did Atari become synonymous with video games instead of Magnavox? It was skillful maneuvering by Bushnell.

Since he couldn't win in court, Bushnell paid a flat fee of $700,000 for a license to use Baer's patents. That meant that Atari bought the rights free and clear and would never have to pay a penny in royalties to Magnavox. And because Magnavox was now the undisputed patent holder, they *had* to sue Atari's competitors in court whenever competing game systems infringed the patents. Atari didn't even have to chip in for the legal fees.

Magnavox had Odyssey on the market while Atari was still years away from manufacturing a home version of Pong. But Magnavox wouldn't capitalize on their exclusive market. Their first mistake was selling the product exclusively through their own network of dealers, when it would have been smarter to sell them in huge chain stores like Sears and Kmart. Their second mistake was implying in their advertising that Odyssey would only work with Magnavox TVs. That wasn't true, but the company was hoping to increase TV sales. All they ended up doing was hurting sales of Odyssey.

In 1975 they discontinued the 12-game system and introduced a table tennis-only home video game to compete against the home version of Pong. Then in 1977 they introduced Odyssey$^2$ to compete against Atari's 2600 system.

Yet in spite of all the effort—and in spite of the fact that they, not Atari, owned the basic video game patents—Magnavox was never more than a me-too product with a marginal market share. Magnavox finally halted production in 1983.

***Turn to page 292 for the story of how video games found their way into the home.***

*  *  *

## CELEBRITY GOSSIP

**Meryl Streep.** After the 1979 Academy Awards, she lost the Oscar statuette she'd won for *Kramer vs. Kramer*. Where was it found? On the back of a toilet in the ladies room, where she had left it.

**Thomas Edison.** As a boy he tried to invent a way for people to float by feeding his friend "gas-producing powder." It didn't work.

**Jimmy Stewart.** His father was so disgusted with Stewart's role in *Anatomy of a Murder*, he took out a newspaper ad urging people not to see it.

**Richard Burton.** "When I played drunks I had to remain sober because I didn't know how to play them when I was drunk."

**Tom Cruise.** He enrolled in seminary school at age 14 to become a priest. He dropped out when he was 15.

**Joan Crawford.** She was married five times. Weird habit: Every time she remarried, she replaced all of the toilet seats in her mansion.

**...of spring, they're wrong 72% of the time.**

# THEY WENT THAT-A-WAY

*Sometimes the circumstances of a famous person's death are as interesting as their lives. Take these folks, for example.*

## BUDDHA (SIDDHARTHA GAUTAMA)

**Claim to Fame:** Founder of Buddhism

**How He Died:** From indigestion, following a meal of spicy foods

**Postmortem:** Like many spiritual people who search for enlightenment, Prince Siddhartha Gautama hoped to find it by fasting, eating only mosses and roots. When that didn't work, he went back to eating a normal diet…and soon acquired the huge belly that became as famous as the religion he founded.

He also acquired what modern historians believe were ulcers—he suffered terrible stomach and intestinal pains—and they caught up with him in 483 B.C. when he sat down to a lavish meal of *sukara-maddava* (spicy pork) in the village of Pava, India. While eating, Gautama suffered an attack of stomach pain so severe that he wasn't able to finish the meal. He and his followers promptly left the banquet and began walking to the village of Kusinara. Along the way, Gautama collapsed from dehydration and may have worsened his condition by drinking tainted water. By the time he arrived at Kusinara, the Buddha—or Enlightened One—was bleeding, vomiting, and near death. Fading in and out of consciousness, he finally passed away after instructing his followers, "Try to accomplish your aim with diligence." He was 80.

## PRESIDENT JOHN QUINCY ADAMS

**Claim to Fame:** Sixth president of the United States

**How He Died:** Shouting the word "No!"

**Postmortem:** Adams served as president from 1825 to 1829. In 1831 the ex-president was elected to the House of Representatives. He was still there 17 years later, when the House took up the matter of honoring U.S. Army officers who had fought in the Mexican-

American war. Adams was vehemently opposed to the idea.

When the vote was taken and the House erupted into a chorus of "Ayes" in favor of the idea, Adams stood up and shouted, "No!" Right then and there he suffered a stroke, collapsing into the arms of another congressman. Four of his colleagues carried him out to the capitol rotunda for some air, and he regained consciousness long enough to thank them for their effort. He drifted in and out of consciousness for the next two days before dying on February 23, 1848.

## WILLIAM THE CONQUEROR

**Claim to Fame:** William, Duke of Normandy, conquered England in 1066, in what became known as the Norman Conquest

**How He Died:** From a riding injury

**Postmortem:** In 1087 William and his soldiers attacked the French town of Mantes, destroying an enemy garrison and burning the town to the ground. Rather than waiting for the fires to go out, William decided to survey the ruins while they were still burning. Big mistake—his horse stepped on a hot coal and lurched violently, lifting William up off his saddle and plopping him on top of the *pommel*, the hard metal protrusion in the front of the saddle. The injury ruptured William's intestine, causing a severe infection that spread across his entire abdomen. He spent the next five weeks in excruciating pain, finally dying on September 9, 1087.

## ELEANOR ROOSEVELT

**Claim to Fame:** Former First Lady, wife of President Franklin D. Roosevelt, U.S. Ambassador to the United Nations

**How She Died:** From a stroke, possibly the result of medical errors made while she was being treated for anemia

**Postmortem:** In April 1960, the 75-year-old Mrs. Roosevelt was found to be suffering from aplastic anemia, which means her bone marrow wasn't producing enough red blood cells. By April 1962, she was also suffering from a shortage of white blood cells and platelets, so doctors prescribed prednisone, a drug that stimulates the bone marrow to produce more blood cells. But prednisone has a side effect: it suppresses the body's ability to fight off infections.

In August 1962, Mrs. Rooselvelt was back in the hospital, this

**The average American home has 15 cookbooks.**

time with a fever and a cough. Her doctors considered the possibility that she was suffering from tuberculosis, but when a chest X-ray showed no signs of the disease, they declined to do any further tests.

Mrs. Roosevelt was discharged from the hospital...but six weeks later she was back again, this time in even worse shape and still suffering from a "fever of unknown origin." On September 27, her doctors finally took a bone marrow sample and sent it to a laboratory to test for tuberculosis, a process that takes four to six weeks.

By October 18, Mrs. Roosevelt was so miserable and so convinced her end was near that she had herself discharged so that she could die at home. Her test results came back on October 26: she had tuberculosis...and months of treatment with prednisone had made it impossible for her body to fight it off. Not only had the doctors' diagnosis been wrong, but the medication was the worst possible thing they could have given her.

Nine days after finally receiving the correct diagnosis, Mrs. Roosevelt, still at home, suffered a stroke and slipped into a coma. She died three days later.

*    *    *

## TWO (VERY) DUMB CROOKS

"Charged with murder in Fort Lauderdale, Florida, Donald Leroy Evans wanted a little respect. Evans filed a motion which would allow him to wear a Ku Klux Klan robe during his court appearance. The motion also requested that Evans's name be officially changed on all court documents to 'the honorable and respected name of Hi Hitler.' Apparently, Evans thought Hitler's subjects were chanting 'Hi Hitler' instead of 'Heil, Hitler.'"

***—Presumed Ignorant***

"A man was sentenced to two years in prison for trying to break *into* the Rideau Correctional Center. Shane Walker, 23, was believed to be bringing drugs to his friends last week when he was foiled by striking corrections workers who heard bolt-cutters snapping the wire fence and apprehended him."

***—National Post***

**An astronaut orbiting Earth can see as many as 16 sunrises and sunsets every 24 hours.**

# A ROOM WITH A FISH

*Do you select a hotel for the amenities it offers? Well, forget mints on your pillow. Here are a few examples of how far some hotels will go to get you into their rooms.*

**HOTEL:** Hotel Monaco, Chicago
**AMENITY:** Goldfish
**ROOM SERVICE:** The hotel is proud to be pet-friendly—so much so that if you didn't bring one of yours, they'll lend you one of theirs. (On your next visit you can even ask for a specific goldfish by name.)

**HOTEL:** Hotel Monasterio, Cuzco, Peru
**AMENITY:** Oxygen
**ROOM SERVICE:** Cuzco is the home of the famed Inca ruins at Machu Picchu and sits at about 10,890 feet above sea level. For the altitude-weary visitor, oxygen pumps are supplied. Every room has one.

**HOTEL:** The Clift Hotel, San Francisco
**AMENITY:** Live music
**ROOM SERVICE:** If you're having trouble sleeping, this hotel has a string quartet on call. And they'll come to your room at bedtime to play you a lullaby. (Cost: $1,000)

**HOTEL:** The Jailhouse Inn, Preston, Minnesota
**AMENITY:** Steel bars
**ROOM SERVICE:** The old Fillmore County Jail, built in 1869, was converted into a hotel in 1989. For $129 (starting rate) you can spend the night in an actual cell.

**HOTEL:** A proposed hotel in Bozeman, Montana
**AMENITY:** Grizzly bears
**ROOM SERVICE:** Plans for this hotel include rooms in underground caverns—that are also grizzly bear dens. You'll get a TV, a kitchenette, and a one-way window to watch your roommates in their natural habitat.

**Down to Earth: Caesar salad used to be known as "aviator's salad."**

# BOX OFFICE BLOOPERS

*We all love bloppers...er...we mean bloopers. Here are some great ones from the silver screen.*

**Movie:** *The Bridge on the River Kwai* (1957)
**Scene:** The film's opening credits.
**Blooper:** This blockbuster won seven Oscars, but not for spelling. They misspelled the star's name, Alec Guinness, as "Guiness."

**Movie:** *Clueless* (1995)
**Scene:** A close-up shot of Cher's (Alicia Silverstone) report card.
**Blooper:** The name on the report card is Cher Hamilton, not the character's name, Cher Horowitz.

**Movie:** *Vanilla Sky* (2001)
**Scene:** Julie (Cameron Diaz) and David (Tom Cruise) are in the car. Julie goes crazy and drives it off a bridge.
**Blooper:** The exterior shot reveals there's no one in the car.

**Movie:** *Die Hard* (1989)
**Scene:** When Sgt. Al Powell (Reginald VelJohnson) crashes his squad car, his forehead is bleeding pretty badly.
**Blooper:** Throughout the remainder of the film, no evidence of the wound is present.

**Movie:** *Double Indemnity* (1944)
**Scene:** Fred MacMurray plays a bachelor.
**Blooper:** Then why is he wearing a wedding ring?

**Movie:** *North by Northwest* (1959)
**Scene:** In a restaurant, Eve (Eva Marie Saint) pulls a gun on Thornhill (Cary Grant).
**Blooper:** Just before the shot is fired, a boy sitting at a table in the background puts his fingers in his ears to muffle the sound of a gun he has no way of seeing...but obviously knows is there.

**Model president: As a struggling actor, Ronald Reagan once posed nude as an artist's model.**

**Movie:** *Twister* (1996)

**Scene:** The story chronicles one of the biggest tornadoes in Oklahoma's history.

**Blooper:** Most of the road signs are from Texas.

**Movie:** *Shrek* (2001)

**Scene:** Shrek (Mike Myers) and Fiona (Cameron Diaz) blow up some balloons and let them go.

**Blooper:** The balloons fly up in the air. (Okay, we know they're fairy tale characters, but that doesn't explain how they could exhale helium.)

**Movie:** *Independence Day* (1996)

**Scene:** Inside a tunnel, Jasmine (Vivica A. Fox) and her son, Dylan (Ross Bagley), escape through a service door just before they're overtaken by a wall of fire. Then Jasmine calls the dog.

**Blooper:** Even allowing Hollywood its usual "artistic license," the fact that Jasmine and Dylan make it out is barely plausible. But the dog? A shockwave is tossing cars like toys, yet somehow superdog manages to jump out of the way barely a few feet in front of it.

**Movie:** *Kate & Leopold* (2001)

**Scene:** Spectators on a bridge are waving American flags.

**Blooper:** The flags have all 50 stars... in 1876.

**Movie:** *Pulp Fiction* (1994)

**Scene:** Vincent (John Travolta) and Jules (Samuel L. Jackson) are in an apartment when someone bursts out of the bathroom and starts shooting at them.

**Blooper:** The bullet holes are in the wall *before* the gunman starts shooting.

**Movie:** *Cocktail* (1988)

**Scene:** Tom Cruise goes into the Regency Theatre in Manhattan and gets into a fight.

**Blooper:** It must have been a long fight—when he went into the theater, *Barfly* appeared on the marquee. When he exited, it was *Casablanca*.

**As big as they are, ostriches only have two toes on each foot. Most other birds have four.**

# IN MY EXPERT OPINION

*Think the experts and authorities have all of the answers? Well, they do... but they often have the wrong ones.*

"Anyone who expects a source of power from the transformation of the atom is talking moonshine."
**—Lord Rutherford, *scientist and Nobel laureate, 1933***

"No woman will in my time be prime minister."
**—Margaret Thatcher, *1969, 10 years before being elected prime minister***

"I applaud President Nixon's comprehensive statement, which clearly demonstrates again that the president was not involved with the Watergate matter."
**—George Bush, *1974***

"No matter what happens, the U.S. Navy is not going to be caught napping."
**—Frank Knox, *Secretary of the Navy, Dec. 4, 1941, 3 days before Pearl Harbor***

"We're going to make everybody forget The Beatles."
**—Bee Gee Barry Gibb, *on his group's 1976 movie,* Sgt. Pepper's Lonely Hearts Club Band, *which flopped***

"No flying machine will ever fly from New York to Paris."
**—Orville Wright, *1908***

"Novelty is always welcome, but talking pictures are just a fad."
**—Irving Thalberg, MGM *movie producer, 1927***

"Airplanes are interesting toys but of no military value."
**—Maréchal Foch, *French military strategist, 1911***

"I cannot conceive of anything more ridiculous, more absurd, and more affrontive to all sober judgment than the cry that we are profiting by the acquisition of New Mexico and California. I hold that they are not worth a dollar."
**—Daniel Webster, *senator of Massachusetts, 1848***

"It will be gone by June."
**—Variety, *referring to rock 'n' roll, 1955***

"Sensible and responsible women do not want to vote."
**—President Grover Cleveland, *1900***

# ELVIS BY THE NUMBERS

*Elvis may have left the building, but his memory lives on... and on... and on. Here are tidbits from the BRI Elvis file.*

**Five Foods Served at Elvis' Wedding Breakfast:**

1. Suckling pig
2. Fried chicken
3. Oysters Rockefeller
4. Champagne
5. Wedding cake

**Nine Songs Elvis Recorded But Never Released:**

1. "Also Sprach Zarathustra"
2. "Fool, Fool, Fool"
3. "Funky Fingers"
4. "Love Will Keep Us Together"
5. "Mexican Joe"
6. "Nine-Pound Hammer"
7. "Oakie Boogie"
8. "What a Friend We Have in Jesus"
9. "You Are My Sunshine"

**Seven Dogs Elvis Owned:**

1. Baba (Collie)
2. Getlo (Chow)
3. Muffin (Great Pyrenees)
4. Sherlock (Basset Hound)
5. Snoopy (Great Dane)
6. Stuff (Poodle)
7. Teddy Bear of Zixi Pom-Pom (Poodle)

**Thirteen Songs Elvis Sang in Concert, but for Which There Is No Known Recording:**

1. "Bad Moon Rising"
2. "Blowin' in the Wind"
3. "Chain Gang"
4. "Happy Birthday to You"
5. "House of the Rising Sun"
6. "I Can See Clearly Now"
7. "I Write the Songs"
8. "It Ain't Me Babe"
9. "Jingle Bells"
10. "Lodi"
11. "Mr. Tambourine Man"
12. "Susie Q"
13. "That's Amore"

**The King's Four Favorite Reading Materials:**

1. The Bible
2. *The Prophet*, by Kahlil Gibran
3. *Captain Marvel* comics
4. *Mad* magazine

**Three Elvis Aliases:**

1. John Burrows
2. Dr. John Carpenter
3. Tiger (his karate name in tae kwon do)

**As of 2001, there were 43,429,000 single men in the U.S. and 50,133,000 single women.**

# FOR POSTERITY'S SAKE

*Look around you. What do you see? A toothbrush, some deodorant, a digital watch, an* Uncle John's Bathroom Reader. *They may look like everyday items to you, but to an archaeologist in the distant future, they'll tell a fascinating story of what life was like at the beginning of the third millennium. They're perfect for a time capsule.*

**TALES FROM THE CRYPT**

The modern craze of saving things began when scientists opened the Egyptian pyramids in the 1920s. Dr. Thornwell Jacobs, president of Oglethorpe University in Atlanta, was inspired by all of the valuable information society learned. He decided to create a similar vault of records and items to be opened by "any future inhabitants or visitors to the planet Earth."

Jacobs called his swimming pool–sized container the "Crypt of Civilization." It was sealed on the campus on May 28, 1940, with instructions not to open it until the year 8113. Jacobs didn't just include a few everyday items in the crypt, but a collection he hoped would represent our entire civilization. There are over 640,000 pages of microfilmed material, hundreds of newsreels and recordings, a set of Lincoln logs, a Donald Duck doll, and thousands of other items. There is even a device designed to teach the English language to the crypt's finders.

**TIME AND AGAIN**

Jacobs's idea, published in a 1936 *Scientific American* article, created a new fad of "keeping time." For the 1939 New York World's Fair, Westinghouse Electric filled a seven-foot-long cylindrical vault with modern amenities and sealed it with instructions that it not be opened for 5,000 years. A company executive named G. Edward Pendray came up with a name for the highly publicized promotion: *time capsule*. The term entered the English language almost overnight. (He also invented the word *laundromat*.)

Westinghouse designed a second capsule for the 1964 New York World's Fair. Here are just a few of the hundreds of included items:

- a bikini
- a Polaroid camera
- plastic wrap
- an electric toothbrush
- tranquilizers
- a ballpoint pen
- a 50-star American flag
- superconducting wire
- a box of detergent
- a transistor radio
- an electric watch
- antibiotics
- contact lenses
- reels of microfilm
- credit cards
- a ruby laser rod
- a ceramic magnet
- filter cigarettes
- a Beatles record
- irradiated seeds
- freeze-dried foods
- a rechargeable flashlight
- synthetic fibers
- the Bible
- a computer memory unit
- birth-control pills

Also included was a bound "Book of Records." Many scientists and world leaders put messages in the book. Albert Einstein wrote, "I trust that posterity will read these statements with a feeling of proud and justified superiority."

## NOW WHERE DID I PUT THAT?

The International Time Capsule Society (ITCS) was formed in Atlanta in 1990. They believe that only a small fraction of time capsules will ever be recovered. Why? Partly because of thievery and partly because of secrecy. But mostly because of poor planning—people just plain forget where they buried it. The ITCS's mission is to document every time capsule to give it a better chance of being opened someday. "People often think that in the future people are going to be more efficient than we are," said ITCS co-founder Knute Berger, adding that it's not so. "If we have incompetent bureaucracy, they will too. You have to plan for that."

The ITCS has created a list of the 10 most-wanted time capsules. (Two have been found—here are the other eight.)

**1. Bicentennial Wagon Train Time Capsule.** This holds the signatures of 22 million Americans. President Gerald Ford arrived for the sealing ceremony in Valley Forge, Pennsylvania, on July 4,

1976, but someone had already stolen it from an unattended van.

**2. MIT Cyclotron Time Capsule.** In 1939 a group of MIT engineers placed a brass time capsule beneath an 18-ton-magnet used in a brand-new, state-of-the-art cyclotron. It was supposed to be opened in 1989, but by then the cyclotron had been deactivated and the capsule all but forgotten. When the capsule's existence was discovered, the brains at MIT had no clue how to get a time capsule out from underneath a 36,000-pound lid. They still don't.

**3. Corona, California, Time Capsules.** The citizens of Corona have lost not just 1, but 17 time capsules since the 1930s. In 1986 they tried, unsuccessfully, to recover them. "We just tore up a lot of concrete around the civic center," said a spokesperson.

**4. *M*A*S*H* Time Capsule.** In January 1983, the hit TV show wrapped for good. In a secret ceremony, the cast members buried a capsule containing props and costumes from the set. Where it was buried is a mystery—no one will say. But it's somewhere in the 20th Century Fox parking lot. The lot, however, has shrunk somewhat over the last 20 years, so the time capsule may be located underneath a Marriott Hotel.

**5. George Washington's Cornerstone.** In 1793 George Washington, a Mason, performed the Masonic ritual of laying of the original cornerstone of the U.S. Capitol. Over the years, the Capitol has undergone extensive expansion, remodeling, and reconstruction, but the original George Washington cornerstone has never been found. It is unknown whether there is anything inside it.

**6. Gramophone Company Time Capsule.** In 1907 in Hayes, Middlesex, England, sound recordings on disk were deposited behind the foundation stone of the new Gramophone Company factory by the opera singer Nellie Melba. During reconstruction work in the 1960s, the container was officially removed, but before it could be reburied, someone stole it.

**7. Blackpool Tower.** In Blackpool, Lancashire, England, a foundation deposit was interred in the late 19th century with the customary ceremony. When a search was organized recently in preparation for new building work, not even remote sensing equipment or a clairvoyant could find the lost capsule.

**Wishful thinking: The wishbone of the turkey used to also be known as the merrythought.**

**8. Lyndon, Vermont, Time Capsule.** The capsule is an iron box containing proceedings of the town's centennial celebration in 1891, scheduled to be opened a century later. But when the time came, the townsfolk couldn't find it. They looked in the town vault, the bank, and the library for clues, to no avail. So they created a new one, which they vowed not to lose.

## WANT TO CREATE YOUR OWN TIME CAPSULE?

It's not as easy as you might think. The ITCS has created a list of guidelines to follow:

**1. Select a retrieval date.** A 50-year or less time capsule may be witnessed by your own generation. The longer the duration, the more difficult the task.

**2. Choose an "archivist" or director.** Committees are good to share the workload, but one person should direct the project.

**3. Select a container.** A safe is a good choice. As long as the interior is cool, dry, and dark, artifacts can be preserved. For more ambitious (century or more) projects, there are professional time capsule companies.

**4. Find a secure indoor location.** It is recommended that time capsules not be "buried"—thousands have been lost in this way. Mark the location with a plaque describing the "mission" of the time capsule.

**5. Secure items for time storage.** Many things your committee selects will have meaning into the future. Try to have a mix of items from the sublime to the trivial. The archivist should keep an inventory of all items sealed in the time capsule.

**6. Have a solemn "sealing ceremony."** Christen the time capsule with a name. Invite the media and keep a good photographic record of your efforts, including the inside of your completed project.

**7. Don't forget your time capsule!** You would be surprised how often this happens, usually within a short time. Try to "renew" the tradition of memory with anniversaries and reunions.

**8. Inform the ITCS of your completed time capsule project.** The ITCS will add your time capsule to its database in an attempt to register all known time capsules. (They can be reached on the Web at *www.oglethorpe.edu/itcs/*.)

## SOME IDEAS TO GET YOU STARTED

Deciding what to include is the most difficult part. There are the obvious choices: a cell phone, a *Bathroom Reader*. But what about things like barbed wire or a Twinkie (don't worry—it'll last). Need suggestions? Here are some of the items the *New York Times* put in their "Millennium" time capsule in 1999:

- a Purple Heart medal from the Vietnam War
- a Beanie Baby
- UPC bar codes
- a firearms registration form
- a pager
- a cellular phone
- a battery
- a friendship bracelet
- an advertisement for an SUV
- food stamps
- a copy of the *The New York Times Magazine*
- an LP record containing sounds of the late 20th century
- a New York Yankees baseball
- greeting cards
- Post-It Notes
- a video rental card
- a phone card
- a David Letterman top 10 list
- a Y2K Bug stuffed toy
- wild apple seeds from Kazakhstan
- a Macintosh mouse
- St. John's Wort capsules
- the Holy Bible in multiple translations
- a *Weight Watchers Magazine*
- a Butt Blaster instruction manual
- the *National Enquirer*
- Alcoholics Anonymous pamphlets
- a Dr. Seuss book
- a *Dictionary of American Slang*
- *The Guinness Book of World Records*
- a reservation list for the Four Seasons restaurant
- an IRS 1040 tax form
- a hair sample from Dolly the cloned sheep
- a Garry Trudeau cartoon sketch

**...your butt 100 times a day fights depression.**

# "A GOOD EXAMPLE IS THE BEST SERMON"

*Benjamin Franklin: Founding Father, renaissance man, and...world-class hypocrite? His advice in the pages of Poor Richard's Almanack is timeless—but did Dr. Franklin always practice what he preached?*

**What Poor Richard Said:** "God helps those who help themselves."

**What Franklin Did:** It probably wasn't what he meant, but Franklin wasn't above helping himself to the work of others. One of the things Franklin is best known for is *Poor Richard's Almanack*, which he wrote and published for 25 years. What's less well-known is the extent to which Franklin "borrowed" from the work of others: He appropriated his journal's title from his own brother James, publisher of *Poor Robin's Almanack*, and took the pen name Richard Saunders ("Poor Richard") from a dead astrologer and doctor of the same name.

• Only a handful of Franklin's most famous quotes are truly his ("Experience keeps a dear school, yet fools will learn in no other" is one example); the rest he lifted without permission, compensation, or apology from *Lexicon Tetraglotton*, *Outlandish Proverbs*, and other popular journals of the day. "Why should I give my Readers bad lines of my own, when good ones of other People's are so plenty?" he liked to joke. And with no copyright laws in place to stop him, there was nothing the other writers could do.

• To his credit, whenever possible, Franklin tried to improve upon the writing he stole from others, either by making it more to the point ("God restoreth health and the physician hath the thanks" became "God heals and the doctor takes the fee"), or by adding coarse references to sex, flatulence, or bodily functions. ("He that lives upon hope, dies farting," "The greatest monarch on the proudest throne is obliged to sit upon his own arse," and "Force sh*ts upon reason's back.")

**What Poor Richard Said:** "Dally not with other folks' women or money."

**What Franklin Did:** Franklin had a lifelong habit of engaging in "foolish intrigues with low women," as he put it, a tendency that began in his teenage years and continued through his married life. He amazed friends and associates with the number and variety of his conquests; it wasn't unusual for visitors to happen upon Franklin in a compromising state with a parlor maid, cleaning girl, or someone else who had consented to the great man's advances. According to legend, when he was young and short of funds, he got his rent lowered by taking his elderly landlady as a lover.

• Why settle for one woman at a time? When Franklin lived in London, he became close friends with the postmaster general of England, Sir Francis Dashwood, with whom he co-authored a revised edition of the *Book of Common Prayer*. But Sir Dashwood also had a naughty side—he was the founder of the Order of St. Francis, a society of orgiasts better known as the Hellfire Club. The club met regularly at Dashwood's country house in Buckinghamshire, and its proceedings usually began with blasphemy, usually a black mass or some other obscene religious ceremony, before turning to fornication, which usually involved women dressed as nuns.

• To be fair, there's no proof that Franklin ever went to a single Hellfire Club orgy. But "it is certainly known that he was a frequent, not to say eager, visitor to Dashwood's house," Bill Bryson writes in *Made in America*, "and it would take a generous spirit indeed to suppose that he ventured there repeatedly just to discuss postal regulations and the semantic nuances of the *Book of Common Prayer*."

**What Poor Richard Said:** "One good Husband is worth two good Wives; for the scarcer things are, the more they're valued."

**What Franklin Did:** Technically speaking, even Franklin's marriage was a form of adultery. He never officially married his "wife," Deborah Read Franklin, who was still legally married to her first husband, a potter named John Rogers. Rogers had left her years earlier and run off to the West Indies, where it was rumored that he had died in a fight. But nobody knew for sure, and that presented a serious problem for Ben and Deborah when they decided to marry: what if Rogers came back? In those days, even unintentional bigamy was punishable by 39 lashes for both husband and wife, along with life imprisonment doing hard labor. Even if Rogers really was dead, if Franklin married Deborah he risked becoming legally obligated to repay Rogers's substantial debts.

• For these reasons, Ben and Deborah never formally married; instead, on September 1, 1730, they simply began presenting themselves to the community as man and wife. Such a "common law" marriage, as it was called, was (barely) formal enough to satisfy community standards and Deborah's family, yet it spared Franklin the risk of being branded a bigamist or having to assume Rogers's debts.

**What Poor Richard Said:** "He that lieth down with dogs shall rise up with fleas."

**What Franklin Did:** Not long after he and Deborah were "married," Franklin brought home an infant son, William, that he'd fathered by another woman. Out of that one indiscretion would flow years of pain for the Franklin family: Deborah's relationship with her stepson was predictably strained; by the time he reached his twenties they barely spoke and she had taken to calling him "the greatest villain upon earth." Years later William sided with the English during the revolutionary war, opening a breach between father and son that would never heal. When Ben Franklin died in 1790, he disinherited his son, "leaving him no more of an estate he endeavoured to deprive me of."

**What Poor Richard Said:** "A good Wife and Health is a Man's best Wealth."

**What Franklin Did:** So what thanks did Deborah get for raising Franklin's illegitimate son as her own? Not much—in addition to cheating on her throughout their long "marriage," Franklin virtually abandoned her in her old age, leaving her alone for five years while he went off to live in London from 1757 to 1762, and again in 1764, this time for more than a decade. He never returned home to visit, not even when Deborah suffered a stroke in the winter of 1768–69. When she died in 1774, she had not seen him in more than 10 years.

**Benjamin Franklin was America's first newspaper cartoonist.**

# THE LEGEND OF GORGEOUS GEORGE

*If you like professional wrestling, you've probably already heard of The Rock, The Iron Sheik, and Hulk Hogan. But have you heard of Gorgeous George? He was TV's first big wrestling villain. TV made him a star, and in many ways, he made television. Here's his story.*

## IN THIS RING, I THEE WED

In 1939 a 24-year-old professional wrestler named George Wagner fell in love with a movie theater cashier named Betty Hanson and married her in a wrestling ring in Eugene, Oregon. The wedding was so popular with wrestling fans that George and Betty reenacted it in similar venues all over the country.

With the sole exception of the wedding stunt, Wagner's wrestling career didn't seem to be going anywhere. After 10 years in the ring, he was still an unknown, and that was a big problem: Nobodies had a hard time getting booked for fights.

## THE ROBE OF A LIFETIME

Wagner might well have had to find something else to do for a living had his wife not happened to make him a robe to wear from the locker room to the ring before a fight, just like a prizefighter. Wagner was proud of the robe, and that night when he took it off at the start of his fight, he took such care to fold it properly that the audience booed him for taking so long. That made Betty mad, so she jumped into the crowd and slapped one of the hecklers in the face. That made George mad, so he jumped out of the ring and hit the guy himself. Then the whole place went nuts.

"The booing was tremendous," wrestling promoter Don Owen remembered:

> And the next week there was a real big crowd and everyone booed George. So he just took more time to fold his robe. He did everything to antagonize the fans. And from that point he became the best drawing card we ever had. In wrestling they either come to like you or to hate you. And they hated George.

## PRETTY BOY

Out of this hatred, George discovered the shtick he was looking for—and over the next several years gradually changed his look. Where other wrestling villains had always been dirty and ugly, "Gorgeous George," as he began to call himself, set out to become the prettiest, daintiest pro wrestler the sport had ever seen. He grew his hair long, curled it, and bleached it platinum blond. And before each fight, he secured it in place with golden bobby pins and a golden hair net. He amassed a collection of more than 100 frilly, purple robes, made of satin and silk and trimmed with sequins, lace, and fur. He made sure to wear one to every match, and before he would enter the ring, he insisted that his tuxedoed "valet" be allowed to spray the mat, the referee, and his opponent with perfume.

Then, as the lights were dimmed and "Pomp and Circumstance" played over the loudspeaker, George would enter the hall under a spotlight and slowly traipse his way to the ring. He made such a show of climbing into the ring and removing (with the assistance of his valet) his robe, his hair net, and his golden bobby pins, that his entrances sometimes took longer than his fights, giving wrestling's blue-collar fans one more reason to hate him.

## FIGHTING DIRTY

Appearances aside, Gorgeous George was no sissy—not out of the ring and certainly not in it. He fought hard and he *always* cheated—gouging eyes, biting ears, butting heads, punching kidneys, kicking crotches, and pulling every other dirty stunt he could think of. He gloated when he was winning, squealed and begged for mercy when he was losing, and bawled like a baby when his opponents mussed his hair, which they did every fight. All of this was fake, of course, but the crowds either didn't know or didn't care. They ate it up, fight after fight.

Gorgeous George's antics may not sound like much compared to the wrestling of today, but at the time, they were mind-boggling. He became famous in the late 1940s, not long after the end of World War II. Many wrestling fans were veterans, and the boys who landed at Omaha Beach on D-Day or battled their way across the Pacific, and raised the flag at Iwo Jima had some pretty rigid ideas about what it meant to be a man. And bobby pins, frilly bathrobes, and platinum blond hair were definitely *not* considered manly. Gorgeous George broke all the rules, and these guys hated him for it. They *loved* to hate him for it. People got in their cars and drove for hours to see him fight, just so they could hate him in person. Gorgeous George made 32 appearances at the Los Angeles Olympic Auditorium in 1949; he sold it out 27 times.

## A BOOB FOR THE BOOB TUBE

But what was most remarkable about Gorgeous George was the impact he had on TV sales. In Los Angeles, wrestling matches—many featuring Gorgeous George—were broadcast on TV as early as 1945, and they proved so popular that by the late 1940s, many TV stations around the country were broadcasting live pro wrestling every night of the week. It was the perfect sport for television—the ring was small and easy to film and the action was larger than life, so viewers had no problem following the fights at home on their tiny black-and-white screens. Baseball and football players looked like ants by comparison.

TV turned Gorgeous George into a national star, even for people who didn't watch wrestling. And in the process, he helped make television the centerpiece of the American living room. Appliance dealers put TVs in their store windows and pasted pictures of Gorgeous George onto their screens. People who'd never owned a TV before came in and bought TVs...just so they could watch Gorgeous George. As Steve Slagle writes in *The Ring Chronicle*,

> In a very real sense, Gorgeous George single-handedly established the unproven new technology of television as a viable entertainment medium that could reach literally millions of homes all across the country. Pro wrestling was TV's first real "hit"...and Gorgeous George was directly responsible for all of the commotion. He was probably responsible for selling more television sets in the early days of TV than any other factor.

## YOU'RE MY INSPIRATION

As we told you in *Uncle John's Legendary Lost Bathroom Reader*, a young pro boxer named Cassius Clay, soon to change his name to Muhammad Ali, reinvented his public persona after he happened to meet Gorgeous George on a radio show in Las Vegas in 1961. "That's when I decided I'd never been shy about talking, but if I

**Legal capacity of the bar in TV's *Cheers*: 75. How we know: It was posted over the door.**

talked even more, there was no telling how much people would pay to see me," Ali remembered. That's when he started calling himself "The Greatest"... just like Gorgeous George.

Muhammad Ali wasn't the only one—Gorgeous George is credited with inspiring Little Richard... and even Liberace. "He's imitating me," George groused to a reporter in 1955.

## THE FINAL BELL

There was, however, a limit to how long American TV viewers could stand to watch live pro wrestling every single night of the week, and by the mid-1950s, the craze had died down. George continued to wrestle until 1962, when a liver ailment—brought on by heavy drinking—forced him into retirement. Nearly broke from two expensive divorces, George had a heart attack on Christmas Eve 1963 and died two days later. He was 48.

Ironically, the fame that made Gorgeous George a national celebrity may have also contributed to his death. Believe it or not, he was a reticent person, and for years he had used alcohol to stiffen his spine and give him the courage to be Gorgeous George.

"He really didn't have the nerve to do all those things," his second wife, Cherie, remembered. "That's why he drank. When he was sober, he was shy."

* * *

## SIGNATURE WRESTLING MOVES

**Lord Blears:** The Oxford Leg Strangle

**The Leduc Brothers:** The Lumberjack Bearhug

**Baron Michele Scicluna:** The Maltese Hangman

**Leo "The Lion" Newman:** The Diamond-Drill Neck Twist

**Hard-Boiled Haggerty:** The Shillelagh Swing

**Johnny Valentine:** The Atomic Skullcrusher

**Cowboy Bob Ellis:** The Bulldog Headlock

**Danny Dusek:** The Filipino Guerrilla Hold

**Lord Athol Layton:** The English Octopus

**The Shiek:** The Camel Clutch

**Big Mess:** The sun spews out more than a million tons of matter every second.

# CARTWHEEL KICKS

*These wrestling moves have very colorful names, but boy are they violent. In fact, they're so violent that you wonder why wrestlers don't get killed. Oh! It's because THEY'RE FAKE! But just to be safe, please don't try them at home—somebody's brain might get busted.*

**Forward Russian Leg Sweep.** Stand next to your opponent, facing in the same direction. Wrap one arm around his (or her) neck, and step in front of his nearest leg, hooking it. Then fall forward, and cause your opponent to fall face first onto the mat.

**Airplane Spin.** Lift your opponent over your head and hold him so he is facing up toward the ceiling. Then spin around and around to make him dizzy, and then drop him on the mat.

**Brainbuster.** Lift your opponent up across your shoulders, hooking one of his legs with one arm, and cradling his neck in your other arm. Then fall to the side that your opponent's head is on, and release his legs, causing him to fall head first onto the mat.

**Tilt-a-Whirl Pile Driver.** Grab your opponent around the waist, lift him, and spin his body until he is upside down, then wrap your arms around his body to hold him in place. Then sit or kneel, dropping your opponent on his head.

**Atomic Drop.** Stand behind and to the side of your opponent. Grab his midsection with one arm, and hook one of his legs with the other. Lift him up over your shoulder so that he is parallel with the mat, then drop him tailbone first on your knee.

**Gutbuster Drop.** Bend your opponent over in a crouch, then grab him by one leg and across his chest. Lift him up so that his body is facing downward, then drop him stomach first across your knee.

**Cartwheel Kick.** Do a cartwheel in the direction of your opponent, taking care to kick him in the head with the side of your foot as it contacts his body.

**Shooting Star Press.** Climb up onto the top rope, then do a backflip, landing on your opponent.

**By the time you reach age 60, your eyes will have been exposed to more…**

# WRESTLING LINGO

*Had enough of wrestling yet? But wait, there's more. If you want to sound like a pro, you have to know the special lingo. Here's a sample.*

**Face** (noun). A "good guy." (Wrestlers with *pretty faces* are often cast as good guys.)

**Heel** (noun). A "bad guy." Someone who cheats and breaks the rules to win.

**Feud** (noun). A grudge match, frequently between a face and a heel.

**Turn** (noun or verb). When a heel changes his persona and becomes a face, or vice versa.

**Potato** (verb). Injure a wrestler by hitting them on the head or causing them to hit their head.

**Stiff** (adjective). A move intended to cause real injury.

**Run-in** (noun). Intervention in a match by an audience member or other nonparticipant.

**Blade** (verb). Intentionally cut yourself with a hidden piece of razorblade in order to produce "juice" (see below).

**Juice** (noun or verb). Blood. Usually caused by blading.

**Job** (noun). A staged loss.

**Post** (verb). Run someone into the ringpost.

**Hardway juice** (noun). Blood from an unintentional injury.

**Heat** (noun). The level of the crowd's enthusiasm for a fight.

**Pop** (noun or verb). A sudden rise in the heat of the crowd, such as when a popular wrestler makes his entrance.

**Bump** (noun). A fall or other move that results in the wrestler falling out of the ring.

**Jobber** (noun). A wrestler who does a job—he's hired to lose to the featured wrestler. Also known as redshirts or PLs, short for "professional losers."

**Clean job** (noun). A staged loss that doesn't involve illegal wrestling moves.

**Screw-job** (noun). An ending that isn't clean—someone, usually the heel, wins by cheating.

**Shoot** (noun). The opposite of a job—one wrestler really is trying to hurt another.

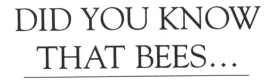

# DID YOU KNOW THAT BEES...

*Some scientists think that after a nuclear holocaust, bees might become the predominant species on Earth. True? We hope we never find out, but look at some of the astonishing things bees can do.*

## ...COMMUNICATE BY DANCING

Studies show that bees are far more complex than you might think, with a sophisticated system of communication. They report the location of food sources to other bees using a kind of waggling dance. The dances always show the direction of the food in relationship to a reference point—the sun.

In 1919 an Austrian zoologist named Karl von Frisch became one of the first people to study and understand the dancing language of bees. In a series of trials, he found that if the bee's view of the sun was entirely blocked by artificial means, the dances became disoriented. If the view of the sky was replaced with a mirror that reflected the sky's scenery backward, the dances were reoriented to the sun's reflection. When von Frisch moved the hive into a darkened room and provided only the light of a flashlight, the dances were oriented to that artificial sun. Bees raised indoors with only a stationary electric light to guide them became hopelessly lost when their hive was moved outdoors under a constantly moving sun.

## ...SEE IN COLOR

Popular theory once held that bees could see only in black and white. Von Frisch designed an experiment to test this. First he trained bees to feed at a clear glass container full of sugar water located on a brightly colored card. Then, when the bees left to return to their hive, an array of empty glasses was set out on cards of many different colors, as well as cards that were various shades of gray. Would the returning bees be able to distinguish the container that was sitting on the correct color, or would they be confused and go to the wrong dish? Over and over the bees returned without hesitation to the correct color, proving that they see in color. (The only exception was when the sugar water sat on a red card. Bees would often go to a dark gray card instead, showing that they are unable to distinguish the color red.)

How do they do it? In a test to see whether they could distinguish shades of gray, the experimenter was surprised to find that bees were able to differentiate between two gray cards that looked absolutely identical to him. He eventually discovered that different companies manufactured the cards, and one reflected more ultraviolet light than the other—an important visual clue for a bee. Think of this: If bees were color-blind, flowers would not be so colorful.

### ...HEAR

One experiment testing the hearing of bees involved rigging a feeding station with an electrical current. A tone sounded three seconds before an electrified current was passed through the station. A different tone sounded when the current stopped, and would sound again periodically until the juice was turned back on. The bees soon learned the meaning of both sounds. They ignored the "safe" noise and reacted immediately to the "warning" noise.

### ...ANTICIPATE

Princeton University ethologist (animal behavior specialist) James Gould, one of the world's foremost authorities on bee behavior, performed an experiment in which he placed a source of food next to a beehive. Once the bees discovered it, he moved it 164 feet (50 meters) away to see how long it would take the bees to relocate the supply. After only one minute, they found the food. Gould then moved it another 164 feet, and again the bees tracked it down again in less than a minute. Every time Gould moved the food another 164 feet, the bees found it without delay. Then he noticed that the bees were flying on to the next station before he had even moved the food.

In the next experiment, Gould placed a bowl of sugar water near a beehive and then, after it had been discovered by the bees, started moving it. Every few minutes, he moved the dish, but each move was four times longer than the previous move. He moved it 1 inch, then 4 inches, then 16 inches, and so on. Soon he was moving the dish more than 100 feet in a single jump. Amazingly, the bees soon caught on...and were waiting for him when he got there.

## ...SENSE TIME

Bees like the nectar of the buckwheat flower, which exudes nectar in the morning. Bees know this and visit the flowers only during the morning hours. This led scientists to wonder if bees had a built-in sense of time, so they did some experiments. In the first experiment, they put out a bowl of sugar water from 10:00 a.m. to noon every day. After only a few days, the bees learned exactly what hours to come for the food and didn't waste time coming early or late.

So next time you're at a picnic and are tempted to swat a curious bee, remember how astonishing the honeybee is and leave it...bee.

## RANDOM BEE FACTS

• Honeybees are not native to North America. They were introduced here from Europe in the 1600s by the Puritans.

• Different bees have different dialects. A German bee cannot understand an Italian bee.

• Honey never spoils. In fact, honey placed in tombs in Southampton, England, over 400 years ago was still good when the tombs were opened.

• A typical American consumes about a pound of honey per year. A typical worker bee lives for one month and in that time collects enough nectar to make about one-twelfth a teaspoon of honey.

• Bees use ultraviolet vision—a specialized vision that allows them to see which flowers have the largest amounts of nectar.

• Honey comes in different colors and flavors—there are more than 300 unique kinds of honey in the United States alone. Why? Honey is made from diverse flower sources—clover, eucalyptus, or orange blossom, for example—and soil chemistry and honeycomb quality also influence how it tastes and looks.

• Another experiment: Will bees feed from water that's been artificially sweetened with Sweet 'N' Low? No.

**Q: How many U.S. states have a royal palace? A: One—Hawaii (Iolani Palace).**

# AFTER THE QUAKE: THE HEROES

*Disasters often bring out the best in people. At 5:13 a.m., April 18, 1906, an earthquake rocked San Francisco (see page 27). For the next four days, fire ravaged the city (page 176). City fathers, the army, police, and firefighters all worked together to put the fires out. But the city might not have survived without the extraordinary efforts of ordinary people who stepped up and helped out. Here are some of their stories.*

The **Post Office** remained standing after the quake but was soon threatened by the growing blaze. Many brave postal workers risked their lives by beating out the smaller fires with wet mail sacks. As soon as the danger was past, they fervently began sorting the tons of mail city residents needed to get out to worried relatives. Survivors scribbled messages on boards, newspapers, even shirts, and as long as it had a legible address, it was delivered—no stamp needed.

The Western Union lines were down, but the Postal Telegraph office managed to stay open for business, providing a link of communication with the outside world.

• Of the city's five newspapers, one, the ***Daily News***, actually managed to put out an edition Wednesday afternoon. The other four newspapers, long bitter rivals, joined forces with the *Daily News* to put out a combined issue on Thursday. The editors never bothered to ask permission of the owners, knowing it would be denied. The most important task at that moment was to get out the information that citizens needed to find food, shelter, services, and loved ones.

• The **Southern Pacific Railroad Station** depot was saved by brave men with one pumper, a single stretch of hose, some wet gunny sacks, and a few buckets. Volunteers carried water from the bay three blocks away. Through this depot in the next few days passed millions of tons of food, blankets, clothing, and medical supplies—as well as 300,000 refugees fleeing the city. All traveled free of charge.

**Mama mia! Domino's Pizza sells a reindeer sausage pizza...but only in Iceland.**

• The **San Francisco Mint** was built of steel and concrete with metal windows. It was fireproof on the outside, but the rampaging fires blew out the windows and set fires inside. Firemen and employees frantically hauled water from a cistern to put out fires in interior woodwork and on the tarpaper roof. Seven hours later, the mint—and all the money inside—was safe.

• The **Hopkins Art Institute** contained thousands of dollars worth of paintings and statues. Throughout Wednesday, teachers and students removed hundreds of pictures to the lawn, where they were carried in wheelbarrows, wagons, and on shoulders to safe spots around the city. Navy men arrived to help Wednesday night, and a young lieutenant used his service pistol to encourage other folks from the passing crowds to assist.

• **Bank owner Amadeo Giannini** walked 17 miles to inspect the damage of his livelihood, the Bank of Italy. When he arrived, the fire was approaching fast. His clerks swore the fire would never reach that far, but Giannini disagreed. He loaded all the bank's funds into two wagons and hauled them to his house, where he hid the money behind his fireplace. When the fires were out, Giannini hauled the money to a new location in the financial district. Giannini's bank later expanded to become one of the largest in the nation—the Bank of America. Another bank president, **Charles Crocker**, had workers load all of his bank's cash into sacks, stack them in a wagon, and take it to the docks. Then he put the money on a boat, which took it out to the middle of San Francisco Bay until all the fires were out. So why is this important? It meant that survivors would be able to withdraw much-needed funds.

• **Alice Eastwood** made her way downtown to the California Academy of Sciences. She was the curator of botany and managed to save many treasured plants while her own home burned to the ground. She could have saved her own possessions, but decided it was easier for her to buy new furniture than to replace the botanical specimens. All she had left after the fire was the dress she wore.

• **The Ultimate Sacrifice:** Police Sergeant Behan saved much of the city's paperwork by wetting it down with beer collected from nearby stores.

**Odds that a polished diamond weighs more than a carat: one in a thousand.**

# GREETINGS FROM EARTH

*We told you about time capsules on page 238. When you see* Star Wars *or* Star Trek *you probably think space travel is way off in the future. You're wrong—we're already out there. Here's some information about our time capsule in outer space.*

## TO BOLDLY GO

The Voyager mission continues. Launched in 1977, the twin Voyager 1 and Voyager 2 spacecraft will soon leave our solar system and become emissaries from Earth. NASA placed a message aboard Voyagers 1 and 2, a time capsule intended to communicate a story of our world to extraterrestrials.

The Voyager message is carried by a phonograph record—a 12-inch gold-plated copper disk containing sounds and images selected to portray the diversity of life and culture on Earth. A committee led by Dr. Carl Sagan of Cornell University assembled:

- 115 images
- A variety of natural sounds
- Musical selections from different cultures and eras
- Spoken greetings from Earth-people in 55 languages—beginning with Akkadian, spoken in Sumer about 6,000 years ago, and ending with Wu, a modern Chinese dialect.

Each record is encased in a protective aluminum jacket, together with a cartridge and a needle. Instructions, in symbolic language, explain the origin of the spacecraft and indicate how the record is to be played. The images are encoded in analog form. The remainder of the record is in audio, designed to be played at $16\frac{2}{3}$ revolutions per minute.

Here's a list of the contents of the record:

### THE PHOTOS (PARTIAL LIST)

Earth
DNA structure
Human sex organs
Diagram of conception

Fetus diagram
Diagram of male and female
Birth
Nursing mother

Father & daughter (Malaysia)
Group of children
Family portrait
Seashore

Ansel Adams' photos of Snake River and Grand Tetons

Forest scene with mushrooms

Sequoia tree

Flying insect with flowers

Diagram of vertebrate evolution

Seashell

Dolphins

Tree toad

Crocodile

Eagle

Jane Goodall and chimps

Page of book (Newton's *System of the World*)

Bushmen hunters

Guatemalan man

Balinese dancer

Supermarket

Turkish man with beard and glasses

Schoolroom

Sunset with birds

Elephant

House (Africa)

Taj Mahal

Sydney Opera House

Rush-hour traffic

Violin

Underwater scene with diver and fish

Demonstration of licking, eating and drinking

Great Wall of China

## MUSIC

- Bach's *Brandenburg* Concerto no. 2 in F, first movement
- Bach's "Gavotte en rondeaux" from the Partita no. 3 in E-major
- Mozart's *The Magic Flute*, "Queen of the Night" aria, no. 14
- Stravinsky's *Rite of Spring*, "Sacrificial Dance"
- Bach's *The Well-Tempered Clavier*, Book 2, prelude and fugue in C
- Beethoven's Fifth Symphony, first movement
- Beethoven's String Quartet no. 13 in B-flat, Opus 130, Cavatina
- Holborne, Paueans, Galliards, Almains and Other Short Aeirs, "The Fairie Round" (Ireland)
- Court gamelan (Java)
- Percussion (Senegal)
- Pygmy girls' initiation song (Zaire)
- Aboriginal songs, "Morning Star" & "Devil Bird" (Australia)
- "El Cascabel" (Mexico)
- "Johnny B. Goode" (USA)
- "Melancholy Blues," performed by Louis Armstrong (USA)
- "Dark Was the Night," by Blind Willie Johnson (USA)
- Panpipes and drum (Peru)
- Men's house song (New Guinea)
- "Tchakrulo" (Georgia S.S.R.)
- "Flowing Streams" (China)
- "Tsuru No Sugomori" (Japan)
- "Izlel je Delyo Hagdutin" (Bulgaria)
- Panpipes (Solomon Islands)
- Night Chant (Navajo)
- Wedding song (Peru)
- Raga: "Jaat Kahan Ho" (India)
- Bagpipes (Azerbaijan)

**What's the slang term for an emergency room patient who isn't sick enough to...**

## THE SOUNDS OF EARTH

| | | | |
|---|---|---|---|
| Hyena | Volcanoes | Mother and child | Train |
| Elephant | Earthquake | Herding sheep | Bus |
| Wild dog | Thunder | Sawing | Auto |
| Tame dog | Mud pots | Tractor | F-111 flyby |
| The first tools | Wind | Riveter | Frogs |
| Footsteps | Rain | Morse code | Saturn 5 lift-off |
| Heartbeats | Surf | Ships | Kiss |
| Laughter | Crickets | Horse and cart | Life signs |
| Fire | Birds | | Pulsar |
| Speech | Blacksmith | | |

## THE INTERSTELLAR MESSAGE

Speakers were given no instructions on what to say other than that it was to be a greeting to possible extraterrestrials and that it must be brief. Here's a sample:

• "Greetings to our friends in the stars. We wish that we will meet you someday."

**—Arabic**

• "Hello to everyone. We are happy here and you be happy there."

**—Rajasthani (Northwest India)**

• "Hello from the children of planet Earth."

**—English**

• "Friends of space, how are you all? Have you eaten yet? Come visit us if you have time."

**—Amoy (Eastern China)**

Here are some (not all) of the languages in which they spoke: Sumerian, Urdu, Italian, Ila, Romanian, Hindi, Nguni, Hittite, French, Vietnamese, Sotho, Swedish, Hebrew, Burmese, Amoy, Sinhalese, Akkadian, Ukrainian, Aramaic, Spanish, Greek, Korean, Wu, Persian, Indonesian, Latin, Armenian, Serbian, Portuguese, Kechua, Polish

It will be forty thousand years before the Voyagers make a close approach to any other planetary system.

*The spacecraft will be encountered and the record played only if there are advanced civilizations in interstellar space. But the launching of this bottle into the cosmic ocean says something very hopeful about life on this planet.*

**—Carl Sagan**

**...justify being there? Gomer—short for "Get out of my emergency room."**

# NATURE'S REVENGE

*What happens when we mess around with nature, trying to get it to do our bidding? Sometimes it works...but sometimes nature gets even. Here are a few instances when people intentionally introduced animals or plants into a new environment—and regretted it.*

**Import:** English sparrows

**Background:** One hundred sparrows were brought from England to Brooklyn, New York, in 1850. Reason: to control canker worms that were killing trees in city parks.

**Nature's Revenge:** The sparrows did their job—for a while. Then they got a taste for native insects, then they had a lot of babies, and then they took off. By 1875 the sparrows had made it to San Francisco, stealing nesting sites from native birds and ravaging crops and livestock feed along the way. In 1903 noted ornithologist W. L. Dawson said, "Without question the most deplorable event in the history of American ornithology was the introduction of the English sparrow." Today they number about 150 million in North America. *Note:* They're not even sparrows—they're from the weaverbird family.

**Import:** Cane toads

**Background:** The cane toad can grow up 9 to 10 inches long and weigh as much as 4 pounds. Its croak is said to sound like a dog's bark. This bizarre species is native to Central America but was imported to Australia in 1935. Australian farmers wanted it to eat two types of beetle that were damaging their sugarcane crops.

**Nature's Revenge:** Nobody seemed to notice that the cane toad lives on the ground—so they were only able to eat beetles that fell off the sugarcane. The experiment was a failure, then a disaster. The toads feasted on other native insect species—many to the point of extinction—and spread into neighboring habitats. They are large enough to eat any insect, as well as frogs and other toads, and have even been known to eat from dog and cat food bowls. And, to make matters worse, they're poisonous. Whatever tries to eat them dies—even if they only eat the tadpoles. The situation continues to be dire: people who spot a cane toad are advised to contact toad hotlines and websites.

**Import:** Rats

**Background:** In the 16th and 17th centuries, hoards of people were leaving Europe on ships bound for the New World. Tyranny, poverty, horrendous filth, and epidemics drove boatload after boatload of settlers across the Atlantic seeking wide-open spaces, better resources, more freedom, and less disease.

**Nature's Revenge:** The settlers found a pristine paradise—and quickly infested it with rats. Early ocean-crossing ships were famously rat infested, the vermin often numbering more than the humans onboard. The adaptable rodent made itself at home and spread all over the continent. According to a study by Cornell University, by 1999 there were approximately a billion rats in the United States—on farms alone, and rats do an estimated $19 billion in economic damage every year.

**Import:** Rabbits, opossums, and stoats

**Background:** New Zealand's landscape had evolved for 60 to 80 million years with only four mammals—all bats. In this unique ecosystem, exceptionally unique flora and fauna, such as flightless birds, prospered. Then, in the early 1800s, Europeans arrived bringing sheep, pigs, and goats as livestock, and rabbits and opossums as game for sportsmen.

**Nature's Revenge:** Rabbits multiply... like rabbits. By 1894 more than 17 million rabbit pelts were being exported annually. While that made money for some, the rabbits' effect on the land, competing wildlife, and sheep farmers was devastating. The opossum did similar damage by eating massive amounts of native plant life in the exotic canopy.

Desperate farmers imported the stoat, a weasel-like creature that eats rabbits and opossums. That worked for a while, but birds, insects, and bats were easier for the stoats to catch. They quickly decimated bird populations, especially that of the kiwi. Thanks to the stoat, today several other species are either endangered or already extinct. New Zealand's government spends millions every year trying to stop the continuing rampage. And what of the stoat's intended targets, the rabbit and opossum? As of 2001, they were still the number one and number two pests in the country.

# WORD ORIGINS

*Ever wonder where words come from?*
*Here are some more interesting stories.*

**POSTHUMOUS**

**Meaning:** Something that arises or occurs after one's death

**Origin:** "*Posthumous* comes from the Latin *postumus*, 'last' or 'last-born,' which, strictly speaking, could be applied to the last child born of a particular mother and father, without reference to death. The *h* crept into *postumus* by association with *humus* (earth or ground) and perhaps with some help from *humare* (to bury). The modern spelling and meaning were fixed by Posthumus Leonatus, hero of Shakespeare's *Cymbeline*, who received this name, as the audience is informed at the start of the play, because he was born after his father died." (From *Devious Derivations*, by Hugh Rawson)

**YANKEE**

**Meaning:** A nickname for Americans or New Englanders

**Origin:** "The exact origin is uncertain, but the idea that enjoys the largest following is that it came from Dutch *Jan Kees*—a variant of *John Kaas*, which literally meant 'John Cheese,' an ethnic insult for a Hollander. Other ideas abound. According to James Fenimore Cooper, Indians sounded the word 'English' as *Yengees*; whence *Yankees*. Or the word may be derived from the Scottish *yankie*, 'dishonest person.'" (From *The Story Behind the Word*, by Morton S. Freeman)

**TYCOON**

**Meaning:** A wealthy and powerful business person

**Origin:** "A trumped-up Japanese title, *taikun* was a word used to magnify the role of the shogun or military commander of the country, especially when he was addressing foreigners, the point being to suggest that he was more potent and important than the emperor himself. The word meant 'emperor' or 'great prince,' borrowed from the Chinese *t'ai kiuen* ('great prince')." (From *The Secret Lives of Words*, by Paul West)

**When your dog drags his rear end across your floor, that's known as "sleigh riding."**

## SABOTAGE

**Meaning:** To deliberately destroy or obstruct

**Origin:** "*Sabots* are great, clumsy wooden shoes, worn by French peasants at the time of the Revolution. But *sabotage* was not invented until about 1910, during the great French railway strikes, and meant, figuratively, to throw a wooden shoe in the gears; deliberate destruction of plant and machinery by dissatisfied workers." (From *More About Words*, by Margaret S. Ernst)

## SINISTER

**Meaning:** Evil or ominous

**Origin:** "In Latin, the word had two meanings: 'on the left side,' and 'unfavorable.' According to Greek tradition people faced north while prophesying, so west—the left side—became the unlucky one. By the early 15th century the interpretation was 'dishonest'; later in the 15th century it became 'evil.' The sense 'threatening' or 'ominous' does not arise until the 18th century." (From *Jesse's Word of the Day*, by Jesse Sheidlower)

## LUKEWARM

**Meaning:** Barely warm

**Origin:** "*Luke* was a Middle English word, now obsolete, meaning 'warm,' which was based on *lew*, another word for 'warm.' *Lew*, in turn, was derived from the Old English word *hleow*, meaning (guess what?) 'warm.' You have probably realized by now that lukewarm actually amounts to saying 'warm-warm,' but this sort of redundancy is common when obsolete words are carried over into modern usage." (From *The Word Detective*, by Evan Morris)

## HAMMOCK

**Meaning:** A hanging bed of cloth tied between two supports

**Origin:** "The airiness and cleanliness of Taino (Native American) houses impressed the Europeans. The people slept in *hamacas*, hanging beds which Columbus described as 'nets of cotton.' By the 17th century, these practical beds were being used by sailors onboard ship. The spelling *hammock* did not prevail until the 19th century." (From *The Chronology of Words and Phrases*' by Linda and Roger Flavell)

**A tree planted near a streetlight will keep its leaves longer into the fall than other trees.**

# I WANT TO RIDE MY BICYCLE! PART III

*Toward the end of the 19th century, America was in the middle of an Industrial Age. Factories everywhere were mass-producing products using Eli Whitney's revolutionary "American System." (See page 167.) It was only a matter of time before somebody would apply it to bicycles. (Part II is on page 205.)*

## MADE IN THE USA

Why import a product when you can build it yourself? That was the thinking of Colonel Albert Pope, a wealthy Civil War veteran. He saw the obvious demand for the penny-farthing bicycle from England and decided that he would be the one to supply it.

First he studied the mechanics of an entire fleet of European bicycles, and then hired engineers to copy their style and design. Pope's first bicycle, which he named the "Columbia," was a durable, lightweight penny-farthing with wire spokes and rubber tires. In 1878 he rented a sewing-machine factory and started production.

The true genius behind Pope's Columbia was his use of "interchangeable parts" technology. The bicycles that were produced in Europe were handmade and welded by individual mechanics—a costly, time-consuming process that produced a slightly different bike every time. Pope standardized bicycle parts so they could be used interchangeably, making bikes easy to build and easy to repair. Soon thousands of mass-produced bicycles started rolling off Pope's assembly line. Now all he had to do was sell them.

## GETTING THE WORD OUT

Pope began spending money to promote the bicycle—a lot of money. He started a publication called *The Wheelman* and paid well-known journalists to write encouraging articles about the bicycle; he paid doctors to write about the health benefits associated with riding; and he helped start riding clubs. He hired Charles Pratt, a lawyer and popular author, to write a set of guidelines for the clubs. Pratt referred to bicycling as "manly" and composed a set of rules that included proper dress, position, and responsibilities. He also established a national organization called the League of American Wheelmen.

It worked. By the 1880s, the bicycle industry was flourishing. But in creating a demand for bikes, Pope's success sparked competition—and Pope didn't like competition. So he and Pratt purchased as many bicycle patents as they could. The patents ranged from Lallement's original design for the veloce (Lallement was then back in America working as a mechanic at one of Pope's factories) to various patent improvements on wheels, spokes, and pedals. Then Pope sent Pratt across the country charging retailers licensing fees for selling Pope's products and threatening lawsuits if they refused to pay. Since most small-time shop owners couldn't afford to go to court against a big-time baron like Pope, they paid up.

But while Pope and Pratt were busy fighting to keep their newly acquired patents alive, a British engineer named James Starley was developing a breakthrough that would make Pope's high-wheeled bicycles obsolete.

## BACK ON THE CHAIN GANG

In 1884 Starley developed a special chain that could connect the pedals to the axle of the bicycle's rear wheel. This development, known as "gearing," allowed manufacturers to shift the pedals of the bicycle from the front wheel to the middle of the crossbar, eliminating the need for a high front wheel. In fact, now both wheels could be the same size—about three feet in diameter—lowering the risks to the rider. Starley dubbed his new machine the "Rover," but the public called it the "safety bike."

This innovation would soon combine with another: In 1888 Scottish veterinarian John Dunlop invented rubber pneumatic (air-filled) tires, making bicycles ride much smoother than ever before. The entire industry was changed overnight, and the modern bicycle was born.

## CATALYST FOR CHANGE

The 1890s were known as the "Golden Age of Bikes." On both sides of the Atlantic, the "miracle machine" provided people freedom they'd never before known. And the world hasn't been the same since.

• Now that the crossbar was lower, women were able to ride (the bike had been primarily designed by men…for men). But now, women had a means of escaping the house. The bike would soon become an excuse for women everywhere to shed their more restrictive clothing—such as corsets and dresses—in the pursuit of more comfortable riding. These seemingly small social changes would soon help pave the way for women's suffrage.

• In 1892 two brothers bought a pair of safety bikes. They loved them so much that they opened up a shop and started building and repairing bikes for a living. But they wouldn't be dabbling in bikes for long—Wilbur and Orville Wright would, however, incorporate the bicycle's design into their new invention: the airplane.

• The new bicycles also caught the attention of another young man. Many of their features intrigued him: interchangeable parts, assembly line production, chain-propelled gear shifts, inflatable rubber tires. In 1896 he teamed them up with a new design for a gasoline engine, added two more wheels, and called it the "Quadricycle." The man's name: Henry Ford.

* * *

## BATHROOM MISCELLANY

• In medieval Europe, wedding ceremonies often took place in baths. Participants stood in a large tub as food was passed around on small boats.

• Some 19th-century chamber pots were decorated with portraits of popular enemies on the inside. One popular target: Napoleon.

# GANDER

*Far too few people know the heartwarming story about what happened in a small town on a remote island in the North Atlantic on September 11, 2001. Canadian air traffic controller (and BRI member) Terry Budden told us about it, and we decided to share it with you.*

## THE TOWN OF GANDER

Gander is located in Newfoundland, Canada's easternmost province. The town is central to Newfoundland Island, and the home of Gander International Airport. The decision to build an airport on Gander was made in 1935 because aircraft couldn't make the long flight from New York to London without stopping to refuel. Newfoundland falls on the Atlantic Ocean right under the flight path between these two points, making it the ideal stopover location. The town itself formed around the airport and was mostly populated by people who worked in support of the aviation industry. They referred to Gander as "the crossroads of the world."

Today, of course, aircraft can fly farther without refueling, making Gander an unnecessary stop. With the exception of local and cargo flights, very little international traffic stops there anymore. Gander has since become a quiet town. Until September 11, 2001.

## GROUNDED

Less than an hour after the terrorist attacks of September 11, the U.S. Federal Aviation Administration grounded all flights and closed their airspace for the first time in history. Transport Canada (Canada's equivalent to the FAA) followed suit, ordering all aircraft to the ground. There were approximately five hundred planes arriving over the east coast of Canada with nowhere to go. Air traffic controllers quickly started directing these flights to the closest airports. Before long, 38 planes were parked wingtip to wingtip on Gander's taxiways and runways—and more than 6,500 passengers and crew suddenly found themselves stranded.

## THE LOGISTICAL NIGHTMARE

Town officials and coordinators immediately scrambled to assess the situation thrust upon them, still reeling from the images on CNN. The Emergency Coordination Center at the airport and the Emergency Operations Center at the town hall were activated, and the situation was discussed. Gander has many contingency plans for all sorts of different situations—there is even a contingency plan for an emergency space-shuttle landing at the airport—but no plan for accommodating and feeding so many people for an undetermined amount of time. The town's 500 hotel rooms were no match for 6,500 unexpected visitors.

Des Dillon of the Canadian Red Cross was asked to round up beds. Major Ron Stuckless of the Salvation Army became the coordinator of a mass collection of food. Murray Osmond, the only Citizenship and Immigration officer on site, began the arduous task of processing thousands of passengers. "There was also the issue of security," Osmond told reporters. "We didn't know which planes out there might have individuals aboard like the ones who attacked the World Trade Center." He worked with a planeload of U.S. soldiers who had arrived to help maintain order.

While airport officials made preparations to process everyone, the passengers had to remain on board—some for as long as 30 hours—worried, confused, and cut off from the outside world. They couldn't see the attacks that kept the rest of the world glued to their televisions and still had no idea why they had been forced to land. Before long, though, passengers with cell phones and portable radios began spreading the word that the United States was under attack. If so, what would be the passengers fate? Were they war refugees? How long would it be until they saw home again?

## JUST PLANE FOLKS

When the passengers finally disembarked, they received a warm welcome. Although Newfoundland is the poorest province in Canada, everyone helped out:

• It was quickly decided that the majority of the rooms would go to the flight crews so they would be well rested and ready to travel on short notice. The decision as to where to house everyone else had to be faced next: the town of Gander, even with all its residents, churches, schools, and shelters opening their doors, could

**Frequent fly-er: A common housefly beats its wings about 20,000 times per minute.**

handle only about half of the stranded passengers. The rest would have to be transported to the surrounding communities of Gambo, Lewisporte, Appleton, Glenwood, and Norris Arm. But transporting these people seemed to be a problem as well—the local bus drivers had been on strike for weeks. They weren't for long: the striking bus drivers put down their picket signs and manned 60 buses to drive the passengers to their destinations.

• Families were kept together. Many places set up special rooms for families with babies and small children where portable cribs were assembled, and boxes were filled with toys and games. Diapers, bottles, and formula were provided, all free of charge.

• When calls went out for food and bedding, people emptied their cupboards, refrigerators, and closets and went to the airport. "They were there all night long, bringing food and standing at the tables, passing it out," said Captain Beverly Bass from American Flight 49. Asked who was manning the tables, a passenger from Air France Flight 004 responded, "They were the grocer, the postman, the pastor—everyday citizens of Gander who just came out."

• The passengers weren't allowed to take their luggage off the flights; they were there with just the clothes on their backs. So, responding to radio announcements, the residents and businesses of Gander supplied deodorant, soap, blankets, spare underwear, offers of hot showers and guestrooms—even tokens for the local laundromat and invitations to wash their clothes in people's homes.

• A lot of the guests didn't speak English and had no idea what was happening. Locals and U.S. soldiers were put to work as translators.

• The local phone company set up phone banks so that all the passengers could call home. They strung wires and cables so those staying in schools, churches, and lodges would also have access to television and the Internet. Passengers participated, too—those who had cell phones passed them around for others to make calls until the batteries ran dead.

• Hospitals added extra beds and sent doctors to the airport, just in case. Anyone with a medical background worked with the local doctors and pharmacies to tend to those with special needs. People in need of prescriptions received what they required at no cost.

• Residents of Twillingate, a tiny island off the northeast coast of

**In the time it takes to turn a page, you'll lose 3 million blood cells and make 3 million more.**

Newfoundland, prepared enough sandwiches and soup for at least 200 people, then delivered them to the mainland.

• To keep their spirits up, the passengers were given a choice of excursion trips, such as boat cruises of the lakes and harbors, while others went to see the local forests and memorials. Whale and iceberg watching were also popular activities. Newfoundlanders brought in entertainers who put on shows and grief counselors to talk to those who needed it.

After the airspace reopened, with the help of the Red Cross the passengers were delivered to the airport right on time. Not a single person missed a flight. Many of the "plane people," as they were sometimes called, were crying and sharing stories with each other. Many people exchanged phone numbers and addresses with newfound friends.

## THE AFTERMATH

Many travelers have since shown their thanks with donations to local churches, libraries, and charitable organizations.

• Lufthansa Airlines was so moved by the townspeople's reaction that they named one of their new aircraft after the town, an honor never before given to any place outside of Germany.

• The passengers from Delta Flight 15 started a scholarship fund and raised more than U.S. $30,000 for the school that housed them.

• The Rockefeller Foundation, which had used a small computer lab at a school in Lewisporte as the nerve center for their philanthropic activities, supplied the school with a brand new state-of-the-art computer lab.

• Gander Academy, which housed the passengers of Sabena Flight 539, Lufthansa Flight 416, and Virgin Flight 21, has received $27,000 in donations from the passengers that stayed there. The school is using the funds to finance a new six-year global peace awareness program.

• On the one-year anniversary, Canadian Prime Minister Jean Chretien traveled to Gander to honor the townsfolk. "You did yourselves proud," he told a crowd of 2,500 people who had gathered on the tarmac. "And you did Canada proud."

**In a typical diamond mine, you have to dig 23 tons of ore to find a single one-carat diamond.**

# A NOTE FROM GANDER

*Here is a great letter we found posted on the Internet from Gander resident Scott Cook, reprinted with his permission.*

"It's been a hell of a week here in Gander. The stories are amazing. We had 38 aircraft with a total of 6,656 people drop by for coffee. They stayed for three or four days. Our population is just under 10,000, so you can imagine the logistics involved in giving each of these people a place to sleep and a hot meal three times a day.

"Many of us spent our time bringing people home so they could get a shower or, once the rain started on the third day, driving them to the mall or sightseeing to relieve their boredom. The diversity of the people who have been in my car and in my shower over the past few days is pretty wild.

"You should have seen the look on my little girl's face when three Muslim women came home with me for a shower. With their robes, she could only see their faces, hands and feet. Their hands and feet were covered with henna paint and two of them didn't speak English. There was a king from the Middle East here, a British MP, the Mayor of Frankfurt, Germany, etc., etc.

"There were also immigrants from all over the world, some of whom didn't have two pennies to rub together. They all slept side by side in schools and church halls. Except the Irish, of course! A flight from Ireland was put up at a couple of local drinking establishments! The Royal Canadian Legion and the Elks Club. One woman here gave a driving tour to a fellow from the U.S. When she brought him back to his gymnasium cot, they exchanged cards. She looked at his and said, 'So you work with Best Western?' He replied, 'No, I own Best Western.'

"You should have been here, but of course, there wouldn't have been room."

* * *

"We make a living by what we've got, but we make a life by what we give." **—Winston Churchill**

# NAPOLEON'S CODE

*Although he stood only 5'6", Napoleon Bonaparte was one of the most important figures in history. Emperor of France and conqueror of Europe, he created new standards for civil law, the French educational system, and much more. Here are some snippets of his wisdom.*

"History is the version of past events that people have decided to agree upon."

"There is no place in a fanatic's head where reason can enter."

"The best way to keep one's word is not to give it."

"The most dangerous moment comes with victory."

"In politics...never retreat, never retract...never admit a mistake."

"In politics stupidity is not a handicap."

"A man will fight harder for his interests than for his rights."

"From sublime to ridiculousness there is only one step."

"If you wage war, do it energetically and with severity. This is the only way to make it shorter and consequently less inhuman."

"Public morals are the natural complement of all laws: they are by themselves an entire code."

"An order that can be misunderstood will be misunderstood."

"If you wish to be a success in the world, promise everything, deliver nothing."

"Ten people who speak make more noise than ten thousand who are silent."

"Adversity is the midwife of genius."

"The word 'impossible' is not in my dictionary."

"Men are moved by only two levers: fear and self-interest."

"Governments keep their promises only when they are forced, or when it is to their advantage to do so."

"He who fears being conquered is sure of defeat."

**What do Swiss steak and Russian dressing have in common? Both were invented in the U.S.**

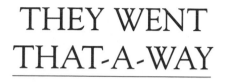

# THEY WENT THAT-A-WAY

*So how did the Spanish master painter Francisco de Goya die? Modern analysis suggests that he literally painted himself to death.*

**FRANCISCO DE GOYA (1746–1828)**

**Claim to Fame:** Art historians consider Goya a master painter—one of the greatest who ever lived. He became a "court" painter for Spanish royalty in 1786. But after an illness in 1792 he abandoned his conventional portrait-painting style and his work became cynical and dark; it is this later work that made him famous and inspired later painters like Edouard Manet and Pablo Picasso.

**How He Died:** He was killed by his own paints.

**Postmortem:** In 1792 Goya, 46, was struck by a sudden mysterious illness that manifested itself in symptoms including convulsions, paralysis of the right side of his body, poor balance, alternating giddiness and chronic depression, ringing in his ears, hallucinations, mental confusion, blindness (temporary), deafness (permanent), and impaired speech.

He almost died. In fact, he was so incapacitated that he had to give up painting for a time. Then, after a period of convalescence, the symptoms disappeared just as mysteriously as they had appeared, and he was able to resume his work.

Thus began a pattern that plagued Goya for the rest of his life: He would paint until he became too ill to work; then he'd rest and the symptoms would disappear. He'd start painting again, and the symptoms would return. The cycle continued for more than 30 years until 1828, when his illness is believed to have triggered the stroke that finally killed him.

For generations, historians assumed that Goya was felled by syphilis or some similar illness, but with syphilis the symptoms don't usually go away. In the early 1970s, a physician, Dr. William Niederland, concluded that Goya most likely died from exposure to the lead and mercury in his paints.

But why did *he* die from poisoning when so many of his contemporary artists did not? One reason is that Goya's luminous, mother-of-pearl painting style required huge amounts of white paint, which contained lead. He also used it to prime his canvases. Not only that, Goya had to mix all of his paints himself. In those days, artists couldn't buy their paint ready made, so Goya ground lead white and a mercury compound called cinnabar into his paints.

And because Goya was one of the fastest of the great portrait painters, he used *a lot* of paint, thus inhaling as much as triple the amount of mercury and lead as his contemporaries, Niederland speculates. His contemporaries didn't inhale enough to even become ill, but Goya inhaled enough to kill himself.

**Final Irony:** The poisonous paint that killed him may also have been what turned Goya into one of the greatest painters in history. The 1792 attack was so severe that Goya never painted the same again—and it was this later painting style that made him famous. "In terms of artistic greatness," Charles Panati writes in *The Browser's Book of Endings,* "had the painter's career ended prior to his major 1792 ailment, it would have survived with only passing mention, the work of a gifted artist, popular in his day, who missed greatness by a wide margin."

* * *

## RULES OF LIFE THEY DON'T TEACH IN SCHOOL
### (But you can learn on the Internet)

**1.** Never give yourself a haircut after three margaritas.

**2.** You need only two tools. WD-40 and duct tape. If it doesn't move and it should, use WD-40. If it moves and shouldn't, use the tape.

**3.** Everyone seems normal until you get to know them.

**4.** If he or she says that you are too good for him or her—believe them.

**5.** Never pass up an opportunity to pee.

**6.** Be really nice to your friends. You never know when you are going to need them to empty your bedpan.

# THE MAGIC SCREEN

*"As new as 1960!" That was the slogan on Uncle John's first Etch A Sketch. It provided hours of mindless fun (just like TV), even though he couldn't figure out how it worked (he still can't).*

## A HUMBLE BEGINNING

In 1958 a 37-year-old Parisian garage mechanic named Arthur Granjean invented an amazing new toy. He called it *L'Ecran Magique*—Magic Screen.

The Magic Screen was an unusual toy for its time—it didn't have a lot of little pieces that could get lost and didn't need batteries. Granjean felt sure his creation would interest someone at the International Toy Fair in Nuremberg, Germany. But everyone passed on it...until executives from a small American toy firm, the Ohio Art Company, convinced their boss to take a second look. That did it. Ohio Art bought the rights for $25,000 and renamed it Etch A Sketch. Then they advertised it on TV—just in time for the 1960 Christmas season—and sales took off. The response was so great that they kept the factory open until noon on Christmas Eve desperately trying to fill orders.

## A CLASSIC TOY

How does Etch A Sketch work? There's a stylus, or pointer, mounted on two rails behind the screen. Using a system of wires and pulleys connected to the knobs on front, one rail moves back and forth, and the other moves up and down. The gray stuff is powdered aluminum mixed with tiny plastic beads. The powder sticks to the glass screen because aluminum powder sticks to *everything*. The beads help the powder flow easily. When the stylus moves, it touches the glass and scrapes the aluminum powder off. Shake it, and the aluminum is redistributed evenly. To prevent it from breaking, a clear plastic film covers the glass.

The basic Etch A Sketch design hasn't changed since 1960, although variations have been introduced:

- Pocket-sized models, travel-sized models, and glow-in-the-dark

**Cockfighting is still legal in three states: Oklahoma, Louisiana, and New Mexico.**

models (only the frame glows).

• The new Zooper model makes weird noises—beeps, boops, squeaks, and squawks—as the knobs turn.

• There's also an Etch A Sketch "action pack," which offers various puzzles and games printed on overlays placed on top of the screen.

• To celebrate the toy's 25th anniversary in 1985, Ohio Art came out with an Executive model made of silver. The drawing knobs were set with sapphires and topaz. Price: $3,750.

## ETCH A SKETCH TRIVIA

• **How many?** Eight thousand Etch A Sketches are sold every day.

• **World's largest Etch A Sketch.** Steve Jacobs created it at the Black Rock Arts Festival in California in 1997. He placed 144 regulation-sized Etch A Sketches in a huge square and surrounded them with a huge red Etch A Sketch frame, including huge white knobs. It qualified for a Guinness World Record.

• **Robot Etch A Sketch.** A Canadian computer programmer named Neil Fraser pulled the knobs off a standard Etch A Sketch and hooked it up to two motors that were attached to the port of his computer. The motors worked by remote control, enabling Fraser to draw pictures without ever touching the toy. Other robotic components tilt the Etch A Sketch upside down and shake it.

• **Extreme Etch A Sketch.** George Vlosich was ten years old in 1989 when, on a long drive from Ohio to Washington, D.C., he brought along his Etch A Sketch. On the way home, he drew a sketch of the Capitol that was so good his parents photographed it. An artist was born. He soon began sketching portraits of his favorite sports heroes, then waited after games to get them to autograph his Etch A Sketch. The "Etch A Sketch Kid" started getting so much media attention that in 2000, Ohio Art sent someone to his home to see if he lived up to his reputation. They were so impressed by his talent that they've been supplying him with free Etch A Sketches ever since.

It takes George between 40 and 60 hours to complete a single Etch A Sketch masterpiece. After it's done, he carefully unscrews the back and removes the excess aluminum powder to preserve the picture forever. His Etch A Sketch artworks sell for up to $5,000 each.

**Cost of a ticket to a Beatles' concert in 1966 (corrected for inflation): $31.**

# AMAZING COINCIDENCES

*We're constantly finding stories about amazing coincidences. Here are a few more of Uncle John's favorites.*

## MESSAGE IN A BOTTLE

Charles Coghlan was born on Prince Edward Island in 1841. He became a successful stage actor and toured the world, but the island was always his home. In 1899, during an appearance on Galveston Island, Texas, he fell ill and died, and was buried in a Galveston cemetery. On September 8, 1900, a hurricane struck Galveston, washing away most of the town and swamping all the cemeteries. Seven years later, a fishermen from Prince Edward Island noticed a large box in the water. He towed it to shore, chipped off the barnacles, and discovered the coffin of Charles Coghlan, beloved native son. It had floated into the Gulf of Mexico, been caught by the West Indian current, carried into the Gulf Stream, and deposited on shore only a few miles from his Canadian birthplace.

## MONSTER TRUCK

Christina Cort lived in Salvador, Brazil, in 1966 when an out-of-control truck crashed into her house. In 1989, she was still living in the same house when another out-of-control truck crashed into it. It was the same truck driver who had barreled into her home 23 years earlier.

## TELL-TALE SKULL

In 1983, a man cutting peat for fuel near Cheshire, England, uncovered a human skull, which he took to the police. Forensic scientists examined the remains and announced they belonged to a European middle-aged woman who had been buried for not less than five but not more than 50 years. After investigating, the police found that a Mrs. Malika Reyn-Bardt had mysteriously disappeared from the area in 1961. When police confronted Peter Reyn-Bardt with the evidence, he broke down and confessed to murdering her and burying pieces of her body at various locations. Before the trial, however, the skull was sent to Oxford University's lab for additional testing. Those tests revealed that the skull actually belonged to a woman who had died around 410 A.D. Reyn-Bardt pleaded not guilty, but was convicted and sentenced to life imprisonment. No trace of his dead wife has ever been found.

### THE LONG WAY HOME

Actor Anthony Hopkins, while playing a role in a movie based on a book called *The Girl from Petrovka* by George Feifer, looked all over London for a copy of the book but was unable to find one. Later that day he was waiting in a subway station for his train when he noticed someone had left a book on a bench. Picking it up, Hopkins found it was... *The Girl from Petrovka.* Two years later Hopkins was filming another movie in Vienna when he was visited on the set by author George Feifer. Feifer complained that he no longer had even a single copy of his own book because he'd loaned his last one to a friend who had lost it somewhere in London. Feifer added that it was particularly annoying because he had written notes in the margins. Hopkins, incredulous, handed Feifer the copy he had found in the subway station. It was the same book.

*   *   *

## THREE STRANGE COINCIDENCES FROM INSIDE THE BRI

• We once printed a fact that said: "Moo. Country star Lyle Lovett is afraid of cows." Not long after the book was released, Lyle Lovett was attacked by a bull.

• Our 2002 Page-A-Day calendar was written in 2001. The page for March 27, 2002, had a funny story about Milton Berle, who just so happened to die on...March 27, 2002.

• Sad coincidence: In 2000, we put together a page of odd holidays for our *All-Purpose Extra Strength Bathroom Reader.* We found a great one called "No News is Good News Day." The date of the holiday: September 11.

**That's gotta hurt: Actor Jackie Chan once dislocated his cheek bone filming an action movie.**

# ONE GOOD TURN DESERVES ANOTHER

*Here's a gut-wrenching story with a happy ending.*

## TOOL TIME

One day in 1964, an 18-year-old high school kid named Peter Roberts was tinkering around in his dad's garage. His father repaired lawn mowers in his spare time to earn pocket money and sometimes Peter helped him. Repairing lawn mowers would be a lot easier, he thought, if his socket wrench had a button that would release the socket from the grip of the wrench. So he kept tinkering and by the end of the day he had invented the ratchet wrench.

Peter worked part-time at the local Sears-Roebuck, so he took his new wrench to his boss...who showed it to his boss...who showed it to all the execs at Sears headquarters in Chicago.

## GETTING SCREWED

Nearly a year went by and Roberts never heard back from them, so he assumed no one was interested in his invention. Then one day a lawyer showed up and informed him that Sears was prepared to offer him two cents for every one of his ratchet wrenches they sold—with the stipulation that they wouldn't owe him any further royalties after he reached the $10,000 mark. The lawyer said it was going to be difficult and time consuming for Sears to manufacture the wrenches, so it might take Roberts years to collect the maximum amount of royalties. He signed over the patent to Sears.

A year later, he was amazed to receive the entire $10,000 in a single check. Suspecting that he'd been had, Roberts hired his own lawyer and took Sears to court in 1969. They argued that Sears was guilty of fraud—they'd led Roberts to believe that they'd only be able to sell a few wrenches a year when in reality they'd already sold more than a million. More importantly, Roberts had been a minor (under 21) when he'd signed the contract. After 20 years of legal wrangling, they finally settled...and Roberts collected $8.2 million.

# A LIGHT IN THE NIGHT

*Before radio, sonar, and GPS, lighthouses provided the only way for sailors to visually locate the shore at night or in foul weather. Here are a few facts about a forgotten piece of history.*

No one knows for sure when or where the very first lighthouse was built. Early lighthouses were too simple to be recorded; some were little more than candles placed in the windows of tall buildings at night. Others were hilltop structures on which large fires could be built. The earliest *known* lighthouses were built on the Mediterranean Sea in the seventh century B.C.

• The Great Lighthouse at Alexandria, Egypt, was one of the Seven Wonders of the ancient world. Completed around 280 B.C., it stood about 450 feet high on the island of Pharos in the Alexandria harbor. Still in operation as late as 1115, it was destroyed by earthquakes in the 1300s.

• The oldest American lighthouse is the Boston Light, in Boston's outer harbor. Built in 1716 on Little Brewster Island, it was destroyed by the British during the American Revolution. It was rebuilt in 1783 and still stands today.

• The oldest working lighthouse in the world is Spain's Tower of Hercules, built by the Romans in 20 B.C.

• Before electricity, lighthouses provided light via wood or coal fires, or even candles. These were replaced by whale-oil lanterns, which gave way to kerosene lanterns in the 1800s. Keeping such a light continually lit wasn't easy. In the United States, most lighthouses had a full-time keeper (nicknamed "wickies" because they kept the lantern wicks trimmed), who lived at the lighthouse and made sure it stayed lit.

• No more—now every working lighthouse in the United States is automated. The last manned lighthouse, Maine's Goat Island Light, became automated in 1990.

• First American lighthouse to use electricity: the Statue of Liberty, which served as a lighthouse in New York Harbor until 1902.

**Michigan borders no ocean...but has more lighthouses than any other state.**

# THE VIDEO GAME HALL OF FAME

*Today most video games are played in the home, but in the 1970s and 1980s, if you wanted to play the newest, hottest games, you went to an arcade. Here are the stories of a few of the classics we played back in the golden age of arcade games.*

**SPACE INVADERS (Taito, 1978)**

**Object:** Using a laser cannon that you scroll back and forth across the bottom of the screen, defend yourself from wave after wave of aliens descending from the top of the screen.

**Origin:** Space Invaders started out as a test that was used to measure the skill of computer programmers, but someone decided that it might also work well as an arcade game. They were right—the game became a national craze in Japan.

Introduced to the U.S. market by Midway in October 1978, Space Invaders became the biggest hit of the year. It made so much money—a single unit could earn back its $1,700 purchase price in as little as four weeks—that it helped arcade games break out of arcades and smoky bars into nontraditional venues like supermarkets, restaurants, and movie theaters.

**TEMPEST (Atari, 1981)**

**Object:** Shoot the moving shapes—red brackets, green spikes, yellow lines, and multicolored balls, before they climb up and out of the geometrically shaped "well" they're in and get you.

**Origin:** Atari game designer Dave Theurer needed an idea for a new video game, so he went to the company's book of potential themes compiled from brainstorming sessions. The idea he chose to develop was "First Person Space Invaders"—Space Invaders as seen from the perspective of the laser cannon at the bottom of the screen.

Theurer created a game and showed it to his superiors...and they told him to dump it unless he could "do something special with it." Theurer told them about a nightmare he'd had about monsters climbing out of a hole in the ground and coming to get him. "I can put it on a flat surface and wrap that surface around to

**Theater spotlights used to burn lime for light. That's where the term *limelight* comes from.**

make a cylinder, and rotate the cylinder," Theurer suggested. As he conceived it, the cylinder would move while the player stood still... but he abandoned that idea when the rotating cylinder started giving players motion sickness. "I switched it so the player moved around," Theurer says. "That fixed it."

**PAC-MAN (Namco, 1980)**

**Object:** Maneuver Pac-Man through a maze and eat all 240 dots without getting caught by one of the four "ghosts"—Inky, Blinky, Pinky, and Clyde.

**Origin:** In 1979 a game designer named Toru Iwatani decided to make a game that would appeal to women, who were less interested in violent, shoot-the-alien games like Space Invaders. Iwatani thought that eating things on the computer screen would make a good nonviolent alternative to shooting them. He came up with the idea for the Pac-Man character over lunch. "I was having pizza," he says. "I took one wedge and there it was, the figure of Pac-Man." Well, almost: Pac-Man was originally supposed to be called Puck-Man, because the main character was round like a hockey puck... but the name was changed to Pac-Man, because Namco officials "worried about American vandals changing the 'P' to an 'F'."

**DONKEY KONG (Nintendo, 1980)**

**Object:** Get the girl.

**Origin:** One of Nintendo's first video games was a Space Invaders knockoff called Radarscope. It flopped in the United States, nearly bankrupting the distributor—who wanted to stop doing business with Nintendo. What could Nintendo do? They promised to ship new chips to American distributors so the unsold Radarscope games could be turned into new games.

There was just one problem—they didn't have any new game chips. So Nintendo president Hiroshi Yamauchi told the company's staff artist, Shigeru Miyamoto, to come up with something, *fast*.

Miyamoto had never made a game before, and he hated tennis games, shooting games, and most games that were popular at the time. So he invented a game about a janitor who has to rescue his girlfriend from his pet ape, who has taken her to the top of a construction site. Miyamoto wanted to name the game after the ape,

**If you plant bamboo today, it may not sprout flowers and produce seeds for 100 years.**

so he looked up the words for "stubborn" and "ape" in his Japanese/English dictionary…and found the words "donkey" and "Kong." Donkey Kong went on to become one of the most successful video games in history, giving Nintendo the boost it needed to build itself into a multibillion-dollar company and an international video game juggernaut. And it might never have succeeded if Radarscope hadn't failed.

**DEFENDER (Williams Electronics, 1980)**

**Object:** Use your spacecraft to shoot hostile aliens while saving humanoids from being kidnapped and turned into mutants.

**Origin:** Another game helped along by a dream: Defender was supposed to make its debut at the 1980 Amusement & Music Operators of America (AMOA) convention, but less than two weeks before his deadline, creator Eugene Jarvis had only the rough outlines of a game—the name, Defender, and a spaceship attacking aliens, all against a planetary backdrop dotted with humanoids who didn't really do anything. What was the defender defending?

"The answer came to him in a dream," Nick Montfort writes in *Supercade*. "Those seemingly pointless little men, trapped on the surface below, *they* were the ones to be defended."

Jarvis made his deadline, but the AMOA was afraid the game was too complicated. They were wrong. Defender became one of the most popular games of the year and made so much money that in 1981 the AMOA voted it Video Game of the Year.

**LEGENDARY FLOP: LUNAR LANDER (Atari, 1979)**

**Object:** Find a flat spot on the lunar surface and use your booster engines to slow your spaceship (without running out of fuel) and land it safely on the moon.

**Origin:** The game was adapted from a computer simulation used in college physics courses to teach students about lunar gravity. Atari had high hopes for the game, even designing a special two-handled lever that controlled the booster engines. It flopped. So did the special lever: "Springs on the lever made it snap back in place when it was released," Steven Kent writes in *The Ultimate History of Video Games*. "Unfortunately, some younger players got their faces too close to the lever, resulting in complaints about children being hit in the face."

**Odds of being killed by a bolt of lightning are about the same as being killed falling out of bed.**

# DUMB CROOKS

*More proof that crime doesn't pay.*

## THE RIGHT TO REMAIN STUPID

"An Illinois woman, when asked to walk a straight line after being pulled over for weaving across a highway divider, told the state trooper, "You'll have to give me a little longer. This is tougher when you've been drinking."

**—Bloomington-Normal *Daily Pantograph***

## OVERNIGHT SENSATION

HELSINGBORG, Sweden—"A 20-year-old man developed what he thought to be a foolproof robbery plan. He hid in a store, waited for employees to leave for the night, and proceeded to rob the place. All was going according to plan until, as he was stuffing items in a sack, he realized he was locked in the store. He tried using a crowbar to open the front door and then attempted to break through a wall in the restrooms, but to no avail. He finally gave up and called the police."

**—*Bizarre News***

## OUT OF THE FRYING PAN...

SAN JOSE, California—"According to the Department of Corrections, Arnold Ancheta, 25, apparently escaped from Elmwood Correctional Facility by squeezing through the bars on the roof of his cell, breaking out through the skylight, and jumping down from the roof. But then, instead of heading toward the fence that leads to the road, he jumped a smaller fence and ended up on the women's side of the facility. Female inmates saw Ancheta running around the yard and alerted correctional officers. He was taken to a hospital and then back to jail."

**—San Diego *Union-Tribune***

## PATIENCE IS A VIRTUE?

"A bank robber in Fresno, California, made a withdrawal from his own account, then demanded all the money in the bank vault. When they told him it would take 15 minutes to empty the vault,

**Tickly fact: The U.S. produces 2 to 4 billion lbs. of chicken and turkey feathers every year.**

he went outside to wait patiently on the curb, according to police, who found him sitting there, still waiting."

—***Fresno Bee***

### JUST DESSERTS

"In Lafayette, Louisiana, a man robbed a bank with his head covered in whipped cream. His disguise melted before he could collect the loot, however, and he was later arrested."

**—"The Edge," *The Oregonian***

### PISTOL-PACKIN' IDIOT

"Gilbert MacConnell went to the West Hartford, Connecticut, police station in February 2002 for a job interview. He wanted to become a cop. MacConnell, age 35, had already passed the written exam, the oral exam, and the physical agility test. But during an interview with police chief James Strillacci, MacConnell admitted owning an unlicensed gun. Officers found the .45-caliber handgun in his car. 'Does this mean I'm not getting the job?' he asked as he was booked and charged with carrying a pistol without a permit and having a concealed weapon in a car. He didn't get the job."

—***Hartford Courant***

### YOU REAP WHAT YOU SEW

"Los Angeles sheriff's deputies investigating the break-in of a sewing shop discovered the theft of a large industrial sewing machine, then noticed a thick thread snagged on the floor. They followed the thread out the door, down the alley, across the street, through a backyard, up some steps, and under a door. After kicking in the door, they discovered the sewing machine in the kitchen and nabbed three surprised thieves."

—***Maxim***

### PRINTS CHARMING

"When John Michell's home was broken into, he did what anyone would do—he called the police. To distinguish his prints from the crook's, citizen Michell allowed investigators to fingerprint him. Police quickly discovered that Michell himself had been wanted for burglary for three years. Michell is now serving a 12-month sentence."

—***Fortean Times***

**The glue that barnacles use to stick themselves to ship hulls is twice as strong as epoxy resin.**

# THE DEATH OF A PRINCESS

*She was called the "people's princess." Beautiful, kind, and caring, Princess Diana captured the hearts of people around the world. But she was also outspoken and, in the eyes of some very powerful people, a troublemaker. Her worst "offense" may have been her love affair with Egyptian millionaire Dodi Al-Fayed. When the princess and her lover died in a tragic car crash, many were quick to wonder whether it was really an accident.*

**The Deceased:** Diana, Princess of Wales

**How She Died:** In the early hours of Sunday, August 31, 1997, a black Mercedes S280 carrying Princess Diana and her soon-to-be fiancé Dodi Al-Fayed left the Paris Ritz Hotel. The pair were on their way to Dodi's Paris apartment. In the front seat Dodi's bodyguard, Trevor Rees-Jones, sat beside the driver, Henri Paul, deputy chief of security at the Ritz. As usual, Diana's vehicle was pursued by "paparazzi"—tabloid photographers with the reputation of doing anything to get a lucrative photograph. At least one photographer was snapping pictures from the back of a high-powered motorcycle.

Minutes later the Mercedes entered the Place de L'Alma tunnel. Some eyewitnesses report hearing an explosion, then a crash. Many of the first people to arrive after the crash described a grisly scene—photographers crowding within inches of the crumpled car, which had hit a support pillar, shooting pictures of the dying princess and the other bloodied victims.

Dodi and Henri Paul were killed instantly. Diana was taken by ambulance to a hospital, where she died three and a half hours after the crash. The only survivor was Trevor Rees-Jones—the one person in the car who had fastened his seatbelt.

Early reports blamed the crash on the paparazzi. According to stories, Henri Paul was driving at high speeds trying to evade them. Or perhaps he was blinded by a flash and swerved into the pillar. An outraged public accused the photographers not only of causing the crash, but also of interfering with the efforts of rescue

**The first American cookbook, *The Compleat Housewife*, was published in 1746.**

personnel. (A doctor who came upon the wreck about a minute after the crash says those reports are false—the photographers were not obstructing efforts to help the victims.)

Several photographers and a motorcyclist were detained for investigation. The photographers admitted to the chase but denied any responsibility for causing the crash. According to them, the Mercedes had outrun them before they got to the tunnel. They were quickly released.

A blood test on the driver, Henri Paul, raised other possibilities. He had more than three times the legal limit of alcohol in his blood, as well as the antidepressant Prozac. Inexplicably, there were also high levels of carbon monoxide.

Was the crash caused by a mix of zealous photographers and a drunk driver? For some, including French officials who concluded their investigation two years later, it was simply a tragic accident. But others remain convinced there's more to the story.

## UNANSWERED QUESTIONS

✔ **Was Diana pregnant?** Almost immediately after the crash, rumors began to circulate that Diana had been six weeks' pregnant with Al-Fayed's child. She had hinted to the press earlier that she was going to "surprise" them. Could she have been planning to announce her engagement or her pregnancy—or both? One person who believes both is Dodi's father, billionaire businessman Mohamed Al-Fayed. He has charged that the CIA has tapes from phone taps indicating that Diana was pregnant, and that she and Dodi intended to marry.

An autopsy, which may have revealed the truth, was not performed until her body was returned to England. When asked if Diana had been pregnant, the coroner replied, "No comment."

✔ **Why was there no traffic-camera video of the Mercedes?** Paris has one of the most sophisticated video traffic surveillance systems in the world. When Mohamed Al-Fayed asked to see the tapes from the 17 cameras that covered the route the Mercedes took from the Ritz to the tunnel, French officials told him no tapes existed for those cameras at that time. What would the video have shown?

✔ **Why did the Mercedes take an indirect route to Dodi's apartment?** The tunnel where the Mercedes crashed was not on the

**Myth-understood: The *low man* on a totem pole is the most important man in the tribe.**

most direct route between the Ritz and Dodi's apartment. An eyewitness reports seeing a car blocking an exit, forcing the Mercedes to take the road through the tunnel.

✔ **Was Henri Paul hired to keep Diana and Al-Fayed under surveillance?** A former British intelligence agent claims Henri Paul was an informant for MI6, the British equivalent of the CIA. There are reports that Paul had multiple bank accounts with balances that are hard to explain, based on his salary as a security officer at the Ritz. Was Paul an expendable part of the network keeping track of Diana and Al-Fayed?

✔ **Was Henri Paul really drunk?** According to one expert, to account for the amount of alcohol reportedly in Paul's blood, he would have had to drink the equivalent of 10 ounces of whisky (eight shots) within a few hours of leaving the hotel—uncharacteristic behavior according to friends and co-workers. On security camera tapes recorded just before the Mercedes left the hotel, Paul does not appear drunk. His co-workers have also testified that he was not drunk, nor did he have a reputation for heavy drinking.

The sole survivor of the crash, Rees-Jones, received head injuries and claims the last thing he remembers was leaving the Ritz. He told investigators that Paul did not act drunk at the hotel. As Al-Fayed's bodyguard, Rees-Jones would have had the responsibility to note whether the driver was in a condition to drive safely.

Was the blood test rigged? Was Henri Paul a scapegoat?

✔ **Did Rees-Jones expect trouble?** Rees-Jones was the only person in the Mercedes wearing a seatbelt. Did the former British paratrooper know something?

✔ **Was another car involved?** Investigators found evidence that the Mercedes had been grazed by another vehicle just before the crash. Pieces of a taillight and flecks of white paint embedded into the front bumper of the Mercedes probably belonged to a white Fiat Uno, according to their investigations.

Witnesses report seeing a small car cut in front of the Mercedes moments before the crash. Some speculate that the car intentionally slowed down in front of the fast-moving Mercedes as it rounded a slight corner in the tunnel, causing Henri Paul to swerve. The white Fiat has never been found.

✔ **Was there an explosion in the tunnel *before* the crash?**

Eyewitnesses report hearing a loud bang in the tunnel just before the crash. Others say they saw a bright light, much brighter than that made by a photographer's flash. Was someone trying to disorient or blind the driver of the Mercedes?

✔ **Why did it take so long to get Diana to the hospital?** The doctor who arrived at the site about a minute after the crash quickly noted the conditions of the passengers, then called emergency services. The first ambulance didn't arrive until 15 minutes later. Diana was treated at the scene for more than 30 minutes after rescue personnel pulled her from the car. The closest hospital with 24-hour emergency service was only a few miles away, normally a 5- to 10-minute drive. The ambulance carrying Diana took 40 minutes to reach the hospital, finally arriving almost two hours after the crash.

## CONSPIRACY THEORIES

✔ **Diana was killed by British intelligence.** Richard Tomlinson, a former British intelligence agent, claims British intelligence had the expertise to fake Diana's crash. He knew of a British plan to assassinate Serbian leader Slobodan Milosevic by faking a car crash similar to the one that killed Diana. According to that plan, the crash would take place in a tunnel and the driver would be disoriented with a powerful strobe light.

Mohamed Al-Fayed has said he is "99.9% certain" Diana and his son were murdered. According to Al-Fayed, British and American intelligence agencies had Diana under surveillance for years and were following her and Dodi for three months before the crash.

Al-Fayed has stated that he believes British intelligence killed Diana and Dodi, and that the CIA has documents directly implicating Prince Philip, Queen Elizabeth's husband. According to Al-Fayed, a document quotes Philip as saying of the relationship between Diana and Dodi, "Such an affair is racially and morally repugnant and no son of a Bedouin camel trader is fit for the mother of a future king."

In many ways Diana was an annoyance to the Royal Family and its supporters. After the end of her "fairy tale" marriage to Prince Charles, she aired her uncomplimentary views of the queen, her former husband, and the rest of the Royal Family in

**...to cry in the movies than non-popcorn-eaters.**

the press. And the public took Diana's side against the Royals. Some felt Diana was a real threat to the monarchy. Maybe her intent to marry Dodi Al-Fayed was the last straw.

✔ **Diana was killed by the CIA.** Mohamed Al-Fayed claims the CIA has a secret dossier of more than 1,000 pages on Diana. The princess personally campaigned against the use of landmines, visiting injured victims in Angola and Bosnia. Her high-profile involvement led to an international treaty banning landmines that has been ratified by 125 nations. The United States, a major producer of landmines, has not signed the treaty. Diana was a nuisance to the American arms industry... but would she have been targeted for assassination?

✔ **Diana was killed by Israeli agents.** England, along with the United States, has been a strong supporter of Israel in the ongoing conflicts between that country and its Arab neighbors. If Diana—mother of a future king of England, Prince William—married an Egyptian, gave birth to half-Arab children, or even converted to Islam, public opinion and official policy may have turned against Israel.

## ONE OTHER POSSIBILITY

**Diana faked her own death.** In spite of overwhelming evidence that Diana died in the crash, some observers believe that she wanted to escape the pressures of her public life so badly that she staged her own death.

✔ Could the driver of the Mercedes have dropped Diana and Al-Fayed off somewhere before entering the tunnel? The army-trained bodyguard, Rees-Jones, may have had the expertise to make a switch. Is Diana really living somewhere in blissful anonymity?

✔ Still other people believe Diana planned to set up the accident... but something went wrong and the plan backfired.

Because the princess was so beloved and died under such strange circumstances, some people will always question the official reports of what happened. Whether Diana faked her death, was murdered, or was actually the victim of a tragic accident, the world may never know.

**26% of American men say their workplace filing system consists of "putting things in piles."**

# SMART ALECKS

*One of the privileges of fame is you get to say nasty things about other people and get away with it. Here's a few of our favorite zingers.*

"Do you mind if I smoke?"

**—Oscar Wilde, to Sarah Bernhardt**

"I don't care if you burn."

**—Sarah Bernhardt**

"Do you mind if I sit back a little? Because your breath is very bad."

**—Donald Trump, to CNN host Larry King**

"Michael Jackson's album was only called *Bad* because there wasn't enough room on the sleeve for "Pathetic."

**—Prince**

"Ernest Hemingway has never been known to use a word that might send a reader to a dictionary."

**—William Faulkner**

"Poor Faulkner. Does he really think emotions come from big words?

**—Ernest Hemingway**

"He's racist, he's homophobic, he's xenophobic, and he's a sexist. He's the perfect Republican candidate."

**—Commentator Bill Press, on Pat Buchanan**

"Boy George is all England needs: another queen who can't dress."

**—Joan Rivers**

"What other problems do you have besides being unemployed, a moron, and a dork?"

**—Tennis pro John McEnroe, to a spectator**

"McEnroe was as charming as always, which means that he was about as charming as a dead mouse in a loaf of bread."

**—Journalist Clive James**

"Never trust a man who combs his hair straight from his left armpit."

**—Alice Roosevelt Longworth, on Gen. Douglas MacArthur**

"He has so many fish hooks in his nose, he looks like a piece of bait."

**—Bob Costas, on Dennis Rodman**

"Why, this fellow don't know any more about politics than a pig knows about Sunday."

**—Harry Truman, on Dwight Eisenhower**

**Bad old days: Dentures used to be made with teeth pulled from the mouths of dead soldiers.**

# THE RISE AND FALL OF ATARI

*On page 225 we told you the story of how Atari "invented" Pong, the first commercially successful video game. Here's the story of how they came to dominate the American home video game industry...and then lost it all.*

## KING PONG

From the moment it was introduced in 1972, Atari's arcade game, Pong, was a money maker. Placed in a busy location, a single Pong game could earn more than $300 a week, compared to $50 a week for a typical pinball machine. Atari sold more than 8,000 of the machines at a time when even the most popular pinball machines rarely sold more than 2,500 units.

Atari would have sold a lot more machines, too, if competing game manufacturers hadn't flooded the market with knockoffs. But there was no way that Atari could fight off all the imitators.

Instead, Atari founder Nolan Bushnell managed to stay one step ahead of the competition by inventing one new arcade game after another. (One of these games, Breakout, in which you use a paddle and a ball to knock holes in a brick wall, was created by an Atari programmer named Steve Jobs and his friend Steve Wozniak, an engineer at Hewlett-Packard. Do their names sound familiar? They should—a few years later, they founded Apple Computer.)

## THE ATARI 2600

In 1975 Atari entered the home video game market by creating a home version of Pong. Selling its games through Sears Roebuck and Co., Atari sold 150,000 games that first season alone.

Bushnell was ready to introduce more home versions of arcade games, and he'd decided to do it by copying an idea from a competing video game system, Channel F. The idea: game cartridges. It was a simple concept: a universal game system in which interchangable game cartridges plugged into a game player, or "console."

There was just one problem: inventing a video game cartridge

Each year in the U.S., 30,000 dog bites are serious enough to require medical attention.

system from scratch and manufacturing it in great enough volume to beat out his competitors was going to cost a fortune. The only way that he could come up with the money was by selling Atari to Warner Communications (today part of AOL Time Warner) for $28 million in 1976. Bushnell stayed on as Atari's chairman and continued to work on the cartridge system.

Introduced in mid-1977, the Atari Video Computer System (VCS)—later renamed the Atari 2600—struggled for more than a year. Atari's competitors didn't do much better, and for a while it seemed that the entire video game industry might be on its last legs—the victim of the public's burnout from playing too much Pong.

### ALIEN RESURRECTION

Then in early 1979, Atari executives hit on the idea of licensing Space Invaders, an arcade game manufactured by Taito, a Japanese company. The game was so popular in Japan that it actually caused a coin shortage, forcing the national mint to triple its output of 100-yen coins.

Just as it had in Japan, Space Invaders became the most popular arcade game in the United States, *and* the most popular Atari game cartridge. Atari followed up with other blockbuster cartridges like Defender, Missile Command, and Asteroids; by 1980 it commanded a 75% share of the burgeoning home video game market. Thanks in large part to soaring sales of the VCS system, Atari's annual sales grew from $75 million in 1977 to more than $2 billion in 1980, making Atari the fastest growing company in U.S. history. But it wouldn't stay that way for long.

### THE BEGINNING OF THE END

Within months of bringing the VCS to market, Bushnell was already pushing Warner to begin work on a next-generation successor to the system, but Warner rejected the idea out of hand. They had invested more than $100 million in the VCS and weren't about to turn around and build a new product to compete with it. Warner's determination to rest on their laurels was one of the things that led to Bushnell's break with the company.

By the time Space Invaders revived the fortunes of the VCS, Nolan Bushnell was no longer part of the company. Warner Com-

**The Three Stooges appeared in more movies than any other comedy team in U.S. film history.**

munications had forced him out following a power struggle in November 1978.

If Bushnell had been the only person to leave the company, Atari's problems probably wouldn't have gotten so bad. But he wasn't—Warner also managed to alienate nearly all of Atari's best programmers. While Atari made millions of dollars, Warner paid the programmers less than $30,000 a year, didn't share the profits the games generated, and wouldn't even allow them to see sales figures.

The programmers didn't receive any public credit for their work, either. Outside of the company, few people even knew who had designed classic games like Asteroids and Missile Command; Warner was afraid that if it made the names public, the programmers would be hired away by other video game companies.

## BREAKOUT

So Atari's top programmers quit and formed their own video game company, called Activision, then turned around and began selling VCS-compatible games that competed directly against Atari's own titles.

Activision dealt a huge blow to Atari, and not just because Activision's games were better. Atari's entire marketing strategy was based around pricing the VCS console as cheaply as possible—$199—then reaping huge profits from sales of its high-priced game cartridges. Now the best games were being made by Activision.

Atari sued Activision several times to try to block it from making games for the VCS but lost every time, and Activision kept cranking out hit after hit. By 1982 Activision was selling $150 million worth of cartridges a year and had replaced Atari as the fastest growing company in the United States.

## THE ATARI GLUT

Activision's spectacular success encouraged other Atari programmers to defect and form *their* own video game companies, and it also prompted dozens of other companies—even Quaker Oats—to begin making games for the VCS.

Many of these games were terrible, and most of the companies that made them soon went out business. But that only made things worse for Atari, because when the bad companies went out

**Partly foggy? The first TV weather chart was broadcast in Britain on November 11, 1936.**

of business, their game cartridges were dumped on the market for as little as $9.99 apiece. If people wanted good games, they bought them from Activision. If they wanted cheap games, they pulled them out of the discount bin. Not many people bought Atari's games, and when the cheap games proved disappointing, consumers blamed Atari.

Meanwhile, just as Bushnell had feared, over the next few years, new game systems like Mattel's Intellivision and Coleco's ColecoVision came on the market and began chiseling away at Atari's market share. With state-of-the-art hardware and computer chips, these game systems had higher-resolution graphics and offered animation and sound that were nearly as good as arcade video games…and vastly superior to the VCS. Adding insult to injury, both ColecoVision and Intellivision offered adapters that would let buyers play the entire library of VCS games, which meant that if consumers wanted to jump ship to Atari's competitors, they could take their old games with them.

## EATEN BY PAC-MAN

But what really finished Atari off was Pac-Man. In April 1982, Atari released the home version of Pac-Man in what was probably the most anticipated video game release in history. At the time, there were about 10 million VCS systems on the market, but Atari manufactured 12 million cartridges, assuming that new consumers would buy the VCS just to play Pac-Man.

Big mistake—Atari's Pac-Man didn't live up to its hype. It was a flickering piece of junk that didn't look or sound anything like the arcade version. It wasn't worth the wait. Atari ended up selling only 7 million cartridges, and many of these were returned by outraged customers demanding refunds.

## ATARI PHONE HOME

Then Atari followed its big bomb with an even bigger bomb: E.T., The Extra-Terrestrial. Atari guaranteed Steven Spielberg a $25 million royalty for the game, then rushed it out in only six weeks so that it would be in stores in time for Christmas (video games typically took at least six *months* to develop). Then they manufactured five million cartridges without knowing if consumers would take any interest in the game.

**Q: What do you get when you cross a sheep with a goat?…**

They didn't. The slap-dash E.T. was probably the worst product Atari had ever made, worse even than Pac-Man. Nearly all of the cartridges were returned by consumers and retailers. Atari ended up dumping millions of Pac-Man and E.T. game cartridges in a New Mexico landfill and then having them crushed with steamrollers and buried under tons of cement.

## TOO LITTLE, TOO LATE

That same year Atari finally got around to doing what Nolan Bushnell had wanted to do since 1978: they released a new game system, the Atari 5200.

But in the face of stiff competition from ColecoVision, which came out with Donkey Kong (the 5200 didn't) and had better graphics and animation, it bombed. Staggering from the failures of Pac-Man, E.T., and the 5200, Atari went on to lose more than $536 million in 1983.

## THE LAST BIG MISTAKE

In 1983 Atari had what in retrospect might have been a chance to revive its sagging fortunes... but it blew that opportunity, too. Nintendo, creators of Donkey Kong, decided to bring its popular Famicom (short for Family Computer) game system to the United States. The Famicom was Nintendo's first attempt to enter the American home video game market, and rather than go it alone, the company wanted help. It offered Atari a license not just to sell the Famicom in every country of the world except Nintendo's home market of Japan, but also to sell it under the Atari brand name. Consumers would never even know that the game was a Nintendo. In return, Nintendo would receive a royalty for each unit sold and would have unrestricted rights to create games for the system.

Atari and Nintendo negotiated for three days, but nothing ever came of it. Nintendo decided to go it alone—and it was a good choice.

***Free replay. Turn to page 347 for more video game history: "Let's Play Nintendo!"***

* * *

"When things go wrong... don't go with them." —**Anonymous**

# NO CAN(ADA) DO

*Many of our Canadian readers have sent us items about life in the Great White North... including some strange Canadian laws. Here are a few examples.*

In Canada, it's illegal to jump from a flying airplane without a parachute.

In Nova Scotia, you're not allowed to water the lawn when it is raining.

In Toronto, it's illegal to drag a dead horse along Yonge Street on Sunday.

A maritime law in Canada specifies that two vessels cannot occupy the same space at the same time.

In Quebec, margarine must be a different color from butter.

The city of Guelph, Ontario, is classified as a "no-pee zone."

In Montreal, you may not park a car in such a way that it is blocking your own driveway.

It's illegal to ride a Toronto streetcar on Sunday if you've been eating garlic.

In Alberta, wooden logs may not be painted.

It is illegal to kill a Sasquatch in British Columbia.

An Etobicoke, Ontario, bylaw states that no more than 3.5 inches of water is allowed in a bathtub.

In Charlottetown, Prince Edward Island, you can only buy liquor with a doctor's prescription.

Burnaby, BC, has a 10 p.m. curfew—for dogs.

An anti-noise ordinance in Ottawa makes it illegal for bees to buzz.

Pedestrians on Toronto sidewalks must give a hand signal before turning.

In Vancouver, BC, it's illegal to ride a tricycle over 10 mph.

It is illegal to sell antifreeze to Indians in Quebec.

Tightrope walking over the main streets of Halifax is prohibited. (Side streets are okay.)

**40% of the world's newspapers are printed on paper that comes from Canadian forests.**

# THE WORLD'S FIRST DISPOSABLE DIAPER

*With everything we've sent through the pipeline in 15 years of* Bathroom Readers, *it's amazing that we've never gotten around to telling the story of the disposable diaper. Here it is at last.*

## NOT AGAIN

One afternoon in the late 1940s, a young mother named Marion Donovan changed her daughter's cloth diaper... only to see the baby wet the new diaper, her clothes, and her crib bedding all over again just a few minutes later. Traditional cloth diapers weren't like modern disposable diapers—the wetness and goo immediately soaked through, soiling everything the baby came in contact with. Rubber baby pants could be used to hold in the moisture, but they caused terrible diaper rash because they didn't allow the baby's skin to breathe.

## CURTAIN CALL

There weren't any other solutions... until Donovan glanced over at her waterproof shower curtain and something clicked. She realized the curtain material would make an excellent outer cover for cloth diapers. If the cover was made properly, it would hold in moisture but would also breathe better than rubber, preventing diaper rash. She cut out a piece of the shower curtain, took it to her sewing machine, and started sewing.

It took Donovan three years (and a lot of shower curtains) to perfect her design for waterproof diaper covers. She ended up switching to nylon parachute cloth instead of shower curtains. She also added snaps, so that mothers didn't have to worry about sticking their babies with safety pins.

Donovan jokingly named her diaper covers Boaters—since the covers didn't leak they kept babies "afloat"—and she convinced Saks Fifth Avenue to begin carrying them in 1949. They were an immense hit, and in 1951 Donovan sold the rights to her diaper covers for $1 million.

**Trying to call a ship in the eastern Atlantic? Use area code 871. Western Atlantic? Try 874.**

## SO CLOSE...AND YET SO FAR

But she wasn't done yet. Donovan then came up with the idea that turned out to be the Holy Grail of modern motherhood: diapers made from absorbant paper instead of cloth, allowing them to be thrown away instead of washed and reused.

So are today's disposable diapers direct descendants of Donovan's idea? Nope—when Donovan went around to the big paper companies and tried to get them interested in paper diapers, they all thought she was nuts.

Disposable diapers had to wait until 1959, when a Procter & Gamble employee named Vic Mills invented his own disposable diaper for his grandson, apparently without even knowing that Donovan had beaten him to the task by nearly a decade. It was Mills's diaper, not Donovan's, that P&G introduced as "Pampers" in 1961.

No matter—Donovan was number one, and she's the person historians credit as the inventor of the world's first disposable diaper.

*    *    *

## THE OLD REVOLVING-TROOPS TRICK

In September 1864, Civil War General Nathan Forrest was leading his Confederate troops north from Alabama toward Tennessee. He planned to attack the Union post in Athens, Alabama, having heard that Union reinforcements were approaching and wanted to take the fort before they arrived. The problem: the post was well manned and heavily fortified. Forrest was greatly outnumbered, but he had a plan.

He sent a message to Union commander Campbell requesting a personal meeting. Campbell agreed to the meeting. Forrest then escorted Campbell on a tour of the Confederate troops, during which Campbell silently calculated the number of troops and artillery surrounding his fort. What he didn't realize was that Forrest's men—after being inspected and tallied—were quietly packing everything up and quickly moving to a new position, to be counted again. Campbell was seeing the same troops over and over again. Assuming he was vastly outnumbered by the Confederates, he returned to his fort, pulled down the Union flag and gave up without a fight.

**High pressure: A pumping human heart can squirt blood as far as 30 feet.**

# *SNL* PART IV: "WELL ISN'T THAT SPECIAL"

*Part III of our history of* Saturday Night Live *(page 220) ended with the show once again in shambles—no producer, low ratings, an unhappy cast. It needed a lot of help. Who better to save it then the man who created it?*

## NEW BEGINNING

Lorne Michaels returned to NBC in 1984 to develop a new show for Friday nights called…*The New Show.* He was having trouble trying to make it as good as *SNL* without copying his original show—and it showed. *The New Show* limped along for 12 weeks getting low ratings and poor reviews. Michaels decided he'd had enough of television. A film that he co-wrote with Randy Newman and Steve Martin, *The Three Amigos*, had just started filming when NBC president Brandon Tartikoff called and offered him his old job back at *SNL*. Michaels initially turned him down, but when Tartikoff threatened to cancel the show instead, he relented and moved back into his old office on the 17th floor of Rockefeller Plaza. The first order of business: hiring a new cast.

## SATURDAY NIGHT DEAD #2

NBC called the 1985–86 season a rebuilding year—most fans and critics called it a disaster. Michaels experimented with established Brat Pack stars Robert Downey, Jr., Anthony Michael Hall, and Joan Cusack, as well as veteran actor Randy Quaid. Everyone else he added was a no-name. Nothing seemed to click.

What went wrong? Among other things, NBC executives had decided that the show was too important to leave alone, so the 17th floor was invaded by "strange men with clipboards" scribbling secret notes to take back upstairs. The writers now had to get network approval for any even slightly taboo subject. They blamed their unfunny scripts on an un-funny cast.

Was it the scripts or the cast? Either way, what resulted was a string of shows met with dead silence from the studio audience and shrinking ratings from the television audience. Toward the season's end, Tartikoff couldn't take it anymore—he decided to put *Saturday Night Live* out of its misery. Michaels flew to Los Angeles to reassure Tartikoff that the show would rebound, that there were bright spots emerging. Tartikoff agreed to give him one more season to turn it around.

The bright spots Michaels was referring to were the only three cast members who would survive that season: Nora Dunn, Jon Lovitz, and Dennis Miller.

## BACK TO THE DRAWING BOARD

Having learned his lesson of hiring names over talent, Michaels returned to his 1975 tactics and once again scoured the improv circuit. Now his main goal was to see not only who was funny, but also who worked well with others.

The first new cast member hired for the 1986 season was stand-up comedian Dana Carvey. Michaels was impressed by Carvey's talent for impressions, as well as his brain full of ideas and characters. Michaels also found Jan Hooks, Victoria Jackson, Kevin Nealon, and a young Canadian comic named Mike Myers. (As a boy in 1972, Myers had starred in a TV commercial—his mother was played by Gilda Radner.)

The cast was completed by Phil Hartman. His versatility in front of the camera is well documented, but what was even more important for the show's renewed success was what he added backstage. "Phil was a rock," remembers Jan Hooks. Jon Lovits called him a "big brother." "He was my mentor," said Mike Myers. Now Studio 8H had something it had sorely been lacking: a family atmosphere—and it showed in front of the camera.

## SCHWING!

As in the past, memorable recurring characters and political satire propelled the show, and *Saturday Night Live* enjoyed its third golden age. A few standouts:

• Dana Carvey's Church Lady, Garth, and George Bush. On Bush: At first, "I couldn't do him at all…but then one night I just sort of hooked it, and it was that phrase 'that thing out there, that guy out there, doin' that thing,' and from there on it was easy."

• Mike Myers's Simon, Sprockets, and *Wayne's World*. Conan O'Brien, a writer for the show from 1988 to 1991, recalls Myers's first week: "He came to us and said he had this character named Wayne who had a cable show in his basement. We politely told him that we didn't think it was his best idea...I felt sorry for him. I thought, 'This poor kid is going to have to learn the hard way.'" But Michaels liked the character and later worked with Myers in 1992 to produce a feature film based on it. *Wayne's World* was the only movie derived from an *SNL* sketch to earn over $100 million.

• John Lovitz's compulsive liar Tommy Flannagin and Master Thespian. He created the character when he was 18 but never thought it would work on *SNL*. "I was just goofing around," he remembers, "saying 'I'm Master Thespian!' And now they've built an entire set for it."

• Phil Hartman's Frank Sinatra. Joe Piscopo, who'd done Sinatra on the show 10 years before, says that the Sinatra family hated Hartman's impression. "I think there's some kind of law: Don't even attempt to do Sinatra unless you're Italian."

## TOO MANY PEOPLE

In his quest to create stars, Michaels continued packing the stage with featured players. He struck gold in 1990 and 1991 by adding a slew of comics who had grown up watching *SNL*: Tim Meadows, Adam Sandler, Rob Schneider, David Spade, Chris Rock, Chris Farley, Ellen Cleghorne, and Julia Sweeney. The opening credits in 1991 seemed to go on forever, and there were more people backstage than ever before.

In fact, viewers barely noticed when Carvey, Lovitz, and Hartman left the show because the new, younger performers were catering to a new, even younger audience, taking on subjects such as shopping malls, frat parties, and MTV.

Sandler, Rock, and Farley emerged as the new big stars. In addition to bringing back much of the rebellious anything-can-happen comedy that recalled the early days, the young cast members brought back another backstage tradition: drugs. Especially Farley, who did everything in excess. (Unfortunately for him, his hero was John Belushi. Both died of drug overdoses at the age of 33.)

Most critics called *SNL* in the early-1990s a "juvenile" show, but that was fine by NBC. The 18 to 34 demographic brought in the highest advertising dollars—and the show remained high in the ratings...for a while.

**When you do something on the "Q.T." you are using an abbreviation of the word quiet.**

## SATURDAY NIGHT DEAD #3

By 1995 the writers were finding it increasingly tough to find new material for overused characters, which resulted in yet another a succession of seemingly endless and pointless skits. Once again, the show had become difficult to watch. The network pressured *SNL* to clean house one more time, and Michaels agreed:

> No one anywhere was saying, "*SNL* is doing what it's supposed to be doing," or "These people are funny." So we had to let Adam Sandler go with two years on his contract, and Farley with a year. And Chris Rock had gone on to do *In Living Color*.

It was time for a new cast.

***The roller-coaster ride continues. To read about SNL's long crawl back to the top, go to page 338.***

*    *    *

## DEEP THOUGHTS BY JACK HANDEY

• The face of a child can say it all, especially the mouth part of the face."

• "For mad scientists who keep brains in jars, here's a tip: Why not add a slice of lemon to each jar, for freshness."

• "I wish I had a kryptonite cross, because then you could keep both Dracula and Superman away."

• "Can't the Marx Brothers be arrested and maybe even tortured for all the confusion and problems they've caused?"

• "The crows were all calling to him, thought Caw."

• "Why do the caterpillar and the ant have to be enemies? One eats leaves, and the other eats caterpillars.... Oh, I see now."

• "Consider the daffodil. And while you're doing that, I'll be over here, looking through your stuff."

• "Instead of a Seeing Eye dog, what about a gun? It's cheaper than a dog, plus if you walk around shooting all the time, people are going to get out of the way. Cars, too."

# NAME THAT CITY

*Here's a game: a lot of American cities have had other names throughout their histories. Can you guess which are which?*

| FORMER NAME | PRESENT NAME |
|---|---|
| **1.** Fort Dallas | **a.** Austin, TX |
| **2.** Hot Springs | **b.** Cleveland, OH |
| **3.** Yerba Buena | **c.** New York, NY |
| **4.** Fort Dearborn | **d.** Baltimore, MD |
| **5.** Lancaster | **e.** Charleston, SC |
| **6.** Terminus | **f.** Atlanta, GA |
| **7.** Cole's Harbor | **g.** Chicago, IL |
| **8.** Waterloo | **h.** Miami, FL |
| **9.** Willingtown | **i.** Minneapolis, MN |
| **10.** Quinnipiac | **j.** Truth or Consequences, NM |
| **11.** Assunpink | **k.** Reno, NV |
| **12.** Rumford | **l.** Milwaukee, WI |
| **13.** Oyster Point | **m.** Lincoln, NE |
| **14.** New Netherland | **n.** San Francisco, CA |
| **15.** St. Charles | **o.** Denver, CO |
| **16.** Fort Pontchartrain | **p.** Wilmington, DE |
| **17.** All Saints | **q.** Concord, NH |
| **18.** Juneautown | **r.** Detroit, MI |
| **19.** Lake Crossing | **s.** Trenton, NJ |
| **20.** New Connecticut | **t.** New Haven, CT |

**Answers**

1. h; 2. j; 3. n; 4. g; 5. m; 6. f; 7. d; 8. a; 9. p; 10. t; 11. s;
12. q; 13. e; 14. c; 15. o; 16. r; 17. i; 18. l; 19. k; 20. b

**In St. Louis, Missouri, it's illegal to drink beer from a bucket when you're sitting at the curb.**

# AS SEEN ON TV

*It wasn't long ago that when you saw a product advertised on TV, you went to the store to buy it. Then came the infomercial. Here's the quintessential infomercial success story, the true tale of a washed-up producer who paired a washed-up product with a washed-up celebrity...and made a fortune.*

## THE WANDERER

For most people it isn't easy figuring out what to do with your life. For Peter Bieler, a Canadian who graduated from college in the mid-1960s, it was next to impossible.

First he wanted to devote his life to spiritualism and lived a monk-like existence of prayer, meditation, and self-denial. But he got tired of that after a couple of years, so he found a job with the consumer products giant Procter & Gamble. He tired of that a few years later, so he went to film school, then managed a rock concert hall in Los Angeles, then landed a job with a TV producer.

After that he got a job at the American Film Institute, after which he decided to become an independent film producer. That turned out to be harder than he thought it would be, so he tried out a job with a company making specialty videos. VCRs were still pretty new, and he was hoping to cash in on the boom.

By now it was 1986. Bieler had spent about 20 years figuring out what to do with his life, and he still hadn't figured it out.

## DOWN THE HALL

Bieler struggled at making videos, too; even his most successful production, *The Eight-Week Cholesterol Cure*, hosted by Larry King, was a dud. His whole division was losing money. "I had no budget for promotion or marketing," Bieler writes in his book *This Business Has Legs*. "All this hard work, and the videos just sat on the shelf and collected dust. It was frustrating."

The company where Bieler worked also had its own production studio that it rented to outside producers. It was constantly buzzing with activity, and one day Bieler went to see what was going on.

## EASY MONEY

The studio was being rented by a man named Tony Hoffman to produce a two-hour infomercial called *Everybody's Money Matters*. Hoffman and his co-host Bob Braun sold their own books and also interviewed other authors selling the same kinds of get-rich-quick books and tapes: how to buy property with no money down, how to get low-interest loans from the government, etc. The show aired on cable at night when airtime was cheap, so it cost only about $7,500 to broadcast the two-hour show nationwide.

And on a good night the show generated more than $80,000 in cash sales of books and tapes direct to the public through the show's 800 number—a heck of a lot more than Bieler's division was making by selling videos to retail outlets.

Bieler went to his boss and suggested that the company itself get into the infomercial business instead of just renting out the studio to outside producers. His boss wasn't interested, so Bieler formed his own company, which he named Ovation. But what would he sell?

Rather than try and invent something on his own, Bieler went to county fairs, home and garden shows, any place where he thought pitchmen might be demonstrating new products to live audiences. He finally settled on a chemical powder that turned spilled liquids into dried slush, which could then be vacuumed or scooped up by hand. He named the product "Gone." It was interesting stuff, but it couldn't do anything that paper towels couldn't do for a lot less money. The infomercial bombed.

## THE V-TONER

Bieler looked around for another product to sell. He found it with help from an entrepreneur named Josh Reynolds, who had made a fortune in the 1970s inventing the "mood ring," a ring that changed colors according to changes in body temperature, supposedly revealing your mood.

Reynolds wasn't having much luck with a new product he was trying to market, an exerciser invented by a Los Angeles chiropractor to help skiers with broken legs maintain the tone in their good leg while the broken one healed. Called the "V-Toner," the product was little more than two foam-padded triangular handles extending from a central steel spring to form a V-shaped angle.

**The swine flu vaccine of 1976 caused more sickness and death than the flu itself did.**

When you squeezed the two handles together, the spring in the center provided resistance, which helped build muscle tone.

The original inventor had managed to sell a few V-Toners, but Reynolds's advertising campaign, which marketed it as a "gym-in-a-bag," was a dud. Even though the product was an old dog, he still thought it had potential. Looking for new investors and new ideas, he found Bieler, who agreed to give it a shot.

## THE MAIN SQUEEZE

Bieler took home the commercials that Reynolds had already made and watched them to figure out what had gone wrong. They weren't bad, but they weren't great, either. Bieler decided to make some changes.

• Rather than pitch it as an all-in-one, gym-in-a-bag product, he decided to emphasize one particular benefit: the fact that women could use it to tone and improve the appearance of their hips and thighs. (He also thought that video footage of sexy women exercising their thighs would make for compelling television.)

• The product's new name: ThighMaster.

• Its new spokesperson: Suzanne Somers. Somers was a familiar face who would get the channel-surfers to stop and pay attention. He wanted someone in her mid-forties, the same age as the customers he was targeting. Somers was famous for her role as Chrissy on the TV show *Three's Company*. She was written out of the show in 1980 over a pay dispute, and since then her TV career had been struggling. Her sitcom *She's the Sheriff* had failed miserably, and by 1986 it was questionable whether she would ever get another shot at primetime again. Still, for Bieler's purposes she was the right age, the viewers knew who she was, and she was in great shape. She was perfect, and she took the job.

## UP, UP AND AWAY

Two measures are used to gauge the success of an infomercial: 1) the number of broadcasting markets in which it earns more money than it costs to put the infomercial on the air, and 2) how well it works in different time slots. "ThighMaster was a colossal hit by both definitions," Bieler says. "It worked everywhere. All the time." ThighMasters started out selling at a rate of 2,000 units a week, then grew to 7,500 a week. But Bieler wanted more.

**Speedy delivery: For every post office the in U.S., India has four.**

## OFF THE SHELF

Bieler knew from his research that only a fraction of viewers who see an infomercial will actually want to buy the product, and only 20% of these willing buyers will actually order the product over the phone. The rest—80%—wait until the product arrives in retail stores…and if it never arrives, they never buy.

Bieler wanted that 80%, so he took his infomercial profits and set up a nationwide sales force that would help to place the ThighMaster in stores like Wal-Mart, Kmart, and Target. The job was made easier by the fact that infomercial viewers all over the country were walking into retailers asking to purchase Thigh-Masters, only to go home empty-handed…and disappointed. When the salespeople came knocking, the retailers jumped at the chance to stock ThighMasters.

## LARGER THAN LIFE

Sales soared again—this time to 75,000 units per week. The product broke sales records at Wal-Mart, Kmart, Target, and Woolworths, and in the process it became a cultural phenomenon: David Letterman and Jay Leno joked about it in their monologues, and it began popping up as a pop-culture reference in movies and sitcoms. Suzanne Sommers became a popular guest on talk shows again; even President George H. W. Bush joked to reporters that his chubby press secretary, Marlin Fitzwater, should use the Thigh-Master.

## DISASTER-MASTER

In its first two years in business, Bieler's company sold more than $100 million worth of ThighMasters, an unprecedented success.

• So where's Bieler now? In 1993 he had a falling-out with his business partner and left Ovation forever.

• Where's Suzanne Somers now? She never did get another hit TV series, but she's done very well with infomercials for products like the Torso Track and the Facemaster.

• And where's Ovation now? It's gone. In 1995 the company, which launched one of the most successful infomercial products in history, closed its doors and filed for bankruptcy. How did *that* happen? Your guess is as good as ours…or Bieler's.

"I don't know," he laments. "I wish I did."

**Celebrity sighting: Drew Carey once worked in Las Vegas. He was a waiter at Denny's.**

# WHERE THERE'S A WILL...

*Ben Franklin is famous for the maxim "A penny saved is a penny earned." But for Ben, that was a lot easier in death than it had been in life.*

## DO AS I SAY, NOT AS I DO

For all his preaching about the importance of frugality, Franklin never practiced it. As U.S. ambassador to France in the late 1700s, he was living in Paris at taxpayer expense. And that expense ran to an astonishing $12,000 per year, including a collection of more than 1,000 bottles of the finest French wines and lavish gifts of carpets, fine china, and other luxuries that he sent to friends and loved ones back home. Spending money wisely, Franklin admitted in 1782, was "a virtue I never could acquire myself."

...at least not while he was alive.

## INVESTING IN THE FUTURE

In 1785 a French mathematician named Charles-Joseph Mathon de la Cour wrote *The Testament of Fortunate Richard*, a parody of the folksy American optimism in Franklin's *Poor Richard's Almanack*. In the parody, Fortunate Richard sets aside a small amount of money in his will with instructions that it be put to good use only after it has collected interest for 500 years.

When Franklin read the story, rather than being offended, he wrote back to Mathon de la Cour *thanking* him for the idea. Sure enough, when the 83-year-old Franklin updated his will in 1789, he left £1,000 (about $4,400) to his hometown of Boston, and another £1,000 to Philadelphia, where he'd worked as a printer and made much of his fortune. (Why British pounds? They were still the most popular currency in the United States in the 1780s.)

In the will, Franklin gave these specific instructions as to how his money should be managed over the next 200 years:

- For the first 100 years, each city was supposed to lend the

**Only 1% of Americans say they are "much worse" at raising kids than their parents were.**

money out to apprentice tradesmen "under the age of twenty-five years," to assist them in setting up their own businesses. (Franklin had set up his own printing business with money borrowed from two benefactors, and he wanted to repay the favor by doing the same thing for other tradesmen.)

• The loans were to be repaid over 10 years with interest and the money lent right back out again.

• Franklin estimated that after a century of earning interest, the Boston and Philadelphia funds would grow to £131,000 ($576,400) each.

• For the second 100 years, Franklin's will directed each city to spend 75% of the fund (about £100,000 or $440,000) on public works, and continue to lend out the remaining 25% as before.

## ROUND TWO

Franklin estimated that over the second 100 years, the £31,000 ($136,400) in each fund would grow to £4 million at which point he wanted each city to turn over 75% of the money to its respective state—Boston to Massachusetts, and Philadelphia to Pennsylvania—to spend without restriction. Each city could keep the remaining 25% also to spend without restriction.

Franklin died on April 17, 1790, at the age of 85. That would mean that the money came due in the 1990s...so what happened to it?

## WILL-POWER

Both Boston and Philadelphia accepted Franklin's money, but things didn't go as Franklin had hoped. The will specified that the money had to be lent to apprenticed tradesmen. But the apprentice system faded away during the Industrial Revolution, and tradesmen increasingly went to work for large industrial companies instead of setting up their own shops.

The number of loan applicants dropped sharply, even when the program was expanded to include tradesmen who *weren't* apprentices. And the loans they did make were seldom repaid. By 1831 the Boston fund was averaging only one new loan a year.

By the end of the first 100 years, nothing had worked out according to Franklin's plan. The Boston fund was worth only

**Top 3 things men lie about on a date: 1) willingness to commit, 2) interest in more than sex...**

70% of what Franklin had expected, and the funds shrank even further because politicians were dipping in it to pay for "business trips." In 1904, 75% of the fund was used to found a trade school called the Franklin Union, now known as the Benjamin Franklin Institute of Technology. The rest was loaned out and reinvested.

Philadelphia's fund fared even worse—it was only worth $173,000, less than half the value of the Boston fund. The city spent $133,000 on a museum called the Franklin Institute and continued lending the balance out for another 100 years, just as Franklin had instructed.

## STILL, NOT BAD

A hundred years later, in 1991, the money in the Boston fund had grown to $5 million. The Philadelphia fund wasn't as lucky: its investments had only grown to $2.2 million. Since the term of Franklin's will had expired, all the money was to be divided up and spent. What happened to it?

• After a legal fight, nearly all of the Boston funds—both the state's share and the city's—were donated to the Franklin Institute of Technology.

• The state of Pennsylvania distributed its share of the money to community foundations and gave $165,000 to the Franklin Institute Museum.

• Philadelphia Mayor Wilson Goode proposed spending his city's share of the money on a huge party celebrating Franklin's contributions. But so many people attacked that idea as being against the spirit of Franklin's bequest that he backed off and appointed a panel of Franklin scholars to think of something better. They set up a scholarship program for graduating Philadelphia high school graduates who want to study crafts, trades, and applied sciences.

Ultimately, Franklin got a lot of bang for his buck, and 200 years after his death, he finally proved that a penny saved really *is* a penny earned.

*   *   *

## A TALE OF TWO PRESIDENTS

President Jimmy Carter had solar panels installed to heat water in the White House. President Ronald Reagan had them taken out.

**...and 3) income. More bad news: The prettier the date, the more likely the man will lie.**

# THE PROFESSOR'S "INVENTIONS"

*It's one of TV's eternal mysteries: Here he was stranded on Gilligan's Island with no tools and no power. Yet the Professor was such a genius that he could invent virtually anything... except a boat. Stupefying. Well, here's a list of some of the things he* did *invent.*

• Lie detector (made from the ship's horn, the radio's batteries, and bamboo)

• Bamboo telescope

• Jet pack fuel

• Paralyzing strychnine serum

• "Spider juice" (to kill a giant spider)

• Nitroglycerine

• Shark repellent

• Helium balloon (rubber raincoats sewn together and sealed with tree sap)

• Coconut-shell battery recharger

• Xylophone

• Soap (made from plant fats, it's not really so far-fetched)

• Roulette wheel

• Geiger counter (*that's* far-fetched)

• Pedal-powered bamboo sewing machine

• Pedal-powered washing machine

• Keptibora-berry extract (to cure Gilligan's double vision)

• Pedal-powered water pump

• Pedal-powered telegraph

• Hair tonic

• Pedal-powered generator

• Various poisons and antidotes

• Pool table (for Mr. Howell)

• Lead radiation suits and lead-based makeup (protection against a meteor's cosmic rays)

# WHAT'S ALL THE BUZZ ABOUT?

*Most people are afraid of bees—hey, they sting. But bees aren't merely pests—they're an essential part of the ecosystem. Consider this: One-third of the average human diet comes from plants that depend on insects to pollinate them, and honeybees perform 80% of that pollination.*

## BUSY AS A BEE

Honeybees are real workhorses. A typical bee visits—and pollinates—between 50 and 100 flowers in a single foraging trip from the hive... and never visits the same flower twice. On average, a honeybee flies 500 miles over the course of its lifetime at an average speed of 15 mph—the human equivalent to traveling twice around the circumference of Earth. And they carry loads up to half their body weight while doing it. There's one simple reason for all that activity: They're collecting food.

## MOTHER NATURE'S PLAN

Here's how it works: Honeybees fly from flower to flower to collect nectar. At a flower, they use their proboscis, or long sucking mouth, to drink the flower's nectar. They store the nectar in a special "honey stomach," which sits next to their regular stomach, then fly back to their hive. Once back in the hive, they spit the nectar into one of the honeycomb cells. Other bees then suck it up and regurgitate it—a process that gets repeated up to 50 times. The combination of water evaporation and enzymes from the bees' saliva creates honey.

In the process of collecting nectar, honeybees also collect pollen. They do this by rubbing up against the flower's *anther*—its male apparatus. Their body hairs brush the pollen into pollen "baskets," which sit on the bees' hind legs; some of the pollen also gets stuck to their body hair. Back in the hive, the pollen that's stuck on their hair gets mixed with different types of pollen by brushing against other bees; outside the hive, it gets mixed by entering different flowers. Either way, the process contributes to

**32% of managers say being "too young-looking" can make a salesperson's job more difficult.**

cross-pollination—the fertilizing of one flower with pollen from another flower... which produces fruit.

## THINKING AHEAD

It also contributes to the bees' diet. Honeybees eat both the pollen and the nectar they collect from flowers. The pollen provides their protein, fat, vitamins, and minerals for growth and reproduction; the nectar provides sugar for energy. Adult bees convert some of the pollen into a milk that they secrete from glands in their heads to feed to their larvae.

And what do the bees do with their honey? They store it for use as food during seasons when flowers don't bloom—winters in temperate climates; rainy spells or droughts in tropical climates. When lots of nectar-producing flowers blossom, bees store much more honey than they could ever eat.

## SWEET HARVEST

Honey harvested by beekeepers is collected in at least two ways: liquid honey is extracted from honeycombs by machine; comb honey is collected while it's still in the original wax combs made by the bees (this honey is less adaptable to cooking but is preferred by connoisseurs).

* * *

# I WANNA BEE AN ENGINEER

Bees collect not only nectar and pollen but also water. They don't drink the water—they use it to air-condition the hive on hot days by spreading it on every surface and fanning it with their wings. When a worker bee arrives back at the hive bearing a load of food, house bees meet it and take the food from him to be stored. Generally, returning bees bearing food are relieved of their loads immediately; those carrying only water have to wait. However, researchers once deliberately turned up the heat under a hive. As the temperature slowly and steadily rose, bees bringing water were greeted at once while those bringing food were ignored. So effective is the evaporative method of air-conditioning that a bee colony on a lava field kept their hive at a constant temperature of 97°F as the surrounding air temperature soared to 140°F.

**In 2002 runner Tom Johnson ran an 80-km. race against a horse... and beat it by 10 seconds.**

# YAH-HAH, EVIL SPIDER WOMAN!

*Until recently, law required all movies made in Hong Kong to have English subtitles. But producers spent as little on translations as possible... and it shows. These gems are from the book* Sex and Zen & a Bullet in the Head, *by Stefan Hammond and Mike Wilkins.*

"Take my advice, or I'll spank you without pants."

"Fatty, you with your thick face have hurt my instep."

"You always use violence. I should've ordered glutinous rice chicken."

"Who gave you the nerve to get killed here?"

"This will be of fine service for you, you bag of the scum. I am sure you will not mind that I remove your toenails and leave them out on the dessert floor for ants to eat."

"A normal person wouldn't steal pituitaries."

"That may disarray my intestines."

"The bullets inside are very hot. Why do I feel so cold?"

"Beware! Your bones are going to be disconnected."

"I am darn unsatisfied to be killed in this way."

"If you don't eat people, they'll eat you."

"She's terrific. I can't stand her."

"Darn, I'll burn you into a BBQ chicken."

"I'll cut your fats out, don't you believe it?"

"Sex fiend, you'll never get reincarnated!"

"How can I make love without TV?"

"I got knife scars more than the number of your leg's hair!"

"Yah-hah, evil spider woman! I have captured you by the short rabbits and can now deliver you violently to your doctor for a thorough extermination."

"What is a soul? It's just a toilet paper."

**As of 2001, 2% of Americans still didn't have 911 service.**

# THE COTTON WAR

*Here's Part III of our story on Eli Whitney.*
*(Part II starts on page 167.)*

## NOT GONNA HAPPEN

Eli Whitney's cotton gin played a pivotal part in creating the pre–Civil War south as an economic power. Cotton had transformed the South from an underdeveloped, underpopulated wilderness into the home of America's largest cash crop. It enriched not only the South, which grew it, but also the North, which had its own fledgling textile industry, and whose merchants shipped it to England.

One of the ironies of the invention is that the wealth it helped create ultimately led to the Civil War and doomed the South to defeat. King Cotton gave Southerners a false sense of security. The North *needed* cotton, the thinking went, so how could it go to war against the South?

## THE BRITISH ARE COMING...AGAIN

And what about England, which imported 90% of its cotton from the South? Cotton fueled its economy too, and Southern leaders like Jefferson Davis (who would become president of the Confederacy in 1861), were convinced that if war did come, England would side with the South. England would have little choice but to use the Royal Navy to keep Southern ports open, so that its access to cotton would be guaranteed. The North knew this as well, the Southerners reasoned, and that made it even less likely that the Northern states would ever go to war over slavery. Fighting the South was one thing; fighting England *and* the South was another.

"You dare not make war upon our cotton," South Carolina Senator James Henry Hammond proclaimed in 1858. "No power on Earth dares make war on it. Cotton is King."

But when the war finally did come in April 1861, England didn't hesitate—it immediately declared its "strict and impartial neutrality" and then sat on the sidelines. Why? England didn't have to worry about cotton—the long, slow buildup to the Civil War had given English mills plenty of time to stockpile extra cotton. When that ran out, they would make do with what they could buy from countries like Egypt and India. And unemployment resulting from cotton shortages was tolerated, because many English textile workers opposed slavery and were willing to go without jobs to help end it.

## SLIP-SLIDING AWAY

Another nail in the coffin: The South's failure to expand its economy beyond a single cash crop left it vulnerable. The invention of the cotton gin had encouraged cotton cultivation not just in the southern United States, but all over the world, and as cotton plantations sprang up in other countries, the price of cotton began a long, steady slide throughout the 1850s.

For decades, Southern planters had reinvested their profits into expanding cotton production instead of diversifying into factories, textile mills, or anything else. As the price of cotton fell, plantations lost money. By the late 1850s, there was little cash available to diversify the Southern economy, even if the South had wanted to. It was too late.

## MASS PRODUCTION

In the North, things were different. Manufacturers of everything from doors and windows to nuts, bolts, shoes, plows, and grandfather clocks had adopted the principles of Eli Whitney's "American system," and were now using machine tools to mass-produce their wares. Soaring profits encouraged further investment and growth; from 1840 to 1860, the 100-mile-long region between Delaware and New York was the most rapidly industrializing region on Earth.

With the growth of industry came increased economic and military strength. By the start of the Civil War, factories in the North were producing goods at a rate of 10 times that of the South. For every ton of iron produced in the South, the North produced 15; for every firearm the South produced, the North manufactured 32. Northern states had more than twice the population of Southern states, and three times the wealth.

And though the South grew 24 times as much cotton as the North, the North had 14 times as many textile mills. So when war

**...A: So bad that as many as 4,000 people died from it.**

came in April 1861, it was the Union soldiers, not the Confederates, who were best outfitted for battle. Though the Civil War dragged on from 1861 to 1865, its outcome was a virtual certainty from the very beginning.

## ELI WHITNEY'S LEGACY

For a person who had never discovered a continent, never commanded an army, and never served as president, Eli Whitney had about as big an impact on American history as anyone. And unlike his fellow inventors Henry Ford and Alexander Graham Bell, *two* of his inventions altered the course of history, not just one.

Cotton gave the South its wealth and strengthened the institution of slavery, sparking the tensions that would lead to the Civil War. At the same time, cotton convinced Southerners that if war did come, its importance guaranteed that the South would never lose. And that made the South all the more willing to fight.

With the invention of mass production, Whitney gave the North the military might and economic strength that it used to destroy the South that the cotton gin had built.

"If Whitney's cotton gin enabled the slave-system to survive and thrive," writes historian Paul Johnson, "his 'American System' also gave the North the industrial muscle to crush the defenders of slavery in due course.... He is a fascinating example of the complex impact one man can have on history."

* * *

## SPECIAL DELIVERY

"Rome post-office workers were confronted by a group of men delivering a very big package, too big for the security hole that packages are normally slipped through. Ignoring security rules, employees asked the group to go to a service window behind the counter. As soon as they brought the package inside, a robber burst out of the carton, waved a gun, and shouted, 'It's a holdup.' The criminals escaped with 115,000 lira."

**—*Townsville Bulletin* (Australia)**

**Two most dangerous countries for journalists between 1992 and 2001: Algeria and Colombia.**

# THE REST OF THE REST OF THE UNITED STATES

*On page 147, we gave an overview of the commonwealths and territories owned by the United States. Here are some of the smaller, uninhabited islands and their stories. (Well, they may have a few inhabitants, but no natives.)*

## UNINHABITED U.S. TERRITORIES

### *Wake Island*

**Location:** North Pacific Ocean, between Hawaii and the Northern Mariana Islands

**Size:** Two and a half square miles

**Population:** 300

**Background:** Wake Island is an atoll made up of three islets around a shallow lagoon. It was discovered in 1796 by British sea captain William Wake. The United States annexed it in 1899 for a telegraph cable station. An airstrip and naval base were built in late 1940, but in December 1941 the island was captured by the Japanese and held until the end of World War II. Today the facilities are under the administration of the Federal Aviation Agency.

### *Kingman Reef*

**Location:** North Pacific Ocean, between Hawaii and American Samoa

**Size:** Less than one-half square mile

**Population:** Uninhabited

**Background:** The U.S. annexed this reef in 1922. There's no plant life on the reef (which is frequently under water) but it does support abundant and diverse marine life. In 2001 the waters surrounding the reef were designated a National Wildlife Refuge.

### *Midway Islands*

**Location:** North Pacific Ocean, north of Hawaii

**Size:** Less than two and a half square miles

**Population:** 150 U.S. Fish and Wildlife Service personnel

**When asked to name the odor that best defines America, 39% of Americans said "barbecue."**

**Background:** Part of the Hawaiian island chain, Midway was first discovered by a Hawaiian sea captain in 1859. At the urging of the North Pacific Mail and Steamship Company, which was looking for a coal depot for its Asian mail run, the U.S. Navy claimed the atoll for the United States in 1867. Midway is best known as the site of a U.S. naval victory over the Japanese fleet in 1942, one of the turning points of World War II. The naval station closed in 1993. Today the island is a wildlife refuge open to eco-tourists.

## GUANO ISLANDS

What is guano? Bird droppings. Fish-eating birds have been dropping their poop in the same spots for thousands of years. The result: huge deposits of guano, rich in nitrogen and phosphorous and highly valued as an agricultural fertilizer.

The Guano Act was enacted by the U.S. government in 1856. It authorized Americans to take "peaceable possession" of any uninhabited, unclaimed islands for the purpose of mining the guano. Nearly 100 islands were claimed for the United States under the act, mostly in the South Pacific. The U.S. still owns a half dozen—the others were abandoned or given up to other countries that claimed them. They're not really anybody's idea of paradise, so don't expect to see any postcards from these tiny islands. But some of these poop-covered rocks have interesting histories.

### *Navassa Island*

**Location:** Caribbean Sea, between Haiti and Jamaica

**Size:** Less than two and a half square miles

**Population:** No permanent residents

**Background:** The Baltimore-based Navassa Phosphate Company began mining guano in 1865, using convicts at first, then former slaves. In deplorable living conditions, the ex-slaves were forced to mine one and a half tons of guano per day for a daily wage of 50 cents. In 1889 they revolted, killing 15 white overseers. Forty workers were taken to Baltimore for trial. Acknowledging the basis for the uprising, the court sentenced only one worker to death—the rest were given life imprisonment. The Navassa Phosphate Company continued to mine guano until 1898.

In 1998 a California entrepreneur named Bill Warren filed a

claim under the Guano Act, obtained a deed from heirs of the Navassa Phosphate Company, and claimed ownership of the island. Predictably, the U.S. government denied his claim.

There is also a dispute between the U.S. and Haiti, which maintains that the island lies within its territorial boundary.

### *Howland Island*

**Location:** North Pacific Ocean, between Hawaii and Australia

**Size:** A little more than one-half square mile

**Population:** Uninhabited

**Background:** Claimed by the American Guano Company in 1858. Its other claim to fame: in 1937 an airstrip was built on the island as a stopover for aviation pioneer Amelia Earhart on her round-the-world flight. Earhart and her navigator took off from Lae, New Guinea, but never reached Howland. (The unexplained disappearance still intrigues conspiracy buffs.) Today Howland Island is a National Wildlife Refuge.

### *Baker Island*

**Location:** North Pacific Ocean, between Hawaii and Australia

**Size:** One-half square mile

**Population:** Uninhabited

**Background:** Named by an American whaler, Michael Baker, who found the island in 1832. Presently, it is a National Wildlife Refuge run by the U.S. Department of the Interior.

### *Johnston Atoll*

**Location:** North Pacific Ocean, 800 miles southwest of Hawaii

**Size:** One square mile of dry land; 50 square miles of shallow water

**Population:** 1,000 military and support personnel

**Background:** The four tiny islands were discovered in 1796 by an American sea captain.

During World War II, the military used Johnston Island, the largest of the four outcroppings, as a refueling point for aircraft and submarines. A few days after the attack on Pearl Harbor, Japanese submarines fired on military facilities there but caused no casualties.

The U.S. Air Force took over in 1948 and used the site for

**Snoring is legal in Massachusetts *only* when all bedroom windows are closed and locked.**

high-altitude nuclear tests in the 1950s and 1960s. In 1964 a series of open-air biological weapons tests were conducted near the atoll using several barges loaded with rhesus monkeys. Chemical weapons have been stored on Johnston Island since 1971, but the U.S. Army began destroying them in 1981. Munitions destruction is reportedly complete, and the Army plans to turn over the atoll to the U.S. Fish and Wildlife Service in 2003.

***Jarvis Island***

**Location:** South Pacific, between Hawaii and the Cook Islands

**Size:** Less than two square miles

**Population:** Uninhabited

**Background:** Discovered by the British in 1821; claimed by the American Guano Company in 1858; abandoned in 1879; annexed by Britain in 1889; abandoned soon after. Reclaimed by the United States in 1935. The island is currently a National Wildlife Refuge; a small group of buildings are occasionally occupied by scientists and weather researchers.

***Palmyra Atoll***

**Location:** North Pacific Ocean, 1,000 miles south of Hawaii

**Size:** Four and a half square miles

**Population:** Uninhabited

**Background:** This group of 54 islets is known for its lush natural beauty and biological diversity.

The first to land on the atoll were sailors from the American ship *Palmyra*, which was blown ashore during a storm in 1852. Though the American Guano Company claimed it, guano was never mined there. In 1862 King Kamehameha IV of Hawaii took possession of the atoll, which is actually a part of the Hawaiian archipelago. The United States included it when it annexed Hawaii in 1898, but when Hawaii became a state in 1959, Palmyra was excluded.

The 1974 murder of a yachting couple on Palmyra became the subject of a 1991 novel by Vincent Bugliosi (and a subsequent TV movie) entitled *And the Sea Will Tell*. Today the atoll is privately owned by the Nature Conservancy, which is managing it as a nature preserve.

# MR. GAME BOY

*You've probably never heard of Gumpei Yokoi, but if you've ever played a Game Boy, a Color Game Boy, Donkey Kong, or just about any other Nintendo product made between 1970 and 1996, you have him to thank for it. Here's his story.*

## IN THE CARDS

In the mid-1960s, an electronics student named Gumpei Yokoi graduated from Doshisha University in Kyoto, Japan, and got a job as a maintenance engineer with the Nintendo company, a manufacturer of playing cards.

Keeping the playing card printing machines in good working order must have been boring work, because Yokoi started passing the time building toys—with company materials, using company machines and equipment, on company time.

That didn't exactly fit into his job description, so when Nintendo's president, Hiroshi Yamauchi, found out what he was up to and called him into his office, Yokoi figured that he'd soon be looking for a new job.

Not quite—Nintendo was making so much money selling children's playing cards that it had decided to create an entire games division. Yamauchi transferred Yokoi to the new division, and told him to come up with a game that Nintendo could manufacture in time to sell for Christmas.

Yokoi went home and got one of the toys he'd already made: an extendable grabbing "hand" that he made out of crisscrossing pieces of wooden latticework. When you squeezed its handles together like a pair of scissors, the latticework extended and the hand closed its grip.

## YOU'VE GOT TO HAND IT TO HIM

Yamauchi was impressed, and production on the Ultra Hand, as they named it, began right away. The company ended up selling more than 1.2 million of the hands at a price of about $6 apiece—the games division's first toy was also its first big hit.

Yokoi's team followed with a series of other toys, including the Ultra Machine (an indoor pitching machine), the Ultra Scope (a periscope), and a "Love Tester" that supposedly measured how much love existed between a boy and a girl. All the Love Tester really did was give people an excuse to hold hands, but that was enough—it was a huge success too. So was the Beam Gun, a gun that shot beams of light at optical targets.

Nintendo spent a fortune converting old bowling alleys and shooting galleries into Beam Gun shooting galleries…and nearly went bankrupt. But it recovered after Yamauchi noticed how much money Atari, Magnavox, and other companies were making in the video game business. He licensed their technology and came out with Color TV Game 6, the company's first video game.

### GAME & WATCH

As video games were becoming more successful, Yamauchi started pressing Yokoi for a competing product. So the design team came up with the Game & Watch, a series of dozens and eventually hundreds of pocket-sized video games that also displayed the time at the top of the screen.

The games used simple calculator technology—LCD screens and tiny buttons that served as game controllers—and they weren't much bigger than credit cards. Kids could play them anywhere: in cars, at school during recess, or in their rooms before bedtime. Nintendo ended up selling more than 40 million of the devices all over the world between 1980 and 1989.

### GAME BOY

As we told you on page 296, Nintendo introduced the Famicom (short for Family Computer)—its first cartridge-based videogame system—in 1983 and then released it in the United States as the Nintendo Entertainment System (NES) in 1985. The system established the company as the dominant world player in the video game business. By 1988, however, the NES was getting a little old and Nintendo's rival Sega was preparing to launch a new system called the Mega Drive. Nintendo's new Super NES system was still in the works, so the company needed a product that would generate revenue and keep fans of the company's products occupied until Super NES was ready.

Lucky for Nintendo, Yokoi had one. Called the Game Boy, it sought to combine the best that the Game & Watch series and the NES had to offer. The Game Boy was portable, about the size of a transistor radio, and it was a cartridge-based system like the NES. With the Game & Watch series, anytime you wanted to play a new game, you had to buy a whole new Game & Watch. With a Game Boy, all you had to do was buy a new cartridge. Better yet, Game Boys could be linked together so that two players could compete against each other.

## LOW TECH

The Game Boy wasn't exactly state of the art. It didn't have a color screen or a backlight, because those drained the batteries too quickly and added too much to the cost. You couldn't play it in the dark. The screen was so crude, in fact, that when Atari's engineers saw it for the first time, they laughed. Over at Sony, the response was different. "This Game Boy should have been a Sony product," one executive complained.

The Game Boy went on to become hugely successful, thanks in large part to the fact that the game appealed to adults in a way that the NES didn't. The original Game Boy was packaged with Tetris, an adult-friendly, maddeningly addictive game in which the player has to maneuver and interlock blocks that fall from the top of the screen. Game Boys became a fixture on subways, on airplanes, in company lunchrooms, any place adults had a few free moments. When President George H. W. Bush went into the hospital in May 1991, the leader of the free world was photographed playing a Game Boy. Kids liked to play Game Boys too…whenever they could pry them away from their parents.

## NEW AND IMPROVED

Yokoi led the effort to keep the Game Boy product line fresh and profitable over the years. In 1994 his design team came up with an accessory that allowed Game Boy cartridges to be played on the Super NES system. That was followed by the Game Boy Pocket and the first Pokémon (short for Pocket Monsters) cartridge in 1996.

Pokémon was the first game that allowed players to exchange items from one linked Game Boy to another, and though Nintendo's expectations for the game weren't particularly high, the game became an enormous industry unto itself, spawning other toys, trading cards, clothing, an animated TV series, a movie, and even

**Food claim: Four tablespoons of ketchup contain as much nutrition as a medium-sized tomato.**

food. It's estimated that Pokémon merchandise has racked up more than $20 billion worth of sales for Nintendo since 1996, *not including* the video games. As for the Game Boy product line (which saw the addition of the Game Boy Color in 1998), by 2001 it had sold more than 115 million units and 450 million cartridges, making it the most popular game system of all time.

## DOWN AND OUT

Needless to say, Yokoi made Nintendo a lot of money over the years. What did he have to show for it? Not much—in 1995 his Virtual Boy, an addition to the Game Boy line that was kind of like a 3D View-Master—bombed. The red LED display gave so many players headaches and dizziness that when the product was released in the United States it came with a warning label. One reviewer called it a "Virtual Dog."

Nintendo lost a lot of money on the Virtual Boy, and Yamauchi apparently decided to humiliate Yokoi publicly by making him demonstrate the game system at the company's annual Shoshinkai trade show, even though it was all but dead. "This was his punishment, the Japanese corporate version of Dante's Inferno," Steven Kent writes in *The Ultimate History of Video Games*. "When employees make high-profile mistakes in Japan, it is not unusual for their superiors to make an example out of them for a period of time, then return them to their former stature."

## EARLY EXIT

Yokoi must have decided not to wait around for his restoration. He left the company in August 1996 after more than 27 years on the job, and founded his own handheld game company called Koto (Japanese for "small town"). It produced a game system similar to the Game Boy, only with a bigger screen and better speakers. We'll never know what kind of gains he might have made against the Game Boy, because on October 4, 1997, he was killed in a car accident. He was 56.

* * *

"When you come to a fork in the road, take it."
***—Yogi Berra***

**Neil Armstrong stepped on the Moon with his left foot. (Or did he? See page 560.)**

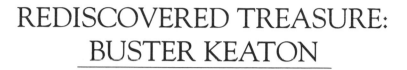

# REDISCOVERED TREASURE: BUSTER KEATON

*Any list of the greatest movie comedians has to include Buster Keaton. Never heard of him? You don't know what you're missing. Here's the story of one of Hollywood's comic treasures.*

## THE GREAT STONE FACE

Today filmmakers have nearly a century of history to build on. But that wasn't always the case—in the early days of Hollywood, directors had to invent their craft as they went along. How do you film a romantic scene? A car chase? An Old West shootout? An invasion from Mars? Somebody had to do it first—and they had to figure it out for themselves.

One such innovator was the silent film star Buster Keaton, one of the three most popular comedians of the 1920s (Charlie Chaplin and Harold Lloyd were the other two). His unsmiling "Great Stone Face" was said to be as recognizable at the time as Abraham Lincoln's, but his work behind the camera made a larger contribution to the art of filmmaking than his brilliant performances in front of it.

## WHAT MADE HIM DIFFERENT

• Before Keaton, the standard practice for filming a comedian was to set up a camera in a fixed position and then have them perform in front of it, just as they had performed before live audiences in vaudeville. Keaton made the camera his partner in the action of storytelling, instead of just a passive, immobile recorder of events.

• In his silent short film *The Playhouse* (1921), for example, Keaton figured out how to film a dream sequence where he plays every role in a vaudeville theater—the orchestra members, the performers onstage, and all the men and women in the audience. Nine characters on screen at the same time, all of them played by Buster Keaton himself.

• In his 1924 film *Sherlock Jr.*, Keaton plays a movie theater projectionist who—literally—walks into the movie screen and becomes a participant in the film being shown there.

• Audiences were thrilled with Keaton's work—and so were filmmakers. They went to see his movies over and over again, just to try to figure out how he filmed his scenes.

• Like Chaplin and Lloyd, Keaton routinely risked his life performing virtually all of his own stunts. He nearly drowned while filming a river scene in *Our Hospitality* (1923) when a safety line broke, and he actually broke his neck filming a scene in *Sherlock Jr.* (1924), when he fell onto a railroad track while dangling from a water tower. Both of these scenes were used in the final films. (Keaton didn't even realize he'd broken his neck until 11 years later, when he finally got around to having it X-rayed.)

• Keaton had a very distinctive onscreen persona—he *never* smiled on camera. His legendary "Great Stone Face" was something that dated back to his childhood in vaudeville. "If I laughed at what I did, the audience didn't," he told an interviewer in the 1960s. "The more serious I turned the bigger laugh I could get. So at the time I went into pictures, that was automatic. I didn't even know I was doing it."

## IN THE BEGINNING

Keaton spent nearly his entire life in show business, first in vaudeville and then in film and television. He was born Joseph Frank Keaton, Jr. in Piqua, Kansas, on October 4, 1895, while his parents were performing in a traveling medicine show with magician Harry Houdini. His father, Joe Keaton, Sr., was a dancer and acrobatic comic; his mother Myra played the saxophone.

Joe Jr. got his nickname from Houdini, following an accident in a hotel when he was only six months old. "I fell down a flight of stairs," Keaton told an interviewer in 1963. "They picked me up… no bruises, didn't seem to hurt myself, and Houdini said, 'That's sure a Buster.'" (In vaudeville, pratfalls were known as "busters.")

The name stuck and so did Buster's ability to survive accidents. Family legend has it that he also lost his right index fingertip (true), nearly lost an eye (unknown), and was sucked out of a hotel room window by a cyclone (unlikely) in three separate incidents all on the same day. True or not, three-year-old Buster got into enough trouble backstage that his parents decided the safest

**Longest railway on Earth: the Transiberian Railway (Russia), nearly 6,000 miles long.**

thing to do was to put him in their act, so they could keep an eye on him when they were working.

## SO *THAT'S* WHY THEY CALL IT SLAPSTICK

It wasn't long after they added little Buster to the act that they realized *he* was getting all the laughs. So they reworked the act. In one skit, Joe would demonstrate how to make children obey their parents while Buster tripped his dad up and hit him with a broom. Joe would pretend to lose his temper and then hit, kick, and throw little Buster all over the stage—into the scenery, into the orchestra pit, and even into the audience—using a hidden suitcase handle and a harness sewn into Buster's costume. The Keatons billed their son as "The Human Mop" and "The Little Boy Who Can't Be Damaged."

## SCHOOL OF HARD KNOCKS

Keaton claimed that in all his years of performing in vaudeville, he was rarely if ever injured during the act. It *seemed* violent, but he'd learned at a very early age how to perform pratfalls and other stunts without getting hurt. "I learned the tricks so early in life that body control became pure instinct with me," he remembered. Still, the Keatons had to hustle to stay one step ahead of child welfare groups, who kept trying to have the act shut down.

"The law read that a child can't do acrobatics, walk a wire, can't juggle, a lot of those things, but there was nothing in the law that said you can't kick him in the face or throw him through a piece of scenery," Keaton explained. "On that technicality, we were allowed to work, although we'd get called into court every other week."

## ON TO HOLLYWOOD

The Three Keatons toured until 1917. By then Joe, drinking heavily, really *was* starting to beat 21-year-old Buster onstage. The act split up and Buster got a job as an actor in film comedian Roscoe "Fatty" Arbuckle's studio.

Say what you will about Buster's "abusive childhood," but when he walked into Arbuckle's studio for the first time at the age of 21, he had more than 17 years of experience performing pratfalls two shows a day, six days a week. He was a master of physical

**Six weeks after an aluminum can is recycled, it's back on the shelf in the form of a new can.**

comedy and improvisation, someone perfectly suited to make his mark in the movie business.

Arbuckle knew it, too. He let Keaton perform in a movie called *The Butcher Boy* his first day at the studio. And Keaton—already wearing his trademark flat porkpie hat—was such a polished performer that he filmed his scene in just one take.

## WHAT GOES UP...

After just two more films, Keaton was promoted to assistant director and soon after that he was writing and co-starring in Arbuckle's films. The pair made 12 short comedies together between 1917 and 1920. When Arbuckle left to work in full-length feature comedies, Keaton inherited his studio, and after making a single introductory feature-length film called *The Saphead,* he began directing and starring in his own movies. These were the films that established Keaton as a star in his own right, and one of Hollywood's most brilliant comedic talents.

He made 19 comedy shorts between 1920 and 1923, including *The Boat* (1921), *Cops* (1922), and *The Electric House* (1922), which are considered some of his finest work. In 1923 he switched to feature films, making 10 in five years, including *Three Ages* (1923), *Sherlock Jr.* (1924), *The Navigator* (1924), and *The General* (1926).

## ...MUST COME DOWN

Ironically, the film that is now considered his greatest masterpiece and one of the finest comedies ever made, *The General*, ruined Keaton's career as an independent filmmaker. The film was based on an actual incident that took place during the Civil War, when Northern raiders stole a Confederate train called *The General.* Keaton plays the Southern engineer who tried to steal it back.

Keaton shot the film on location in Oregon using real locomotives and more than 400 members of the Oregon National Guard. It was one of the most expensive silent films at the time and though it is now considered a classic, it flopped after its release. So did Keaton's next film, *College* (1927). Those two failures forced his distributor, United Artists, out of the independent film distribution business altogether.

Keaton then made what he would later call "the worst mistake of my career," when he closed his film studio and signed with Metro-Goldwyn-Mayer in 1928. Keaton, 34, was at the height of his creative powers and had 45 films to his credit. He didn't realize it at the time, but his creative career was largely over.

## FROM BAD TO WORSE

Buster's first movie with MGM, *The Cameraman* (1928), is considered the last of his great films. But MGM reneged on its promise to give Keaton creative control and proceeded to stick him in one terrible picture after another.

It was at this point that Keaton's life—both onscreen and off—began to fall apart. As his career plummeted, he began drinking heavily; his long-troubled marriage fell apart and in the subsequent divorce he lost custody of his two sons. By the time he started work on the ironically titled *What, No Beer?* (1933), he was drinking more than a bottle of whiskey a day and was frequently too drunk to show up for work. MGM sent him to alcohol rehabilitation clinics more than once, but he continually relapsed and in February 1933, the studio fired him. He would never star in another major Hollywood film; he was only 37.

## AS SEEN ON TV

It took Keaton years to get his drinking under control, but he never gave up. Whenever he was sober enough to work, he did. Between 1934 and 1949, he appeared in 3 foreign films and more than 20 low-budget films he called "cheaters" because they were slapped together in three or four days. They were the worst films of his career.

Still, because the "cheaters" were produced by Columbia Pictures, they got wide distribution, and that helped Keaton get small parts in feature films. And *that* helped him get his first television appearance—on *The Ed Wynn Show* in 1947—at a time when many other film stars were shunning the new medium. He landed his own TV show in Los Angeles the following year, all the while continuing to act in feature films.

## NOW PLAYING

Remember, this was before movie channels, VCRs and DVD players made it possible to view old movies, so it may be difficult to imagine how important these TV and film appearances were to reviving Keaton's popularity. He was the only silent film star still working regularly; other greats like Charlie Chaplin and Harold Lloyd were largely unknown to younger audiences because their best films had not been seen in movie theaters for more than 20 years.

Not so with Keaton: by the early 1950s, he was popping up regularly on TV and in films, and this regular exposure helped generate new interest in his old silent films. As they were restored and rereleased they played to huge adoring audiences.

Keaton died from lung cancer in 1966 at the age of 70. By then he'd won an honorary Academy Award and had lived to see his reputation reestablished as one of the legends of the silent screen.

* * *

## CAMEO APPEARANCES

Even if you've never seen any of Buster Keaton's silent classics, you may have seen some of his cameo appearances. Look for him in the following films:

- ***Sunset Boulevard* (1950).** Gloria Swanson plays Norma Desmond, a faded silent screen star who takes in a down-on-his-luck screenwriter played by William Holden. Keaton is one of the "wax works"—the old Hollywood stars who play bridge at Desmond's house.

- ***Limelight* (1952).** Charlie Chaplin plays a washed-up music hall clown who tries to revive his career; Keaton is his piano-playing sidekick.

- ***Pajama Party* (1964).** Fourth of the "Beach Party" movies starring Annette Funicello. Keaton plays an indian chief named Rotten Eagle.

- ***A Funny Thing Happened on the Way to the Forum* (1966).** Keaton's last major cameo. His character Erronius spends much of the film going from horse to horse collecting mare's sweat for a love potion.

**60% of Americans say they'd be willing to walk barefoot down the streets of New York City.**

# STRANDED!

The Adventures of Robinson Crusoe *is a wonderful story, but would you really want to be stranded on a raft in the middle of the ocean? Here are four true stories of shipwrecks and castaways.*

## L'HERETIQUE

Alain Bombard was a 27-year-old French doctor who thought it strange that shipwreck survivors on life rafts tend to die quickly. A person can live up to six weeks without food and go up to 10 days without water, so why do so many castaways die within days of being set adrift? The common belief was that they drank salt water, which robs their body's tissues of water. Bombard disagreed. He felt sure that the reason people died was because they waited until their bodies were already dehydrated before drinking the seawater out of desperation.

In 1952 Bombard set out to prove that the ocean will support a castaway indefinitely and that drinking seawater is not detrimental to one's health. He decided to cross the Atlantic Ocean alone in a rubber raft without food or water, taking only emergency supplies in a sealed container to be used as a last resort.

Bombard set out from the Strait of Gibraltar in a 15-foot inflatable sailboat dubbed *L'Hérétique*, French for "The Heretic." He sailed first to Casablanca, which took a week, then to the island of Grand Canary, which took 18 days. From there, he set out to cross the Atlantic, leaving on October 19, 1952.

**Recipe for Survival**

Bombard caught fish, drank seawater, and even ate a bird that landed on his boat. By straining seawater through fabric, he collected plankton, which provided vitamin C and warded off scurvy. Bad weather resulted in constant bailing, but storms brought fresh rainwater, a welcome change after drinking nothing but saltwater for the first 23 days. He lost weight, began to suffer from saltwater boils, got diarrhea, and became depressed.

On December 6, he wrote out his last will and testament. Then, 53 days after leaving Grand Canary, he encountered the freighter *Arakaka*. But instead of asking to be rescued, Bombard

**On average, every square meter of the surface of the planet receives 240 watts of sunlight.**

only wanted to know where he was—and his location turned out to be 600 miles away from where he thought he was. It meant he had at least another 20 days to go. Bombard was miserable, but he refused all assistance except the offer of a hot shower and fresh batteries for his radio. Then he went back to his rubber raft.

### Christmas Present

Two weeks later, he made landfall on Barbados. It was the day before Christmas. After surviving on nothing but fish, seawater, rain (and a bird), Bombard had lost 55 pounds—a little less than a pound per day, typical for castaways. He developed a slight case of anemia, he had diarrhea, weak spells, blurry vision, he'd lost of a few toenails, and had a skin rash. But overall he was in fairly good health. And he proved that a person can indeed survive on salt water (most survival experts still insist that it's better to drink nothing at all).

## THE AURALYN

Maurice and Maralyn Bailey were aboard their 31-foot sloop *Auralyn* on their way to the Galapagos Islands on March 4, 1973, when their boat was struck by a wounded sperm whale. The *Auralyn* started sinking—an hour later it was gone. They left the ship in a four-foot inflatable life raft tied to a nine-foot inflatable dinghy. They had all their survival supplies with them with one exception—they forgot the fishing gear. Still, they had a 20-day supply of food and water.

Three hundred miles from the Galapagos Islands, the Baileys spent three nights rowing as hard as they could trying to reach land, but it was futile and they gave up, allowing the current to sweep them farther out to sea. On the eighth day, a ship passed nearby but failed to see them, and they wasted three of their six flares. When food ran out, they survived on sea turtles. Then, using turtle scraps as bait and safety pins as hooks, they were able to catch some fish. To pass the time, they played cards and dominoes.

### Don't Pass Me By

On the 25th night, another ship went by without seeing either their flare or their flashlight. On the 37th day, another ship passed, and two days later another one. They set off an improvised smoke

**In 1997, 4,824 British people were treated for injuries caused by opening cans of corned beef.**

bomb—kerosene-soaked cloth strips in a turtle shell—but weren't spotted. Another ship went by on the 45th day, but they couldn't get their "smoke bomb" to light. One of the main float tubes of their raft collapsed on the 55th day and couldn't be repaired—after that, they needed to pump it up every 20 minutes. Gradually, their health began to fail.

In June torrential rains came, providing fresh water to drink but the deteriorating canopy above their raft failed to keep them dry. By their 100th day afloat, they had to eat the birds that constantly landed on their raft. They even began catching and eating sharks. On June 30, a Korean ship appeared and saw them waving their jackets. Amazingly, after 118 days at sea, they were able to climb aboard under their own power.

## THE PETRAL

In August 1985, Gary Mundell set out to sail solo from California to Hawaii aboard his boat *Petral*. Everything went well for the first few days. But then one night, he was jolted awake by a bump. Getting up to investigate, he discovered that the boat had run aground on Caroline Island, one of the most remote pieces of real estate in the Pacific. Mundell had gone to bed thinking the island was at least 15 miles away. Had he miscalculated? It didn't matter now—he was stranded on a deserted island. The island, seven miles long and one mile wide, was completely uninhabited. He couldn't get the boat free and couldn't reach anyone on the radio.

He transferred absolutely everything movable from the boat to the shore using his inflatable raft, and set up camp under a grove of coconut trees. As the days passed, Mundell found plenty of food: coconuts, crabs, and fish. He caught rainwater in his sail and filled the many discarded bottles and jugs that washed up on the beach until he had more than 60 gallons. He never had to ration water—and even filled his raft and had a bath.

### Setting Priorities

After the first month passed without spotting a ship or plane, Mundell considered sailing to the nearest inhabited island 460 miles away, but decided to stay put…where at least he had food and water.

On the 50th day, he spotted a ship a few miles away. Taking no chances, he did everything he could to get the crew's attention—flares, smoke signals, and mirror flashes. The ship, the French

**Hot stuff: Oysters can change gender according to the temperature of the water they live in.**

research vessel *Coriolis*, answered with their searchlight. Rescue! Once aboard the *Coriolis*, he discovered how he had miscalculated his location: he hadn't—Caroline Island was actually 15 miles east of its charted position.

## THE SPIRIT

In 1974 Ray and Ellen Jackson, experienced sailors, bought a 42-foot yacht called *Spirit* and spent the next year outfitting her with every safety feature money could buy. They left California in 1975 and cruised 8,000 miles all over the Pacific. But after Ray injured his back in Hawaii, they decided to fly home and asked Ellen's brother, Jim Ahola, to sail the boat back to California.

Ahola had considerable experience with the *Spirit* but still decided to hire more experienced help, Bruce Collins to captain and Durel Miller to crew. His girlfriend, Camilla Arthur, and her friend, Nancy Perry, asked to come along, too. On September 12, 1976, the *Spirit* left Hawaii bound for California.

### Sinking Spirit

On the morning of September 27, without warning, there was a huge bang and the ship keeled over. Had the boat been hit by whales? Did it strike floating debris? Had a submarine surfaced beneath them? They never found out. Although the *Spirit* righted itself, there was a hole in the bow and it quickly began to sink. Flying debris had smashed the radio—so no SOS could be sent. There were two life rafts on board, but the survival kits had been washed away. Collins, Ahola, and Arthur got into one raft and Miller and Perry took the other. Five minutes later the *Spirit* was gone. They were 750 miles from land.

The castaways tied the two rafts together and distributed the meager supplies. They had no food, no fishing gear, and little water. Eleven hours later, the tether broke and the two rafts drifted apart. The raft carrying Miller and Perry drifted for 22 days. Miller was an experienced seaman but Perry was a complete stranger to the sea and was debilitated by seasickness. By the 12th day, she was incoherent and helpless. By the time they were rescued, she had lost 43 pounds (she only weighed 113 pounds to start with). Miller lost 55 pounds but cared for her constantly, kept a lookout, and flagged down a ship called the *Oriental Financier* on the 22nd day.

**The average American woman thinks about politics 12 min. a day. Average man: 6 min.**

### Another Survivor

A subsequent search for the second raft covered nearly 200,000 square miles. On the sixth day of the search it was found, but with only one survivor on board, Captain Bruce Collins—Ahola and Arthur were dead. Collins reported that they ran out of fresh water on the 12th day and he had survived by drinking the foul-tasting rainwater he collected from the canopy of the raft. The others had refused to drink it, fearing it was poisonous. Ahola died on the 19th day. His death devastated his girlfriend, and she died two days later.

Camilla's mother sued the Avon life raft company for failing to provide enough survival gear to keep her daughter alive. A court awarded her $70,000, but the company appealed. It was settled out of court.

* * *

## PIZZA FACTS

• **First takeout pizza.** In 1889 King Umberto and Queen Margherita of Italy wanted to sample the Neapolitan street food but didn't want to go out. So she asked pizzeria owner Raffaele Esposito to bring the pizzas to her. He made three kinds, including one with tomato paste, fresh basil, and a new ingredient, mozzarella cheese.

• **First pizzeria in the United States.** Opened by Gennaro Lombardi in 1905, on Spring Street in New York's Little Italy.

• **The first mozzarella cheese.** It was made from the milk of water buffaloes, first brought to Italy from India in the seventh century.

• **The first deep-dish pizza.** Invented in the 1940s by Chicago's Pizzeria Uno.

• **The first commercial pizza-pie mix.** Called Roman Pizza Mix, was produced in Worcester, Massachusetts, in 1948 by Frank A. Fiorello.

• **The first frozen pizza.** Marketed by Celentano Brothers in 1957.

• **The first Pizza Hut.** Opened in 1958 by two brothers attending Wichita State University.

**Oops! Herbicide use has created at least 48 "superweeds" that are resistant to chemicals.**

# *SNL* PART V: SPARTANS RULE!

*We've noticed in writing this long piece about* Saturday Night Live *that it probably drops more names than any other article in the BRI's history. Here are some more.* *(Part IV is on page 300.)*

## OUT WITH THE OLD

Michaels weathered the latest storm of critical attacks and did yet another shake-up after the disastrous 1995 season. The only surviving cast member was Tim Meadows (against NBC's wishes). And the revolving door kept on bringing in new faces: Impressionist Darrell Hammond; MTV's Colin Quinn; stand-up comics Tracy Morgan and Jim Breuer; and from the Los Angeles-based improv group, The Groundlings, Cheri Oteri, Jimmy Fallon, Chris Kattan, Ana Gasteyer, Chris Parnell, and Will Ferrell.

In the late 1990s, *SNL* entered its fourth golden age. How? By getting back to basics. Tom Shales and James Miller explain the resurgence in their book *Live from New York*:

> In 1996 and again to an even greater degree in 2000, *Saturday Night Live* returned to its richest vein of humor, American politics, and in the process rejuvenated itself for the umpty-umpth time. The cast was prodigious, the writing team witty and self-confident, and the satire biting.

Will Ferrell, according to many critics and cast members, emerged as one of the funniest people in *SNL*'s history. His George W. Bush, along with Darrell Hammond's Bill Clinton and Al Gore, kept the *SNL*'s presidential-bashing alive and well. Even the real Al Gore studied *SNL*'s send-up of the 2000 presidential debates "to help understand where he had gone wrong with his own debate performance."

## SATURDAY WHITE LIVE

While *SNL* has been hailed for its no-holds-barred takes on politics and television, it's had less then a stellar track record when it comes to dealing with women and minorities. Many who were there refer to the 17th floor as a "good ole' boys" organization, which is no surprise considering that most of the writers and cast have been white men. And as uneven as the comedy has been over the years, so too has been its take on racial relations.

## TOKEN PLAYERS

In the 1970s, Garrett Morris's biggest complaint was that the all-white writing team only gave him stereotypically black roles (he once performed "Proud Mary" dressed as Tina Turner). "I was hired under the terms of the Token Minority Window Dressing Act of 1968," he half-joked. "I get to play all parts darker than Tony Orlando."

But that began to change when Eddie Murphy first got exposure as a commentator on "Weekend Update" in 1981. "There's a different kind of black man on *Saturday Night Live* now," he announced to the world as he held up a photo of Garrett Morris. The next season, Murphy produced and starred in a short film for the show in which he was made up to look like a white man... to see how "the other half" lived. That, along with his portrayals of James Brown and Stevie Wonder, brought the show a black audience.

Damon Wayans joined as a featured player in 1985, thinking that he would take over where Murphy left off. He was wrong. Wayans wanted to improvise his in-your-face brand of racial comedy; the writers wanted him to read his "one line per skit" off of the cue cards. He protested when he purposely flubbed a skit on live television—a cardinal sin according to Michaels—and was fired that night. Wayans would soon get to showcase his talents on Fox's variety show *In Living Color,* which was a huge hit for the fledgling network. And NBC noticed.

## READY TO ROCK

"I got hired because *In Living Color* was on," said Chris Rock, who joined in 1991. "*SNL* hadn't had a black guy on in eight years, and *In Living Color* was hot, so they had to hire a black guy." Rock fared somewhat better than Wayans, most notably with his break-out character, urban talkshow host Nat X: "This week's list—the top five reasons why white people can't dance," he would say wearing a huge afro wig, "Why only five? Because THE MAN won't give me ten!"

**...size between a subatomic particle and the planet Earth.**

That joke hit pretty close to the mark, though, as Rock watched Farley and Sandler each get in twice as many skits. Like Wayans before him, Rock didn't really get to showcase his talents until *after* he left the show.

Tim Meadows has the distinction of being on the show longer than anyone else, and though he had some popular characters (such as the Ladies' Man), the writers never gave him anything too controversial to say. Why? Meadows's heyday fell between the Rodney King riots in 1992 and the O. J. Simpson Trial in 1995—a time when race relations in the United States were tense.

In recent years, Tracy Morgan has added his brand of street comedy to *SNL*. Like Rock and Wayans before him, Morgan was heavily inspired by Eddie Murphy. And like Murphy, he's getting to speak his mind on "Weekend Update" commentaries: "Racial profiling? I'm all for it—if ya' ax me, I say, 'Shake 'em down!'"

## BROADENING HORIZONS

While there have been more women then black people on *SNL* (and only two black women, Ellen Cleghorne and Danitra Vance), very few have been given equal footing with the men—and thus very few memorable characters.

But that trend, too, has been changing. The two stand-outs in recent years: Cheri Oteri's cheerleader (with Will Ferrell) and Molly Shannon's neurotic Catholic student Mary Catherine Gallagher. And although she had no breakthrough characters, Ana Gasteyer showed as much impressionistic range and musical talent as anyone on the show since Phil Hartman—a talent that landed her in a lot of sketches.

In 1999 Tina Fey took over as head writer (the first woman to do so). She completely revamped the struggling "Weekend Update" segment by co-anchoring it with Jimmy Fallon, reminding viewers of the chemistry that Dan Aykroyd and Jane Curtin had back in the 1970s. *Saturday Night Live* was as funny and current as ever, but would soon face one of its most daunting tasks.

## FROM THE RUBBLE

Only two weeks after the September 11 terrorist attacks in 2001, *Saturday Night Live* began its 27th season on uncharted ground. Lorne Michaels knew that the words "Live from New York" would

**The calories in a bagel with cream cheese can run an electric toothbrush for 52 hrs., 20 min.**

have a greater resonance than ever before, so he planned the opening very carefully. After an emotional speech by Mayor Rudolph Giuliani, who was surrounded by New York firefighters, longtime *SNL* friend Paul Simon performed a soulful rendition of his song "The Boxer." Then an unsure Lorne Michaels asked the mayor, "Can we be funny?" After a brief pause, Giuliani returned with, "Why start now?" It was perhaps the first good laugh on TV since the tragedy and a sign that life would return to normal.

## SIX DEGREES OF SATURDAY NIGHT

After nearly three decades, hundreds of the entertainment industry's biggest names have crossed paths with *Saturday Night Live*, from Robin Williams to Oprah Winfrey to Paul McCartney to Madonna. It's tough to flip through the channels for too long without seeing some evidence of *SNL's* impact: (click) *The Chris Rock Show;* (click) David Spade on *Just Shoot Me;* (click) *Stripes* with Bill Murray; (click) a commercial for *Austin Powers;* (click) "Tonight on *Conan*: Steve Martin, followed by Molly Shannon, with musical guest Elvis Costello" (who made his U.S. television debut on *SNL*).

As *Saturday Night Live* enters its fourth decade, the show continues to collect Emmys and praise from critics, who marvel at the show's longevity. Tom Shales continues to hail *SNL*, calling it a "weekly miracle." When asked how he's kept the show funny in the 21st century, Lorne Michaels answered: "I think that we've got those non-suck devices working again."

*  *  *

## RANDOM *SNL* FACTS

- Youngest host: Drew Barrymore, on Nov. 20, 1982, 7 years old.
- Five hosts cast members most liked working with: Steve Martin, Tom Hanks, John Goodman, Alec Baldwin, Christopher Walken.
- Short list of wanted hosts that have never appeared (so far): Johnny Carson, Tom Cruise, Bill Clinton.
- Other *SNL* alums: Ben Stiller (1989), Janeane Garofalo (1994), Kevin Meaney (1986), Jay Mohr (1993–94), Chris Elliot (1994).

**Who figured out that the rings reveal the age of a tree? Leonardo da Vinci.**

# MICROCARS

*One day in the early 1960s, young Uncle John was waiting in line at a Dairy Queen when he happened to see a strange little car pull into the parking lot. It looked like a refrigerator on wheels. That car—the Isetta—was Uncle John's introduction to an unusual class of foreign car known as microcars. If you aren't familiar with them, here's yours:*

## SIZE MATTERS

In post-World War II Europe, economic realities were forcing car designers to rethink the idea of the automobile. Europeans were already accustomed to smaller cars. More densely populated than America, many of its cities had narrow streets that predated the automobile by centuries. As early as 1923, smaller, more easily maneuverable cars were being built by manufacturers such as Alfa-Romeo and Fiat.

After World War II, fuel was expensive and materials were in short supply. The damaged economy made even these small cars out of reach for most people. In contrast to America's postwar optimism—which was expressed by materialism and a "bigger is better" attitude—Europeans tightened their belts and looked for ways to get by on less. Many people used bicycles or motorcycles for transport, but these left a lot to be desired in inclement weather and were of little use for carrying much more than the driver.

## CREATIVE SOLUTIONS

In the late 1940s and early 1950s a number of unconventional inventors began designing vehicles that were a sort of hybrid—more than motorcycles, but not quite cars. Many were designed to use motorcycle engines, particularly the early models. Later versions used more powerful proprietary engines. But one thing all the new cars had in common was size: they were very small. As a group, they became known as "microcars."

Some had four wheels, making them more carlike. But many had just three—usually two in front and one in back—which brought the cost down. According to British law, for example, a vehicle with fewer than four wheels (and without a reverse gear) was considered a motorcycle and was taxed at a lower rate than regular cars. Another plus: A less-expensive motorcycle license was all that was needed to drive the three-wheelers.

More than 50 different microcar brands were produced in Europe after the war. Some had a great deal of success; others barely got off the drawing board. With names such as Atom, Frisky, Scootacar, Trojan, and Wolf, it was difficult to take some of them seriously. But Europeans seemed to find the names and many of the wacky designs endearing. The vehicles were cheap to buy, economical to operate, and, as one ad said, "Why walk when you can ride?"

## SMALL BEGINNINGS

Some of the diminutive vehicles were designed and built by companies with automotive backgrounds, such as British Reliant, which expanded on its prewar line of three-wheeled vans. (Reliant made three-wheelers until early 2001.) But many others were produced by inventive entrepreneurs with little or no experience in vehicle design.

Bavarian businessman Hans Glas manufactured agricultural machinery. When demand for his equipment dropped sharply in the late 1940s, Glas thought there might be a market for a well-built scooter, so he began manufacturing one in 1951. He was right. After the success of the scooter, he went on to design a tiny car, the four-wheeled Goggomobile, first sold in 1955 for about $750. It was as rugged as its agricultural heritage might suggest—one reviewer noted that "the only way to flip a Goggomobile is to drive it over a land mine." With more than 280,000 sold by the end of production in 1969, the Goggomobile became the most successful small car produced in Germany.

## LUFTWAFFE CHIC

Another well-known microcar started out as a wheelchair. Shortly after the war, German aeronautical engineer Fritz Fend, a former Luftwaffe technical officer, began experimenting with some ideas he had for a hand-powered tri-cycle for disabled servicemen. His design evolved into a motorized version, with two wheels in front, the single wheel in the rear. When he started producing the vehicles, he was surprised to find that he was swamped by requests for it—not from disabled servicemen, but from ordinary people looking for cheap transportation.

**Ulysses S. Grant sometimes smoked as many as 20 cigars a day. (He died of throat cancer.)**

Fend was more of an inventor than a businessman, so to meet the demand for the new vehicles, he turned to his aviation contacts at the Messerschmitt aircraft company. The Messerschmitt factory, which had built fighter planes for the Nazis, was closed after the war. They were banned from making aircraft, so it was sitting idle... until it was put back to use making Fend's little cars. The first production model of the eight-foot-long Messerschmitt, which the makers preferred to call the Kabinroller, was introduced to the public in 1953.

With flowing lines and a clear, plastic dome top, it resembled a cockpit on wheels—and some people thought the Cabin-Scooter was made of old fighter plane parts. Reinforcing that misconception, the top opened upward and its two seats were in tandem, one behind the other. With a 191cc engine and a top speed of more than 50 mph, the Cabin-Scooter got 60 to 75 miles per gallon. Some 45,000 were sold by the end of production in 1964. A more powerful sibling, the Messerschmitt Tiger, had four wheels, a 500cc engine, and claimed a top speed of 90 mph.

## TINY BUBBLES

Just before World War II, Italian businessman Renzo Rivolta purchased Isothermos, a small company that specialized in making refrigerators. After the war he added scooters and motorcycles to his line, then three-wheeled minitrucks, and then in 1952 his first car, the Isetta ("Little Iso").

Though the Isetta and the Messerschmitt were called "bubble cars" because of their rounded enclosures, the Isetta bore little resemblance to the Messerschmitt—there was no chance anyone could mistake it for a fighter plane. Sometimes called "an Easter egg on roller skates," it was distinctly ovoid, 54 inches wide by 90 inches long.

The *entire* front end of the Isetta served as its single front door, much like a refrigerator door. With the door open, occupants would step into the car, turn around, and sit down on the single seat. The driver closed the door by pulling on the steering wheel, which was attached to the door and would pivot into place. The car had a canvas pullback sunroof, which made motoring around the countryside more pleasant on sunny days, but the real reason for it was that in the event of a front-end collision, passengers could use it as an emergency escape.

Though versions of the Isetta were made in Brazil, France, Spain, and Belgium, it was BMW of Germany that refined the little car and contributed most to its success. In the postwar economy, BMW was having trouble selling its more expensive models and was looking for an economy car to manufacture. BMW scouts were impressed by the Isetta's performance in Italy's Mille Miglia (1,000-mile) race. One reportedly finished with an average speed of almost 50 mph and with a fuel efficiency of 60 miles per gallon.

BMW bought the manufacturing rights, replaced the original engine with a more powerful 13-horsepower 247cc motorcycle engine and made several design improvements, such as better suspension and sliding side windows. At a cost of just 20% of its least-expensive luxury cars, BMW sold more than 160,000 Isettas in Germany. Another 30,000 were made in Great Britain under the BMW license. Some critics called it "a death trap," but many historians actually attribute the survival of BMW to the success of the Isetta.

BMW built Isettas until 1962, when competition from sturdier, more carlike microcars, especially the British-built Mini, was making bubblecars obsolete.

## MILLIONS OF MINIS

In the late 1950s, microcars enjoyed a second surge of popularity. Egypt had seized the Suez Canal in 1956, and Britain was rationing gasoline. Sir Leonard Lord, head of British Motor Corporation, asked designer Sir Alec Issigonis to come up with something revolutionary—a car to "wipe those blasted bubble cars off the road." And that's exactly what happened.

At roughly 4½ feet by 10 feet, the Mini was only a little larger than most of the earlier microcars, but with proper car-like side doors and a front and rear seat. The engine was in its own compartment, in the front over the drive wheels. But the real revolution was the drive train—by turning the 848cc engine sideways and putting the gearbox underneath it, Issigonis fit all the mechanical parts into just 18 inches. That left plenty of room for four passengers and even luggage.

With its four-cylinder 37-horsepower engine, the Mini could hold its own on the highway among larger cars. The early models had a top speed of 72 mph, but later performance modifications boosted

**Look it up (Chuck): Each year, U.S. airlines use more than 20 million airsickness bags.**

that figure to over 100 mph, a remarkable speed considering the Mini rode on 10-inch wheels. The combination of size, power, and maneuverability made the car the best in its class, and sales figures reflected its successful design: during the 25 years after its introduction in 1959, more than five million Minis were built.

But in spite of its long popularity, the Mini gradually fell victim to the times. It was competing with small but more powerful sports cars and the economical Volkswagon Beetle. By the mid-1980s sales had fallen off dramatically. A new owner, the British auto manufacturer Rover, tried to revive the Mini by offering a number of special editions. Strong sales in Japan helped to keep it going for a while, but as the end of the millennium approached, it looked like the Mini would finally join the Isetta and other legendary little cars on the scrap heap of history.

But history was about to repeat itself.

## BACK TO THE FUTURE

In 1994 BMW was seeking to expand its line and bought the four-wheel-drive Land Rover. It turned out to be a bad match. English investors didn't like the idea of a German company owning Rover, and the Rover division cost more money than it made. BMW sold off most of Rover in 2000, but the head of the company was a fan of the Mini…so they kept it.

In 2001 BMW unveiled a new Mini, built in an English factory, sporting BMW styling and engineering. With a motor nearly twice the size of the original and more than twice the horsepower, top speed is estimated at 125 mph. Automotive reviewers think it is both a blast from the past—and a peek at the future.

Though giant SUVs and luxury cars abound today, many car manufacturers with a grasp of history are preparing smaller, more fuel-efficient models. And if the BMW Mini is any indicator, modern microcars will feature high-tech advancements with new designs, materials, and fuels. Meaning: the future may hold mini more surprises.

* * *

"I was hitchhiking the other day and a hearse stopped. I said, 'No thanks—I'm not going that far.'"

***—Steven Wright***

**Organ donor: J. S. Bach played the cathedral organ. So did 100 of his descendants.**

# LET'S PLAY NINTENDO!

*Today's video game business is less about boing! and crash! than it is about ka-ching! and cash! Here's part V of the story of video games.*

## NO SALE

As we told you on page 292, back in 1981, Atari was the world leader in video games. In 1983 Nintendo offered to sell Atari the licenses to their Famicom game system, but they couldn't come to an agreement, so Nintendo decided to go it alone. They renamed the American version the Advanced Video System (AVS) and in January 1985, introduced it at the Consumer Electronics Show in Las Vegas, one of the largest such trade shows in the world.

They didn't get a single order.

Nintendo's problem wasn't so much that the AVS was a bad system, but more that the American home video game industry was struggling. After several years of impressive growth, in 1983 sales of video game consoles and cartridges suddenly collapsed without warning. Video game manufacturers, caught completely off guard, lost hundreds of millions of dollars as inventory piled up in warehouses, never to find a buyer. Atari's loss of $536 million prompted Warner Communications to sell the company in 1984. Mattel sold off its version, Intellivision, the same year and shut down their entire video game division. Many other companies went out of business.

## GOODBYE VCS, HELLO PC

Meanwhile, computer technology had finally advanced to the point that companies were able to manufacture and sell home computers at prices that families could afford. By 1982 a computer called the Commodore 64 could be bought for as little as $200, which was $100 less than the cost of an Atari 5200.

Why buy just a game system when you could buy a whole computer—which also played video games—for the same price or lower? Just as the video game industry had evolved from dedicated Pong-only games to cartridge-based multigame systems, game systems were giving way to the personal computer. Stand-alone video games were dead... or so most people thought.

Hiroshi Yamauchi, the president of Nintendo, didn't see things that way. His company didn't make personal computers and he didn't know much about the American market. But Famicom game systems were selling like crazy in Japan, and he didn't see any reason why they shouldn't also sell well in the United States. So what if the company didn't receive a single order at the Consumer Electronics Show? He told his American sales team to keep trying.

## WORD GAMES

Nintendo's American sales team was headed by Minoru Arakawa, who also happened to be Yamauchi's son-in-law. Arakawa *had* to keep trying. He didn't have any choice—he was a member of the family.

One of the problems the AVS was up against was that retailers had been badly burned by the video game crash of 1983. They weren't about to put any more nonselling video games on their shelves. Arakawa decided that the best way to proceed was to conceal the fact that the AVS was a video game. He couldn't do that while it was still called the Advanced Video System, so he renamed it the Nintendo Entertainment System, NES for short.

He added a light pistol and some shooting games, so that he could say it was a "target game." (Guns and target games still sold well in toy stores.) Then he added the Robot Operating Buddy (ROB), a small plastic "robot" that interacted with a couple of the games played on the NES. "Technologically speaking," Steven Kent writes in *The Ultimate History of Video Games*, "ROB offered very little play value. It was mostly a decoy designed to prove that the Famicom was not just a video game."

## DEJA VU

With a new name, a light gun, and a robot, Arakawa was sure the NES would sell. He rented a booth at the Summer Consumer Electronics Show and set the ROB out in front, where everyone could see it.

He didn't get a single order.

Why didn't retailers want to buy? Were consumers turned off too? Arakawa didn't know for sure, so he set up a focus group where he could watch young boys—Nintendo's target market—play NES games. Observing the scene from behind a two-way mirror, Arakawa heard for himself how much the kids disliked the NES. "This is sh*t!" as one kid put it.

## ONE MORE TRY

Arakawa was ready to throw in the towel. He called his father-in-law, told him the situation was hopeless, and suggested that Nintendo pull the NES out of the U.S. market. But Yamauchi refused to hear a word of it. He didn't know much about the Consumer Electronics Show and he didn't know much about focus groups. One thing he did know was that the Famicom was *still* selling like crazy in Japan, so why couldn't it sell well in the United States? There was nothing wrong with the NES—he was certain of that.

Yamauchi told Arakawa to test it one more time—in New York City. This time Arakawa left nothing to chance. There were about 500 retailers in the city, and Arakawa and his staff visited every one. They made sales pitches, delivered the game systems, stocked store shelves, and set up Nintendo's in-store displays themselves. They made plans to spend $5 million on advertising during the Christmas shopping season, and—without permission from Yamauchi—promised retailers they would buy back any game systems that didn't sell. And they *never, ever* referred to their video game as a video game. The NES was an "entertainment system."

## IS NINTENDO THE NEXT ATARI?

With the buyback guarantee, retailers had nothing to lose, so they agreed to stock Nintendo, even though they didn't think it would sell. They were wrong—more than 50,000 games sold by Christmas, prompting many stores to continue stocking the NES after the holidays. Arakawa launched similar tests in Los Angeles, Chicago, and San Francisco. The NES sold well in each city.

In 1986 Nintendo expanded its U.S. marketing push nationwide and sold 1.8 million game consoles, and from there sales grew astronomically. They sold 5.4 million consoles in 1987 and 9.3 million in 1988. By 1990 American sales of the NES accounted for 10% of the entire U.S./Japan trade deficit.

But if there's one thing that video game makers have learned the hard way, it's that *staying* ahead in the business can be a lot harder

**What do baby humans have that baby rattlesnakes don't? Rattles.**

than *getting* ahead. For all their successes, Nintendo has made their share of blunders, too. They clung to the NES a few years longer than they should have, on the assumption that its market dominance would allow it to keep ahead of its rivals. They were wrong.

When a rival company called Sega introduced their Genesis system in 1989, Nintendo ignored it, even though the Genesis was twice as powerful as the NES. They shouldn't have—Genesis introduced a character called Sonic the Hedgehog, an edgy, anti-Mario character who appealed to older kids *and* adults the same way that Donkey Kong's Mario had appealed only to kids. In late 1991, Nintendo introduced SuperNintendo, but it was too late. Sonic's appeal, combined with six years of waiting for Nintendo to update their system, helped Sega get a toehold in the market…and outsell Nintendo.

### SONY'S PLAYSTATION

But Nintendo's biggest mistake of all came in 1992. The industry was gearing up for yet another generation of game systems—using CD-ROM disks instead of cartridges. CD-ROMs were cheaper to make and stored more than 300 times more information than a Super NES cartridge, allowing for much more sophisticated graphics.

Nintendo had no experience with CD-ROMs, so they made plans to partner with Sony Corporation to make the new system. But there was a problem—Sony had already announced plans to introduce its own game system (Play Station), and Nintendo executives were worried about revealing Nintendo's technological secrets to a competitor as large and powerful as Sony. So what did they do? For some reason, Nintendo waited until the day *after* Sony announced the partnership. Then they made an announcement of their own: they were ditching Sony and partnering with the Dutch electronics giant, Philips.

### REVENGE!

Though the company had lost ground to Sega in the U.S. market, Nintendo was still the world leader in video game sales, and many Sony executives were reluctant to challenge Nintendo's dominance. The consensus: scrap the Play Station project because Nintendo will wipe it out. But Sony CEO Norio Ohga was so furious at being humiliated by Nintendo that he almost singlehandedly forced the company to continue work on the project.

**The ball that drops in Times Square every New Year's Eve is named the "Star of Hope."**

The Sony Play Station was introduced in Japan in 1994 and in the United States in 1995. Nintendo eventually scrapped its CD-ROM–based system and introduced the Nintendo 64, yet another cartridge game system.

## BRAVE NEW WORLD

The Nintendo 64 was a blunder of Atari proportions. Compared to the Play Station, it had poor sound, poor graphics... and poor sales. By August 1997, the Play Station had surged past both Sega and Nintendo to become the industry leader. Sega, which spread their resources over too many game systems at once—Genesis, Saturn, and another one called Dreamcast—fell to a distant third and in January 2001 got out of the hardware business altogether. Today they only make game software.

Nintendo's decision to stick with cartridges for the Nintendo 64 continues to haunt them today. When Sony introduced the Play Station 2 in 2000, they were careful to make it "backward compatible," so that virtually all 800 of the Play Station 1 games could be played on the new station. Extra bonus: Because the PlayStation 2 uses a DVD player instead of a CD-ROM player, you can also watch movies on it.

The Nintendo Game Cube, introduced in 2001, is another story. It uses a *mini* DVD-ROM system that doesn't play movies and isn't compatible with Nintendo 64 game cartridges. That means Nintendo 64 owners have no incentive to buy the Game Cube, because their old games will be just as obsolete whether they buy Game Cube or PlayStation 2.

Even worse for Nintendo is the new kid on the block: the Microsoft Xbox. Considered even more technologically advanced than the PlayStation 2, Xbox is giving both Nintendo and Sony a run for their money.

## FORTUNE-TELLING

Who will be the next Atari? Will Nintendo's game systems slip to third place behind Sony and Microsoft, or even disappear entirely? Will the PlayStation 2 stay on top, or is the Xbox the new king of the hill? What comes next?

Stay tuned—if there's one thing to be learned from the video game industry, it's that the game is *never* over.

**Odds that an American worker won't tell their spouse after they receive a raise: 36%.**

# YOU'RE MY INSPIRATION

*It's always interesting to find out where the architects of pop culture get their ideas. These may surprise you.*

**PRINCESS LEIA'S HAIR:** According to *Star Wars* creator George Lucas, "I was trying to create something different, so I went with a kind of Southwestern Pancho Villa woman look. The buns are basically from turn-of-the-century Mexico."

**SCOOBY-DOO:** Modeled after Bob Hope's movie persona, "in which he played the coward for laughs before ending up the reluctant hero."

**"DOUBLE VISION":** The title of Foreigner's 1978 hit song came from a hockey injury. Frontman Lou Gramm was at a New York Rangers game when the goalie was knocked in the head with a stick. After the dazed player was taken off the ice, the arena announcer reported that he was "suffering double vision."

**ELLIE ARROWAY:** The protagonist in Carl Sagan's novel *Contact* (played by Jodie Foster in the movie) was based on a real-life SETI (Search for Extra-Terrestrial Intelligence) member Jill Tarter, who "has logged more telescope hours in the search for cosmic company than any other human on the planet."

**CAPTAIN JACK SPARROW:** Johnny Depp based his character in *Pirates of the Caribbean* on a mix of Rolling Stones guitarist Keith Richards and the amorous cartoon skunk, Pepe LePew.

***THE EXORCIST*:** Both the novel and film were based on reports of an actual exorcism performed on a 14-year-old boy in Missouri in 1949, the last official case of exorcism in the United States.

**"ME AND BOBBY MCGEE":** Songwriter Kris Kristofferson got his inspiration from a scene in Fellini's movie *La Strada*. When Anthony Quinn realizes that Giulietta Masina is dead, "he suddenly realized he was free but he was also the loneliest son of a bitch in the world. It showed the two sides of freedom—that freedom is just another word for nothing left to lose."

**A human eyeball weighs about an ounce.**

# FUN WITH NAMES

*We've always been fascinated by strange (real) names. Lucky for us there doesn't seem to be a shortage of them.*

## PEOPLE

**Derek Tuba,** band teacher in Winnipeg, MB

**Milo Shocker,** electrician in Oak Creek, Wisconsin

**Mr. Fillin,** substitute teacher in Woodside, CA

**Brie Mercis,** works at a cheese shop in Burlingame, CA

**Cardinal Rapsong,** Vatican spokesman against pop music

**Drs. French & Fry,** two dentists who share an office in Montgomery, AL

**Dr. Chin,** runs the Chin Ear, Nose & Throat Clinic in Malaysia

**Mr. David Dollar,** head of research, World Bank, NYC

## PLACES

**Pinch** and **Quick,** neighboring towns in West Virginia

**Pickles Gap,** Arkansas

**Oddville,** Kentucky

**Coolville,** Ohio

**Bowlegs,** Oklahoma

**Smartt,** Tennessee

**What Cheer,** Iowa

**Smut Eye,** Alabama

**Telephone,** Texas

**Bingo,** Maine

## BUSINESSES

**Deadman Funeral Home,** Manchester, TN

**Gamble Insurance Agency,** Central, SC

**Crummy Plumbing Company,** Ocean Shores, WA

## STORES

**A Pane in the Glass,** Naples, FL

**Wok-N-Roll,** Chinese restaurant, Yarmouth Post, MA

**The Hairtaker,** Los Angeles

**Great Buns,** bakery, Las Vegas

**Bye Bye Bifocals,** optician, Dallas

**Franks A Lot,** restaurant, Kansas City, MO

## MORE PEOPLE

Mary Rhoda Duck

Wavva White Flag

Janet Isadore Bell

Diana Brown Beard

Mary Hat Box

Eartha Quake

Dorothy May Grow

Alvin Will Pop

**Very punny: Who won the 1995 Procrastinator of the Year award? Congressman Tom Delay.**

# LONELY PHONE BOOTH

*In the 1960s, some miners put a phone booth in the middle of the Mojave Desert. Long after they left, the booth remained...waiting for someone to call.*

## HELLO? ANYBODY THERE?

Miles from the nearest town, the old phone booth stood at the junction of two dirt roads. Its windows were shot out; the overhead light was gone. Yet the phone lines on the endless rows of poles still popped and clicked in anticipation—just as they'd been doing for nearly 30 years. Finally, in 1997, it rang.

A guy named Deuce had read about the booth and called the number...and continued to call until a desert dweller named Lorene answered. Deuce wrote a story about his call to nowhere, posted it on his website...and the word spread through cyberspace. Someone else called. Then another person, and another—just to see if someone would answer. And quite often someone did. Only accessible by four wheel drive, the lonely phone booth soon became a destination. Travelers drove for hours just to answer the phone. One Texas man camped there for 32 days...and answered more than 500 calls.

## REACH OUT AND TOUCH SOMEONE

Someone posted a call log in the booth to record where people were calling from: as close as Los Angeles and as far away as New Zealand and Kosovo. Why'd they call? Some liked the idea of two people who've never met—and probably never will—talking to each other. Just sending a call out into the Great Void and having someone answer was reward enough for most.

Unfortunately, in 2000 the National Park Service and Pacific Bell tore down the famous Mojave phone booth. Reason? It was getting too many calls. The traffic (20 to 30 visitors a day) was starting to have a negative impact on the fragile desert environment.

The old stop sign at the cattle grate still swings in the wind. And the phone lines still pop and click in anticipation. But all that's left of the loneliest phone on Earth is a ghost ring.

So if the urge strikes you to dial (760) 733-9969, be prepared to wait a very, very long time for someone to answer.

**Polite tip from etiquette experts: If no one answers the phone after 6 rings, hang up.**

# THAT'S RICH!

*Some interesting facts about gold and gemstones.*

Where was the first U.S. Gold Rush? Not California—North Carolina, in 1803. (Started when a boy found a 17-pound nugget on his father's farm.) It supplied all the gold for the nation's mints until 1829.

It is estimated that only about 100,000 tons of gold have been mined during all of recorded history.

The word *garnet* comes from the Latin word for "pomegranate" (garnets were thought to resemble pomegranate seeds)

Legend says that one day Cupid cut Venus' fingernails while she was sleeping and left the clippings scattered on the ground. So that no part of Venus would ever disappear, the Fates turned them into stone. The stone: onyx, Greek for "fingernail."

The chemical formula for lapis lazuli: *(Na,Ca)8(Al,Si)12O24-(S,SO4)*. The chemical formula for diamond: C.

The name "turquoise" comes from the fact that it was first brought to Europe from the Mediterranean by Levantine traders, also known as...Turks.

The California Gold Rush yielded 125 million ounces of gold from 1850 to 1875—more than had been in the previous 350 years and worth more than $50 billion today.

From 330 B.C. to 1237 A.D., most of the world's emeralds came from "Cleopatra's Mine" in Egypt.

Organic gems:

- Amber (petrified tree sap, at least 30 million years old)
- Coral (exoskeletons of sea creatures—*coral polyps*—used as a gem since the Iron Age)
- Pearl (from oysters)
- Ivory (elephant tusks)
- Tagua nut (very hard, small blue-white nut of the tagua palm—a substitute for ivory)

Ancient Greeks named amber from the word "electron," because rubbing amber gives off static electricity.

Rarest gem: Painite, discovered in Burma. Fewer than 10 specimens exist in the world.

Gold is recycled. Result: jewelry purchased today may contain gold mined in prehistoric times.

**Pearl of wisdom: A baby oyster is called a *spat*.**

# OOPS!

*Everybody enjoys reading about somebody else's blunders. So go ahead and feel superior for a few minutes.*

## BUM WRAP

"Jean Baptiste de Chateaubrun (1685–1775) spent 40 years polishing and refining two plays, virtually his life's work, only to discover that his housekeeper had carelessly used the pages as wrapping paper, losing them forever."

—***The Best of the Worst***

## MAJOR-LEAGUE DUST UP

"A deceased Seattle Mariners fan's last wishes went awry when the bag containing his cremated remains failed to open as a plane attempted to scatter them over Safeco Field, the Mariners' home stadium. Instead, the entire bag of ashes fell onto the closed roof of the stadium in one piece, bursting into a puff of gray smoke as it hit. A startled eyewitness called 911, and officials ordered the stadium to be evacuated.

"It took more than an hour for sheriff's deputies to trace the tail number of the plane and determine that the mysterious substance on the stadium roof was the ashes of a Mariners fan, not anthrax or some other kind of terrorist attack."

—***Seattle Times***

## HARD OF EAR-ING

"A Russian criminal who tried to flee from Western Ukraine to Slovakia using another person's identity papers was unmasked when the fake ears he had used for a disguise fell off at passport control. They had been attached with cheap Russian medical glue."

—***The Fortean Times***

## CALL HIM CHUCK

WATERTOWN, Conn., August 2002—"Mario Orsini, 73, faces assault charges for shooting and wounding his brother, Donato, 66, after mistaking him for a woodchuck, police said."

—***USA Today***

**Earliest use of the flashback in Western literature: Homer's *Odyssey*.**

## ALL WET

"A Philadelphia television weatherman whose dire predictions convinced countless viewers to take a snow day off work in March 2001, was inundated with hate mail and death threats after his 'Storm of the Decade' turned out to be a teapot-sized tempest. John Bolaris' heavily promoted forecasts, complete with graphics and theme music, did not envision the possibility that the storm would change course, which it did. An avalanche of angry e-mails and phone messages, which included such warnings as 'If I owned a gun, there would be one less person to worry about,' started almost immediately. Said Mr. Bolaris, 'I felt like leaving town.'"

**—*The National Post***

## GETTING SOME SHUT-EYE

"A Long Island woman accidentally squeezed a drop of glue in her daughter's eye, thinking she was holding a tube of prescription eye drops. Christine Giglio of Massapequa, New York, reached for the drops, a treatment for nine-year-old Nikki's pinkeye, but instead grabbed a tube of fingernail glue. When she realized what she had done, she called for emergency help. Giglio said she made the mistake because the two tubes looked very similar. Fortunately, the eye's protective mechanisms of blinking and tearing often prevents any lasting damage, said Dr. Richard Bagdonas, the attending emergency room surgeon. (Nikki made a full recovery.)"

**—Associated Press**

## GOTTA KEEP 'EM SEPARATED

"Dean Sims, 26, was left unable to use the toilet after undergoing an operation at Woolwich Hospital to remove an abscess from his left buttock. The former factory worker returned home and was amazed to find that his buttocks had been taped together with surgical tape. Said Mr. Sims, 'How disgusting is that?' Sims phoned the hospital, only to be told he'd have to wait until the next day to have the bandage removed by a nurse. 'I've got to let them do it—I don't want it to get infected,' he added. 'Gangrene could set in.'

"His mum, Rita, said, 'He's in agony and getting cramps—he wants to go to the loo badly but can't.' A hospital spokesman said the bandaging was a mistake. Sims is demanding an apology."

**—*News Shopper* (UK)**

**How about you? The average person owns 25 T-shirts.**

# LET'S DO A STUDY!

*If you're worried that the really important things in life aren't being researched by our scientists, keep worrying.*

• Researchers at Georgetown University found that caterpillars can "shoot" their feces a distance of 40 times their body length.

• A 2002 study in Saudi Arabia concluded that women were responsible for 50% of the car accidents in the country. (Women aren't allowed to drive in Saudi Arabia.)

• In 2003 researchers at Plymouth University in England studied primate intelligence by giving macaque monkeys a computer. They reported that the monkeys attacked the machine, threw feces at it, and, contrary to their hopes, failed to produce a single word.

• Psychologists at the University of Texas conducted a study in 1996 to determine if calling children "boys" or "girls" is harmful.

• In 2001 scientists at Cambridge University studied kinetic energy, centrifugal force, and the coefficient of friction… to determine the least messy way to eat spaghetti.

• In 2002 food industry researchers reported that when children were told they couldn't have junk food, they wanted it even more. Industry spokespeople said that the study showed that children should decide for themselves how much junk food they should eat.

• Researchers at Northwestern University in Illinois used their federal grant money to study female sexuality…by paying female students to watch pornographic films ($75 per film).

• A 2001 study found that 60% of men in the Czech Republic do not buy their own underwear.

• According to a *British Medical Journal* report in 2003, Korean researchers have proven that karaoke is bad for your health.

• A 2002 study by the Department of Veterans Affairs Medical Center in Vermont found that studies are often misleading.

**Q: What is the most nutritious "food" in the world? A: Blood.**

# COME HEAR BERTHA BELCH

*What's the difference between good and evil? Maybe just a little grammar. The following are excerpts from real church bulletins.*

"Ladies Bible Study will be held Thursday morning at 10:00. All are invited to lunch in the Fellowship after the B.S. is done."

"Evening Massage—6 p.m."

"The pastor would appreciate if the ladies of the congregation would lend him their electric girdles for pancake breakfast next Sunday."

"For those of you who have children and don't know it, we have a nursery downstairs."

"The pastor will preach his farewell message, after which the choir will sing 'Break Forth Into Joy.'"

"Barbara remains in the hospital and needs blood donors for more transfusions. She is also having trouble sleeping and requests tapes of Pastor Jack's sermons."

"Our youth basketball team is back in action Wednesday at 8 p.m. in the recreation hall. Come out and watch us kill Christ the King."

"Bertha Belch, a missionary from Africa, will be speaking tonight at Calvary Methodist. Come hear Bertha Belch all the way from Africa."

"The peacemaking meeting scheduled for today has been cancelled due to a conflict."

"The Lutheran Men's Group will meet at 6:00 p.m. Steak, mashed potatoes, green beans, bread, and dessert will be served for a nominal feel."

"Attend and you will hear an excellent speaker and heave a healthy lunch."

"The church will host an evening of fine dining, superb entertainment, and gracious hostility."

"This evening at 7 p.m. there will be a hymn sing in the park across from the church. Bring a blanket and come prepared to sin."

"Mrs. Johnson will be entering the hospital this week for testes."

**Shortest verse in the Bible: John 11:35. ("Jesus wept.")**

# Q & A: ASK THE EXPERTS

*Everyone's got a question they'd like answered—basic stuff, like "Why is the sky blue?" Here are a few questions, with answers from the nation's top trivia experts.*

## SUGAR PIE, HONEY BUNCH

**Q:** *Are brown sugar, raw sugar, molasses, and honey healthier than refined white sugar?*

**A:** "Nutritionists agree that there is no significant amount of vitamins or minerals in any of these alternative sweeteners. So you can't ease your guilty sweet tooth with the justification that you're using 'health foods.' Honey has an additional problem in that it can cause botulism toxin to grow in the intestinal tracts of infants. It should *never* be given to children under one year old.

"These days, foods can contain many other forms of sugar, such as sucrose, fructose, high fructose corn syrup and corn sweeteners. These may be hyped to seem as if they're more nutritious...but they aren't." (From *Old Wives' Tales*, by Sue Castle)

## NOW HEAR THIS

**Q:** *What makes our ears ring?*

**A:** "Sometimes, even in a quiet room, we hear noise that seems to come from inside our heads.

"Behind the eardrum is a bony chamber studded with three tiny, movable bones. These bones pick up vibrations from the eardrum. Deeper in the ear is a fluid-filled channel called the *cochlea*. Vibrations from the bones make waves in the fluid, where thousands of hair cells undulate in the sloshing fluid.

"These hair cells are crucial. Somehow, the ripples that pass through them trigger electrical impulses, which travel along the auditory nerve—the hearing nerve—to the brain. The brain translates the signals into sound.

"Hair cells can get hurt by loud noises, or by a knock on the head, impairing their ability to send electrical impulses through the hearing nerve. But some hair cells will be hurt in such a way that they continuously send bursts of electricity to the hearing nerve. In effect, these hair cells are permanently turned on. When the brain receives their signals, it interprets them as sound and we hear a 'ringing,' even in a silent room." (From *How Come?*, by Kathy Wollard)

## NUKE 'EM

**Q:** *Can the microwaves leak out of the box and cook the cook?*

**A:** "There is extremely little leakage from today's carefully designed ovens. Moreover, the instant the door is opened, the magnetron shuts off and the microwaves immediately disappear.

"What about the glass door? Microwaves can penetrate glass but not metal, so the glass door is covered with a perforated metal panel so you can see inside, but the microwaves can't get through because their wavelength (4¾ inches) is simply too big to fit through the holes in the metal panel. There is no basis for the belief that it is hazardous to stand close to an operating microwave oven." (From *What Einstein Told His Cook*, by Robert L. Wolke)

## POLLY WANT A FRIEND?

**Q:** *How do parrots talk?*

**A:** "Exactly why parrots can change their calls to make them sound like words is still not understood. Their ability to mimic may possibly be linked with the fact that they are highly social birds. A young parrot in captivity learns the sounds it hears around it and quickly realizes that repeating these sounds brings attention and companionship. This is perhaps a substitute for its normal social life.

"Although they are such good mimics in captivity, parrots do not imitate other sounds in the wild. There are, however, many other species that do: mynah birds and lyrebirds, for example, do mimic the sounds they hear in their everyday lives." (From *What Makes the World Go Round?*, edited by Jinny Johnson)

## CAN YOU HEAR ME NOW?

**Q:** *Is there sound in space? If so, what's the speed of sound there?*

**A:** "No, there is no sound in space. That's because sound has to travel as a vibration in some material such as air or water or even stone. Since space is essentially empty, it cannot carry sound, at least not the sorts of sound that we are used to." (From *How Things Work*, by Louis A. Bloomfield)

**Tallest monument in the U.S.: The Gateway Arch in St. Louis, at 630 feet.**

# CLASSIC PUBLICITY STUNTS

*Advertising costs a lot of money. So why pay for it when you can get the press to spread the word for free? All it takes is a combination of imagination, determination, and no shame whatsoever. These guys were masters at it.*

**STUNTMAN:** P. T. Barnum

**STUNT:** "That is not a real bearded lady," cried a paying customer at Barnum's Museum. "It's a bearded man wearing a dress!" The customer then had Barnum served with a subpoena and took him to court.

**IT WORKED!** The trial was a public spectacle as the bearded lady, her husband, and a doctor each testified as to her femininity. Meanwhile, thousands flocked to the museum to judge for themselves. After the trial it came out that Barnum had actually hired the man to sue him...solely to drum up business.

**STUNTMAN:** Press agent Marty Weiser

**STUNT:** In 1974 Weiser leased a drive-in theater in Los Angeles and invited the press to attend a movie premiere...for horses. Weiser featured a "horsepitality bar" full of "horse d'oeuvres" (popcorn buckets filled with oats). And true to his word, more than 250 horses and their riders paraded into the theater, "parked" in the stalls, and watched the movie.

**IT WORKED!** The odd story ran in every newspaper and newscast in town, which attracted huge crowds to the film Weiser was promoting, Mel Brooks's Western comedy spoof, *Blazing Saddles*.

**STUNTMAN:** Press agent Milton Crandall

**STUNT:** In 1923 Denver newspapers were tipped off that a whale had been sighted on top of Pikes Peak, a 14,000-foot-high mountain in Colorado. The reporters raced up to the site to see the whale. Sure enough, just beyond the peak, occasional sprays of water shot into the air, while hundreds of spectators gathered below, shouting, "Thar she blows!"

**How did the ancient Egyptians discover leavened bread? One theory...**

**IT WORKED!** The "whale" was actually Crandall hiding just behind the peak shooting sprays of seltzer in the air. And the shouting people were all paid to stand there in the cold for an hour. But it was worth it—for Crandall, anyway. He got just the publicity he was looking for to promote the 1922 movie, *Down to the Sea in Ships*.

**STUNTMAN:** A "researcher" calling himself Stuart Little
**STUNT:** In the 1940s, Mr. Little started a massive letter-writing campaign to the editors of newspapers across the nation. His beef: He refused to believe government statistics that claimed the average life span of a crow was only 12 years. Little was certain that crows lived longer than that. So in the letters he asked people from all over to send him authenticated reports of old crows. Little just wanted to set the record straight.
**IT WORKED!** Thousands responded. Soon *everyone* was talking about old crows. And the makers of Old Crow bourbon whiskey—and the press agent responsible for Stuart Little's letters—were smiling all the way to the bank.

**STUNTMAN:** Publicist Harry Reichenbach
**STUNT:** A group of teenage boys walked up to a store window in 1913 and saw a lithograph of a naked young woman standing in a lake. They ogled it for hours. Reichenbach complained to the head of the anti-vice society about the picture's effect on the young, demanding they come see the outrage. They did, and began a moral crusade against it.
**IT WORKED!** The picture was titled *September Morn*. The artist, Paul Chabas, had hired Reichenbach to drum up interest in it. Pretty soon the artist was unable to meet demand. The image showed up in magazines, on calendars, and on cigarette packs. Sailors had the woman tattooed on their forearms. The lithograph sold seven million copies, and the original painting is on display today in the Metropolitan Museum of Art in New York.

**STUNTMAN:** Publicist Jim Moran
**STUNT:** "Don't change horses in midstream," says the old adage. Moran set out to prove it wrong. Wearing an Uncle Sam top hat and tails, he was photographed in the middle of the Truckee

**... By kneading dough with their feet—the yeast between their toes made it rise.**

River, where he successfully leapt from a black horse to a white one. He'd had been hired by the Republican Party to inspire voters in the 1944 presidential campaign to change parties after three consecutive terms of Democrat Franklin D. Roosevelt.

**IT WORKED!** Actually, no, it didn't. FDR easily defeated Republican Thomas Dewey in the election.

**STUNTMAN:** Surrealist Salvador Dalí

**STUNT:** In 1939 Dalí was commissioned to create a window display for New York City's prestigious department store Bonwit Teller. The artist's design incorporated a female mannequin with a head of roses, ermine fingernails, a green feathered negligee, and a lobster telephone. A male mannequin wore a dinner jacket with 81 glasses of crème de menthe attached to it. Each glass was topped off with a dead fly and a straw. The only furniture in the window was a fur-lined claw-foot tub filled with water and floating narcissi (flowers).

**IT WORKED!** When the window was unveiled, the Bonwit Teller staff was outraged; they took it upon themselves to alter the scene without asking the artist. A furious Dalí stomped into the store, tipped the water out of the tub, and pushed it through the plate-glass window. After the police showed up and arrested him, the newspapers wrote about it and radio commentators talked about it. And Dalí's one-man show—which just happened to be opening that very evening—was packed.

**STUNTMAN:** Washington Irving

**STUNT:** In October 1809, a notice appeared in the New York *Evening Post*, describing "a small elderly gentleman dressed in an old black coat and cocked hat by the name of KNICKERBOCKER" who had gone missing. In November a notice from Knickerbocker's landlord stated that he had found a "very curious book" among the old gent's belongings and if the rent wasn't paid soon, he would sell it.

**IT WORKED!** Soon everyone in New York was talking about the missing author and his mysterious book. When Diedrich Knickerbocker's book, *A History of New York*, was published in December, everyone wanted to read it. Only later did they discover there was no Knickerbocker, lost or found. The real author of the book, the notices, and the publicity stunt… was Washington Irving.

**Windmills originated in Iran.**

# LITTLE THINGS MEAN A LOT

*"The devil's in the details," says an old proverb. It's true—the littlest things can cause the biggest problems.*

## A PIECE OF TAPE

In the early morning of June 17, 1972, an $80-a-week security guard named Frank Wills was patrolling the parking garage of an office complex in Washington, D.C., when he noticed that someone had used adhesive tape to prevent a stairwell door from latching. Wills removed the tape and continued on his rounds ...but when he returned to the same door at 2:00 a.m., he saw it had been taped *again*. So he called the police, who discovered a team of burglars planting bugs in an office leased by the Democratic National Committee. This "third-rate burglary"—and the coverup that followed—grew into the Watergate scandal that forced President Richard M. Nixon to resign from office in 1974.

## A CONVERSION ERROR

On July 23, 1983 the pilots of Air Canada flight 143 was preparing to fly from Montreal to Edmonton, Canada. The device that calculates the amount of fuel needed wasn't working, so the pilots did the calculations by hand. Part of the process involved converting the volume of fuel to weight. They used the conversion factor of 1.77 pounds/liter...not realizing that on a Boeing 767, fuel is measured in *kilograms*, not pounds. (They should have used the conversion factor of .8 kilograms/liter.) Result: they didn't load enough fuel to get them to Edmonton. While the plane was cruising at 41,000 feet over Red Lake, Ontario, it suddenly ran out of fuel and both engines quit. The pilots had no choice but to *glide* the 767 to an emergency landing at a former airbase at Gimli, Manitoba, something that the pilots had never trained for and that was not covered in the 767's emergency manual, since no one ever thought that pilots would be dumb enough to let the plane run out of fuel in mid-air. No one was injured.

**Geologically speaking, we live in the Cenozoic era, which began 65 million years ago.**

# YOU CALL THIS ART?

*Ever been in an art gallery and seen something that made you wonder: "Is this really art?" So have we. Is it art just because someone puts it in a gallery? You decide.*

**THE ARTIST:** Richard Lomas, a New Zealand painter
**THE WORKS:** *Bug Paintings*
**THIS IS ART?** In 1991 Lomas was distressed by a comment made by a fellow artist, that painting was dead. Lomas was traveling by van across North America at the time but still wanted to prove his friend wrong. So he strapped a still-wet canvas to the front of his van and drove and drove... and drove. When he finally stopped, the canvas had been reshaped by wind, sun, and a lot of splattered bugs. Inspired by his creation, he has since driven more than 8,000 miles making more "masterpieces." He's even strapped his canvases to the front of trains. "My paintings may contain dead matter," he says, "but they stimulate lively debate."

**THE ARTIST:** SAW Gallery in Ottawa, Canada
**THE WORK:** *Scatalogue: 30 Years of Crap in Contemporary Art*
**THIS IS ART?** The gallery's curator, Stefan St. Laurent, was lamenting that "people who live in this Western society can't really deal with their own excrement." So to help them, he commissioned works for an unusual exhibit. The pieces include a sculpture of former prime minister Brian Mulroney holding feces in his outstretched hand, a performance video featuring actors posing with toilets, and last (but not least), a genuine pair of soiled trousers. According to St. Laurent, the show tackled such issues as racism, homophobia, sexism, anti-Semitism, globalization, and consumerism. Visitors were also invited to check out the Scatalogue Boutique, where they could purchase cow-pie clocks.

**THE ARTIST:** Michael Landy, a London conceptual artist
**THE WORK:** *Break Down*
**THIS IS ART?** By age 37, Landy had become so fed up with materialism that he gathered every single thing he owned—7,006 items in all—and staged their destruction in a 14-day exhibit he

**The Venus flytrap only grows wild in one place: a 100-mile stretch of Carolina swampland.**

called an “examination of consumerism.” As Landy supervised, 12 workers systematically destroyed everything from family heirlooms to dirty socks to his Saab 900. They smashed the big stuff with hammers and shredded the smaller stuff, reducing all of it to piles of pebble-sized trash, destined to end up in a landfill. More than 45,000 spectators witnessed the “art piece.” His next work: Getting new credit cards, new keys, a new passport, a new birth certificate, new shoes, and a new suit. “I found it a bit soul-destroying,” he said. “I really didn’t want to buy anything.”

**THE ARTIST:** Marilene Oliver, a London art student

**THE WORK:** *I Know You Inside Out*

**THIS IS ART?** In 1993 a convicted killer named Joseph Jernigan was put to death by lethal injection. After the execution, Jernigan’s body was frozen, then sliced (crosswise) into 1,871 micro-thin cross-sections and photographed for medical students. The images were also posted on the Internet, which is where Marilene Oliver found them in 2001. She printed them out, cut them to shape, and stacked them to create a life-size figure of the murderer.

Still not satisfied, Oliver scanned her own skin on a flatbed scanner and created a touch screen display next to the Jernigan figure, kind of like Adam and Eve. This one she called *I Know Every Inch of Your Body.*

**MORE “ART”**

**How to Make a Quick Buck:** First, get a cup of coffee in a Styrofoam cup. Drink the coffee. Attach the coffee-stained cup to a piece of wood. Find a dead ladybug. Attach that to the same piece of wood. Call the piece *Untitled* and enter it into a New York City art auction. That’s what modern artist Tom Friedman did in 1999. The winning bid: $29,900.

**How to Get Rid of a Stack of Newspapers:** At the same auction an unnamed artist entered a piece that consisted of a stack of newspapers. He called it *Stack of Newspapers.* Unfortunately for him, no bids were made on the “artwork.”

And the idea wasn’t even original—the previous year, artist Robert Gober had entered a tied stack of newspapers into a Sotheby’s auction which he called, *Newspaper, 1992.* It sold for $19,000.

**Bad sign: Mozambique has an AK-47 assault rifle on its flag.**

# THE TIME IT TAKES

*It takes the average bathroom reader one minute and fifteen seconds to read the average page of a* Bathroom Reader. *Here are some more examples of how long things take (or took).*

• **.05 second** for a human muscle to respond to stimulus

• **.06 second** for an automotive airbag to fully inflate

• **.2 second** for the Int'l Space Station to travel 1 mile

• **.46 second** for a 90-mph fastball to reach home plate

• **.6 second** for an adult to walk one step

• **1 second** for a hummingbird's wings to beat 70 times

• **1.25 seconds** for light to travel from the moon to Earth

• **3 seconds** for 475 lawsuits to be filed around the world

• **4 seconds** for 3,000,000 gallons of water to flow over Niagara Falls

• **10 seconds** for 50 people to be born

• **20 seconds** for a fast talker to say 100 words

• **58 seconds** for the elevator in Toronto's CN Tower to reach the top (1,815 feet)

• **1 minute** for a newborn baby's brain to grow 1.5 mg

• **45 minutes** to reach an actual person when calling the IRS during tax time

• **4 hours** for the *Titanic* to sink after it struck the iceberg

• **4 hrs, 30 min** to cook a 20-pound turkey at 325°F

• **92 hrs** to read both the Old and New Testaments aloud

• **96 hours** to completely recover from jet lag

• **6 days,** according to the Bible, to create the universe

• **7 days** for a newborn baby to wet or soil 80 diapers

• **19 days** until baby cardinals make their first flight

• **25 days** for Handel to compose "The Messiah"

• **29 days, 12 hrs, 44 mins, and 3 secs** from a new moon to a new moon

**Dough doe? Animal Crackers come in 18 different "species."**

• **30 days** for a human hair to grow half an inch

• **35 days** for a mouse to reach sexual maturity

• **38 days** for a slow boat to get to China (from New York)

• **12 weeks** for a U.S. Marine to go through boot camp

• **89 days, 1 hour,** for winter to come and go

• **91 days, 7 hrs, 26 mins, and 24 secs** for the Earth to fall into the Sun if it loses its orbit

• **258 days** for the gestation period of a yak

• **1 year** for Los Angeles to move two inches closer to San Francisco (due to the shifting of tectonic plates)

• **2 years** for cheddar cheese to reach its peak flavor

• **4 yrs, 8 mos** to receive your FBI file after making the appropriate request

• **6 years** in a snail's life span

• **25 years** equals the time the average American spends asleep in a lifetime

• **27 years** was the length of Nolan Ryan's pitching career

• **33 years** was the life expectancy of a Neanderthal man

• **69 years** for the Soviet Union to rise and fall

• **95 years** to count to a billion

• **100 years** for tidal friction to slow Earth's rotation by 14 seconds

• **1,800 years** to complete the Great Wall of China

• **500,000 years** for plutonium-239 to become harmless

• **45.36 million years** to reach the nearest star, Proxima Centauri, in a car going 65 mph

• **1 billion years** for the sun to release as much energy as a supernova releases in 24 hours

* * *

## POLITICAL DARWINISM

"In my lifetime, we've gone from Eisenhower to George W. Bush. We've gone from John F. Kennedy to Al Gore. If this is evolution, I believe that in 12 years, we'll be voting for plants."

**—Lewis Black**

**How long American drivers wait at traffic lights in their lifetime: 14 days.**

# THE WILHELM SCREAM

*Have you ever heard a sound effect in a film—a screeching eagle, a car crash, or a laughing crowd—that you swear you've heard before in other movies? You're probably right. Here's the story behind Hollywood's most famous "recycled" sound effect.*

## SOUNDS FAMILIAR

Like most American kids growing up in the 1950s, Ben Burtt went to the movies... *a lot*. Movie budgets were much smaller back then, and film studios reused whatever they could—props, sets, stock footage, sound effects, everything. If you watched and listened to the movies carefully, you might have noticed things you'd seen and heard in other movies.

Burtt noticed. He was good at picking out sounds—especially screams, and especially one scream in particular. "Every time someone died in a Warner Bros. movie, they'd scream this famous scream," he says.

By the 1970s, a grown-up Burtt was working in the movie business himself, as a sound designer—the guy who creates the sound effects. Years had passed, but he'd never forgotten that classic Warner Bros. scream. So when he got the chance, he decided to track down the original recording. It took a lot of digging, but he eventually found it on an old studio reel marked "Man Being Eaten by an Alligator." It turns out it had been recorded for the 1951 Warner Bros. western *Distant Drums* and used at least twice in that movie: once in a battle with some Indians, and then—of course—when a man is bitten and dragged underwater by an alligator.

## A STAR IS BORN

No one could remember what actor had originally been hired to record the scream, so Burtt jokingly named it after a character in the 1953 movie, *Charge at Feather River*. The character, named Wilhelm, screams the scream after he is struck in the leg by an arrow. The "Wilhelm Scream" was used two more times in that film: once when a soldier is struck by a spear, and again when an Indian is stabbed and then rolls down a hill.

The Wilhelm Scream is now more than 50 years old, but if you

**Top 5 causes of home accidents: stairs, glass doors, cutlery, jars, power tools (in that order).**

heard it you'd probably recognize it, because Burtt, who's worked on almost every George Lucas film, uses it often—including in his Academy Award-winning sound design for *Star Wars*. "That scream gets in every picture I do, as a personal signature," he says.

So when you hear a Wilhelm Scream in a film, can you assume that Burtt did the sound effects? No—when other sound designers heard what he was doing, they started inserting the scream into their movies, too. Apparently, Burtt isn't the only person good at noticing reused sound effects, because movie buffs have caught on to what he is doing and discovered at least 66 films that use the Wilhelm Scream. A few examples:

## AHHHHHHHHHEEEEEIIIIII!!!

***Star Wars* (1977)** Just before Luke Skywalker and Princess Leia swing across the Death Star's chasm, a stormtrooper falls in.

***The Empire Strikes Back* (1980)** 1) In the battle on the ice planet Hoth, a rebel soldier screams when his big satellite-dish laser gun is struck by laser fire and explodes. 2) As Han Solo is being frozen, Chewbacca knocks a stormtrooper off of the platform.

***Return of the Jedi* (1983)** 1) In the desert scene, Luke slashes an enemy with his light saber. The victim screams as he falls into the Sarlac pit. 2) Later in the film, Han Solo knocks a man over a ledge. The man is Ben Burtt himself, making a cameo appearance—and that's him impersonating the Wilhelm Scream... with his own voice.

***Batman Returns* (1992)** Batman punches a clown and knocks him out of the way. The clown screams.

***Toy Story* (1995)** Buzz Lightyear screams when he gets knocked out of the bedroom window.

***Titanic* (1997)** In the scene where the engine room is flooding, a crew member screams when he's hit with a jet of water.

***Spaceballs* (1987)** Barf uses a section of tubes to reflect laser bolts back at four guards. The last one screams.

***Lethal Weapon 4* (1998)** A gunshot turns a terrorist's flamethrower into a jet pack, and he flies into a gasoline truck.

***Lord of the Rings: The Two Towers* (2002)** A soldier falls off the wall during the Battle of Helm's Deep... and lets out a Wilhelm.

**Insomniac: A giraffe only sleeps about 4 hours a day.**

# NOT WHAT THEY SEEM TO BE

*Things (and people) aren't always what they seem. Here are some peeks behind the image.*

## JOHN JAMES AUDUBON

**Image:** Considered a pioneer of American wildlife conservation, this 19th-century naturalist spent days at a time searching for birds in the woods so he could paint them. The National Audubon Society was founded in 1905 in his honor.

**Actually:** Audubon found the birds, then shot them. In addition to painting, he was an avid hunter. According to David Wallechinsky in *Significa*, "He achieved unequaled realism by using freshly killed models held in lifelike poses by wires. Sometimes he shot dozens of birds just to complete a single picture."

## WASHINGTON CROSSING THE DELAWARE

**Image:** One of the most famous paintings of American history depicts General George Washington—in a fierce battle against the redcoats—leading his men across the Delaware River on Christmas Eve 1776.

**Actually:** It was painted 75 years after the battle by a German artist named Leutze. He used American tourists as models and substituted the Rhine River for the Delaware. He got the style of boat wrong; the clothing was wrong; even the American flag was incorrect. Yet the drama of the daring offensive was vividly captured, making it one of our most recognized paintings.

## *WEBSTER'S DICTIONARY*

**Image:** The oldest and most trusted dictionary in the United States, created in 1828 by Noah Webster.

**Actually:** "The truth is," says M. Hirsh Goldberg in *The Book of Lies*, "is that any dictionary maker can put *Webster's* in the name, because book titles can't be copyrighted." And a lot of shoddy publishers do just that. To know if your *Webster's* is authentic, make sure it's published by Merriam-Webster, Inc.

**Widest waterfall in the world: Victoria Falls in Africa (almost a mile wide).**

# FLUBBED HEADLINES

*These are 100% honest-to-goodness headlines. Can you figure out what they're trying to say?*

INFERTILITY UNLIKELY TO BE PASSED ON

**CRITICS SAY SUNKEN SHIPS NOT SEAWORTHY**

*STUDY FINDS SEX, PREGNANCY LINK*

**AIR HEAD FIRED**

Safety Experts Say School Bus Passengers Should Be Belted

**SURVIVOR OF SIAMESE TWINS JOINS PARENTS**

**State Says Cost of Saving Money Too High**

*LUNG CANCER IN WOMEN MUSHROOMS*

Man Steals Clock, Faces Time

***Bank Drive-in Window Blocked by Board***

ELIZABETH DOLE HAD NO CHOICE BUT TO RUN AS A WOMAN

DEER AND TURKEY HUNT FOR DISABLED PEOPLE

*Axe For Media School's Head*

***Summer Schools Boost Scrores***

***Study Says Snoring Drivers Have More Accidents***

WOMEN BOWLERS VOTE TO KEEP THEIR SKIRTS ON

**Hillary Clinton on Welfare**

***IF STRIKE ISN'T SETTLED QUICKLY, IT MAY LAST A WHILE***

ASTRONAUT TAKES BLAME FOR GAS IN SPACECRAFT

NEW STUDY OF OBESITY LOOKS FOR LARGER TEST GROUP

**COLD WAVE LINKED TO TEMPERATURES**

*Pataki Proposes Allowing Pickups on State Parkways*

Montezuma Mourns Banker Slain in Attack with Flowers

**REAL ESTATE EXECUTIVE SOLD ON CITY MARKET**

PECAN SCAB DISEASE CAUSING NUTS TO FALL OFF

**The meaning of "cool" as in "that's really cool, man" has been in use since the 1880s.**

# UNCLE JOHN'S STALL OF FAME

*Uncle John is amazed—and pleased—by the creative way people get involved with bathrooms, toilets, toilet paper, etc. That's why he created the "Stall of Fame."*

**Honoree:** The Reverend Susan Brown, minister at the Church of Scotland's cathedral in Dornoch, Scotland
**Notable Achievement:** Giving the roll with a hole a holy role.
**True Story:** When she performs a marriage, Reverend Brown always gives the same wedding gift to the newlyweds: a twin-pack of toilet paper. Why toilet paper? And why a pack of *two* rolls, instead of one or three?

It's symbolic, Reverend Brown explains. "There are two rolls together, just like the couple. And the toilet paper is soft, gentle, long, and strong, which is what I hope their marriage will be." Reverend Brown married Madonna and director Guy Ritchie in December 2000; they got toilet paper, too.

**Honoree:** Dr. Tom Keating, also known as "Bathroom Man," a former teacher from Decatur, Georgia
**Notable Achievement:** Taking his daughter's restroom complaint and turning it into a personal crusade to clean up America's school bathrooms.
**True Story:** In the late 1980s, Dr. Keating's daughter, an eighth-grader, complained to him about the messy state of the bathrooms at her school. First he addressed the problem at her school... then he started checking the restroom conditions at other schools. It turned into an obsession, and soon Keating had founded a group called Project C.L.E.A.N.—Citizens, Learners, and Educators Against Neglect—which works with students, teachers, and administrators to improve the condition of their restrooms.

In a typical school visit, Keating tours the restrooms, notes all the problems—messiness, vandalism, missing toilet paper and other supplies—and works with school officials to come up with a strategy. Then, with the help of students, bathrooms are painted, lighting is improved, damage is repaired, and any fixtures prone to vandalism—such as soap and toilet paper dispensers—are replaced with vandal-resistant models.

"It all comes down to respect," Keating says. "Kids have to respect their school restrooms as if they were their own, and faculty, staff, and administration have to respect the students as young adults who can be trusted to take care of their basic, biological needs in an acceptable setting." And there's a bonus—Keating believes that cleaner bathrooms can lead to better grades. "Students will pay closer attention in class if they're not worried about 'holding it in' until school is over," he says.

**Honoree:** Monell Chemical Senses Center, a research facility in Philadelphia

**Notable Achievement:** Turning sour smells into sweet success

**True Story:** In November 2002, the U.S. National Research Council called for a massive increase in the amount of money the Pentagon spends on nonlethal weapons. So the army is now looking into malodorants, substances so stinky that the military can use them to disperse crowds, empty buildings, and keep enemies away from sensitive areas. And Monell is at the cutting edge of research. They cook up the stinkiest smells they can think of, then let volunteers of all nationalities and cultures sniff them to make sure they have worldwide dis-appeal. Monell's worst odors:

• "Who Me?" which smells like the odorant added to natural gas (if you've ever smelled a gas leak, that's the smell), combined with the smell of rotting mushrooms.

• "Bathroom Malodor," a nasty, poopy smell that's mixed with the smell of rotting rodents. The lab also sells this smell to makers of bathroom cleansers, who use it to test the effectiveness of new products.

• "Stench Soup," a combination of "Who Me?" and "Bathroom Malodor."

So which of these three smells is considered most offensive by the most people? "Bathroom Malodor," hands down—nothing else comes close. "We got cursed in a lot of different languages when we tested that," says researcher Pamela Dalton.

# IT'S A WEIRD, WEIRD WORLD

*Proof that truth really is stranger than fiction.*

## WHITE ON!

"A University of Northern Colorado intramural basketball team has been inundated with T-shirt requests since naming itself 'The Fightin' Whites.' The team, made up of Native Americans, Hispanics, and Anglos, chose the name because nearby Easton High refused to change *its* nickname from 'Reds' and drop its American Indian caricature logo. The team plans to donate profits from the shirts to an American Indian organization. The shirts show a 1950s-style caricature of a middle-aged white man with the phrase 'Every thang's gonna be all white!'"

**—*USA Today***

## OUT TO LUNCH

"At a hospital in Nashville, Tennessee, on election day, nurses went into the room of a 72-year-old woman to prepare her for open-heart surgery, only to find the woman wasn't there. Instead they found a note which read, 'Gone to vote, back in 30 minutes.' An election official later confirmed an elderly woman with IVs coming out of her arms had indeed come in to vote."

**—Bloomington-Normal *Pantagraph***

## FISHY BEHAVIOR

"A student at Carnegie Mellon University in Pittsburgh, Pa., has arranged an 'external study' in lieu of regular classes, consisting of his dressing as a lobster, building a shelter on campus from scrap lumber and living in it. Fine-arts major Bill Kofmehl III, also known as 'Lobster Boy,' moved into the shelter February 1, vowing not to speak to anyone for three months. He did, however, occasionally climb to the roof in his lobster costume and make noises through a cardboard tube and a bullhorn."

**—*Chicago Sun-Times***

**Hey, sweetie: Aspartame is 200 times sweeter than sugar; saccharin is 500 times sweeter.**

## HONEY, I'M HOME

"Trish and Vincent Caminiti of Bayport, NY, returned from a three-week vacation to find that 20,000 bees had established a hive in the walls of their home. According to neighbors, the swarm arrived in a dense, black, 10-foot-wide funnel cloud that buzzed so loud some thought it was an aircraft. The swarm then entered the home one at a time through a hole only a half-inch in diameter in the wall of the house."

**—*Strange Tails***

## DON'T BE CHICKEN

"The Associated Press reported that some Pittsburgh parents recently held chicken pox "parties" for their kids. The parties involve having one kid with a current outbreak of the disease mingle with other kids to infect them, too, so that they would acquire a lifetime immunity. These parents apparently want their kids to avoid standard immunizations because of the side effects."

**—*News of the Weird***

## TALIBAN(G)

"Hoping to defend his nation's honor, former Taliban foreign minister Wakil Ahmed Muttawakil challenged U.S. president George Bush and British prime minister Tony Blair to a duel, suggesting that they fight former Afghan leader Mullah Omar with Kalashnikov assault rifles. Needless to say, they didn't take him up on the offer."

**—*National Post***

## DUCK!

"Workers from White's Mobile Home Supply were hanging axles under a trailer when lightning struck nearby. They came out from under the home only to be greeted by a sight they'll never forget.

"'About 20 to 30 seconds after the lightning struck, stuff started falling from the sky,' owner Ron White said. 'At first they thought it was tennis shoes. Then they realized it was ducks.'

"The workers collected 20 mallards from the mobile home park. "'Lightning can hit ducks, but it is rare,' said Arkansas Game and Fish Commission biologist Mike Checkett. 'I think this is something they'll remember for the rest of their lives.'"

**—*SFGate***

**Water can flow through a plant at 4 mph.**

# ICKY LICKY STICKS

*We were saving this page for our next* Bathroom Reader for Kids Only, *but then thought that everyone should be warned. These are 100% real.*

**SNOT SHOTS.** Green bits of supersour, fruit-flavored bubble gum (also available: Blood Balls—gumballs filled with powdered candy that colors the mouth red).

**CRAPPIN' CRITTERS.** These are models of cows, sheep, and other animals, which emit chocolate-brown jelly beans.

**TOXIC WASTE HAZARDOUSLY SOUR CANDY.** Hard candies packaged in an industrial drum. After sucking through the supersour outer layer, you get a sweet center. But then—*yow!*—you get an even more painfully sour hidden center.

**EVERY FLAVOR BEANS.** Inspired by *Harry Potter*, these look like ordinary jelly beans... until you take a bite. Some of the 38 flavors—like banana, root beer, chocolate pudding, and buttered toast—are tasty. But there's also sardine, horseradish, grass, black pepper, dirt, vomit, and booger. *Warning:* The horseradish and coconut beans are both white.

**ICKY LICKY STICKS.** "Tasty sweet liquid candy packaged in grotesque human body parts! A wart-covered foot seeps cherry toe jam candy, a bloodshot eyeball oozes cherry eye mucous candy, and a runny, wart-covered nose leaks sour apple snot candy."

**INSECTNSIDE.** Made to look like fossilized amber—it's really a clear amber-colored toffee candy... with a *real* cricket sealed inside.

**OH RATZ.** It's a gummy rat, which you're supposed to dip into candy powder contained in a tiny plastic garbage can.

**SOUR FLUSH.** Candy powder in a plastic toilet bowl.

**RAT PIZZA.** A gummy pizza with a gummy rat on top. (They also make Worm Wiener, a gummy worm in a gummy hot dog bun.)

**CHOCKA CA-CA.** A piece of chocolate fudge that comes in a baby diaper. Packaged in a gift box—pink for girls, blue for boys.

**The automobile was invented in 1886; the used car lot (17 cars) was invented in 1897.**

# THE IG NOBEL PRIZES

*Too dumb to win a Nobel Prize? Don't feel too bad—there's still the Ig Nobel prizes. The science humor magazine* Annals of Improbable Research *awards them at Harvard University every year, to honor people whose achievements in science, medicine, or technology "cannot or should not be reproduced." Bonus: If you win, your prize is handed to you by a genuine Nobel laureate!*

**IG NOBEL PRIZE:** Public Health (2001)

**AWARD-WINNING TOPIC:** "A Preliminary Survey of Rhinotillexomania in an Adolescent Sample," by Chittaranjan Andrade, et al. *Journal of Clinical Psychiatry*, June 2001. ***Translation:*** "We studied nose-picking behavior in a sample of 200 adolescents from four urban schools."

**FINDINGS:**

• "Nose picking is common in adolescents.... Almost the entire sample admitted to nose picking, with a median frequency of four times per day."

• "Nearly 17% of subjects considered that they have a serious nose-picking problem."

• "Nose picking may merit closer nosologic scrutiny."

**IG NOBEL PRIZE:** Psychology (1995)

**AWARD-WINNING TOPIC:** "Pigeons' Discrimination of Paintings by Monet and Picasso," by Shigeru Watanabe, et al. *Journal of the Experimental Analysis of Behavior,* 1995.

**FINDINGS:**

• "Pigeons successfully learned to discriminate color slides of paintings by Monet and Picasso. Following this training, they discriminated novel paintings by Monet and Picasso that had never been presented during the discrimination training."

• The pigeons "showed generalization from Monet's to Cezanne's and Renoir's paintings [all Impressionist painters], or from Picasso's to Braque's and Matisse's paintings [Cubists and Fauvists]."

**A poem written to celebrate a wedding is called an *epithalamium.***

• "Upside-down images of Monet's paintings disrupted the discrimination, whereas inverted images of Picasso's did not."

**IG NOBEL PRIZE:** Public Health (2000)

**AWARD-WINNING TOPIC:** "The Collapse of Toilets in Glasgow," by Jonathan Wyatt, et al. *The Scottish Medical Journal*, 1993.

**FINDINGS:**

• "Three cases are presented of porcelain toilets collapsing under body weight, producing wounds serious enough to require hospital treatment."

• "The excessive age of the toilets was a causative factor."

• "As many such toilets get older, episodes of collapse may become more common, resulting in further injuries."

**IG NOBEL PRIZE:** Psychology (2001)

**AWARD-WINNING TOPIC:** "An Ecological Study of Glee in Small Groups of Preschool Children," by Lawrence W. Sherman. *Child Development*, March 1975.

**FINDINGS:**

• "A phenomenon called group glee was studied in videotapes of 596 formal lessons in a preschool. This was characterized by joyful screaming, laughing, and intense physical acts which occurred in simultaneous bursts or which spread in a contagious fashion from one child to another."

• "While most events of glee did not disrupt the ongoing lesson, those which did tended to produce a protective reaction on the part of teachers [i.e., the teacher called the class back to order]."

• "Group glee tended to occur most often in large groups (seven to nine children) and in groups containing both sexes."

**OTHER IG NOBEL LAUREATES**

• **Physics (2002):** "Demonstration of the Exponential Decay Law Using Beer Froth," by Arnd Leike, *European Journal of Physics*, January 2002.

• **Mathematics (2002):** "Estimation of Total Surface Area in Indian Elephants," by K. P. Sreekumar, et al. *Veterinary Research Communications*, 1990.

**The ears of an African elephant can weigh up to 110 pounds each.**

# THE HALIFAX EXPLOSION

*In late 1917, World War I was raging in Europe. Back in North America, the port of Halifax, Nova Scotia, was the hub of Canada's war effort. All the ships heading out to the Atlantic brought prosperity to the small town... but they also brought disaster.*

## UNLIKE TWO SHIPS PASSING IN THE NIGHT

In December 1917, the French cargo ship *Mont Blanc* took on 5,000 tons of explosives in New York, including more than 400,000 pounds of TNT. The 300-foot-long ship was headed into Halifax Harbor to await a convoy of ships that would accompany it to England. The *Mont Blanc*'s captain, Aime Le Medec, should have been flying a red flag to warn other ships of the dangerous cargo, but he was afraid that enemy ships might see the flag and start shooting.

At the same time, a 440-foot Norwegian ship, called the *Imo*—much faster and larger than the *Mont Blanc*—was leaving Halifax for New York. The *Imo*'s captain, Haakon From, knew he was behind schedule and ordered the ship full speed ahead.

Halifax Harbor has, roughly, an hourglass shape. The "waist" of the hourglass is a slim channel of water called the Narrows. Halifax is on the southern side of this narrow channel; the town of Darmouth sits on the north side. Two ships passing through the Narrows must do so with caution—as the *Imo* and the *Mont Blanc* were soon to learn.

## COLLISION

On the cold, clear morning of December 6, shortly before nine, the *Imo* and the *Mont Blanc* both entered the Narrows: the *Imo* going east toward open sea (too fast, some said), the *Mont Blanc* was going west to moor up. Harbor rules say that ships must pass port to port—left side to left side—just like cars on the road. But the *Imo* was veering too far north; it was headed directly toward the *Mont Blanc* like a truck in the wrong lane. Captain Le Medec, aboard the *Mont Blanc*, signaled the other ship, but, strangely, Captain From didn't stop—he signaled that he was continuing farther north. After repeated and confused attempts to communicate with horns and flags, Le Medec finally steered his ship south-

In 1986 *Down and Out in Beverly Hills* became the 1st Disney film to use the "F" word.

ward... but Captain From did the same thing at the same time. Result: The smaller ship was broadsided. The collision sent the *Mont Blanc* straight toward the city of Halifax.

The impact started a fire on the deck of the *Mont Blanc*. Her crew, knowing the ship could blow up at any second, went straight to the lifeboats... without alerting the harbor patrol of the dangerous cargo. They rowed north toward Dartmouth, leaving the floating bomb heading straight for Halifax.

It was an astounding sight: a flaming ship drifting slowly toward shore. All morning activity stopped as people watched the spectacle—kids on their way to school, dockworkers on shore, shopkeepers, and homemakers who could see the harbor from their windows. The *Mont Blanc* drifted for about 20 minutes until it came to rest against Pier 6 in the Richmond district, the busy, industrial north end of Halifax. As firefighting crews rushed to put the fire out, the flames were getting closer and closer to the massive stores of TNT on the lower decks.

## EXPLOSION

Then, shortly before 9:05 a.m., a blinding, white flash filled the harbor. The *Mont Blanc* exploded into bits and a giant mushroom cloud rose up over the town. More than 1,600 people were killed instantly. Thousands more were injured, many blinded from the glass and shrapnel that rained down on Halifax and Dartmouth. Schools, homes, factories, and churches were leveled by the ensuing shockwave. A 30-foot tidal wave swept away what was left of the waterfront, drowning many of the initial survivors and sinking dozens of ships in the harbor. Shattered pieces of the *Mont Blanc* were hurled as far as three miles away. A tugboat was thrown from the middle of the harbor onto the Dartmouth shore. The wave also rushed over the shores of Dartmouth and up Tufts Cove, where it completely washed away the settlement of an indigenous tribe called the Micmac.

The blast was so strong that windows were broken even in Charlottetown—120 miles away. It was the largest man-made explosion in human history, and its size and devastation wouldn't be eclipsed until the atomic bomb was dropped on Hiroshima in 1945.

More than 1,600 homes were gone; 12,000 more were damaged from the fires that spread through Halifax after the explosion. At least 6,000 people were left homeless at the onset of a powerful winter storm that would drop more than a foot of snow within the next 24 hours. Hundreds who had survived the blast, the tidal wave, and the ensuing fires would end up freezing to death.

## RELIEF

Rescue efforts were slow at first. Power, water, gas, telephone, telegraph, and railroad lines were all obliterated. The dead and dying lined the streets, while thousands of others were buried under debris. And medical supplies were in pitifully short supply. But help was on the way. Money started pouring in from all over the world, from as far away as China and New Zealand. The Canadian government appropriated $18 million for relief efforts, and surrounding towns donated shelters, blankets, and other necessities. But much of the immediate help came from Massachusetts. A train full of supplies and medical personnel left for Halifax the day of the explosion. In all, Bostonians donated $750,000 through the Massachusetts-Halifax Relief Committee. (To this day, Halifax sends an annual Christmas tree to the city of Boston in gratitude.)

## THE BLAME GAME

The survivors of the explosion were stunned. Something this horrible had to be somebody's fault. First, they blamed the Germans, because if Germany hadn't started the war, the disaster would not have happened. Every surviving German in town was rounded up and arrested, in spite of the fact that they had suffered the same as everyone else. But as rebuilding began and cooler heads prevailed, people realized that if anyone was to blame, it was the ships' captains.

Captain From and most of the crew of the *Imo* perished in the blast; Captain Le Medec of the *Mont Blanc* survived and was brought to trial. After months of inquiry and many civil suits, there was insufficient evidence to establish criminal negligence. Captain Le Medec's license was revoked, but in the end, no one was ever convicted.

On January 22, 1918, Canada appointed the Halifax Relief Commission to handle pensions, insurance claims, rehousing, and rebuilding, as well as the rehabilitation of survivors. The extent of the damage was so great that the Commission would remain open until 1976.

**...man-made loss of life on North American soil...until 9/11/01.**

# COMIC RELIEF

*Our annual salute to those who stand up so we may laugh while sitting down.*

"I met a beautiful girl at a barbeque, which was exciting. Blonde, I think—I don't know. Her hair was on fire. And all she talked about was herself. You know those kind of girls. It was just me, me, me. Help *me*. Put *me* out."

**—Garry Shandling**

"You can say, 'Can I use your bathroom,' and nobody cares. But if you ask, 'Can I use the plop-plop machine,' it always breaks the conversation."

**—Dave Attell**

"I can bend forks with my mind, but only the ones at Denny's. And you have to look away for a little while."

**—Bobcat Goldthwaite**

"*Frisbeetarianism* is the belief that when you die, your soul goes up on the roof and gets stuck."

**—George Carlin**

"Did you hear they finally made a device that makes cars run 95% quieter? It fits right over her mouth."

**—Billy Crystal**

"My parents only had one argument in forty-five years. It lasted forty-three years."

**—Cathy Ladman**

"First the doctor told me the good news: I was going to have a disease named after me."

**—Steve Martin**

"I think I'm a pretty good judge of people, which is why I hate most of them."

**—Roseanne**

"It's strange, isn't it. You stand in the middle of a library and go '*aaaaagghhhh*' and everyone just stares at you. But you do the same thing on an airplane, and everyone joins in."

**—Tommy Cooper**

"I'm against picketing... but I don't know how to show it."

**—Mitch Hedburg**

"A study in the *Washington Post* says that women have better verbal skills than men. I just want to say to the authors of that study: *Duh*."

**—Conan O'Brien**

**500 pairs of false sideburns were used in the making of *Gone With the Wind*.**

# HOW PAPER BECAME MONEY

*Today we take it for granted that a $20 bill is worth 20 dollars. But convincing people that paper can be just as valuable as gold or silver took centuries and involved many false starts. Take this one, for example.*

## SPOILS OF WAR

In 1298 a Venetian traveler named Marco Polo signed on as "gentleman commander" of a Venetian galley and led it in battle against the fleet of its rival city, Genoa.

Lucky for us, Polo lost. After he was captured and thrown into prison, he spent the next two years dictating a detailed account of his 24 years of travel in India, Africa, and China (then part of the Mongol empire ruled by Kublai Khan).

Until then, very little was known about that part of the world. Few Europeans had been to the Far East, and even fewer had written about their experiences. Polo's memoirs changed everything. *The Travels of Marco Polo* was widely read all over Europe and is considered the most important account of the "outside" world written during the Middle Ages.

## HARD TO BELIEVE

But not everyone believed it. In its day, *The Travels of Marco Polo* was also known as *Il Milióne*, or "The Million Lies," because so many of the things that Polo described seemed preposterous to his European readers. He told of a postal system that could transport a letter 300 miles in a single day, fireproof cloth that could be cleaned by throwing it into a fire (it was made from asbestos), and baths that were heated by "stones that burn like logs" (coal).

But one of Polo's most preposterous-seeming claims: In Kublai Khan's empire, people traded *paper* as if it were gold.

Here's how Polo described it:

> In [the] city of Kanbalu, is the mint of the Grand Khan, who may truly be said to possess the secret of the alchemists, as he has the art of producing paper money.... When ready for use, he has it cut

> into pieces of money of different sizes.... The coinage of this paper money is authenticated with as much form and ceremony as if it were actually of pure gold or silver... and the act of counterfeiting it is punished as a capital offence.
>
> This paper currency is circulated in every part of the Grand Khan's dominions; nor does any person, at the peril of his life, refuse to accept it in payment. All his subjects receive it without hesitation, because, wherever their business may call them, they can dispose of it again in the purchase of merchandise they have occasion for, such as pearls, jewels, gold, or silver. All his majesty's armies are paid with this currency, which is to them of the same value as if it were gold and silver.

*Paper* money? Europeans had never seen anything like it.

## MADE IN CHINA

Kublai Khan's paper currency may have been news to Europeans, but for the Chinese it was just the latest attempt to establish paper as a legitimate form of money:

- Felted paper made from animal fibers was invented in China in about 177 B.C., and less than 40 years after that, the Chinese Emperor Wu-Ti (140–87 B.C.) began to issue the first notes made from paper. They were intended only as a temporary substitute for real money—precious metals and coins—when real money was in short supply. These first bills were more like cardboard than the foldable bills we use today.

- Another emperor, Hien Tsung, issued his own notes during a copper shortage in the early 800s. These, too, were intended only as temporary substitutes, but the idea caught on. More currency was issued in the year 910; after that, paper money came to be issued on a more regular basis.

- By 1020 so many paper notes were in circulation that China became the first country to experience "paper inflation." That's what happens when too much money is printed: it takes more currency to buy the same goods than it used to, so the purchasing power of each individual note goes down. If enough paper money is printed, the currency eventually becomes as worthless as... paper. To counteract the inflation, government officials began spraying the bills with perfume to make them more attractive. It didn't do any good—and neither did anything else they tried.

**Finland has more islands than any other country: 179,584.**

• When one issue of currency became worthless, government officials would replace it with a new issue of currency; but since they kept printing new bills, in time the new ones would become worthless too, and the cycle would repeat itself.

• By the time of the Mongol invasion in the early 13th century, China had already endured several rounds of paper inflation, but that didn't stop the Mongols from adopting the concept of paper money and spreading it across the entire Mongol empire.

• Kublai Khan issued his own series of paper notes in 1260. These were the ones that Marco Polo encountered when he visited China. By 1290, they were worthless, too.

## THE END OF THE PAPER TRAIL

Although the Chinese used paper money over the next 150 years, by 1455 they were so disillusioned with it that it disappeared altogether and did not reappear in China for another 450 years.

"The Chinese people lost all faith in paper money and became more than ever convinced of the virtues of silver," historian Glyn Davies writes in *A History of Money*, "a conviction that lasted right up to the early part of the twentieth century."

***Turn to Part II of "How Paper Became Money" on page 544.***

* * *

## WISDOM THEY DON'T TEACH IN SCHOOL
### (but you can learn on the Internet)

• Scratch a dog and you'll find a permanent job.

• No one has more driving ambition than the boy who wants to buy a car.

• There are worse things than getting a call for a wrong number at 4 a.m. It could be a right number.

• Money may buy a dog; only kindness can make him wag his tail.

• The great thing about the future is that it always starts tomorrow.

• Seat belts are not as confining as wheelchairs.

• Learn from the mistakes of others. You won't live long enough to make them all yourself.

# PHONE PHUNNIES

*Riddle: What's the difference between a phone booth and a bathroom? (If you don't know, please don't use our phone booth.)*

## OVER THE HUMP

Next time you find yourself in rural India and need to phone home, don't bother looking for a phone booth; there are none—the cost of laying telephone cable in rural areas is prohibitive. Yet there are millions of potential customers, so enterprising telecommunications companies have to be creative. Enter Shyam Telelink. The solution: They own 200 mobile phones. Every day they send the phones out into the back country... mounted on camels. Customers say the service is very user-friendly. Cost: 2 cents a call.

## DIAL-A-DOLPHIN

Stressed out and stuck in traffic with only your cell phone to keep you company? Call a dolphin. As you listen to their underwater clicks and whistles, your stress will disappear. At least that's what scientists at Ireland's Dolphin and Wildlife Foundation hope will happen once they've installed underwater microphones in the Shannon estuary, where dolphins reside year round. They're working with telecom giant Vodaphone to make it possible for cell phone users worldwide to "reach out and touch" the dolphins.

Some kinks still need to be worked out, though—dolphins use a wide frequency band to communicate... most of which is beyond the human range of hearing.

## CALL ME STUPID

Michael LaRock, a thief who had been on the run for over a year, called the police in Ticonderoga, New York, to boast that he would never be caught. Apparently it didn't occur to him that the police might have caller I.D. The cops tracked the call to Auburn, Georgia, and quickly contacted the local police. While Officer Dan Charlton in New York was talking to LaRock on the phone, he heard the doorbell ring in the background. The next thing he heard was the Georgia police coming through the door to arrest the thief... right in his own home.

# DUMB CROOKS OF THE OLD WEST

*Here's proof that stupidity is timeless (and sometimes deadly).*

**THE DALTON BROTHERS**

In the little town of Coffeyville, Kansas, in 1890, Bob, Emmett, and Gratton Dalton, along with two other men, formed a gang of outlaws. Inspired by the exploits of their cousins the Younger Brothers—who 15 years earlier had stolen nearly half a million dollars from trains and banks with the James Gang—the Daltons pulled a few small-time robberies. But they wanted a big payoff and the fame that goes with it—and that could only come from a bank heist. So they planned it all out...all wrong:

1. The Daltons aimed to rob two banks at once: two men would rob the First National Bank, while the other three hit Condon & Co. across the street. They thought they'd get double the loot, but they only doubled their chances of getting caught.

2. Instead of traveling to another town where no one knew them, they chose Coffeyville—where everyone knew them.

3. The street in front of the banks was being repaired the day of the heist. They could have postponed it, but went ahead anyway. Now they had to hitch their horses a block away, making a clean getaway that much more difficult.

4. *Smart:* They wore disguises. *Dumb:* The disguises were wispy stage mustaches and goatees. Locals saw right through them.

The bank robberies were a disaster. The townsfolk saw the Dalton boys coming and armed themselves. The Daltons did get $20,000 from First National, but came up empty at the other bank when a teller said she couldn't open the safe. When they emerged from the banks, an angry mob was waiting for them in the street. A hail of bullets followed, killing every member except Emmett Dalton, who spent the next 15 years in prison. He emerged from the penitentiary to discover that the Dalton Gang's story had indeed been immortalized, but not as legendary outlaws...only as hapless screwups.

# LUCKY FINDS

*Have you ever found something valuable? It's one of the best feelings in the world. Here's another installment of a regular* Bathroom Reader *feature—a look at some folks who found really valuable stuff... and got to keep it.*

## IT MAY BE UGLY, BUT IT'S MINE

**The Find:** Painting by Jackson Pollack

**Where It Was Found:** In a thrift shop

**The Story:** Retired truckdriver Teri Horton, 70, of Costa Mesa, California, bought an abstract painting for a friend at a local thrift shop. The price was $8, but Horton thought it was ugly and told the store owner, "I ain't paying eight dollars for this thing." She got it for $5. As it turned out, the painting wouldn't fit through her friend's front door, so Horton kept it. When another friend, an art professor, saw the painting, he told her it might actually be an original work by the 20th-century master Jackson Pollack. He was right: in July 2003, forensic specialists found one of Pollack's fingerprints on it—making it worth $20 million. "I still think it's ugly," Horton said, "but now I see dollar signs."

## SHELL SHOCK

**The Find:** 40-carat emerald

**Where It Was Found:** In a conch shell

**The Story:** An elementary school teacher and part-time salvage diver was searching the wreck of a Spanish galleon that had sunk off the coast of Florida during a hurricane 380 years ago. Finding nothing of value, the diver collected a bucketful of seashells for his students instead. Later, as he was washing the shells, a 40-carat emerald estimated to be worth millions rolled out of a queen conch shell. According to Doug Pope, president of Amelia Research & Recovery, the man didn't even know what he'd found. "He thought it might be a piece of a Heineken bottle."

## PRICEY WATERHOUSE

**The Find:** Victorian masterpiece painting

**Where It Was Found:** In an old farmhouse

**The Story:** In 1973 a British couple bought a run-down farmhouse in Canada. They requested that an old painting in the house be included in the sale—because they thought it looked nice on the wall. Nineteen years later, they decided to have the painting appraised by Odon Wagner, an art dealer in Toronto. "Odon nearly fell off his chair," said a spokesman for Christie's auction house. It was *Gather Ye Rosebuds While Ye May*, a 1909 work by the Victorian master John William Waterhouse that had been missing for almost a century. "Nobody knew where it was," he said, "and we still don't know how it got to Canada." It was expected to sell for about $5 million. He said the couple was "very, very pleased."

### YEAH! YEAH! YEAH!

**The Find:** More than 500 unknown photos of the Beatles

**Where They Were Found:** At a university in Scotland

**The Story:** Dundee University in Scotland was working to digitize its archives in 2002 when someone came across a cache of 130,000 photos by the late Hungarian photographer Michael Peto. Peto's son had given the collection to the university in 1971. Included were hundreds of black and whites of the Beatles from 1965, including candid shots of the band eating, drinking tea, and relaxing between takes on the set of the movie *Help!* Many of the images had never been seen by the public before. A spokesperson for Christie's auction house wouldn't put a dollar figure on the photos, but expected them to be worth a "significant" amount.

* * *

## IT'S THE THOUGHT THAT COUNTS

Joe Purkey of Knoxville, Tennessee, lost his high school ring in 1964. Then he got a phone call about it…37 years later. It was Bob's Septic Service on the line. It seems that between when he bought the ring and when it was delivered, Purkey had lost 40 pounds. The ring was too loose and slipped off his finger…into the toilet *just as he was flushing it.* An employee of the septic service found it in their filtering system. She cleaned it off, researched the date and initials, and in November 2001 gave it back to its original owner. Purkey claimed to be grateful, but wasn't thrilled about wearing it again. "It was never really lost," he said, "I just didn't wanna go get it."

**Worldwide, about 20% of all married couples are first cousins.**

# PRIMETIME PROVERBS

*Reflections on life from some of today's most popular shows.*

## ON LAWYERS

**Corporal Cortez:** "They're not going to be glad to see us."

**Harm:** "I'm a lawyer, Corporal, no one's ever glad to see me."

—***J.A.G***

## ON LISTENING

**Kelly:** "Dad, you haven't heard a single word I've said!"

**Ozzy:** "Can I explain something? You haven't been standing in front of 50 billion decibels for the past thirty years! Leave me a note!"

—***The Osbournes***

## ON ENDANGERED SPECIES

**Stan:** "Dolphins are intelligent and friendly."

**Cartman:** "Intelligent and friendly on rye bread with some mayonnaise."

—***South Park***

## ON LOVE

"My love for you is like this scar: ugly, but permanent."

—**Grace, *Will and Grace***

## ON EATING

"Cheese: it's milk that you chew."

—**Chandler, *Friends***

## ON DEATH

**Frasier:** "There's nothing you can do when the cold hand of Death comes knocking on your door..."

*(knock at door)*

**Frasier:** "Would you get that?"

**Niles:** "I most certainly will not!"

—***Frasier***

## ON HIGHER EDUCATION

"College is for ugly girls who can't get modeling contracts."

—**Kelso, *That '70s Show***

## ON ANIMALS

"If frogs could fly...well, we'd still be in this mess, but wouldn't it be neat?"

—**Drew, *The Drew Carey Show***

## ON HIGH SCHOOL

**Andie:** "You guys are a bunch of cynics, you know that? I mean, what kind of high school memories will you have if all you did in high school was bitch and moan about everything?"

**Joey:** "Bitching memories."

**Dawson:** "Moaning memories."

—***Dawson's Creek***

# NAME THAT SLEUTH

*It took us a while, but using time-tested sleuthing techniques, we finally solved... The Mystery of the Fictional Detective Names.*

**PERRY MASON** (1933)
As a youngster, author Erle Stanley Gardner subscribed to a boy's fiction magazine, *The Youth's Companion*, and learned a lot about writing from the stories he read. *The Youth's Companion* was published by... Perry Mason and Company.

**SPENSER FOR HIRE** (1973)
Robert B. Parker first introduced his streetwise, Chaucer-quoting, beer-drinking, gourmet-cooking, Bostonian, ex-boxer private investigator in *The Godwulf Manuscript*. Parker saw Spenser as a tough guy but also as a knight in shining armor and named him after the English poet (and Shakespeare contemporary) Edmund Spenser.

**MIKE HAMMER** (1947)
Writer Mickey Spillane had been in and out of the comic book business for years when he tried to sell a new detective strip to some New York publishers in 1946. The character's name was Mike Danger. When no one would buy, he decided to turn it into a novel and changed the name to Mike Hammer, after one of his favorite haunts, Hammer's Bar and Grill.

**SHERLOCK HOLMES AND DR. JOHN WATSON** (1887)
Dr. Watson is believed to have been inspired by author Arthur Conan Doyle's friend Dr. James Watson. It's less clear how he named the famous sleuth whom he originally named *Sherringford* Holmes. Most experts say Doyle took "Holmes" from American Supreme Court justice, physician and poet Oliver Wendell Holmes, well-known for his probing intellect and attention to detail. Sherringford was changed to Sherlock, Doyle enthusiasts say, for a famous violinist of the time, Alfred Sherlock. Fittingly, Doyle made his detective an amateur violinist.

**INSPECTOR MORSE** (1975)

Morse's creator, Colin Dexter, was once a Morse Code operator in the English army—but that's not where he got the name for his character. Sir Jeremy Morse, the chairman of Lloyd's Bank, was a champion crossword-solver in England. Dexter, once a national crossword champion himself, named his melancholy inspector after Sir Jeremy.

**HERCULE POIROT** (1920)

Some say the meticulous Belgian detective was named after a vegetable—*poireau* means "leek" in French. But it's more likely that Poirot's creator, Agatha Christie, took the name from the stories of another female author of the time, Marie Belloc Lowndes. Her character: a French detective named Hercules Popeau.

**TRAVIS MCGEE** (1964)

John D. MacDonald began working on his Florida boat-bum character in 1962, calling him Dallas McGee. The next year, President John Kennedy was shot—in Dallas—and MacDonald changed the name to Travis.

**KINSEY MILLHONE** (1982)

Sue Grafton spent 15 years as a Hollywood scriptwriter before the birth of her first Kinsey Millhone novel, *A Is for Alibi.* Where'd she get the name? From the birth announcements page of her local newspaper.

**JOHN SHAFT** (1970)

Ernest Tidyman was trying to sell the idea of a bad-ass black detective to his publisher, but was stymied when the publisher asked the character's name—he didn't have one ready. Tidyman absent-mindedly looked out the window and saw a sign that said "Fire shaft." He looked back at the publisher and said, "Shaft. John Shaft."

* * *

"Ninety-eight percent of the adults in this country are decent, hard-working, honest citizens. It's the other 2% that get all the publicity. But then, we elected them."

**—Lily Tomlin**

# CELEBRITY LAWSUITS

*It seems that people will sue each other over practically anything. Here are a few real-life examples of unusual legal battles involving celebrities.*

**PLAINTIFF:** President Theodore Roosevelt
**DEFENDANT:** Newspaper publisher George Newett
**LAWSUIT:** In 1912 Newett wrote an editorial in his Ishpeming, Michigan, paper, *The Iron Ore*. "Roosevelt lies, and curses in a most disgusting way," he wrote. "He gets drunk too, and that not infrequently, and all of his intimates know about it." Roosevelt happened to be campaigning for another presidential term at the time and jumped at the opportunity to be the center of a big news story. He sued Newett for libel, insisting that he hardly drank alcohol at all. Roosevelt arrived in the small town with a phalanx of security, some famous friends to act as character witnesses, and a horde of reporters and photographers. Huge crowds showed up for the trial. *The National Enquirer* even gave the start of arguments a banner headline: DRUNKEN ROOSEVELT TRIAL BEGINS! On the stand, Roosevelt mesmerized the judge, the jury, and the crowd with long stories about his many adventures around the world.
**VERDICT:** Newett must have realized he was outgunned. After five days, he gave up, reading a statement to the court admitting that he had wronged the former president. Roosevelt, having proved his point, asked the judge that he be awarded the lowest legal sum—6¢. The judge agreed. Asked by a reporter what he would do with his winnings, he replied, "That's about the price of a good paper." Cost of *The Iron Ore*: 3¢.

**PLAINTIFF:** Judy Z. Knight, aka JZ Knight
**DEFENDANT:** Julie Ravel
**LAWSUIT:** Knight claimed she could go into a trance and "channel" the spirit of a 35,000-year-old warrior from the lost continent of Atlantis named Ramtha. She charged fees of up to $1,500 per séance. By the 1980s she had attracted thousands of followers (including actresses Shirley MacLaine and Linda Evans), had pub-

lished books and videotapes, and had become very wealthy. When Ravel, also a clairvoyant, started channeling the same ancient Atlantian in 1992, Knight sued her in an Austrian courtroom. "I've had spiritual contact with Ramtha since 1978," Knight said. "I need him and he needs me."

"Ramtha feeds his thoughts and energies through me and me alone," Ravel replied. "I am his keeper."

**VERDICT:** Knight won. The judge ordered Ravel to stop using the Ramtha "brand" and to pay Knight $800 for interfering with her transmissions and for creating her subsequent period of "spiritual limbo."

**PLAINTIFF:** Shenandoah South Theater

**DEFENDANT:** Singer Wayne Newton

**LAWSUIT:** In 1994 Newton filed suit against the Branson, Missouri, theater for failing to pay him his full fee. Shenandoah owner Gary Snadon immediately filed a countersuit. Newton had appeared at the Shenandoah in 1993 and had been paid $5 million, Snadon said, while the theater had lost $500,000. Snadon's suit charged that Newton had ruined the theater's reputation. How? Because the singer told too many "fat" jokes and jokes about people from Pennsylvania.

**VERDICT:** Newton paid an undisclosed amount in a settlement before the trial ended. The Shenandoah South closed down later that year.

* * *

## RANDOM FACTS TO BUG YOU

• The praying mantis is the only insect that can turn its head like a human.

• The word *bug* started out as the Anglo-Saxon word *bugge* or *bough*, meaning "a terror, a devil, or a ghost."

• The hairs on the butt of a cockroach are so sensitive that they can detect air currents made by the onrushing tongue of a toad.

• The praying mantis is the official state insect of Connecticut.

• Mating soapberry bugs remain locked in embrace for up to 11 days, which exceeds the life span of many other insects.

**President Gerald R. Ford's birth name was Leslie Lynch King, Jr. (He was adopted.)**

# FLYING FLOPS

*Okay, so the last thing you want to read about is airplane trouble. But it's better to read about it in the bathroom than in an airplane. What? You took this book with you on a flight to Hawaii? Oh, well, our advice: skip this article for now and read it when you're back on solid porcelain.*

## CAPRONI CA-60 TRANSAEREO (1921)

If a plane with two wings is called a biplane, and a plane with three wings is called a triplane, what do you call a plane with nine wings? A *very* bad idea.

Count Gianni Caproni was an Italian nobleman who owned an airplane factory and built bombers for the Italian Air Force in 1914 and 1915. Yet for some reason, when he set out to build a seaplane that could fly from Italy all the way to New York, he ignored all of his practical experience. Instead of building a *plane* that could land on water, he took a *houseboat* and added wings—nine wings (three in the front, three in the middle and three in the back)—and eight engines (four on the front wings to pull the plane, and four on the back wings to push it).

On March 4, 1921, his test pilot fired up the engines, taxied across Lake Maggiore, and took off...sort of.

The craft got about 60 feet into the air, then suddenly nose-dived, broke into pieces, and slammed into the lake. The pilot survived, but Count Caproni's image did not. "His reputation for commercial aircraft thoroughly blackened," Bill Yenne writes in *The World's Worst Aircraft*, "Caproni skulked away into oblivion."

## THE BREWSTER BUFFALO

In the 1930s, the U.S. Navy checked out prospective new fighter planes by putting them through a rigorous test flight. A test pilot would fly the prototype to its maximum altitude and then take it into a long, steep dive at full speed. If the pilot could pull out of the dive without ripping the plane's wings off, the Navy would consider buying it.

Reasonable or not, the test encouraged airplane manufacturers to build planes stronger than necessary, which made them heavy.

That, in turn, made them slow and difficult to maneuver—bad qualities for aircraft whose speed and agility could mean the difference between victory and defeat.

The worst example of this was the 2.5-ton Brewster Buffalo. It was so overbuilt in its structure that the manufacturer *under*built other parts of it—landing gear and machine guns, for example—just to save on weight.

England's Royal Air Force bought 150 Buffaloes, but then found them so worthless against the fast German fighters that it sent them to Britain's Far East colonies, to go up against Japanese fighters (considered "antiquated junk"). Big mistake—Japan's Mitsubishi Zeros proved to be faster, more maneuverable and better armed. They flew circles—literally—around the Buffaloes, whose four tiny machine guns were no match for the Zero's two larger machine guns and 20-millimeter cannons.

According to one expert, within a few months of the start of the war, "every Buffalo in the Far East had been lost, giving Brewster the distinction of having handed the Japanese complete air superiority over Southeast Asia on a silver platter."

Only a few American Buffaloes saw action and they didn't see it for long—13 of the 19 sent into combat during the Battle of Midway in June 1942 were shot out of the sky in less than half an hour. "It is my belief," wrote one Buffalo pilot who survived, "that any commander who orders pilots out for combat in a Brewster should consider the pilot as lost before leaving the ground."

### CONVAIR XFY-1 POGO

One of the problems with flying an airplane, especially in a war, is that there isn't always a runway where you need one. The Convair Pogo, developed in the mid-1950s, was designed to be an airplane that didn't *need* a runway. It looked just like an ordinary plane, except that it was tilted up vertically on its tail like a rocket. It had an engine and propeller so powerful that it could take off straight up in the air and land the same way, just like a helicopter…or a pogo stick.

Taking off wasn't too difficult, but landing vertically was another story: the pilot had to literally set the plane back down on the ground while looking over his shoulder, which was almost impossible.

It was the same with a similar plane, the XFV-1, being developed at Lockheed. "We practiced landing looking over our shoulders," remembers Lockheed designer Kelly Johnson, "but we couldn't tell how fast we were coming down, or when we would hit. We wrote the Navy: 'We think it is inadvisable to *land* the airplane.' They came back with one paragraph that said, 'We agree.'"

### CONVAIR XF2Y-1 SEA DART

The Sea Dart was built in the 1950s when it was easy to get money from the Pentagon and defense contractors were willing to try anything. So how about a supersonic jet fighter…on water skis?

Only five prototypes were ever made, only three were ever flown, and only two made it back safely. Vibration caused by the retractable skis made the Sea Dart unstable, but what really killed it was common sense. With the Pentagon's approval, Convair had pumped millions into the Sea Dart program without having any idea *why* such planes should be built in the first place. They never did come up with a reason, either.

"The program was terminated," Yenne writes, "without ever having demonstrated any operational rationale."

* * *

## THOUGHTS FOR THE THRONE

*If you could shrink the world down to 100 people—keeping the same ratios—there would be:*

- 51 female, 49 male
- 57 Asians, 21 Europeans, 14 from the Americas, and 8 Africans
- 70 nonwhite, 30 white
- 70 non-Christian, 30 Christian
- 50% of the wealth in the hands of 6 people—all in the U.S.
- 80 living in substandard housing
- 70 who are illiterate
- 50 suffering from malnutrition
- 1 person near death, 1 near birth
- 1 with a college education
- Not one who owned a computer…or a *Bathroom Reader*

# BOX OFFICE BLOOPERS

*Some of our favorites from new and classic films.*

**Movie:** *E.T. The Extra-Terrestrial* (1982)

**Scene:** When Elliott (Henry Thomas) first meets E.T. in his backyard, a crescent moon can be seen overhead.

**Blooper:** In the famous bike-flying scene, the silhouettes of Elliott and E.T. pass in front of a full moon, yet it's only three days later.

**Movie:** *Braveheart* (1995)

**Scene:** In the beginning of the film, young William Wallace (James Robinson) is throwing rocks with his left hand.

**Blooper:** In the next scene, a grown-up William Wallace (Mel Gibson) is throwing rocks with his right hand.

**Movie:** *Terminator 3: Rise of the Machines* (2003)

**Scene:** At the veterinary hospital, Kate (Claire Danes) is hiding only a few feet away from the T-X (Kristanna Loken).

**Blooper:** The T-X is *the* state-of-the-art Terminator, with heightened sensory awareness all around: sight, hearing, smell, even the ability to sense body heat. Yet somehow Kate—heavy breathing, sweating, and all—stays under the T-X's radar and escapes.

**Movie:** *Titanic* (1997)

**Scene:** The passengers are all boarding the lifeboats.

**Blooper:** One of them is wearing a digital watch.

**Movie:** *Maid in Manhattan* (2002)

**Scene:** Near the beginning of the movie, it's six days before Christmas. There's a fresh blanket of snow in the foreground.

**Blooper:** Someone forgot to tell the trees—in the next scene they all have green leaves.

**Movie:** *L.A. Confidential* (1997)

**Scene:** Toward the end of the movie, Lynn Bracken (Kim Basinger) is talking to Detective Exley (Guy Pearce).

**Makes sense:** ***Frito*** **means "fried" in Spanish.**

**Blooper:** An establishing shot shows them facing each other, but in each of their close-ups, the sun is behind their heads. Are there two suns in Los Angeles?

**Movie:** *Forrest Gump* (1994)

**Scene:** After Jenny (Robin Wright) dies, Forrest (Tom Hanks) is visiting her grave. He says, "You died on a Saturday."

**Blooper:** The gravestone reads March 12, 1982 (it's a Friday).

**Movie:** *Galaxy Quest* (1999)

**Scene:** When Commander Taggert (Tim Allen) and Lieutenant Madison (Sigourney Weaver) first encounter the "chompers," Madison exclaims, "Oh, screw that!"

**Blooper:** That's what we *hear*, but it doesn't take a professional lip reader to see that she actually says... a word other than "screw."

**Movie:** *The Rocky Horror Picture Show* (1975)

**Scene:** The audience is told that it is a "late November evening."

**Blooper:** In the very next scene, when Brad (Barry Bostwick) and Janet (Susan Sarandon) are in the car, Richard Nixon's resignation speech is playing on the radio. Nixon resigned in August.

**Movie:** *Pearl Harbor* (2001)

**Scene:** When Evelyn (Kate Beckinsale) first arrives at Pearl Harbor, she walks past a tall building.

**Blooper:** The building has a sign that says "Est. 1953"—12 years after the actual attack.

**Movie:** *When Harry Met Sally* (1989)

**Scene:** During a car ride when Harry (Billy Crystal) first gets to know Sally (Meg Ryan), Harry is spitting seeds out of an open window.

**Blooper:** An exterior shot shows that Harry's window is closed.

**Movie:** *There's Something About Mary* (1998)

**Scene:** Ted Stroehmann (Ben Stiller) gets "stuck" in his zipper.

**Blooper:** While trying to get free of the zipper, Ted somehow manages to alternate between wearing his tuxedo jacket and not wearing it, from close-ups to wide shots.

# LAND OF THE GIANTS

*Back in the early 1960s, little Uncle John saw a giant statue of Paul Bunyan at Freedomland USA, an amusement park outside New York City. Freedomland closed in 1964, but the Paul Bunyan statue is still around—standing behind a gas station in nearby Elmsford, New York. And it turns out there are a lot more Paul Bunyans around the country...if you know where to find them.*

## WHO'S THAT MAN?

If you've taken a lot of car trips you've seen them—18- to 25-foot figures of dark-haired, square-jawed men, dressed in a short-sleeved shirt and work pants. Their arms are extended at the elbow, with the right hand facing up and the left hand facing down, often holding something, like a muffler or a roll of carpet.

What you might not know is that there are more than 150 of these gigantic fiberglass figures dotting America's highways, advertising everything from tires to burger joints to amusement parks. Almost all of them were made by one man.

## BIRTH OF THE BIG BOYS

It all started in 1962, when the Paul Bunyan Cafe on Route 66 in Flagstaff, Arizona, wanted a statue of their namesake to stand by the highway and attract hungry motorists. Prewitt Fiberglass in Venice, California, was happy to supply a figure of the giant lumberjack and created a molded Paul Bunyan character wearing a green cap, a dark beard, a red shirt, and jeans, and holding an axe.

That was it as far as Prewitt Fiberglass was concerned—one customer, one Paul Bunyan. But then owner Bob Prewitt decided to sell his business to a fiberglass boat builder named Steve Dashew. Dashew renamed the company International Fiberglass and, wanting to make a success of his new venture, started looking for business opportunities.

The leftover Paul Bunyan mold caught his eye. It was such an odd asset, he thought it might have value. Dashew began calling retail businesses around the country and asking them if they could use a giant advertising figure. A few said they could. When a story about one of Dashew's customers appeared in a retail trade magazine, stating that sales had doubled after the Paul Bunyan went up, business in the giant fiberglass figures began to boom.

## PAUL BUNYAN'S FRIENDS

Dashew started to aggressively market the big statues across the country, and sold them by the score. At first they were all Paul Bunyans, but Dashew soon discovered he could modify the basic mold slightly to create other figures.

• He turned them into cowboys, Indians, and astronauts. All of the figures had the same arm configuration as the first Paul Bunyan, so they were almost always holding something, like a plate or some tires.

• International Fiberglass made other figures, too—such as giant chickens, dinosaurs, and tigers—selling each for $1,800 to $2,800.

• They made 300 "Big Friends" for Texaco, figures of smiling Texaco service attendants in green uniforms with green caps.

• They built Yogi Bear figures for Yogi Bear's Honey Fried Chicken restaurants in North and South Carolina.

• To advertise Uniroyal Tires, they made a series of hulking women who looked a lot like Jackie Kennedy, holding a tire in one of her upraised hands. These women were issued with a dress, which could be removed to reveal a bikini.

But the figures made from the original Paul Bunyan mold proved to be the most popular, not to mention the most cost-effective for Dashew, who used the same mold over and over again. By the mid-1960s, the figures had made their way into hundreds of towns across the United States and were great attention-getters for retail stores and restaurants of all kinds.

## BYE-BYE, BUNYAN

But by the 1970s, the big figures that had seemed so impressive years earlier were getting dingy, weather-beaten, and silly looking to the next generation of consumers. As sales of the statues slowed, Dashew concentrated his energies on other business ventures. In 1976 he sold the business and the Paul Bunyan mold was destroyed.

Today, most of the fiberglass colossi are also gone, having been destroyed, removed, or beaten down by the elements. But they haven't all disappeared. In fact, almost every state in the Union has at least one. With businesses changing hands, the figures have been modified over the years:

• One Bunyan in Malibu, California, used to hold an immense hamburger. When a Mexican food joint bought out the burger place, he was given a sombrero and a serape, and his hamburger was replaced with a taco.

• A Bunyan at Lynch's Super Station in Havre de Grace, Maryland, was dressed in desert fatigues in 1991 to show support for the Gulf War.

• One former Uniroyal Gal stands in front of Martha's Cafe in Blackfoot, Idaho, holding a sandwich platter.

• Another Uniroyal Gal, in Rocky Mount, North Carolina, has been dressed in a pair of Daisy Duke shorts, given a beach ball to hold, fitted with a queen-size stainless-steel belly button ring, and placed in front of the Men's Night Out "private club."

**BIG MEN IN THE MEDIA**

If you can't get to see one of the giant statues in person, you can look for them in movies and on TV:

• A Paul Bunyan was featured in the 1969 movie *Easy Rider*.

• A modified Bunyan is pictured in the opening credits of the TV show *The Sopranos*. The figure, which holds a giant roll of carpet to advertise Wilson's Carpet in Jersey City, New Jersey, is now a stop on the New Jersey Sopranos bus tour.

• Bunyans have also made appearances in the TV show *The A-Team*, in the 2000 John Travolta flick *Battlefield Earth*, and in commercials for Saturn cars and Kleenex Tissues.

*    *    *

## PATRIOTIC PAUL

In the small town of Cheshire, Connecticut, a Paul Bunyan statue ignited controversy because zoning laws declared him too tall for any purpose other than holding a flag. The statue now functions as a flagpole.

# A PASSING FANCY

*Creativity—why should it be wasted on the living? Now, thanks to some imaginative "grief counselors" (see page 512), our dearly departed have quite a few options as to where to spend eternity.*

## OUT OF THIS WORLD

The remains of more than 100 people have been shot into space by Celestis of Houston, Texas. They pack a small portion of cremated remains (or "cremains") into a lipstick-sized aluminum container, load it into a NASA spacecraft, and blast it into an Earth or moon orbit. Timothy Leary and *Star Trek* creator Gene Roddenberry both chose this after-death option. Cost: $995 to $12,500.

## DIAMONDS ARE FOREVER

LifeGem of Chicago came up with a brilliant idea: They compress portions of cremated remains into manufactured diamonds. It sounds like a hoax but it's for real: after all, diamonds are carbon—the same stuff humans are made of—and it's been possible to manufacture diamonds from carbon since the 1970s. So far they've made the blue-tinted diamonds (which get their hue from the boron present in human remains) for 50 clients, whose loved ones usually have the diamonds set into jewelry. Cost: $4,000 and up.

## PUSHING UP DAISIES

San Francisco's Creative Cremains mixes cremated ashes and flower seeds into the paper they use to make their handmade death-announcement cards. The cards are intended for grieving friends or relatives, who can cut them into pieces and plant them to create a flowering garden memorial. Cost: $300 and up.

## SPEND ETERNITY WITH YOUR GOLF CLUB

A dizzying variety of companies will pack a portion of human ashes into keepsake items, from fishing rods to pendants to musical instruments. The objects can also be engraved with details of the deceased's life. Cost: $150 and up.

## GOING OUT WITH A BANG

Celebrate Life of Lakeside, California, will pack the cremated remains of your loved one into fireworks and then explode them on a beach or off a boat at sunset. Fireworks shows can be coordinated to music ("When Irish Eyes Are Smiling," "Wind Beneath My Wings," etc.) and can even be rendered in red, white, and blue. Cost: $500 to $3,750.

## GOOD G-REEF

Since late 1999, Georgia's Eternal Reefs Inc. has mixed the ashes of more than 200 ocean lovers with eco-friendly concrete to create artificial "reef balls." Once lowered into the ocean, the balls provide refuge for fish and other sea life. Eternal Reefs attempts to place the balls near areas of damaged coral to give plants a new home to cling to. Cost: $1,495 to $4,950.

## DIG THIS!

The nutrients a decaying body gives off are typically wasted when enclosed in a traditional wood or metal coffin. The "green burial" movement encourages the deceased to go out in environmental style instead, buried in a biodegradable cardboard box or a simple shroud. This method is widely embraced in the United Kingdom, where some 150 burial grounds offer green burial. The United States has been slower to follow, but Memorial Ecosystems in South Carolina has buried 18 unembalmed bodies in biodegradable caskets on its 33-acre site since 1998. Cost: $3,000 or less.

## HANGING AROUND

Mississippi's Eternally Yours incorporates cremated remains into paintings, sprinkling a few tablespoons over original works of art that can be customized to match home decor or the deceased's interests. Cost: $350 to $950.

## FREE AT LAST

Donated bodies, called "anatomical gifts" in the funeral biz, are used for research at medical schools across the country. Many medical facilities will pick up the "gift" at no charge to the deceased's estate. Once the research is complete, the body is cremated. Cost: Free.

# DIE-HARD CHICKEN

*Readers have been asking us to tell this story for years. It was so weird even we had a hard time swallowing it... but it's true.*

## OFF WITH HIS HEAD!

On September 10, 1945, Mike the rooster was making his usual rounds in the Olsen farmyard in Fruita, Colorado. He paused for a moment to join the other Wyandotte chickens as they hunted and pecked for grain outside the chicken coop. Mike didn't notice the dark shadow that fell across his path. It was Lloyd Olsen.

Clara Olsen had sent her husband out to the chicken coop on a mission: catch the rooster and prepare him for dinner. Lloyd Olsen grabbed Mike and put the rooster on the chopping block. Remembering that his mother-in-law (who was coming to dinner) loved chicken necks, Lloyd took special care to position the ax on Mike's neck so a generous portion of neck would remain. He gave that rooster one strong whack and cut off his head.

Mike the now-headless rooster ran around in circles, flapping his wings. At this point, most chickens would have dropped dead. Instead, Mike raced back to the coop, where he joined the rest of the chickens as they hunted and pecked for food.

Lloyd Olsen was flabbergasted. He kept expecting the rooster to keel over. It never happened. The next morning he checked again and found the feathered fellow—minus his head—asleep in the henhouse with the hens.

## ONE FUNKY CHICKEN

Lloyd decided that if Mike was so determined to live, even without a head, he would figure out a way to give him food and water, so Lloyd used an eyedropper to drip food and water into Mike's gullet.

When Mike had managed to live an entire week, Lloyd and Clara took their headless wonder to scientists at the University of Utah to determine how it was possible for the bird to stay alive without a head. The scientists determined that the ax had missed the jugular vein, and a clot had kept Mike from bleeding to death. Although his head was gone, his brainstem and one ear were left on his body. Since a chicken's reflex actions are controlled by the brain stem, Mike's body was able to keep on ticking.

## MIRACLE MIKE

Sensing that Mike had the possibility of becoming a real cash cow (or chicken), the Olsens hired a manager and took him on a national tour. Audiences in New York, Los Angeles, Atlantic City, and San Diego paid a quarter each to see "Miracle Mike." *Time* and *Life* magazines ran feature articles on the amazing fowl. Mike even made it into the *Guinness Book of World Records*. This "Wonder Chicken" was so valuable, he was insured for $10,000.

For 18 happy months Mike was a celebrity. Then one night in a motel in Arizona, Mike the headless chicken started choking on some food. Lloyd tried to save him, but he couldn't find the syringe he had often used to clear Mike's throat. Moments later Mike was dead—this time for real.

Those who knew Mike, which included many of the residents of Fruita, remembered him as a "robust chicken, and a fine specimen, except for not having a head." One recalled that Mike seemed "as happy as any other chicken."

## GONE BUT NOT FORGOTTEN

Mike's been dead for almost 60 years, but his spirit lives on in Fruita. In 1999 the Chamber of Commerce was looking for something more interesting than "pioneers" as the theme for Colorado Heritage Week, when someone suggested Mike. Now, every third weekend in May, folks in this town of 6,500 gather to celebrate the remarkable rooster at the "Mike the Headless Chicken Festival."

The two-day-long celebration features the 5K Run Like a Chicken race, egg tosses, Pin the Head on the Chicken, a Cluck Off, Rubber Chicken Juggling, and the Chicken Dance. Chicken Bingo is played with chicken droppings on a grid and there is a Famous Fowl Pet Parade, for which owners dress their dogs, cats, and horses like chickens. Of course, great quantities of chicken—fried or barbecued—are enjoyed by all.

In 2000 Mike was memorialized in a statue made out of rakes, axes, and farm implements by artist Lyle Nichols, who said, "I made him proud-looking and cocky." And he gave the chamber a discount on the sculpture... because it didn't have a head.

**If you have *alektorophobia,* you're chicken...of chickens.**

# NAME THAT COUNTRY

*See if you can guess the name of the country before reading all the clues. (Answers on page 748.)*

## SAVED

1. It was originally inhabited by the Pipil tribe.
2. The Pipil are believed to be direct descendants of the Aztecs.
3. The Pipil were defeated by Spanish explorers looking for gold.
4. The Christian Spaniards named it in honor of Jesus.

*Name the country.*

## NOTHING TO IT

1. The local Nama people call it "an area where there is nothing."
2. The name describes the coastal desert area of the country.
3. It has been governed at different times by the British, the Germans, and the South Africans.
4. It gained independence in 1990 from South Africa.

*Name the country.*

## THE NAMELESS NAME

1. It got its European name long before Europeans knew it existed.
2. Early geographers insisted it must be there—if not, the Earth would "wobble."
3. The early name was Latin for "The Unknown Southern Land."
4. Captain James Cook "discovered" it in 1770.

*Name the country.*

## OVER THERE WHERE THE SUN COMES UP

1. Our word for this country originally comes from China.
2. It combines the words "sun" and "east," meaning "sunrise," or "sun's origin."
3. Portuguese traders learned the name from Malaysians in the 1500s.
4. Inhabitants of this country call it Nippon.

*Name the country.*

**It takes 16,550 kernels of durum wheat to make a pound of pasta.**

## GRECIAN FORMULA

**1.** Early inhabitants called themselves the Pritani.

**2.** The Greek sailor Pytheas named it after the inhabitants in 300 B.C.

**3.** When enemy tribes attacked in the 400s, many inhabitants fled this island, taking the name with them to the mainland.

**4.** To differentiate between the new "lesser" settlement on the mainland, the word "Greater" was added to the name of the island.

*Name the island.*

## ACUTE COUNTRY, BUT A BIT OBTUSE

**1.** This country, when grouped with two other countries, is known by another name.

**2.** When grouped with three other countries, it's known by yet another name.

**3.** The name comes from a Germanic tribe that invaded the country about 1,500 years ago.

**4.** It is believed that the tribe's name referred to their homeland in present-day Germany, which was shaped like a fishhook.

*Name the country.*

## WHY DON'T THEY SPEAK GERMAN?

**1.** This country was also named after an invading Germanic tribe.

**2.** The tribe's name came from a Latin word meaning "masculine."

**3.** Their allegiance with Rome, and use of its written Latin language, are two reasons why their language is so different from German.

**4.** They controlled so much of Europe at one point that the Arabic and Persian words for "European" are based on their name.

*Name the country.*

## OVERCOATIA

**1.** This country was named by the Portuguese in the 1470s.

**2.** The name comes from the Portuguese word for a traditional overcoat: *Gabao*.

**3.** The French gained control of this equatorial country in the late 1800s and helped to end its slave trade.

**4.** It's in western Africa.

*Name the country.*

**Myth conception: Rice thrown at weddings *won't* kill the birds that eat it.**

# MADE IN JAPAN: WEIRD GAME SHOWS

*Reality shows like* The Bachelor, Survivor *and* Fear Factor *prove that people will do just about anything for money...and they'll do it on national television. But even those shows don't compare to crazy programs on Japanese television.*

**ZA GAMAN**

**Object of the Game:** University students compete in contests to see who can stand the most pain, eat the most unpleasant foods, and perform the most humiliating tasks.

**Anything for Money:** In one episode, "contestants were taken to an icy location, made to drink huge amounts of beer, and kept jogging up and down as their bladders swelled. The dubious winner was the drinker who lasted longest" without having to pee. (A restroom was provided.) In another segment, contestants rolled down a steep hill inside barrels; in another, they did headstands in the desert while officials with magnifying glasses focused sunlight on their nipples.

**Update:** *Za Gaman* was the inspiration for the British game show *Endurance U.K.*, in which eight players compete in humiliating and disgusting contests—bobbing for false teeth in buckets of pig eyeballs, eating quiches full of maggots—to win valuable prizes.

**TAKESHI'S CASTLE**

**Object of the Game:** This show was inspired by the obstacle courses in 1980s-era video games like Donkey Kong. One hundred players start each game—they're the "soldiers" of a character called "General Lee" and their goal is to storm Count Takeshi's castle, which is guarded by Takeshi and his henchmen. Wearing helmets and knee pads, the contestants scream out, "I'll do my best!" as they begin several rounds of physical challenges, with each successive round being harder than the one before it. Each round puts them closer to Takeshi's Castle.

In the first round, players might have to scale a wall or, with their hands tied behind their backs, bite a bun that is hanging on

**British peerage, from lowest to highest rank: baron, viscount, earl, marquis, duke.**

a string dangling over their heads. In the next round, they might play tag wearing giant blueberry suits or climb a steep hill while Takeshi's henchmen shoot water guns at the targets on their helmets. Then contestants might ride a giant rice bowl down a waterslide into a pond—if they fall out of the bowl, they're out.

Players who fail to complete a round lose the game. Prize for making it to the final round and storming the castle: 1 million yen—about $8,500.

**Anything for Money:** So how hard is it? The list of injuries suffered by contestants is long: broken arms, legs, fingers, toes, and jaws; concussions; bruises; and lacerations galore. Usually only 5 or 6 contestants out of the original 100 make it to the final round and attempt to storm Takeshi's Castle. And most of these attempts fail—the castle has been taken only a handful of times. Want to see the show for yourself? In mid-2003 it began airing on the Spike network under the name *MXC—Most Extreme Elimination Challenge*.

## TV CHAMPION

**Object of the Game:** A different type of competition is aired each week—sushi rolling, cake baking, flower arranging, speed eating, trivia quizzes, etc. Some contests are screwier than others.

**Anything for Money:** In the "Lung Man Championship," contestants bowled by blowing a bowling ball into the pins; in the "Sweat King Championship," they collected their own sweat in a bottle.

## FOOD BATTLE CLUB

**Object of the Game:** This show is like *TV Champion*, except that all of the contests are "gluttony" contests—players gorge themselves on food or beverages to see who can consume the most.

**Anything for Money:** "Contestants, mostly young men, double-fist platefuls of sushi, drain glasses of milk, and slurp up bowls of steaming ramen noodles. Some visibly hold back a vomit reflex as the cameras zoom in on the food and saliva dribbling down their chins."

Japan's craze for speed-eating shows took off in 1996, when a 144-pound speed-eating champ named Hirofumi Nakajima went to New York and won the Nathan's Famous Hot Dog eating contest by downing 24¼ hot dogs in 12 minutes, beating out 320-pound American Ed Krachie. Nakajima, who reportedly had never eaten a hot dog before, went on to win the contest three years in a

**Experts say cats watch more TV than dogs do. (Cats are more visual; dogs rely more on smell.)**

row. Speed-eating contest shows like *The King of Gluttons* and *The National Big Eaters' Tournament* flooded Japanese airwaves after Nakajima's success, and they're still popular today.

## MUSCLE RANKING

**Object of the Game:** This hour-long, primetime Saturday night show featured regular people "pitted against celebrities and athletes in offbeat tests of agility and strength." If you won a round you moved up in the "Muscle Ranking." Michael Jordan appeared on an episode in 1999.

**Anything for Money:** One week contestants might have to springboard over a 10-foot pyramid; on another, they'd have to hit baseballs through small holes in a wooden tic-tac-toe board. Then there was the time they flung themselves into Velcro-covered walls while wearing Velcro-covered suits.

**Update:** *Muscle Ranking* was pulled from the airwaves in May 2002 after two contestants suffered spinal injuries while taping the show—one was hurt when he fell into a moat while jumping on a giant styrofoam ball, the other while trying to stop a different giant ball from rolling down a slope. "The purpose of the show is to entertain, but if people are getting hurt in its making, the audience can't enjoy it," a spokesman told reporters.

* * *

## CELEBRITY REVENGE

In 1938, legendary film producer David O. Selznick held auditions for a lead role in his upcoming film, *Gone With the Wind.* He wanted a redhead. A young starlet named Lucille Ball came in to audition, but it was raining outside and she was soaked. She was led to the producer's office and left alone to wait. Selznick walked in as she was trying to dry her hair. He had her quickly read the lines and dismissed her. She didn't get the part.

**Revenge!** Lucy never forgot. In 1957 Lucy and her husband, Desi Arnaz, by then two of the country's biggest stars, bought Selznick's old studio, renamed it Desilu, and set up their headquarters…in the office that Lucy remembered so well.

**Got a *complex*? Psychologist Carl Jung coined the term in the early 1900s.**

# LOCAL HEROES

*Here are the stories of ordinary people who were faced with an extraordinary situation... and did something about it.*

## SPILT MILK

**Local Hero:** Steve Leech, a milkman in Cornwall, England

**Heroic Deed:** Putting out a dangerous fire

**The Story:** Leech was making his regular deliveries one morning when he noticed smoke pouring out of a gift shop along his route. He called 999 (the English equivalent of 911) but then decided not to wait for the fire fighters to arrive. "I saw the row of apartments up above the shop," he explains, "and I thought, bloody hell, I'd better do something!"

What did Leech do? He kicked open the door of the shop and started pouring milk on the fire. By the time the firefighters arrived 15 minutes later, the fire was under control—and Leech is credited with saving the row of eight shops, as well as the lives of the people living in the apartments above them. "It was hard work opening all those bottles, since they have tamper-proof lids," he says, "but it was even harder trying to explain to my boss where all the milk (320 pints) had gone."

**Update:** Leech needn't have worried about his boss—he not only kept his job, in January 2002 England's National Dairymen's Association named him the "Hero Milkman of the Millennium."

## FIRST-RATE THIRD GRADER

**Local Hero:** Austin Rosedale, a third-grader at Sunny Hills Elementary School in Issaquah, Washington

**Heroic Deed:** Saving his teacher from choking

**The Story:** Austin was in the computer lab one day in November 2001 when his teacher, Mrs. Precht, started choking on a cough drop. She was just about to pass out when he sprang into action.

Luckily for Precht, Austin's parents had given him a Day Planner organizer that happened to have an instructional diagram of the Heimlich maneuver printed on the cover. Austin had read it so many times that helping Mrs. Precht was a snap. With two thrusts to her abdomen, he dislodged the cough drop. "I just visualized the

**Birmingham, England, has 22 more miles of canals than Venice, Italy.**

pictures," he says, "and remembered what I'd read."

**BLUE'S BROTHER**

**Local Hero:** Art Aylesworth, a Montana insurance agent

**Heroic Deed:** Helping to save the mountain bluebird and the western bluebird from extinction

**The Story:** A longtime conservationist, Aylesworth had worked on a few wildlife habitat restoration projects. But in the mid-1970s he became alarmed when he learned that extensive logging in the state was pushing the bluebirds—which nest in the cavities of old trees—toward extinction. So he got some scrap lumber and built some nest boxes for the birds; then he founded an organization called the Mountain Bluebird Trails Group and recruited hundreds of volunteers to do the same thing.

The organization gave the boxes to anyone willing to put them up and keep an eye on them; it estimates that over the next 25 years, it gave away more than 35,000 boxes. Did it work? Yes—when Aylesworth started handing out the boxes in 1974, only a handful of the bluebirds were thought to still exist; by 1998 the count had grown to more than 17,000.

**GUN CONTROL**

**Local Hero:** Dale Rooks, a crossing guard at Suter Elementary School in Pensacola, Florida

**Heroic Deed:** Finding a unique way to get speeding motorists to slow down in front of the elementary school

**The Story:** For years Rooks had tried everything he could think of to get drivers to slow down in front of the school—including waving his hands and yelling—but nothing worked. Then inspiration struck him—he got an old hair dryer and covered it with gray duct tape so that it looked like a radar gun, and started pointing it at speeders. That did the trick. "People are slowing down, raising their hands at me apologetically," he says. "It's amazing how well it works."

**Update:** Inspired by his example, fifth-graders at the school set up a lemonade stand and raised $93 to buy Rooks a *real* radar gun. "I don't mean it to be funny," he says, "but it looks just like a hair dryer."

# SORRY ABOUT THAT

*There are a few lessons we all learned when we were kids—be courteous to others, share your toys, and when you screw up, say you're sorry. Some people got it...and apparently some didn't.*

**HO! HO! HO!**

**Incident:** In December 2002, Reverend Lee Rayfield of Maidenhead, England, had to send out letters of apology to his parishioners. Reverend Rayfield had held a special Christmas service just for children. A horrified shock went through the room when Rayfield delivered an unexpected message: Santa Claus, he told the kids, is *dead*. In order to deliver presents to all the children in the world, he explained, the reindeer would have to travel 3,000 times the speed of sound—which would make them all burn up in less than a second. The audience included "a lot of young children who still believe in Santa Claus," said one angry parent, "or did until last night."

**Apology:** "I guess I made a serious misjudgment," said Rayfield.

**HOT WATER**

**Incident:** After American-turned-Taliban John Walker Lindh was captured in Afghanistan in November 2002, the press reported that he was from Marin County, California. That prompted former President Bush to describe Lindh as "some misguided Marin County hot-tubber." Jackie Kerwin, editor of the *Marin Independent Journal*, took exception to the insult and urged readers to write letters about it. And they did. Letters poured in, prompting newspapers, radio, and TV news programs to spread the story across the country.

**Apology:** "Dear Ms. Kerwin," Bush wrote to her, "Call off the dogs, please. I surrender. I will never use 'hot tub' and 'Marin County' in the same sentence again." He even made a personal phone call. "He gets on the phone and says 'Hot tubs for sale,'" Kerwin said, "and that pretty much set the tone for the rest of the conversation. But I think he was genuinely sorry."

**HERE'S MUD (SLINGING) IN YOUR EYE**

**Incident:** In the 2000 media guide for their men's basketball team, Ohio State University displayed photographs of some distinguished

**Why do we all know Ann Turner Cook? Her face is on Gerber Baby Food jars.**

alumni, including comedian Richard Lewis, who had graduated in 1969. But it turned out to be a dubious honor: the caption below his name said, "Actor, Writer, Comedian, Drunk." This was particularly insulting because Lewis is a recovering alcoholic. "I was really depressed that I would be so defamed," he said.

**Apology:** Red-faced officials apologized profusely...and then fired the editor, Gary Emig, who had put in "drunk" as a joke in an early draft, but forgot to take it out.

## AN INFIELD HIT

**Incident:** Between innings at a June 2003 baseball game, the Milwaukee Brewers were staging one of their fans' favorite events: the Sausage Race. Dressed up as a bratwurst, a hot dog, an Italian sausage, and a Polish sausage, four Brewer employees raced around the infield. But as they passed the opposing team's dugout, Pittsburgh Pirate first baseman Randall Simon reached out and playfully whacked one of the runners with his bat. The employee fell to the ground, causing another runner to fall, too. The costumes were padded, so the victims received only minor knee scrapes, but Simon was taken from the park in handcuffs, charged with disorderly conduct, and fined $438.

**Apology:** An embarrassed Simon later called the injured sausages—Mandy Block and Veronica Piech—to personally apologize. Block, the Italian sausage that took the hit, accepted the apology and asked for an autographed bat from Simon—the one that he used to hit her. (She got it.)

## I APOLOGIZE IN YOUR GENERAL DIRECTION

**Incident:** In an exhibit called "The Roman Experience," the Deva Museum in Chester, England, invited visitors to stroll through streets constructed to look as they did during Roman times. Hoping to provide an authentic experience, staff added an odor to the Roman latrines. They got one called "Flatulence" from Dale Air, a company that makes aromas for several museums. Unfortunately, it was too authentic: several schoolchildren immediately vomited.

**Apology:** Museum supervisor Christine Turner publicly apologized, saying, "It really was disgusting." But Dale Air director Frank Knight was somewhat less contrite. "We feel sorry for the kids," he said, "but it is nice to see that the smell is so realistic."

**The world's youngest-ever mother was five years old and lived in Peru in the 1950s.**

# CRÈME *de la* CRUD

*The best of the worst of the worst.*

## WORST MATADOR

***"El Gallo" (Raphael Gomez Ortega), an early-20th-century bullfighter***

El Gallo employed a technique called the *espantada* (sudden flight) that was unique in the history of professional bullfighting—when the bull entered the ring, he panicked, dropped his cape, and ran away. "All of us artists have bad days," he would explain. His fights were so hilarious that he was brought out of retirement seven times; in his last fight in October 1918, he claimed he spared the bull because "it winked at him." (The audience thought it was a big joke, but Ortega's relatives didn't—his brother was so ashamed during that last fight that he entered the ring and killed the bull himself...just to salvage the family's honor.)

## WORST DRUG-SNIFFING DOG

***"Falco," at the County Sheriff's Office, Knoxville, Tennessee***

In August 2000 David and Pamela Stonebreaker were driving through Knoxville in their recreational vehicle when sheriff's deputies pulled them over for running a red light. The cops were suspicious and called for backup: a drug-sniffer named Falco. The dog sniffed outside the vehicle and signalled "positive," so deputies immediately searched the inside of the RV...and found more than a *quarter ton* of marijuana.

But in court, the Stonebreakers' attorney challenged the search—the dog couldn't be trusted. It turned out that between 1998 and 2000 Falco had signalled "positive" 225 times and the cops found drugs only 80 times. In other words, the dog was wrong nearly 70% of the time. Falco, the defense argued, was too incompetent to justify searching vehicles based on his "word" alone. The judge agreed and the Stonebreakers (their real name) went free.

## LEAST-WATCHED TV SHOW IN HISTORY

"In 1978 an opinion poll showed that a French television program was watched by no viewers at all. The great day for French broad-

The thyroid cartilage is more commonly known as the Adam's apple.

casting was August 14, when not one person saw the extensive interview with an Armenian woman on her 40th birthday. It ranged over the way she met her husband, her illnesses, and the joy of living....The program was broadcast in primetime."

—***The Incomplete Book of Failures*, by Stephen Pile**

## WORST JOCKEY

***Beltran de Osorio y Diez de Rivera, "Iron" Duke of Albuquerque***

The duke developed an obsession with winning England's Grand National Steeplechase horse race when he was only eight years old, after receiving a film of the race as a birthday present. "I said then that I would win that race one day," the amateur rider recounted years later.

• On his first attempt in 1952, he fell from his horse; he woke up later in the hospital with a cracked vertebra.

• He tried again in 1963; bookies placed odds of 66–1 against him finishing the race still on his horse. (The duke fell from the horse.)

• He raced again in 1965, and fell from his horse after it collapsed underneath him, breaking his leg.

• In 1974, having just had 16 screws removed from a leg he'd broken after falling from the horse in another race, he fell while training for the Grand National and broke his collarbone. He recovered in time to compete (in a plaster cast) and actually managed to finish the race while still on his horse—the only time he ever would. He placed eighth.

• In 1976 the duke fell again during a race—this time he was trampled by the other horses and suffered seven broken ribs, several broken vertebrae, a broken wrist, a broken thigh, and a severe concussion, which left him in a coma for two days.

• He eventually recovered, but when he announced at the age of 57 that he was going to try again, race organizers pulled his license "for his own safety."

The Iron Duke never did win the Grand National, as he promised himself he would, but he did break another record—he broke more bones trying to win it than any jockey before or since.

# FAMILIAR PHRASES

*Here's one of our regular features—the origins of some common terms and phrases.*

**THE BALL'S IN YOUR COURT**

**Meaning:** It's your turn; it's up to you

**Origin:** "This term comes from tennis, where it signifies that it is the opponent's turn to serve or play the ball. A British equivalent is 'the ball's at your feet,' which comes from football (soccer), and has been in use much longer. How much longer? Lord Auckland used it figuratively in a letter written in about 1800: 'We have the ball at our feet.'" (From *Southpaws & Sunday Punches*, by Christine Ammer)

**TO BEAR DOWN**

**Meaning:** To put pressure on someone or something

**Origin:** "For centuries sailors used the word *bear* in scores of expressions to describe a ship's position in relation to the wind, the land, or another ship. Most are still used by sailors today. *Bear up*, for instance, means to head the ship into the wind. *Bear off* means to head away from the wind, a phrase sailors came to use figuratively whenever they wanted anything thrust away from their person. *Bear down* in the original nautical sense meant to approach from the weather, or windward, side. It later came to mean to approach another ship rapidly, pressuring them to yield." (From *Scuttlebutt*, by Teri Degler)

**BY THE SKIN OF ONE'S TEETH**

**Meaning:** By an extremely narrow margin; just barely

**Origin:** "A literal translation of a biblical phrase from Latin. The biblical source is the passage where Job is complaining about how illness has ravaged his body: 'My bone cleaveth to my skin and to my flesh, and I am escaped with the skin of my teeth.' The point is that Job is so sick that there's nothing left to his body. The passage is rendered differently in other translations; the Douay Bible, for example—an English translation of the Vulgate (St. Jerome's fourth-century translation)—gives: 'My bone hath cleaved to my skin, and nothing but lips are left about my teeth.' The phrase first appeared in English in a mid-16th-century translation of the Bible. It did not become common until the 19th century." (From *Jesse's Word of the Day*, by Jesse Sheidlower)

## TO EAT ONE OUT OF HOUSE AND HOME

**Meaning:** To eat large quantities of someone else's food

**Origin:** "Its first recorded use in English was by William Shakespeare, who used it in his play *Henry IV*, written in 1597–98. In Act II, Hostess Quickly of the Boar's Head Tavern is complaining about Sir John Falstaff, who has been lodging with her, eating huge quantities of food, and avoiding paying his bill: 'He hath eaten me out of house and home, he hath put all my substance into that fat belly of his...' The phrase *out of house and home* was in use as early as the 13th century, and during the 15th century people often said 'he hath eaten me out of house and harbor.' Shakespeare combined the two phrases." (From *Inventing English*, by Dale Corey)

## NOT UP TO SNUFF

**Meaning:** Below standard

**Origin:** "Englishmen were so fond of finely powdered tobacco, or snuff, that its use was nearly universal throughout the kingdom. Connoisseurs would pride themselves on knowing their snuff. One derided as *not up to snuff* was considered an amateur at judging powdered tobacco. But soon the phrase expanded to any person or product considered to be less than discerning." (From *Everyday Phrases*, by Neil Ewart)

## TO PAY THE PIPER

**Meaning:** To accept the consequences

**Origin:** "Street dancing was a common form of amusement during medieval times. Strolling musicians, including flute players, would play for a dance wherever they could gather a crowd.

"Frequently a dance was organized on the spur of the moment. Persons who heard the notes of a piper would drop their work and join in the fun. When they tired of the frolic, they would pass the hat for the musician. It became proverbial that a dancer had better have his fun while he could; sooner or later he would have to pay the piper." (From *I've Got Goose Pimples*, by Marvin Vanoni)

**...hold its head above water to observe activity on the surface.**

# DUBIOUS ACHIEVERS

*Here are some of the most bizarre world records we could find. How bizarre? One of the record holders is a bacterium.*

**I'M SENSING...SURGERY.** Since 1979, Fulvia Celica Siguas Sandoval, a transsexual TV clairvoyant from Peru, has had plastic surgery 64 times. More than 25 of the operations have been to her face.

**LIKE A ROCK.** St. Simeon the Younger lived from 521 to 597 AD in Antioch, Syria. He spent his last 45 years sitting on top of a stone pillar.

**CONAN THE BACTERIUM.** *Deinococcus radiodurans* can withstand 10,000 times the radiation it would take to kill a human, earning it the title of "World's Toughest Bacterium." It was discovered living in swollen tins of irradiated meat in Oregon in the 1950s.

**SOCK IT TO ME!** Britain's Kirsten O'Brien managed to wear 41 socks at once...all on one foot. She performed the "feet" on the BBC's *Big Toe Radio Show* on May 20, 2003.

**THE HOLE-IEST OF RECORDS.** Having 600 body piercings is pretty impressive in itself, but in 2002, 28-year-old Kam Ma of Whitburn, England, got 600 piercings in 8 hours and 32 minutes.

**CRIME AGAINST HUMANITY?** On June 1, 2000, 566 accordion players gathered at the International Folklore Festival in the Netherlands. For 22 minutes they played folk songs in unison—becoming history's largest accordion ensemble ever (hopefully).

**PANTS ON FIRE.** John Graham (if that *is* his real name) holds the title "World's Biggest Liar." He earned it by telling the most tall tales at the Annual Lying Competition held in Cumbria, England. He's won the contest five times (or so he says).

# POLITALKS

*Politicians aren't getting much respect these days—but then, it sounds like they don't deserve much, either.*

"That is true...but not absolutely true."

**—Montreal Mayor Jean Drapeau**

"My colleagues and I are upset by this blatant attempt to replace diversity with fairness."

**—N.J. assemblyman Joseph Doria**

"Solar energy is not something that is going to come in overnight."

**—Gerald Ford**

"Have we gone beyond the bounds of reasonable dishonesty?"

**—CIA memo**

"You can't just let nature run wild."

**—Gov. Wally Hickel (AK)**

"I intend to open this country up to democracy, and anyone who is against that, I will jail!"

**—President Joao Baptiste Figueiredo, Brazil**

"Things happen more frequently in the future than they do in the past."

**—Gov. Booth Gardner (WA)**

"Sometimes in order to make progress and move ahead, you have to stand up and do the wrong thing."

**—Rep. Gary Ackerman**

"If you let that sort of thing go on, your bread and butter will be cut right out from under your feet."

**—British foreign minister Ernest Bevin**

"If we don't succeed, we run the risk of failure."

**—Dan Quayle**

"We're going to move left and right at the same time."

**—Gov. Jerry Brown (CA)**

"Facts are stupid things."

**—Ronald Reagan**

"First they tax our beer, then they tax cigarettes. Now they are going to increase the tax on gasoline. All that's left are our women."

**—Sen. John East**

"Sixty years of progress, without change."

**—Saudi government's anniversary slogan**

**"Gin" comes from the French *genièvre*, for "juniper." (Gin is made from juniper berries.)**

# THE FABULOUS FLYING FLEA

*If you designed and built your own airplane, would you name it after a small, bloodsucking insect? Believe it or not, one man did.*

## UPS AND DOWNS

One day during World War I, a young French soldier named Henri Mignet talked an airplane mechanic into letting him climb into the cockpit of an airplane and taxi down the runway.

Taxiing an airplane is simple enough, even for people (like Mignet) with no flying experience. But rather than stop at the end of the runway as he'd been told, Mignet gunned the engine and tried to fly the plane. He managed to get airborne but not for long: moments later both he and the plane were on their backs in a nearby cornfield.

## JUST PLANE NUTS

Mignet was sent back to his unit and punished for wrecking the plane. Maybe he never lived down the humiliation, or maybe he bumped his head harder than people thought. Whatever the case, he spent the rest of his life trying to prove that the accepted scientific principles of aviation were a sham, and that people who built planes were liars and con men. He set out to prove that ordinary people could build airplanes themselves, without any help from the so-called experts.

In 1928 he wrote an article titled "Is Amateur Aviation Possible?" for a French aviation magazine. The timing couldn't have been better. Charles Lindbergh's famous flight from New York to Paris in May 1927 had generated huge worldwide interest in aviation, and Mignet's article told people exactly what they wanted to hear: that they could build their own airplane for next to nothing and learn to fly it themselves. "It is not necessary to have any technical knowledge to build an aeroplane," Mignet wrote. "If you can nail together a packing crate, you can construct an aeroplane."

The article generated so much attention that Mignet followed up with a second article, including diagrams that people could use to build an airplane he called the HM 8.

Like the first seven planes he'd designed (and given his initials), number 8 could not actually fly. But Mignet's readers didn't know that—and he wouldn't admit it—and anyway he kept designing new planes, even after serious aviators banned him from local airfields.

By 1935 Mignet had progressed all the way to HM 14, which actually could fly a little. He named the aircraft *Pou du Ciel* (Sky Louse) and published his plans in a book called *Le Sport de l'Air.* The English edition was titled *The Flying Flea.* (Why name his creations after lice and fleas? Because, Mignet proudly explained, like his designs, these insects "made people scratch their heads.")

## ON A WING AND A PRAYER

Built from wood scraps, held together by nails and glue, powered by an old motorcycle engine, and resembling "a coffin with an outboard motor in front," Mignet's Sky Louse lacked many features of conventional airplanes—ailerons, rudder pedals, engine cowls—that were necessary for safe flight but that he found offensive. "I cut them out!" he exclaimed. "No more sheet metal which flies off or rattles!" Mignet *did* like wings, so he gave his plane an extra set behind the cockpit.

People in Europe and the United States bought copies of Mignet's book by the thousands, and many of these enthusiasts built their own Sky Lice in their garages and barns. Thankfully, Mignet's designs were so awful (and his admirers so inept) that not many of these planes ever left the ground. Those few pilots unlucky enough to take to the air soon learned that Mignet's design had a fatal flaw—if they sent a Sky Louse into a steep enough dive, it either locked into the straight-down position or flipped upside down and locked into *that* position until the pilot ran out of gas or crashed.

Mounting casualties ended the Sky Louse craze by the late 1930s, but they didn't kill the movement entirely. In fact, Mignet's admirers are still at it: amateur aeronautic engineers in Europe, America, Australia, and New Zealand are still building—and flying—Flying Fleas today.

# THE WHO?

*Ever wonder how bands get their names? So do we. After some digging around, we found the stories behind these famous names.*

**GENESIS.** Named by producer Jonathan King, who signed the band in 1967. He chose the name because they were the first "serious" band he'd produced and he considered signing them to mark the official beginning of his production career.

**HOLE.** Named after a line in the Euripides play *Medea*: "There's a hole burning deep inside me." Singer Courtney Love chose it because she says, "I knew it would confuse people."

**THE BLACK CROWES.** Originally a punk band called Mr. Crowe's Garden (after singer Chris Robinson's favorite kid's book). They later shortened the name and switched to southern rock.

**AC/DC.** Chosen because it fit the band's "high-voltage" sound.

**CREAM.** Eric Clapton, Jack Bruce, and Ginger Baker chose the name because they considered themselves the cream of the crop of British blues musicians.

**THE CLASH.** A political statement to demonstrate the band's antiestablishment attitude? No. According to bassist Paul Simonon: "I was looking through the *Evening Standard* with the idea of names on my mind, and noticed the word *clash* a few times. I thought The Clash would be good."

**GUNS N' ROSES.** The band chose Guns N' Roses by combining the names of two bands that members had previously played in: L.A. Guns and Hollywood Rose.

**ELTON JOHN.** Born Reginald Kenneth Dwight, he joined the backing band for blues singer Long John Baldry. Dwight later changed his name by combining the first names of John Baldry and saxophonist Elton Dean.

**THE O'JAYS.** Originally the Triumphs, they changed their name to the O'Jays in 1963 to honor Eddie O'Jay, a Cleveland disc jockey who was the group's mentor.

**"I've got all the money I need… if I die by 4 o'clock this afternoon." —Henny Youngman**

**JANE'S ADDICTION.** According to band legend, Jane was a hooker and heroin addict whom the band members met (and lived with) in Hollywood in the mid-1980s.

**THEY MIGHT BE GIANTS.** Named after an obscure 1971 B-movie starring George C. Scott and Joanne Woodward.

**DAVID BOWIE.** David Robert Jones changed his last name to Bowie to avoid being mistaken for Davy Jones of the Monkees. He chose Bowie after the hunting knife he'd seen in American films.

**BAD COMPANY.** Named after the 1972 Western starring Jeff Bridges.

**THE POGUES.** Began as Pogue Mahone, which is Gaelic for "kiss my arse."

**ELVIS COSTELLO.** Born Declan MacManus, he changed his name at the urging of manager Jake Riviera. According to Costello: "It was a marketing scheme. Jake said, 'We'll call you Elvis.' I thought he was completely out of his mind." Costello is a family name on his mother's side.

**THE B52S.** Not named after the Air Force jet. *B52* is a southern term for tall bouffant hairdos, which the women of the band wore early in the band's career.

**THE POLICE.** Named by drummer Stewart Copeland as an ironic reference to his father, Miles, who had served as chief of the CIA's Political Action Staff in the 1950s.

**MÖTLEY CRÜE.** Comes from Motley Croo, a band that guitarist Mick Mars worked for as a roadie in the early 1970s. According to bassist Nikki Sixx, they changed the spelling and added the umlauts because they "wanted to do something to be weird. It's German and strong, and that Nazi Germany mentality—'the future belongs to us'—intrigued me."

**RADIOHEAD.** Originally called On A Friday (because they could practice only on Fridays), EMI signed them in 1992. But EMI execs feared that On A Friday might be confusing to some. So the band quickly chose a new name. Their inspiration: an obscure Talking Heads song called "Radio Head."

# AT THE AUCTION

*What do you think the very first G.I. Joe is worth? How about Orson Welles's Oscar for writing Citizen Kane? Elvis's tooth? (How much are the answers worth to you?)*

## AMERICA'S FIGHTING MAN

What would you pay for the very first action figure ever made? When G.I. Joe's creator, Don Levine, put it up for auction, he was certain it would fetch a lot—perhaps even break records.

The former Hasbro executive and Korean War veteran designed the toy in 1963 as a boy's answer to Mattel's Barbie Doll. And to make sure boys wouldn't be too embarrassed to play with a doll, Levine coined the term "action figure."

Forty years later, he decided to put his one-of-a-kind prototype, made of hand-painted ceramic plastic and wearing hand-sewn clothes and boots, up for sale at Heritage Comic's auction at the 2003 Comic-Con convention in San Diego. He expected to get about $600,000—which would have been more than any toy ever auctioned.

How much did he get? Nothing. The few bids the toy received didn't even meet the reserve price of $250,000. A disappointed Levine put it back in his display cabinet.

**But wait!** A month later, a comic book distributor named Stephen Geppi contacted Levine and offered him a whopping $200,000 for Joe #1. "I remember playing with G.I. Joe when I was a kid, and who'd have thought some 40 years later I would be buying the actual prototype," Geppi said. "What a coup."

## AND THE LOSER IS...

In 1998 the American Film Institute rated *Citizen Kane* as the greatest American film ever made. Yet when the film was released in 1941, it won only one Academy Award—writer/director Orson Welles and co-writer Herman J. Mankiewicz received an Oscar for Best Original Screenplay.

Knowing that it would be highly prized in any Hollywood memorabilia collection, Welles's daughter Beatrice decided to put

**Amharic, the language of Ethiopia, has an alphabet of 267 letters.**

the *Kane* Oscar on Christie's auction block in June 2003. Ronald Colman's Best Actor Oscar for *A Double Life* netted a whopping $174,500 when Christie's sold it in 2002, and the auction house estimated that the *Kane* Oscar might bring as much as $400,000.

But everything came to a screeching halt when the Academy of Motion Picture Arts and Sciences stopped the auction, citing an obscure 1951 Academy bylaw. They claimed that Beatrice Welles had no right to sell the Oscar because the bylaw stipulates that if an Oscar winner (or the winner's heirs) ever offer the statuette for sale, it has to be offered to the Academy first…for $1.

### The Plot Thickens

How was it possible that Ronald Colman's family could sell their Oscar but Orson Welles' daughter couldn't sell hers, even though both prizes were awarded before 1951?

When Orson Welles died in 1985, the *Kane* Oscar was not among his effects. Believing it lost, his daughter asked the Academy for a replacement. They gave her one but made her sign a waiver promising to return it if she ever decided she didn't want it.

Then in 1994, the original Oscar surfaced at Sotheby's. It turned out that Welles had given the Oscar to cinematographer Gary Graver as a gift during the shooting of his unfinished film, *The Other Side of the Wind*, in 1974. Twenty years later, Graver, who had not signed a waiver (neither had Ronald Colman), sold the Oscar for $50,000 to Bay Holdings, who then auctioned it at Sotheby's. When Beatrice Welles learned of the other statuette's existence, she sued Graver and Bay Holdings and won.

Graver was not pleased. "He gave it to me and told me to keep it," he said in a newspaper interview. "She never saw it before in her life. Orson had given it to me and she went to court and said, 'I want it.'"

But Beatrice Welles got a taste of her own medicine when the Academy forced her to withdraw the *Kane* Oscar from the auction block. She is now stuck with two Oscars, her father's original and the duplicate, together worth exactly…$2.

## STAYIN' ALIVE

In 1977, 23-year-old John Travolta strutted into disco history in the film *Saturday Night Fever*. Besides being a blockbuster hit—the film made $145 million at the box office—it also enjoyed critical success. Gene Siskel, the Chicago film critic known for his "thumbs up" TV show with Roger Ebert, declared it his favorite film. In fact, he loved the film so much that when the famous white polyester suit Travolta wore came up for sale at a charity auction in the 1980s, he leapt at the chance to own it. His final bid of $2,000 beat out Jane Fonda. The suit was his.

Though some chuckled at Siskel's purchase, Siskel got the last laugh. In 1995 Christie's sold the suit at auction for $145,500—the highest amount ever paid for an article of clothing at that time. Ironically, the record was broken in 1997 by the $225,000 paid for Princess Di's blue velvet evening dress—the one she wore the night she danced with John Travolta at the White House.

* * *

## OTHER CELEBRITY ITEMS UP FOR AUCTION

**Elvis's tooth.** In July 2003, Flo and Jesse Briggs, owners of a hair salon in Fort Lauderdale, Florida, put the King's tooth up for auction. The tooth purportedly once belonged to an old girlfriend, Linda Thompson (the Briggses got it from Startifacts, a company that sells celebrity memorabilia). Minimum bid for the tooth: $100,000. Number of legitimate bidders: 0. The tooth was pulled from auction.

**JFK's boxer shorts.** Former First Lady Jacqueline Kennedy's personal secretary and her personal attendant auctioned off 300 "intimate" items belonging the Kennedys, including a yellowed pair of President Kennedy's World War II Navy-issue cotton underwear. (No, not *that* kind of yellow.) They sold for $5,000. Also in the auction was a pair of JFK's pajama bottoms, which went for $2,000.

**Carly Simon's secret.** As part of a charity fundraiser, Simon offered to reveal who the song "You're So Vain" was written about. The catch: She agreed to tell only the highest bidder…and he's not allowed to tell anyone else. NBC exec Dick Ebersol paid $50,000 for the privilege (he also gets a live rendition of the song, a peanut butter-and-jelly sandwich, and a vodka on the rocks). Now he knows…and he's not telling.

**El norte: Norway consumes more Mexican food than any other European nation.**

# HOAXMEISTER

*Think everything you read in the newspaper or see on the news has been checked for accuracy? Think again. Sometimes the media will repeat whatever they're told... and this guy set out to prove it.*

**MONKEY SEE, MONKEY SAY**

Joey Skaggs's career as a hoax artist began in the mid-1960s when he first combined his art training with sociopolitical activism. He wanted to show that instead of being guardians of the truth, the media machine often runs stories without verifying the facts. And in proving his point, he perpetrated some pretty clever hoaxes.

**HOAX #1:** A Cathouse for Dogs

In 1976 Skaggs ran an ad in the *Village Voice* for a dog bordello. For $50 Skaggs promised satisfaction for any sexually deprived Fido. Then he hosted a special "night in the cathouse for dogs" just for the media. A beautiful woman and her Saluki, both clad in tight red sweaters and bows, paraded up and down in front of the panting "clientele" (male dogs belonging to Skaggs's friends). The ASPCA lodged a slew of protests and had Skaggs arrested (and indicted) for cruelty to animals. The event was even featured on an Emmy-nominated WABC News documentary. But the joke was on them—the "dog bordello" never existed.

**HOAX #2:** Save the Geoduck!

It's pronounced "gooey-duck" and it's a long-necked clam native to Puget Sound, Washington, with a digging muscle that bears a striking resemblance to the male reproductive organ of a horse. In 1987 Skaggs posed as a doctor (Dr. Long) and staged a protest rally in front of the Japan Society. Why? Because according to "Dr. Long," the geoduck was considered to be an aphrodisiac in Asia, and people were eating the mollusk into extinction. Although neither claim had the slightest basis in fact, Skaggs's "Clamscam" was good enough to sucker WNBC, UPI, the German news magazine *Der Spiegel*, and a number of Japanese papers into reporting the story as fact.

**HOAX #3:** Miracle Roach Hormone Cure

Skaggs pretended to be an entomologist from Colombia named Dr. Josef Gregor in 1981. In an interview with WNBC-TV's *Live at Five*, "Dr. Gregor" claimed to have graduated from the University of Bogota, and said his "Miracle Roach Hormone Cure" cured the common cold, acne, and menstrual cramps. An amazed Skaggs remarked later, "Nobody ever checked my credentials." The interviewers didn't realize they were being had until Dr. Gregor played his theme song—*La Cucaracha*.

**HOAX #4:** Sergeant Bones and the Fat Squad

In 1986 Skaggs appeared on *Good Morning, America* as a former Marine Corps drill sergeant named Joe Bones, who was determined to stamp out obesity in the United States. Flanked by a squad of tough-looking commandos, Sergeant Bones announced that for "$300 a day plus expenses," his "Fat Squad" would infiltrate an overweight client's home and physically stop them from snacking. "You can hire us but you can't fire us," he deadpanned, staring into the camera. "Our commandos take no bribes." Reporters from the *Philadelphia Enquirer*, *Washington Post*, *Miami Herald*, and the *New York Daily News* all believed—and ran with—the story.

**HOAX #5:** Maqdananda, the Psychic Attorney

On April 1, 1994, Skaggs struck again with a 30-second TV spot in which he dressed like a swami. Seated on a pile of cushions, Maqdananda asked viewers, "Why deal with the legal system without knowing the outcome beforehand?" Along with normal third dimension legal issues—divorce, accidental injury, wills, trusts—Maqdananda claimed he could help renegotiate contracts made in past lives, sue for psychic surgery malpractice, and help rectify psychic injustices. "There is no statute of limitations in the psychic realm," he said. Viewers just had to call the number at the bottom of their screen: 1-808-UCA-DADA. In Hawaii, *CNN Headline News* ran the spot 40 times during the week. When people called the number (and dozens did), they were greeted by the swami's voice on an answering machine, saying, "I knew you'd call." Skaggs later revealed that the swami—and his political statement about the proliferation of New Age gurus and ambulance-chasing attorneys—was all a hoax.

# FILTHY WATER PEOPLE

*Did you ever get a lousy nickname that stuck? You're in good company. Many Native American tribes are known today by unflattering names given to them by their neighbors. Here are a few examples.*

**CHEYENNE**

**Meaning:** Red-Talkers

**Origin:** This Great Plains tribe called themselves the *Tsitsistas*, which means the "Beautiful People." The neighboring Dakota people may have agreed, but they couldn't understand what the Tsitsistas were saying, because they spoke a different language. They called the Tsitsistas the "Red-Talkers," meaning "those who speak unintelligibly," or, in Dakota, the *Cheyenne*.

**APACHE**

**Meaning:** Enemy

**Origin:** Like many Native American tribes, this one, famous for legendary chief Geronimo, called themselves "the People"—*Dine* (di-nay) in their native language. But the neighboring tribe, the Zuni—victim of many of their war parties—called them "the enemy," or *apachu*. Over time, that evolved into their permanent name, the *Apache*.

**ARAPAHO**

**Meaning:** Tattooed People

**Origin:** These Plains Indians called themselves the *Inuna-ina*, which translates to "the People." Their neighbors, the Crow, identified them by their distinctive body markings and called them "Tattooed People," or, in their language, *Arapahos*.

**HURON**

**Meaning:** Boar's Head

**Origin:** This tribe lived in the area between Lakes Huron and Ontario and called themselves the *Wyandot*, meaning "Those from the Peninsula." But the French called them *Hures*, or "Boar's Head," because the men in the tribe wore their hair in bristly spikes that resembled boar's hair—and *Hures* eventually became *Huron*.

### WINNEBAGO

**Meaning:** Filthy Water People

**Origin:** These Great Lakes Indians were named by the *Chippewa* people. Their own name was *Horogióthe*, or "Fish-Eaters." But the Chippewa called them the *Winnebago*—the "Filthy Water People," possibly because the Horogióthe painted themselves with clay when going to war, which made them appear to have bathed in muddy water.

### MOHAWK

**Meaning:** Man-Eaters

**Origin:** This tribe from upper New York State and eastern Canada called themselves *Kaniengehagaóthe*, or "Flint People." That proved to be a very difficult word to pronounce for Europeans, who called them what their neighbors, the Narragansett, called them: *Mohawk*, or "Man-Eaters." Why? They engaged in ritualistic cannibalism.

### GROS VENTRES

**Meaning:** Big Bellies

**Origin:** This tribe from what is now Montana and Saskatchewan called themselves the *Ahahninin*, or "White Clay People." When early French fur trappers and traders asked members of neighboring tribes about the name, they responded—in Native American sign language—by sweeping their hand out from their chest and downward, making what appeared to be a "belly" shape. What were they saying? Historians believe they were saying "Waterfall People," referring to the part of the Saskatchewan River where they lived. The French mistook the gesture and called them the name they are still called today, the *Gros Ventres*—"Big Bellies."

* * *

"Names are not always what they seem. The common Welsh name Bzjxxllwcp is pronounced Jackson."

**—Mark Twain**

# WHAT IS LOVE?

*We have no idea. Here's what some other people think.*

"Love is a fire. But whether it is going to warm your heart or burn down your house, you can never tell."

**—Joan Crawford**

"Love doesn't make the world go 'round. Love is what makes the ride worthwhile."

**—Franklin P. Jones**

"Love is the irresistible desire to be desired irresistibly."

**—Louis Ginsburg**

"Love is the great beautifier."

**—Louisa May Alcott**

"Love is the triumph of imagination over intelligence."

**—H. L. Mencken**

"All love is transference, nothing more than two normal neurotics mingling their infantile libidos with one another."

**—Sigmund Freud**

"Brief is life, but love is long."

**—Alfred, Lord Tennyson**

"Love is everything it's cracked up to be."

**—Erica Jong**

"Life is a flower of which love is the honey."

**—Victor Hugo**

"Love is an ideal thing, marriage a real thing; a confusion of the real with the ideal never goes unpunished."

**—Goethe**

"Love is only a dirty trick played on us to achieve the continuation of the species."

**—W. Somerset Maugham**

"Love is the reason you were born."

**—Dorothy Fields**

"The magic of first love is our ignorance that it can never end."

**—Benjamin Disraeli**

"True love is like ghosts, which everybody talks about and few have seen."

**—La Rochefoucauld**

"Love is life. All, everything that I understand, I understand only because I love."

**—Leo Tolstoy**

"Love stinks."

**—J. Geils Band**

**Q: What has 18 legs and catches flies? A: A baseball team.**

# FOUNDING FATHERS

*You already know the names. Here's who they belong to.*

## JOHANN ADAM BIRKENSTOCK

**Background:** Birkenstock was an 18th-century German shoemaker.

**Famous Name:** Birkenstock's family kept the shoemaking tradition going. In 1897 his grandson Konrad Birkenstock introduced a revolutionary concept in footwear: the first shoe with a contoured insole that reflected the shape of the human foot. In 1965 Konrad's grandson Karl took the idea further and created the Birkenstock sandal. Introduced to the United States in 1966, it became the unofficial official footwear of the hippie generation.

## ELMER (THE BULL)

**Background:** In the 1930s, Elsie the Cow was the logo for Borden dairy products. The company had a live cow named Elsie for personal appearances. There was so much demand for Elsie that Borden had to find another cow to make appearances, too. They found a bull instead, named him Elmer, and called him Elsie's "husband."

**Famous Name:** Borden's chemical division originally wanted to use Elsie as "spokescow" for their new white glue. But the dairy division didn't want Elsie to be associated with a nonfood product (especially one that *looked* like milk). So they decided to use Elsie's husband... and called it Elmer's Glue-All.

## THOMAS JACOB HILFIGER

**Background:** Born in Elmira, New York, in 1951, Tommy knew what he wanted to do from an early age: design clothing.

**Famous Name:** While still in high school, he worked at a gas station, saved his money to buy used jeans, which he resold to other kids. He used the money he earned to open a chain of hip clothing stores called People's Place and got his start as a designer by telling the jeans-makers what styles would sell better. (He was right.) After working for other clothing companies for several years (Jordache fired him—they were wrong), he struck gold in 1985 with a line of urban-preppy clothing—Tommy Hilfiger.

**P. T. Barnum staged the first international beauty contest.**

## RUDOLF DIESEL

**Background:** Born in Paris in 1858, Diesel studied mechanical engineering in college. He then dedicated his life to creating efficient heat engines, and in 1893 published his design for a new internal combustion engine.

**Famous Name:** At his wife's suggestion, Diesel named the engine after himself. But the moderate fame and fortune he received from his design were short-lived. Plagued by ill health and legal battles over his patents, he lost most of his money. While traveling on a ship to England in 1913, Diesel threw himself overboard.

## MARGE SPENCER

**Background:** In 1947 a man named Max Adler decided to start a mail-order gift company. When designing his new catalog, he decided that Adler Gifts didn't sound quite right.

**Famous Name:** So he asked his secretary, Marge Spencer, if she wouldn't mind lending her name to the catalog. She agreed and Spencer Gifts was born.

## ENZO FERRARI

**Background:** The man who created one of the world's most sought-after sports cars began his transportation career shoeing mules for the Italian army in World War I.

**Famous Name:** In the 1920s, Ferrari became one of Italy's most famous race car drivers and a designer for the Alfa Romeo racing team. In 1929 he started his own racing team, building sports cars only to help finance the team. When he died in 1988, Ferrari had sold fewer than 50,000 cars.

## TADAO KASHIO

**Background:** In 1946 Tadao founded Kashio Seisakusho, a company that specialized in manufacturing aircraft parts.

**Famous Name:** His younger brother Toshio suggested they work on developing a calculator instead. So the Kashio brothers—there were four of them—used technology from telephone relay switching equipment to create an all-electric "gearless" calculator. (Up until that time, calculators used electricity to drive internal gears.) It took a decade of tinkering, but they introduced the Model 14-A calculator in 1957 and changed their name to…Casio Computer.

**That stings! Human DNA and jellyfish DNA are 90% identical.**

# THE MAD BOMBER, PT. I

*From our Dustbin of History files, the story of a city, a criminal psychiatrist, and a psycho with a grudge.*

## SPECIAL DELIVERY

On November 16, 1940, an unexploded bomb was found on a window ledge of the Consolidated Edison Building in Manhattan. It was wrapped in a very neatly hand-written note that read,

CON EDISON CROOKS—THIS IS FOR YOU.

The police were baffled: surely whoever delivered the bomb would know that the note would be destroyed if the bomb detonated. Was the bomb not meant to go off? Was the person stupid...or was he just sending a message?

No discernable fingerprints were found on the device and a brief search of company records brought no leads, so the police treated the case as an isolated incident by a crackpot, possibly someone who had a grievance with "Con Ed"—the huge company that provided New York City with all of its gas and electric power.

## WAKE-UP CALL

Nearly a year later, another unexploded bomb was found lying in the street a few blocks from the Con Ed building, this one with an alarm clock fusing mechanism that had not been wound. Again the police had no leads and again they filed the case away—there were larger problems at hand: the war in Europe was escalating and U.S. involvement seemed imminent. Sure enough, three months later, the Japanese attacked Pearl Harbor, triggering America's entry into World War II.

Shortly thereafter a strange, neatly written letter arrived at police headquarters in Manhattan:

> I WILL MAKE NO MORE BOMB UNITS FOR THE DURATION OF THE WAR—MY PATRIOTIC FEELINGS HAVE MADE ME DECIDE THIS—I WILL BRING THE CON EDISON TO JUSTICE—THEY WILL PAY FOR THEIR DASTARDLY DEEDS...F. P.

True to his (or her) words, no more bombs showed up during the war, or for five years after that. But in that time at least 16 threat

**Huh? Number of U.S. marine wildlife sanctuaries where fishing is illegal: zero.**

letters, all from "F. P.", were delivered to Con Ed, as well as to movie theaters, the police, and even private individuals. Still, there were no bombs... until March 29, 1950.

## CITY UNDER SIEGE

That day, a third unexploded bomb much more advanced than the previous two was found on the lower level of Grand Central Station. "F. P." seemed to be sending the message that he (or she) had been honing his (or her) bomb-building skills over the last decade. Still, so far none of them had exploded. And police wondered: were these all just empty threats? That question was answered a month later when a bomb tore apart a phone booth at the New York Public Library. Over the next two years, four more bombs exploded around New York City. And try as they might to downplay the threat, the police couldn't keep the press from running with the story. "The Mad Bomber" started to dominate headlines.

More bombs were found, and more angry letters—some neatly written, others created from block letters clipped from magazines—promised to continue the terror until Con Edison was "BROUGHT TO JUSTICE."

Heading up the case was Police Inspector Howard E. Finney. He and his detectives had used every conventional police method they knew of, but the Mad Bomber was too smart for them. In December 1956, after a powerful explosion injured six people in Brooklyn's Paramount Theater, Inspector Finney decided to do something unconventional.

## PSYCH-OUT

Finney called in Dr. James A. Brussel, a brilliant psychiatrist who had worked with the military and the FBI. Brussel had an uncanny understanding of the criminal mind, and like everyone else in New York, this eloquent, pipe-smoking psychiatrist was curious about what made the Mad Bomber tick. But because none of the letters had been released to the press, Brussel knew very little about the case. That all changed when police handed him the evidence they had gathered since 1941.

The pressure was on: citizens were growing more panicked with each new bomb, and more impatient with the cops' inability to catch the Mad Bomber. After poring through letters, phone call transcripts and police reports, and studying the unexploded bombs, Dr. Brussel presented this profile to Inspector Finney:

> It's a man. Paranoiac. He's middle-aged, forty to fifty years old, introvert. Well proportioned in build. He's single. A loner, perhaps living with an older female relative. He is very neat, tidy, and clean-shaven. Good education, but of foreign extraction. Skilled mechanic, neat with tools. Not interested in women. He's a Slav. Religious. Might flare up violently at work when criticized. Possible motive: discharge or reprimand. Feels superior to his critics. Resentment keeps growing. His letters are posted from Westchester, and he wouldn't be stupid enough to post them from where he lives. He probably mails the letter between his home and New York City. One of the biggest concentration of Poles is in Bridgeport, Connecticut, and to get from there to New York you have to pass through Westchester. He has had a bad disease—possibly heart trouble.

## GOING PUBLIC

Finney was impressed... but skeptical. His team had drawn some of the same conclusions, but even so, there had to be thousands of middle-aged men who fit that profile. What good would it do?

"I think you ought to publicize the description I've given you," suggested Dr. Brussel. "Publicize the whole Bomber investigation, in fact. Spread it in the newspapers, on radio and television." Finney disagreed. It was standard procedure to keep details of investigations away from the press. But Brussel maintained that if they handled the case correctly, the Mad Bomber would do most of the work for them. He said that, unconsciously, "he wants to be found out." Finney finally agreed. And as he left the office, Brussel added one more thing: "When you catch him, he'll be wearing a double-breasted suit, and it will be buttoned."

So the papers published the profile and the chase went into high gear. As Finney predicted, "a million crackpots" came out of the woodwork, all claiming to be the Mad Bomber, but none of them had the Mad Bomber's skill or his distinctively neat handwriting. A slew of legitimate leads came from concerned citizens about their odd neighbors, yet nothing solid surfaced. Still, Brussel was confident that the real Bomber's arrogance would be his undoing.

***Did Brussel's strategy work? Turn to Part II on page 596 to find out.***

# UNCLE JOHN'S SECOND FAVORITE ROLL

*A friend of Uncle John's recently called to report that her son had just made a backpack...completely out of duct tape. That started us wondering about other ways people use duct tape. Here's a small fraction of what we found.*

## DUCK TAPE

Originally called "duck" tape (because it was made from a kind of cotton canvas known as "duck"... and it was waterproof), this household staple was developed for the military to keep moisture out of ammunition cases. Don't have any leaky ammo cases? You can use it for a Band-Aid or to repair a tent, even as a fly strip. Russian cosmonauts used it to help keep the aging *Mir* space station lashed together. And now it even comes in a rainbow of designer colors, including camouflage.

Here are some other creative uses people have found for the tape:

• Researchers say it's good for removing warts. Duct tape irritates the wart, which causes the immune system to kick in and attack the virus that created it. Recommended course of treatment: Tape the wart for six days, then rip off the tape, soak the area in water, and file the wart with a pumice stone or emery board. Reapply duct tape and keep it on for another six days. Repeat the cycle for two months or until the wart goes away.

• The Tesoro Iron Dog is a 2,000-mile snowmobile race in Alaska. With temperatures hovering around -20°F, racers apply duct tape to their exposed skin to protect it from frostbite.

• When one of his cows suffered a deep cut that caused "some of its insides to fall out," a farmer in Maine used duct tape to close the wound. He found that medical tape couldn't hold the gash together under all the conditions a cow faced on the farm—but duct tape did. Another farmer stuffed the innards back into an injured hen and taped her up with duct tape. When the duct tape finally fell off (months later), the hen was as good as new.

**The U.S. national flowers are the goldenrod and the columbine.**

• When calves are born in severely cold weather, their ears sometimes freeze. Instead of using fleece-lined earmuffs, which the cows scratch off, a Canadian rancher duct tapes the calves' ears to their heads. The ears stay warm and the cows can't get the tape off.

• During the 2002 Winter Olympics at Salt Lake City, snowboarder Chris Klug broke a boot buckle just before his final race. After having survived a liver transplant only 19 months earlier, Klug wasn't about to let a broken buckle stop him. With less than two minutes to spare, he grabbed a roll of duct tape, jury-rigged a quick repair, and went on to win a bronze medal in the giant slalom event.

• On the NASCAR pro circuit, a special grade of duct tape is used for split-second auto body repairs. In fact, some cars are literally covered in it, which is why this grade is known as the "200-mph tape." (Another grade of duct tape, known as "nuclear tape," is used to repair nuclear reactors.)

• Starlets, beauty queens, and fashion models have long used duct tape to enhance cleavage in low-cut gowns. First they apply surgical tape across their breasts to protect them, then duct tape, which is strong and flexible enough to lift, shape, and hold everything in place. The technique was once demonstrated on *Oprah*.

## SPACE CASES

• When *Apollo 17* astronauts Harrison Schmitt and Eugene Cernan drove their lunar vehicle across the moon, the fine grit kicked up by the vehicle's wheels wreaked havoc on their equipment. They fixed the problem by building extended fenders out of spare maps, clamps, and duct tape. (Or did they? See page 560.)

• After a month of living on the International Space Station without a kitchen table, astronaut Bill Shepherd and cosmonauts Sergei Krikalev and Yuri Gidzenko began piecing together scraps of aluminum. Once they got a frame together, they covered the top with duct tape. The table became the social center of the space station—the best place to eat, work, or just hang out.

* * *

"Duct tape is like the Force: It has a dark side and a light side—and it holds the universe together."

**—Pop philosopher Carl Zwanzig**

# UNCLE JOHN'S PAGE OF LISTS

*Some random facts from our files.*

**5 Roman Delicacies, circa 200 A.D.**

1. Parrot tongue
2. Ostrich brain
3. Thrush tongue
4. Peacock comb
5. Nightingale tongue

**8 Things Rupert Murdoch Owns**

1. *The N.Y. Post*
2. *The Times* (London)
3. *The Australian* (Sydney)
4. *TV Guide*
5. Twentieth-Century Fox
6. Madison Square Garden
7. Fox News Channel
8. L.A. Dodgers

**4 Jell-O Flavor Flops**

1. Cola
2. Coffee
3. Apple
4. Celery

**5 Greatest American Generals (Gallup Poll, 2000)**

1. George Patton
2. Dwight Eisenhower
3. Douglas MacArthur
4. Colin Powell
5. George Washington

**5 States with the Most Nuclear Waste Sites**

1. Illinois—10
2. California—9
3. New York—9
4. Michigan—6
5. Pennsylvania—6

**4 Most Expensive Ad Spots on a Race Car**

1. Hood
2. Lower rear quarter panel
3. Behind rear window
4. Behind driver's window

**10 Animals That Have Been in Space**

1. Dog
2. Chimp
3. Bullfrog 4. Cat
5. Tortoise
6. Bee 7. Cricket
8. Spider 9. Fish
10. Worm

**4 Most Copied Hollywood Noses (Beverly Hills plastic surgeons)**

1. Heather Locklear
2. Nicole Kidman
3. Marisa Tomei
4. Catherine Zeta-Jones

**7 Actors in *The Magnificent Seven***

1. Robert Vaughn
2. Steve McQueen
3. Brad Dexter
4. James Coburn
5. Horst Bucholz
6. Yul Brynner
7. Charles Bronson

# LET'S PLAY TOILET GOLF

*It may be heresy for us to say, but sometimes you just don't want to read in the bathroom. For those rare moments, here are a few products that will help make your next pit stop as fun as a trip to a theme park.*

**NOW *THAT'S* A BATHTUB**

In 2003 the Jacuzzi company introduced "La Scala," a bathtub spa with a built-in, 43-inch flat-screen TV, a CD player, a DVD player, and a floating remote control. Price: $29,000 (installation is extra).

But what about the rest of us, who don't have $29,000 to spend on a tub? Shouldn't we be able to have fun in the bathroom, too? Never fear—the BRI is here! We've been looking around for things that anyone can use to turn their bathroom into an entertainment center. Here's what we found:

**ROLL MODEL**

**Product:** Don't P Me Off Roll Playing Puzzle

**Description:** Have you ever solved one of those puzzles where you have to separate a couple of twisted pieces of metal that seem impossibly locked together? This is that kind of puzzle—only with a sadistic twist. The cylindrical wooden box completely encases a roll of toilet paper, so your houseguests can't get at it...unless they solve the puzzle. How hard is it? The manufacturer's advice: "We suggest that you have an extra roll on hand."

**STREAM OF CONSCIOUSNESS**

**Product:** Peeball

**Description:** You need a urinal to play, so unless your bathroom is well equipped, your Peeball career will be limited to away games. Peeball is a little smaller than a Ping-Pong ball and is made of bicarbonate of soda, similar to the stuff that Alka-Seltzer is made of.

**How to Play:** Toss the ball into the urinal, aim, and fire! The player who dissolves their Peeball in the shortest amount of time is the winner.

**Background:** Peeball was developed by England's Prostate Cancer Charity. Because "difficulty peeing and weak flow" are typical symptoms of prostate cancer, Peeball educates players about the disease and encourages anyone who has the symptoms to get a checkup. "The message is that if men can't dissolve the Peeball in a certain period of time, they might need to see a doctor," says spokesperson Gina Growden.

### LOO-TERATURE

**Product:** Toilet Paper Literature

**Description:** Klo-Verlag, a German publishing company, takes novels, detective stories, fairy tales, poetry, and other written works and publishes them on rolls of toilet paper. The company prefers shorter pieces that can be printed several times on the same roll, so that when one "end user" finishes off part of the roll, the next person in the bathroom will still find the remaining material interesting to read. "We want our books to be used," company head Georges Hemmerstoffer explains. "That's our philosophy."

### TEE PEE

**Product:** Toilet Golf

**Description:** The game consists of a green bathroom rug shaped like a putting green, a miniature putter, and two golf balls. The rug wraps around the base of a toilet, so you can practice your putt while on the pot. (Also available: Toilet Bowling and Toilet Fishing.)

### SOUND SYSTEMS

- **Talking Toilet Paper.** A digital voice recorder is built into the spool of this toilet paper holder. Record any message you want—then, every time someone touches the toilet paper, they'll get a surprise. Manufacturer's suggested messages: "This is a bathroom, not a library" or "Whoa! Somebody light a match!"

- **Fart Clock.** Every hour on the hour the Fart Clock lets out one of 12 different fart sounds. Includes a light sensor to turn it off when the room darkens.

- **Fart Phone.** It farts instead of rings. This phone will provide a mystery every time someone calls—is that the phone, or did somebody step on a duck?

**There are 4.5 million wild turkeys in the U.S. (Not including the ones in liquor stores.)**

# THE PARANOID'S FIELD GUIDE TO SECRET SOCIETIES

*Secret societies actually do exist. In fact, there are dozens of them, from the Freemasons to the Ku Klux Klan. But are they really responsible for the world's ills, as some people believe? Probably not, but on the other hand, you never know...*

## THE ILLUMINATI

**Who They Are:** This group was founded in 1776 by Adam Weishaupt, a Jesuit priest, in Bavaria. His mission: to advance the 18th-century ideals of revolution, social reform, and rational thought (the name means "the Enlightened Ones" in Latin). Weishaupt and his cronies were fiercely opposed by the monarchs of Europe and by the Catholic Church, which is why they had to meet and communicate in secret. German author Johann Goethe was a member. In the United States, both Benjamin Franklin and Thomas Jefferson were accused of being members and denied it, but both wrote favorably about Weishaupt and his efforts.

**What They're Blamed For:** This group has been associated with more conspiracy theories than any other. Considered the silent evil behind such paranoid bugaboos as One World Government and the New World Order, the Illuminati have been blamed for starting the French and Russian revolutions, as well as both world wars, and almost every global conflict in between. They are said to use bribery, blackmail, and murder to infiltrate every level of power in society—business, banking, and government—to achieve their ultimate goal: world domination.

## BILDERBERG GROUP

**Who They Are:** Founded in 1952 by Prince Bernhard of the Netherlands, the Bilderberg Group (named after the hotel in Oosterbeck, Holland, where the first meeting was held) was founded to promote cooperation and understanding between

Western Europe and North America. To that end, leaders from both regions are invited to meet every year for off-the-record discussions on current issues. The list of attendees has included presidents (every one from Eisenhower to Clinton), British prime ministers (Lord Home, Lord Callaghan, Sir Edward Heath, Margaret Thatcher), captains of industry like Fiat's Giovanni Agnelli, and financiers like David Rockefeller. Invitees are members of the power elite in their countries, mostly rich and male. Meetings are closed. No resolutions are passed, no votes are taken, and no public statements are ever made.

**What They're Blamed For:** The fact that so many of the world's most powerful players refuse to disclose anything about the group's meetings strikes many outsiders as downright subversive. What are they doing? The group has been accused of hand picking Western leaders to be their puppets, pointing to circumstantial evidence like the fact that Bill Clinton was invited to attend a meeting before he became president, as was Britain's Tony Blair before he became prime minister. Conspiracy buffs have even accused the Bilderbergers of masterminding the global AIDS epidemic as a way of controlling world population to the benefit of the European/American elite.

## TRILATERAL COMMISSION

**Who They Are:** Founded in 1973 by David Rockefeller and former National Security Council chief Zbigniew Brzezinski, this organization is composed of 350 prominent private citizens (none currently hold government positions) from Europe, North America, and Japan (the tri-lateral global power triangle). Like the Bilderberg Group, their stated goal is to discuss global issues and to promote understanding and cooperation. Unlike other groups, this one is more visible: it publishes reports, and members are identified. It's also more diverse, with women and ethnic groups represented. However, membership is by invitation only, usually on the recommendation of serving members, making it one of the most exclusive private clubs in the world. There are no representatives from developing nations.

**What They're Blamed For:** Many conspiracy theorists view the Trilateral Commission as the "sunny" face of the evil machinations of international bankers and business moguls who are working to

**The average public swimming pool contains more urine than fluoride.**

make the world their own little oyster, with one financial system, one defense system, one government, and one religion—which they will control. Again, all members are major players in business and government. Americans of note include Bill Clinton, Jimmy Carter, Henry Kissinger, and George Bush (the elder), former Federal Reserve Chairman Paul Volcker, former Speaker of the House Tom Foley, and former U.S. Trade Representative Carla Hills, to name a few. Since there is considerable crossover between the Trilateral Commission and the Bilderberg Group, the commission is thought by some to be under the control of the Illuminati. That it is completely private, with no direct role in government (read "no accountability"), only adds fuel to the fires of suspicious minds.

## SKULL & BONES SOCIETY

**Who They Are:** This society was founded at Yale University in 1833. Only 15 senior-year students are admitted annually; they meet twice a week in a grim, windowless building called the Tombs. Unlike most campus fraternities, Skull & Bones appears to focus on positioning its members for success after college. But no one knows for sure, because members are sworn to total secrecy for life. The names of past and current members include many of America's power elite: both George Bushes, William Howard Taft, as well as the descendants of such famous American families as the Pillsburys, Weyerhausers, Rockefellers, Vanderbilts, and Whitneys.

**What They're Blamed For:** What's wrong with a little good ol' boy networking? Nothing, perhaps, but Skull & Bones members have also been accused of practicing satanic rites within the walls of the Tombs. Initiation reportedly requires pledges to lie down in coffins, confess sordid details of their sex lives, and endure painful torture so that he may "die to the world, to be born again into the Order." Like the Illuminati, the Order (as it's called by its members) supposedly works to create a world controlled and ruled by the elite—members of Skull & Bones.

## BOHEMIAN GROVE

**Who They Are:** Founded in 1872 by five San Francisco *Examiner* newsmen as a social boozing club, the Bohemian Grove has been called "one of the world's most prestigious summer camps" by *Newsweek*. Prospective members may wait up to 15 years to get in and then have to pony up a $2,500 membership fee. The Grove

**_Buculets_ are those little bumpers on the underside of your toilet seat.**

itself is a 2,700-acre retreat set deep in a California redwood forest. Members' privacy is zealously guarded: no strangers are allowed near the site, and reporters are expressly forbidden entry. The Bohemian Grove motto is from Shakespeare: "Weaving spiders come not here," a reminder that all deal making is to be left at the gates. The members relax and entertain each other by putting on plays, lecturing on subjects of the day, and wining and dining lavishly.

So why does anyone care about the Bohemian Grove? Well, the membership is a virtual Who's Who of the most powerful people (mostly Republican) in American government and business. Members past and present include Dick Cheney, Donald Rumsfeld, Karl Rove, George W. Bush, Richard Nixon, Gerald Ford, Henry Kissinger, Caspar Weinberger, Stephen Bechtel, Joseph Coors, Alexander Haig, Ronald Reagan, and hundreds more. Critics claim there is no way men like these (no women are allowed) can hang out together and *not* make back-room deals.

**What They're Blamed For:** Conspiracy theorist claim that the Manhattan Project was set up at the Grove and that the decision to make Eisenhower the Republican presidential candidate for 1952 was hammered out between drinks on the lawn.

Darker charges have been made against the Grove as well. Members are purported to practice some odd rituals, such as wearing red hoods and marching in procession like ancient druids, chanting hymns to the Great Owl. Members say it's all in good fun, but outsiders wonder at the cultlike overtones. Outrageous rumors were rampant in the 1980s: sacrificial murders, drunken revels, even pedophilia, sodomy, kidnapping, and rape. Of course, none of this has ever been proven, but as limousines and private jets swoop into this secret enclave in the woods, the "big boys" continue to party and the rest of the world remains in the dark about just exactly what goes on.

* * *

## THE SECRET RECIPE FOR ~~COCA~~ COLA

The Bathroom Readers' Institute is pleased to reveal the closely-guarded secret recipe of ~~Coca~~ *Cola*. Here it is: 3½ [illegible] of [illegible], 2 [illegible] of [illegible], 14 [illegible], 13⅓ [illegible] of [illegible], and a dash of salt. (Now you know—don't tell anyone.)

# THE RHINOCEROS PARTY

*Who says politics has to be stodgy and humorless? Not Canada.*

## BACKGROUND

In the early 1960s, Quebec was wracked by violent protests against the federal government and the Anglo-Saxon establishment that dominated the province. In the midst of this turmoil, Dr. Jacques Ferron, a physician and writer, launched a new political party—a satirical alternative "to serve as a peaceful outlet for disgruntled Quebecois." And he chose the rhinoceros as the party's symbol. Why a rhino? Ferron said it epitomized the professional politician—"a slow-witted animal that can move fast as hell when in danger."

It existed for only 30 years, but the Rhinoceros Party "put the 'mock' back in 'demockracy.'" And for a fringe group, it attracted a surprising number of votes. Here are some of their more creative campaign promises:

• They vowed to sell Canada's Senate at an antiques auction in California.

• They promised to plant coffee, chocolate, and oranges in southern Ontario, so Canada could become a banana republic.

• In the 1980 election, the Rhinos promised to break all their promises and introduce an era of "indecision and incompetence."

• Fielding candidates with names like "Richard the Troll" and "Albert the Cad," the Rhinos ran on a platform of "sex, drugs, and rock 'n' roll" for the masses.

• Other parties talked about a guaranteed annual income; the Rhinos vowed to introduce a "Guaranteed Annual Orgasm" and to sell seats in Canada's Senate for $15 each.

• In 1988 they made national headlines by running a candidate named John Turner against the incumbent opposition leader… John Turner. Turner was not amused (everyone else was).

• They promised to repeal the law of gravity, provide free trips to bordellos, and nationalize all pay toilets.

• When the Canadian government was trying to decide where to

**Q: Why aren't there any zebras in Prague? A: Czechs and stripes don't mix.**

locate its embassy in Israel, the Rhinoceros Party proposed to locate it in a Winnebago, which could travel continuously between Jerusalem and Tel Aviv.

## MORE PROMISES AND PROPOSALS

• As an energy-saving measure, they proposed larger wheels for the backs of all cars, so they would always be going downhill.

• They proposed legislating a lower boiling point of water (another energy-saving measure).

• They also proposed moving half the Rockies one meter to the west, as a make-work project.

• They promised to make bubble gum the currency of Canada and to provide tax credits for enthusiastic sleepers.

• They promised to spend $50 million on reform schools for politicians.

• They pledged that "None of our candidates will be running on steroids."

• Another promise: to have the Rocky Mountains bulldozed so that Alberta could get a few extra minutes of daylight.

• They promised to turn the parliamentary restaurant into a national franchise operation.

• One Rhino candidate proposed "to create a cartel of the world's snow-producing countries, call it Snow-pec, and export snow to cool down the Middle East conflict."

• They promised to bring back "the good old English system of driving on the left-hand side of the road, but in the first year only, buses and trucks will drive on the right-hand side."

## END OF AN ERA

When the government passed a law in 1993 requiring a $50,000 deposit from every party in a national election—essentially killing off the Rhinoceros Party—the Rhinos asked Canadians to write their own names on the ballot and vote for themselves.

"We cannot fool all of the people some of the time or even some of the people all of the time," said Charlie McKenzie, the party's general secretary, "but if we can fool a majority of the people at election time, that's all the time we need."

**The only American praised by Hitler in *Mein Kampf*? Henry Ford.**

# HOUSEHOLD ORIGINS

*Some things are so commonplace that it's difficult to imagine life without them. Here's where these everyday items came from.*

## PLASTIC WRAP

Invented by accident in 1933, when Ralph Wiley, a researcher at Dow Chemical, was washing his lab equipment at the end of the day and found that a thin plastic film coating the inside of one vial wasn't coming off. The stuff was polyvinylidene chloride, and after further experimentation, Wiley found that the stuff was clingy, resisted chemicals, and was impervious to air and water. It was so tough, in fact, that he wanted to call it "eonite," after an imaginary indestructible substance in the *Little Orphan Annie* comic strip. Dow decided to call it Saran Wrap instead.

## WATER BEDS

Believe it or not, people have been sleeping on water-filled bags for more than 3,500 years. The Persians were apparently the first—they sewed goatskins together, filled them with water, and left them in the sun to get warm. The direct ancestor of the modern water bed was invented in 1853 by Dr. William Hooper of Portsmouth, England, who saw the beds as a medical device that could be used to treat bedridden patients suffering from bedsores, as well as burn victims, and arthritis and rheumatism sufferers. His water bed wasn't much more than a rubber hot water bottle big enough to sleep on. It wasn't until 1967 that San Francisco design student Charles Hall made an improved model out of vinyl and added an electric heater to keep the bed warm all the time.

## ELECTRIC PLUGS AND SOCKETS

Electricity was first introduced into homes in the 1880s, but every lamp or appliance had to be "hard-wired" into the wall by an electrician. That lasted until 1904, when a Connecticut inventor named Harvey Hubbell was in a penny arcade and noticed a janitor struggling to disconnect the wires of a boxing game so that he could clean behind it. Hubbell knew there had to be a better—not to mention a safer—way to detach and reattach wires to walls.

After experimenting with metal and wood (which served as an insulator before plastic came into use), he came up with a two-pronged plug-and-socket system that isn't all that different from the one used today. In fact, since then there have only been two major updates to his design, both safety features: 1) many plugs and sockets have a third prong that serves as a ground, and 2) one prong is wider than the other so that the plug can only be plugged into the socket one way—keeping "neutral" on the correct side.

## BINOCULARS

In 1608 a Dutch maker of eyeglasses named Hans Lippershey noticed that when he held up two lenses and looked through both of them at a church steeple, the steeple looked bigger—it was magnified. So he made a tube, fitted a lens at each end, and tried to obtain a patent for this telescope, which he called a "looker." The patent application was rejected by Dutch authorities because other people had noticed the same thing before he did and made their own telescopes. (To this day it is not certain who invented the very first telescope.) In addition to rejecting Lippershey's patent, Dutch authorities complained that squinting through one eyepiece gave them eyestrain, and they asked him to join two telescopes together so that using it wouldn't give them such a headache. He took their suggestion, and the first binoculars were invented.

## STAPLERS

The hardest part about inventing the stapler wasn't the device itself, it was getting all those little staples to stick together. The precursors of modern staplers were invented in the 19th century and were used by printers to bind pages of books and magazines together. These machines used rolls of wire instead of staples, which the machine cut and bent into shape as it was binding the pages together. The first machines to use pre-bent, U-shaped pieces of wire came in the 1860s, but they held only one staple at a time and had to be reloaded by hand before each use. The first stapler to hold more than one staple was invented in 1894, but it used staples set onto a wooden core that came loose easily and jammed the stapler. In 1923 Thomas Briggs, founder of the Boston Wire Stitcher Company (later shortened to Bostitch), figured out a way to glue the staples together into a long strip that could be loaded into a stapler. Bostitch still makes staplers today.

**Half the world's population lives in temperate zones, which make up 7% of Earth's land area.**

# DIAMOND GEMS

*Why does Uncle John love baseball? It's loaded with facts, stories, odd characters, obscure histories, and weird statistics...just like a* Bathroom Reader. *Even if you're not a fan, you might like these gems.*

## ONE IN A MILLION

Ever heard of Bob Watson? He has the distinction of scoring major-league baseball's one millionth run. It happened on May 4, 1975, while he was playing for the Houston Astros. His prize: one million Tootsie Rolls.

## THE FIRST...AND HOPEFULLY LAST

The only major leaguer ever to be killed playing baseball was the Cleveland Indians' shortstop Ray Chapman. On August 16, 1920, before players wore batting helmets, Chapman was beaned in the head by a pitch from Yankee's hurler Carl Mays. He fell, slowly stood up, walked around in a daze, then collapsed again. Chapman was pronounced dead at 4:40 a.m. the next morning. Mays, who had always had a surly reputation, lamented about it after his playing days. "I won over 200 big-league games, but no one remembers that. When they think of me, I'm the guy who killed Chapman."

## INFLATION

After fan Sal Durante caught Roger Maris's historic 61st home run in 1961, he tried to return the ball to the quiet Yankee, but Maris told the truck driver to keep the ball and sell it if he wanted to. Durante sold it for $5,000. Maris' record stood for 37 years until Mark McGwire broke it in 1998, hitting 70 home runs. The 70th was caught by 26-year-old Phil Ozersky, who sold the ball for $3 million.

## THE OTHER ROBINSON

Jackie Robinson, as most people know, broke major-league baseball's color barrier in 1947. But few people outside baseball have heard of Frank Robinson (they're not related). In his Hall of Fame career, Frank Robinson won the Most Valuable Player award (in both the American and the National League), was a Triple Crown winner (led the league in homers, RBIs, and batting average), and won the All-Star Game and World Series MVP awards. But he

**Out of this world: In Sanskrit, *nirvana* literally translates to "going out."**

wasn't done yet: In 1974 he became the first African American to manage a big league ball club, and in 1989 became the first African American to be named Manager of the Year.

## HUMBLE BEGINNINGS

Superstar slugger Sammy Sosa was once a shoeshine boy. At only eight years old, he gave the money he earned to his widowed mother so she could buy food for the family.

## BY THE NUMBERS

The Baltimore Orioles' Cal Ripken Jr. played in a record 2,632 consecutive major-league games from 1982 to 1998. During Ripken's streak:

- 3,695 major leaguers went on the disabled list.
- 522 shortstops started for the other 27 teams.
- 33 second basemen played second base next to Ripken at shortstop (including his younger brother Billy Ripken).

Ripken also holds the record for the most consecutive innings played, with 8,243. He didn't miss a single inning from June 5, 1982, to September 14, 1987. His potential wasn't recognized early on, though—47 players were selected ahead of Ripken in the June 1978 draft.

## A LEAGUE OF HER OWN

On July 31, 1935, the Cincinnati Reds oversold tickets for their night game. To avoid a potential riot, they allowed the extra fans—8,000 in all—to stand along the foul lines. It was so packed that the players had to muscle their way through the crowd to get to the field. When Reds batter Babe Herman was trying to make his way to the plate in the bottom of the eighth, a nightclub singer named Kitty Burke grabbed the bat from the surprised player and told her friends, "Hang on to him, boys, I'm going to take his turn at bat." Sure enough, she went to the plate against Cardinal Paul "Daffy" Dean. The bewildered pitcher shrugged and lobbed a ball to the blonde bombshell. Burke swung ferociously but only hit a slow roller toward first base. Dean scooped up the ball and tagged her out (to a round of boos from the crowd). Although the at-bat didn't officially count, it was—and still is—the only time a woman has hit in a major-league game.

# STRANGE LAWSUITS

*These days, it seems that people will sue each other over practically anything. Here are some real-life examples of unusual legal battles.*

**THE PLAINTIFF:** Tom Morgan, a Portland, Oregon, grocery cashier

**THE DEFENDANT:** Randy Maresh, a cashier at the same store

**THE LAWSUIT:** Apparently Morgan believed that Maresh lived to torment him. He sued Maresh for $100,000, claiming that his co-worker "willfully and maliciously inflicted severe mental stress and humiliation by continually, intentionally, and repeatedly passing gas directed at the plaintiff." Maresh's lawyer didn't sit quietly—he argued that farting is a form of free speech and protected by the First Amendment.

**THE VERDICT:** Case dismissed. The judge called the defendant's behavior "juvenile and boorish" but conceded that there was no law against farting.

**THE PLAINTIFF:** John Cage Trust

**THE DEFENDANT:** Mike Batt, a British composer

**THE LAWSUIT:** In 1952 composer John Cage wrote a piece he called "4'33"." It was four minutes and 33 seconds of silence. In 2002 Batt included a track called "A One Minute Silence" on an album by his rock band The Planets, crediting it to "Batt/Cage." That's when Cage's estate came in—they accused Batt of copyright infringement.

Batt's response: "Has the world gone mad? I'm prepared to do time rather than pay out." Besides, he said, his piece was much better than Cage's because "I have been able to say in one minute what Cage could only say in four minutes and 33 seconds."

**THE VERDICT:** The suit ended with a six-figure out-of-court settlement. "We feel that honour has been settled," said Nicholas Riddle, Cage's publisher, "because the concept of a silent piece is a very valuable artistic concept."

**THE PLAINTIFF:** James Crangle

**THE DEFENDANT:** District of Columbia, a.k.a., "Police State Leviathan"

**THE LAWSUIT:** On December 22, 1989, Crangle found himself accidentally driving the wrong way down a one-way street in Washington, D.C. When the District police tried to pull him over, Crangle attempted to elude them…and ended up crashing into a utility pole. Still unwilling to give up, he climbed on top of a mailbox, claiming sanctuary. After his arrest, he filed suit against the cops, saying that local police had no authority to arrest him since he was on "federal property"—the mailbox.

**THE VERDICT:** The suit was dismissed.

**THE PLAINTIFF:** Kimberly M. Cloutier

**THE DEFENDANT:** Costco Wholesale Corp.

**THE LAWSUIT:** In 2001 Costco fired Cloutier for wearing an eyebrow ring—a violation of their dress code, which bars facial jewelry. All she had to do was remove the ring while she was at work, but she refused. Why? She considers wearing the ring an essential part of her religion, the "Church of Body Modification." Costco managers were unwilling to accommodate the church's view that piercings "are essential to our spiritual salvation," so Cloutier filed a religious discrimination charge under the 1964 Civil Rights Act and sued Costco for $2 million.

**THE VERDICT:** Despite voicing "grave doubts" about the viability of the case, a judge threw out an early challenge by Costco to the lawsuit. The case is still pending.

**THE PLAINTIFF:** Coca-Cola Co.

**THE DEFENDANT:** Frederick Coke-Is-It of Brattleboro, Vt.

**THE LAWSUIT:** Born Frederick Koch, he pronounced his name "kotch," but got fed up with people pronouncing it "Coke." Out of frustration he had his name legally changed to Frederick "Coke-Is-It." When the Coca-Cola Company heard about Mr. Coke-Is-It, they sued him on the grounds that he changed his name specifically to "infringe on their rights."

**THE VERDICT:** They settled out of court…and amazingly, Koch, er, Coke-Is-It, is *still* it—he won the right to keep his new name.

**The first Rolls-Royce sold for $600 in 1906. Today they sell for more than $200,000.**

# I ♥ THE '80s!

*Yo, Rambo, remember the Gimme Decade? The Teflon President and "Who Shot JR?" Relax, it's like, totally awesome!* *(Part 2 is on page 648.)*

### 1980

- Ronald Reagan elected 40th U.S. president (defeats Jimmy Carter)
- John Lennon assassinated
- Mount St. Helens erupts
- #1 movie: *The Empire Strikes Back*
- U.S. hockey team wins Olympic Gold over Finland
- Country Grammy: Willie Nelson's "On The Road Again"
- 1% of American homes have a PC

### 1981

- President Reagan and Pope John Paul II shot; both recover
- Prince Charles weds Lady Diana
- Sandra Day O'Connor becomes first woman appointed to Supreme Court
- 52 U.S. hostages released from Iran
- AIDS identified for the first time
- MTV debuts
- Best Picture Oscar: *Chariots of Fire*

### 1982

- Falklands War begins and ends
- First issue of *USA Today* hits stands
- Graceland opens to the public (adults: $6.50; kids: $4.50)
- First permanent artificial heart transplant performed on Barney Clark
- *Time* magazine man of the year: Pac-Man
- *Late Night with David Letterman* debuts on NBC
- #1 movie: *E.T.: The Extra-Terrestrial*

### 1983

- U.S. invades Grenada
- President Reagan first proposes SDI (Star Wars) program
- Vanessa Williams becomes first black Miss America
- America's first poet laureate: Robert Penn Warren
- Truck bomb in Lebanon kills 284 U.S. Marines
- Michael Jackson's *Thriller* becomes bestselling album of all time
- *M*A*S*H* ends after 251 episodes
- *Terms of Endearment* wins 5 Oscars

### 1984

- First photos of missing children on milk cartons
- Bishop Desmond Tutu awarded the Nobel Peace Prize
- Indian Prime Minister Indira Gandhi assassinated
- Soviet Union boycotts summer Olympics in L.A.
- Dan Marino (Miami Dolphins) throws single-season record 48 TD passes
- #1 movie: *Ghostbusters*
- #1 single: Prince's "When Doves Cry"
- *Newsweek* magazine dubs 1984 the "Year of the Yuppie"

**Q: On what sitcom did Nancy Reagan appear to tell kids to "Just Say No?" A: *Diff'rent Strokes.***

# DUMB CROOKS

*Here's proof that crime doesn't pay.*

## REVOLVING DUMMIES

"In August 1975 three men were on their way in to rob the Royal Bank of Scotland at Rothesay, when they got stuck in the revolving doors. They had to be helped free by the staff and, after thanking everyone, sheepishly left the building.

"A few minutes later they returned and announced their intention of robbing the bank, but none of the bank employees believed them. When they demanded £5,000, the head cashier laughed at them, convinced that it was a practical joke.

"Disheartened, the gang leader reduced his demand first to £500, then to £50 and ultimately to 50 pence. By this stage the cashier could barely control her laughter.

"Then one of the men jumped over the counter and fell awkwardly on the floor, clutching at his ankle. The other two attempted a getaway, but got trapped in the revolving doors for a second time, desperately pushing the wrong way."

***—The Incomplete Book of Failures***

## SMILE

"A Mexico City mugger known to police as 'Teeth' stopped a news photographer at gunpoint, demanding everything the photographer was carrying, including his camera. But first, Teeth wanted his picture taken. The lensman clicked away... and then ran. The next day his newspaper, *Reforma*, ran the 'mug shot' on page one."

***—Christian Science Monitor***

## PHOTO FINISH

"Sheriff's detectives arrested 28-year-old Einetta Denise Brown of Tampa, Florida, on identity theft charges. They said Brown, who is unemployed, has made her living since 1996 off credit card scams worth tens of thousands of dollars, leaving behind scores of angry victims.

"Detective Skip Pask said he first learned of Brown in 1998, but he was unable to catch up with her until December 2000, when

**Q: What is a *bilateral periorbital hematoma*? A: A black eye.**

she foolishly used a stolen credit card to pay for Christmas portraits of herself and her two young daughters.

"'She had been doing it for so long, she got comfortable,' Pask said. 'And careless.'"

***—St. Petersburg Times***

## "I AM A CROOK"

"William Nixon did not know he had carried out a robbery—he was drunk at the time. Then he saw himself on a security video tape on television. Nixon, 36, immediately surrendered himself to police and admitted robbing the Carrickfergus, Northern Ireland, filling station several weeks earlier. He pled guilty to the robbery of about £250 ($400) from two women assistants, using an imitation firearm. Nixon had already spent the full amount from his welfare check on drink and could be seen staggering during the robbery. The proceeds of the robbery also went to alcohol.

"After the hold-up, he left the shop with a cigarette in his hand saying: 'All the best,' to the women, and sauntered off down the road."

***—Belfast News Letter***

## TRY ACTING SMART

"Actor Brad Renfro (*The Client* and *Sleepers*) and a pal were charged with grand theft after trying to take a $175,000 yacht on a joy ride. Catching them might have been harder if they hadn't forgotten to untie the boat, causing it to smash back into the dock."

**—*Stuff* magazine**

## BOOK HIM

"Gregory Roberts, 43, of Las Cruces, New Mexico, was arrested at the public library shortly after 2 a.m. Tuesday, for breaking and entering. Officers found his shoeprints on broken glass where he allegedly entered by kicking in a windowpane.

"Once inside the library, Roberts got himself trapped between the outer and inner doors of the foyer. He couldn't get back in, and he couldn't get back out. What could he do? He called police from a pay phone in the foyer. They got him out, but now Roberts is trapped behind another door: a jail door."

***—Albuquerque Journal***

**A flea can jump 30,000 times in a row without taking a break.**

# FAMOUS CLOSE CALLS

*Too many world leaders—Gandhi, JFK, and Anwar Sadat to name a few—have lost their lives to assassins. But the death toll would be even higher if fate hadn't thwarted a few assassination plots. Here are some intriguing examples.*

**GENERAL ULYSSES S. GRANT (1822–1885)**

**THE ATTEMPT:** On April 14, 1865, Abraham Lincoln invited General Grant and his wife, Julia, to accompany him and Mrs. Lincoln to Ford's Theatre. The Grants declined. That night, of course, Lincoln was assassinated. "Had his assassination plot gone according to plan," Carl Sifakis writes in *The Encyclopedia of Assassinations*, John Wilkes Booth "would have killed not only the president, but a future president as well, General Ulysses S. Grant."

**WHAT HAPPENED:** Why didn't the Grants go? Because Julia Grant *detested* Mary Lincoln. A few weeks earlier while touring Grant's headquarters together, Mary snubbed Julia so many times in front of so many important people that she refused to spend another night in her company. Grant, biographer William S. McFeely writes, "was left to make to the president the most classic—and limp—of excuses: He couldn't go because of the children."

**PRESIDENT CHARLES DE GAULLE (1890–1970)**

**THE ATTEMPT(S):** De Gaulle, president of France from 1959 to 1969, may have set a record as the modern world leader with the most attempts on his life—31. Some examples:

• **September 1961.** Assassins planted plastic explosives and napalm at the side of a road and set the bomb to go off when de Gaulle's car approached. But they detonated it too soon. De Gaulle's driver sped the undamaged car straight through the flames to safety.

• **August 1962.** A team of assassins, using submachine guns and hand grenades, planned to attack de Gaulle's motorcade. But the lookout failed to spot the cars until they were already speeding by. The killers only managed to shoot out a window and a tire on de Gaulle's car, and de Gaulle escaped unharmed…except for a cut on his finger that he got brushing broken glass off his clothes.

In 1910 about 32 million Americans lived on farms. Today, fewer than 5 million do.

• **July 1966.** The last attempt made on de Gaulle's life and perhaps his luckiest break. Would-be assassins packed more than a ton of dynamite into a car and parked it on the road to Orly Airport. They made plans to set it off as de Gaulle was driven to the airport for a flight to the USSR.

**WHAT HAPPENED:** At the appointed time, de Gaulle's car drove past the car bomb... and nothing happened. Why not? The night before the attack was to take place, the "assassins" decided to commit a robbery to raise the money they would need to make their getaway. But they got caught—and were sitting in jail, unable to trigger the bomb.

## KING HASSAN II (1929–1999)

**THE ATTEMPT:** On August 16, 1972, King Hassan of Morocco was flying home from France aboard his private Boeing 727. As the plane approached the airport in the capital city of Rabat, it was attacked by four jet fighters of the Royal Moroccan Air Force.

**WHAT HAPPENED:** In the middle of the attack, someone claiming to be a mechanic on the royal plane radioed to the attackers, "Stop firing! The tyrant is dead!" The fighters backed off, and the royal 727 was allowed to land.

The "mechanic" turned out to be the king himself. Unharmed, he exited the plane and then participated in the scheduled welcoming ceremonies as if nothing had happened. When the plotters realized they'd been fooled, eight more fighter planes attacked the ceremonies with machine gun fire, killing 8 people and wounding more than 40... but missing the king (he hid under some trees). Later that day still more fighters attacked a guest house next to the royal palace, where it was thought the king was hiding. Hassan survived all three attempts, executed the general behind the plot, and remained on the throne until July 1999, when he died from a heart attack at age 70.

## CZAR ALEXANDER II (1818–1881)

**THE ATTEMPT:** In 1879 a violent anarchist group called Will of the People tried to bomb the czar's train outside Moscow.

**WHAT HAPPENED:** It was common for the czar's entourage to consist of two trains—one in front to test the rails and a second in back to carry the czar. So when the first train rolled by, the attackers let it go and blew up the second train... only to learn later that Alexander had been riding on the *first* train. The second one was a decoy.

**AFTERMATH:** In 1881 Will of the People made another attempt, as Alexander was returning by carriage to the Winter Palace. They tunneled under a road along the czar's intended route and packed the space with explosives. But they were thwarted at the last minute when the czar's guards changed the route.

This time, however, there were backup bombers, and as the czar passed by, one of them tossed a bomb at the imperial carriage, blowing it apart and killing two of the czar's guards. Alexander somehow escaped unscathed and might well have survived the entire attack had he not lingered at the scene to tend to the wounded. But moments later a second bomb killed him.

So in murdering Alexander II, did the anarchists get the revolution they were hoping for? No—the czar, a reformer by czarist standards, was succeeded by his son Alexander III, considered one of the most repressive czars of the 19th century.

### PRIME MINISTER MARGARET THATCHER (1925– )

**THE ATTEMPT:** Four weeks before a scheduled meeting of Thatcher's Conservative Party in the seaside town of Brighton, an Irish Republican Army bomber named Patrick Magee checked into the Grand Hotel, where Thatcher and numerous other high government officials would be staying. He then rented a room five stories above Thatcher's and planted 30 pounds of explosives.

**WHAT HAPPENED:** The bomb was programmed to explode at 3:00 a.m. on the last night of the conference. It was assumed that Thatcher would be in bed. She might have been, too, had her speechwriters done a better job preparing the speech she was to deliver the next day. But at 3:00 a.m. she was still working on it. Just moments after she left of her room, the powerful bomb ripped through the hotel, destroying much of the building... including part of Thatcher's suite. By then, however, she was in another part of the hotel, unharmed.

Five people, including a member of Parliament, were killed in the blast and 30 more were injured. Authorities speculated that the death toll would have been much higher had so many officials not been downstairs in the hotel bar.

**Hostess Twinkies are 68% air.**

# WEIRD CANADA

*Canada: land of beautiful mountains, clear lakes, bustling cities... and some really weird news reports. Here are some of the oddest entries from the BRI news file.*

## WHO WOULD HAVE SUSPECTED?

In April 2001, police in Vancouver, British Columbia, ended a three-year crime spree when they arrested 64-year-old Eugene Mah and his 32-year-old son, Avery. The Mahs had been stealing assorted lawn and garden items from homes in their neighborhood, including garbage cans, lawn decorations, recycling boxes, and realty signs. Why did they steal them? Nobody knows. Eugene Mah is a real estate tycoon worth a reported $13 million. One local psychiatrist said the thefts may be due to an obsessive-compulsive hoarding disorder. They reportedly stole a neighbor's doormat... and each of the 14 other doormats the neighbor bought as replacements.

## BEAVER FEVER!

In June 2003, two disc jockeys in Toronto caused a SARS panic—in the Dominican Republic. Z103.5 Morning Show hosts Scott Fox and Dave Blezard thought it would be funny to call the resort where their co-worker, Melanie Martin, was vacationing. They told the desk clerk that Martin had smuggled a "rare Canadian beaver" into their country. But the desk clerk, who didn't speak much English, thought he'd heard the word "fever." With SARS (Severe Acute Respiratory Syndrome) being big news at the time and Toronto being one of the cities where the disease had spread, the clerk panicked—and locked the woman in her room. The entire hotel wasn't quarantined, according to the station's news manager, but staff were at the point of contacting medical authorities when the disc jockeys finally convinced them that it was all a misunderstanding. Martin was released from her room that afternoon.

## COMING IN FOR A LANDING

Lucette St. Louis, a 66-year-old woman from Corbeil, Ontario, was rounding up three runaway pigs owned by her son, Marc, when she became the victim of a bizarre accident. One of the 180-pound pigs had wandered into the road and a passing car hit it. The impact sent the pig airborne, landing on top of Mrs. St. Louis and breaking her leg in two places. "Well, at least," she said, "I can tell my grandchildren that pigs really do fly."

## DEATH MERCHANT

Roman Panchyshyn, a 47-year-old Winnipeg retailer, upset some of his fellow residents when he started selling $65 sweatshirts that read "Winnipeg, Murder Capital of Canada—Escape The Fear" in his store. The shirts showed the city skyline dripping in blood. "We spend hundreds of thousands of dollars yearly to promote Winnipeg to the world," complained City Councillor Harry Lazarenko, "and I don't want this to give us a black eye." So he contacted the premier to see if Panchyshyn could be stopped. He couldn't—the shirts are accurate. Winnipeg has the highest murder rate in Canada. Said the unapologetic Panchyshyn, "The truth hurts."

## WEIRD CANADIAN RECORDS

• On August 30, 1995, Sean Shannon of Canada recited Hamlet's "To be or not to be" soliloquy in 23.8 seconds—an average of 655 words a minute.

• On August 17, 1991, 512 dancers of the Royal Scottish Dance Society (Toronto branch) set the record for the largest genuine Scottish country dance (a reel).

• In 1988 Palm Dairies of Edmonton created the world's largest ice cream sundae—24,900 kg. (54,895 lbs.).

• In 1993 the Kitchener-Waterloo Hospital Auxiliary filled a bowl with 2,390 kg (5,269 lbs.) of strawberries.

• Four hundred mothers in Vancouver broke the record for mass breast feeding in 2002.

• In Feb. 2000, 1,588 couples at the Sarnia Sports Centre broke the record for most kissing in one place at one time.

• Dave Pearson holds the record for clearing all 15 balls from a standard pool table in 26.5 seconds at Pepper's Bar in Windsor, Ontario, in 1997.

• In 1998 1,000 University of Guelph students formed the longest human conveyor belt, laying down in a row and rolling a surfboard over their bodies. In 1999 they set the record for simultaneous soap-bubble blowing.

**A regulation tennis ball must weigh between 2 and 2 $^{1}/_{16}$ ounces.**

# URBAN LEGENDS

*Hey—did you hear about the guy who invented a car that can run for months on a single tank of gas? We've looked into some urban legends to see if there's any truth to them.*

**LEGEND:** If you eat a lot of cup-of-soups, you *must* remove the noodles from the Styrofoam cup and put them in a bowl before you add boiling water. Why? There's a layer of wax lining the cup that will liquefy when you pour in hot water. The wax can accumulate in your system, causing a deadly "waxy buildup."

**HOW IT SPREAD:** Via word of mouth, for more than 20 years. The latest version is an e-mail that describes how a college student lived on the stuff for months to save money, only to die when so much wax built up in his stomach that surgeons were unable to remove it.

**THE TRUTH:** Cup-A-Noodle cups and those of similar soups don't have a wax lining—they're just ordinary Styrofoam cups. And even if the cups *did* contain wax, wax is so easy to digest that it's a fairly common ingredient in candy and other foods.

**LEGEND:** On the day he retires, a longtime General Motors employee is invited down to the factory lot to pick out any car he wants as a retirement gift. He picks a Chevy Caprice. But after weeks of long drives in the country he finds he still hasn't used up the first tank of gas. When he calls GM to praise the car's performance, they react suspiciously...and the very next morning he looks out into his driveway and sees two mysterious men in white lab coats working under the hood of his car. The retiree chases the men away, but from then on his car gets only normal gas mileage.

It turns out that the car he picked was actually a 200+ mpg prototype that GM is hiding from consumers, so that they have to buy more gas than is really necessary. When GM realized the Caprice had gotten out of the factory, they dispatched two company engineers to "fix" it.

**HOW IT SPREAD:** The story has been floating around since the 1920s, spreading first by word of mouth, then by photocopies posted on bulletin boards and lately by e-mail. The tale resurfaces every few years with fresh new details—new auto companies and updated makes of car—that keep it believable.

**THE TRUTH:** This story fails the common sense test: why would any auto company suppress technology that would give it such a huge advantage over its competitors? If GM could make a 200+ mpg car using patented technology that its competitors didn't have, it would dominate the industry.

This legend has been kept alive by generations of con artists who claim to have invented 200+ mpg carburetors or magic pills that can turn tap water into auto fuel. When frustrated investors demand to see proof that the "inventions" really do work, the con artists frequently claim that the invention has been stolen by mysterious men in black suits or that it's been suppressed by the auto industry. Rather than admit they've been conned, gullible investors sometimes pass these claims along as true.

(Similar urban legends haunt the tire industry, which is supposedly suppressing tires that will last for a million miles, and the drug industry, which is accused of buying up the patents to electric headache cures so that the public has to keep buying aspirin.)

**LEGEND:** The screams of a UCLA coed being sexually assaulted are ignored because the assault takes place during a midnight "scream session," when students scream out their dorm windows to relieve the stress of final exams. The attack forced a change in university policy: "To this day, anyone screaming unnecessarily during finals week at UCLA is subject to expulsion."

**HOW IT SPREAD:** Originally by word of mouth, then by e-mail, from one college student to another.

**THE TRUTH:** No such attack ever happened—and UCLA doesn't expel students for screaming during finals. This legend, which has been attributed to many different universities around the country, is kept alive by the insecurities of incoming freshmen, nervous about living away from home for the first time.

**LEGEND:** On October 2, 1994, Lauren Archer let her three-year-old son Kevin play in the "ball pit" of a McDonald's play area. Afterward Kevin started whimpering, telling his mommy, "It hurts." That night when Archer bathed her son, she noticed an odd welt

**Lost in translation: A French kiss is known as an English kiss in France.**

on his butt. It looked like he had a large splinter. She immediately made an appointment with the doctor to have it removed the next day, but when Kevin became violently ill later that evening—she rushed him to the emergency room.

Too late. Kevin died from what an autopsy revealed to be a heroin overdose…and the "splinter" in his rear end turned out to be the broken-off needle of a drug-filled syringe. How did it get there? Police investigators emptied out the McDonald's ball pit and found, according to one version of the story, "Rotten food, several hypodermic needles, knives, half-eaten candy, diapers, feces, and the stench of urine."

**HOW IT SPREAD:** First by e-mail beginning in the mid-1990s, then by word of mouth from one frightened parent to another. The story's credibility is supported by the fact that the original e-mail gives specific names and dates, and even cites a newspaper article that supposedly appeared in the October 10, 1994 issue of the *Houston Chronicle*.

**THE TRUTH:** It's a hoax. No such incident ever happened and no such article ever appeared in the *Houston Chronicle*. Don't take our word for it—after years of denying the rumors, the *Chronicle* finally printed an official denial in February 2000. A similar story about rattlesnakes in a ball pit—at Burger King—is also false.

* * *

## CELEBRITY EXCUSES

"Crack is cheap. I make too much money to use crack."

**—Whitney Houston,** ***on why crack wasn't on the long list of drugs she admitted to having used***

"I was told that I should shoplift. My director said I should try it out."

**—Wynona Ryder,** ***to the security guard who busted her at Saks Fifth Avenue***

"I've killed enough of the world's trees."

**—Stephen King,** ***on why he's quitting writing***

**The Tin Woodsman's real name in the *Oz* books was Nick Chopper.**

# BUDDHA'S WISDOM

*Siddhartha Gautama, known as the Buddha, or "Enlightened One," died in 480 B.C., but his wisdom lives on.*

"Do not dwell in the past, do not dream of the future, concentrate the mind on the present moment."

"Nothing ever exists entirely alone; everything is in relation to everything else."

"Believe nothing, no matter where you read it, or who said it, unless it agrees with your own reason and your own common sense."

"Holding on to anger is like grasping a hot coal with the intent of throwing it at someone else; you are the one who gets burned."

"Better than a thousand hollow words, is one word that brings peace."

"Every human being is the author of his own disease."

"In the sky, there is no distinction of east and west; people create distinctions out of their own minds and then believe them to be true."

"It is a man's own mind, not his enemy or foe, that lures him to evil ways."

"We are what we think."

"Let us be thankful, for if we didn't learn a lot today, at least we learned a little, and if we didn't learn a little, at least we didn't get sick, and if we got sick, at least we didn't die. So, let us all be thankful."

"There are only two mistakes one can make along the road to truth; not going all the way, and not starting."

"Work out your own salvation. Do not depend on others."

"Thousands of candles can be lighted from a single candle, and the life of the candle will not be shortened. Happiness never decreases by being shared."

"Your work is to discover your world and then with all your heart give yourself to it."

# THE BIRTH OF THE DEMOCRATIC PARTY

*Major political parties aren't born overnight. They usually begin when a group of dissenters gets so fed up with the party they belong to that they break away to form a new one.*

## ONE-PARTY SYSTEM

The two-party political system was a basic element in the founding of the United States, right? Wrong. As we told you in *Uncle John's Supremely Satisfying Bathroom Reader,* America's Founding Fathers were vehemently opposed to the idea of political parties. Why? England's political parties seemed to spend their time battling one another instead of working together to advance the national interest, and the Founding Fathers hoped to avoid that.

But they couldn't—by 1787, as the Constitutional Convention was being held in Philadelphia to draw up the country's new constitution, political factions were already beginning to emerge. There were "Federalists," who wanted to create a strong federal government by giving it powers that had previously belonged to the state governments. And there were "Anti-Federalists," who opposed the new constitution, which in its final form promised to do just that.

The Federalists won that debate, and the new constitution went into effect on March 4, 1789. In 1796 they succeeded in electing Vice President John Adams president after George Washington, who was non-partisan, declined to run for a third term.

## THE JEFFERSONIAN REPUBLICANS

And who did Adams beat? The leader of the Anti-Federalists: Thomas Jefferson (he lost by only three electoral votes). As the Federalists won one debate after another, Jefferson's supporters decided to make a clean break and resurfaced as the "Democratic-Republican" Party, also known as the "Republicans" or the "Jeffersonian Republicans." Ironically, these Republicans are considered the direct antecedents of the modern *Democratic* Party, not the Republican Party.

The Jeffersonian Republicans opposed the Alien and Sedition

Acts, new laws that outlawed associations whose purpose was "to oppose any measure of the government of the United States." The Acts also imposed stiff punishments for writing, printing, or saying anything against the U.S. government. The Republicans saw these acts as targeted at them and also as a grave threat to democracy. Jefferson put his hat in the ring for the 1800 presidential election, and after the Republicans mounted a fierce campaign, he won.

## SWAN SONG

The Federalists went on to lose again in 1804, then again in 1808, and again in 1812. That year they made the mistake of publicly opposing the War of 1812, and even secretly discussed seceding from the Union because of it. When this came to light in 1814, they were finished as a political force. They lost the presidency again in 1816, and by 1820 they were so far gone that they didn't even field a candidate for president. That year, President James Monroe ran for reelection unopposed.

For the moment, it seemed that American democracy might be returning to a one-party system. What prevented that from happening? The fact that four men—Secretary of War John C. Calhoun, Secretary of the Treasury William Crawford, Secretary of State John Quincy Adams, and Speaker of the House Henry Clay all wanted to succeed Monroe as president.

Calhoun and Crawford were not above using the patronage and other perks of their offices to gain an advantage in the race. And both of them leaked details of the other's doings to news reporters. In the process, the entire Monroe administration became tainted with a reputation for corruption.

## ACTION JACKSON

Many Americans were outraged by Calhoun's and Crawford's scheming. One such man was General Andrew Jackson, hero of the Battle of New Orleans in 1815 and a man so tough his soldiers called him Old Hickory after "the hardest wood in creation." As the first war hero since George Washington, Jackson was the most popular living American, and for years his admirers had urged him to run for president. For years he had turned them down.

But the corruption of the Monroe administration changed his mind. It convinced Jackson that it was "his public duty to cam-

**Jupiter is large enough to fit all the planets of the solar system inside it.**

paign for the presidency and engage in what he called 'a general cleansing' of the federal capital," historian Paul Johnson writes in *A History of the American People*. "Jackson became the first presidential candidate to grasp with both hands what was to become the most popular campaigning theme in American history—'Turn the rascals out.'"

Jackson became the fifth candidate to enter the race for president in 1824. Although he was the least politically experienced of the candidates, he was the most popular man in the country. Result: on election day, Jackson won more votes and carried more states than any other candidate.

But amazingly, it wasn't enough.

## POLITICAL SCRAMBLING

Because the electoral college vote was split among four candidates, none of them, not even Jackson, won an absolute majority of electoral votes. According to the Twelfth Amendment to the Constitution, that meant that the House of Representatives would have to choose between the top three finishers: Jackson, Adams, and Crawford. Each state's delegation would get one vote.

Because he came in fourth, Henry Clay was excluded from consideration for the presidency. But as Speaker of the House, he was well positioned to steer it to the candidate of his choice, and his choice was John Quincy Adams. Crawford had suffered a stroke during the campaign and was in no condition to assume presidential duties, and Clay saw Jackson as "a mere military chieftain" with a bad temper and not nearly enough political experience to be president. By comparison, Adams was the Harvard-educated son of a former president, and had served stints as secretary of state and U.S. ambassador to Russia.

Clay worked hard to deliver the presidency to Adams, but when the time came to vote in the House of Representatives, he was still one vote short—he needed New York. But the New York delegation was evenly split, which, according to the rules, meant that its vote wouldn't even be counted unless someone in the delegation changed their vote.

## THAT'S THE TICKET

Henry Clay put enormous pressure on an elderly New York congressman named Stephen Van Rensselaer to change his vote in favor of Adams... but Van Rensselaer couldn't make up his mind. So when the vote was called, he lowered his head, closed his eyes, and whispered a short prayer, asking for divine guidance.

When Van Rensselaer opened his eyes, the first thing he saw was a ticket for John Quincy Adams on the floor beneath his desk. That was all he needed—Van Rensselaer picked up the ticket, carried it over to the ballot box, and put Adams in the White House.

Jackson, who'd won more votes and carried more states than anyone else, was convinced that he'd just been cheated out of the presidency. The Adams presidency, he charged, was the result of a "corrupt bargain": essentially Henry Clay had delivered the presidency to Adams and Adams appointed Clay Secretary of State, which in those days was considered heir apparent to the presidency. Jackson and his supporters vowed to get revenge.

The Jeffersonian Republican Party was so deeply divided over the election of 1824 that it split in two. Jackson's supporters now began to refer to themselves as the "*Democratic*-Republican" Party—Democrats for short. Adams's supporters called themselves the "*National* Republicans."

The two-party system was back, this time to stay.

## MUD FIGHT

What followed was one of the nastiest political battles in the history of the United States. Adams, his reputation tarnished by the charges of corruption, was determined to muddy Jackson's reputation as well. Adams's supporters attacked Jackson's military career, accusing him of misconduct during the War of 1812. They also dug up an old charge (possibly true) that he'd married his wife Rachel before her divorce from her first husband was final. That made her a bigamist, which was not only illegal but scandalous.

Nothing was sacred. Adams's people even attacked Jackson's deceased mother. The pro-Adams *National Journal* called her "a *Common Prostitute*, brought to this country by British soldiers! She afterwards married a *Mulatto Man*, by whom she had several children of which number *General Jackson is one!*"

Jackson's forces fought back, attacking President Adams as an out-of-touch, elitist aristocrat, as well as an alcoholic and a "Sabbath-breaker" who, when he did go to church, went barefoot.

**... at about the same time Christians now celebrate Christmas.**

## LIFE OF THE PARTY

But what really made the election of 1828 remarkable was that it was the first truly *national* presidential campaign. Traditionally, the slow pace of communication across the U.S. necessitated that political campaigns be run at the state and local level, with no national strategy or tactics. That began to change in 1826, when Senator Martin Van Buren, the political boss of New York known as "the Little Magician," joined forces with the Jackson camp.

Van Buren launched a centrally controlled communications strategy. The campaign formed its own newspaper, called the *United States Telegraph*, and hired a staff of writers to write pro-Jackson articles that were then published in the *Telegraph* and 50 other pro-Jackson papers around the country.

At the same time, local and state committees organized pro-Jackson dinners, barbecues, parades, and other events where local politicos would deliver stump speeches written by the national campaign. Campaign workers sang campaign songs—another innovation for 1828—planted hickory trees in town squares and along major roads, and distributed hickory brooms, hickory canes, and even hickory leaves that people could wear to show their support for Old Hickory. Then, on election day, local Jackson organizations marched their voters to the polls under banners reading "Jackson and Reform."

## DEMOCRATS IN POWER

The old-fashioned Adams campaign could not match the strategy or intensity of the Jackson campaign. Old Hickory won 56% of the popular vote and 178 out of 261 electoral votes, including every state west of New Jersey and south of the Potomac River. "Organization is the secret of victory," one pro-Adams newspaper observed, and "by want of it, we have been overthrown."

"Jackson's victory brought a full-blown party system into existence," Arthur Schlesinger writes in *Of the People*. "Martin Van Buren... was the champion of the organized party with party machinery, national conventions and national committees, all held together by party discipline and the cult of party loyalty."

***The Democrats were the first to benefit from Van Buren's system, but other parties would soon follow. Read about the birth of the Whig party on page 701.***

# FIRST EDITIONS

*As you might imagine, Uncle John is a book hound. He loves "first editions." So you can imagine how flushed he got when he found a list of some real first editions.*

• **World's First Dictionary:** *Explaining Words, Analyzing Characters* (100 A.D.), by Xu Shen. Chinese words and definitions.

• **World's First Fantasy Story:** *The Castaway*, published in Egypt circa 1950 B.C. The story of a man who is shipwrecked on an island ruled by a giant bearded serpent with a deep voice and an ability to predict the future.

• **World's First Sci-Fi Story:** *True History*, by Lucian of Samosata, published in the second century A.D. Adventures in outer space, in unknown seas, and on the moon. Everyone in space speaks Greek.

• **World's First Book of Firsts:** *Origins of Ages* (100 B.C.), author unknown. Lists the founders of the ruling families of China.

• **World's First Novel:** *Cyropaedia* (360 B.C.), by the Greek author Xenophon. An account of the life of Cyrus, founder of the Persian empire. The book offers "an idealized account of Persian society, contrasting with the unsympathetic views of most Greeks."

• **World's First Autobiography:** *Memoirs of Aratus of Sicyon*, published after his death by poisoning in 213 B.C. Critics commend Aratus for admitting his own weaknesses in the book, but fault him for being "insultingly critical of people he disliked."

• **World's First Book of Ghost Stories:** *Tales of Marvels* (early third century), by Chinese author Tsao Pi. Stories include a haunted house and a man who convinces a ghost that he's a ghost, too.

• **World's First Joke Book:** *Forest of Jokes*, by Harn Darn Jun, a Chinese author, around 200 A.D. Here's one of the jokes:

> In Lu, a man with a long pole tried to go in through a city gate. But whether he held the pole upright or side on, he couldn't get through. He was at his wit's end. Then an old man came up and gave him advice which he acted on: "I may not be a sage, but I have had plenty of experience. Why don't you saw the pole in half and carry it through that way?"

**Humorist Will Rogers once served as honorary mayor of Beverly Hills.**

# BEFORE THEY WERE INFAMOUS

*Great leaders make choices early in life that pave the way for their illustrious careers. But what about the world's worst tyrants? Here's a look at the early lives of some rotten apples in the history barrel.*

## JOSEPH STALIN (1879–1953)

**Place in History:** Soviet ruler from 1924 to 1953. Fueled by a mad paranoia, Stalin is responsible for the murder and mass starvation of millions of Soviet citizens. His forced collectivization of Soviet agriculture starved as many as 5 million people from 1932 to 1933; the political purges that followed from 1936 to 1938 may have killed as many as 7 million more. His diplomatic and military blunders leading up to World War II contributed mightily to the 20 million Soviet military and civilian casualties during the war.

**Before He Was Infamous:** Born Iosif Vissarionovich Dzhugashvili, young Joseph entered a Russian Orthodox seminary in 1894, but he was kicked out at the age of 20. He went underground, became a Bolshevik revolutionary, and later adopted the pseudonym Stalin, which means "Man of Steel." Between 1902 and 1913, the man of steel was arrested and jailed seven times, and sent to Siberia twice. In 1917, he became the editor of *Pravda*, the Communist Party newspaper. Stalin did not play a prominent role in the communist revolution of November 1917, but in 1922 he was elected general secretary of Communist Party, a post that became his power base. Vladimir Lenin died in 1924, but it wasn't until after six years of maneuvering against opponents that Stalin emerged as Lenin's unrivaled successor in 1930.

## MAO TSE-TUNG (1893–1976)

**Place in History:** Leader of the Chinese Communist Party (1935) and founder of the People's Republic of China, which he ruled from 1949 until his death in 1976. Under such disastrous programs as The Great Leap Forward (1958-60) and The Cultural Revolution (1966-76), more than 30 million people starved to death or were murdered outright by Mao's government and its policies.

**Snot funny: The Japanese have been blowing their noses on tissue paper for over 300 years.**

**Before He Was Infamous:** At 13, this child of peasant farmers left home to get an education. He tried police school, soap-making school, law school, and economics before settling on becoming a teacher. He attended the University of Beijing, where he became a Marxist and in 1921, at the age of 27, a founding member of the Chinese Communist Party. In 1927 he alienated orthodox Marxists by arguing that peasants, not workers, would be the main force in the communist revolution. It wasn't until 1935, following the 6,000 mile "Long March" to escape the Chinese government's brutal campaign against the communists, that he emerged as the party's leader.

## ADOLF HITLER (1889–1945)

**Place in History:** Elected German Chancellor in 1933 and ruled Nazi Germany from 1933 until his death in 1945. The Nazis murdered an estimated 6 million Jews and other people it considered inferior, including Gypsies, Jehovah's Witnesses, communists and homosexuals. Hitler also started World War II, which killed as many as 55 million people.

**Before He Was Infamous:** As a small boy, Hitler dreamed of becoming a priest, but by age 14 he'd lost his interest in religion. As a young man he enjoyed architecture and art and dreamed of becoming a great artist, but when he applied for admission to the Academy of Fine Arts in Vienna, he was turned down—twice—for lack of talent. He bummed around Vienna until 1913, living off an orphan's pension and what little money he made from odd jobs like beating carpets, and from selling paintings and drawings of Viennese landmarks. When World War I broke out in 1914 he was living in Munich, where he volunteered for the Bavarian Army and was later awarded the Iron Cross.

Germany lost the war in 1918; the following year Hitler joined the German Workers Party at a time when it had only about 25 members. He soon became its leader, and in 1920 the party changed its name to the National Socialist German Workers' Party—better known as the Nazis.

## POL POT (1925–1998)

**Place in History:** Leader of the Cambodian *Khmer Rouge* guerrilla movement, which seized control of the Cambodian government in

1975 and ruled the country until January 1979. On Pol Pot's orders the cities were emptied and the urban population forced out into the countryside to work on collective farms that became known as "killing fields." Nearly 1.7 million Cambodians—20% of the entire population—were starved, worked to death or murdered by the Khmer Rouge.

**Before He Was Infamous:** Born Saloth Sar, Pol Pot lived in a Buddhist monastery for six years, and was a practicing monk. He worked briefly as a carpenter before moving to Paris at the age of 24 to study radio electronics on a full scholarship. While there he joined the French Communist Party. He later lost his scholarship and returned home in 1953, the same year that Cambodia won independence from France. Over the next decade Sar rose through the ranks of the Cambodian Communist Party (the Khmer Rouge), and in 1963 he became its head. In the mid 1970s he adopted the pseudonym, Pol Pot.

### IDI AMIN DADA (ca. 1924–2003 )

**Place in History:** Ugandan dictator from 1971 to 1979. In those years he expelled the entire Asian population of Uganda (more than 70,000 people) and is believed to have murdered as many as 400,000 people during his eight-year reign of terror. In 1979 he invaded the neighboring country of Tanzania; when the invasion failed and the Tanzanians counterattacked he fled into exile, eventually settling in Saudi Arabia. He died there in August 2003.

**Before He Was Infamous:** Amin, a member of the small Kakwa tribe of northwestern Uganda, was born in 1925 and raised by his mother, a self-proclaimed sorceress. As a child he sold doughnuts (*mandazi*) in the streets. In 1943 he joined the King's African Rifles of the British colonial army and went on to serve in the Allied Forces' Burma campaign during World War II. After the war he became a boxer and was the heavyweight champion of Uganda for nine years (1951–1960).

Amin continued his rise through the ranks of the military, and by the time Uganda became independent from England in 1962 he was one of only two African officers in the entire Ugandan armed forces. President Milton Obote appointed him head of the army and navy in 1966; five years later Amin seized power in a coup and declared himself president for life.

**The phrase "the sky's the limit" comes from Cervantes' *Don Quixote*.**

# MANEKI NEKO

*There are countless superstitions involving cats, most of them focused on the bad luck that they supposedly bring. In Japan and other Asian countries, however, the cat is a symbol of good fortune.*

## THE BECKONING CAT

If you've ever walked into a Chinese or Japanese business and noticed a figure of a cat with an upraised paw, you've met Maneki Neko (pronounced MAH-ne-key NEH-ko). "The Beckoning Cat" is displayed to invite good fortune, a tradition that began with a legendary Japanese cat many centuries ago.

According to legend, that cat, called Tama, lived in a poverty-stricken temple in 17th-century Tokyo. The temple priest often scolded Tama for contributing nothing to the upkeep of the temple. Then one day, a powerful feudal lord named Naotaka Ii was caught in a rainstorm near the temple while returning home from a hunting trip. As the lord took refuge under a big tree, he noticed Tama with her paw raised, beckoning to him, inviting him to enter the temple's front gate. Intrigued, the lord decided to get a closer look at this remarkable cat. Suddenly, the tree was struck by lightning and fell on the exact spot where Naotaka had just been standing. Tama had saved his life! In gratitude, Naotaka made the little temple his family temple and became its benefactor. Tama and the priest never went hungry again. After a long life, Tama was buried with great respect at the renamed Goutokuji temple. Goutokuji still exists, housing dozens of statues of the Beckoning Cat.

## LUCKY CHARMS

Figures of Maneki Neko became popular in Japan under shogun rule in the 19th century. At that time, most "houses of amusement" (brothels) and many private homes had a good-luck shelf filled with lucky charms, many in the shape of male sexual organs. When Japan began to associate with Western countries in the 1860s, the charms began to be seen as vulgar. In an effort to modernize Japan and improve its image, Emperor Meiji outlawed the production, sale, and display of phallic talismans in 1872. People still wanted lucky objects, however, so the less controversial Maneki Neko figures became popular.

Eventually the image of the lucky cat spread to China and then to Southeast Asia. How popular did the Beckoning Cat become? In Thailand, the ancient goddess of prosperity, Nang Kwak, was traditionally shown kneeling with a money bag on her lap. Now she's usually shown making the cat's raised-hand gesture and occasionally sporting a cat's tail.

In Europe and North America, images of Maneki Neko can be found in Asian-owned businesses, such as Chinese restaurants. And back in Japan, a new cat icon adorns clothing, toys, and various objects: Hello Kitty—a literal translation of Maneki Neko, or "Beckoning Cat."

**MANEKI NEKO FACTS**

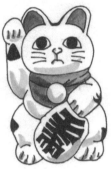

• Sometimes Maneki Neko has his left paw up, sometimes the right. The left paw signifies that the business owner is inviting in customers. The right invites in money or good fortune.

• Most Maneki Nekos are calico cats; the male calico is so rare it's considered lucky in Japan. But Maneki Neko may be white, black, red, gold, or pink to ward off illness, bad luck, or evil spirits and bring financial success, good luck, health, and love.

• Maneki Nekos made in Japan show the palm of the paw, imitating the manner in which Japanese people beckon. American Maneki Nekos show the back of the paw, reflecting the way we gesture "come here."

• The higher Maneki Neko holds his paw, the more good fortune is being invited.

* * *

"I don't need a reading lamp in my living room. I don't have a toilet in there."

**—Norm Macdonald**

# THE DUSTBIN OF HISTORY

*Leon Livingston had many titles—A-No.1, the Rambler, Emperor of the North—but none fit him better than "King of the Hoboes."*

**Forgotten Figure:** Leon Ray Livingston

**Claim to Fame:** Being King of the Hoboes

**Background:** Leon began his hobo lifestyle when he ran away from home in San Francisco in 1883. Only 11 years old, the boy was too young to find work, so he took up with a hobo named Frenchy, an ex-convict and experienced wanderer who taught little Leon the ways of the open road:

- How to survive on handouts from local charities.
- Where to sleep—parks, freight cars, or the "hobo jungles" outside railroad yards.
- How to make "mulligan stew," a traditional hobo meal consisting of a stolen chicken and whatever few vegetables they could gather, all cooked in a large tin can on a campfire.
- How to move about the country for free: generally in empty freight cars.
- Ways to avoid the railroad police, known as "bulls," who patrolled the train yards looking for freeloaders. Being caught usually meant getting a beating with the bulls' nightsticks. Worse, sometimes it meant being tossed off a moving train.

## FAME (BUT NO FORTUNE)

Leon, who became known as A-No.1, got to be adept at hopping a train after it had left the station (other "brethren of the road" who weren't as skilled often lost their lives, falling under the wheels of the train). He loved the hobo life and kept a scrapbook of the travels that took him from the Klondike to the Amazon. And everywhere he went, he wrote his name, "A-No.1," on fences, on barns, on storefronts, and in train yards. Every bare wall he encountered bore witness to the fact that A-No.1 had been there.

Word of mouth turned him into America's most famous tramp. And because he neither drank nor smoked, because he valued honesty and cleanliness, the other hoboes looked up to A-No.1, and gave him another nickname, "King of the Hoboes."

## ROAD SCHOLAR

As he got older, A-No.1 rambled from coast to coast with the famous writer Jack London, whose hobo moniker was "Sailor Jack." London inspired A-No.1 to become a writer himself. His first published book was *The Life and Adventures of A-No.1*, followed closely by *Hobo Camp Fire Tales*. He wrote 12 books in all.

A-No.1 claimed that his only real goal in life was to keep American boys and girls from running away from home and living the sort of life he led. He gave lectures on the evils of the vagabond life and used the money he made from his books to send runaway kids back home.

"When I started out, the wanderlust was upon me and I enjoyed the zest of adventure," A-No.1 said. "Later I traveled because it became a habit, and now, although I hate the life, I travel because I cannot stop."

A-No.1 died in 1944 and was buried in the place he had come to love most—a small town in Pennsylvania called Cambridge Springs. On his tombstone is written, A-NO.1 AT REST AT LAST.

* * *

## FAMOUS LAST WORDS

"I have just had to tell your mother that I shall be dead in a quarter of an hour. Hitler is charging me with high treason. In view of my services in Africa I am to have the chance of dying by poison. The two generals have brought it with them. It is fatal in three seconds. If I accept, none of the usual steps will be taken against my family. I'm to be given a state funeral. It's all been prepared to the last detail. In a quarter of an hour you will receive a call from the hospital in Ulm to say that I've had a brain seizure on the way to a conference."

**—Suicide note of "Desert Fox" Erwin Rommel after participating in a plot to assassinate Hitler**

**In Arabic countries, *Sesame Street* is known as *Iftah Ya Simsim.***

# MYTH-CONCEPTIONS

*"Common knowledge" is frequently wrong. Here are some examples of things that many people believe—but that according to our sources, just aren't true.*

**Myth:** If you touch a baby bird, its mother will abandon it.

**Fact:** Whether or not a mother can detect the scent of a human depends on the animal's sense of smell. Birds have a poor sense of smell and would never know from it whether a human had touched their nest.

**Myth:** Julius Caesar was a Roman emperor.

**Fact:** In Caesar's time, Rome was a republic and had no emperor. The Roman Empire didn't exist until 17 years after Caesar's death.

**Myth:** You should drink at least eight 8-ounce glasses of water a day.

**Fact:** The bottled-water industry loves this myth, but according to kidney specialist Dr. Heinz Valtin, there is no scientific evidence to support the claim.

**Myth:** Diamonds are the most valuable gem.

**Fact:** Carat for carat, rubies are far more valuable than diamonds.

**Myth:** Ticks are insects.

**Fact:** Insects have six legs and three body parts. Ticks, on the other hand, have eight legs and two body parts, which classifies them as arachnids, not insects.

**Myth:** The chameleon changes color to match its background.

**Fact:** Chameleons really *can* change color instantaneously, but it's a reaction to fear or to extreme temperature and light changes—it has nothing to do with matching the colors of its background.

**Myth:** Arabic numerals come from Arabia.

**Fact:** The numbering system we use today actually originated in India. It was later brought to Arab lands, where westerners first encountered them and labeled the numbers "Arabic."

# THE MAN FROM C.R.A.P.

*An acronym is a word made up of the initial letters of other words—and some of them end up being pretty funny. And if you don't like them, don't blame us—see someone at* C.R.A.P. *(the* **C***ommittee to* **R***esist* **A***cronym* **P***roliferation)*.

EGADS

**Stands For:** Electronic Ground Automatic Destruct System (*military command given to destroy a missile already in flight*)

BOGSATT

**Stands For:** Bunch Of Guys Sitting Around The Table (*Pentagonese for where the important decisions are made*)

CHAOTIC

**Stands For:** Computer-Human-Assisted Organization of a Technical Information Center

LIE

**Stands For:** Limited Information Estimation *(it's true)*

MANIAC

**Stands For:** Mathematical Analyzer, Numerical Integrator, And Computer

OOPS

**Stands For:** Occasionless Ordered Preemptive Strike (*World War III begun by accident)*

SIMPLE

**Stands For:** Simulation of Industrial Management Problems with Lots of Equations

NO FUN

**Stands For:** NO First Use of Nuclear Weapons

BUFF

**Stands For:** Big Ugly Fat Fellow (*Air Force slang for a B-52 bomber*)

WOMBAT

**Stands For:** Waste Of Money, Brains, And Time (*A computer programmer "wrestles with a wombat" when the solution proves more complex than the problem*)

OOH, OOH

**Stands For:** On the One Hand, On the Other Hand

WOE

**Stands For:** Withdrawal Of Enthusiasm (*The bored tone of an airline pilot's "Welcome aboard" on the third or fourth straight flight*)

**Do you get ingrown toenails? It's hereditary—odds are someone else in your family does, too.**

# I GOT IT BACK!

*Have you ever lost something special? Well, don't give up hope—you may find it again. These folks did.*

**ON GUARD**

**Lost Item:** A wallet

**The Story:** In November 2002, a Swedish man named Holger Granlund got a call from the army saying that they had found his wallet...the one he'd lost 56 years earlier. It was found in the hayloft of a stable where Granlund had been on guard duty in 1946. Amazingly, almost everything was still in it—his driver's license, a food ration card, and photos of young women he'd known. The only item missing: a 20-kroner bill (worth about $2).

**RING ME LATER**

**Lost Item:** A University of Notre Dame class ring

**The Story:** When Robert Lensing graduated from Indiana's Notre Dame University in 1959, he received the traditional sapphire class ring...which mysteriously disappeared from a jacket pocket. (He suspected his mother's cleaning lady.) A few years later, a landscaper named Frank Foster bought a used camper from a family in Petersburg, Indiana. Foster and his wife found the ring under some seat cushions, put it in a jewelry box, and forgot about it—for almost four decades. Not long after Foster's wife died in 2000, he remarried. His new wife found the ring and insisted they return it to the owner. They contacted Notre Dame, who used the ring's inscription to find Lensing, and in February 2002, 42 years after it was lost, he got his ring back. "This just shows that there's a lot of good in people," said Lensing.

**A NOT-SO-BRIEF CASE**

**Lost Item:** A briefcase

**The Story:** In September 1989, Frank Keating got on a United Airlines flight from Washington, D.C., to Tulsa, Oklahoma. But, when he got off, he inadvertently left his briefcase on the plane. The airline sent it to him... in November 2002. "I had forgotten all about it," said Keating, who had become governor of Oklahoma in the meantime. The case had been sitting on a shelf in a security closet in San Francisco. United spokesman Jeff Green said, "We're glad we got it back to him. Sorry it took 13 years." Contents of the case: some papers, wrapped birthday presents for his mother-in-law, and a calculator (the batteries were dead).

## PYRAMID SCHEME

**Lost Item:** A cat

**The Story:** Cathryn Chartez really likes her cat. So much so that she took it with her on vacation to Egypt in October 2002. But the cat escaped in the Cairo airport as she was headed home to the United States. The Egyptian tourist police tried to help her find it, to no avail. Chartez went home catless. Two months later, she went back to Egypt to look for her cat again, putting up posters, taking out advertisements, and offering a $110 reward. It worked. A week later an electrical worker found the kitty hiding from the rain in a nearby terminal and notified the police…and the worker refused to accept any reward money.

## THANKS!

**Lost Item:** A gold ring

**The Story:** In 1945 the mayor of Jersey City, New Jersey, gave the sheriff a gift: a gold ring, inscribed "From Mayor Frank Hague to Sheriff Teddy Fleming 1945." Years later Fleming passed the ring on to his son, the historian Thomas Fleming. In 1968 Fleming was visiting the famous French battlefield, the Argonne, on the 50th anniversary of his father's service there during World War I. While climbing a steep hill, he slipped and fell—and lost the ring.

In 1985 Frenchman Gil Malmasson was metal-detecting in the Argonne and found it. He immediately contacted the American embassy, but couldn't track down the Flemings. Thirteen more years passed. Then in 1998 Malmasson was surfing the Internet and found the website for Jersey City…and the name "Mayor Frank Hague." He got in touch with the current mayor, Bret Schundler, who made some phone calls and located Fleming within hours. Fleming flew to Paris and met Malmasson—who happily put the ring back on his finger.

**Not as fragile as you thought: Egg shells are proportionately as strong as bone.**

# JUST PLANE WEIRD

*Close calls, close encounters, and other strange events in the sky.*

## GOT JUICE?

During the landing phase of Aeroflot Flight #2315 on May 9, 1994, over Arkhangelsk, Russia, loss of hydraulic fluid caused the landing gear system to fail; the right leg of the plane would not come down. In desperation, the crew poured every beverage they could find into the hydraulic system—soda, water, wine, milk, juice, and liquor. That made it possible for the crew to lower the gear, but only partway. When the plane landed, it veered to the right and went off the side of the runway, but a serious crash had been avoided. (According to experts, in an emergency any fluid will help—even urine.)

## YOU SNOOZE, YOU LOSE (ALTITUDE)

On February 17, 1994, the pilot of a private Piper PA-34 fell asleep at the controls as he was flying from Springfield, Kentucky, to Crossville, Tennessee. This was normally a short flight, but five hours later he woke up over the Gulf of Mexico, with only 20 minutes of fuel remaining. Lucky break: He was able to reach the Coast Guard by radio just as he ran out of fuel. A helicopter pulled him out of the water 70 miles west of St. Petersburg, Florida.

## BLINDED BY THE LIGHT

On October 30, 1995, a Southwest Airlines flight was climbing after takeoff from McCarran International Airport in Las Vegas when a blinding beam of light swept into the cockpit. The first officer, who was piloting the aircraft, was completely blinded for 30 seconds. For another two minutes he suffered flash blindness in the right eye and after-image effects in his left eye. He was unable to focus or interpret any of the instrument readings and was "completely disoriented."

The source of the beam: an outdoor laser light show at one of the Vegas hotels. But because so many hotels entertain guests with nightly light shows, it was impossible to determine which one was responsible. The captain (who was not affected) took over the controls until the first officer recovered.

**Looney law: In Oklahoma, you can be fined for making funny faces at dogs.**

## BETTER LATE THAN STUPID

America West Flight #6361 had been in the air less than two minutes one day in 2003, when the pilot received a call from the tower: there was a bomb onboard. The pilot immediately returned to the Medford, Oregon, airport where the passengers and crew were evacuated. A bomb squad searched the plane and luggage, but found nothing.

A little while later, when a man arrived at the check-in counter and insisted that he be allowed to board the delayed flight, America West clerks became suspicious. It turned out that the man had been on his way to the airport when he realized he was going to miss the flight. Brilliant solution: He called in the bomb threat on his cell phone, hoping to delay the plane a few minutes. The police were notified, the call was traced, and the man was promptly arrested. (The plane took off without him... again.)

## WHERE THERE'S SMOKE...

While taxiing for takeoff in Detroit, Michigan, on April 17, 1986, a TWA passenger saw some mist coming out of the plane's air vents. It was nothing abnormal, just condensation from an overheated air conditioner pack. But the passenger, believing that the plane was on fire, panicked and shouted, "Open the door!" The lead flight attendant responded to the emergency orders (which she thought came from the cockpit) and opened an exit door. Passengers sitting near exit doors also prepared for evacuation by opening *their* doors. Fortunately, the plane was still on the ground—21 passengers jumped off before the captain could intervene.

* * *

## "IT WAS MY CADDY...REALLY"

"At the 1959 Memphis Invitational Open, pro golfer Tommy Bolt was assessed one of the strangest fines in PGA tour history. Just when his playing partner was about to putt, Bolt loudly passed gas. Officials were not amused and fined him $250 for unsportsmanlike behavior."

—***Dubious Achievements in Golf's History***

# UNSCRIPTED

*When actors have to come up with their own lines…*

"I have no experience, but I guess they're different from dogs and horses."

**—Bo Derek, on children**

"If I'm androgynous, I'd say I lean toward macho-androgynous."

**—John Travolta**

"I loved making the movie *Rising Sun*. I got into the psychology of why she liked to get tied up in plastic bags. It has to do with low self-esteem."

**—Tatjana Patitz**

"The only happy artist is a dead artist, because only then you can't change. After I die, I'll probably come back as a paintbrush."

**—Sylvester Stallone**

"Good looking people turn me off. Myself included."

**—Patrick Swayze**

"There is no capital of Uruguay, you dummy—it's a country."

**—Lorenzo Lamas, to Jon Stewart on *The Daily Show***

"I feel my best when I'm happy."

**—Winona Ryder**

"Sure the body count in this movie (*Die Harder*) bothers me, but it's what everybody likes. At least it's not an awful body count—it's a fun body count."

**—Bonnie Bedelia**

"In an action film you act in the action, in a drama film you act in the drama."

**—Jean-Claude Van Damme**

"You can hardly tell where the computer models finish and the real dinosaurs begin."

**—Laura Dern, on *Jurassic Park***

"I think that the film *Clueless* was very deep. I think it was deep in the way that it was very light. I think lightness has to come from a very deep place if it's true lightness."

**—Alicia Silverstone**

"He's the chief, right? What else is there to say? It's not bad sleeping with Einstein."

**—Lara Flynn Boyle on then-boyfriend Jack Nicholson**

"My main hope for myself is to be where I am."

**—Woody Harrelson**

# THE FEDERAL WITNESS PROTECTION PROGRAM

*If you've ever wondered what being in the federal government's witness protection program is like, check out the book* WITSEC: Inside the Federal Witness Protection Program, *by Pete Earley and Gerald Shur. It will tell you everything you ever wanted to know... and more.*

## DOUBLE CROSS

In 1967 a Mafia hitman named Joe "The Animal" Barboza was arrested on minor charges and thrown in jail. His boss, Massachusetts mobster Raymond Patriarca, was supposed to bail him out, but Patriarca turned on Barboza instead, having three of Barboza's friends assassinated.

Barboza figured he was next and decided he wasn't going to just sit around and wait for someone to kill him. He immediately contacted the FBI and offered to testify against Patriarca... on one condition: the government had to protect Barboza, his wife, and their daughter against retaliation from the Mafia. For the rest of their lives. Breaking the Mafia's code of silence was an automatic death sentence, not just for Barboza but for his family as well. The FBI agreed and handed the job over to the U.S. Marshals Service, the federal agency charged with overseeing the security of the federal courts.

## ON THE MOVE

Once the deal was made, deputies transferred Barboza to a new jail and registered him under a false name, so that nobody would know who he was. Another team of deputies set up a 24-hour guard at his house, an arrangement that lasted until Patriarca took out a $300,000 "contract" on Barboza. Fearing for the family's safety, the marshals moved the Barbozas to an abandoned lightkeeper's house on a small island off the coast of Massachusetts and stationed 16 armed guards there to protect them 24 hours a day. They stayed on the island until a Boston newspaper found out and revealed where they were hiding. Then they moved again.

**Ernest Hemingway rewrote the final page of A *Farewell To Arms* 39 times.**

## YOUR TAX DOLLARS AT WORK

Barboza and his family remained in hiding and under round-the-clock protection for more than a year before Barboza testified against Patriarca in court. In the months that followed, he testified against more than a dozen other mobsters as well. By the time all the trials were over, Patriarca was behind bars and his criminal organization had been crippled.

It was an impressive victory for the Justice Department, but protecting Barboza had cost a fortune—more than 300 deputies had rotated in and out of two-week shifts guarding the family, and now that the trials were over, a way had to be found to protect the Barbozas for the rest of their lives.

But how? For now the Barbozas were hiding out in military housing at Fort Knox, Kentucky, but they couldn't stay there forever. A lifetime of 24-hour guards was out of the question: It cost too much money, consumed too much manpower, and put too many lives at risk. There had to be a better way.

## HIDING IN PLAIN SIGHT

Gerald Shur, an attorney with the Justice Department's organized crime division, had been thinking about the problem for several years and came up with an answer: Why not just give the witnesses new identities and move them to a new part of the country?

In those days, mobsters were pretty territorial—they rarely left the cities where they lived. A witness from the New York City mob was a dead man if he stayed in New York, but if he moved to Portland, Oregon, he'd probably be safe—nobody there would know who he was. And if he changed his name and avoided contact with friends and relatives back home, nobody would be able to track him down. Round-the-clock armed guards would be unnecessary.

Shur was convinced that this was the best way to protect government witnesses like Barboza. He knew it could work because some deputies in the Marshals Service were already beginning to move mobsters around the country on their own initiative. But Shur wanted to put an official program in place. He figured that if potential witnesses knew that such a program existed, they were more likely to cooperate with prosecutors.

Not many people agreed with Shur. But when President Lyndon Johnson's political opponents accused Johnson of being soft

**Glenn Burke of the L.A. Dodgers is credited with inventing the "high-five" in 1977.**

on crime, a presidential commission on law enforcement started looking for new ways to nab criminals. In 1967 Shur pitched his witness protection idea to the commission. They recommended it to President Johnson, but it didn't become law until President Nixon signed the Witness Security Program (WITSEC) as part of the Organized Crime Control Act of 1970.

## WITSEC BY THE NUMBERS

Initially Shur figured that no more than a few dozen new witnesses would enter the program each year. His guess was way off. For one thing, government prosecutors were eager to use witness testimony to win convictions. But just as importantly, every time a mob witness was able to break *omertà*—the Mafia's code of silence—and survive, it became more likely that other disgruntled or imprisoned mobsters would agree to rat out their crime bosses. By 1972 witnesses were entering the program at a rate of 200 a year; two years later the number had doubled.

To date, WITSEC has relocated more than 7,000 government witnesses and 9,000 of their family members. The Marshals Service estimates that more than 10,000 convictions have been obtained with the help of WITSEC witnesses. So far none of the witnesses in the program have been murdered in retaliation for their testimony, although 30 witnesses who left the program have been murdered... including the mobster who helped to start it all: In February 1976, Joe "The Animal" Barboza left the program and returned to a life of drug dealing, extortion, and murder. He was gunned down in San Francisco, California, in a drive-by shooting that police believe was a mob hit.

Though WITSEC was originally set up to battle the Mafia, today more than half of the people who enter the program are witnesses in drug trials; fewer than one in six are connected to the Mafia.

## STARTING OVER

• *Any* relatives or loved ones of a witness are eligible to enter the program if they are potential targets. This includes grandparents, in-laws, girlfriends, boyfriends, even mistresses.

• When a witness enters WITSEC, they get a new name, assistance moving to a new city, and help with rent and other expenses until they find a job. They also get a new birth certificate, social

**Have you heard? According to experts, a dog can't hear the lowest key on a piano.**

security card, and driver's license, but that's about it. The Marshals Service doesn't create elaborate fake pasts or phony job histories, and it doesn't provide fake credit histories, either.

## GETTING A JOB

• It's not easy finding a job without a résumé or job history. "You go to get a job, you got no references and they're not going to lie for you," says former mobster Joseph "Joe Dogs" Iannuzzi. "They don't help you get references for an apartment. You have to go and muscle it for yourself."

• But the Marshals Service does what it can to help. It has compiled a list of companies whose CEOs have agreed to provide jobs to government witnesses.

• When a witness is placed with a company only the CEO or some other high corporate official knows that the employee is a government witness, and even they are not told the person's true identity. They are, however, given details of the employee's criminal history. "You go to the head of the corporation," says retired deputy marshal Donald McPherson, "and you tell him the crimes. You have that obligation. You're not going to help a bank robber get a job as a bank teller."

## STAYING IN TOUCH

• Witnesses are strictly forbidden from revealing their new identities, addresses, or even the region of the country they live in to friends and loved ones back home. If family members don't know the names and whereabouts of their relatives in the program, the mob is less likely to come after them and try to get the information.

• It's a myth that when witnesses enter the program they are forbidden from ever contacting loved ones outside the program again. They're only forbidden from making *direct* contact—letters and phone calls can be forwarded through the Marshals Service. In-person meetings can be arranged at safe, neutral sites, such as federal buildings or safehouses.

• Does the program work? It's estimated that as many as one in five return to a life of crime after entering the witness protection program. That's about half the recidivism rate of convicts released from prison.

**Don't be cruel! On an average day, 4 people call Graceland and ask to speak to Elvis.**

# FABULOUS FLOPS

*Some folks have an eye for business, and some businesses have an "i" for idiot.*

## YOU SAY TO-MA-TO, I SAY TO-BLAH-TO

In 1994 a small biotech company called Calgene got FDA approval for the first genetically engineered whole food to hit the stores in the United States—the *Flavr Savr* tomato. It was genetically altered to delay ripening, which allowed growers to keep the plant on the vine longer, shippers to keep it in the trucks longer, and grocers to keep it on shelves longer. It sounds good, but the tomatoes had problems: they didn't taste very good; crop yields were below expectations; and the machines used for packing them, built for still-green and firm tomatoes, mashed the Flavr Savrs to mush. After two years on the market, the original "Frankenfood" was pulled from stores. Calgene's loss: an estimated $150 million.

## PUT A SOCK IN IT

Remember the Pets.com sock puppet? He appeared in 2000 in TV commercials for the online pet store and was wildly popular. He showed up on *Good Morning America* and floated in the Macy's Thanksgiving Day parade as a 36-foot balloon. Unfortunately, Pet.com's concept—selling pet supplies over the Internet—wasn't as popular as the puppet. After little more than a year, Pets.com was gone… and so was $100 million in start-up funds.

**Flop-Flip:** And the sock puppet? He reappeared in 2002 in ads for 1-800-BarNone, a company that offered loans to people with bad credit, and has written an autobiography, *Me By Me*.

## BEERZ IN THE HOOD

In June of 1991, G. Heileman Brewing Company, makers of Colt 45, came out with a new beverage: PowerMaster, a malt liquor with a 5.8% alcohol content (the average American beer has 3.5%; most malt liquors have 4.5%.) Black community leaders immediately protested, charging that the product was aimed specifically and irresponsibly at urban African Americans. For proof, they pointed to the billboard ads for the beverage that were popping up in black neighborhoods. The protests quickly spread around the country, and by July the Bureau of Alcohol, Tobacco and Firearms ruled that the "Power" in PowerMaster had to go. A beer's name, they said, cannot reflect the strength of its alcohol content (even though they had approved the name just a month earlier). Heileman was forced to pull PowerMaster, at a marketing loss of more than $2 million.

**Flop-flip:** A year later, the brewer quietly introduced Colt 45 Premium, a malt liquor with a 5.9% alcohol content. The can was black with a red horse on it—the same design as PowerMaster.

### HOPE SPRINGS ETERNAL

Pharmaceutical giant Pfizer Inc. spent 10 years and tons of money developing a "fountain of youth" drug designed to slow the aging process and keep people feeling young and vital well into old age. Initial research showed promise, prompting the company to pour even more money into the project. The reasoning was obvious: if it worked, the drug could make them millions, or even billions of dollars. In 2001 an independent testing lab performed a study that Pfizer executives expected would vault the drug toward FDA approval... but it didn't work out that way. The study actually concluded that people who took the "fountain of youth" drug had about the same results as those who'd taken sugar pills. By June 2002, the project had been canned. Cost of the decade of work: $71 million.

### FELT TIP FOLLIES

In late 2001, Sony Music came out with a "copy-proof" CD. It was a much-heralded step toward preventing the piracy of their artists' music, which they claimed hurt sales. Sony spent millions developing the technology and in the first few months of 2002 shipped more than 11 million of the discs. But by May the innovation proved to be a total flop. Word had spread like wildfire on the Internet that the high-tech copy-proofing could be thwarted... by scribbling around the rim of the CDs with an 89¢ felt-tip marker.

* * *

"Wise men learn by other men's mistakes, fools by their own."

—**Anonymous**

# KIBBLE ME THIS

*What would Porter the Wonder Dog have eaten 200 years ago, before there was Alpo or Dog Chow? Here's the history of the multi-billion-dollar dog food industry.*

## CHOW DOWN

• More than 2,000 years ago, Roman poet and philosopher Marcus Terentius Varro wrote the first farming manual. In it he advised giving farm dogs barley bread soaked in milk, and bones from dead sheep.

• During the Middle Ages, it was common for European royalty to have kennels for their hounds. Kennel cooks would make huge stews, mostly grains and vegetables with some meat or meat by-products—the hearts, livers, and lungs of various livestock.

• Dogs in common households had meager diets. They were fed only what their owners could spare. A normal domesticated dog's diet consisted of crusts of bread, bare bones, potatoes, cabbage, or whatever they could scrounge on their own.

• In the 18th century, farm dogs, which had to be fairly healthy to do their jobs, were regularly fed mixes of grains and lard. In cities, you could make a living by searching the streets for dead horses, cutting them up, and selling the meat to wealthy dog owners.

• There were exceptions: The very wealthy, throughout history, have fed their pet dogs fare that was much better than what most humans ate. In the 1800s Empress Tzu Hsi of China was known to feed her Pekingese shark fins, quail breasts, and antelope milk. European nobility fed their dogs roast duck, cakes, candies, and even liquor.

## LUXURY FOOD

Then in the mid-1800s, as the Industrial Revolution created a growing middle class with more money and more leisure time, pets began to be regarded as "luxury items" by everyday folk. Result: pet food became more closely scrutinized.

More pets and more money meant a new profession: veterinary medicine. It was officially founded in the United States in 1895, but many self-styled experts were already giving advice on dog diets. Many said that dogs needed to be "civilized," and since wild dogs ate raw meat, domesticated dogs shouldn't. (That advice influenced the pet food industry for decades after.)

In the late 1850s, a young electrician from Cincinnati named James Spratt went to London to sell lightning rods. When his ship arrived, crew members threw the leftover "ship's biscuits" onto the dock, where they were devoured by hordes of waiting dogs. That gave Spratt an idea. "Ship's biscuits," or hard tack, were the standard fare for sailors for centuries. Flour, water, and salt were mixed into a stiff dough, baked, and left to harden and dry. The biscuits were easily stored and had an extremely long shelf life, which was important in the days before refrigeration. And they looked a lot like today's dog biscuits.

Spratt had the idea that he could make cheap, easy-to-serve biscuits and sell them to the growing number of urban dog owners. His recipe: a baked mixture of wheat, beet root, and vegetables bound together with beef blood. When Spratt's Patent Meal Fibrine Dog Cakes came on the market in 1860, the pet-food industry was born. Spratt's Dog Cakes were a hit in England, so in 1870 he took the business to New York…and began the American pet food industry.

## A GROWING TREND

Others followed in Spratt's footsteps:

• In the 1880s, a Boston veterinarian introduced A.C. Daniels' Medicated Dog Bread.

• The F. H. Bennett Biscuit company opened in 1908, making biscuits shaped like bones. Bennett also made the first puppy food, and was the first to package different-sized kibble for different breeds.

• In 1931 the National Biscuit Company (Nabisco) bought Bennett's company and renamed the biscuits Milkbones. Then they hired 3,000 salesmen with the specific goal of getting Milkbones into food stores—and the national consciousness. For the first time, dog biscuits were part of regular grocery shopping.

• In 1922 Chappel Brothers of Rockford, Illinois, introduced Ken-L Ration, the first canned dog food in the United States. It was horse meat. In 1930 they started sponsoring a popular radio show, *The Adventures of Rin Tin Tin*. Ken-L Ration became such a success that by the mid-1930s they were breeding horses just for dog food and slaughtering 50,000 of them a year.

**Many restaurants in France allow dogs and even offer special menus for them.**

## AW, DRY UP

By 1941 canned dog food had a 90% share of the market...until the United States entered World War II and the government started rationing tin and meat. Then dry dog food became popular again.

In 1950 the Ralston Purina Company started using a cooking extruder to make their Chex cereal. Here's how it worked: ingredients were pushed through a tube, cooked under high pressure, and puffed up with air. This allowed Chex to stay crisp when milk was added.

At about the same time, manufacturers were getting complaints about the appearance, texture, and digestibility of dry dog food. Purina's pet food division borrowed an extruder from the cereal division and experimented with it in secret for three years. The result: Purina Dog Chow. Dogs loved it, it digested well, and it quickly became the number one dog food in the nation—and still is today.

## NO PEOPLE FOOD FOR YOU

In the early 1950s, Ken-L Ration made the jump from radio to TV advertising, running commercials on wholesome shows like *The Adventures of the Ozzie and Harriet*. ("This dog food uses only USDA, government-inspected horse meat!")

In 1964 the Pet Food Institute, a lobbying group for the now-gigantic pet food industry, began a campaign to get people to stop feeding their dogs anything *but* packaged dog food. They funded "reports" that appeared in magazines, detailing the benefits of processed dog food, and even produced a radio spot about "the dangers of table scraps."

The dog food industry was spending an incredible $50 million a year on advertising. Commercials centered around the "beef wars," with competing companies all claiming to have the most pure beef. (*Bonanza* star Lorne Greene did a TV commercial for Alpo...holding a sirloin steak.)

In the 1960s and 1970s, factors such as increased numbers of breeds and rising crime rates made dog ownership skyrocket. By 1975 there were more than 1,500 dog foods on the market.

Today, more than 1,600 square miles of soybeans, 2,100 square miles of corn, and 1.7 million tons of meat and poultry products are made into pet food every year. There are more than 65 million dogs in the U.S., and pet food is an $11 billion industry...and growing.

**Drew Barrymore's first acting role: A commercial for *Gaines Burgers*. (She was 11 months old.)**

# COOL BILLIONS

*There are 1,000,000,000 reasons to read this page.*

• If you had $1 billion and spent $1,000 a day, it would take 2,740 years to spend it.

• One billion people would fill roughly 305 Chicagos.

• It took from the beginning of time until 1800 for the world's population to reach one billion, but only 130 years more for it to reach two billion—in 1930.

• One billion people lined up side by side would stretch for 568,200 miles.

• First magazine in history to sell a billion copies: *TV Guide*, in 1974.

• More than one billion people on Earth are between the ages of 15 and 24.

• One Styrofoam cup contains one billion molecules of CFCs (chlorofluorocarbons)—harmful to the Earth's ozone layer.

• Nearly one billion Barbie dolls (including friends and family) have been sold since 1959. Placed head to toe, the dolls would circle the Earth more than three times.

• To cook one billion pounds of pasta, you'd need two billion gallons of water—enough to fill nearly 75,000 Olympic-size swimming pools.

• The first billion-dollar corporation in the U.S. emerged in 1901—United States Steel.

• The ratio of billionaires to the rest of the U.S. population is 1 to 4.5 million.

• A single ragweed plant can release a billion grains of pollen.

• One teaspoon of yogurt contains more than one billion live and active bacteria.

• The first year in which the U.S. national debt exceeded $1 billion was 1863.

• There are about one billion red blood cells in two to three drops of blood.

• It's estimated that by 2005 there will be more than one billion cell phone users.

• Earth's oceans will completely disappear in about one billion years due to rising temperatures from a maturing sun.

# DUMB JOCKS?

*Sports stars say the darnedest things. Are they trying to be funny...or just not all there? You be the judge.*

"My wife doesn't care what I do when I'm away as long as I don't have a good time."

**—Lee Trevino**

"Be sure to put some of them neutrons on it."

**—Mike Smith, baseball player, *instructing a waitress on how to prepare his salad***

"This taught me a lesson, but I'm not sure what it is."

**—John McEnroe**

"I want all the kids to do what I do, to look up to me. I want all the kids to copulate me."

**—Andre Dawson, Chicago Cubs outfielder**

"They shouldn't throw at me. I'm the father of five or six kids."

**—Tito Fuentes, baseball player, *after getting hit by a pitch***

"That's so when I forget how to spell my name, I can still find my clothes."

**—Stu Grimson, hockey player, *on why he has a photo of himself above his locker***

"I've won on every level, except college and pro."

**—Shaquille O'Neal**

"I could have been a Rhodes Scholar, except for my grades."

**—Duffy Daugherty, Michigan State football coach**

"People think we make $3 million and $4 million a year. They don't realize that most of us only make $500,000."

**—Pete Incaviglia, baseball player**

"If history repeats itself, I think we can expect the same thing again."

**—Terry Venables, professional skier**

"After a day like this, I've got the three Cs: I'm comfortable, I'm confident, and I'm seeing the ball well."

**—Jay Buhner, outfielder, *after a perfect 5-for-5 day***

"Just remember the words of Patrick Henry—'Kill me or let me live.'"

**—coach Bill Peterson, *giving a halftime pep talk***

# CELEBRITY RUMORS

*Oh, those poor celebrities. Just because they're out in the public eye, people want to make up weird stories about them. At the BRI we hear rumors about celebrities all the time, and we decided to look into some to see if they were true.*

**RUMOR:** Movie critic Gene Siskel, half of TV's Siskel and Ebert, was buried with his thumb pointing upward ("Two Thumbs Up" was the Siskel and Ebert trademark), as he'd requested in his will.

**HOW IT SPREAD:** From a UPI news story that began circulating over the Internet shortly after Siskel's death in February 1999. "Gene wanted to be remembered as a Thumbs-Up kind of guy," Siskel's attorney was quoted as telling the wire service.

**THE TRUTH:** The "news" article is fake. It was probably intended as a joke, but at some point people started passing it around as if it were true. Just to be safe, though, reporters at *Time Out New York* obtained a copy of Siskel's will from the Chicago court where it was filed. Their finding: "There are no digit-placement requests in the critic's last wishes."

**RUMOR:** Vanna White of *Wheel of Fortune* fame starred in a stage version of *The Diary of Anne Frank*. Her performance was so bad that when the Nazis came in the house, people in the audience stood up and shouted, "She's in the attic!"

**HOW IT SPREAD:** By word of mouth and on the Internet.

**THE TRUTH:** Another example of a story that started out as a joke but came to be passed along as true. White has never played Anne Frank on stage, on TV, in the movies, or anyplace else. Over the years, the "She's in the attic!" story has been attributed to numerous actresses of questionable talent, including Pia Zadora.

**RUMOR:** Cher had her lowest pair of ribs surgically removed to make her waist look slimmer.

**HOW IT SPREAD:** In 1988 *Paris Match* magazine published a story claiming that she'd had the procedure done. From there the story was published in newspapers and magazines all over the world. (Jane Fonda, Tori Spelling, Janet Jackson, and even Marilyn Manson are rumored to have had the same procedure.)

**THE TRUTH:** Neither Cher nor anyone else could have the procedure done even if they wanted to, because no such procedure exists. Cher got so fed up with the rumor that she sued *Paris Match* (they retracted the story). She even hired a physician to examine her for evidence of the "procedure" (there was none) and release his findings to the public. It didn't do any good—the rumor persists to this day.

**RUMOR:** *Playboy* magazine founder Hugh Hefner used to place a number of small stars on the cover of his magazine to indicate how many times he'd slept with that month's cover girl. If he found her satisfactory, he placed them *inside* the "P" of the magazine's masthead. If he was disappointed, he placed them *next* to the "P."

**HOW IT SPREAD:** By word of mouth from one fantasizing *Playboy* reader to another. The story was helped along by the fact that from 1955 until 1979, there really *were* a series of small stars on the cover, sometimes inside the "P"... and sometimes alongside it.

**THE TRUTH:** The stars were marketing codes—*Playboy* was published in several different regional editions, and the company used different numbers of stars to identify the different editions. The stars were always printed in a dark color. If the cover was a dark color, the masthead was white and the stars went inside the "P." But on a light-colored cover, the stars went alongside it.

**RUMOR:** Iron Eyes Cody, the famous "crying Indian" of the Keep America Beautiful anti-littering ad campaign of the 1970s... was actually Italian.

**HOW IT SPREAD:** By word of mouth. Cody, who died at the age of 94 in 1999, went to his grave insisting his father was a member of the Cherokee tribe and his mother was full-blooded Cree.

**THE TRUTH:** When reporters from the *New Orleans Times-Picayune* went to Cody's hometown of Kaplan, Louisiana, in 1996 to check birth records, they found that he'd actually been born Espero DeCorti, to Italian immigrant parents. DeCorti assumed Indian identities in the 1920s to get jobs in Hollywood westerns. Once "Iron Eyes" became a Native American, he never stopped pretending. As DeCorti's half-sister May Abshire remembered of their childhood, "He always said he wanted to be an Indian."

# REAL TOYS OF THE CIA

*Uncle John loves those clever spy gadgets in the James Bond movies devised by Q. It turns out that some of them are real. Here are a few actual spy tools.*

**IT LOOKS LIKE:** A cigarette
**BUT IT'S REALLY:** A .22-caliber gun
**DESCRIPTION:** This brand of cigarette packs a powerful puff. Intended as an escape tool, the weapon only carries a single round, but with good aim it can inflict a lethal wound from close range. To fire the cigarette, the operator must twist the filtered end counterclockwise, then squeeze the same end between the thumb and forefinger. Warning: Don't shoot the weapon in front of your face or body—it has a nasty recoil.

**IT LOOKS LIKE:** A pencil
**BUT IT'S REALLY:** A .22-caliber pistol
**DESCRIPTION:** Like the cigarette gun, this camouflaged .22 comes preloaded with a single shot. The weapon is fired in the same manner as the cigarette: simply turn the pencil's eraser counter-clockwise and squeeze. The only difference between the weapons is that the pencil has a greater firing distance—up to 30 feet.

**IT LOOKS LIKE:** A belt buckle
**BUT IT'S REALLY:** A hacksaw
**DESCRIPTION:** Fitted inside a hollow belt buckle is a miniature hacksaw. When the buckle is opened, a small amount of pressure is released from the saw's frame, exerting tension on the blade. This makes the saw a more efficient cutting machine, keeping the blade taut when sawing through, for example, handcuffs. The belt buckle saw will cut through anything from steel to concrete in about 15 minutes and will tear through rope and nylon. Don't wear belts? Buckles can be put on coats and luggage, too.

**IT LOOKS LIKE:** Eyeglasses
**BUT IT'S REALLY:** A dagger
**DESCRIPTION:** Concealed in the temple arms of these CIA

**"Q" stands for *quartermaster*, a military name for the officer in charge of supplies.**

glasses are two sharp blades. Disguised as the reinforcing wire found in most eyeglass frames, the daggers are designed to be used once and broken off at the hilt, inside the victim. The lenses are cutting tools, too. The lower edges are ground to razor sharpness and can be removed by heating or breaking the frames.

**IT LOOKS LIKE:** A felt-tip marker
**BUT IT'S REALLY:** A blister-causing weapon
**DESCRIPTION:** Don't mistake this pen for your Sharpie, and be careful: you wouldn't want it leaking in your pocket. A little over three inches long, the marker distributes an ointment that creates blisters on the skin. In order to activate the applicator, press the tip down on a surface for one minute—then simply apply a thin coating of the colorless oil over any area, such as a keyboard or door handle. The ointment will penetrate clothing and even shoes, and will cause temporary blindness if it comes in contact with the eyes. Blisters will cover the skin wherever contact is made within 24 hours and will last for about a week.

**IT LOOKS LIKE:** Dentures
**BUT IT'S REALLY:** A concealment device (and much more)
**DESCRIPTION:** What could possibly fit inside a dental plate? A lot more than you'd think. Items such as a cutting wire or a compass can be placed in a small concealment tube and hidden under a false tooth. A rubber-coated poison pill can be carried in the same manner. The poison can either be ingested to avoid capture or poured into an enemy's food and utilized as a weapon. Radio transceivers can be placed in dental plates, with audio being transmitted through bone conduction. The CIA has even created a dental plate that alters the sound of one's voice. If all of these gadgets prove ineffective, then the dental plate itself can be removed and its sharp scalloped edge used for digging, cutting, or engaging in hand-to-hand combat.

*     *     *

**James Bond:** "They always said, 'The pen is mightier than the sword.'"
**Q:** "Thanks to me, they were right."

***—Goldeneye***

# LIFE IMITATES ART

*Everyone loves the movies. They're entertaining—usually a good escape from reality. No one expects the story to come true... but sometimes it does. Here are a few examples.*

## *THE BIRTH OF A NATION* (1915)

**THE MOVIE:** *The Birth of a Nation* is considered one of the greatest American movies ever made—and one of the most racist. Director D. W. Griffith's classic tells the triumphs and travails of a white southern family before and after the Civil War. The film also uses cinematic techniques that were revolutionary for the time, such as tracking shots, extreme close-ups, fade-outs, extensive cross-cutting, and panoramic long shots.

Yet unfortunately, *The Birth of a Nation* offers an incredibly demeaning portrayal of African Americans. It depicts black northern soldiers (actually white actors in blackface) as sex-crazed rapists and glorifies the Ku Klux Klan for keeping former slaves "in their place" (i.e., away from the ballot box).

**REAL LIFE:** The original Klan was a secret society founded after the Civil War to enforce white supremacy in the South. And it only lasted a few short years before dying out in the 1870s.

But in the fall of 1915, following the release of *The Birth of a Nation*, a Methodist preacher named William Simmons decided to revive the Ku Klux Klan in Georgia. By the , the revitalized Klan boasted of three million members across the United States, thanks in large part to the popularity of the groundbreaking silent film.

## *THE MANCHURIAN CANDIDATE* (1962)

**THE MOVIE:** This Cold War classic features Laurence Harvey as a brainwashed U.S. soldier who finds himself at the center of an elaborate conspiracy involving Communists and conservatives. The goal of this conspiracy: to kill a presidential candidate. To achieve this end, Harvey smuggles a rifle with a telescopic sight into a political rally where the man will be speaking.

**REAL LIFE:** A year after the film was released, President John F. Kennedy was assassinated in Dallas, allegedly by former Marine Lee Harvey Oswald using a rifle with a telescopic scope. And in the decades that followed, speculation abounded that more than one person was involved in the shooting, that Oswald was a mere dupe, and that just like the movie, the president's murder was actually engineered by a shadowy cabal of extremists. To make things even weirder, *The Manchurian Candidate* co-starred Kennedy's buddy, Frank Sinatra, as a fellow soldier who unravels the assassination conspiracy.

Following the film's release, a contractual dispute between Sinatra and the filmmakers forced *The Manchurian Candidate* to be withdrawn from theaters and not shown to the public for decades. The suppression of the film only enhanced its reputation as an eerily prophetic political thriller.

## *DEATH WISH* (1974)

**THE MOVIE:** This film stars Charles Bronson as a mild-mannered guy who turns into a pistol-wielding vigilante after his family is brutally assaulted by thugs. In one pivotal scene, Bronson is sitting by himself on a New York City subway car and is accosted by a mugger. Instead of handing over his cash, Bronson shoots the mugger and then casually walks out of the car.

**REAL LIFE:** On December 22, 1984, Bernhard Goetz, a meek, self-employed electrical engineer, smuggled a five-shot .38-caliber revolver onto the New York subway. Goetz took a seat near a group of four young men. When one of the youths approached him and demanded money, Goetz stood up, drew his gun, and shot all four of them. Goetz then pocketed his gun and walked off the subway. He later surrendered to police.

While Goetz appears to have been motivated by fear (he had been mugged previously), his actions eerily paralleled those of Bronson's character. Like Bronson in *Death Wish*, Goetz was seen by many as a hero, an "ordinary Joe" who lashed out in justifiable rage against deserving creeps.

The outcome of the two men's actions, however, couldn't have been more different: at the end of *Death Wish*, Bronson is free and eager to impose lethal justice on a fresh batch of miscreants. Goetz stood trial for his crimes and although acquitted of attempted murder, he served eight months in jail for illegal gun possession.

**Shoeless Joe Jackson's shoes are in the Baseball Hall of Fame.**

# STAR TREK WISDOM

*Is there intelligent life in TV's outer space? You decide.*

"Is there anyone on this ship who, even remotely, looks like Satan?"

**—Kirk**

**Tuvok:** "The phaser beam would ricochet along an unpredictable path, possibly impacting our ship in the process."
**Janeway:** "All right, we won't try that."

"Mr. Spock, the women on your planet are logical. That's the only planet in the galaxy that can make that claim."

**—Kirk**

"I'm a doctor, not an escalator."

**—McCoy**

"I must say, there's nothing like the vacuum of space for preserving a handsome corpse."

**—Doctor**

"I'm attempting to construct a mnemonic memory circuit, using stone knives and bearskins."

**—Spock**

"The best diplomat I know is a fully-loaded phaser bank."

**—Scotty**

"Mr. Neelix, do you think you could possibly behave a little less like yourself?"

**—Tuvok**

"What am I, a doctor or a moon shuttle conductor?"

**—McCoy**

"Time travel, from my first day on the job I promised myself I'd never let myself get caught up in one of these God-forsaken paradoxes. The future is the past; the past is the future. It all gives me a headache."

**—Janeway**

"It's difficult to work in a group when you're omnipotent."

**—Q**

**Data:** "Tell me, are you using a polymer-based neuro-relay to transmit organic nerve impulses to the central processor of my positronic net?"
**Borg Queen:** "Do you always talk this much?"

"The weak innocents... they always seem to be located on the natural invasion routes."

**—Kirk**

"I'm a doctor, not a bricklayer."

**—McCoy**

**Survival of the fittest? Charles Darwin and Albert Einstein married their first cousins.**

# CURTAINS!

*When you go to the theater, you expect to see a well-rehearsed play, but that's not always what you get. Sometimes actors forget lines or the scenery falls and the cast has to find a way to keep the show going... sometimes with hilarious results.*

## A KNOCKOUT PERFORMANCE

During a performance of *Rumplestiltskin* at The Afternoon Players of Salt Lake City, the actor playing Rumplestiltskin made an unscripted leaping exit—and knocked himself out on a door frame. The actress playing the Princess had no idea that he'd been hurt. According to the plot, the Princess has to guess Rumplestiltskin's name by midnight or he'll take away her baby. The actress sat onstage and waited for the Rumplestiltskin character to reappear. When he didn't, she began to improvise.

"I wonder where that funny little man is?" she asked, loudly. "That funny little man was supposed to come back here and I was supposed to guess his name." Still no Rumplestiltskin. While she improvised, the actors backstage were frantically trying to think of what to do. Finally two of them put on silly hats and ran onstage. "You know that funny little man?" one of them said, in a very meaningful way. "Well, he's *never* coming back."

The Princess's eyes widened in horror. "You mean, he's *never* coming back?"

"No. He's *never* coming back." The three stood there in dead silence. Finally the other actor spoke. "But he told us to tell you that he knew you had guessed his name. It's Rumplestiltskin. And now you can keep your baby! Hooray!" Curtain down. End of play.

## "IT'S A MIRACLE!"

*The Miracle Worker* tells the story of Helen Keller, who was deaf, dumb, and blind. In one production in the Midwest, the actor playing the Doctor was discovered to have a drinking problem. But as his character was only in the first scene, the director took pity on him and cast him anyway.

At the start of the play, the Doctor is supposed to inform the Keller family that a fever has left their infant without the use of her eyes, ears, or vocal chords. Unfortunately, on opening night, the actor drunkenly blurted, "Mr. and Mrs. Keller, I've got bad news. Your daughter is... dead."

The other actors were stunned. If Helen was dead, the play couldn't go on. Thinking quickly, the actress playing Mrs. Keller ad-libbed, "I think we need a second opinion."

The curtain came down, and the drunken actor was yanked off the stage. The stage manager put on the Doctor's white coat and took his place on stage. When the curtain went up again, the new Doctor declared, "Your baby is alive, but she'll be deaf, dumb, and blind for the rest of her life."

The actor playing Mr. Keller was so relieved to hear the correct lines that he clasped his hands together and cried, "Thank God!"

## A CROSS TO BEAR

Every summer, Passion plays are performed throughout the South. These spectacles tell the story of Jesus using huge casts, massive sets, and lots of special effects. In one production in Texas, an actor playing a Roman guard was supposed to stab the actor playing Jesus with a spear that had a special retractable blade. Oops—the guard grabbed the wrong prop backstage and poked a *real* spear into Jesus' ribcage. Jesus cried out in agony, "Jesus Christ! I've been stabbed!"

The stage manager quickly brought down the curtain and called an ambulance. As sirens wailed in the distance, the curtain rose to reveal a new Jesus—a 260-pound stagehand in a loincloth.

When the time came for him to be lifted to heaven on special ropes, the new actor said, "And now I shall ascend!" The ropes were attached to a special counterweight system—that had been rigged for a man who weighed 100 pounds less. The stagehand pulling the rope couldn't lift him. He added more weights to the system as the actor repeated, "And now I shall ascend." This time Jesus was lifted a few feet above the cross, but quickly dropped back down again. The desperate stagehand quickly put all the weights he could find onto the system and pulled the rope as the actor playing Jesus said, "And now I shall... AAAAIIIIEEEEE!"

Jesus' scream could be heard across town as he was catapulted straight up into the metal grid at the top of the theater and knocked senseless.

Another ambulance was called, and the show was canceled.

**_WHOOSH!_ Olympic downhill skiers reach 80 mph.**

# POP CULTURE QUIZ

*So you're an avid bathroom reader and you think you know a thing or two. Well, see if you can match wits with Uncle John—he knew almost all of these.*

**1.** What beer did E.T. the Extra-Terrestrial drink in the 1982 film?

**a)** Budweiser **b)** Miller Genuine Draft
**c)** Coors Light **d)** Milwaukee's Best

**2.** What country's flag consists of one solid color?

**a)** Zimbabwe **b)** Costa Rica **c)** Greece **d)** Libya

**3.** Whose autobiography is entitled *Wheel of Fortune*?

**a)** Pat Sajak **b)** Vanna White **c)** Edith Piaf **d)** B. F. Goodrich

**4.** What's an *ananym*?
**a)** A name someone uses to remain anonymous
**b)** A name spelled backward
**c)** A word that means the opposite of another word
**d)** A quotation that precedes a book, chapter, or article

**5.** How long did the 1991 Persian Gulf War last?
**a)** 32 days—January 16 to February 17
**b)** 39 days—January 16 to February 24
**c)** 43 days—January 16 to February 28
**d)** 54 days—January 16 to March 11

**6.** Who was the first ghost to visit Scrooge in Charles Dickens's *A Christmas Carol*?

**a)** Bob Cratchit **b)** Jacob Marley
**c)** The Ghost of Christmas Past **d)** Tiny Tim

**7.** The first African American to win a Nobel prize for peace:

**a)** Ralph Bunche **b)** Martin Luther King Jr.
**c)** Frederick Douglass **d)** Louis Armstrong

**Big Bird's address: 123 1/2 Sesame Street (Zip Code unknown).**

**8.** In Denmark, the "Peanuts" comic strip is known as:

**a)** "Karl Brun und Venindes" **b)** "Horned Toads"
**c)** "Gud Gryf" **d)** "Radishes"

**9.** Who once boxed under the name "Packy East?"

**a)** Frank Sinatra **b)** Bob Hope
**c)** Mickey Rourke **d)** Ronald Reagan

**10.** What is the name of the dog on the box of Cracker Jacks?

**a)** Crackers **b)** Bozo **c)** Bingo **d)** Porter

**11.** When M&Ms introduced their blue candies in 1995, what color did they discontinue?

**a)** tan **b)** orange **c)** purple **d)** white

**12.** Who was the shortest Beatle?

**a)** John **b)** Paul **c)** George **d)** Ringo

**13.** The only member of the *Lord of the Rings* movie cast to have actually met the author of the books, J. R. R. Tolkien, was:

**a)** Ian Holm (Bilbo Baggins) **b)** Ian McKellan (Gandalf)
**c)** Christopher Lee (Saruman) **d)** John Rhys-Davies (Gimli)

**14.** What does the "L" stand for in Samuel L. Jackson's name?

**a)** Lawrence **b)** Leroy **c)** Luscious
**d)** Nothing—he has no middle name, but added an initial for "mystique."

## Answers

**1.** c; **2.** d; **3.** c (Piaf was a French singer, known as "The Little Sparrow."); **4.** b (Ananyms are often used as pseudonyms, as in Oprah Winfrey's production company: Harpo); **5.** c; **6.** b; **7.** a; **8.** d; **9.** b; **10.** c; **11.** a; **12.** d (He's 5'8". He's also the oldest, born on July 7, 1940.); **13.** c (Lee also knew the books better than anyone else on the set, and was a creative consultant to director Peter Jackson.); **14.** b.

**The Cartheginians fought off Roman ships in 300 B.C. by catapulting live snakes at them.**

# "PAGING MR. POST"

*The funeral business (known as "the dismal trade" in the 18th century) necessarily deals with concepts that many people find distasteful. That led to the evolution of a unique set of euphemisms in the death biz.*

**Passed into the arms of God.** Dead. Other euphemisms: *passed away, gone to meet his/her Maker, expired, deceased.*

**Temporary preservation.** Embalming—the common treatment of dead bodies in which bodily fluids are replaced with preservative fluid. Other euphemisms: *sanitary treatment, hygienic treatment.*

**Grief therapy.** The "therapeutic" effect of having an expensive funeral "viewing."

**Burn and scatter.** Slang for services that scatter cremated remains at sea. Also known as *bake and shake.*

**Casket coach.** Hearse.

**Consigned to earth.** Buried.

**Pre-need sales.** Funeral services sold to someone who hasn't died yet.

**Corpse cooler.** A specialized coffin with a window, once used to preserve the body for viewing. An ice compartment kept the corpse cool.

**Interment space.** A grave. Used in phrases such as *opening the interment space* (digging the grave) and *closing the interment space* (filling the grave).

**Cremains.** Cremated remains; ashes.

**Babyland.** The part of a cemetery reserved for small children and infants.

**Slumber room.** The room in which the loved one's body is displayed.

**Memorial park.** Cemetery.

**Lawn-type cemetery.** A cemetery that bans headstones in favor of ground markers, allowing caretakers to simply mow the lawn rather than trim each grave by hand.

**Funeral director.** Undertaker.

**O-sign.** A dead body sometimes displays what hospital workers call the "O-sign," meaning the mouth is hanging open, forming an "O." The "Q-sign" is the same—but with the tongue hanging out.

**Gotta hand it to her: Queen Elizabeth I owned 2,000 pairs of gloves.**

**Protective caskets.** Coffin sealed with rubber gaskets to keep out bugs and other invaders. Unfortunately, methane gas has been known to build up inside such caskets, causing them to explode and spew out their contents. This prompted the introduction of *burping caskets* that allow gas to escape.

**Grief counselor.** Mortuary salesperson.

**Mr. Post.** Morgue attendant. Used by many hospitals to page the morgue when a body has to be removed from a room.

**Nose squeezer.** Flat-topped coffin.

**Beautiful memory picture.** An embalmed body displayed in an expensive casket.

**Body.** This term for a dead person is generally discouraged, along with *corpse*. Preferred: the dead person's name, or *remains*.

**Plantings.** Graves.

**Selection room.** Room in which buyers look at displayed caskets. This term replaces *back room, showroom, casket room.*

**Companion space.** An over/under grave set for husband-and-wife couples; one body is placed deep in the ground and the second buried above it.

* * *

## LET'S DO ANOTHER STUDY

• Colorado State University scientists concluded that Western Civilization causes acne.

• A 2003 study carried out by scientists at Edinburgh University found that fish feel pain.

• In 1994 the Japanese meteorological agency concluded a seven-year study into whether or not earthquakes are caused by catfish wiggling their tails. (They're not.)

• Physicists at the University of Nijmegen in the Netherlands released a report in 2000 on their study of diamagnetics, during which they claimed to have "levitated" a frog, a grasshopper, a pizza…and a sumo wrestler.

**"His mother should have thrown him away and kept the stork." —Mae West**

# ANIMAL NAME ORIGINS

*When we came up with the idea for this page we figured that after 15* Bathroom Readers, *we must have done it before. We were wrong.*

**GORILLA**

"First used in a Greek translation of 5th century BC Carthaginian explorer Hanno's account of a voyage to West Africa. He reported encountering a tribe of wild hairy people, whose females were, according to a local interpreter, called gorillas. In 1847 the American missionary and scientist Thomas Savage adopted the word as the species name of the great ape and by the 1850s it had passed into general use." (From *Dictionary of Word Origins*, by John Ayto)

**FERRET**

"*Ferret* comes from Latin *furritus*, for 'little thief,' which probably alludes to the fact that ferrets, which are related to pole cats, like to steal hens' eggs. Its name also developed into a verb, *to ferret out*, meaning 'to dig out or bring something to light.'" (From *Cool Cats, Top Dogs, and Other Beastly Expressions*, by Christine Ammer)

**SKUNK**

"Because the little striped mammal could squirt his foul yellow spray up to 12 feet, American Indians called him *segankw*, or *segonku*, the Algonquin dialect word meaning simply 'he who squirts.' Early pioneers corrupted the hard-to-pronounce Algonquin word to *skunk*, and that way it has remained ever since." (From *Animal Crackers*, by Robert Hendrickson)

**HOUND**

"Before the Norman conquest of England, French hunters bred a keen-nosed dog that they called the St. Hubert. One of their rulers, William, took a pack to England and hunted deer—following the dogs on foot. Saxons had never before seen a dog fierce enough to seize its prey, so they named William's animals *hunts*, meaning 'seizure.' Altered over time to *hound*, it was long applied to all hunting dogs. Then the meaning narrowed to stand for breeds that follow their quarry by scent." (From *Why You Say It*, by Webb Garrison)

**Literally translated, *hors d'oeuvre* means "outside of work."**

**LEOPARD**

"It was once wrongly believed that the leopard was a cross between a 'leo' (a lion) and a 'pard' (a white panther)—hence the name 'leopard.'" (From *Why Do We Say It?*, by Nigel Rees)

**PYTHON**

"According to Greek legend, the god Apollo's earliest adventure was the single-handed slaying of Python, a flame-breathing dragon who blocked his way to Pytho (now Delphi), the site he had chosen for an oracle. From the name of this monster derives the name of the large snake of Asia, Africa, and Australia, the python." (From *Thou Improper, Thou Uncommon Noun*, by Willard R. Espy)

**CARDINAL**

"One would think that such an attractive creature would have given its name to many things, but in fact it is the other way around. The bird's name comes from the red-robed official of the Roman Catholic Church, who in turn was named for being so important—that is, from the adjective *cardinal*, from the Latin cardo, meaning 'hinge' or 'pivot.' Anything cardinal was so important that events depended (hinged or pivoted) on it." (From *It's Raining Cats and Dogs*, by Christine Ammer)

**MOOSE**

"Captain John Smith, one of the original leaders at Jamestown, wrote accounts of the colony and life in Virginia, in which he defined the creature as *Moos, a beast bigger than a stagge*. *Moos* was from Natick (Indian) dialect and probably derived from *moosu*, 'he trims, he shaves,' a reference to the way the animal rips the bark and lower branches from trees while feeding." (From *The Chronology of Words and Phrases*, by Linda and Roger Flavell)

**FLAMINGO**

"This long-legged pink wading bird is named for the people of Flanders, the *Flemings*, as they were called. Flemings were widely known for their lively personalities, their flushed complexions, and their love of bright clothing. Spaniard explorers in the New World thought it was a great joke naming the bird *flamingo*, which means 'a Fleming' in Spanish." (From *Facts On File Encyclopedia of Word and Phrase Origins*, by Robert Hendrickson)

**Florence, Italy, was the first city to have all of its streets paved...in 1339 B.C.**

# BIRTH OF THE BAGEL

*Uncle John was in his office munching on a bagel (toasted, with cream cheese) when he realized that the last time he wrote about that fabulous food was all the way back in the very first* Bathroom Reader! *And that wasn't the (w)hole story!*

## WHAT EXACTLY IS A BAGEL?

There are lots of different kinds of bagels made today, but to the purist, real bagels contain only flour, water, yeast, malt, and salt. No sugar, no eggs, no raisins, no onions, no sesame seeds, no cinnamon, no garlic, no jalapeño peppers, no cheddar cheese, and no sun-dried tomatoes.

The dough is rolled into a cylinder and then twisted into a ring with a hole in the middle. The rings are allowed to rise, and then (the key to making real bagels) they're cooked quickly in boiling water before they're baked. The boiling process gelatinizes the gluten in the dough, giving the bagel its unique hard and shiny surface and thus sealing the inside to preserve its density and chewiness.

## WHERE DID BAGELS COME FROM?

Bagels are believed to have been invented in the 17th century, but there is some debate about their exact origin. They might be Polish—text from Kraków, Poland, written in 1610 refers to *beygls* being good gifts for new mothers—possibly because they make good teething rings, which many people still use them for today.

Another theory says that an Austrian baker wanted to make a gift for King John III Sobieski of Poland after he saved the city of Vienna from Turkish invaders in 1683. King John was famous for his horsemanship, so the baker made a roll in the shape of a stirrup. (Bagels used to be much thinner, with bigger holes.) The Austrian-German word for stirrup: *beugel*, or *bügel*.

However they began, bagels were a hit. They spread all through Eastern Europe over the next two centuries—even into Russia, where they were called *bubliki*. Many different peoples baked bagels in the old days, but over time, Jewish bakers became bagel specialists.

**French flies: *Entomophagy* is the practice of eating insects.**

## BAGELS IN THE NEW WORLD

In the 1880s, thousands of eastern European Jews emigrated to North America, bringing the bagel with them. The chewy bread soon became a staple in stores and street markets on New York's Lower East Side, as well as in Montreal and Toronto. (Each of these cities claims to have the best bagels today.)

In 1907 the International Bakers Union was founded in New York City. By 1915 bagels had become so popular that bagel-makers formed their own union: Bagel Bakers Local #338. It was a very exclusive group (the only way to get in was to be the son of one of the 300 members). Their recipes were closely guarded secrets, and bagel-baking techniques—hand rolling and twisting—remained unchanged for decades.

## THE THOMPSON MACHINE

It wasn't until the early 1960s that this process changed. Dan Thompson—whose father started baking bagels in Los Angeles in the 1920s—started tinkering with a bagel-making contraption after watching his dad try in vain to invent one. In 1963 he succeeded. The Thompson Bagel Making Machine was the first commercially-practical bagel-making device. Using nonunion, unskilled workers, Thompson's machine could make over 1,000 bagels an hour.

Who leased the first one? Lender's Bagels, a small shop that had been in operation in New Haven, Connecticut, since 1927. In 1963 they were going into the frozen bagel business, and Dan Thompson's invention came along at just the right time. Lender's Bagels became a familiar item in supermarkets across the country, and Lender's became the biggest bagel maker in the world.

## MODERN-DAY BAGELS

Today there are bagel shops all over the country and bagels come in all different flavors, shapes, and sizes: there are chocolate-chip bagels, spinach bagels, pumpkin bagels, miniature bagels, pizza bagels, and even square bagels. Bagel-making machines can now turn out more than 50,000 bagels an hour.

But nostalgia is affecting business today too, so many shops have gone back to the old style, making all their bagels by hand or with simple machines, boiling them in a bagel kettle, and using the sim-

**Price of an Alberta Ferretti hamster-fur skirt suit in 2000: $6,300.**

ple authentic recipe. If you ever get to Englewood, New Jersey, stop by Englewood Hot Bagels. That's where Uncle John got his bagels as a boy, and he hasn't found a better one since. Enjoy.

## BAGEL BITS

• Classic combo: Cream cheese was invented in 1872; Philadelphia Cream Cheese hit the market in 1880. But it wasn't until Joseph and Isaac Breakstone began selling their Breakstone Cream Cheese brand in 1920 that New York bagel eaters discovered it—and cream cheese became *the* bagel spread.

• In 2000 several rioters at a Fourth of July celebration in Morristown, New Jersey, were arrested for throwing "dangerous" projectiles into the crowd and at police. The projectiles: "batteries, golf balls, and stale bagels."

• According to the *Guinness Book of World Records*, the world's largest bagel was made by Larry Wilkerson and Jeff Maninfior in 1998, at the Lender's Bagel Bakery in Mattoon, Illinois. Weight: 714 pounds. Diameter: 6 feet. Flavor: blueberry.

• During the 2002 American League Championship Series between the New York Yankees and Anaheim Angels, Anaheim mayor Tom Daly bet New York mayor Michael Bloomberg a crate of oranges and chilies that the Angels would win. Bloomberg's bet: a crate of Nathan's hot dogs and 48 H&H bagels. (Daly won.)

• In 2002 John and Cecelia O'Hare sued a McDonald's restaurant in Panama City Beach, Florida, claiming that an improperly cooked bagel damaged Mr. O'Hare's teeth...and somehow ruined their marriage as well. They sued for $15,000 in damages. (Case pending.)

* * *

## BIRTH OF A STRANGE LAW

To attract patrons to his circus, P. T. Barnum would often hitch a plow to an elephant and have it work fields next to the big top. One farmer got so angry about his field being torn up that he pushed a bill through the state legislature. To this day it's illegal to plow a field with an elephant in North Carolina.

# EYE OF THE HURRICANE

*Hurricanes are the largest, most powerful, most unpredictable, and deadliest phenomena on Earth. (Kind of like Uncle John about an hour after dinner on "bean night"—but that's another story.)*

## WHAT'S IN A NAME?

*Hurricanes*, *typhoons*, and *cyclones* are the same thing—it just depends on what part of the world you're from. The word *hurricane* comes from "Hurikan," the Mayan name for the god of evil. The Mayans believed the Hurikan was a huge winged serpent whose breath could flatten trees and dry up oceans. In the Northwest Pacific, meteorologists use the Chinese word *typhoon* (from *taaifung*, which means "big wind") for the same kind of weather system. Meteorologists also use the term *cyclone* (from the Greek word for "coil"), especially for smaller hurricanes and typhoons. Cyclone describes the way a hurricane's wind coils around a low pressure system. (See page 614 to find out how hurricanes are named.)

## HOW THEY'RE BORN

The mother of all hurricanes is the sun. Hurricanes are born when a unique set of circumstances come together in exactly the right order. For a hurricane to form, several conditions must be met:

• First the sun must heat up a large area of tropical ocean where the water temperature is a minimum of 80°F (the 80-degree layer has to be 150 feet deep or the storm will die). Billions of tons of water start to evaporate and rise into the atmosphere.

• The winds coming from different directions have to converge on the rising air, forcing it further upwards.

• As the warm air rises, it meets cooler air above. The moisture in the air mass condenses and turns into heavy rain. The heat energy created during condensation is pumped back into the air mass, making it rise even faster.

• The next step, according to Jack Williams in *The USA Today Weather Book*, is a violent mid-air collision.

> The air in such high pressure areas is flowing outward. That helps disperse the air that's rising in the storm, which creates a

semi-vacuum and encourages even more air to rise from the ground. A hurricane's winds are formed by air near the ocean rushing inward to replace air that's rising in the storm.

• Result: a huge doughnut-shaped weather system that continues to grow as long as the sun and ocean feed in energy and moisture.

• Finally, the rotation of the earth causes this enormous cloud to spin from a force known as the Coriolis Effect.

**Weather in Motion**

The Coriolis Effect is named after Gustave Gaspard Coriolis, a 19th-century French scientist who is credited with explaining why Napoleon's cannon balls always deflected slightly to the right of the targets at which they were fired. The reason, Coriolis determined, is that the rotation of the earth affects objects in motion. The Coriolis Effect gives northbound air masses a counterclockwise spin—and southbound air masses a clockwise spin.

## HOW HURRICANES KILL

Over the past 30 years the damage and loss of life from hurricanes has diminished as meteorologists have become better at tracking storms. The hurricane death toll has also decreased, but there are still hundreds of victims every year, sometimes even thousands. Here are the three major ways people die during hurricanes:

**Storm surge.** As a hurricane approaches land, the storm's rushing winds push a wall of water ahead of it like a tank moving forward through a muddy ditch. Some hurricanes are capable of producing a storm surge 15 feet high. This can be extremely hazardous because some of the most densely-populated—and hurricane-prone—parts of the Atlantic and Gulf coastlines are less than 10 feet above sea level.

Coupled with normal tides, a hurricane can create a "storm surge" super-tide which can rise as high as a three-story building. Shoreline communities can be engulfed in a matter of minutes while huge wind-driven waves pound buildings to kindling, and boats, houses, and people are dragged miles out to sea as the surge retreats. In 1900 more than 6,000 people died in Galveston, Texas, when a 15-foot storm surge overwhelmed the entire city. In 1995 a 24-foot storm surge caused $3 billion worth of damage to beachfront property near Pensacola, Florida, although thanks to early warning from meteorologists, no lives were lost.

**Moving Air.** Hurricane winds can reach sustained speeds in excess of 150 mph for hours at a time. That's enough to level most buildings, overturn a bus, and turn virtually any seemingly harmless object into a deadly projectile. But if that isn't bad enough, tornadoes will often form on the fringes of hurricanes, raising hurricane-related wind speeds to more than 300 mph.

**Floods.** As hurricanes come ashore, they almost always encounter cold weather systems on higher ground. Warm humid air colliding with huge masses of cold air causes torrential rainfall. In a matter of hours, millions of tons of water can be deposited over an inland community creating flash floods in places where residents never expect high water. To make matters worse, people often underestimate the power of moving water. They are tempted to wade through a knee deep stream or drive over a flooded bridge, unaware that 18 inches of water moving at 20 mph can sweep away an 18-wheeler. Over the past 30 years, nearly 60% of all hurricane fatalities were caused by inland flooding.

## THE NUMBERS

• In an average year, hurricanes cause nearly five billion dollars of damage to the United States.

• The highest storm surge ever recorded was a 42-foot surge in Bathurst Bay, Australia, in 1899.

• The largest amount of rain in less than 12 hours was 45 inches dumped on La Reunion Island by tropical Cyclone Denise in 1966. La Reunion Island is a good place to live if you like rain—it holds five world records for cyclone-induced rain including 97.1 inches over a 48-hour period (unnamed cyclone, 1958) and 223.5 inches over a 10-day period (Cyclone Hyacinthe, 1980).

• What was the most destructive hurricane of the 20th century? In 1992 Hurricane Andrew damaged or destroyed nearly 100,000 homes and caused $26 billion worth of property damage. But that's not the record—in 1926 an unnamed hurricane rampaged through Florida and Alabama. If that storm's damage were measured in today's dollars, it's estimated that it would have cost more than $84 billion.

**...National Christmas Tree lighting ceremony on the White House lawn.**

# I'VE BEEN CORNOBBLED!

*You won't find these archaic words in most dictionaries, but take our word for it—they're real. And just for fun, try to use them in a sentence. (We did—check out page 706.)*

**Hobberdehoy,** A youth entering manhood

**Faffle,** To stutter or mumble

**Dasypygal,** Having hairy buttocks

**Cornobbled,** Hit with a fish

**Collieshangie,** A noisy or confused fight

**Wem,** A stain, flaw, or scar

**Calcographer,** One who draws with chalk

**Bodewash,** Cow dung

**Twiddlepoop,** An effeminate-looking man

**Liripoop,** A silly creature

**Leptorrhinian,** Having a long narrow nose

**Bridelope,** When the new bride is "both symbolically and physically swept off on horseback" to the husband's home

**Mundungus,** Garbage; stinky tobacco

**Chirogymnast,** A finger-exercise machine for pianists

**Toxophily,** love of archery

**Pismire,** An ant

**Valgus,** Bowlegged or knock-kneed

**Xystus,** An indoor porch for exercising in winter

**Jumentous,** Having a strong animal smell

**Saprostomous,** Having bad breath

**Balbriggan,** A fine cotton used mainly for underwear

**Atmatertera,** A great-grandfather's grandmother's sister

**Anisognathous,** Having the upper and lower teeth unlike

**Whipjack,** A beggar pretending to have been shipwrecked

**Spodogenous,** Pertaining to or due to the presence of waste matter

**Crapandina,** A mineral such as toadstone or bufonite said to have healing properties

**Galligaskin,** Baggy trousers

**What's for dinner, honey? A hive of honeybees eats up to 30 pounds of honey over the winter.**

# BATHROOM NEWS

*Here are a few fascinating bits of bathroom trivia that we've flushed out from around the world.*

## OPEN AND SHUT CASE

In March 1997, a Russian Antonov-24 charter plane broke apart in midair and crashed just 30 minutes after takeoff. Investigators looking into the crash concluded that moisture leaking from a toilet had damaged the structural integrity of the plane. Then, apparently somebody on the fatal flight slammed the restroom door a little too hard, "causing a chain reaction of disintegration in the structure beneath the toilet, which was rotten due to the prolonged water leakage."

## KEEP IT CLEAN

In July 2003, Vietnam's Ministry of Culture and Information banned the broadcast of commercials for toilet paper between the hours of 6:00 p.m. and 8:00 p.m. Reason: Viewers complained that seeing T.P. commercials at dinnertime caused them to lose their appetite. Airing such ads at the dinner hour "is not suitable to the national psychology, manners, and customs" of Vietnam, the country's state-controlled *Tien Phong* newspaper reported. The ban also applies to commercials for condoms, sanitary napkins, and skin disease medications.

## SHELTER FROM THE STORM

The town of Van Wert, Ohio, was struck by not one but *four* tornadoes on November 11, 2002. One of the tornadoes bore down on the town movie theater just as a matinee crowd of about 50 people were getting ready to watch *The Santa Clause 2*. The twister ripped the roof off the theater and tossed two automobiles into the seats, where patrons had been sitting just moments before. Amazingly, no one was injured because the management had evacuated everyone into the only part of the building strong enough to withstand the tornado—the restrooms. "Could have been a real tragedy," said Jack Snyder, spokesman for the Van Wert County Emergency Management Agency. "We consider ourselves very lucky."

## THE NIGHT SHIFT

In June 2003, Danish researchers released a scientific study on a medical condition known as *nocturia*—having to get up several times a night to pee. Their findings:

• Sleep deprivation caused by nocturia can result in "daytime sleepiness, depression…poor memory, and difficulties managing work."

• The average worker with nocturia suffers a 10% drop in productivity. Estimated cost to the European economy: nearly $16 million per year.

## MORE THAN HE CAN BEAR

Ed Yurkovich made a trip to the bathroom at his home in Willard, Wisconsin, in June 2003. His pit stop would have been unremarkable except for two things: 1) he left the bathroom window ajar, and 2) there are bears in Willard, Wisconsin.

Yurkovich left the house, and while he was gone a 300-pound bear pried the bathroom window completely open and climbed into the house. Once inside, the bear couldn't figure out how to get back out, so it roamed from room to room, pooping on the floor and scratching at other windows, trying to get out. When Yurkovich returned home, the bear was lying on the living room floor. As soon as he opened the front door the bear ambled out and disappeared into the trees. Estimated damage: $1,000.

* * *

## GOING OUT WITH A BANG

What happens when a congressman running for reelection accidentally discharges a gun at a neighborhood reception? He loses. In 2002, Republican Congressman Bob Barr attended a rally hosted by Bruce Widener, a local lobbyist and gun collector. As Widener handed Barr an antique .38-caliber pistol from his collection, it suddenly went off, shattering a glass door. Barr, a board member of the National Rifle Association, was in a tight primary battle against another congressman, John Linder, and the incident helped Linder paint Barr as an extremist. "We were handling it safely," Widener explained. "Except that it was loaded."

**Q: What is an *undecennial*? A: An 11th anniversary.**

# GROANERS

*A good pun is its own reword.*

Dijon vu—the same mustard as before.

Marathon runners with bad footwear suffer the agony of defeat.

A lot of money is tainted. It taint yours and it taint mine.

When two egoists meet, it's an I for an I.

Every calendar's days are numbered.

The reading of a will is a dead giveaway.

It was an emotional wedding. Even the cake was in tiers.

When chemists die, we barium.

Why couldn't the bicycle stand on its own? Because it was two-tired.

She had a boyfriend with a wooden leg... until she broke it off.

A chicken crossing the road is poultry in motion.

Those who jump off a Paris bridge are in Seine.

Energizer Bunny arrested—charged with battery.

When a clock gets hungry, it goes back four seconds.

When the actress saw her first strands of gray hair, she thought she'd dye.

Reading while sunbathing makes you well-red.

Without geometry, life is pointless.

A man's home is his castle, in a manor of speaking.

A pessimist's blood type: always B-negative.

Show me a piano falling down a mine shaft, and I'll show you A flat minor.

Once you've seen one shopping center, you've seen a mall.

What you seize is what you get.

* * *

A man walks into a bar with a salamander in his hand. The bartender asks the man what he calls it. "Tiny" replies the man. "Why's that?" asks the barkeep. "Because he's my newt!"

**World's muddiest river: Yellow River, in China.**

# MADE A FORTUNE...

*Uncle John grew up near an old, crumbling outhouse way out in the woods... but now he has a lavish two-holer right in his backyard. Here are some other people who have come from humble beginnings to achieve great wealth.*

## JIM CARREY

**From Rags...** He had to drop out of high school and take a job as a janitor in a factory. In fact, his entire family worked in that factory, living in a small cottage on the grounds. At his lowest low, Carrey wrote a $10 million check to himself... to be redeemed when he made the big time.

**...to Riches:** After working the comedy circuit for years, Carrey landed a role on *In Living Color*, which led to a movie deal. In 1996 he became the highest paid actor ever when he received $20 million to star in *Cable Guy*. When his father died, Carrey placed the check he had written to himself in his dad's burial suit.

## J. K. ROWLING

**From Rags...** As a single mother living on public assistance, Rowling started writing *Harry Potter and the Philosopher's Stone* in a café while her baby daughter napped. Why the café? Because it was warmer than the tiny flat she lived in. When Bloomsbury Books bought her manuscript in 1996, she was thrilled. The £1,500 (about $2,400) she was advanced was more money than she'd ever received at one time in her life.

**...to Riches:** Four years and three more books later, Rowling was worth more than $400 million... and she's not done yet.

## OPRAH WINFREY

**From Rags...** Born in Mississippi to unwed teenage parents, Winfrey grew up in poverty. While living in Milwaukee, she was molested by relatives. Not knowing what else to do, her mother sent her to live in a detention home.

**To Riches:** Fortunately, the detention home was full and Winfrey went to live with her father. He nurtured her abilities and helped her get to college. Now, as the queen of the talk show, Winfrey is worth an estimated $1 billion.

**Baby seals are called *weaners*.**

# ...LOST A FORTUNE

*Like the celebrities on the opposite page, these people came from humble beginnings. But we think what happened to them after they made their fortunes is much more interesting.*

## WILLIE NELSON

**From Riches...** By 1988 Willie Nelson had been a country music star for nearly 20 years and had two multiplatinum albums under his belt.

**...to Rags:** Due to years of "creative" accounting, in 1990 Nelson owed the IRS $16.7 million. To pay it, he had to auction off just about everything he owned.

## M. C. HAMMER

**From Riches...** "U Can't Touch This," released in 1990, became a pop phenomenon, making Hammer an overnight superstar. A world tour and endorsement deals with Pepsi and KFC followed.

**...to Rags:** Hammer went on a $30 million spending spree that included mansions and a $500,000-a-month payroll. After two mediocre follow-up albums and some poor investments, Hammer declared bankruptcy in 1996, more than $13 million in debt.

## NIKOLA TESLA

**From Riches...** In his heyday in the 1890s, Tesla was a rich and famous inventor and held more than 700 patents. He is best-known for developing alternating current (AC) electricity.

**...to Rags:** He was also naive. Thomas Edison, who saw Tesla as competition, did all he could to undermine Tesla's work. It worked. A series of patent lawsuits left Tesla with no money or credit, despite his many inventions. He died broke in 1943.

## MIKE TYSON

**From Riches...** The youngest heavyweight champion in boxing history had earned $300 million.

**...to Rags:** By 2003 it was all gone. Tyson blames his former promoter, Don King, for mismanaging his earnings. King claims that Tyson blew the money himself. The two will duke it out in court.

**Willie Nelson's first gig: playing guitar in a polka band.**

# LACROSSE

*What's the national sport of Canada? If you said "hockey" you're half right. Hockey is Canada's national* winter *sport, but Canada's national* summer *sport is lacrosse. (It's also the oldest known sport in North America.)*

### BAGGATTAWAY

In 1636 French Jesuit missionary Jean de Brebeuf watched Huron Indians of southeastern Canada play an unusual game called *baggattaway,* meaning "little brother of war." He wrote in his journal that the players used curved sticks with net pouches on the end to hurl a small ball. The stick reminded him of the cross carried by French bishops, called the crosier, or *la crosse.* That's the first documented mention—and the origin of the modern name—of one of the fastest-growing sports in the world today, lacrosse. Its roots go back at least to the 1400s and possibly much earlier. Today, organized lacrosse is played in more than 20 countries on five continents, with teams in such diverse places as Japan, Germany, Argentina, South Korea, and the Czech Republic.

And, it's still an important game to Native Canadians.

### THE BIG LEAGUES

At the time Europeans discovered it, baggattaway was already a very popular sport in North America. Different versions with different names were being played by tribes throughout southeastern Canada, around the Great Lakes, and all the way into the southeastern United States. The rules and equipment varied from region to region, but in general the game was as follows:

Players used a wooden stick about three to four feet long with a big curve on one end, kind of like a shepherd's staff. A mesh pouch made of strips of boiled bark was attached to the curve and tied back down the handle of the stick. The stick could be used to pick up, carry, bat, throw, or catch a small ball, which was made of wood, baked clay, or deerskin stuffed with hair. (They could also use the stick to whack their opponents.)

Players would move down the field, then organize strategies, sometimes using all-out attacks, trying to put the ball through a

**First sport on film: boxing (Thomas Edison filmed it in 1894).**

goal. Goal markers could be a pole or two poles, or rocks or trees at either end of the playing field. As for the playing field: there were no sidelines, and the goals could be hundreds of yards—or several miles—apart. The games could last as long as three days, and, in probably the most stunning aspect of the early game, the teams could number from 5 to *1,000* players on each side.

## SPORTS MEDICINE

Baggattaway wasn't just a game to native North Americans, it was an important part of spiritual life as well. Tribal mythology says that the sport was a gift given to them by the Creator. Its purpose was healing, and it was (and still is) known as a "medicine game," because it promoted good health, mental toughness, and community teamwork. It was traditionally played by men, but entire villages would take part in the contests, which were often prepared for with elaborate rituals led by spiritual leaders.

Often it was a war ritual, and the games were prepared for by chanting, dreaming, and dancing—the same way a tribe prepared for battle. The Cherokee in the southeast even named the game accordingly: "Little Brother of War." Its grueling nature and violent style of play—which often resulted in serious injuries—was seen as perfect training for warriors. French fur trader Nicholas Peffot wrote in the late 1600s, "legs and arms are sometimes broken, and it has happened that a player has been killed."

Sometimes it even substituted for battle, with tribes settling disputes with a game—although that strategy didn't always work. One account says that a game was played in 1790 between the Choctaws and the Creeks to settle a territorial dispute. When the Creeks were declared the winners, the unhappy Choctaw players attacked them, and they ended up in a full-scale war.

## ALL LACROSSE THE WORLD

But it wasn't until 200 years after Father de Brebeuf first noted the game that Europeans became active players. In 1834 the Canadian Caughnawaga tribe played a demonstration game for European settlers in Montreal, and lacrosse started its worldwide spread. After it was reported in the newspapers, interest grew among non-natives, and leagues started to form. Then it got its biggest boost: in 1856 Dr. George Beers, a dentist from Montreal, founded the Montreal

**Wild turkeys can run 30 mph and fly at speeds up to 55 mph.**

Lacrosse Club. He wrote down the rules, setting field size, team size, etc., campaigned tirelessly, and set lacrosse on the path to becoming the highly organized and successful sport it is today. Beers is still called the "Father of Lacrosse." It became so popular that by 1859, an act of Canadian Parliament named lacrosse Canada's national sport.

In 1867 white Canadian and native teams did an exhibition tour throughout Great Britain. People loved it, and leagues started to spring up around the British Isles. The Caughnawaga even played for a special audience: Queen Victoria. She gave the game her blessing, and by the end of the century it had spread to Australia, New Zealand, and South Africa. It had also spread to the United States, becoming part of high school and university programs in the Northeast, with the first intercollegiate tournament held at the Westchester Polo Grounds in New York in 1881. In 1904 and 1908, lacrosse was played in the Olympic Games in St. Louis and London.

## LACROSSE FACTS

• The official name for the lacrosse stick: the crosse. In men's lacrosse, it's still legal to whack your opponent with it.

• In the 1960s, Czech Boy Scout groups saw pictures of Native Americans playing lacrosse in *National Geographic* magazine. They made their own sticks, wrote their own rules, and began playing "Czech-lacrosse." It was actually closer to baggattaway than today's official lacrosse game.

• NFL Hall of Fame running back (and movie star) Jim Brown is considered by many the best football player to ever play the game. Many say the same thing about his lacrosse play: he was an All-American at Syracuse University in the 1950s and is a member of the Lacrosse Hall of Fame.

• In 1763 the Chippewa and Sauk tribes played a game outside Fort Michilimackinac, a British stronghold in Michigan. When the ball was "accidentally" kicked over the fort walls, the players all rushed after it and, as planned, attacked the soldiers inside. When it was over, 20 British soldiers had been killed, 15 taken prisoner, and the fort belonged to the Indians.

• The Iroquois Nationals, a multi-tribe team from the New York–Ontario area, is the only team from an indigenous nation participating in international sports competition.

**Say it three times fast: *Geschwindigkeitsbegrenzung* is German for "speed limit."**

# THE ADVENTURES OF EGGPLANT

*On page 602 we told you about the first reality TV show. On page 411 we told you about Japanese game shows. Mix them together with the plot of the movie* The Truman Show, *and you've got this unbelievable true story.*

## MADE IN JAPAN

In January 1998, a struggling 23-year-old standup comedian known only by his stage name Nasubi (Eggplant) heard about an audition for a mysterious "show business–related job" and decided to try out for it.

The audition was the strangest one he'd ever been to. The producers of a popular Japanese TV show called *Susunu! Denpa Sho-Nen (Don't Go for It, Electric Boy!)* were looking for someone who was willing to be locked away in a one-bedroom apartment for however long it took to win one million yen (then the equivalent of about $10,000) worth of prizes in magazine contests.

Cameras would be set up in the apartment, and if the contestant was able to win the prizes, the footage would be edited into a segment called "Sweepstakes Boy." The contestant would be invited on the show to tell his story and, with any luck, the national TV exposure would give a boost to his career. That was it—that was the reward (along with the magazine prizes).

## SUCH A DEAL

As if that wasn't a weak enough offer, there was a catch—the contestant would have to live off the prizes he won. The apartment would be completely empty, and the contestant wouldn't be allowed to bring anything with him—no clothes, no food, nothing. If he wanted to eat, he had to win food. If he wanted to wear clothes, he had to win those, too. Nasubi passed the audition and agreed to take the job.

On day one of the contest, the producers blindfolded him and took him to a tiny one-bedroom apartment in an undisclosed location somewhere in Tokyo. The apartment was furnished with a magazine rack and thousands of neatly stacked postcards (for entering the contests), as well as a table, a cushion to sit on, a telephone, notepads, and some pens. Other than that, it was completely empty.

Nasubi stripped naked and handed his clothes and other personal effects to the producers. He stepped into the apartment, the door was locked behind him, and his strange adventure began.

## HOME ALONE

Nasubi spent his days entering magazine sweepstakes, filling out between 3,000 and 8,000 postcards a month. It took him two weeks to win his first prize—a jar of jelly. Two weeks later, he won a five-pound bag of rice.

But how could he cook it? He hadn't won any cooking utensils. He tried eating the rice raw, and when that failed he put some in a tin can, added some water, and put it next to a burner on the stove. Using this method, he cooked about half a cup of rice each day, and ate it using two of his pens for chopsticks. (The producers are believed to have given Nasubi some sort of food assistance, otherwise he would not have eaten anything for the first two weeks of the show. To this day it is unclear exactly how much assistance he received, but judging from the amount of weight he lost during the show, it wasn't much.)

## SECRET ADMIRERS

Nasubi didn't know it at the time, but he was being watched. Sure, he knew about the cameras in the apartment, but the producers had told him that the footage would be used on *Susunu! Denpa Sho-Nen* after (and if) he completed his mission. And he had believed them.

But the producers had lied—he'd been on TV from the very beginning. Each Sunday night, edited highlights of the week's activities were broadcast in a one-hour show on NTV, one of Japan's national networks. The show was a big hit, and in the process Nasubi became a national celebrity, one of the hottest new stars in Japan. A naked star at that, albeit one whose private parts were kept continuously concealed by a cartoon eggplant that the producers superimposed on the screen.

## NASUBI'S BOOTY

Viewers were there when Nasubi won each of his two vacuum cleaners, and they were there when he won each of his four bags of rice, his watermelon, his automobile tires, his belt, and his ladies underwear (the only articles of clothing he won during months in captivity), his four tickets to a Spice Girls movie (which he could not leave the apartment to see), his bike (which he could not ride outside), and countless other items, including chocolates, stuffed animals, headphones, videos, golf balls, a tent, a case of potato chips, a barbecue, and a shipment of duck meat.

Nasubi also won a TV, but the joy of winning it was shattered when he discovered that his apartment had neither antenna nor cable hookup. (The producers feared that if he watched TV, he'd find out he was *on* TV.)

And he won a few rolls of toilet paper—10 *months* after his ordeal began.

Nasubi sang a song and danced a victory dance every time a new prize came in the mail; when he did, many viewers at home sang and danced with him. When his food ran out, they gagged and sobbed with him as he ate from the bag of dog food he won; when he prayed for a new bag of rice, viewers prayed, too.

## ROUND-THE-CLOCK EXPOSURE

Nasubi was such a media sensation that reporters tried to find out where he was living. It took six months, but someone finally located his apartment building in June 1998. Before they could make contact with him, however, the producers whisked Nasubi off to a new apartment in the dead of night, telling him the move was intended "to change his luck."

In July the producers set up a live website with a video feed and a staff of more than 50 people (many of whom were there just to make sure the moving digital dot stayed over Nasubi's private parts at all times). Now people could watch Nasubi 24 hours a day.

Finally, in December 1998, one year after he was first locked into the apartment, Nasubi won the prize—a bag of rice—that pushed his total winnings over a million yen. So was he free? Not exactly: The show's producers gave him his clothes, fed him a bowl of ramen noodles, and then whisked him off to Korea, where he couldn't speak the language and no one would recognize him.

**Was it a mis-de-mooo-ner? In 1740 a French judge found a cow guilty of sorcery.**

Then he was placed in *another* empty apartment, where he had to win prizes to pay for his airfare back home.

When Nasubi finally accomplished *that*, he was flown back to Tokyo, taken to a building, and led into another empty room (it was really just a box, but he didn't know it).

## INSTANT CELEBRITY

Out of habit, he stripped naked and waited for something to happen. Suddenly the roof lifted, the walls fell away, and Nasubi found himself, still naked, his hair uncut and his face unshaved for more than 15 months (he never did win clippers or a shaver), standing in an NTV broadcast studio in front of a live audience. Seventeen million more people were watching at home.

More than 15 months had passed since Nasubi had been locked into his apartment, and it was only now, as he held a cushion over his privates, that he learned he'd been on TV since day one. His weekly show had made him Japan's hottest new star, the producers explained to him. The diary he'd kept? It had already been published and was a bestselling book, one that had earned him millions of yen (tens of thousands of dollars) in royalties. That bowl of ramen soup the producers fed him the day he came out of isolation? The footage had been turned into a popular soup commercial. They told him about the website—it made money, too. All of this resulted in a lot of money for Nasubi.

It took quite a while for all of this information to sink in. "I'm so shocked," Nasubi finally said. "I can't express what I feel."

## ONE OF A KIND

Today Nasubi is a happy, successful celebrity. Nevertheless, as crazy as Japanese game shows can be, it's unlikely that any other person will experience what he went through. Even if someone were crazy enough to agree to be locked in an apartment for such a long time, they would know from the beginning what was up.

But there's another reason: that much isolation just isn't healthy. Sure, he looked relatively happy on the show, and he certainly had moments of joy. But the footage had been edited to make Nasubi's experience seem better than it really was. In press interviews, he admitted there were times when he thought he was going to go nuts. "I thought of escaping several times," he told reporters later. "I was on edge, especially toward the end."

**An American living in Japan in 1869 invented the rickshaw to transport his invalid wife.**

# FUNNY BUSINESS

*Big corporations play by an interesting set of rules: their own.*

## THE ANTI-ANTISMOKING CAMPAIGN

In the early 1980s, Merrell Dow, a subsidiary of Dow Chemical, released Nicorette, a cigarette-substitute chewing gum. To promote it they published *The Smoking Cessation Newsletter*, which they sent to doctors' offices, did studies on the dangers of cigarettes, and even encouraged their own employees to quit smoking. Meanwhile, tobacco giant Philip Morris was spending millions annually on chemicals for the manufacture of their tobacco products, which they purchased from... Dow Chemical. Using their economic muscle to squash Nicorette, in 1984 Philip Morris ceased all purchasing from Dow. It worked. An internal memo later revealed that Merrell Dow president David Sharrock personally assured Philip Morris executives that he would screen all advertising and eliminate any anti-tobacco statements. Result: The newsletter was reduced to a one-sentence blurb: "If you want to quit smoking for good, see your doctor."

## THE CHICKEN SAYS "MOO"

Given up eating red meat? Next time you're in England you may want to think twice before you order chicken. Recent tests by the British *Food Standards Agency* on imported chicken show they're not exactly what you'd expect. Poultry companies in Holland and Belgium have been pumping water into their birds to inflate their weight and then advertising it as "more meat." But how do you artificially inflate chickens? Inject the birds with extra protein, which allows the meat to retain more water. Chicken protein? No—the tests revealed that pork and beef protein had been put into the chickens.

## SMOKE AND MIRRORS

Remember the huge tobacco lawsuits of the late 1990s? Threatened with having to foot the bill for *all* smoking-related illnesses, the nation's largest tobacco companies agreed to pay 46 states an unbelievable $206 billion. The idea was that the states would use the money 1) to pay for smoking prevention programs, and 2) to defray

***Kwanzaa* means "first fruits" in Swahili.**

the costs of health care for smokers who got ill. So far, however, less than 5% of the $33 billion paid out has gone to prevent smoking. And it gets worse: several states have earmarked their share of the money to help…the tobacco industry. In North Carolina, for example, $43 million of the $59 million they've received has gone to marketing and producing tobacco, the state's biggest crop. They bought equipment for farmers, built a new tobacco auction hall, and put $400,000 toward a new tobacco processing plant. Other states have used the money won from tobacco companies to buy stock—in tobacco companies.

## THE HOMELAND LAWSUIT SECURITY AGENCY

In November 2002, just before President Bush signed the Homeland Security Bill into law, an interesting one-page "rider" was found buried in the bill: a provision that would protect companies that manufactured vaccine *ingredients* from being sued (vaccine makers were already protected). What does that have to do with homeland security? Nothing. Who would benefit from the provision? Pharmaceutical giant Eli Lilly. A vaccine ingredient they manufactured was suspected of causing autism in thousands of children, and Lilly was facing hundreds of lawsuits that could potentially cost them millions—maybe billions—of dollars. It was as if the law were tailor-made for Eli Lilly. Parents of autistic children, medical experts, and many lawmakers were outraged.

And nobody would admit to adding the rider to the bill.

Finally, weeks later, House Majority Leader Dick Armey (R-Texas) admitted he had done it, explaining, "It's a matter of national security. We need vaccines if the country is attacked with germ weapons." Adding to the intrigue, he said he had put the rider in at the request of the White House. What connection did the White House have to Eli Lilly? In the 1970s, former President George H. W. Bush sat on the board of Eli Lilly; White House budget director Mitch Daniels was a former Eli Lilly exec; and current Eli Lilly CEO Sidney Taurel served on the president's Homeland Security Advisory Council.

**UPDATE:** In January 2003, amid complaints from parents of autistic children and growing media speculation about corporate influence on lawmaking, Republicans announced that the rider would be repealed.

# IF MURPHY WERE A...

*BRI member Aaron Allerman sent us these "laws." For more great axioms, check out Arthur Bloch's collection in* Murphy's Law.

## ...LAWYER

**Alley's Axiom:** Justice always prevails...three times out of seven.

**Green's Rule:** What the large print giveth, the small print taketh away.

**First Law of Negotiation:** A negotiation shall be considered successful if all parties walk away feeling screwed.

**Power's Principle:** If the law is on your side, pound on the law. If the facts are on your side, pound on the facts. If neither is on your side, pound on the table.

**Potter's Parking Principle:** The person you beat out of a prime parking spot will be the judge in your first case of the day.

**Goulden's Law of Jury Watching:** If a jury in a criminal trial stays out for more than 24 hours, it is certain to vote not guilty, save in those instances when it votes guilty.

**Bloom's Law:** The judge's jokes are always funny.

**Andrew's Law:** Honesty is almost the best policy.

## ...DOCTOR

**Dolman's First Law:** The first time you screw up a colonoscopy, your patient will definitely be a lawyer.

**First Rule for Interns:** Never say, "I'm new at this," to a patient.

**The HMO Principle:** The necessary procedure will not be allowed.

**Edd's Law of Radiology:** The colder the X-ray table, the more of the body the patient is required to place on it.

**The First Rule for Ob/Gyns:** All babies are born between midnight and 5:00 a.m.

**Morse's Law of Online Research:** Any search for medical information will yield at least one porno site.

**Law of Laboratory Work:** Hot glass looks exactly the same as cold glass.

**Stettner's Law for Surgeons:** Never say "oops," while your patient is conscious.

**Breezy's Translation:** When the doc says, "That's interesting," he really means, "Oops."

# MISSING PARTS

*Parts is parts—you can't let a missing finger, leg, or eye get you down. These folks didn't.*

**TYCO BRAHE** (1546–1601)

**Missing Part:** Nose

Known as the father of astronomy, Tyco Brahe compiled the world's first accurate and complete set of astronomical tables. While a student at the university in Rostock, Germany, he and a fellow student, Manderup Parsbjergh, began quarreling over an obscure mathematical point. The argument went on for weeks, until they decided to settle it with a duel... in the dark... with swords! Result: Parsbjergh sliced off a chunk of Brahe's nose. Brahe's vanity wouldn't let the disfigurement stop him from achieving greatness—in public he wore an artificial nose made of gold and silver.

**MORDECAI BROWN** (1876–1948)

**Missing Part:** Index finger

As a pitcher for the Chicago Cubs, Brown helped win four championships in the early 1900s. When he was seven his right hand had gotten caught in a corn shredder—his index finger had to be amputated; his thumb and pinkie were permanently impaired. Three weeks later, while chasing a pig, he broke his other two fingers, which never healed properly. With little more than a stub to pitch with, Brown—known as "Three Finger"—learned to throw a sharp curveball and went on to win 239 major-league games. He was elected into the Baseball Hall of Fame in 1949.

**HERBERT MARSHALL** (1890–1966)

**Missing Part:** Leg

The British actor lost a leg fighting in World War I. But being an amputee didn't stop him from acting. Marshall spent 50 years as a romantic lead on the stage and on the screen starring opposite such stars as Marlene Dietrich in *Blonde Venus* and Greta Garbo in *The Painted Veil.* Audiences never even knew that he wore an artificial leg—film directors kept his onscreen movements to a minimum to hide it.

**Weird fact: Hawaii has 3 Interstate Highways. (Think about it.)**

**JERRY GARCIA** (1942–1995)

**Missing Part:** Finger

He was four years old when it happened: Jerry and his older brother, Tiff, were splitting wood and playing "chicken" with the ax. Jerry mistimed removing his finger from the block, and Tiff accidentally chopped Jerry's finger off. It didn't hold him back, in 1957, at the age of 15, Jerry discovered the guitar and went on to become guitarist and singer for the Grateful Dead.

**SARAH BERNHARDT** (1844–1923)

**Missing Part:** Leg

Probably the most famous actress at the turn of the 20th century, Sarah Bernhardt suffered from a festering knee injury and had to have her leg amputated while touring in a production of *Jeanne Dore* in 1915. But this didn't stop her. Fitted with a wooden leg, "the Divine Sarah" continued to tour in plays, acted in movies, and even performed at the front during World War I.

**HAROLD LLOYD** (1893–1971)

**Missing Parts:** Thumb and index finger

One of the greatest comedians of the silent movies, Harold Lloyd was posing for a photograph in 1919 when he grabbed a prop—a papier-mâché "bomb"—and lit it with his cigarette. The prop turned out to be a real bomb: it exploded, taking the thumb and index finger from Lloyd's right hand. But he didn't let it ruin his career—he just started wearing gloves. And ultimately, Lloyd's gloves, like his horn-rimmed glasses, became part of his comic persona.

**LANA TURNER** (1921–1995)

**Missing Parts:** Eyebrows

For her role as an exotic handmaiden in the 1938 film *The Adventures of Marco Polo*, Turner shaved off her natural eyebrows and replaced them with fake straight, black ones. Her real eyebrows never grew back, so from that point on Lana Turner either painted or glued on fake eyebrows in every film she made.

*   *   *

**Q:** What was the original name of the Jordanian city Amman?

**A:** Philadelphia.

**In 1924 a new Ford cost $265.**

# HOST WITH THE MOST

*The Academy Awards is showbiz's premier event. Almost as important as selecting the nominees is selecting a celebrity host who can make or break the entire evening.*

**THE WRITE STUFF**

The host of the Academy Awards is expected to be perfect. He's supposed to be smooth and gracious, funny but not too irreverent; ready with a witty ad-lib if something goes wrong, and most importantly, properly respectful of the evening's events. And he's supposed to do it all on live television in front of millions of people. It may look easy from the audience, but it takes *a lot* of preparation.

When Steve Martin was asked to host the 2003 Academy Awards, he assembled a team of top-notch comedy writers six months in advance of the event. They met at his home in Los Angeles eight times before the big night to prepare "the greatest opening monologue ever." Martin had a list of nominees, presenters, and stars who might be attending the ceremonies. At each meeting he sat at his laptop while the team of seven jokesmiths tossed out ideas. So who made the team?

• **Dave Barry,** Pulitzer Prize–winning columnist for the *Miami Herald* since 1983. He has written 24 bestselling humor books and is the subject of the CBS TV show *Dave's World.*

• **Bruce Vilanch,** *Hollywood Squares* regular and award-winning writer for the Oscar, Emmy, Tony, and Grammy shows as well as for Bette Midler and Whoopi Goldberg.

• **Rita Rudner,** standup comic and TV host.

• **Dave Boone,** head writer for *Hollywood Squares*. An Academy Award veteran, he also wrote material for Billy Crystal and Whoopi Goldberg.

• **Andy Breckman,** writer for David Letterman and *Saturday Night Live*. He also created the TV show *Monk.*

• **Beth Armogida,** joke writer for Jay Leno and for Drew Carey on *Whose Line Is It Anyway?*

**Average temperature at the South Pole: –56°F. At the North Pole: –21°F.**

• **Jon Macks,** staff writer for *The Tonight Show with Jay Leno* and an Academy Award veteran.

## THE BIG NIGHT

On Oscar night, while Martin stood at the microphone onstage, his comedy advisors were gathered in a small room, just offstage. As he delivered lines like, "A movie star is many things: tall, short, thin, or skinny," they sat in a semi-circle facing a wall of television screens that showed the audience and the stage. Martin would introduce a presenter and then run to join the team for instant feedback and new jokes. When something unusual happened during the presentation, the writers wrote a few funny lines about it and Martin delivered them seconds later. For example, when Sean Connery appeared in a tuxedo accented with a frilly white front, Martin quipped, "So many people here tonight are wearing Armani but Sean is wearing Red Lobster."

Martin's team even handled the most controversial moment of the night with ease. When the outspoken filmmaker Michael Moore accepted his Oscar for *Bowling for Columbine*, Martin hurried to join his writers backstage. As Moore criticized President Bush for his handling of the war in Iraq, drawing cheers and catcalls in equal measure, the backstage writers went to work. From a list of possible jokes, the writers picked one, refined it, and sent Martin back onstage to ease the tension: "Backstage, it's so sweet. The Teamsters are helping Michael Moore into the trunk of his limo."

* * *

Will Rogers, Frank Sinatra, Whoopi Goldberg, Jimmy Stewart, Fred Astaire, Jerry Lewis, Robin Williams, Chevy Chase, David Letterman, and even Paul Hogan hosted the Academy Awards. But who hosted the most?

• **Bob Hope** hosted 17 times—the most ever. "Welcome to the Academy Awards, or as they're known at my house, Passover," he said, referring to his failure to win an Oscar.

• **Billy Crystal** hosted 7 times, 1990–1993, 1997–1998, 2000.

• **Johnny Carson** hosted 5 times, 1979–1982, 1984: The first non-movie star to host, he called the ceremony "two hours of sparkling entertainment spread over a four-hour show."

**Of the Seven Ancient Wonders of the World, six are lost. Only the pyramids of Egypt remain.**

# CELEBRITY LAWSUITS

*Here are a few more real-life examples of unusual legal battles involving celebrities.*

**PLAINTIFF:** Michael Costanza
**DEFENDANT:** Jerry Seinfeld
**LAWSUIT:** In 1998 Costanza filed a $100 million lawsuit against Seinfeld and the producers of the show *Seinfeld*, TV's "show about nothing." He claimed that the character George Costanza, played by Jason Alexander, was actually based on him. He and Seinfeld had been friends at Queen's College, he said, and his privacy rights had been violated when his "name, likeness, and persona" were used to create the neurotic George without his permission. He and George even had some of the same jobs, he said. Seinfeld never denied knowing Costanza, but spokesmen for the show insisted that the character was based on the show's producer, Larry David, not on Costanza. David called Costanza, who was "never that close of a friend to the star," a "liar" and a "flagrant opportunist." (Which actually does sound kind of like George.)

**VERDICT:** Michael Costanza lost. In June 1999, Justice Harold Tompkins wrote, "While a program about nothing can be successful, a lawsuit must have more substance."

**PLAINTIFF:** Painter James Abbott McNeill Whistler
**DEFENDANT:** Critic John Ruskin
**LAWSUIT:** In July 1877, Ruskin, England's most famous art critic, wrote a vicious attack on Whistler's Impressionist painting *Nocturne in Black and Gold: The Falling Rocket.* Ruskin was not a fan of the still-new, non-traditional style of Impressionism and accused Whistler of trying to sell "unfinished paintings." He went on to write, "I have seen, and heard, much of Cockney impudence before now; but never expected to hear a coxcomb [a fool] ask two hundred guineas for flinging a pot of paint in the public's face." Whistler, an expatriate American who was already famous in his own right for paintings such as *Arrangement in Grey and Black* (better known as Whistler's Mother), sued for libel. In one heated exchange, Ruskin's

At its deepest point, the Pacific Ocean is 36,198 feet deep (about 6.85 miles).

lawyer asked, "The labor of two days is that for which you ask two hundred guineas?" Whistler responded, "No. I ask it for the knowledge I have gained in the work of a lifetime." Ruskin himself refused to appear in the courtroom, but his lawyer reported Ruskin's promise to retire from criticism forever if he lost the case.

**VERDICT:** Ruskin lost the case. He lived the rest of his years in seclusion. But Whistler lost, too: the jury gave him a dubious award—one farthing and no court costs. He had to declare bankruptcy, losing his home and most of his personal property to pay the fees.

**PLAINTIFF:** The states of Arizona, Arkansas, Connecticut, Florida, Illinois, Michigan, Missouri, North Carolina, Ohio, Pennsylvania, Washington, West Virginia, and Wisconsin, and the District of Columbia

**DEFENDANT:** Robin Leach

**LAWSUIT:** In 1999 Leach, former host of the television show *Lifestyles of the Rich and Famous*, appeared in ads hawking vacation packages for three Florida-based travel companies. Residents of various states received letters suggesting they had "won" a vacation to Florida and a cruise to the Bahamas. Anyone who claimed the prize received a video in which Leach promised "world-class" vacations and "an experience you'll never forget." That last claim turned out to be true. "Winners" ended up paying up to $1,100 for their "free" vacation and instead of ritzy beachfront hotels, got roach-infested motels miles from shore. The "cruise" turned out to be an uncomfortable one-day ferry ride; the "Las Vegas entertainment" was a bingo game. Customers complained, and attorneys general across the country filed suit.

**VERDICT:** The three travel companies paid millions in restitution to their customers. Leach paid, too: Federal Trade Commission rules say a spokesperson must believe that any claims they make are true, and those beliefs must be based on personal experience. Leach agreed to an undisclosed settlement. "Next time Robin Leach puts his name behind a vacation package promising champagne wishes and caviar dreams," said Washington attorney general Christine Gregoire, "he'd better know those promises are true."

# HOW PAPER BECAME MONEY, PART II

*For most of history, people felt that gold and silver were "real" money and that paper money was worthless. (If you feel that way, too, please take all the worthless paper money you can find and mail it to Uncle John at the address listed in the back of this book.) Here's how paper money became established in Western civilization.*

*(Part I of the story is on page 385.)*

## MY MONEY OR YOUR LIFE

The concept of paper money originated in China as early as 140 B.C. But it wasn't until the late 1200s, when the Italian traveler Marco Polo wrote about it in his memoirs, that the idea was introduced to Europe.

So did paper money catch on in Europe soon after that? Not a chance—in China despots like Kublai Khan were quick to kill anyone who refused to accept the notes. Under that kind of pressure, paper money caught on fast.

In Europe things were different. Sure, there were plenty of European tyrants, but none of them tried to force paper money on their subjects the way Kublai Khan did. Paper notes had to earn their way into the public's confidence, via a very gradual process of evolution. Here's how it happened.

## DON'T LEAVE HOME WITHOUT THEM

Many travelers use *traveler's checks* instead of cash. Merchants all over the world accept them just as if they were cash, yet they have no value to thieves because once they're reported stolen, they can't be used. The traveler gets a new book of checks and the thief ends up with nothing.

It turns out there was a way to avoid traveling with cash even before traveler's checks were invented. As far back as the Middle Ages, when people went on business trips they could deposit gold coins or other valuables with a trusted merchant—frequently a jeweler, or *goldsmith*—when they traveled outside of their home town. The traveler carried a note from the goldsmith that stated how much money had been left on deposit and promised to release the gold to anyone who presented the note for payment of a debt, provided that 1) the traveler had signed the note over to the debtor by name, and 2) he had endorsed it with his signature.

## SAFE AT HOME

If the goldsmith was well known and trusted, this note was literally as good as gold. If the note was stolen, it didn't matter, because the gold was still safely locked in the goldsmith's vault and would not be released without the owner's signature. These early "promissory notes," as they came to be called, were the forerunners of modern banknotes.

Goldsmiths soon realized that people tended to deposit more money than they withdrew, and that the difference could be lent out temporarily to borrowers who agreed to repay the money with interest. Storing gold and other valuables, lending money, and other services (such as exchanging foreign coins) proved to be so lucrative that by the mid-1600s, some goldsmiths had gotten out of the goldsmithing business altogether, focusing exclusively on financial services. They were the first modern bankers.

## MAKING CHANGE

At first each promissory note was unique and read something like, "John Cooper has deposited 20 pounds, 6 shillings, and 10 pence and promises to pay any debts he incurs out of these funds." But by the late 1600s, the volume of transactions had increased over the years and goldsmith bankers found that it was much easier to issue standardized notes in nice round amounts like £100, £50, £20, £10, £5, and £1. So instead of getting one note for exactly 20 pounds, 6 shillings, and 10 pence, John Cooper would get one note for 20 pounds, another for 5 shillings, another for 1 shilling, and would probably have to carry the 10 pence (similar to a dime) in cash.

These standardized "banknotes" were made payable to the bearer and no longer required the traveler to endorse it with his signature. This made banknotes more convenient. But if you wanted the security of a signature, there was another new invention: checks.

## PASS IT ON

Standardized banknotes were used as money, but they were still thought of as receipts, having no intrinsic value in themselves. Merchants accepted the notes as payment and then went to the bank, claimed the gold, and brought it home for safekeeping.

But what happened when *this* person wanted to take a trip? He had to gather up his gold and trudge right back to the bank and exchange it for banknotes all over again. Why even bother? As people came to trust the banknotes more and more, they stopped redeeming them for gold. They just traded the banknotes. A single banknote might pass from person to person to person for months or even years before being redeemed for gold.

There would be some more fine-tuning to produce the bills we use today (that story is in *Uncle John's Absolutely Absorbing Bathroom Reader*), but for all intents and purposes...paper currency had arrived.

## FOOTNOTE

So you can take paper money down to your local bank or to the U.S. Treasury and redeem it for gold, right?

Wrong. At one time, the U.S. government pegged the value of a dollar to a fixed amount of gold (the gold standard). In 1933, for example, the value of $1 was set at exactly 1/35 of one ounce of gold. But that year the federal government began easing away from the gold standard, in the hope that it might help end the Great Depression (it didn't). The government continued to define the value of the dollar in terms of gold but outlawed the circulation of gold coins. Until 1933 there were six denominations of U.S. gold coins: $1, $2.50 (quarter eagle), $3, $5 (half eagle), $10 (eagle), and $20 (double eagle).

In 1971 the government took another step away from the gold standard when it stopped the free exchange of U.S. gold for foreign-owned U.S. dollars, which was depleting U.S. gold reserves.

Finally, in 1978, Congress removed the dollar from the gold standard entirely. You can still *buy* gold with dollars, but you can't *redeem* dollars for gold. The amount of gold that a single dollar can buy changes all the time, and that's true of all the major currencies of the world. Governments today don't want their economies directly tied to the price of any commodity—including gold.

**Life expectancy for men in the U.S.: In 1900, 46.6 years; in 2000, 72.7 years....**

# SAM'S BRAINTEASERS

*BRI members are always asking for more of these tricky questions. We aim to please. Think you can figure them out?* *(Answers on page 747.)*

**1.** Mr. Red, Mr. White, and Mr. Blue met at a coffee shop. One man was wearing a red suit, one a white suit, and the other a blue suit. After a short while, Mr. White exclaimed, "Why, I just noticed that none of us is dressed in the same color as his own last name."

"Really?" remarked the man in the red suit. "So?"

Can you figure out what color suit each man is wearing?

**2.** What do the following words have in common? (It's really not that difficult if you chip away at them for a while.)

*Sheath Pirate Ashamed Brandy*

**3.** Mr. Tidball purchased two clocks from Gordo's Repair Shop and set them at the same time. He soon discovered, however, that one clock was two minutes slow per hour and the other was one minute fast per hour. The next time Tidball looked, one clock was exactly an hour ahead of the other. How long had it been since he last set the clocks?

**4.** Uncle John's cousin, "Bozo" Newman, was about to board a city bus with his newly purchased, five-foot-long novelty toothbrush, when the bus driver informed him of a city ordinance prohibiting packages more than four feet tall. Bozo only had enough money to take the bus home so he tried returning the toothbrush—but the store wouldn't take returns. Five minutes later, Bozo was on the bus riding home…with the big toothbrush in one piece.

How'd he do it?

**5.** Uncle John was in the "reading room" when he came across a word puzzle in the daily newspaper. After some active thinking, he solved it. Can you? It read, "Which is the odd word out and why?" Here's the word list:

*Brush Taste Shampoo Stench Flush Wash Seat*

**…Life expectancy for women in the U.S.: In 1900, 48.7 years; in 2000, 76.1 years.**

**6.** What's the closest relation the son of your father's brother's sister-in-law could be to you?

**7.** A long time ago in a faraway land, there lived a queen called Bubbles and her gorgeous daughter, Princess Porcelain. The princess wished to be married, but Queen Bubbles would not allow it—she never wanted Porcelain to leave the throne room.

So Bubbles devised a scheme to rid the palace of suitors. All a suitor had to do to win Porcelain's hand was to draw a piece of paper from a golden bowl. But there was a catch: there were two pieces of paper in the bowl. One said "My Child," resulting in marriage to the princess, while the other said "The Snakes," which meant the suitor would be thrown into a pit of venomous snakes, never to be seen again. Somehow, the suitors always seemed to end up in the snake pit.

One day a handsome knight named Sir Flushalot came along and Porcelain fell head over heels for him. The princess pulled him aside and whispered, "I think my mother is a cheat. I believe both pieces of paper say 'The Snakes.'" Flushalot assessed the situation and said, "Fear not—I've got a plan." Aware that he cannot expose the queen as a cheater, how does Sir Flushalot win Princess Porcelain's hand in marriage?

*   *   *

## ANOTHER LUCKY FIND

**The Find:** A Victorian masterpiece painting

**Where It Was Found:** In a Colorado building

**The Story:** In the 1960s, a man (he refused to release his name to the media) bought a building in Colorado. Inside the building was a painting, signed "Waterhouse," depicting a sultry Cleopatra reclining on a chair. He thought it was "pretty and rather sexy." Nearly 40 years later he heard about a "Waterhouse" being sold for millions of dollars, so he called Christie's and sent a photo. Christie's senior director, Martin Beisly, immediately flew from London to Colorado and confirmed that it was a painting that hadn't been heard of since 1889. "Scholars knew about the picture," he said, "but had no idea where it was and even thought it might have been destroyed." Estimated worth: $900,000.

**Toys "R" Us was originally called the "Children's Supermart."**

# WISE WOMEN

*Some thoughtful observations from the stronger sex.*

"You can have it all. You just can't have it all at once."

**—Oprah Winfrey**

"When I stand before God at the end of my life, I would hope that I would not have a single bit of talent left and could say, 'I used everything you gave me.'"

**—Erma Bombeck**

"The only time a woman really succeeds in changing a man is when he's a baby."

**—Natalie Wood**

"If you think you can, you can. And if you think you can't, you're right."

**—Mary Kay Ash**

"You may be disappointed if you fail, but you are doomed if you don't try."

**—Beverly Sills**

"I have become my own version of an optimist. If I can't make it through one door, I'll go through another door—or I'll make a door. Something terrific will come no matter what."

**—Joan Rivers**

"If you don't like something, change it. If you can't change it, change your attitude. Don't complain."

**—Maya Angelou**

"You gain strength, courage, and confidence by every experience in which you really stop to look fear in the face."

**—Eleanor Roosevelt**

"The greater part of our happiness or misery depends on our dispositions and not our circumstances."

**—Martha Washington**

"When you get into a tight place and everything goes against you till it seems you could not hold on a minute longer, never give up then—for that is just the place and time that the tide will turn."

**—Harriet Beecher Stowe**

"Difficult times have helped me to understand better than before, how infinitely rich and beautiful life is in every way, and that so many things that one goes worrying about are of no importance whatsoever."

**—Isak Dinesen**

**Sheryl Crow's two front teeth are fake—the real ones got knocked out when she tripped onstage.**

# (B)AD PROMOTIONS

*When a company comes up with a sales promotion, the idea is to attract potential customers and make a bunch of money. But sometimes it doesn't work out that way.*

**Brilliant Marketing Idea:** In 1994 Prudential Securities was trying to improve its image, tarnished by allegations that agents had been lying to customers for years. Their $20 million campaign started with a "straight talk" newspaper ad highlighting the honesty of their agents. A full-page photo of real-life Prudential broker Susan B. Gooding featured the caption, "From where I sit, preserving integrity is not a lost art." Underscoring her integrity, the ad finished with, "One of my clients is my father."

**Oops!** Gooding's father had been dead since 1991 and, the *Chicago Sun Times* reported, he was never her client. Prudential claimed it was an honest mistake and pulled the ads immediately.

**Brilliant Marketing Idea:** In January 2002, CNN ran a TV commercial for news anchor Paula Zahn's new show, *American Morning*. In it the announcer says, "Where can you find a morning news anchor who's provocative, super-smart, and oh, yeah, just a little sexy? CNN...Yeah, CNN." And as he says "sexy," the word appears on the screen—and the sound of a zipper opening can be heard.

**Oops!** CNN was immediately slammed by rival networks for using sex to sell a news broadcast. "It was a major blunder by our promotions department," said Chairman Walter Isaacson. " The spot was pulled after being shown only twice.

**Brilliant Marketing Idea:** In March 2003, the Hong Kong Tourism Board put their new slogan—"Hong Kong Will Take Your Breath Away"—in ads in several major publications in England.

**Oops!** In a bizarre coincidence, just as the ad campaign began, Hong Kong was hit by an outbreak of SARS (*Severe Acute Respiratory Syndrome*). The outbreak led to a rapid decline in tourism, severely damaging the economy. "As soon as the outbreak began," said a Tourism Board spokesman, "we realized it would be pretty embarrassing, but it was too late to pull the ads." What was so embarrassing? One of SARS' main symptoms is shortness of breath.

**The bestselling tie colors in the U.S.: blue and red.**

# TAWK O' DA TOWN

*While looking through the book* New Yawk Tawk *by Robert Hendrickson, we were surprised to find out that many words and phrases in the English language were born in the Empire State.*

**SENT UP THE RIVER.** Slang for "sent to prison." The river is the Hudson and the prison is Sing Sing, which is upriver from New York City.

**DEPARTMENT STORE.** It didn't invent the concept of one store with different departments, but the first store to actually call itself this was H. H. Heyn's Department Store in 1887.

**COCKAMAMIE.** Meaning "worthless" or "absurd," this word may come from the inability of early 20th-century kids in Manhattan's Lower East Side to pronounce *decalcomania*, a cheap picture to be transferred onto wood or china (a decal).

**FLEA MARKET.** It got its name because secondhand items have fleas, right? Guess again. Downtown Manhattan was home to *vallie* (valley) *markets* in Dutch Colonial days. The term was abbreviated to *vlie* (pronounced "flee") *market*, and was eventually anglicized to *flea market*.

**COWBOY.** Sounds like a word from Wyoming, but it was actually the term given to bands of men who rustled cows in New York in the 1800s.

**REUBEN.** This grilled sandwich of corned beef, Swiss cheese, sauerkraut, and Russian dressing on rye bread was invented at Reuben's Delicatessen in Manhattan at the turn of the 20th century.

**ALMIGHTY DOLLAR.** Coined by New Yorker Washington Irving in 1836: "The almighty dollar, that great object of universal devotion throughout the land..."

**PUNK ROCK.** Attributed to *Punk* magazine editor Legs McNeil, describing the 1970s music scene that started in lower Manhattan.

**MULTIMILLIONAIRE.** At his death in 1848, New York fur trader John Jacob Astor was worth $20 million (about $80 billion in today's dollars). The term was first applied to him.

**RUSH HOUR.** First used to describe commuter gridlock on New York streets in 1890.

**OUT IN LEFT FIELD.** Far from the action. *Right* field might be more fitting, because that's where the fewest baseballs go. But at Yankee Stadium, the seats in left field were far away from the biggest player of the day, *right* fielder Babe Ruth.

**PORTERHOUSE STEAK.** Named in 1814 for the New York restaurant that popularized it, Martin Morrison's Porterhouse.

**YUPPIE.** An acronym of "*y*oung *u*rban *p*rofessional." This term comes from New York City in the 1980s. Possibly coined by Jerry Rubin, one of the founders of the 1960s *yippie* movement.

**THREEPEAT.** Coined in 1990 by San Francisco 49ers running back Roger Craig, describing his hopes for a third Super Bowl win the following year. (They didn't threepeat.)

**PUBLIC RELATIONS.** First used by publicity writer Edward Bernays, nephew of Sigmund Freud, for his 1920 wedding announcements in an attempt to make his occupation sound more respectable.

**BUNT.** A baseball term meaning to hit the ball softly. Most likely a corruption of the word *butt* (as in "butting" the ball with the bat). The first known utterance of *bunt* was in 1872 by a player named Pearce on the Brooklyn Atlantics.

**BLAST FROM THE PAST.** Made popular by NYC disc jockey Murray the K in the 1960s, referring to old records.

**KEEPING UP WITH THE JONESES.** Created by New York cartoonist "Pop" Momand in 1913 as the title of a comic strip that showed middle-class people living beyond their means. It was originally going to be called "Keeping Up with the Smiths," but Momand changed it because he thought "Joneses" sounded better.

**HEADLINE.** The first one appeared on the October 27, 1777, edition of the *New York Gazette*.

**SIDEKICK.** New York writer O. Henry first recorded the term in 1904. It was street slang for "buddy." Why? Men's side pants pockets—called *sidekicks*—were the most difficult for pickpockets to reach and therefore reliable, like a trusted friend, always at your side.

# TRUE GLUE

*It's been used on elephant tusks, racing cars, space shuttles—even human wounds. It's* cyanoacrylate, *better known as superglue. Here's its story.*

## ACCIDENTAL INVENTION

Dr. Harry Coover was a researcher working for Kodak Research Labs in 1942. While trying to develop a clear plastic gun sight for use during World War II, he discovered something else: cyanoacrylates. But it was no good for what he needed—it stuck to everything, which created a huge mess. So he set it aside and moved on.

Nine years later Dr. Coover was working at the Tennessee Eastman Chemical Company. This time he was trying to find a tough polymer for jet canopies. While experimenting, he remembered the cyanoacrylate and wondered about its ability to refract light. A fellow researcher named (ironically) Dr. Fred Joyner spread a film of ethyl cyanoacrylate between two prisms of a refractometer. Not only did it not refract light, but it once again left a big sticky mess. And no matter how hard they tried, the two scientists couldn't pry the expensive prisms apart.

Embarrassed, they sheepishly told company execs about the ruined equipment. But instead of ridicule, they received praise—and orders to begin developing the adhesive for commercial use. Eastman Compound #910 hit the market in 1958, but initial sales were low. Why? People didn't believe Eastman's claims about the glue. So to prove its worth, Dr. Coover appeared on the TV quiz show *I've Got a Secret* and lifted host Gary Moore completely off the floor...using only a single drop of the glue.

## HOW IT WORKS

Here's how it works: Cyanoacrylate, CA for short, is a highly reactive liquid, and when left to its own devices will quickly solidify. The addition of an acid stabilizer prevents the CA from reacting and keeps it in a liquid state. When the acid stabilizer comes into contact with a catalyst, its stabilizing effect is neutralized. This allows the CA molecules to react with each other, forming long polymer chains. The catalyst for the acid stabilizer is hydroxyl ions, which are conveniently located in every molecule of water. So do you have to mix CA with water? No. Most surfaces already have a tiny bit of water on them. If they don't, there are always minuscule amounts of water available in the air. The water acts like a trigger, allowing the molecular structure of the CA to change. The molecules join up like a long series of popper beads. What was a thin liquid becomes a hard mass of molecular spaghetti noodles, bonding to whatever it contacts.

## HELPFUL TIPS FOR USING SUPERGLUE

• Make sure the parts being glued don't move *at all* during the formation of the chains. If so, the chain will break and the glue won't hold.

• A little dab'll do ya. Superglue bonds best when it's used at the rate of one drop per square inch. More than that requires a much longer bonding period, which may result in a weaker bond.

• If you're gluing two flat surfaces together, rough them up with sandpaper first. That'll give the glue more surface area to bond to. But make sure you blow off any dusty residue first.

• Glued your fingers together? Use nail polish remover. Don't have any? Try warm soapy water and a little patience. Your sweat and natural skin oils will soon loosen the bond.

## STICKY FACTS

• Superglue is so strong that a single square-inch bond can lift a ton of weight.

• Why doesn't superglue stick to the bottle? Because it needs moisture to set and there is no moisture in the bottle.

• What's the difference between superglue and Krazy Glue? Nothing. Krazy Glue is just one of many brands available. It first went on sale in 1973. Some other brands: SuperBonder, Permabond, Pronto, Black Max, Alpha Ace, and (in Mexico) Kola Loka.

• Cyanoacrylate products are a $325 million-a-year industry. Approximately 90% of U.S. homes have at least one tube.

• During the Vietnam War, tubes of superglue were put in U.S. soldiers' first-aid kits to help seal wounds. Special kinds of superglue are now used in hospitals worldwide, reducing the need for sutures, stitches, and staples. (It doesn't work on deep wounds or on wounds

**The odds of someone winning a lottery twice in four months is about 1 in 17 trillion....**

where the skin does a lot of stretching, such as over joints.)

• Superglue is now used in forensic detection. When investigators open a foil packet of ethyl-gel cyanoacrylate, the fumes settle on skin oils left behind in human fingerprints, turning the invisible smears into visible marks.

## STICKY SITUATIONS

• **Lovers use it.** An ex-con who violated his parole glued himself to his girlfriend so the police couldn't arrest him. An Algerian woman tried the same trick with her husband to keep him from being deported. Neither attempt was successful.

• **Pranksters use it.** An Atlantic City man sued a casino after he got stuck to a glue-smeared toilet seat and had to waddle through the casino for help.

• **Veterinarians use it.** A tortoise that cracked its shell falling from a second-floor window was successfully glued back together. Other superglued animals: racing pigeons have had their feathers glued together for better aerodynamics, fish have had their fins reattached, and horses have had their split hooves mended.

• **Protestors use it.** A man protesting tax laws that left people penniless in Bristol, England, took matters into his own hands. After more than 200 attempts to contact the Inland Revenue helpline, he went down to the local tax office armed with a tube of superglue. When they wouldn't help him, he glued his hand to a desk, vowing to stay attached until he got some answers. After finally getting unstuck, he was allowed to voice his views on a local radio station.

• **Fishers use it.** The winner of the "How Krazy Glue Saved the Day Contest" was a woman who fell asleep while fishing in a small rowboat on a Minnesota lake. More than a mile from shore, she was awakened when her feet started getting wet. Frantically, she mopped up the water with an old shirt, but it was still coming in through a small leak in the bottom of the boat. So she took a tube of Krazy Glue out of her tackle box (she used it to make fishing lures), cut a thick piece of leather from her boot, and glued the leather over the leak. "The leak stopped and I kept on fishing," she said. "By the way," she added, "I can't swim—Krazy Glue saved my life!"

# REVENGE!

*We all have fantasies of getting even with people who annoy us…but we seldom actually go through with them. Here are some examples of what could happen if we did.*

## REVENGE OF THE PHONE CLERK

**Background:** In early 2002, New Zealander James Storrie called New Zealand Telecom Corporation to complain that his cell phone had been disconnected. When the representative informed him that the phone had been reported stolen, Storrie insisted that he still had the phone and that he had not reported its theft. The mistake was cleared up, but the representative (identity unknown) was apparently offended by Storrie's attitude.

**Revenge Gone Wild!** When Storrie received his next phone bill, he found that he'd been charged an extra $140. What for? The explanation was printed right on the bill: "penalty for being an arrogant bastard." N.Z. Telecom apologized profusely, offered Storrie some undisclosed financial compensation, and promised to investigate the vengeful billing.

## REVENGE OF THE BAD WAITER

**Background:** One evening in June 2003, Wayne and Darlene Keller of Corona, California, took their two children to a Sizzler's restaurant. Mrs. Keller requested vegetables with her dinner, instead of potatoes. According to the family, the waiter, Jonathan Voletner, rudely told her that she had to choose between French fries or a baked potato. "When I told him my wife can't eat potatoes," said Mr. Keller, "he brought back a really small salad, practically threw it at her, and told her to go get the dressing herself." After the meal, the Kellers left—and they didn't leave a tip.

**Revenge Gone Wild!** Voletner had his girlfriend follow the Kellers home to get their address. When he got off work, he, his girlfriend, and his brother went to the Keller home, waited until 1 a.m., and then doused their house, yard, and mailbox with a gallon of maple syrup, smashed eggs, toilet paper, duct tape, and plastic wrap. They might have gotten away with it, but in a state of heightened stupidity, Voletner rang the doorbell. Then he hid in the bushes and waited to see their reaction. Their reaction: They called the police.

Officers found Voletner in the bushes and his co-conspirators in a nearby car. When they presented the suspects to the Kellers, Mrs. Keller said, "Oh my God! It's the waiter from the restaurant!" They were all charged with vandalism, with Voletner receiving an extra charge of child endangerment because his girlfriend was a minor. He was also fired by Sizzler's. "The company doesn't allow this sort of thing," the manager said.

## REVENGE OF THE POSTMASTER

**Background:** On October 17, 2001, 62-year-old James Beal was fired from his job as relief postmaster in Empire, Michigan.

**Revenge Gone Wild!** The next day, Beal showed up at the post office carrying two five-gallon buckets full of worms, grubs, and porcupine poop. He proceeded to splatter several of his former co-workers with the putrid concoction, completely saturating two of them. He was on his way to his car for another bucket when police arrived. For his bizarre act of revenge, he was charged with four counts of assaulting a federal worker. "I let my anger sort of overrule my judgments," Beal told the court. He was sentenced to 18 months in federal prison.

## REVENGE OF THE NON-WITNESS

**Background:** Jane White was upset that Jehovah's Witnesses had come to her house once a month, every month, for 12 years. At first, she politely told them that she wasn't interested. Finally, after a visit on a Saturday in January 2002, she had had enough.

**Revenge Gone Wild!** White went to the group's local Kingdom Hall in Peacehaven, England, the following morning, carefully timing her visit for the middle of the Sunday service. She banged on the door loudly, again and again, until someone answered, and then proceeded to offer members of the congregation religious literature that she had brought along. "I tried to hand out free magazines just like the Jehovah's Witnesses hand out," she said. "Nobody seemed to want them, though." She continued her "mission" for 30 minutes until the police showed up and asked her to leave.

## REVENGE OF THE SPAM HATERS

**Background:** In November 2002, *Detroit Free Press* columnist

Mike Wendland wrote a story about a man named Alan Ralsky. Ralsky had become a multimillionaire through marketing spam on the Internet. How much spam? His company sent up to 250 million e-mails a day. The story told readers about Ralsky's new 8,000-square-foot, $740,000 home. The spammer bragged that one entire wing of the house was paid for by a single weight-loss e-mail.

**Revenge Gone Wild!** A group of spam haters decided to give Ralsky a dose of his own medicine. They posted his home address on hundreds of websites, and Ralsky started getting tons—literally—of junk mail. Then they posted his e-mail address and his phone number, and the mega-junkmailer got inundated with the very thing he had made his millions from—spam. And, no surprise: *He was annoyed!* Ralsky later complained, "They've signed me up for every advertising campaign and mailing list there is. These people are out of their minds! They're harassing me!"

*　　*　　*

## THE WORLD'S LARGEST...

• Roanoke, Virginia, has the "World's Largest Man-Made Illuminated Star," an 88-foot electric wonder set atop a mountain.

• Artichoke-growing region Castroville, California, proudly trumpets its "World's Largest Artichoke."

• Vegreville, Alberta, is home to the world's largest egg sculpture, a Ukranian Easter egg that stands 25.7 feet tall.

• The owner of a Magnolia, Arkansas, grill store constructed a working 70-foot "World's Largest Charcoal Grill."

• "The World's Largest Wind Chime" has been removed from Lakeside, California, because locals said it was too loud.

• Though many towns claim they're home to the "World's Largest Peanut," only Ashburn, Georgia, has constructed a towering 10-foot peanut atop a 15-foot brick stack, leaving the lesser peanuts of Pearsall and Floresville, Texas; Durant, Oklahoma; and Dothan, Alabama, behind. Those wishing for an all-peanut day of tourism can see the Ashburn peanut and then check out the nearby big-toothed 13-foot "Jimmy Carter Peanut" of Plains, Georgia.

**The black widow spider's bite has a 1% fatality rate.**

# GO DIRECTLY TO JAIL

*Four stories of dumb crooks who saved us all a lot of trouble.*

## SELF HELP

"A 22-year-old Green Bay man led police on a chase that moved as slowly as 20 mph and ended in the Brown County Jail's parking lot. The man parked his pickup in the jail's lot, smoked a cigarette, got out of the truck, and lay face-down on the ground to be arrested, police said. He told the officers he knew he was drunk and was going to be sent to jail, so he just drove himself there."

—***Milwaukee Journal Sentinel***

## SUPPLY-SIDE ECONOMICS

"Sylvain Boucher of Quebec was spotted by prison guards standing between the prison wall and an outer fence. Assuming he was trying to escape, they grabbed him, but soon discovered he was not an inmate…and he was carrying a large amount of illegal drugs. Boucher was trying to break *in*, thinking the prison would be a good market for his drugs. He'll get to find out. Before he had the supply, but no market. Now he has the market, but no supply."

—***Moreland's Bozo of the Day***

## IS THIS WHY THEY CALL IT "DOPE"?

"Philomena A. Palestini, 18, of Portland, Maine, walked into Salem District Court to face one criminal charge, but walked out in handcuffs with two. Court Security Officer Ronald Lesperance found a hypodermic needle and two small bags of what police believe is heroin in her purse as she walked through the security checkpoint. 'This doesn't happen very often,' said Lesperance."

—***Eagle Tribune***

## THE "IN" CROWD

"A man who tried to break *into* a Rideau correctional center with drugs and tobacco was sentenced to two years in prison yesterday. Shane Walker, 23, was believed to be bringing drugs to a jailed friend last week when he was foiled by corrections workers who heard bolt-cutters snapping the wire fence and apprehended him."

—***The National Post***

**Only country in the Middle East without a desert: Lebanon.**

# MOON SCAM?

*Is nothing sacred? Those conspiracy nuts won't leave anything alone. They attack our most sacred institutions. (On the other hand, they could be right.)*

**MOONSTRUCK**

On July 20, 1969, millions of television viewers around the world watched as Neil Armstrong stepped down from a lunar landing module onto the surface of the moon and spoke the now famous words, "That's one small step for man, one giant leap for mankind."

In western Australia a woman named Una Ronald watched. She saw the images of the moon landing in the early hours of the morning. But as the camera showed Armstrong's fellow astronaut Edwin "Buzz" Aldrin demonstrating his moon walk technique, Ronald swears she saw something else. She swears she clearly saw a Coke bottle kicked into the picture from the side. The scene was edited out of later broadcasts, she says.

Was this alleged "blooper" evidence of a giant hoax?

**MISSION IMPOSSIBLE**

If Una Ronald was the first to suspect the moon landing wasn't quite what it appeared to be, she certainly wasn't the last. And there was a lot more than just the Coke bottle to excite skeptics.

Ten years before Apollo 11 supposedly went to the moon, Bill Kaysing was head of technical publications at Rocketdyne Systems, a division of Boeing that still makes rocket engines for the space program. In his book *We Never Went to the Moon,* Kaysing says that in 1959 Rocketdyne estimated that there was about a 14% chance we could safely send a man to the moon and back. According to Kaysing, there is no way the space program could have advanced enough in the following 10 years to send the three Apollo 11 astronauts to the moon, followed by five more moon landings in the next three years.

NASA experts recently admitted that they currently do not have the capability of sending manned missions to the moon. So how could they have done it more than 30 years ago? Even simulations these days require powerful computers, but the computer onboard the *Columbia* had a capacity smaller than many of today's handheld calculators.

Kaysing and others think they know the answer, and cite a number of anomalies that lead them to conclude that the Apollo missions were faked:

4 **The Fluttering Flag:** In 1990 a New Jersey man named Ralph Rene was reviewing old footage of the moon landing. As he watched the American flag fluttering in the airless atmosphere of the moon, it suddenly dawned on him: how can there be a breeze if there is no air?

Rene's suspicions led him to research inconsistencies in the Moon landing story, and to publish a book called *NASA Mooned America*. The fluttering flag was just the beginning.

4 **Phony Photos:** A close look at the thousands of excellent still photos from the moon landings reveal some very odd features. For one thing, they are a little too good. The astronauts seem to be well lit on all sides, regardless of where the sunlight is coming from, almost as if there were some artificial light source.

• Defenders claim that light was reflected from the lunar surface, bouncing back to light the shadow side of the astronauts. Oddly, that same reflective light does not illuminate the dark side of lunar rocks, which are even closer to the ground.

• Shadows seem to fall in different directions and look to be different lengths even for objects of a similar height, such as the two astronauts. This leads some to conclude that there were multiple light sources—possibly some man-made ones.

• Even when everything else is in shadow, the American flag and the words "United States" are always well lit, and sometimes seem to be in a spotlight. Was someone trying to squeeze extra PR value out of fake photos?

4 **Starlight, Star Bright:** Some skeptics cite the absence of stars in photos of the lunar sky as evidence that they were not taken on the moon. After all, in the dark sky of the moon with no atmosphere, stars should be clearly visible.

• Experts agree—to the naked eye, stars in the sky of the moon *should* be magnificently clear. But, the experts say, *stars* wouldn't show up on film that was set to expose the much brighter lunar surface.

• On the other hand, why were there no pictures taken of the stars in the lunar sky? Surely how the stars look from the moon would have interested many people. Was it because astronomers could spot the fake photos too easily?

4 **Where's the Dust?** One of the most memorable images NASA released from Apollo 11 was the imprint of Buzz Aldrin's boot in the lunar dust. But the lunar landing module apparently had less of an impact on the moon's surface.

• Moon photos show no visible disturbance from the high-powered thrust engines the *Eagle* landing module used to land, nor is there any dust in the landing pads.

• If the *Eagle* blew away all the dust, as some speculate, how did Aldrin make such a nice footprint?

4 **Deadly Radiation:** In a recent press conference, a NASA spokesman said that radiation is one of the biggest obstacles to space travel. Wouldn't it have been a problem 30 years ago?

• Two doughnut-shaped rings of charged particles, called the Van Allen Belts, encircle the Earth. To get to the moon, astronauts would have had to pass through the belts, exposing themselves to deadly radiation unless they had a lot more protection than the thin shield the Apollo spacecraft provided.

• Once outside the radiation belts and Earth's protective atmosphere, astronauts would have been exposed to solar radiation. Expert opinions differ as to whether this exposure would have been life-threatening. But inexplicably, *not one* of the astronauts from the seven lunar missions got cancer, a well-known result of overexposure to radiation.

• Even more sensitive to radiation is photographic film. On all those beautiful moon photos there is absolutely no sign of radiation damage. Why not?

4 **Follow the Bouncing Astronaut:** What about the movie footage showing the astronauts demonstrating the moon's low gravity by bouncing around the surface? Skeptics say that could have easily been faked. In the moon's gravity—a sixth of Earth's—the astronauts should have been able to leap 10 feet in the air. But they didn't.

• In fact, in the movie footage they don't get any farther off the

**There are more than 90 different scientific theories on how dinosaurs became extinct.**

ground than they could on Earth.

• And if it looks like they are moving in slow motion, that is because they are—half speed to be exact. Bill Wood, a scientist who worked for the NASA subcontractor responsible for recording Apollo signals and sending them to NASA headquarters in Houston, explains that the original film footage, shot at 30 frames per second, was transferred to video, which runs at 60 frames per second. If the film of the astronauts walking on the surface of the moon is viewed at regular speed their movements look remarkably normal.

4 **Moon Rocks:** Besides the photos and film footage, the only physical evidence we have that astronauts actually went to the moon is lunar rocks.

• NASA points to the fact that scientists around the world have examined the rocks brought back by the Apollo missions and have no doubt that they originated on the moon. But the moon isn't the only place to find such rocks.

• In the ice of Antarctica, scientists have found remnants of lunar rocks blasted off the moon by meteoric impacts. Numerous expeditions have explored the continent for rock samples from the moon, Mars, and comets.

• In 1967, two years before the Apollo mission, such a group visited Antarctica, including ex-Nazi rocket scientist Wernher von Braun, by then working for NASA. Why would a rocket scientist be sent to look for rocks? Was he collecting fake evidence?

## WHY FAKE IT?

These anomalies in the "information" given to the public about the Apollo moon missions have caused many to question whether we really did send anyone to the moon. But if the moon landings were faked, how was it done, and why?

The why is fairly easy to understand. The 1960s were the height of the Cold War. The Space Race was on, and the Soviet Union had already beat the United States by launching the first satellite to orbit Earth, the first man—and woman—in space, and the first space walk, among other important achievements. The United States was clearly behind. In 1961 President Kennedy issued a challenge: "I believe this nation should commit itself to achieving a goal, before this decade is out, of sending a man to the moon and

**Mae West never kissed her leading men on screen.**

returning him safely to the Earth."

The Apollo program was born, and five months before the end of the decade, NASA displayed pictures of Americans on the moon, proof that we had beat the Russians to the most important prize. We won. Mission accomplished.

But was it accomplished by actually sending men to the moon, or just making it look that way?

**A Funny Thing Happened on the Way to the Moon**

Investigative journalist Bart Sibrel claims to have found a mislabeled NASA film showing multiple "takes" of a scene shown to the public as part of the "live" broadcast of the Apollo 11 flight. In the footage the astronauts appear to be rehearsing the lines the public heard. Sibrel claims to have spent half a million dollars investigating the moon landings, and produced a video called *A Funny Thing Happened on the Way to the Moon.*

In 2002 Sibrel, backed by a Japanese film crew, confronted Buzz Aldrin outside a Beverly Hills hotel and challenged him to swear on a Bible that he had really gone to the moon. Aldrin responded by punching Sibrel in the face.

And what about those marvelous still photos? Many believe they were staged, perhaps in a secret location in Nevada, or even in a giant geodesic soundstage in Australia. Either way it would have been much easier to manipulate the lighting to get the results shown in the moon landing photos.

Would such a monstrous hoax have been easy to pull off? Certainly not. But to some people it seems more possible—and cheaper—than actually sending someone to the moon and back. Consider these statistics: Of the seven manned missions to the Moon, only Apollo 13 had trouble, which is an 86% success rate. In the years since, 25 unmanned craft have been sent to Mars. Only seven have succeeded—a 28% success rate. Which figure seems more realistic?

## JUST WHEN YOU THOUGHT IT WAS SAFE

Before you get too comfortable with the idea that the government created a huge hoax because we couldn't have possibly gone to the moon, keep in mind that there are also people who believe the film *is* fake, but that we actually *did* go to the moon. So why fake it? To cover up what we *really* found there. But that's another story…

# NOT-SO-WISEGUYS

*When people enter the federal government's Witness Protection Program they're supposed to hide, right?*

**WISEGUY:** Henry Hill, a member of New York's Lucchese crime family and participant in the $5.8 million Lufthansa heist from New York's Kennedy Airport in 1978, the largest cash theft in U.S. history

**IN THE PROGRAM:** The Witness Protection Program relocated him to Redmond, Washington, in 1980, and Hill, who'd changed his name to Martin Lewis, was supposed to keep a low profile and stay out of trouble. He wasn't very good at either—in 1985 he and writer Nicholas Pileggi turned his mob exploits into the bestselling book *Wiseguy*, which became the hit movie *Goodfellas*.

**WHAT HAPPENED:** When the book became a bestseller, "Martin Lewis" couldn't resist telling friends and neighbors who he really was. Even worse, he reverted to his life of crime. Since 1980 Hill has racked up a string of arrests for crimes ranging from drunk driving to burglary and assault. In 1987 he tried to sell a pound of cocaine to two undercover Drug Enforcement officers, which got him thrown out of the Witness Protection Program for good.

"Henry couldn't go straight," says Deputy Marshal Bud McPherson. "He loved being a wiseguy. He didn't want to be anything else."

**WISEGUY:** Aladena "Jimmy the Weasel" Fratianno, Mafia hit man and acting head of the Los Angeles mob. When he entered the Witness Protection Program in 1977, Fratianno was the highest-ranking mobster ever to turn informer.

**IN THE PROGRAM:** Fratianno has another claim to fame: he is also the highest-paid witness in the history of the program. Between 1977 and 1987, he managed to get the feds to pay for his auto insurance, gas, telephone bills, real-estate taxes, monthly checks to his mother-in-law, and his wife's facelift and breast implants.

**WHAT HAPPENED:** The Justice Department feared the payments made the program look "like a pension fund for aging mobsters," so he was thrown out of the program in 1987. But by that time, Fratianno had already soaked U.S. taxpayers for an estimated $951,326. "He was an expert at manipulating the system," McPherson said. Fratianno died in 1993.

**WISEGUY:** James Cardinali, a five-time murderer who testified against Gambino crime boss John Gotti at his 1987 murder trial. Gotti, nicknamed the "Teflon Don," beat the rap, but Cardinali still got to enter the Witness Protection Program after serving a reduced sentence for his own crimes. After his release, federal marshals gave him a new identity and relocated him to Oklahoma.

**IN THE PROGRAM:** Witnesses who get new identities aren't supposed to tell anyone who they really are, and when Cardinali slipped up and told his girlfriend in 1989, the program put him on a bus to Albuquerque, New Mexico, and told him to get lost.

But Cardinali wouldn't leave quietly. When he got to Albuquerque, he made signs that read "Mob Star Witness" and "Marked to Die by the Justice Department." Then, wearing the signs as a sandwich board, he marched back and forth in front of the federal courthouse, telling reporters he would continue his protest until he was let back into the program or murdered by mobsters, whichever came first. "If I get killed," Cardinali told reporters. "I want everybody to see what they do to you."

**WHAT HAPPENED:** Cardinali flew to Washington D.C. to appear on CNN's *Larry King Live*. But leaving the state violated his parole, so when he got back to New Mexico he was arrested, taken to jail...and released into the custody of the U.S. Marshals Service. Then he vanished. Did he embarrass the Witness Protection Program into letting him back in? The Marshals Service "will neither confirm nor deny" that he did.

**WISEGUY:** John Patrick Tully, convicted murderer and member of the Campisi crime family of Newark, New Jersey

**IN THE PROGRAM:** Tully served a reduced sentence for murder and entered the Witness Protection Program in the mid-1970s. By the early 1980s, he was living in Austin, Texas, where, as "Jack Johnson," he worked as a hot dog and fajita vendor. (It was a "nostalgic" choice—years earlier, he'd robbed a bank and used the money to buy a hot dog cart.)

Tully's business thrived, but he had repeated run-ins with the police and was arrested numerous times for public intoxication and drunk driving. At some point the police figured out who "Mr. Johnson" really was and then, Tully alleges, they started harassing him.

**WHAT HAPPENED:** Tully fought back by publicly revealing his true identity. He wrapped himself—literally—in the American flag, and, standing on the steps of city hall with his seven-page rap sheet in one hand and a beer in the other, announced his entry in the 1991 race for mayor. His reasons for running: 1) As a reformed criminal he was a better candidate than typical politicians who "get into office and *then* start crooking," and 2) "If the police are going to hit me, they're going to have to hit me in the limelight."

Tully actually won 496 votes…but lost the race.

**WISEGUY:** Joseph "Joe Dogs" Iannuzzi, bookie, loan shark, and member of New York's Gambino crime family from 1974 to 1982

**IN THE PROGRAM:** Joe Dogs had a reputation for being an excellent cook—even in the mob. After turning State's evidence in 1982, he supported himself by opening a bagel shop in Florida.

Then in 1993 he wrote *The Mafia Cookbook*. How can someone in the Program promote a book? They can't—witnesses are forbidden from contact with the media, and Joe Dogs had to pass on several offers to appear on TV. But he was a huge fan of David Letterman, so when he was asked to appear on *The Late Show*, he agreed, even though he risked being thrown out of the program. Why would he take the chance? "Dave was my idol," Iannuzzi explained.

**WHAT HAPPENED:** It finally dawned on somebody at *The Late Show* that bringing a man marked for death by the mob into New York City and putting him on TV with Dave in front of a live studio audience might not be such a good idea. At the last minute, just as Joe Dogs was getting ready to cook Veal Marsala, show staffers told him his segment had been cancelled.

Iannuzzi was furious—according to some accounts he even threatened to "whack" Letterman. And although he never actually went on the show, the U.S. Marshals Service kicked him out of the Witness Protection Program anyway.

"What am I going to do now? Well," he told reporters, "I can always cook."

**Duh! A hijacker took over a public bus in Argentina—and insisted on being driven to Cuba.**

# BEHIND THE HITS

*Ever wonder what inspired some of your favorite songs? Here are a few inside stories about popular tunes.*

**The Artist:** Santana

**The Song:** "Smooth" (1999)

**The Story:** One night in 1997, Rob Thomas, lead singer of Matchbox 20, had a dream: he was on the cover of *Rolling Stone* shouting something into the ear of one of his musical heroes, guitar legend Carlos Santana. A month later, Thomas was invited by R&B composer Itaal Shur to contribute a song to Santana's next album. Thomas was thrilled.

They wrote a song (inspired by Thomas's wife, Marisol Maldonado) and sent a rough demo tape to Santana. Thomas recommended English pop star George Michael for the vocals, but Santana liked what he heard on the demo, "I believe it when he sings." So Thomas flew to San Francisco to meet his idol and record the song.

"Smooth" was Santana's first #1 song ever (it was on top for 12 weeks in 1999), was his first to reach the top 10 in 30 years, earned Thomas BMI's Pop Songwriter of the Year award, and won nine Grammies. (Santana made the cover of Rolling Stone in March, 2000...without Thomas.)

**The Artist:** The Charlie Daniels Band

**The Song:** "The Devil Went Down to Georgia" (1979)

**The Story:** Starting his music career in 1959, virtuoso fiddle player Charlie Daniels had enjoyed moderate success as a session musician and songwriter. He was known in music circles but the Charlie Daniels Band couldn't get much radio airplay—he was too country for rock stations, too hard rock for country stations.

In 1979 Daniels decided to write the "ultimate fiddle song." While brainstorming for ideas, he remembered a Stephen Vincent Benet poem he had learned in school called "The Mountain Whippoorwill." In the poem, Hill-Billy Jim enters a fiddlin' contest and then "all hell breaks loose in Georgia."

Daniels modernized the words, but went into the studio with-

**Mark Twain invented a Trivial Pursuit–like game called "Mark Twain's Memory-Builder."**

out any music. Armed with only a poem about a boy who beats the devil, Daniels and his band did something just as improbable—they created a hit right there on the spot.

The record company knew it, too, and released it as a single. Result: The song was a hit on country *and* rock radio stations, turned Daniels into a star, and was named the Country Music Association's Single of the Year for 1979.

**The Artist:** Tag Team

**The Song:** "Whoomp! (There it is)" (1993)

**The Story:** Cecil "DC, the Brain Supreme" Glenn was a DJ at Atlanta's Magic City nightclub. He dreamed of producing a hit rap record. One night he heard another DJ chanting into the mike, "Whoomp! There it is!" When Glenn saw the nightclub crowd's unified response, he knew that was his hit. So he and his best friend, Steve "Roll'n" Gibson, wrote and recorded a song around the phrase.

The song was a hit at the club, but they couldn't sell it to a major label. So they borrowed $2,500 to press the record themselves and founded a small label called Bellmark Records to distribute it. The song took off immediately, hitting the Billboard Top 10 and has been a staple at sports arenas ever since.

**Close Call:** Another rap group, 95 South, recorded "Whoot, There It Is" and actually released it a month earlier. So why did Tag Team's song hit the big time and not 95 South's? According to *Rolling Stone*'s Tracy Hopkins, "Tag Team's version had more crossover appeal. 95 South's chorus of 'Tell me where the booty at/Whoot, there it is!' was just too raunchy."

**The Artist:** Julia Ward Howe

**The Song:** "Battle Hymn of the Republic" (1862)

**The Story:** At the onset of the Civil War, Howe was riding through the streets of Washington, D.C., with her husband one warm summer night, watching Union troops prepare for battle. One group of men was sitting outside an inn singing a sad folk song that began "John Brown's body lies a-mouldering in the grave." Howe couldn't sleep that night. She couldn't get the tune out of her head. So she tried to think about more uplifting words, and out came:

Mine eyes have seen the glory of the coming of the Lord;
He is trampling out the vintage where the grapes of wrath are stored...

Inspired, she got out of bed and stayed up all night finishing the lyrics. A few days later, Howe brought the lyrics to her friend James T. Fields, the editor of *Atlantic Monthly*. He featured the song in the magazine, where it caught the eye of President Lincoln. Lincoln loved it so much that he adopted "Battle Hymn of the Republic" as the theme song of the Union army.

**Irony:** "Dixie," the theme song adopted by Confederate troops, was written by a northerner, Daniel Decatur Emmett, who had never even visited the South.

**The Artist:** Bob Dylan

**The Song:** "Like a Rolling Stone" (1965)

**The Story:** Bob Dylan was fed up with the music business—he was tired of the grueling road schedule, shady promoters, and pressure to keep churning out hit after hit. So in 1965 he hid away in a little cabin in Woodstock, New York, to regroup. He recounted his experience in the book *Bob Dylan: Behind the Shades*.

> I'd literally quit playing and singing, and I found myself writing this song, this story, this long piece of vomit about twenty pages long, and out of it I took "Like a Rolling Stone."...The first two lines, which rhymed "kiddin' you" with "didn't you" just knocked me out.

Dylan was so impressed with the song that he came out of hiding to record it. It was the first single from his seminal album *Highway 61 Revisited* and began the second chapter of his legendary career. Not only was it Dylan's first top 10 hit, peaking at #2, but it was also the first song over six minutes long to reach the Billboard Top 40.

* * *

## CELEBRITY GOSSIP

O. J. Simpson was originally cast for the title role in the movie *The Terminator* but was ultimately rejected because, according to a studio executive, "People would never have believed a nice guy like O. J. could play the part of a ruthless killer."

**Cyndi Lauper's 1984 hit "Girls Just Want to Have Fun" was written by a man.**

# Q & A: ASK THE EXPERTS

*More random questions, with answers from the nation's top trivia experts.*

**OH, DO I HAVE A HEADACHE**

**Q:** *How do woodpeckers avoid brain damage after hitting their heads against trees all day?*

**A:** "The force generated by the woodpecker pecking does not pass through its braincase—it travels along the bird's upper jaw, which connects below the brain and allows shock to dissipate throughout the bird's entire body. Naturally, some of the blow does reverberate back into the cranium, but since the woodpecker's brain surface area is relatively large, the impact is absorbed as a slap, not a punch. And because the avian skull fits tightly around its bird brain—like a bicycle helmet—it prevents internal bruising. Every bit of cushioning helps: According to experts, the acceleration force felt by a common acorn woodpecker measures between 600 and 1,200 g's—enough that its eyeballs would literally pop out on impact if it didn't blink." (From *The Wild File*, by Brad Wetzler)

**A MARK OF DE-STINK-SHUN**

**Q:** *Why does sweat leave a yellowish stain?*

**A:** "The most likely culprits are body secretions called apocrine sweat and sebum, the oily secretion of the sebaceous glands, although deodorants and antiperspirants may also play a role.

"The underarms are rich in apocrine sweat glands, which produce milky secretions. Apocrine sweat contains many chemicals, including the acidic substances that produce underarm odor.

"The sebaceous glands are usually associated with hair follicles. Cells filled with fatty droplets die and burst, providing lubrication for the skin and hair. When the oils are exposed to air, they oxidize, turning yellowish, and if not quickly removed by laundering, they can permanently yellow clothing. Sebaceous glands at the back of the neck cause 'ring around the collar.'" (From *The N.Y. Times Second Book of Science Questions and Answers*, by Claiborne Ray)

**Be careful! Every 45 seconds, a house catches fire in the United States.**

## THE ANSWER IS BLOWIN' IN THE WIND

**Q:** *Where does wind come from?*

**A:** "Wind is the movement of a mass of air, caused by differences in pressure in the atmosphere. A wind always flows from a high- to a low-pressure area, trying to equal out the pressure. Picture the air in a balloon, which is at higher pressure than the air outside. Puncture it: the air rushes out, from the high to the low area of pressure.

"Over the equator is a band of low pressure, and over each of the poles is a band of high pressure. There are alternating bands of high and low pressure over the rest of the planet, and they control wind direction. These patterns, and the effect of the Earth spinning on its axis, create winds which blow east and west, not north and south." (From *What Makes the World Go Round?*, by Jinny Johnson)

## LOSE YOUR BLUES

**Q:** *How does bleach get clothes white?*

**A:** "Most laundry bleaches are oxidizing agents. In the washing machine they release free-roving molecules of sodium hypochlorite or peroxide. The color of a stain or spot is made up of a group of atoms and molecules linked together by a pattern of double and single bonds. The oxidizing agent tears into those bonds, destroying the bond pattern and fading the color or changing it completely to white. The stain is still there, albeit invisible, until detergent and the agitation of the machine lift most of it off.

"Fabric colors are also made up of bonds, so if you add bleach to clothes that aren't colorfast—you'll notice that the colors you liked might also become invisible." (From *More How Do They Do That?*, by Caroline Sutton and Kevin Markey)

## USELESS INFORMATION

**Q:** *Why do our palms sweat when we get nervous?*

**A:** "Palms sweat very easily—they contain more sweat glands than other parts of the body. The reason may go back to the days when our ancestors climbed trees to escape danger. Fear of the danger activated the sweat glands, making the palms moist, and this moisture provided our ancestors with a better climbing grip. As in the case of goose bumps and body hair, sweaty palms no longer serve the same purpose but are still with us even after millions of years of evolution." (From *Ever Wonder Why?*, by Douglas Smith)

**Q: What percent of a dime is silver? A: 0%**

# CHICKEN NUGGETS

*Question: What looks like a chicken, squawks like a chicken, and walks like a chicken? Don't know? Answer: a chicken. (And we thought the* chicken *was dumb.)*

## STICKIN' CHICKENS

What do you do when a hen won't lay eggs? Try acupuncture! That's what researchers in Taiwan have been doing to hens who have turned "broody" (which means they would rather hatch an egg than lay another). A needle is inserted between the nostrils of the hen's beak, and left there for two days. Apparently the treatment works—it "cures" the hen of the desire to hatch her eggs.

## TV DINNERS

"Battery" (egg-laying) hens get depressed and angry. Who can blame them—they spend their entire lives in tiny cages, where they're expected to lay 300 eggs a year. Researchers in Scotland decided to look for a way to make these hens' lives happier. So did they let the birds roam free? No. Scientists at the Roslin Institute introduced the hens to TV. Now they're addicted. Whenever the television is turned on, they sit, mesmerized. Their favorite viewing: screen-saver images of flying toasters and schools of fish that move slowly across the screen.

## SINGING SUPPER

A rural New Zealand woman and her friend were waiting for their dinner to finish cooking when they heard something that sounded like a chicken squawking. They looked around outside, but there wasn't a fowl in sight. They suddenly realized the noise was coming from *inside* the house. They followed the cries into the woman's kitchen. The noise was coming from the oven. When she looked inside, she saw that steam was pouring out of the roasting chicken's neck. The chicken was long dead, but as the steam passed over the bird's intact vocal chords, it caused them to vibrate. The woman and her friend turned off the oven and became vegetarians for the night, having cheese and lettuce sandwiches for dinner.

**Rah-rah-rah! In 1898 all cheerleaders were male. Now 3% are.**

# COMIC RELIEF, TOO

*More funny lines from funny people.*

"I don't see the point of testing cosmetics on rabbits, because they're already cute."
**—Rich Hall**

"My wife's an earth sign. I'm a water sign. Together we make mud."
**—Henny Youngman**

"When authorities warn you of the sinfulness of sex, there is an important lesson to be learned: Do not have sex with the authorities."
**—Matt Groening**

"How come if you mix flour and water together you get glue? And when you add eggs and sugar, you get a cake? Where does the glue go?"
**—Rita Rudner**

"Contraceptives should be used on every conceivable occasion."
**—Spike Milligan**

"My wife asked for plastic surgery; I cut up her credit cards."
**—Rodney Dangerfield**

"Never moon a werewolf."
**—Mike Binder**

"Mario Andretti has retired from racecar driving. He's getting old. He ran his entire last race with his left blinker on."
**—Jon Stewart**

"I buy books on suicide at bookstores. You can't get them at the library, because people don't return them."
**—Kevin Nealon**

"My mother breast-fed me with powdered milk. It was my first do-it-yourself project."
**—Buzz Nutley**

"I like to leave a message before the beep."
**—Steven Wright**

"Of course we need firearms. You never know when some nut is going to come up to you and say something like, 'You're fired.' You gotta be ready."
**—Dave Attell**

"I wonder if the Buddha was married... his wife would say, 'Are you just going to sit around like that all day?'"
**—Garry Shandling**

**Napoleon Bonaparte's emblem was the bumblebee.**

# HOW TO COOK A PORCUPINE

*No kidding—this recipe is real. The next time your dinner party guests ask where you got your recipe for a large rodent with quills, tell them you found it...in the bathroom.*

**INGREDIENTS:**

1 porcupine
1 stalk of celery
1 medium yellow onion, sliced
2 medium carrots, sliced
1/4 tsp. pepper
1 tsp salt
1 bay leaf

**COOKING INSTRUCTIONS**

**1.** Find, catch, kill, skin, and *dress* the porcupine. (Dress means clean the animal by removing the guts). Good luck! Watch out for the quills, and be sure to wear gloves—game animals carry *tularemia*, a fever-causing disease that can be spread to humans.

**2.** Hang the porcupine in a cool, dry place for 48 hours, preferably in your garage or someplace where you won't mind the smell.

**3.** Place the porcupine in a bath of salted water. Soak in the refrigerator overnight.

**4.** Bring water and porcupine to a boil. Discard water. Immerse porcupine in fresh, cool water, bring to boil again. Discard water again.

**5.** Remove meat from porcupine. Chop into small pieces and place in a large pot or dutch oven. Add 3 cups of water or porcupine stock, celery, onions, carrots, pepper, salt, and bay leaf. Simmer until the meat is tender, 2-1/2 hours if the porcupine is young, longer if it is older. Be sure the meat is cooked through—game animals can also harbor the parasitic disease *trichinosis*.

**6.** Remove bay leaf.

Serves 4-6

*Note*: In *Uncle John's Ahh-Inspiring Bathroom Reader* we brought you a recipe for shrunken heads. This year, it's porcupines. Who knows what we'll cook up next year?

# BETS YOU CAN'T LOSE

*BRI stalwart Rhys Rounds often challenges us to some friendly "contests of skill"...and he beats us every time. So for revenge, we're passing along a few of his secrets.*

**I'LL BET...** "I can make you say the word 'black.'"

**SETUP:** Start asking your mark the colors of various objects in the room, making sure that none of them are black or blue. After three or four objects, ask "What are the colors of the American flag?"

**PAYOFF:** When they respond, "Red, white, and blue," you say, "I win! I told you I could make you say 'blue'!" Nine times out of ten they'll come back with, "You didn't say *blue*, you said *black*." Then you say, "Now I really do win!"

**I'LL BET...** "I can make you say what I want you to."

**SETUP:** When the other person agrees to the bet, tell them to say "multifarious verbiage."

**PAYOFF:** When they say that they won't or that they don't know what that means, you've won the bet. Why? To say multifarious verbiage means to say a variety of words...which they've just done.

**I'LL BET...** "I can roll the cue ball underneath a cue stick without holding it and without the ball touching the stick."

**SETUP:** To demonstrate the difficulty, place the cue stick over the two long side rails of the pool table. Then have the sucker try to roll the cue ball underneath the stick, which they won't be able to do—the space between the stick and the tabletop is too small.

**PAYOFF:** But *you* can do it. Pick up the cue ball, put it on the floor under the table, and roll it underneath the table so it passes below the cue stick above. It will never touch the stick.

**I'LL BET...** "You can't lift my hand off the top of my head."

**SETUP:** Put your palm on the top of your head and instruct the person to try to remove it by pushing up on your forearm. It works best when a smaller person challenges a bigger, stronger person.

**PAYOFF:** They won't be able to. We're not sure why; it's one of

**What term did Matisse coin in 1908 as an insult of another painter's work? Cubism.**

those freaks of nature (not you, the trick).

**I'LL BET...** "I can remove this quarter from underneath this napkin without touching the napkin or blowing on it."
**SETUP:** Put a quarter under a napkin. After you've set up the trick, discreetly put another quarter into your hand. Then put that hand underneath the table, say some magical incantations, and after a moment, reveal that the quarter is magically in your hand!
**PAYOFF:** The person will most likely go straight for the napkin to prove you wrong. When they remove it, pick up the quarter and you've won the bet.

**I'LL BET...** "You can't taste the difference between an apple and a raw potato if you close your eyes and plug your nose."
**SETUP:** The best way to ensure success with this one is to make them try it three times. Just once is a 50/50 guess. Three times puts the odds in your favor.
**PAYOFF:** It's not really a trick. According to experts, smell and sight are more important in tasting things than most people realize. Without those two senses, the tastebuds don't have enough info to send to the brain.

**I'LL BET...** "You can't eat eight saltines in 60 seconds."
**SETUP:** Make sure that you stipulate the person isn't allowed to wash them down with anything—and that they have to eat them one by one.
**PAYOFF:** Because of the saltiness of the crackers, most people will get "cotton mouth" and not be able to eat more than five or six. Don't wager too much, though, because there is the occasional big mouth that can pull this one off. But at least you've gotten them to make a fool of themselves.

**I'LL BET...** "I can jump higher than this house."
**SETUP:** Just jump up in the air six inches or so.
**PAYOFF:** You've just jumped higher than any house ever could.

**Kangaroos can't walk.**

# THE WORST BUSINESS DECISION IN U.S. HISTORY

*The worst decision in history? A bold claim, especially when you consider how many bad decisions people make every day (except Uncle John). Still, have you driven a Daisy lately? No, and you never will, either. Here's why.*

## TILTING AT WINDMILLS

In the early 1880s, a Plymouth, Michigan, watch repairman named Clarence J. Hamilton came up with the idea of making windmills from metal instead of wood. Farmers used windmills to pump water for crop irrigation, and in those days most of them built the windmills themselves. Hamilton thought that if he could design a better, sturdier windmill made from iron and sell it at a low enough price, farmers would line up to buy them. So in 1882 the Plymouth Iron Windmill Company opened for business.

It turns out Hamilton was wrong—farmers in the 1880s were loathe to spend money on anything they could make themselves, even if his iron windmills were better. After six years in business, the Plymouth Iron Windmill Company was still struggling, so Hamilton invented something else that he thought would help boost windmill sales: a toy rifle that used compressed air to shoot industrial ball bearings —"BBs" for short—instead of bullets. It wasn't the first BB gun ever invented, but this one was made of metal, which made it sturdier and a better shot than competing guns, which were made of wood. His idea was to give a free BB gun to every farmer who bought a windmill.

## FLOWER POWER

Hamilton showed the air rifle to the company's general manager, Lewis Cass Hough, who shot at the trash can in his office and then went outside and shot an old shingle from 10 feet away. "Boy!" he said. "That's a daisy!" The name stuck... but Hamilton's idea of giving away free BB guns with every windmill didn't—farmers wanted the guns, not the windmills. So the Plymouth Iron Windmill Co. changed its name to the Daisy Manufacturing Co. and started making BB guns full time.

## BB KING

In 1891 Lewis Hough hired his nephew Charles Bennett and made him Daisy's first salesman. Smart move. Thanks to Bennett's hard work, by the turn of the century, Daisy was manufacturing 250,000 air rifles a year.

By 1903 Bennett was president of the company and a pillar of the Plymouth business community. To celebrate his success, that spring he made a trip into nearby Detroit to buy an Oldsmobile, the hottest-selling car in the country.

But before he took his test drive, Bennett happened to stop at a tailor shop to buy a suit, and while there he mentioned he was going to buy a car. A man named Frank Malcomson happened to overhear him, and as Bennett was leaving, Malcomson introduced himself. He explained that his cousin, coal merchant Alex Malcomson, had started his own auto company with the help of a business partner. So far they'd managed to build only one test car, but Malcomson told Bennett that he should really take a ride in his cousin's car before he signed the papers on the Oldsmobile. Bennett agreed to go for a ride that very afternoon.

About an hour later, Alex Malcomson's business partner, a relatively unknown engineer named Henry Ford, pulled up in the test car, which he called the Model A. Bennett hopped in, they went for a drive, and by the time they were through, Bennett had given up his plans to buy an Oldsmobile. The Model A was a better car, he told Ford, and he was willing to wait until it came on the market.

But how long would that take? And how much would it cost? Ford said he wasn't sure and that Alex Malcomson was a better person to ask. So he drove Bennett to Malcomson's office, dropped him off, and then sped off to parts unknown. "He probably had someone else that he was taking for a ride," Bennett reminisced many years later.

## RISKY BUSINESS

Would the Model A ever come to market at all? The *car* may have been impressive, but the company behind it, if it could even be called a company, was a mess. Ford & Malcomson, soon to evolve into the Ford Motor Company, was having trouble coming up with the cash it needed to begin production. Henry Ford deserved a lot of the blame: in less than two years he'd wrecked one auto company and gotten himself thrown out of another. He had a bad habit of sneaking off to tinker on race cars when he should have been designing regular cars to sell to the public. And in the process he'd burned through nearly $90,000 of his investors' money—about $1.8 million today—while managing to build only about a dozen cars.

Malcomson was hardly better. He was the largest coal dealer in the area, but he'd built up his business by borrowing huge sums of money from nearly every banker in Detroit. He was so overextended, in fact, that he had to hide his interest in the Ford company so that his bankers wouldn't know what he was up to.

When Ford and Malcomson made the rounds of Detroit's wealthiest investors to raise funds for yet another auto company, few took them seriously. The two men were reduced to cajoling money out of relatives, suppliers, Malcomson's attorneys, his coal company employees, his landlord, and anyone else they could think of...including Charles Bennett.

## DEAL OF A LIFETIME

When Bennett went into Malcomson's office to talk about buying a car, Malcomson offered him a chance to buy a stake in the company. A *huge* stake in the company. Reports vary as to exactly how much he was offered, but it was at least 25% and may have been as much as 50%—for as little as $75,000.

A 50% stake would have made Bennett the largest individual shareholder, with Ford, Malcomson, and the others dividing up the other 50%. Bringing Bennett into Ford made a lot of business sense: Associating with such a successful businessman would make the Ford Motor Company seem viable, too, making it easier to attract other investors and to borrow money from bankers no longer willing to lend money to Malcomson alone.

Bennett knew a good product when he saw one, and he wanted in. There was only one thing stopping him—he didn't have $75,000. But the Daisy Manufacturing Company did. So when he got back to Plymouth, Bennett told his business partner Ed Hough (Lewis Hough's son) that he was going to invest some of Daisy's money in a car company.

**According to experts, dark chocolate is the candy most likely to cause tooth decay.**

## SLOW DOWN, PARDNER

That was when Daisy's attorneys informed Bennett that the company charter forbade investing its funds in other companies. The reasoning was logical. What would happen if Ford & Malcomson went under like so many other auto companies had? Daisy would lose its investment. And if it merged with the automaker (another idea Bennett was toying with), it might even have to make good on that company's losses. Besides—kids were always going to want BB guns for Christmas. Would anyone still be interested in automobiles five years from now? Maybe cars were just a fad.

"Bennett's fellow directors at Daisy balked at the proposal, on the grounds that there was no reason to diversify from air rifles into something as whimsical as the automobile," writes Douglas Brinkley in *Wheels for the World*.

## THANKS, BUT NO THANKS

Bennett tried everything he could think of to get Daisy's directors to agree to invest in the auto company, but nothing worked—and Daisy never did buy in. Instead of getting half of the company, Bennett had to settle for buying a 3.3% stake for $5,000, which was all he could personally afford.

To be fair, there's a good chance that even if Daisy had been willing to buy half of what would soon become the Ford Motor Company, Henry Ford might not have allowed it. Ford was determined to be his own boss, and when the investors in his earlier auto companies tried to assert themselves, he just walked away, leaving them holding the bag. That as much as anything had caused him to fail. It's questionable whether he would have allowed anyone other than himself to own such a huge stake in the new company.

Plus, there was talk that if Daisy got involved with the new company, Bennett might want to give a BB gun away with each car sold, or even worse, that he would insist the new car be called a Daisy. According to Brinkley, Henry Ford "was not about to see his latest creation named after a flower or a gun."

## DUMB DECISION #2

Bennett owned 3.3% of Ford, so when the company introduced the Model T in 1908 and grew into the largest auto manufacturer

**Benjamin Franklin invented crop insurance.**

on Earth, Bennett became stinking rich, right? Wrong. After he and Malcomson took sides against Henry Ford in a power struggle (never a good idea) and lost, Bennett sold his Ford shares. That was in 1907—the year *before* the Model T changed the world. Bennett got $35,000 for his shares.

### GO AHEAD AND CRY

Had Bennett held onto his 3.3% stake in the Ford Motor Company until 1919—for 12 more years—when Henry Ford bought out the last of the other shareholders and assumed full ownership, he would have earned $4,750,000 ($47 million today) in dividends. His stock would have been worth $12.5 million ($123 million today). Not a bad return on a $5,000 investment.

Had Daisy bought 50% of the company in 1903 (and had Henry Ford not run the company into the ground, as he had done with earlier ventures when he wasn't allowed to call the shots), their half of the Ford Motor Company would have been worth at least $125 million ($1.24 *billion* today), and possibly as much as $500 million ($4.95 *billion* today).

"The original investors in the Ford Motor Company had received the largest return on risk capital in recorded business history," Robert Lacey writes in *Ford: The Men and the Machine*. Thanks to one bad decision, Daisy's investors didn't get a penny of it.

* * *

## SMART CROOKS (for a change)

How do you make sure the police won't interrupt your burglary? Fix it so they can't even leave their headquarters. That's what happened in 2001 in the Dutch town of Stadskanaal. Thieves simply padlocked the front gates of the high fence that surrounds the police compound, then robbed a nearby electronics store. That set off a burglar alarm in the police station, but there was nothing police could do about it—they were all locked in. As the crooks made off with TVs and camcorders, Stadskanaal cops had to sit and wait for reinforcements to arrive from the next town. A police spokesman said, "It's a pity all our officers were at that moment in the police station. Normally most of them are on patrol." They've since taken precautions to make certain it never happens again.

**There are 71 known moons in our solar system (so far).**

# URBAN LEGENDS

*Hey—did you hear about the girl who needed to get a tan in just three days? Urban legends seem to be true…but are they really? Here are a few we've looked into.*

**LEGEND:** McDonald's purchases cow eyeballs from a company called "100% Beef," and adds them as filler to Big Mac patties, claiming they are "100% beef patties."

**HOW IT SPREAD:** By word of mouth, probably for as long as McDonald's has dominated the American fast food industry. In the very first *Bathroom Reader*, we wrote about a similar claim (false) that McDonald's uses worms as ground-beef filler.

**THE TRUTH:** McDonald's *doesn't* add cow eyeballs to hamburgers or use them as a thickener in its milkshakes (another legend). For one thing, the U.S. Department of Agriculture regulates the usage of the term "100% beef." Theoretically, companies can't use it unless their patties really are what they claim to be. Plus, if you think about it, every cow that ends up as beef consists of hundreds of pounds of meat, while two eyeballs weigh less than a Quarter Pounder. Even if McDonald's had wanted to add cow eyeballs to its beef patties (it doesn't) and such a thing were legal (it isn't), there simply aren't enough of them to taint that much meat.

**LEGEND:** A sorority girl wants a dark tan for a formal dance that's just a few days away. She goes to a tanning salon, and they tell her she can't stay under the lamps for more than 30 minutes because any more would be unsafe. You can't get a dark tan in 30 minutes, so she spends the next two days traveling to every tanning salon in town, spending 30 minutes in each.

She gets a beautiful tan and looks great at the formal…but the next morning her sorority sisters find her dead in her room with smoke billowing out of her eyes, ears, and mouth. An autopsy reveals that the tanning rays had cooked her body from the inside out, like a burrito in a microwave oven.

**HOW IT SPREAD:** Like wildfire—the tale first appeared in 1987 and was repeated all over the country. Sometimes the victim is a bride-to-be, sometimes she's a high-school girl getting ready

**Percentage of Americans who say a "unibrow" is a turnoff: 35%.**

for her prom. And she doesn't always die—sometimes she is permanently blinded or has to have a "fried" arm or leg amputated. It was one of the most popular—and most widely believed—urban legends of the 1980s.

**THE TRUTH:** The story is not only false, it's also scientifically impossible. Yes, tanning rays are dangerous—overexposure can cause sunburns, skin cancer, cataracts, and other problems. But tanning beds don't cook the human body from the inside out. This story features two traditional urban legend themes: fear of new technology and excessive vanity that is punished by fate.

**LIFE IMITATES URBAN LEGEND!** In May 1989, two years after the first broiled-girl rumors started, a woman named Patsy Campbell actually did die from burns received after spending just 25 minutes in a tanning bed. Campbell, who had been taking medication that made her skin very sensitive to light, was the first and so far only person ever to receive fatal burns in a tanning bed.

**LEGEND:** A young couple gets married. The reception is held at the bride's grandmother's house, and they continue a family tradition of playing a game of hide-and-seek. When it's the bride's turn to hide, she disappears. After hours of searching, they still can't find her. They finally call the police to assist in the search...but she is never found.

Years later the bride's sister gets married and despite the tragedy, hide-and-seek is played again. The sister decides to hide in a large steamer trunk in the attic and when she pops it open, she finds the dead body of her long-lost sister—who suffocated when the trunk lid slammed shut and locked her in—still in her wedding gown.

**HOW IT SPREAD:** Word of mouth...for almost 300 years. In the 1830s, Thomas Haynes Bayly wrote *The Ballad of The Mistletoe Bride*:

> At length an oak chest, that had long lain hid,
> Was found in the castle—they raised the lid,
> A skeleton form lay mouldering there
> In the bridal wreath of that lady fair!
> O, sad was her fate! in sportive jest
> She hid from her lord in the old oak chest.
> It closed with a spring! and, dreadful doom,
> The bride lay clasped in her living tomb!

**THE TRUTH:** It never happened.

# SIMPLE SOLUTIONS

*How often have you seen a clever solution to a difficult problem and said, "That's so obvious—I wish I'd thought of that!" Here are some simple, but brilliant, inventions that could change the world.*

## MONEYMAKER-PLUS

**Problem:** How can people irrigate crops in impoverished parts of the world? With electric pumps? Nope—electricity is often nonexistent, and where it is available it's too expensive for poor farmers.

**Simple Solution:** A foot-powered irrigation pump

**Explanation:** Approtec, a nonprofit company in Nairobi, Kenya, calls it the MoneyMaker-Plus. Working the pedals like a stair-climbing exercise machine, one person can pull water from a stream, a pond, or a well 20 feet deep, send it to sprinklers, and irrigate up to one and a half acres a day. In underdeveloped countries, such a device can be life-changing. As of 2002, Approtec estimates that 24,000 MoneyMaker-Plus pumps were in use, bringing an average of $1,400 a year more to people who previously earned less than $100 a year. The pumps helped create 16,000 new jobs and generate $30 million a year total in profits and wages. They're made from local materials (creating more jobs), they're easily repaired without special tools, they're lightweight for easy transport (25 pounds), and most importantly, they're affordable—they cost only $38.

## ANTI–CELL PHONE SANDWICH

**Problem:** How can people effectively, cheaply—and legally—stop the ringing of cell phones in designated cell phone–free zones?

**Simple Solution:** Wall panels that jam cell phone signals

**Explanation:** Electronic jamming of cell phone transmissions is illegal in the United States, but Hideo Oka and fellow engineers at Japan's Iwate University figured out a way around that—they invented a nonelectronic method. The system consists of a layer of magnetic material (they use nickel zinc ferrite) sandwiched between two thin layers of wood. It looks like 3/8-inch wood paneling. The nickel-zinc ferrite interferes with the electromagnetic waves that cell phones rely on. That means that theaters or restaurants or homeowners can use it to build "cell-free" zones. Oka believes he can find a way to manufacture the device with recycled materials, which would make it very affordable. Naturally, the cell phone industry isn't happy—observers say a legal battle is looming.

## STAR

**Problem:** Arsenic in drinking water. Scientists say that naturally occurring contamination of groundwater in some developing countries causes as many as 200,000 deaths a year. How can people without access to high-tech filters or water-treatment plants make their water safe to drink?

**Simple Solution:** STAR, a patented—and remarkably cheap—filtration system

**Explanation:** In 2001, Xiaoguang Meng and George Korfiatis, scientists at the Stevens Institute of Technology, successfully tested a system that consisted of two buckets, some sand, and a tea-bag-sized packet of iron-based powder. This filter reduces arsenic levels in well water from 650 parts per billion (deadly) to 10ppb, the level recommended by the World Health Organization. Cost per family: $2 a year.

## KENYA CERAMIC JIKO (KCJ)

**Problem:** In Kenya, most families use small metal charcoal-burning stoves—called *jikos*—for cooking. But they're terribly inefficient. And with the cost of wood and wood-based charcoal skyrocketing, how can people afford to cook for their families?

**Simple Solution:** The highly efficient Kenya Ceramic Jiko stove

**Explanation:** The KCJ is a small, hourglass-shaped metal stove with a ceramic lining in its top half. It uses up to 50% less fuel—saving the average family more than $60 a year. The manufacturer, KENGO (Kenya Energy and Environment Organization), has held workshops all over the country, demonstrating how the stoves work and even teaching villagers how to set up shops to make them. (Several women's groups make the ceramic linings.) The KCJ burns cleaner, reducing emissions, and costs only $3.

# READING TOMBSTONES

*In olden days, families had special symbols carved into gravestones to tell something about their loved ones, to express their grief, or to reflect their belief in eternal life or their faith. So, next time you're strolling through a cemetery, look around—the dead are talking to you.*

**Anchor:** Steadfast hope

**Tree trunk:** The brevity of life

**Birds:** The soul

**Snake in a circle:** Everlasting life in heaven (also called *ouroboros*)

**Cherub:** Divine wisdom or justice

**Broken column:** Early death

**Cross, anchor, and Bible:** Faith, hope, and charity

**Cross, crown, and palm:** Trials, victory, and reward

**Crown:** Reward and glory

**Dove:** Purity, love, the Holy Spirit

**Horseshoe:** Protection against evil

**Gourds:** Deliverance from grief

**Lamb:** Innocence (usually on a child's grave)

**Swallow:** Motherhood

**Hourglass:** Time and its swift flight

**Arch:** Rejoined with partner in heaven.

**Ivy:** Faithfulness, memory, and undying friendship

**Laurel:** Victory

**Lily:** Purity and resurrection

**Mermaid:** Dualism of Christ—half God, half man

**Conch shell:** Wisdom

**Oak:** Strength

**Palms:** Martyrdom

**Shattered urn:** Old age

**Peacock:** Eternal life

**Poppy:** Eternal sleep

**Column:** Noble life

**Garland:** Victory over death

**Rooster:** Awakening, courage, vigilance

**Shell:** Birth and resurrection

**Six-pointed star:** The creator

**Weeping willow:** Mourning, grief

**Triangle:** Truth, equality, trinity

**Olive branch:** Forgiveness

**Dolphin:** Salvation, bearer of souls across water to heaven

**Skeleton:** Life's brevity

**Broken sword:** Life cut short

**Crossed swords:** Life lost in battle

**Heart:** Devotion

**Going out with a bang: Three U.S. presidents have died on the Fourth of July.**

# CHAIR-LEADERS

*Pull up a chair for this one. On page 402 we told you about giant Paul Bunyan statues. Well, it turns out that someone's been building them places to sit down.*

## CLASH OF THE TITANS

Small towns seem to love being the home of "the World's Largest" anything. Oversize statues, balls of string, and other oddities are good for tourism and civic pride. For example:

• Ashburn, Georgia, has been a popular photo op spot ever since 1975, when the "World's Largest Peanut" was erected on I-75.

• Castroville, California, one of the world's top growing centers for artichokes, is the proud home of a 15-foot-tall artichoke, which sits next to an artichoke-shaped restaurant.

• Kissimmee, Florida, has a restaurant shaped like an orange called Orange World.

But what happens when different towns want the same "World's Largest" claim to fame? The battle over who has the world's largest chair has been raging for almost a century.

## HIGH CHAIRS

In the late 1800s, Gardner, Massachusetts, with 20 furniture factories, was becoming a chair-manufacturing center. In 1905 the town decided to draw attention to its manufacturing prowess by erecting a 12-foot Mission-style chair on Elm Street. Postcards and placards soon proclaimed Gardner to be "Chair City of the World."

A few years later, Thomasville, North Carolina, which called itself the "Furniture Capital of the World" built its own giant chair, and at 13-feet, 6-inches, it was just a bit bigger than Gardner's.

Gardner's town fathers were infuriated. Not to be outdone, they quickly built a 15-foot Mission chair. And just to be sure their chair would remain the biggest, in 1935 they replaced that one with a 16-foot Hitchcock chair.

Wartime production needs quelled the giant-chair feud for a few years, but after steel production bans were lifted in 1948, Thomasville built an 18-foot steel chair on a 12-foot pedestal. To bolster

**Claxton, Georgia, claims to be the Fruit Cake Capital of the World.**

their position, they convinced the nearby town of High Point to build the world's largest chest of drawers.

## WE WON'T TAKE THIS SITTING DOWN

Under cover of darkness, furniture makers from Bassett, Virginia, sent a team to North Carolina to measure Thomasville's big chair. The boys from Bassett planned to build their own big chair and wanted to ensure that, at 19 feet tall, it would be big enough to steal Thomasville's thunder.

Various other towns jumped into the fray, too: Bennington, Vermont, built a 19-foot ladderback; Washington, D.C., erected a 19-foot Duncan Phyfe; and Morristown, Tennessee, erected a massive 20-foot green recliner, so large it could seat 10 people across.

Gardner fought back gamely, building a 20-foot, 7-inch chair for the bicentennial celebrations in 1976. But Gardner's chair was eclipsed by a mammoth ladderback built at Pa's Woodshed in Binghamton, New York: 24 feet, 9 inches tall. The monstrous creation (considered an eyesore by some), made it into the 1979 *Guinness Book of World Records*.

## THE CHAIR BATTLE MARCHES ON

• A furniture company in Wingdale, New York, used more than a ton and a half of wood to build its 25-foot-tall Fireside Chair.

• A custom furniture maker in Lipan, Texas, erected a 26-foot rocking chair in 2001.

• Anniston, Alabama, has a 33-foot office chair in the vacant lot next to Miller Office Supply. A spiral staircase leads to the seat of the chair, which was constructed from 10 tons of steel.

• Still after a "World's Largest" title, Bassett Furniture built a 20-foot, 3-inch Mission chair. They sent it on tour to Bassett stores across the United States, calling it the "World's Largest Chair," until Anniston, Alabama, publicly refuted their claim. Now they call it the "World's Largest Chair on Tour."

• But the winner in the battle of the giant chairs is Promosedia in the province of Udine, Italy. Equivalent in size to a 7-story building, it was constructed in 1995 to advertise the chair-building region, known as the "Chair Triangle." Their 65-foot chair is indisputably the largest in the world. (So far.)

**Pull up a stone: The chair was invented in about 2500 B.C.**

# THE GREAT BRINKS ROBBERY

*It was the perfect crime—so well planned and executed that all the gang members needed to do to was lie low until the heat cooled down. But could they?*

## IN AND OUT

The year was 1950. It was a cold January in Boston. At around 7 p.m. on the 17th, a green 1949 Ford truck pulled up in front of the Prince Street entrance of the Brinks Armored Car garage. Millions of dollars in cash, checks, and money orders were stored inside the building. Seven men emerged from the back of the Ford and walked swiftly to the front door. Each man wore a Navy peacoat, gloves, rubber-soled shoes, and a chauffeur's cap.

After a series of blinking flashlight signals from a nearby rooftop, one of the men pulled out a key and unlocked the front door. Once inside, each man donned a Captain Marvel Halloween mask and went to work. They walked up the stairs and encountered a second locked door. Another key was produced, and they entered a room where five surprised Brinks employees were counting money. The gang pulled out handguns and quickly subdued the stunned Brinks men. Once their captives were bound and gagged, the masked men began collecting the loot.

With clockwork precision and very little talking, the gang filled their bags with money. Fifteen minutes after their arrival, the robbers—each carrying two full bags—left the building. Six of them got back into the truck and one got into a Ford sedan parked nearby. As they made their getaway, the employees managed to free themselves and call the police. When it was over, $1.2 million in cash and $1.5 million in checks, money orders, and securities were missing. It was the single largest robbery in U.S. history.

## URBAN HEROES

The daring crime made front-page news all over the country. And the public was sympathetic with the robbers almost as soon as they heard about it. Their nonviolent methods and their audacity to take on a company as huge as Brinks made them cult heroes. Comedians and cartoonists joked about it, mocking the huge security company's apparent lack of security. On his weekly TV variety show, Ed Sullivan announced that he had some very special guests: the Brinks robbers themselves. Seven men wearing Captain Marvel masks walked onstage to thunderous applause. It became more than a passing fad—the press dubbed it the "Crime of the Century."

## COPS...

The Boston police and Brinks were humiliated. How could seven men so easily walk off with more than $2.7 million? The FBI took over the case and immediately found some good news: word on the street was that the caper had been in the works for months, and informants were naming names. Among the prime suspects: some of Boston's most notorious petty criminals, such as Anthony Pino, Joseph McGinnis, Stanley Gusciora, and "Specs" O'Keefe—all men known for pulling off similar crimes, although nothing nearly as big. The bad news: they all had alibis. But when a green Ford truck matching witnesses' descriptions was found in pieces at a dump near where O'Keefe and Gusciora lived, the investigators knew they were hot on the trail. They just needed proof.

## ...AND ROBBERS

The Feds' instincts were correct: O'Keefe and Gusciora *were* two of the key men behind the Brinks job. But what they didn't know was that it was Anthony Pino, an illegal alien from Italy, who first came up with the idea...back in 1947.

Pino had the savvy to do the job, but he couldn't do it alone. So he'd called a meeting of some members of the Boston underworld and put together a gang. By the time they were ready to go, there were 11 members: Pino; his associate, liquor store owner Joseph McGinnis; strong-arms O'Keefe and Gusciora, both experienced criminals with reputations for keeping their cool and handling weapons; Pino's brother-in-law, Vincent Costa, the lookout; Adolph "Jazz" Maffie; Henry Baker; Michael Vincent Geagan; Thomas "Sandy" Richardson; James Faherty; and Joseph Banfield.

It would be the heist of a lifetime, and the gang spent the next two years preparing for it. Pino cased the Brinks building from nearby rooftops, and was amazed at how lax the security was. Still, they would take no chances: They broke in after hours on several different occasions and took the lock cylinders from five doors, had keys made to fit them, and returned the cylinders. And while inside, they obtained the Brinks shipment schedules. It took discipline to not steal anything on those smaller break-ins, but they knew the real score would be on the big break-in, planned for a time when the day's receipts were being counted and the vault was open. They were willing to wait.

By December 1949, Costa, the lookout man, could tell exactly how many employees were in the building and what they were doing by observing which lights were on. After about a dozen dress rehearsals, the gang made their move. The job went down without a hitch.

## THE LONG GOOD-BYE

The robbery was the easy part. Now each gang member had to keep quiet, not spend money like crazy, and lay low for six long years, after which the statute of limitations would run out. If they could do that, they would all be scot-free... and very rich.

A small portion of the loot was split up among the gang members, but most of it was hidden in various places. O'Keefe and Gusciora put their share ($100,000 each) in the trunk of O'Keefe's car, parked in a garage on Blue Hill Avenue in Boston—with the agreement that the money was not to be touched until 1956.

Even though they were careful to destroy any physical evidence tying them to the crime, they were known criminals and couldn't evade suspicion. Many were picked up and questioned by the FBI. All denied involvement; all provided alibis (though more than a few were shaky); and all of their homes and businesses turned up nothing in searches. Still, investigators knew there was something fishy going on. Their best approach would be to get one of the men to sing; they just had to watch closely and wait for someone to slip up.

## SOMEONE SLIPS UP

Less than six months after the Brinks job, O'Keefe and Gusciora were nabbed for robbing an Army-Navy store in Pennsylvania. Police found a pile of cash in the car, but none of it could be tied to the Brinks job. O'Keefe was sentenced to three years in the Bradford County jail; Gusciora was sentenced to five years.

**Flying fish "fly" at 40 mph.**

O'Keefe wanted to appeal but had no money for legal bills, so he talked Banfield into retrieving his share of the money from the car. It was delivered a few weeks later (minus $2,000). But O'Keefe couldn't keep it behind bars, so he sought out another gang member, the only one left on the outside that he thought he could trust—Jazz Maffie. Bad move: Maffie took O'Keefe's money, disappeared, then reappeared claiming it had been stolen. Then Maffie said he had spent the money on O'Keefe's legal bills. O'Keefe, meanwhile, was stuck in jail and getting angrier.

The Feds worked this angle, trying to create a wedge between O'Keefe and the rest of the gang. They told O'Keefe that the gang had ratted him out for the Brinks job. But O'Keefe stuck to his guns and kept denying any involvement.

## THE TENSION MOUNTS

Prior to committing the robbery, the 11 men had agreed that if any one of them "muffed" (acted carelessly), he would be "taken care of" (killed). Sitting in jail, O'Keefe convinced himself that the other members of the gang had "muffed." And he vowed he would get his share of the loot...one way or another.

After he was paroled in the spring of 1954, O'Keefe returned to Boston to ask McGinnis for enough money from the loot to hire a lawyer for his pending burglary charge. But McGinnis wouldn't budge. So O'Keefe kidnapped McGinnis's brother-in-law, Costa, demanding his share as ransom. He only got some of it but still released the hostage. Pino and McGinnis, in the meantime, decided that O'Keefe needed to be "taken care of."

## BULLET-PROOF

That June, O'Keefe was driving through Dorchester, Massachusetts, when a car pulled up next to him and sprayed his car with bullets. O'Keefe escaped unharmed. Days later, fellow gang member Henry Baker shot at him, but O'Keefe escaped again. Fearing retribution, Pino brought in a professional hit man named Elmer "Trigger" Burke. When Burke found his target and shot him in the chest and wrist with a machine gun, Specs O'Keefe lived up to his reputation as one of the toughest crooks in the Boston underworld by surviving. By this point, he was extremely angry.

O'Keefe immediately went to the cops and fingered Burke, who was arrested and convicted for attempted murder. But the plan backfired. While he was talking to police, they discovered that O'Keefe was carrying a concealed weapon, a violation of his parole. He was arrested and sentenced to 27 months in prison. Knowing that there was a contract on O'Keefe's life, the FBI stepped up their interrogations. But he still wouldn't confess.

## THE HEAT IS ON

Time was starting to run out. It had been more than five years since the crime, and the deadline for the statute of limitations was getting closer and closer. Thousands of hours had gone into identifying the suspects, but the FBI still had no hard evidence. As the case remained in the public eye, each passing day without an arrest was an embarrassment.

Through all of it, the Feds knew that O'Keefe was the key, so they kept chipping away at him. When they informed him that a huge portion of the loot had been recovered, he finally gave in. On January 6, 1956, Specs O'Keefe called a meeting with the Feds and said, "All right, what do you want to know?" It was 11 days before the six-year statute of limitations would take effect.

O'Keefe spelled out every detail to the police—except where the rest of the money was hidden. He had no idea. (Neither did the police—they had exaggerated the loot-recovery story as a ruse to get O'Keefe to talk.)

## TRIED AND CONVICTED

Police rounded up all of the remaining members. They were arrested and tried amid a media circus. More than 1,000 prospective jurors had to be excused because they admitted they were sympathetic to the robbers. In the end, a jury found all of them guilty. Each man was sentenced to life in prison. Some died there—others were later released on parole.

For turning state's evidence, O'Keefe was given a reduced sentence. After prison, he changed his name, moved to California, and reportedly worked as Cary Grant's chauffeur.

The Brinks gang stole $2.7 million in cash and securities. The government spent *$29 million* trying to catch them and bring them to justice. But in the end, only 2% of the loot—$51,906—was recovered. What happened to the remaining 98% is a mystery.

**Southernmost state capital in the continental United States: Austin, Texas.**

# RETURN OF THE MAN FROM C.R.A.P.

*More odd acronyms. Submit any complaints to* C.R.A.P.*—the* Committee *to* Resist Acronym Proliferation.

**GHOST**

**Stands For:** Graffiti Habitual Offenders Suppression Team (*Undercover LAPD cops who bust graffiti artists*)

**POETS**

**Stands For:** Piss Off Early, Tomorrow's Saturday (*British slang for "TGIF"*)

**SCAM**

**Stands For:** Southern California Auto Mart

**CACA**

**Stands For:** Canadian Agricultural Chemicals Association

**FIB**

**Stands For:** Fishermen's Information Bureau (*It was* this *big... really.*)

**SAP**

**Stands For:** Society for American Philosophy

**EATM**

**Stands For:** Exotic Animal Training Management

**SWIFT ANSWER**

**Stands For:** Special Word Indexed Full-Text Alpha-Numeric Storage With Easy Retrieval (*The longest true acronym in English... so far*)

**BARRF**

**Stands For:** Bay Area Resource Recovery Facility

**NAPS**

**Stands For:** National Alliance of Postal Supervisors

**RUIN**

**Stands For:** Regional Urban Information Network

**SLUTS**

**Stands For:** School of Librarianship Urban Transportation System

**GORK**

**Stands For:** God Only Really Knows (*How doctors refer to patients they can't diagnose*)

**WUNY**

**Stands For:** Wait Until Next Year (*Said after a losing season*)

# THE MAD BOMBER, PT. II

*When we left the case of the Mad Bomber (page 438), Dr. James Brussel, the original "profiler," had just released his theories to the press, setting the game afoot. Here's how it played out.*

**FOUND OUT**

The Mad Bomber's response to his case being made public: he took his terror a step further. The bombs kept coming and the letters got more brazen. "F. P." even called Brussel on the telephone and told him to lay off or he would "be sorry." Brussel had him exactly where he wanted him.

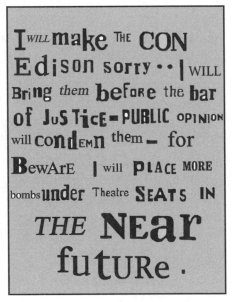

I WILL make THE CON Edison sorry • • I WILL Bring them before the bar of JUSTICE = PUBLIC OPINION will condEMn them – for BewArE I will PLACE MORE bombs under Theatre SEATS IN THE NEar futURe .

The final clue came when police received a letter revealing the date that began the Mad Bomber's misery: September 5, 1931—almost 10 years before the first bomb was found. Brussel immediately ordered a search of Con Ed's personnel files from that era. An office assistant named Alice Kelly found a neatly written letter from a former employee named George Metesky who had promised that Con Edison would pay for their "DASTARDLY DEEDS."

The police traced Metesky to what neighborhood children called the "crazy house" on Fourth Street in Waterbury, Connecticut, just beyond Westchester County, New York. When they arrived, George Metesky was wearing... pajamas. He greeted them warmly and freely admitted to being the Mad Bomber. He even showed them his bomb-making workshop in the garage.

They told him to get dressed for his trip to the station. He

***Judo* translates to "the gentle way."**

returned wearing... a double-breasted suit, buttoned.

## DEDUCTIVE REASONING

So how was Dr. Brussel able to provide such an accurate description?

• It was pretty evident that the Mad Bomber was a man. In those days, very few women would have had the knowledge necessary to make bombs. Bomb-making is, moreover, a classic behavior of paranoid males.

• Because 85% of known paranoids had stocky, muscular builds, Brussel added it to the profile. Metesky had a stocky, muscular build.

• Male paranoiacs have difficulty relating to other people, especially women, and usually live with an older, matriarchal-type woman who will "mother" them. Metesky lived with his two older sisters.

• Another clue to Metesky's sexual inadequacy, Brussel claimed, was his lettering. His script was perfect except for the "W"s—instead of connecting "V"s that would have been consistent with the rest of the letters, Metesky connected two "U"s, which Brussel saw as representing women's breasts.

• Brussel concluded that Metesky was between 40 and 50 years old because paranoia takes years to develop, and based on when the first bomb was found, Metesky had to have already been well down the road. Brussel was close—Metesky was 54.

• What led Brussel to believe that Metesky did not live in New York City was his use of the term "Con Edison"—New Yorkers call it "Con Ed."

• Metesky's language identified him as middle European, too. His use of "dastardly deeds," as well as some other phrases, was a sign of someone with Slavic roots. There was a high concentration of Poles in southern Connecticut, and Brussel connected the dots.

• Paranoids believe that the world conspires against them, so Brussel knew that something traumatic must have happened to Metesky. He was right. On September 5, 1931, Metesky was injured in a boiler explosion at a Con Ed plant. He complained of headaches, but doctors could find no sign of injury. After a year of sick pay and medical benefits, Metesky was fired. A failed lawsuit sent him over the edge, and he began plotting his revenge.

• Brussel also predicted that the Bomber would have a debilitating heart disease. He was close: Metesky suffered from a tubercular lung.

• How did Brussel know what kind of suit Metesky would be wearing when he was arrested? Simple: Paranoids are neat freaks, as was apparent in his letters and bombs. He would wear nothing less than the most impeccable outfit of the day—a double-breasted suit, buttoned.

## AFTERMATH

George Metesky proudly explained everything to the police. In all, he had planted more than 30 bombs, but miraculously, no one was killed. Metesky said that that was never his intention. "F. P.", he explained, stood for "Fair Play."

On April 18, 1957, George Metesky was found mentally unfit to stand trial and was committed to the Matteawan Hospital for the Criminally Insane. In 1973 he was deemed cured and was released. Metesky lived out the remainder of his days in his Waterbury home, where he died in 1994 at the age of 90. Dr. Brussel gained celebrity status for his role in the case; today he's considered the father of modern psychological profiling in criminal investigations.

## TRAGIC LEGACY

Although Metesky's bombs never killed anybody, it was more because of strange luck than "Fair Play." (Police called it a "miracle" that his theater bombs—planted inside the seats—never took any lives.) Even worse, Metesky may have helped pave the way for others who were more successful in their terrible exploits. According to investigators, both the "Zodiac Killer," who killed at least six people—some with bombs—in the San Francisco area in the 1970s, and Ted "Unabomber" Kaczynski, who killed three people in the 1980s and 1990s with package bombs, were inspired by George Metesky, New York City's Mad Bomber.

* * *

"One thing I can't understand is why the newspapers labeled me the Mad Bomber. That was unkind."

**—George Metesky**

**U.S. city that consumes the most ketchup per capita: New Orleans.**

# IRONIC, ISN'T IT?

*There's nothing like a good dose of irony to put the problems of day-to-day life in proper perspective.*

## THE ANIMAL KINGDOM

• The crow population of Woodstock, Ontario, grew so large that residents started complaining to the city council about the noise. The council's solution: frequent bursts of fireworks to scare the crows away.

• Bill Pettit Jr. of Southampton, New Jersey, recently opened his 335-acre farm to bird hunters. Pettit is a veterinarian.

• While driving through Versailles, New York, Wendy Maines saw five dogs attacking a cat. She stopped the car, honked the horn, and scared the dogs away. Then she accidentally ran over the cat.

## UP AND AWAY

Hours after Michael Antinori miraculously walked away from a helicopter crash on June 3, 2002, he climbed into his single-engine plane and took off. Shortly thereafter, the plane went down. He died on impact.

## SEW TOUGH

At Albion State Prison, a new class is being offered to inmates. Guards say it has become so popular among the most violent criminals that there is a waiting list to sign up. What's the subject of the class? Quilting.

## LAW AND ORDER

• Chris Axworthy, Saskatchewan's justice minister, was getting fed up with the car-theft problem in his hometown of Regina so he called a committee meeting to announce a government crackdown on car thieves. When he left his home to go to the meeting, he found that his Chrysler Intrepid had been stolen.

• Two plainclothes German police officers were making their way through a crowd of protesters to meet up with some uniformed cops. But the uniforms met them halfway and beat the two with nightsticks. The bruised officers are suing the department.

**Q: What color are Green Cards (U.S. permanent resident I.D.'s)? A: Surprise! They're yellow.**

• Love Your Neighbor Corp. of Michigan recently sued Love Thy Neighbor Fund of Florida for trademark infringement.

## OCCUPATIONAL HAZARD

Robert Young Pelton wrote a book called *The World's Most Dangerous Places*. In chapter 23 he states that "the most likely place to be kidnapped is Colombia." After the book was released, Pelton traveled to the South American country on a writing assignment for *Adventure* magazine…and was abducted by a paramilitary group. (He was later released.)

## ROCK AND ROLE

Some Hawaiians are questioning the decision to cast wrestler/actor Dwayne "The Rock" Johnson in the lead role for a new movie about Hawaiian king Kamehameha I. What's wrong with that? It turns out The Rock is part Samoan, and historically, Samoans are fierce enemies of the Hawaiians.

## LADIES' MAN

Johnny Hamilton gives $400,000 a year to women's shelters, scholarships, and feminist charities in Michigan. He is the owner of a topless bar in Detroit.

## LOVE AND MARRIAGE

• A 21-year-old man from Rockville, Maryland, was arrested for peeping into a ladies' restroom stall while he was at the county courthouse. He was there to pick up his new marriage license.

• Anne Jonsson of Stockholm, Sweden, viciously attacked her husband, Lars. She fractured his skull, broke his nose, and gave him various cuts and bruises. What did Lars do to deserve all this? He refused to take her to a rally against domestic violence.

## FALSE ADVERTISING

After falling short of its projected profits, *Success* magazine declared bankruptcy in 1999.

* * *

"My mother never saw the irony of calling me a son-of-a-bitch."

**—Richard Jeni**

**Prior to 1953, the slogan of L&M cigarettes was "just what the doctor ordered."**

# CURE FOR WHAT AILS YE

*Uncle John believes that placing this page against your forehead and rubbing vigorously will cure headaches, fever blisters, tennis elbow, planter's warts, swimmer's ear, lazy eye, pinkeye, the evil eye, weak knees, and tired blood. Here are some of Uncle John's other favorite folk remedies:*

To cure lung infections, rub onions on your chest.

To ease arthritis pain, carry a peeled potato in your pocket. If that doesn't work, try a pocketful of buckshot...or the ashes from a turtle shell.

For kidney troubles, eat... kidney beans. If that doesn't work, try chewing the bones from a dogfish head.

To cure a cold, rub your feet with grease. If that doesn't work, eat some bear brains.

Fox fat, when warmed and placed in the ear, will cure an earache.

To get rid of a wart, rub the wart with a peeled apple, then feed the apple to a pig.

To treat a burn, rub it with mashed potatoes.

To cure a child of whooping cough, put them on a donkey and lead the donkey in a clockwise circle nine times.

Eating beaver fat will calm your nerves.

Rubbing a fox tongue on your eyes will cure cataracts.

To cure a headache, tie a string around a buzzard's head and wear it around your neck.

Frostbite? Mix cow milk with cow manure and apply it to the affected area.

To fix a limp, rub the bad leg with skunk or wildcat grease.

To stop a nosebleed, pack your nose with cobwebs.

To reduce fever, eat watermelon or chew turnips.

To cure swollen eyes, put crab eyes on the back of your neck.

A piece of deer hoof worn in a ring will cure epilepsy.

If you touch a sleeping person with a frog tongue, they will reveal their secrets to you.

**Them's the breaks: No insurance company will underwrite Jackie Chan's productions.**

# AMERICA'S FIRST REALITY TV SHOW

*Survivor and The Real World may seem innovative, but they owe a huge debt to a show that hasn't aired since 1973, despite being named one of the greatest shows of all time by TV Guide. Here's the story of the show that started it all.*

## GET REAL

In 1971 a documentary film producer named Craig Gilbert came up with a novel idea for an educational TV show: film the lives of four American families in four different parts of the country—the West Coast, the Midwest, the South, and the East Coast. A different film crew would be assigned to each family and would film their lives for four straight weeks, from the moment the first person got up until the last person went to bed. Many hours of footage would be filmed, then it would be edited and condensed into four one-hour documentaries, one on each family. The documentaries would be broadcast on PBS.

Television programming was a lot different in those days—for years viewers had been fed a steady diet of decidedly *un*realistic family shows like *Ozzie and Harriet, Father Knows Best, The Waltons*, and *The Brady Bunch*. Gilbert figured viewers might be interested in a new aspect of American family life: reality.

## FAMILY SECRETS

For the West Coast family, Gilbert chose the Louds, an upper middle-class family living in Santa Barbara, California—parents Bill and Pat, and their five teenage children: sons Lance, Kevin, and Grant, and daughters Delilah and Michele. "They basically said, 'How would you like to star in the greatest home movie ever made?'" Lance Loud remembered. "We didn't have to do anything, just be our little Southern California hick selves."

Gilbert hired two filmmakers, Susan and Alan Raymond, to film the family. Shortly after production got underway, he decided to dump the four-family concept and focus exclusively on the Louds—for a longer time period. To this day it is unclear whether

Craig Gilbert knew it at the time, but the Louds' marriage was in serious trouble (thanks to Bill's philandering), and their son Lance, who lived in New York, was gay. The Louds had assumed that keeping their family secrets for four weeks wouldn't be that difficult; but now Gilbert was asking them for permission to film for months on end. Could they withstand this invasion of their privacy?

Bill and Pat thought it over…and decided to take a chance. "I thought I might get away with just saying, 'These are my children and my kitchen and my pool and my horses, over and out.'" Pat Loud recalled years later. "What naifs we were!"

## OPEN HOUSE

Bill and Pat need not have worried about protecting Lance Loud's privacy—he was completely open about his sexuality, even when the film crew was present. He was the very first openly gay teenager ever shown on American television; for many viewers, he was the first out-of-the-closet homosexual they had ever seen.

As for the Louds' marital problems, they proved both impossible to hide and impossible to repair. As the weeks passed and Pat became more comfortable around the cameras, she began to open up about the problems she was having with Bill. Their marriage continued to deteriorate until finally, a few months into filming, Pat threw Bill out of the house. The Raymonds were there, and they captured it all on film.

## 12-STEP PROGRAM

By the time the Raymonds wrapped up production, they'd been filming the Louds for seven solid months. They had so much raw footage—more than 300 hours worth—that it took them the better part of two years to edit it down to the 12 one-hour episodes that would air as *An American Family* beginning in January 1973.

One of the reasons the Louds agreed to allow the film crew into their home in the first place was because they didn't think many people would ever see the finished product. This was a documentary, after all, and one being made for educational television at that. PBS wasn't even broadcast in Santa Barbara in 1971 (by 1973, it was); besides, Pat didn't watch much educational television and she didn't think anyone else would, either. "We erro-

**What's the economic acronym DINK stand for? Double Income, No Kids.**

neously believed the series would be a simply interminable home movie that no one in their right mind would watch for more than five minutes," she recalled in 2002. Lance Loud thought of the film as "a very odd, never-to-be-noticed project."

## HITTING THE BIG TIME

But when *An American Family* finally hit the airwaves in January 1973, more than 10 million people tuned in, making it one of the most-watched series in PBS history. The viewers were there for episode 2, when Lance's sexuality was revealed; they were there for episode 9, when Pat Loud asked Bill for a divorce; and they stayed glued to their sets until the series came to an end in episode 12.

Overnight, the Louds became one of the most famous families in America. They were on the cover of *Newsweek* (underneath the banner "Broken Family"), they made the national television talk shows, appearing with Dick Cavett, Dinah Shore, Mike Douglas, and Phil Donahue, and their problems were discussed around the water coolers of every workplace in America. Everyone knew who they were.

## ROUGH GOING

Today, more than 30 years later, the Louds may be remembered with fond nostalgia, but that wasn't the case in 1973. Many viewers were stunned by what they saw. The Louds were an upper middle-class family, more affluent than most of the viewers who watched them. Like the fictional TV families people were used to seeing on the tube, the Louds seemed to have it all: They lived in a big, beautiful house in sunny Southern California; they had steady, high-paying jobs; they had four cars, five beautiful children, three dogs, two cats, a horse, a swimming pool—seemingly everything that anyone could possibly want. So why weren't they happy? Why couldn't Bill and Pat save their marriage? Why was Lance Loud gay? What on Earth was *wrong* with these people?

Many viewers—not to mention pundits and TV critics—came to see Bill and Pat Loud as unfit parents and their family as the personification of everything that was wrong with American families in the early 1970s. *Newsweek* called the Louds "affluent zombies" and described the series as "a glimpse into the pit." *The New York Times Magazine* called Lance Loud a "flamboyant leech," the

**Sounds worse than it is: The medical condition *epistaxis* is...a nosebleed.**

"evil flower of the family," and an "emotional dwarf."

That wasn't at all how the Louds had expected to come across. "People were shocked, and we were shocked that they were shocked," Lance Loud remembered.

> We thought people would be on our side and sympathize with a family responding to all the different moods and trends of the times. But they didn't sympathize; they misunderstood, thinking that we were arrogant in our stupidity. They were totally wrong.

## NO HOLLYWOOD ENDING

In the end, nearly everyone associated with the film ended up regretting ever getting involved. Bill and Pat accused the Raymonds of distorting their family life, zooming in on problems and controversies at the expense of everything else. "It seemed that the entire series was all about Lance being homosexual and my husband and I divorcing," Pat Loud says. "My other four children and their friends seemed to be of no real interest to the editors."

The Raymonds had their own regrets. Though they did make two more films about the Louds—in 1983 and 2003—they swore off making documentaries about any other family. "It was too brutal," Susan Raymond says. "We made films on policemen, on a prison warden, on a principal of a school—people who are public officials. But we didn't do anything on ordinary people or families. We didn't think they could handle that kind of scrutiny."

## FINAL CHAPTER

After the show ended, Lance Loud spent several years as the lead singer of a punk rock band called the Mumps, but though his fame brought the band some notoriety, it also made it harder for them to be taken seriously. The Mumps broke up in 1980 and Lance returned to Southern California, where he worked as a freelance journalist, published in magazines like *The Advocate, Interview,* and *Vanity Fair.* He also abused intravenous drugs for nearly 20 years, which caused him to become infected with hepatitis. In 1987 he learned that he was HIV positive.

In late 2001, his health failing, Lance checked into an L.A. hospice and called the Raymonds to see if they would document his relationship with his family during this final phase of his life. They agreed. Why did Lance want to do it? Felled by years of unsafe sex and drug addiction, he'd come to see his life as a cautionary tale. But he also wanted to show viewers that for all the problems the Louds had gone through, 30 years later they still loved each other and were close. "He could have asked for a priest or a minister, but he called for his filmmakers," Susan Raymond says.

Lance Loud died on December 22, 2001 at the age of 50—the same age his father was when *An American Family* premiered in 1973. *Lance Loud! A Death in an American Family* aired on PBS in January 2003.

After the original series ended, Pat Loud moved to New York and became a literary agent. She has since retired and now lives in Los Angeles. Bill Loud remarried in 1976; he is retired and also lives in Los Angeles. Kevin Loud lives with his family in Paradise Valley, Arizona; Grant, Delilah, and Michele Loud and their families all live in Los Angeles.

## DUBIOUS ACHIEVERS

Alan and Susan Raymond, credited with filming the first-ever reality TV show, are still making documentaries…but they refuse to watch any of the shows their work has inspired. Anthropologist Margaret Mead predicted that *An American Family* would come to be seen "as important a moment in the history of human thought as the invention of the novel," but judging from the shows that have followed it—*The Real World*, *Big Brother*, and *The Osbournes* among them—it's a safe bet she was wrong.

"Like Frankenstein's monster, it's a mixed blessing to be considered someone who spawned this reality TV genre," Alan Raymond says. "I think it's a largely superficial, stupid genre of television programming that I don't think as a documentary filmmaker I take much pride in."

* * *

**A Final Note.** For all it cost them personally, how much money were the Louds paid for letting a crew film them for seven months? Not much. "The family received no compensation for their participation in the film," Pat Loud says. "The only money we got was a check for $400 to repair the kitchen where the gaffer's tape had pulled the paint off the walls."

**Scientists say: An adult must taste a disliked food 10 times before learning to like it.**

# MEAD'S CREED

*When Margaret Mead died in 1978, she was the most famous anthropologist in the world. Her 44 books and more than 1,000 articles helped shape our understanding of human behavior.*

"We are now at a point where we must educate our children in what no one knew yesterday, and prepare our schools for what no one knows yet."

"No matter how many communes anybody invents, the family always creeps back."

"I was brought up to believe that the only thing worth doing was to add to the sum of accurate information in the world."

"Every time we liberate a woman, we liberate a man."

"Always remember that you are absolutely unique. Just like everyone else."

"The solution to adult problems tomorrow depends on large measure upon how our children grow up today."

"What people say, what people do, and what they say they do are entirely different things."

"I learned the value of hard work by working hard."

"Our humanity rests upon a series of learned behaviors, woven together into patterns that are infinitely fragile and never directly inherited."

"One of the oldest human needs is having someone to wonder where you are when you don't come home at night."

"Nobody has ever before asked the nuclear family to live all by itself in a box the way we do. With no relatives, no support, we've put ourselves in an impossible situation."

"Sister is probably the most competitive relationship within the family, but once the sisters are grown, it becomes the strongest relationship."

"Thanks to television, for the first time the young are seeing history made before it is censored by their elders."

"We need to devise a system within which peace will be more rewarding than war."

**Eighty percent of migraine sufferers are women.**

# FAMILIAR PHRASES

*Here are more origins of common phrases.*

## TO BREAK THE ICE

**Meaning:** To start a conversation

**Origin:** "Severe winter weather is a major nuisance to operators of boats. Until the development of power equipment, it was frequently necessary to chop ice at the river's edge with hand tools in order to make channels for plying about the river. The boatman had *to break the ice* before he could actually get down to business." (From *Cassell Everyday Phrases*, by Neil Ewart)

## TO PULL ONE'S OWN WEIGHT

**Meaning:** To do one's share or to take responsibility for oneself

**Origin:** "The term comes from rowing, where a crew member must pull on an oar hard enough to propel his or her own weight. In use literally since the mid-19th century, it began to be used figuratively in the 1890s." (From *Southpaws & Sunday Punches*, by Christine Ammer)

## TO KICK THE BUCKET

**Meaning:** To die

**Origin:** "There are a number of explanations for the origin of this expression, but the most plausible one has to do with the way some people committed suicide in the past. It was once fairly common for a man bent on killing himself to do so by standing on an upturned bucket, putting a noose around his neck, and then 'kicking the bucket.'" (From *Ever Wonder Why?*, by Douglas B. Smith)

## A SHOT HEARD AROUND THE WORLD

**Meaning:** An act of great importance, which has far-reaching consequences

**Origin:** "The shot from which this phrase derives wasn't literally heard around the globe, but its repercussions were certainly felt far from Concord, Massachusetts, where it was fired on April 19, 1775. On that day, British troops marched to Concord to seize a cache of weapons they believed were being hidden there by Amer-

**Something else to look forward to: The ability to taste sweets decreases with age.**

ican patriots. A confrontation between Colonial militiamen and the Redcoats took place at Concord Bridge of which the essayist, Ralph Waldo Emerson wrote, 'Here once the embattled farmers stood, And fired the shot heard 'round the world.' The American Revolution had begun. Not only did that first shot have great significance for the Americans and the British, but it had a tremendous impact on the rest of the world as well." (From *Inventing English*, by Dale Corey)

### THREE SHEETS TO THE WIND

**Meaning:** Very drunk

**Origin:** "The phrase comes from the world of seafaring and the sheets referred to are ropes. The first thing one learns about ropes once aboard ship is that they are never called ropes. They are named according to their particular function: *halyards* (which move or hold things vertically, usually sails), *sheets* (which move or hold things horizontally), and *lines* (which hold things in a static position). The sheets in this case are those ropes that hold the sails in place. If one sheet is loose, the sail will flap in the wind, and the ship's progress will be unsteady. Two sheets loose ('to the wind'), and you have a major problem, and with three sheets to the wind, the ship reels… like a drunken sailor. (*Four sheets to the wind*, by the way, meant 'completely unconscious.')" (From *The Word Detective*, by Evan Morris)

### GET OFF YOUR HIGH HORSE

**Meaning:** Stop being arrogant

**Origin:** "The 14th-century English religious reformer John Wycliffe once described a royal pageant in which high-ranking personages were mounted on *high horses*, or chargers, and these mounts became symbols of their superiority and arrogance. Mounted knights were certainly superior to foot soldiers, and even in 19th-century armies the cavalry regarded itself superior to the infantry. Ever since, telling someone to *get off their high horse* has meant to stop behaving arrogantly, with or without justification." (From *It's Raining Cats and Dogs*, by Christine Ammer)

# ANTE UP!

*Bet you didn't know that poker is a relatively new invention. Think we're bluffing? Read on. (By the way, can you guess Uncle John's favorite poker hand? That's right—the royal flush.)*

## PLACE YOUR BETS

If anyone tells you they know the true origin of poker, they're not playing with a full deck. People have been betting on cards for more than 1,000 years, about as long as cards have been around—and that makes it hard to trace poker back to any one particular game. For that matter, poker may have descended from several different games which were mixed and matched over centuries to create the game played today. Some likely candidates:

• **Domino Cards,** a game played in China as early as 900 A.D. As the name suggests, these playing cards were marked like dominos, with each card representing the scores thrown by a pair of dice—a one and a six, for example.

• **Tali,** a dice game played in the Roman Empire. In Tali throws of the dice are ranked in much the same way as poker: Three of a kind beat a pair, and high numbers are worth more than low ones.

• **As Nas,** a four-player Persian game that used a deck of 20 cards divided into four different suits. (According to some sources, there was also a five-player, 25-card version.) There were five types of cards in the deck: lions, kings, ladies, soldiers, and dancing girls; when played with a modern deck of cards, aces, kings, queens, jacks, and tens are used instead. Each player is dealt five cards, one at a time, per hand.

• **Primero,** an Italian card game played from the 16th century on. Thanks to the Napoleonic Wars (when soldiers weren't fighting, they liked to sit around and play cards), in the early 19th century, Primero spread across much of Europe and evolved into a number of different regional versions: Brag in England, Pochen in Germany, and Poque in France.

**America once issued a 5-cent bill. (Bills worth less than $1 are called "fractional currency.")**

## BORN ON THE BAYOU

Modern poker is all-American—it evolved from card games that were played in New Orleans in the early 19th century. Exactly how it developed isn't entirely clear, but it's possible that poker came about when the French colonists, already familiar with Poque, learned to play As Nas from Persian sailors visiting the port city. In Poque the only hands that counted were pairs, three of a kind, and four of a kind; but As Nas recognized two pairs and the full house. At some point, card historians speculate, players dumped many of Poque's rules and replaced them with those from *as nas* to make the game more interesting.

The name Poque may have been combined with As (from As Nas) to get *poqas*, which when spoken with a Southern accent sounded like "pokah." Steamboats took pokah up the Mississippi and Ohio rivers to the north, where people pronounced it "poker." From there, poker spread by wagon train and railroad across the continent.

## NOT PLAYING WITH A FULL DECK

Have you ever taken notes during a poker game? Hardly anyone ever does—that's one reason why the history of poker is so difficult to trace. Luckily, in 1829 an English actor named Joseph Crowell saw poker being played on a steamboat bound for New Orleans and recorded what he saw, providing a rare glimpse of what poker was like in its earliest form.

Like today, each player was dealt five cards and then placed bets; whoever had the best cards won all the money that was bet. But at that time the deck still had only 20 cards (four suits of aces, kings, queens, jacks, and tens)—it wasn't until the 1840s that the full 52-card deck came into use.

Why were so many cards added? There were two main reasons:

• When the concept of the draw—replacing some of the cards in your hand with new cards taken from the deck—was introduced in the 1840s, a 20-card deck wasn't big enough anymore.

• People who'd been cheated by card sharks playing a crooked game called three-card monte thought a game with 52 cards instead of just 3 would be a lot harder to rig.

The 52-card version of poker (and other games) became so popular that the 20-card deck eventually died out altogether.

**The average spider web weighs 1/27,000th of a pound.**

## WAR GAME

The Civil War was a period of great innovation in poker, thanks to the fact that millions of soldiers learned the game during the war and played it whenever they had a chance. Draw poker became very popular, and a newer variation, *stud-horse* poker (stud poker for short), in which some cards in a hand are dealt face up, and others dealt face down, also became widespread. The straight (five cards of sequential rank, such as 3, 4, 5, 6, and 7) also became a recognized poker hand during the war.

## PLAY CONTINUED

When the Civil War ended and the soldiers went home, they brought poker with them, and the innovations continued:

• The wild card was introduced in about 1875.

• Low ball (the *worst* hand, not the best, wins the pot) followed in about 1900.

• Why settle for playing only one type of poker per game? "Dealer's choice" games—in which the dealer gets to pick any version of poker they want for that hand—also became popular at the turn of the century.

## YOUR GOVERNMENT AT WORK

Were it not for this period of innovation, poker might have faded into obscurity or disappeared altogether. All forms of gambling fell out of favor in many parts of the country at the turn of the 20th century, and many states passed antigambling laws. These laws naturally applied to poker, too...or did they?

In 1911 California's attorney general had to decide whether poker was a form of gambling and thus should be outlawed. His conclusion: standard poker and stud poker, in which you had to play the cards you were dealt, were purely games of chance. That made them a form of gambling, he reasoned, and that made them illegal. *Draw* poker was another story. Drawing new cards from the deck—or deciding not to—made it a game of skill, and games of skill were not illegal under California law. So draw poker not only survived, it thrived—and today hundreds of different variations of draw poker are played all over the world.

**Survey results: The average Nevadan gambles $846 annually in casinos ($2.31 per day).**

## I'LL SEE YOU AND RAISE YOU

*Here's a look at some of the most popular forms of poker. How many have you played?*

• **Seven-Card Stud.** Two down cards (face down) and one up card (face up) are dealt to each player. They bet, and then four more cards are dealt one at a time—three up and the last one down—and bets are placed after each of these cards is dealt.

• **Razz.** Like Seven-Card Stud, except that the lowest hand wins, not the highest.

• **Texas Hold 'em.** Each player gets two down cards, then they place their bets. Three *common* cards are dealt face up to the center of the table, then the players place their bets again. Two more common cards are dealt, with bets being placed after each one. The best combination of five cards you can make from your two cards and the five on the board constitutes your hand; the highest hand is the winner.

• **Omaha High.** Each player gets *four* down cards; then bets are placed.

• **Omaha High-Low.** The same as Omaha High, except that the high hand and the low hand split the pot (the winnings).

• **Five-Card Stud.** Each player is dealt one down card and one up card, then bets are placed. Each player is dealt a second up card, and bets are placed again. A third and then a fourth up card are dealt to each player, each one followed by a round of betting.

• **Five-Card Draw.** Each player is dealt five cards down. Bets are placed, then each player may discard one or more cards and replace them with new cards from the deck, then bets are placed again.

• **Lowball.** The same as Five-Card Draw, except that the lowest hand, not the highest, wins.

• **Indian Poker.** Each player is dealt one card only, which they are not allowed to see. They hold it up against their forehead—supposedly like an Indian feather—so that everyone else can see it, then bets are placed. High card wins. The idea is that this game is the opposite of all the others—you know what everyone else's cards are, but you don't know your own.

**The British Isles have no mountains higher than 5,000 feet.**

# HURRICANES 101

*On page 519 we told you how hurricanes are formed. Here are some more basic facts about one of nature's deadliest creations.*

## HOW HURRICANES ARE NAMED

Hurricane names are chosen years in advance. Here's how meteorologists pick them.

**In the Atlantic Ocean.** Until the 1940s, hurricanes went mostly unnamed. But during WWII long range airplanes began encountering two or more hurricanes in a single flight. So in 1953, to simplify storm tracking, American meteorologists started giving them names—alphabetically to help aviators keep track of whether they were encountering a new storm or one that was dying. As a further refinement, male names were given to hurricanes south of the equator and female names were used for storms north of the equator.

Hurricanes, however, rarely occur in the South Atlantic because the water is too cold for them to form. And because they always move away from the equator, there was no way for a hurricane with a female name to move south and become a him-icane. So, for four decades all the hurricanes that passed over North America had female names. By the 1970s charges of sexism prompted American meteorologists to reconsider the system and in 1979 they began to use male and female names alternatively.

**Pacific Politics.** The Pacific Ocean is so huge and bordered by so many nations that meteorologists divide it into several regions. How a typhoon (in the Pacific, hurricanes are called "typhoons") is named depends on where it was born.

• **The central Pacific** uses Polynesian names: Akoni, Lo, Oke, Peke, and Walaka.

• **Australia** uses English names, such as Fiona, Vance, Graham, and Harriet.

• **The southwest Indian Ocean** uses names an Indian influence plus a few holdovers from the British Raj: Atang, Boura, Kalunde, and Winston.

• **The northwest Indian Ocean** region doesn't use names—

typhoons are numbered.

• **The northeast Pacific** uses names from the Americas: Andres, Carlos, and Kevin.

• **In the northwest Pacific**, there were so many different countries demanding to be included in the naming process that the United Nations had to step in. Names were submitted by Japan, China, Vietnam, Thailand, Malaysia, Cambodia, Micronesia, North and South Korea, the Philippines, and the United States. The current list of 141 names includes: Longwang (a mythological Chinese dragon); Damrey (Cambodian for "elephant"); Kodo ("cloud" in the Marshall Islands); and Higos ("fig" in the Marianas).

## HOW HURRICANES ARE RATED

Hurricanes are classed by wind speed: a category 1 has speeds of 74–95 mph; a category 2 has speeds of 96–110 mph; a category 3 has speeds of 111–130 mph; a category 4 has speeds of 131–155 mph; and the rare category 5 storms have speeds of 156 and up.

The highest known sustained wind speed from a cyclone was Typhoon Tip, located in the northwest Pacific Ocean. Tip's sustained surface wind on October 12, 1979, was estimated at 190 mph. In the Atlantic region, Hurricane Camille in 1969 and Hurricane Allen in 1980 registered winds also estimated at 190 mph. But these are only estimates—category 5 winds are so strong that the instruments used for measuring them are often destroyed, leaving scientists to guess at how fast the wind really was.

## THE FIRST RECORDED HURRICANE

In 1495, while anchored in Hispaniola, Christopher Columbus noted on his ship's log: "When the storm reached the harbor, it whirled the ships round as they lay at anchor, snapped their cables, and sank three of them with all who were on board."

Does this mean that Europeans had never heard of hurricanes before 1495? Actually, it does. Hurricanes can't reach Europe because Earth's rotation always sends them west and north. Typhoons don't make it because they would have to cross Asia. The spent remains of Atlantic hurricanes *have* struck Europe (from the Arctic circle) but before modern meteorology, the Europeans just thought they were big rain storms.

# THE WAY OF THE HOBO

*Have you ever dreamed of hopping on a freight train and living off the land? Trust Uncle John, it's not as glamorous as it sounds. But just in case you do, here's a starter course.*

## HOBO HIERARCHY

*What's the difference between a hobo, a tramp, and a bum?*

**Hobo:** A migratory worker (the most respected of the three). Hoboes are resourceful, self-reliant vagabonds who take on temporary work to earn a few dollars before moving on. Some experts think the word *hobo* comes from *hoe boys*, which is what farmers in the 1880s called their seasonal migrant workers. Others say it's shorthand for the phrase *homeward bound*, used to describe destitute Civil War veterans who took years to work their way home.

**Tramp:** A migratory nonworker. A tramp simply likes the vagabond life—he's never looking for a job.

**Bum:** The lowest of the low; a worthless loafer who stays in one place and would rather beg than work for goods or services.

## HOBO LINGO

**Accommodation car:** The caboose of a train

**Banjo:** A small portable frying pan

**Big House:** Prison

**Bindle stick:** A small bundle of belongings tied up in a scarf, handkerchief, or blanket hanging from a walking stick

**Bull:** A railroad cop (also called a "cinder dick")

**Cannonball:** A fast train

**Chuck a dummy:** Pretend to faint

**Cover with the moon:** Sleep out in the open

**Cow crate:** A railroad stock car

**Crums:** Lice (also called "gray backs" and "seam squirrels")

**Doggin' it:** Traveling by bus

**Easy mark:** A hobo sign, or "mark," that identifies a person or place where one can get food and a place to stay overnight

**Honey dipping:** Working with a shovel in a sewer

**Hot:** A hobo wanted by the law

**Knowledge box:** A schoolhouse, where hobos sometimes sleep

**Moniker:** Nickname

**Road kid:** A young hobo who apprentices himself to an older hobo in order to learn the ways of the road

**Rum dum:** A drunkard

**Snipes:** Other people's cigarette butts (O.P.C.B.); "snipe hunting" is to go looking for butts

**Spear biscuits:** To look for food in garbage cans

**Yegg:** The lowest form of hobo—he steals from other hobos

## HOBO ROAD SIGNS

Wherever they went, hobos left simple drawings, or "marks," chalked on fence posts, barns, and railroad buildings. These signs were a secret code giving fellow knights of the road helpful tips or warnings.

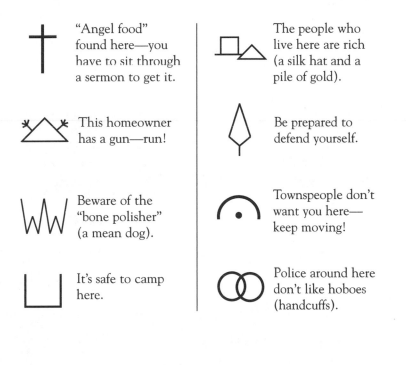

"Angel food" found here—you have to sit through a sermon to get it.

This homeowner has a gun—run!

Beware of the "bone polisher" (a mean dog).

It's safe to camp here.

The people who live here are rich (a silk hat and a pile of gold).

Be prepared to defend yourself.

Townspeople don't want you here—keep moving!

Police around here don't like hoboes (handcuffs).

Can you taste them? The secret recipe for Dr Pepper is said to contain 23 fruit flavors.

# CRÈME *de la* CRUD

*Most really bad movies die a quick death in the theaters and then gather dust on video store shelves. But not this one.*

**RECIPE FOR DISASTER**

• Take two A-list movie stars: Ben Affleck and Jennifer Lopez.

• Add a torrid off-screen love affair that doesn't translate into on-screen chemistry.

• Add a huge dollop of media hype about how great the movie's going to be.

• Mix in a vulgar, inane script.

Stir it all together and you have *Gigli* (pronounced *zheelie*), a movie that rivals *Ishtar* and *Battlefield Earth* for the title of Hollywood's biggest flop. Good news: You don't have to see the picture—you can be entertained just by reading the scathing reviews. Here are some samples.

"Looking for something to praise in *Gigli* is like digging for rhinestones in a dung heap."
—***Northwest Herald***

"Larry and Ricki eventually climb between the sheets in a scene that is insulting to the sexuality of all living creatures, from plankton on up."
—***Boston Globe***

"There is not one iota of dramatic weight to it, and so we just sit, slack-jawed, as *Gigli* unfolds, a cinematic train wreck of distinguished proportions."
—***Entertainment Today***

"If you're going to skip one film this year—make it *Gigli*."
—***Talking Pictures***

"*Gigli* looks like a project that was intended for appreciation by precisely two people in the entire universe: Ben Affleck and Jennifer Lopez. For their sake, I hope they buy a lot of tickets."
—**EFilmCritic.com**

"*Gigli* is a rigli, rigli bad movie."
—**Mercurynews.com**

"This is a film that inspires hatred."
—**FilmThreat.com**

**No wonder they're "big boned"—Elephants spend 18 hours a day eating.**

"Fifty minutes into this bomb, one character yells, 'I'm getting tired of this!' In our theater, one audience member yelled back 'Me too!'"

**—CrankyCritic.com**

"If miscasting was a crime, *Gigli* would be proof of a felony."

**—CNN**

"The rare movie that never seems to take off, but also never seems to end."

***—USA Today***

"*Gigli* is so unrelentingly bad that people may want to see it just as a bonding experience; viewers (read: victims) will want to talk and comfort each other afterwards."

***—San Francisco Examiner***

"Lopez even gives a long, carefully detailed speech about how to not only gouge out someone's eye, but to remove the memory of everything they've ever seen. Which, by the end of the movie, wasn't starting to seem so bad."

***—The Star-Ledger***

"Test audiences reportedly balked at the film's happy ending and wanted Gigli and Ricki to die bloody deaths. And they say critics are harsh."

***—Rolling Stone***

"Not helping things is Lopez's Betsy-Wetsy lisp that transforms a line like 'brutal street thug' into 'bruel threet fug.'"

**—Film Freak Central**

"How on Earth did director Martin Brest envision this film? As *Chasing Amy* meets *Rain Man* meets *Pulp Fiction*? Did anyone think that sounded like a winning combination?"

***—Chicago Tribune***

"Mr. Affleck and Ms. Lopez's combined fees reportedly ran close to $25 million, and they earn their money by hogging as much screen time as possible and uttering some of the lamest dialogue ever committed to film."

***—The New York Times***

"*Gigli* is as awkward as the word itself. I suggest you spell *Gigli* backwards so it sounds like 'ill gig.'"

**—Critic Doctor**

"For two hours, not a single hair moved on Ben's head—not even when every hair in the audience was on end and growing in the direction of the exit's welcoming glow."

**—Movie Juice**

"It wasn't good, and we got buried."

**—Ben Affleck**

**Ted Danson once appeared in a TV commercial as a package of lemon chiffon pie mix.**

# POKER LINGO

*Ever watched rounders and fish splash the pot until they're down to the felt? If so, you've seen some serious poker players. They have their own language, too. Ante up!*

- **All in:** Bet all your chips
- **Down to the felt:** So broke all you see in front of you is the green felt of the poker table
- **Tapioca, or Tap City:** Tapped out; out of money
- **Buy the pot:** Make a bet so large that other players are unlikely to match it
- **Tap:** Bet as much as your opponents have on hand, forcing them to bet everything
- **Catching cards:** On a winning streak
- **Railroad bible:** Deck of cards
- **Toke:** The tip you give to the dealer
- **Splash the pot:** Toss your chips into the pot, instead of just placing them there. It's considered bad form because other players can't see how much you're actually betting
- **Rake:** The house's cut
- **Cowboys:** Kings
- **Ladies:** Queens
- **Rock:** A very conservative player, someone who doesn't take big chances
- **Paint:** A face card
- **Trips:** Three of a kind
- **Berry patch:** A very easy game
- **Underdog:** A weak hand that's likely to lose
- **Rag:** An up facing card so low in value that it can't affect the outcome of the hand
- **Alligator blood:** A player who keeps his cool under pressure has alligator (cold) blood
- **Wheel:** The best hand in lowball poker—6, 4, 3, 2, A
- **Fish:** A very bad poker player. They're only in the game so that you can beat them out of their money
- **George:** A fish
- **Rounder:** A professional poker player. A rounder makes his living parting fishes and georges from their money
- **Base deal:** Dealing from the bottom of the deck
- **In the hole:** In stud poker, the cards dealt face down, so only you can see them
- **Bullets:** Aces in the hole
- **Big slick:** A king and an ace in the hole
- **Boat:** A full house

# COYOTE RINGS THE WRONG BELL

*Every year it happens—we're less than 24 hours from going to press and Uncle John runs over to Jay's desk and says, "Flying Flushes! We have to replace a 3-page article... hurry!" So Jay calmly goes to the ol' folk tale bookshelf and finds one he likes.*

**AGE-OLD ADVERSARIES**

In Mexico there are many tales about animals, but most of them are about Hare and Coyote. These two always argue and try to outwit each other; they are rivals in hunting and everything else. But since Coyote is much the stronger, Hare has to match his wits against Coyote's strength.

Now, one day Hare finished a fine meal and lay down under a tree for his siesta. Sometimes he gazed up at the blue sky, and other times he just closed his eyes. Finally, after a while, Hare fell fast asleep.

Coyote came along very, very quietly, looking for Hare, for Coyote was hungry. When he saw Hare sleeping, he approached very slowly and silently, and when he was near, Coyote took a great jump and *plppp!* he landed squarely on top of Hare with all four paws.

**SURPRISE!**

Hare awoke with a frightened start and saw at once that he was in deep trouble. But he was not afraid.

"Now I have you, Hare!" said Coyote. "You must have had a fine breakfast, for you feel nice and fat. Mmm, what a great meal you will make!"

Hare was thinking fast.

"Yes, I did have a fine meal," he said, "And I don't mind if you eat me, for my flesh is old and dry and I don't have much longer to live anyway. But if you will just be patient and wait a bit, perhaps I can give you something to eat that is much more tender and softer than I am."

"I wouldn't mind having something more tender," replied Coyote, "But I don't see anything better to eat around here. So it will have to be you, Brother Hare, Ha, Ha, Ha!"

Hare did not laugh.

"I know," he said, breathing hard, for Coyote was sitting right on top of him and he was very heavy. "I know you see only me right now, because all the tender, young hares are in school, but that is just a little way from here. They are all there, soft and juicy, and just the right age for eating."

Coyote licked his lips.

## FOR WHOM THE BELL TOLLS

"Yeeeessssss," said Coyote, "I know that these little hares are very soft and juicy. But tell me, where is that school, Brother Hare?"

"Just a little way down the hill. They are waiting for me to ring the bell for them to come out and play. But I can't ring it yet, not until the sun reaches the tops of the trees up on the hill. Then I can ring the bell. See? It's right up here in this tree." And he pointed to a tree under which they were lying and in which there was a big, brown hornets' nest.

"Will those little, plump hares come out when you ring the bell?" asked Coyote.

"They will, indeed, but I have to wait a long time. It's too early now. They must stay there a long time yet."

"Would they come out if you rang the bell now?"

"Sure they would, but I won't ring it now. I must wait for the right time."

"Brother Hare, I'm not really that hungry now anyway, and I promise I won't eat you. You see, I am letting you get up. Why don't you go for a little walk, to stretch and get the stiffness out of your joints? I'll stay and ring the bell for you at the right time, my friend." Coyote got off Hare, and Hare stretched himself slowly.

## DON'T BEE CRUEL

"I don't mind running off if you will promise to stay and ring the bell. But please do not forget, Brother Coyote, you must not ring it until the sun reaches the tops of the trees on the hill."

"I won't forget, but you must tell me how to ring the bell."

**In Bavaria, beer isn't just an alcoholic drink—it's considered a staple food, like bread or eggs.**

"It's very easy—all you have to do is shake the tree very hard. Then they will hear it at the schoolhouse. But shake it violently, so they will be sure to hear it."

"You can be sure I'll shake the tree hard enough, Brother Hare. Now run along!"

Hare was off like a flash. When he was at a safe distance, he shouted, "Be sure to wait for the sun to reach the trees, Brother Coyote."

"I won't forget, Hare. Now please, be on your way!"

Hare ran off, while Coyote watched, licking his lips. No sooner was Hare out of sight than Coyote rushed up the tree and began shaking it with all of his might. He shook it and shook it, but no bell rang. Finally, he threw all of his weight violently against the tree, and *klppp!* down fell the hornets' nest and landed squarely on Coyote's back. Suddenly the air was filled with hornets as they flew out in fury form their nest, stinging Coyote all over his body, from the point of his nose to the tip of his tail. You couldn't see his fur anywhere for all of the hornets.

Coyote ran as fast as he could, howling, but the hornets were after him all the way, stinging him at every step, teaching him a painful lesson for knocking down their nest.

And so greedy Coyote had sharp stings for supper instead of plump, little hares.

*   *   *

## COYOTE ADVICE

*Coyotes thrive throughout Canada, the United States, and Mexico. And contrary to legend, they are actually very clever. They're also predators. Here are a few tips from the Sierra Club to help protect pets and property:*

• If you keep livestock or small animals, confine them in secure pens, especially from dusk to dawn when coyotes are most active.

• Guard dogs and electric fences deter predators.

• Coyotes are attracted to food scraps in garbage. Dispose of trash in a metal can, and secure the lid with a bungee cord or chain.

• It is best not to feed cats and dogs outdoors, but if you have to, do not leave bowls or food scraps outside at night.

**Ernest Hemingway's rules for manhood: plant a tree, fight a bull, write a book, have a son.**

# PLEASED TO MEAT YOU

*Uncle John once saw a sign on an electrician's truck that said "Let us fix your shorts." He's been collecting wacky business mottoes like these ever since.*

**Concrete company:** "We dry harder."

**Taxidermist:** "We really know our stuff."

**Podiatrist:** "Time wounds all heels."

**Butcher:** "Let me meat your needs."

**Pastry shop:** "Get your buns in here."

**Septic services:** "We're number 1 in the number 2 business."

**Dry cleaner:** "Drop your pants here."

**Towing company:** "We don't want an arm and a leg…just your tows!"

**Window cleaner:** "Your pane is our pleasure."

**Restaurant:** "Don't stand there and be hungry, come in and get fed up."

**Diaper service:** "Let us lighten your load."

**Funeral home:** "Drive carefully, we'll wait."

**Chimney sweep:** "We kick ash."

**Trash service:** "Satisfaction guaranteed or double your trash back."

**Garden shop:** "Our business is growing."

**Auto body shop:** "May we have the next dents?"

**Muffler shop:** "No appointment necessary. We'll hear you coming."

**Car wash:** "We take a bite out of grime."

**Massage studio:** "It's great to be kneaded."

**Sod installation:** "We just keep rolling a lawn."

**Auto repair:** "We meet by accident."

**Bakery:** "While you sleep, we loaf."

**Plumber:** "A good flush beats a full house."

**Butcher:** "Pleased to meat you."

**Vacuum cleaners:** "Business sucks."

# THE DOO-DOO MAN

*In our opinion, the ability to take a negative experience and turn it into something positive is a real gift. But what inspired this man could appeal only to bathroom readers.*

## TRAIL HAZARD

In 1985 Dr. A. Bern Hoff stepped in something unpleasant while hiking in Norway's Jotunheim Mountains. The unpleasant "something" had been deposited right in the middle of the hiking trail and, judging from appearances, only minutes before. Maybe it was his keen eyesight, maybe it was his degree in parasitic pathology, but somehow Dr. Hoff knew right away what he'd stepped in: "people droppings," as he delicately puts it.

It wasn't the first time Hoff had trod on people droppings, either: an avid hiker, he'd had similar experiences atop Africa's Mount Kilimanjaro, Hawaii's Haleakala Crater, and the Grand Canyon in Arizona. He stepped into people's "business" so often that it seemed like every hiking trip was turning into a business trip. As a former official with the Centers for Disease Control, he understood that the problem wasn't just disgusting, it was a serious health hazard. Hoff decided it was time for action.

"I got tired of seeing and smelling this stuff on the trail," he says. "Nobody wanted to deal with it, so I said, 'Hey, I'll do it.' This has got to stop." He formed H.A.D.D.—Hikers Against Doo-Doo.

## THE NUMBER TWO PROBLEM

Hoff had stumbled—literally—onto a problem that started growing rapidly in the 1980s and continues today: Record numbers of people are hiking and camping out in the wild. And since most first-timers have never been taught how to properly "do their business" in the backcountry, in many popular outdoor destinations around the country, the results are plain to see, smell…and step in.

To counter this disturbing trend, H.A.D.D. offers a number of different "business plans." It teaches new campers tried-and-true waste-disposal techniques, and serves as an international clearinghouse for new waste-disposal ideas.

## THE CAN

H.A.D.D. has also designed a cheap, sturdy portable privy called "The Can" that can be made from two ordinary 55-gallon drums. At last count, H.A.D.D. members have set up more than 280 Cans in wilderness areas around the world. The organization hopes to one day mount an expedition to bring The Can to the top of Mount Aconcagua, long known as Argentina's "tallest and most defiled peak," and is raising funds to improve the facilities on Russia's Mount Elbrus, which *Outside* magazine dubbed "the world's nastiest outhouse."

When Hoff founded H.A.D.D. in 1990, it consisted of only himself and his soiled hiking boots. Today the organization boasts more than 10,000 members, with chapters all over the world. "We're tongue-in-cheek, of course, but we are serious about trying to clean up the environment," Hoff says.

## BUSINESS SCHOOL

Some tips on how to mind your own business in the wild:

• Pack out what you pack in. Bring several square pieces of paper, a paper bag full of kitty litter, and several zipper-type plastic bags or bags with twist-ties. Do your business onto the paper, then put the paper and your business into one of the plastic bags. Pour in some kitty litter, and seal the bag tightly. Dispose of it properly when you get back to civilization.

• If you do have to bury your business, be sure to do it: 1) at least 200 feet away from the nearest water source, trail, or campsite; 2) in organic soil, not sandy soil; and 3) in a "cat hole" dug at least six inches across and six inches deep. (*Hint:* Bring a small shovel.)

• Don't bury your business under a rock: business needs heat and moisture to decompose properly, and the rock will inhibit both.

• Don't bury it in the snow, either: snow melts...but your business doesn't. When spring comes it will reappear.

• Use toilet paper sparingly if at all; if you do use it, *don't* burn it and *don't* bury it with your business. Keep it in a plastic bag and dispose of it properly at the end of your trip.

• Pee at least 200 feet from the nearest water source, and *don't* pee on green plants—otherwise, when your pee dries, animals will be attracted to the salt.

# ACCORDING TO THE LATEST RESEARCH

*It seems as though every day there's a report on some scientific study with dramatic new information on what we should eat...or how we should act...or who we really are under all the BS. Some are pretty interesting. Did you know, for example, that science says...*

## NIGHT LIGHTS CAUSE CANCER

**Researcher:** Dr. Richard Stevens

**Subjects:** Residents of Beaver Dam, Wisconsin

**What He Learned:** In 2002, citing several studies of women's cancer rates, Dr. Stevens reported to the World Conference on Breast Cancer in Victoria, British Columbia, that artificial night lighting increases the risk of breast cancer. Extended hours of light, he said—night lights, street lights, and even car headlights—rob a person of valuable hours of darkness and disrupt the body's natural clock. That causes the body to make less melatonin, a hormone produced almost exclusively at night. Melatonin limits the body's estrogen levels, and high levels of the female hormone estrogen are known to increase the risk of getting the disease. He recommended red bulbs in night lights—they're less disruptive to sleep patterns.

## THE VATICAN EMITS HAZARDOUS RAYS

**Researcher:** Paola Michelozzi of the Rome health department

**Subjects:** People who live near Vatican City

**What She Learned:** EMFs (electromagnetic field emissions) are produced by electric current. In power lines and large communication antennas, those emissions can be very high—and, some say, dangerous. The Vatican has a huge radio and communications station on the outskirts of Rome, and because the Vatican is an independent country, it's not regulated by Italian law. Dr. Michelozzi's team decided to study the area around the station and the effects of the EMFs. Their finding: The rate of deaths for men due to leukemia was three times higher than the expected rate within a 1.2-mile radius. For children it was double. The Vatican refuses to release any information about their transmissions.

## BEER STINKS

**Researchers:** Chemist Malcolm Forbes, University of North Carolina

**Subject:** Beer

**What He Learned:** Have you ever opened a bottle beer and noticed that it smells "skunky?" Dr. Forbes studied hops, the ingredient that gives beer much of its taste, and found that after exposure to light, a chemical reaction in the hops molecules results in the production of a compound called a *thiol*. Another place thiols can be found: in a skunk's spray gland. "Of course," says Forbes, a beer connoisseur who was happy to do the study, "the best solution we offer is to drink your beer as fast as possible."

## REDHEADED WOMEN ARE MORE SENSITIVE

**Researcher:** Dr. Edwin Liem, University of Louisville

**Subjects:** Redheads and brunettes

**What He Learned:** Anesthesiologists have said it for decades: they have to use more anesthetic to put a redhead "under." Now they have proof. Dr. Liem gave a group of women common anesthetic drugs and monitored their reflex movements in response to being pricked with needles. He found that red-haired women needed 20% more of the drug to numb their pain reflexes completely. Doctors think it may be caused by a genetic glitch in redheads related to melanin, a pigment that affects skin and hair color.

## LONDON CABBIES HAVE BIGGER BRAINS

**Researchers:** Scientists at University College London

**Subjects:** Taxi drivers

**What They Learned:** To get a license to drive the traditional black cab in London, drivers have to pass a very rigorous test called "The Knowledge." Those that do are known to be excellent navigators. This study showed something else: after giving 49 drivers MRI brain scans, researchers noticed that the drivers had an enlarged hippocampus—the part of the brain associated with navigation in birds and other animals. And even more amazingly, like a muscle, the more it's used, the larger it grows. Longtime cabbie David Cohen was surprised by the results: "I never noticed part of my brain growing. It makes you wonder what happened to the rest of it."

**The beer-drinkingest state: Nevada, at 35 gallons per capita....**

# STRANGE LAWSUITS

*Here are more real-life examples of unusual legal battles.*

**THE PLAINTIFF:** Paula Blum, 54-year-old mother
**THE DEFENDANT:** Ephraim Blum, her son
**THE LAWSUIT:** After years of trying (and failing) to get alimony payments from her ex-husband, Blum switched tactics—she sued her son. Not for alimony, though: Blum used the Family Law Reform Act, which states that upon reaching adulthood, a child has an obligation to give his parents financial assistance.
**THE VERDICT:** Incredibly, the court found in her favor, ordering Ephraim to pay his mother $270 a month for life.

**THE PLAINTIFF:** Gerald Mayo
**THE DEFENDANT:** Satan and His Staff
**THE LAWSUIT:** Alleging that Satan had deliberately made his life miserable, placed obstacles in his path, and plotted his doom, Mayo sued the Prince of Darkness in federal court. On what charges? Civil rights violations. Mayo claimed that Satan had "deprived him of his constitutional rights."
**THE VERDICT:** Case dismissed. The judge expressed doubt over whether the defendant was actually a resident of the judicial district and noted that Mayo hadn't included instructions on how to serve Satan with the necessary papers.

**THE PLAINTIFF:** Ralph Forbes, of Russellville, Arkansas
**THE DEFENDANTS:** The National Department of Education, the Russellville School District, the High Priests of Secular Humanism, the Communist Party of the USA, the Church of Satan, the Anti-Christ, and Satan, God of This World System
**THE LAWSUIT:** In 1986, outraged that schools around Little Rock were sponsoring Halloween celebrations, Forbes—a local pastor and candidate for U.S. senator—decided to sue on behalf of Jesus Christ and children everywhere. Calling Halloween activities "rites of Satan," he was determined to stop them.

The Devil's advocate, attorney John Wesley Hall, Jr., argued that the suit should be dismissed because Forbes had failed to

**... Least beer-imbibing state: Utah, right next door, at 13 gallons per person each year.**

prove that Satan owned property or wrote contracts in Arkansas.
**THE VERDICT:** Case dismissed.

**THE PLAINTIFF:** An anonymous 19-year-old man
**THE DEFENDANT:** The New York City Transit Authority
**THE LAWSUIT:** The man tried to commit suicide by jumping off a subway platform into the path of an oncoming train. He lost one arm, a leg, and part of his other arm—but not his life. Frustrated with the futile attempt, the man filed suit against the Transit Authority. His claim: "The motorman was negligent in not stopping the train quickly enough."
**THE VERDICT:** Settled out of court for $650,000. While they were negotiating the settlement, the man tried suicide again, using the same method as before—and once again was unsuccessful. (No word on whether he filed a second lawsuit.)

**THE PLAINTIFF:** "Josef M.", a 62-year-old German man
**THE DEFENDANT:** Josef M.'s butcher
**THE LAWSUIT:** Josef M. sued his butcher for $790...for selling him a loaded bratwurst. He claimed the sausage exploded as he bit into it, and hot fat squirted into his mouth, burning it and the inside of his throat. His major complaint: "I couldn't kiss for four weeks," he said.
**THE VERDICT:** The court rejected the claim as frivolous.

**THE PLAINTIFF:** Robert Paul Rice, an inmate
**THE DEFENDANT:** Utah State Prison
**THE LAWSUIT:** Rice sued the prison for violating his religious freedom, claiming that he listed "the Vampire Order" as his religion and should have his religious needs provided for. According to the suit, prison officials failed to provide a "vampire diet" (only grains and vegetables—no meat) or a "vampiress" with whom he could partake in "the vampiric sacrament." Lawyers for the prison argued that it provides five diets to choose from and "vampire" isn't one of them. And a "vampiress?" Sorry, prisons in Utah do not allow conjugal visits.
**THE VERDICT:** Rice lost. The court ruled that the case "raised questions that are so insubstantial as not to merit consideration."

**Foggiest place on the U.S. West Coast: Cape Disappointment, WA (107 days per year).**

# DUMB JOCKS?

*More verbally challenged sports stars.*

"He treats us like men. He lets us wear earrings."

**—Torrin Polk, University of Houston receiver, *on his coach, John Jenkins***

"Left hand, right hand, it doesn't matter. I'm amphibious."

**—Charles Shackleford, NCSU basketball player**

"[He] called me a 'rapist' and a 'recluse'. I'm not a recluse."

**—Boxer Mike Tyson, *on writer Wallace Matthews***

"In terms of European athletes she is currently second. A Cuban leads the rankings."

**—Paul Dickenson, BBC commentator**

"We can't win at home. We can't win on the road. I just can't figure out where else to play."

**—Pat Williams, Orlando Magic GM, *on his team's poor record***

"It's almost like we have ESPN."

**—Magic Johnson, *on how well he and James Worthy play together***

"Me and George and Billy are two of a kind."

**—N.Y. Yankee Mickey Rivers, *on his relationship with George Steinbrenner and Billy Martin***

"I told [GM] Roland Hemond to go out and get me a big-name pitcher. He said, 'Dave Wehrmeister's got 11 letters. Is that a big enough name for you?'"

**—Eddie Eichorn, White Sox owner**

"Men, I want you just thinking of one word all season. One word and one word only: Super Bowl."

**—Bill Peterson, football coach**

"I want to rush for 1,000 or 1,500 yards, whichever comes first."

**—George Rogers, New Orleans Saints running back**

"Raise the urinals."

**—Darrel Chaney, Atlanta shortstop, *on how management could keep the Braves on their toes***

# OOPS!

*More blunders and screwups to make you feel all smug and superior.*

## HAPPY MEAL

Washington, D.C., June 2002—"Benjamin Crevier recently got a personal invitation from U.S. Vice President Dick Cheney to a $2,500-a-plate dinner with President George W. Bush. Ben, who is five years old, wrote back to decline, saying he had only $11.97 in his piggy bank."

**—*The North County* (Maryland) *Times***

## HOMEWRECKERS

"A wrecking crew that was supposed to demolish an abandoned house accidentally plowed a bulldozer into the headquarters of a group that had tried for months to preserve it. The Dade Heritage Trust had failed to save the 102-year-old home of pioneer doctor James M. Jackson, located next door to the trust's headquarters. But the bulldozer operator made a wrong turn, taking out a porch column, a window and roof tiles of the trust's headquarters. 'What can I say?' said Jesus Ramos, bulldozer operator and owner of Shark Wrecking. 'It was an accident.'"

**—Associated Press**

## NOT *THAT* KIND OF GRASS

"In December 2002, Chicago police got an anonymous tip that a major consignment of illegal drugs was being moved in a truck. When officers stopped the vehicle, they found two small plastic bags with crushed green plants thought to be marijuana. Lab tests found no drugs were present. The 'marijuana' turned out to be hay from a church Nativity scene."

**—*The National Post,* Canada**

## ARMED AND DANGEROUS

"A suspect picked the wrong vehicle to carjack in Hollywood Sunday. Los Angeles police say the suspect took one car, then pulled into a gas station, ditched the vehicle and tried to take a minivan. Big mistake. The minivan was full of judo wrestlers from

Florida International University, who were in town to teach a self-defense class. The wrestlers punched the man in the face and hit him from behind, then held him until police arrived. The suspect was jailed on felony charges."

—*Los Angeles Times*

## OFF WITH THEIR HEAD

"Officials at England's York Dungeon Museum of Horrors are looking for the visitor who purchased an authentic human skull in the museum's gift shop. The skull was accidentally placed on a bookshelf while an exhibit was being renovated. Someone apparently mistook the real skull for one of the replica skulls sold in the gift shop…and sold it as a souvenir."

—**Reuters**

## EGG ON HIS FACE

"A 30-year-old plumber from Perugia in central Italy came up with a novel way of proposing to his girlfriend: He ordered a chocolate Easter egg with an expensive engagement ring, featuring a huge diamond and three rubies set in gold, placed inside. The young man then presented his beloved with the egg, a traditional Easter gift in that part of Italy. He didn't say anything to the girl, wanting her to open it on her own and experience the surprise of her life. Several days went by with no response from the girl, so he finally asked her if she had enjoyed his present. What he heard left him speechless. The girl explained she did not like dark chocolate, of which the egg was made, so she went to a nearby café and exchanged it for an identical egg made of milk chocolate.

"The two rushed to the café, but learned the egg had already been sold to another customer. No trace of the egg or the ring was ever found."

—*Financial Times*

## "OH LORD, WON'T YOU BUY ME A…"

"When a gold Mercedes-Benz sports sedan was delivered by mistake to Ruth Shepard's driveway in Uniondale, New York, in May 2002, she thought it was a surprise Mother's Day present. A short time later, she was arrested for resisting police officers' attempts to get the car back to its rightful owner."

—**Universal Press Syndicate**

Some snakes can go an entire year without eating.

# GRANNY DUMPING

*How do doctors, nurses, and other hospital workers deal with the stress of being exposed to illness and death on a daily basis? They come up with irreverent, occasionally morbid—and very funny—terms for what goes on in the hospital every day.*

**Blood Suckers:** People who take blood samples, e.g., nurses or laboratory technicians

**Gassers:** Anesthetists

**Rear Admiral:** Proctologist

**AGA:** Acute Gravity Attack —the patient fell over

**AGMI:** Ain't Gonna Make It

**Coffin Dodger:** A patient the hospital staff thought was going to die, but didn't

**Gone Camping:** A patient in an oxygen tent

**Shotgunning:** Ordering lots of tests, in the hope that one of them will identify what is wrong with a patient

**GPO:** Good For Parts Only

**D&D:** Divorced and Desperate; someone who isn't sick but comes to the hospital because they need attention

**CTD:** Circling the drain, or close to death

**Rule of Five:** If more than five of the patient's orifices have tubes running out of them, they're CTD.

**UBI:** Unexplained Beer Injury

**Pop Drop/Granny Dumping:** Checking an elderly relative into an emergency room, just so you can go on vacation without them

**ECU:** "Eternal Care Unit" (deceased), as in: "He's gone to the ECU."

**DBI:** Dirt Bag Index—a mathematical formula: the number of a patient's tattoos times the number of missing teeth equals the number of days since they last bathed.

**VIP:** Very Intoxicated Person

**Hand Them a Bible So They Can Study for the Final:** They're going to die.

**UNIVAC:** Unusually Nasty Infection; Vultures Are Circling

**Eating In:** Feeding by way of an intravenous tube

**GTTL:** Gone To The Light (deceased)

**Silver Bracelet Award:** A patient brought in wearing handcuffs

# WORD ORIGINS

*Ever wonder where words come from?*
*Here are some more interesting stories.*

### PANDEMONIUM

**Meaning:** Wild and noisy disorder or confusion

**Origin:** "John Milton's word for the capital of Hell in *Paradise Lost* (1667). He wrote it as 'Pandaemonium'—meaning "all demons" in Greek—having no idea that in the 19th century the word would mean 'uproar.' So when, as he also wrote, 'All Hell broke loose,' all the demons in Hell were scattered, marking the disintegration of the infernal city." (From *The Secret Lives of Words*, by Paul West)

### COOKIE

**Meaning:** A small sweet cake, typically round, flat, and crisp

**Origin:** "The word was borrowed from the Dutch *koekje*, 'little cake,' which is the diminutive of Dutch *koek*, 'cake.' *Cookie* came into American English from the Dutch settlers of New York. It first appears in 1703 in the statement that 'at a funeral, 800 cockies...were furnished.' This early English spelling of the word differs from our modern spelling, but several other spellings also arose, such as *cookey* and *cooky*. The spelling *cookie* may have won out because the word is very common in the plural, spelled *cookies*." (From *Word Mysteries and Histories*, by the Editors of The American Heritage Dictionaries)

### DRAB

**Meaning:** Lacking brightness, dull

**Origin:** "In the 16th century, *drab* was a word for a kind of cloth, coming into English from French *drap*, 'cloth.' From this, the word came to mean the common color of such cloth, which was its natural undyed color of dull brown or gray. Hence the fairly general meaning 'dull,' whether of an object's color (where it usually is brown or gray still, as 'drab' walls) or in a figurative sense, as a 'drab' day or someone's 'drab' existence." (From *Dunces, Gourmands & Petticoats*, by Adrian Room)

**Old softie: Princeton professor John W. Tukey coined the term *software* in 1958.**

## URANIUM

**Meaning:** A dense radioactive metal used as a fuel in nuclear reactors

**Origin:** "In 1781 the brilliant English-German astronomer Sir William Herschel first recognized the seventh planet in our solar system, and named for it Uranus from the Greek god *Ouranos*. Eight years later the German chemist Kloproth discovered element 92, which he named *uranium* in honor of Herschel." (From *Word Origins*, by Wilfred Funk)

## NONCHALANT

**Meaning:** Feeling or appearing casual and relaxed

**Origin:** "The nonchalant person is cool and indifferent, a literal etymology, since the word is from French *nonchaloir*, meaning 'not heated,' which is derived from Latin *noncalere*, 'not to be hot.' *Calor* is Latin for 'heat,' from which we get *calorie*, the amount of food needed to heat you or energize you." (From *More About Words*, by Margaret S. Ernst)

## SALARY

**Meaning:** A regular payment made by an employer to an employee

**Origin:** "A salary, during the great days of the Romans, was called a *salarium*, 'salt-money.' The ancients regarded salt as such an essential to good diet (and before refrigeration it was the only chemical that preserved meat) that they made a special allowance in the wages of soldiers to buy *sal* (Latin for 'salt'). With time any stipend came to be called a *salarium*, from which English acquired the word salary." (From *Hue and Cry and Humble Pie*, by Morton S. Freeman)

## BLINDFOLD

**Meaning:** A piece of cloth tied around the head to cover the eyes

**Origin:** "The name of the folded piece of cloth has only a coincidental resemblance to the way the material is doubled over. *Blindfold* actually comes from the Middle English *blindfeld*, 'to be struck blind.' Walter Tyndale used *blyndfolded* in his English translation of the Bible (1526), and if he was not the first to make the mistake, he was certainly the most influential." (From *Devious Derivations*, by Hugh Rawson)

**Q: What woman's body part would ancient Chinese artists never paint? A: The feet.**

# EH TWO, CANADA?

*While rummaging through the trivia vault here at the BRI, we kept coming across a fascinating fact: Of the 175-plus nations in the world, Canada—the 35th most populous country—comes in second in a surprising number of categories.*

**Canada was the 2nd** country to legalize medical marijuana. (*1st: Belgium*)

**Canada has the 2nd** coldest national capital: Ottawa. (*1st: Ulaanbaatar, Mongolia*)

**Canada is the 2nd** largest foreign investor in Chile. (*1st: United States*)

**Canada has the 2nd** highest University enrollment rate in the world. (*1st: United States*)

**Canada has the 2nd** most tornadoes. (*1st: United States*)

**Canada is the 2nd** in pork exports. (*1st: Denmark*)

**Canada has the 2nd** highest amount of gum chewed per capita. (*1st: United States*)

**Canada has the 2nd** highest broadband Internet access in the world. (*1st: South Korea*)

**Canada was the 2nd** country to publish a National Atlas. (*1st: Finland*)

**Canada has the 2nd** highest fresh water use per capita. (*1st: United States*)

**Canada has the 2nd** highest water quality. (*1st: Finland*)

**Canada is the 2nd** largest per capita emitter of greenhouse gases. (*1st: United States*)

**Canada has the 2nd** most biotech companies. (*1st: United States*)

**Canada is the 2nd** largest exporter of red meat. (*1st: Australia*)

**Canada is the 2nd** biggest market for U.S. seafood. (*1st: Japan*)

**Canada is the 2nd** largest foreign investor in Korea. (*1st: United States*)

**Canada has the 2nd** highest incidence of breast cancer in the world. (*1st: United States*)

**Canada is the 2nd** most workaholic nation in the world. (*1st: Japan*)

**Canada was the 2nd** country with triple platinum sales of *Prodigy's* "Fat Of The Land," featuring the single *Smack My Bitch Up*. (*1st: New Zealand*)

**Only 20% of the Sahara is covered with sand—the rest is rocky.**

Thanksgiving Day in **Canada is the 2nd** Monday in October.

**Canada has the 2nd** most foreign visitors to Texas. (*1st: Mexico*)

**Canada was the 2nd** country to establish a Ministry of the Environment. (*1st: France*)

**Canada was the 2nd** country to require daytime running lights on all new vehicles. (*1st: Norway*)

**Canada has the 2nd** largest oil reserves in the world. (*1st: Saudi Arabia*)

**Canada has the 2nd** highest proportion of immigrant population. (*1st: Australia*)

**Canada was the 2nd** country with a Boy Scout program. (*1st: England*)

**Canada has the 2nd** most civilian pilots in the world. (*1st: United States*)

**Canada has the 2nd** highest cable TV access in the world. (*1st: Belgium*)

**Canada was the 2nd** country in the world to have a nuclear reactor. (*1st: United States*)

**Canada was the 2nd** country to develop a jet airplane. (*1st: Great Britain*)

**Canada is the 2nd** largest country in the world. (*1st: Russia*)

## ALTHOUGH...

- Canada is **1st** in literacy rate.
- Canada is **1st** in waste generated per person.
- Canada was the **1st** country to mine uranium.
- Canada was the **1st** British colony to gain self-government.
- Canada was the **1st** western country to recognize Ukrainian independence.
- Canada was the **1st** country to conduct a national survey on violence against women.
- Canada was the **1st** country to have a domestic communications satellite.
- **Canada is 1st** in ATM usage.
- **Canada was the 1st** to adopt a national multiculturalism policy.
- **Canada is 1st** in hydropower generation.
- **Canada also has...**

...the highest ocean tides (They're in the Bay of Fundy).

...the longest covered bridge (New Brunswick).

...the longest street (Yonge Street, Toronto, at 1,178 miles).

...the largest National Park (Wood Buffalo National Park in Alberta/North West Territories).

**No surprise: Canada is the largest importer of American automobiles.**

# LITTLE THINGS MEAN A LOT

*A few more little things that caused big problems.*

## ANOTHER CONVERSION ERROR

The Mars Climate Orbiter blasted off in December 1998. Ten months later, it suddenly stopped transmitting signals and was presumed lost. An investigation found that the satellite had entered Martian orbit 60 miles too low and was destroyed entering the atmosphere. What caused the error? Lockheed Martin, which operated the satellite for NASA, had been sending maneuvering data to the orbiter in standard English units... unaware that the navigation team had done its calculations in *metric* units. Asked if they knew that NASA used the metric system, a Lockheed spokesman said, "obviously not." Estimated loss: $125 million.

## A COMMA

In 1997 the American Asphalt Co. submitted the winning bid ($27 million) for a contract to build and pave the planned Las Vegas Beltway. But one of the losing bidders noticed something— American had mistakenly put a comma where a period was supposed to be, and road signs that were supposed to be priced at $23.80 per square foot were priced at $23,800 instead. This erroneous amount hadn't been added to the final price—the $27 million bid was still correct—but rather than risk a lawsuit, county officials scrapped all the bids and changed the scope of the bid, delaying construction for weeks...and adding $3.1 million in new costs.

## A CHIP OF PAINT

On April 24, 1990, NASA launched the $1.5 billion Hubble Space telescope into Earth orbit... only to have it send back blurry images. What happened? A single chip of paint flaked off one of the instruments used to measure the shape of the telescope's huge 94.5-inch main mirror. That distorted some of the measurements and caused the mirror to be shaped slightly too flat. NASA eventually fixed the problem, but it took an extra space shuttle mission to do it and cost them millions of dollars.

**Up or down? The Congo is the only river that flows both north and south of the equator.**

# THE ICE WORM COMETH

*The BRI library has an entire wing for books and articles on hoaxes. Here are a few classics.*

## KLONDIKE ICE WORMS

**Background:** In 1898 a young journalist named "Stroller" White got a job in Dawson, Alaska, with the *Klondike Nugget*. The terms of his employment were tough: he had to increase sales...or he was out in the cold. Just then, a fierce storm took hold of the area and it gave him an idea. He wrote an article about "ice worms" that had crawled out of a nearby glacier to "bask in the unusual frigidity in such numbers that their chirping was seriously interfering with the sleep of Dawson's inhabitants."

**What Happened:** Sales of the *Nugget* skyrocketed as people began forming expedition teams to search for the noisy creatures. White got to keep his job and the ice worm story became so popular that bartenders started serving "ice-worm cocktails," in which they added a piece of frozen spaghetti to a customer's drink. Annual ice worm festivals became a local tradition—and are still held today.

**Update:** For years everyone assumed that ice worms were just a figment of White's imagination, but scientists recently claimed to have found real evidence of the existence of ice worms living inside Alaskan glaciers. No word on whether or not they chirp.

## PRINCESS CARABOO

**Background:** One spring morning in 1817, a strange woman strolled into Almondsbury, England. She was five-foot-two and stunning, wearing a black shawl twisted like a turban around her head. She spoke a language no one could understand and had to use gestures to communicate. In those days a homeless woman roaming the street was usually tossed in the poorhouse, so the stranger was directed to see the Overseer of the Poor. But instead of sending her to the poorhouse, he sent her to stay at the home of Samuel Worrall, the county magistrate.

Days later a Portuguese sailor arrived at the Worrall household claiming to speak Caraboo's bizarre language. He translated as Caraboo revealed her secret past: she was no homeless beggar—

**Q: What was *Queen Anne's Revenge*? A: The name of Blackbeard's pirate ship.**

she was a princess from the island of Javasu. Pirates had kidnapped her and carried her across the ocean, but as they sailed through the English Channel, Caraboo jumped ship and swam ashore.

**What Happened:** The Worralls informed the local press and soon all England knew of Princess Caraboo. And for weeks, Caraboo was treated royally…until her former employer came forward.

A woman named Mrs. Neale had recognized the newspaper description of "Princess Caraboo" as her former servant, Mary Baker, a cobbler's daughter. The giveaway: Baker had often entertained Mrs. Neale's children by speaking a nonsense language. "Caraboo" reluctantly confessed to the fraud she and the "sailor" had perpetrated.

Amazingly, Mrs. Worrall took pity on Caraboo and gave her enough money to sail to Philadelphia. Seven years later she returned to England and made a living selling leeches to the Infirmary Hospital in Bristol.

## CROSS-DRESSING KEN

**Background:** In July 1990, Carina Guillot and her 12-year-old daughter, Jocelyn, were shopping at a Toys "R" Us in Florida. As they strolled up and down the store aisles, they caught a glimpse of a peculiar-looking Ken doll. Sealed inside of a cardboard package was Barbie's friend Ken, dressed in a purple tank top and a polka-dotted skirt with a lace apron. As doll collectors, the Guillots immediately knew this one was out of the ordinary and brought it to the front register for closer inspection. Employees determined that the doll hadn't been tampered with and was indeed a genuine Mattel original. The Guillots purchased it for $8.99.

**What Happened:** Word of the "cross-dressing Ken" quickly hit the national media circuit. Newspapers wrote about it; TV talk shows talked about it. Collectors made outrageous bids of up to $4,000 for it. But the Guillots wouldn't sell. Instead they kept the doll long enough for the truth to come out of the closet. Finally, a night clerk at the store, Ron Zero, came forward and confessed to the prank. Apparently Zero had dressed Ken up in Barbie's clothes and then carefully resealed the package with white glue. Toys "R" Us fired him four days later.

# MORE DIAMOND GEMS

*Another collection of fantastic baseball feats. If you like these you can find more in* Who Was Traded for Lefty Grove? *by Mike Attiyeh.*

## HE WHAT?

In 1960 Stan "The Man" Musial of the St. Louis Cardinals did something almost unheard of in today's world of professional sports. After receiving one of baseball's biggest ever contracts—$100,000 a year—in 1958, Musial had a subpar year in 1959 (he failed to bat above .310 for the first time in his 17-year career). So he demanded—and received—a $20,000 pay cut.

## BUSY DAY

Mets center fielder Joel Youngblood showed up at Wrigley Field in Chicago on August 4, 1982, having no idea he was about to make history. In the third inning, he hit a two-run single off the Cubs' Ferguson Jenkins. The following inning, he was told that he'd been traded to the Montreal Expos—and that they were waiting for him. So he packed his stuff and caught a plane to Philadelphia. He joined the Expos' lineup late in the game and singled off Phillies ace Steve Carlton. Youngblood made the record books for being on two different teams, batting against two future Hall of Famers, and getting hits off both of them...all on the same day.

## BET ON PETE

He may have had a gambling problem off the field, but on the field, Pete Rose was a gambler's best friend. Rose has the distinction of being on the winning side in more games than any other player in baseball history: 2,011 games.

## IN LIKE A LION, OUT LIKE A LAMB

When most fans hear the words "Red Sox" and the date "1986," only one thing comes to mind: the infamous ball that went through Bill Buckner's legs, which cost them game 6 of the World Series, which the "cursed" Red Sox then lost in game 7. But the Red Sox season started on a positive note. For the only time in major-league history, Dwight Evans hit the very first pitch of the baseball season over the fence for a home run.

## FROM A TO Z

Hank Aaron holds arguably the game's most coveted record: 755 career home runs. He comes in first in another category as well: alphabetically. Of the more than 15,000 players in the history of the game, Aaron's name comes first. (In case you were wondering, Dutch Zwilling of the 1910 Chicago White Sox comes last.)

## HE COULDN'T KETCH UP

Joe DiMaggio's 56-game hitting streak in 1941 is another one of professional sport's most revered records. But it fell one hit short of landing "Joltin' Joe" a $10,000 sports endorsement. The Heinz Ketchup company was all set to pay DiMaggio to endorse their Heinz 57 Sauce... if the streak went to 57 games. But on July 17, 1941, thanks to stellar plays by Cleveland Indians third baseman Ken Keltner, DiMaggio went 0 for 3, so the streak ended at 56 games. One Heinz exec was quoted as saying, "I'll be damned if I'm going to change the name to Heinz 56 Sauce!"

## KEEPING HIS EYES ON THE BALL

Ted Williams's biggest goal in life was to have people say, "There goes Ted Williams, the greatest hitter who ever lived." Knowing that eyesight was every bit as important to hitting as strength and speed, "Terrible Ted" went to great lengths to protect his peepers. He never read in a moving vehicle, and never chewed gum because it "made his pupils move up and down."

## RECORD COLLECTOR

So who holds the record for the most records in baseball? Nolan Ryan. Arguably the game's best hurler, Ryan pitched in the big leagues from 1966 to 1993. When he retired, he owned or shared more than 40 American League and National League records.

* * *

"Managing a team is like holding a dove in your hand. Squeeze too hard and you kill it, not hard enough and it flies away."

**—Tommy Lasorda,**
**manager, Los Angeles Dodgers**

**Literature quiz: What are Dr. Jekyll's and Mr. Hyde's first names? A. George and Charles.**

# BACK IN THE SADDLE

*Peggy Thompson and Saeko Usukawa have put together a collection of great lines from Westerns called* Tall in the Saddle. *Some samples:*

"Boys who play with guns have to be ready to die like men."

**—Joan Crawford, *Johnny Guitar* (1954)**

"A horse is a man's slave, but treat 'em like a slave and you're not a man. Remember that."

**—James Cagney, *Tribute to a Bad Man* (1956)**

"Honey, you were smelling bad enough to gag a dog on a gut wagon."

**—*The Ballad of Cable Hogue* (1970)**

"I'd like to make a dress for her. Half tar, half feathers."

**—*Destry Rides Again* (1939)**

"There are two kinds of people in this world: those with pistols, and those who dig. You dig."

**—Clint Eastwood, *The Good, the Bad and the Ugly* (1966)**

**Eleanor Parker:** "The women always look beautiful when they get married, and the men always look scared."

**William Holden:** "They both get over it."

**—*Escape from Fort Bravo* (1953)**

"I like grumpy old cusses. Hope I live long enough to be one."

**—John Wayne, *Tall in the Saddle* (1944)**

**Parson:** "I sure hope this town has some pretty girls in it."

**Yellowleg:** "You get this far out in the brush, they're all pretty."

**—*The Deadly Companions* (1961)**

"Faith can move mountains. But it can't beat a faster draw."

**—*El Dorado* (1967)**

"I almost got married once myself. It was all set until her family came West in a covered wagon. If you'd've seen her family, you'd know why the wagon was covered."

**—*Gun Fury* (1953)**

"Don't spill that liquor, son. It eats right through the bar."

**—Walter Brennan, *The Westerner* (1940)**

**Spencer Tracy:** "I'll only be here twenty-four hours."

**Conductor:** "In a place like this, that could be a lifetime."

**—*Bad Day at Black Rock* (1955)**

**The closest black hole, known as V4641 Sgr, is 1,600 light years from Earth.**

# NEWS CORRECTIONS

*Uncle John was thumbing through his local newspaper when he noticed the "Corrections" box. It turned out to be one of the most entertaining sections of the paper.*

"The 'Greek Special' is a huge 18-inch pizza, and not a huge 18-inch penis, as described in an ad. Blondie's Pizza would like to apologize for any confusion Friday's ad may have caused."

**—*The Daily Californian***

"In last week's *Democrat*, some words were transposed through a typesetting error. The paragraph that began 'Occasionally circus elephants spent ninety-five percent of their lives chained by two legs...' should have read 'A majority of circus elephants...' while the paragraph that began 'A majority of circus elephants go mad...' should have read 'Occasionally circus elephants...'"

**—Coös County *Democrat***

"In our story on London Hosts, it was stated that the 'Pub 80' concept probably appealed more to the younger drinker or those looking for bad food. This should, of course, be 'bar food'. We apologize for any embarrassment caused."

**—*Morning Advertiser***

"A book review...quoted a passage from the book incorrectly. It says, 'Your goal should be to help your daughter become a sexually healthy adult'—not 'a sexually active, healthy adult.'"

**—*The New York Times***

"The following corrects errors in the July 17 geographical agent and broker listing: *International*: Aberdeen is in Scotland, not Saudi Arabia; Antwerp is in Belgium, not Barbados; Belfast is in Northern Ireland, not Nigeria; Cardiff is in Wales, not Vietnam; Helsinki is in Finland, not Fiji; Moscow is in Russia, not Qatar."

**—*Business Insurance***

"Due to a typographical error in last week's issue, the words 'Con-Men' appeared on the border of an Ashley & Nephews advertisement. 'Con-Men' was the headline of a story that was not used because of lack of space and is absolutely nothing to do and is in no way connected with Ashley & Nephews."

**—*The Enfield Independent***

**The average child will eat 1,500 peanut butter sandwiches by high school graduation.**

"Just to keep the record straight, it was the famous Whistler's Mother, not Hitler's, that was exhibited at the recent meeting of the Pleasantville Methodists. There is nothing to be gained in trying to explain how the error occurred."

**—*Titusville* (Pa.) *Herald***

"Tuesday's edition called a charge residents pay for 911 service a 'surge' charge. It is, of course, a sir charge."

**—Carlsbad *Current-Argus***

"An article about Ivana Trump and her spending habits misstated the number of bras she buys. It is two dozen black, two dozen beige, and two dozen white, not two thousand of each."

***—The New York Times***

"In our issue of November 30 we reported that the Lubavitch Foundation in Glasgow held a 'dinner and ball' to celebrate its tenth anniversary. This was incorrect. A spokesman explained: 'The Lubavitch movement does not have balls.'"

***—Jewish Chronicle***

"Sunday's Lifestyle story about Buddhism should have stated that Siddartha Gautama grew up in Northern India, not Indiana."

***—Bloomington Herald-Times***

"The following typo appeared in our last bulletin: 'Lunch will be gin at 12:15 p.m.' Please correct to read '12 noon.'"

**—California Bar Association newsletter**

"I would like to point out that what I did in fact write was that the council forced piped TV 'on us' not 'up us' as printed in the *County Times* on October 25. T. A. Wilkinson"

***—County Times & Express***

"November is a heavy publishing month for all newspapers and with large issues misprints inevitably increase. Note, however, that there are 5,000 characters in every full column of type. Even if there are five misprints a column that is only an error of 0,1 percent. We are working constantly on the problem, aiming to keep problem, aiming to keep —Editor"

***—The Johannesburg Star***

* * *

"Newspapers are unable to discriminate between a bicycle accident and the collapse of civilization." **—George Bernard Shaw**

**Light conversation: In Saudi Arabia, there are solar-powered pay phones in the desert.**

# THE BUGS AND THE BEES

*We sometimes wonder about insects creeping and crawling in the garage or out in the garden. What do they do all day? It turns out that even with six or eight legs, they still have a one-track mind.*

## CHEAPSKATE FLIES

The mating ritual of a type of fly called *Hilara*, commonly known as the "dance fly," involves gift-giving. The male catches a small insect, wraps it in silk, and then presents it—along with a wing-waving mating dance—to his potential mate. When she accepts it, he mounts her while she's busy eating the gift. But some dance flies are too lazy to even catch the bug. In one species, the male offers the female what *looks* like a gift-wrapped insect. While she unwraps it, he mates with her, trying to complete the act before she discovers there's no bug in the bag.

## TRICKY ORCHIDS

The female tiphiid wasp can't fly. So she climbs to the top of a tall plant and releases her pheromones into the air. The male flies by, grabs her, and flies away. Mating takes place in midair.

One type of orchid has made an interesting adaptation: its flower looks just like a female tiphiid. Not only that, its scent is almost identical to her pheromones. The unsuspecting male wasp grabs the flower and tries to take off with it; in the struggle, he brushes against the pollen before becoming frustrated and flying away. He goes on to the next orchid and goes through the same routine, thus pollinating the orchids.

## HUNGRY SPIDERS

The female black widow spider is genetically programmed to control the black widow population in her neighborhood, based on available food supply. Here's how she does it: A male approaches her web, sits on the edge, and bobs his abdomen, causing the web to vibrate. If she's not in the mood, she won't respond. If she is willing to mate, she'll send out an answering pattern of vibrations calling him toward her. But if she's hungry, she'll send the male the *exact same* mating response. And when he gets close enough…she eats him.

**At the outbreak of World War I, the American Air Force consisted of only 50 men.**

# I ♥ THE '80s!

*Power Ties? Just say no? Baby on Board? Just do it.*

### 1985

- New Coke flops; Coca-Cola reintroduces "classic" Coke
- Reagan meets Gorbachev in first U.S./Soviet summit
- Pete Rose breaks Ty Cobb's record of 4,191 base hits
- Live Aid concert held in Philadelphia and London simultaneously
- #1 movie: *Back to the Future*
- *Calvin and Hobbes* comic strip premiers
- A *Yugo* costs $3,990

### 1986

- Space shuttle *Challenger* explodes
- Russian space station *Mir* launched
- Martin Luther King Day becomes U.S. holiday
- Soviet nuclear plant Chernobyl has major meltdown
- 20-year-old Mike Tyson becomes youngest heavyweight champ ever
- Album of the Year: Paul Simon's *Graceland*
- On TV: *Miami Vice Cheers, Family Ties*

### 1987

- Televangelist Jim Bakker resigns after sex scandal with secretary Jessica Hahn
- Best Director: Oliver Stone, *Platoon*
- Oct. 19, Black Monday—Stock Market crashes
- #1 single: George Michael's "Faith"
- Van Gogh's painting "Sunflowers" sells for $39 million
- British humanitarian Terry Waite kidnapped in Lebanon
- Yugoslavian baby declared Earth's five billionth inhabitant

### 1988

- George H. W. Bush elected 41st U.S. president (defeats Michael Dukakis)
- After eight years of fighting, Soviet army begins withdrawal from Afghanistan
- Oliver North indicted for his role in Iran-Contra scandal
- Pan Am 103 crashes in Lockerbie, Scotland
- #1 film: *Rain Man*
- *Uncle John's Bathroom Reader* debuts

### 1989

- Iranian Ayatollah Khomeini issues *fatwa* (death sentence) on *Satanic Verses* author Salman Rushdie
- Time, Inc. and Warner Communications announce plans to merge
- Oil tanker Exxon *Valdez* crashes, causing worst oil spill in U.S. history
- Chinese troops squash pro-democracy demonstrators in Tiananmen Square
- Sega *Genesis* released
- Berlin Wall falls
- #1 movie: *Batman*
- Top TV show: *The Cosby Show*

**'80s quiz: In 1987 for the first time live models advertised what on TV? A: Bras (Playtex).**

# UNCLE JOHN'S STALL OF SHAME

*Don't abuse your bathroom privileges...or you may wind up in Uncle John's "Stall of Shame."*

**Honoree:** Joseph Carl Jones, Jr., an alleged burglar

**Dubious Achievement:** Landing in the can after a trip to the can.

**True Story:** On the morning of February 7, 2003, Janie Sidener of Mineral Wells, Texas, arrived to open the store where she worked. She should have been the first one in the building that morning, but shortly after she entered she noticed something unusual, so she looked around. That's when she saw Joseph Carl Jones, fast asleep on a bed that the store had for sale. "Apparently he needed to take a break," said police spokesperson Mike McAllister.

Sidener quietly called her employer, who called the police. They woke the burglar, arrested him, and hauled him off to the slammer. So what was it that alerted Sidener to the fact that something was amiss? Before his nap, Jones had used the bathroom...and hadn't flushed.

**Adding Insult to Injury!** The store Jones had picked to rob was owned by the wife of the district attorney.

**Honoree:** Jon Carl Petersen, 41, head of the Iowa office of the U.S. Bureau of Alcohol, Tobacco and Firearms (ATF)

**Dubious Achievement:** Wrecking his own career with alcohol, toilet paper, and firearms (ATPF).

**True Story:** During Homecoming Week 2002, a pickup truck full of Indianola high school sophomores decided to TP some houses in town, an unofficial Homecoming tradition for many years. Too bad they chose the street where Petersen lived. And too bad Petersen had been drinking.

When he saw the kids throwing toilet paper in his yard, he jumped in his patrol vehicle and chased them with lights flashing and sirens blaring. When they finally stopped, he ordered the sophomores out of their truck and held them at gunpoint until police arrived...and arrested *him.* A sobriety test showed that Petersen had a blood alcohol level of 0.22%, twice the legal limit. He was charged with drunk driving, 10 counts of assault with a weapon, and two counts of simple assault. If convicted on all counts, he faces up to 20 years in prison and a $50,000 fine.

"He deserves what he gets," said one of the kids involved. "It's kind of stupid that he's an Alcohol, Tobacco and Firearms agent, and he was doing two of the things he's trying to prevent."

**Honoree:** Catherine Tarver, the mother of an accused murderer

**Dubious Achievement:** Using a public restroom to influence the outcome of a trial.

**True Story:** In May 2003, Judge Walter McMillan ordered that Tarver be barred from Georgia's Washington County Courthouse. Reason: A courthouse employee saw Tarver cracking open eggs and sprinkling chicken feathers, chicken blood, and what has been described as "voodoo powder" in the restroom. So Judge McMillan imposed a ban, telling her, "If I find any more eggs in this courthouse, you will face criminal charges."

Sheriff Thomas Smith speculates that Tarver was trying to influence the outcome of the trial. "I think it's a curse against the prosecution," he told reporters. "There's been four incidents of it in the courthouse bathroom where brown eggs have been busted. It always happened on the day of Brandon Tarver's hearings."

Tarver denies using voodoo. "I don't even know what that is," she claims.

**Honoree:** Dr. Michael Warren, a South Carolina dermatologist

**Dubious Achievement:** Turning his bathroom into an ICU—a peekaboo ICU.

**True Story:** When the staff restroom went out of order in 2002, Dr. Warren cheerfully allowed female employees to use his private restroom. But when months went by without Dr. Warren making an attempt to get the restroom fixed, his staff became suspicious. That's when they found a hidden camera in the doctor's bathroom. Dr. Warren admits that he installed the camera but claims that he did so "as a security measure, after cash and checks were stolen from his office." (No word on what a thief would steal from the doctor's bathroom.)

**In how many Agatha Christie mysteries did "the butler do it?" None.**

# WORLD-CLASS LOSERS

*Everyone makes mistakes. Some are just better at it than others.*

## PAPER WEIGHT

In 1965 an aspiring English publisher named Lionel Burleigh announced he was starting a newspaper called the *Commonwealth Sentinel,* which he promised would be "Britain's most fearless newspaper." Burleigh did everything it took to make the paper a success—he promoted it on billboards, sold advertising space, wrote articles, and printed up 50,000 copies of the first issue so that there would be plenty to go around. Burleigh remembered every detail, except for one very important thing: distribution.

In fact, he had forgotten it completely until he received a phone call from the police informing him that all 50,000 copies had been deposited on the sidewalk in front of the hotel where he was staying. They were blocking the entrance. Could he please come and remove them?

Britain's "most fearless paper" folded after just one day. "To my knowledge, we only sold one copy," Burleigh remembered years later. "I still have the shilling in my drawer."

## A LOAD OF BULL

In 1958 the town of Lindsay, Ontario, organized the country's first-ever bullfight. There aren't many bullfighting bulls in Canada, and even fewer matadors, so they had to bring in both from Mexico. But the bulls brought ticks with them, and ticks from other parts of the world aren't allowed into Canada. The bulls had to be quarantined for a week. By the time they got out, the matadors had returned to Mexico. Result: no bullfight.

## HORSE SENSE

Horatio Bottomley (great name) was a convicted fraud artist and ex-member of the English parliament. In 1914 he figured out what he thought was a foolproof way to rig a horse race: He bought all six horses in the race, hired his own jockeys to race them, and told them in which order he wanted them to cross the finish line. Then he bet a fortune on the horses he'd picked to win, and also placed bets on the order of finish. Everything went according to plan… until a thick fog rolled in over the track in the middle of the race. It was so thick that the jockeys couldn't see each other well enough to cross the finish line in the proper order. And Bottomley lost every bet he placed.

## MORE LOSERS

*Not to be outdone by civilians, the "military intelligence" personnel of past war machines have had their day in the doghouse as well.*

**Brits in the Pits.** In the early 1940s, the English military came up with what they thought would be a simple but powerful antitank weapon: a four-and-a-half-pound hand grenade covered with sticky adhesive that would help it stick to the sides of tanks. The grenade was withdrawn from service a short time later. Reason: It stuck a little too well…to the soldier who was trying to throw it. It was so sticky, in fact, that the only practical way to put it to use was to run up to the tank and stick the grenade on manually—which was practically a suicide mission because the bomb's short fuse gave its user less than five seconds to get away.

**Peru's Blues.** As part of its Air Force Week celebrations in 1975, the Peruvian military decided to show off the might of its newest fighter planes. Fourteen derelict fishing boats were towed a short distance out to sea to serve as targets. After the crowds had gathered along the coast, a squadron of 30 fighters swooped down and attacked the boats with bombs and machine-gun fire for 15 minutes. They didn't sink a single boat.

**France's Chance.** In 1870 the French military made preparations to use its own new machine gun, called the *mitrailleuse*, in the imminent war against Prussia. Machine guns were new at the time and the government wanted to keep the technology a secret. So it distributed the guns to military units… without instructions for how to use them; the instructions weren't sent until *after* the war had begun. But by then it was too late—France lost.

* * *

"Whoever said, 'It's not whether you win or lose that counts,' probably lost."

**—Martina Navritilova**

There is one slot machine in Las Vegas for every eight inhabitants.

# EVERYDAY OBJECTS

*They once were miracle inventions—now they're so common we throw them in a junk drawer. Here are the stories behind three items that make life just a little bit easier.*

## SAFETY PIN

In 1849 a New York inventor named Walter Hunt had a problem: he was too broke to pay an employee the $15 he owed him. But the employee gave him an out—he'd forgive the $15 debt if he could have the rights to whatever Hunt could invent from a single piece of wire.

Hunt was a prolific inventor—he'd designed a fire engine warning gong, a stove that burned hard coal, and even an early sewing machine (which he decided not to market because he didn't want to put seamstresses out of work). But for all his skill, he seemed unable to profit from any of his inventions.

Hunt had no money, so he had no choice—he accepted the employee's challenge. After three hours of twisting an eight-inch piece of brass wire, Hunt had created the world's first safety pin. It had a clasp at one end, a point on the other, and a coil in the middle to act as a spring and keep the point tucked into the clasp.

So did Hunt hand over his "dress pin," as he called it, to the employee? No—he reneged on the deal and patented the safety pin himself. Then he sold the rights to his new invention for $400 (about $5,000 today), from which he paid his draftsman the $15, keeping the rest. Millions of safety pins have been made and sold since then, but Hunt never made another cent on his invention.

## CAN OPENER

Strange but true: the metal can was invented a full 50 years before the first practical can opener.

Peter Durand, the English merchant who developed the "tin cannister" in 1810, had figured out a way to preserve foods *in* cans, but he neglected to come up with a way to get the food *out*. Early cans carried instructions advising users to cut around the top with a chisel and hammer. British soldiers didn't carry chisels—they had to open their canned rations with bayonets or pocket knives, and, in desperation, sometimes shot them open with their rifles.

In 1858 a man named Ezra Warner came up with a can opener that looked like a bent bayonet, with a large, curved blade that could be driven into the rim of a can and forced around the perimeter to cut off the top. It was unwieldy and dangerous; but grocery stores that sold canned food had to buy them so they could open cans as a service to customers. The customers would then leave the store carrying the opened cans. Not surprisingly, it wasn't a big hit.

Then in 1861 the Civil War broke out, creating a sudden and urgent need for food that could accompany soldiers into battle without spoiling. Union soldiers were issued canned rations…and Warner's bayonet-style can openers. Canned food became so popular with soldiers that after the war, more and more canned goods appeared on market shelves. But people still needed an easier way to open the cans.

Connecticut inventor William Lyman had the answer, and in 1870 patented his "cutting wheel" can opener, a crank-operated gadget that held a circular metal wheel that could cut through can tops. And since then not much has changed. In 1925 the Star Can Company of San Francisco added a serrated wheel to hold the can and rotate it against the cutting wheel. The electric can opener was introduced in 1931. But amazingly, even the most modern versions of the can opener still look and work pretty much like the one Lyman invented… more than 130 years ago.

## DRINKING STRAW

Marvin Stone liked mint juleps. Back in the 1880s, every day after putting in his time manufacturing paper cigarette holders in his Washington, D.C., factory, Stone would stop by the same tavern and order a mint julep—a concoction of bourbon, mint, sugar, and water, served over ice. Keeping the drink chilled was important (warm mint juleps tend to lose some of their minty tang), so mint julep fans would avoid touching the glass with their warm hands. Instead, they sipped the drink through a natural hollow piece of wheat straw.

Stone didn't like the grassy taste the wheat straw imparted to his favorite drink. He also didn't like the way the straw would get

**Stephen King was 19 years old when his first story was published.**

dusty and start to crack as it was used repeatedly. There had to be a better way. One day, as he watched his cigarette holders being wound out of paper, he had an inspiration. Why not make an artificial straw by winding thin strips of paper around a cylinder?

He made a prototype in 1888, winding a continuous strip of paper around a pencil and fastening it with dabs of glue. It worked. Stone made several drinking straws for his own use and asked his favorite bartender to stash them behind the counter. When other customers noticed Stone's invention, they wanted their own, so Stone decided to mass-produce it.

Lemonade was a popular drink in the late 19th century, and Stone reasoned that people might like using straws for lemonade as well as for mint juleps. He fashioned an eight-and-a-half-inch paper straw out of wax-coated manila paper (to resist sogginess) and set the diameter just wide enough to allow lemon seeds to pass through without clogging the straws. By 1890 the Stone Cigarette Holder Factory was producing more drinking straws than cigarette holders.

Most straws today are made of plastic, not paper. But the winding technique Stone invented lives on: most cardboard tubes (like the one at the center of a toilet paper roll) are still made in the same way that Stone wound his first straw. Straws themselves have undergone an evolution: there are straws of colored plastic, with flexible shapes, loop-the-loops, and even flavored straws. But they still do the same basic job: getting liquid into your mouth, fast and cold.

* * *

## INSPECTOR GADGET?

Have you ever been snooping with your binoculars, only to have your arms get tired just when you're sure something really important is about to happen? If so, U.S. Patent #5,131,093—the *Bino Cap*—may be just the invention for you. It's a foldable, lightweight combination binoculars/baseball cap. Just put it on and snoop away; your arms are free to take notes, stir your coffee, or record observations into your voice-activated digital recorder. (Despite the fact that it's been patented, no word on whether the device is actually available yet.)

**Radar was used for the first time in the battle of Britain in 1940.**

# EATIN' THE TIN SANDWICH

*The history of the harmonica will take you to China, Africa, Europe, the Mississippi Delta, and beyond...*

## BLOWING IN THE WIND

When musicians like Bob Dylan and John Lennon became famous in the 1960s, they did it with a little help from the harmonica. And they gave the harmonica a boost, too. Sales of the tiny instrument skyrocketed when folksingers and rock musicians brought it back into the limelight. But it wasn't the first time the "harp" became a sensation.

From the 1920s until the 1940s, the harmonica was one of the most popular instruments in the country. The biggest blues, jazz, country, and hillbilly bands—and even theater companies—had harmonica players as part of their acts. Harmonica classes became a regular part of curriculums in many public schools. By the 1930s, the German company M. Hohner, the biggest maker of harmonicas worldwide, was selling over 25 million a year.

Where did the easy-to-carry instrument originate? That's a very old story.

## THE SOUND OF OLD SHENG-HAI

Most musicologists agree that the earliest predecessor to the harmonica was developed in China between 3,000 and 5,000 years ago. It was a three-foot-long instrument made of bamboo pipes called the *sheng*, which means "sublime voice." Although neither the sheng nor its ancient sisters, the *naw*, the *yu*, and the *ho*, looked anything like a harmonica, they all had one important feature in common: free reeds.

A reed is a thin strip of cane, wood, plastic, or metal that vibrates when air passes over it. A "free reed" instrument, like the accordion or harmonica, produces sound from a reed vibrating inside a chamber—the vibrating reed produces a single note and doesn't touch anything else.

"Fixed reed" instruments, like the clarinet and the saxophone,

**In colonial America, tobacco was legal tender in several Southern colonies.**

use a reed that vibrates against some other part of the instrument. On the clarinet or sax, it's the mouthpiece, which is attached to a tube with holes in it. Cover the holes and you change the pitch.

The *sheng* had multiple free reeds set inside bamboo tubes, which allowed chords (multiple notes that sound good together) to be played. For thousands of years, *sheng* and similar instruments were played all over China and Southeast Asia.

## FREEING THE PITCH

Fixed-reed instruments had been played in Europe for centuries (and some say that even those were introduced from Asia), but free-reeds had not. In 1776 French Jesuit missionary Pierre Amiot sent several *shengs* from China to Paris—and people who heard them loved them. Within a few years European instrument makers were building their own free reed devices, making instruments such as the harmonium and the reed organ.

In 1821, a 16-year-old named Christian Friedrich Ludwig Buschmann was experimenting with different ways to combine pitch pipes in order to create a new instrument. He soldered together 15 pipes of different pitches, similar to the *sheng* and, without knowing it, made the next big step toward the modern harmonica.

## THE INS AND OUTS

Buschmann's harmonica, known as the *aura*, was an immediate hit, and soon other instrument makers began experimenting with the design. In 1825 a man named Richter (his first name is unknown) came up with the idea of a 10-hole, 20-note configuration, one row of reeds activated by inhaling, the other by exhaling.

Richter arranged the notes with the common person in mind: no matter where the mouth is placed, it would always play notes that were in harmony—that sounded good—together, whether inhaling or exhaling. That's why the instrument is called a "harmony-ca"—it's always in harmony. Richter's three-octave model has been changed little since. (Pretty impressive when you consider that a grand piano has an eight-octave range, but weighs about 1,000 pounds—4,000 times as much as a harmonica.)

## HARMONIC CONVERGENCE

In 1857 Matthias Hohner, a clockmaker from Trössingen, Germany, visited a harmonica maker in Vienna, Austria, and decided to make his own instruments. He started making them in his kitchen with the help of his family and sold 650 harmonicas the first year. In 1862 relatives in the United States urged him to export some of the instruments. He did, and by 1887 was producing more than a million harmonicas a year, with sales across Europe and the United States.

## BLEND IT LIKE HOHNER

One of the things that helped make the harmonica so successful was its musical flexibility. It could play romping *Biergarten* music, plaintive European folk songs, and even complex classical music. And it was small and inexpensive, so even poor people could afford one. By the late 1800s, African Americans in the southeast, who had their own musical traditions developed over thousands of years, were inventing a new kind of music: the blues. And the "harp" would be part of it. The trademark "bending" of the notes—using air direction and pressure to slide between notes—would become the trademark sound of the blues. The popularity of the music would soon influence other new styles of American music—jug band, Dixieland, jazz, and swing—and would help carry the harmonica to even greater popularity.

## THE GOLDEN YEARS

The 1920s began the first golden age for the harmonica. Two new technologies were sweeping the country: radio and recording. That meant that people could become national stars relatively quickly—and so could the instruments they played: Vernon Dalhart's 1925 recording "Wreck of the Old 97," with Dalhart singing and playing harmonica, became country music's first million-seller.

By the end of the 1920s, hundreds of artists were making recordings and many of them featured the harmonica. And it wasn't just for accompaniment: all-harmonica bands became hot tickets. Then, in the late 1930s, a musical virtuoso named Larry Adler gave it another boost: Adler played classical and jazz—as a harmonica soloist. How popular was he? From the 1940s until he died in 2001, he regularly played with the biggest stars of the day:

**There are as many molecules in 1 teaspoon of water as there are teaspoons of water in the Atlantic.**

Jack Benny, George Gershwin, Billie Holiday, and later, Sting and Elton John.

## ELECTRIFIED

The harmonica went into decline in the 1950s, but bluesmen like Little Walter, Howlin' Wolf, and Sonny Boy Williamson kept it alive, creating a modern blues-harp sound that would be carried on by James Cotton and Charlie Musselwhite. By the 1960s, the harmonica was back, thanks first to the folk music craze and then to Beatlemania.

Since then, harmonica players like Stevie Wonder, John Mayall, Huey Lewis, Delbert McClinton, Magic Dick (J. Geils Band), Neil Young, Bruce Springsteen, Charlie McCoy, Mickey Rafael (Willie Nelson's band), and John Popper (Blues Traveler) continue to show the world what one little instrument can do.

## HARMONICA TRIVIA

• Nicknames for the harmonica: the *Harp*, the *Tin Sandwich* (Cowboy dialect), the *Mississippi Saxophone* (Blues lingo), and the *Mouth Organ* (from the German *mundharmonika* or *mundorgan)*.

• Presidents Lincoln, Wilson, Coolidge, and Reagan were all harp players of varying ability. Lincoln reportedly wrote a letter to Hohner, telling how he enjoyed playing the harmonica to relax.

• The best-selling record of 1947 was "Peg O' My Heart" by a harmonica trio called The *Harmonicats*. After the *Harmonicats*' success, the musicians union decided to classify the harmonica as an instrument. Before that they called it a toy.

• On December 16, 1965, astronaut Wally Schirra played *Jingle Bells* on the harmonica—from Gemini Six, at an altitude of 160 miles above Earth.

• In 1986 the M. Hohner Company sold their one billionth harmonica.

• Currently, the most expensive harmonica in the Hohner catalog is a "Chord 48" (the size of a baseball bat, with hundreds of reeds). Cost: $1,500.

• More expensive, but not in the catalog: the solid gold, gem-encrusted model that Hohner presented to Pope Pius XI in the 1930s.

**Benjamin Franklin once wrote an essay on the possibility of waterskiing.**

# DEATH ON THE MISSISSIPPI

*Few people know about the* Sultana, *despite the fact that it suffered the worst maritime disaster in U.S. history. For some reason, it is almost completely ignored by history books. Here's the tragic story.*

## HEADING HOME

The Civil War was finally over. It was April 1865, General Robert E. Lee had surrendered; Abraham Lincoln had been shot; and Confederate president Jefferson Davis had been captured. After four years of bloodshed, the war-torn nation was ready to start the process of healing and rebuilding. The first order of business was to get the weary troops home.

Captured Union soldiers were being released from Confederate prison camps. Thousands amassed along the Mississippi River seeking passage on one of the many steamships making their way upriver to the north.

One such riverboat was the *Sultana*, a state-of-the-art sidewheeler that had been built for transporting cotton. But now her cargo was people. By law, she was allowed to carry 376 passengers and a crew of 85, and the ship's captain and owner, J. C. Mason, had a reputation as a careful river pilot. But in the end, the money he stood to make from the Union government for transporting extra troops was too tempting to pass up: $5 for each enlisted man and $10 per officer.

## A SETUP FOR DISASTER

The *Sultana* left New Orleans on April 21 carrying a small number of passengers, about 100, and headed north. Each time she stopped, though, the ship took on more troops. The men who boarded were weak, tired, and homesick. After spending months or even years in brutal prison camps, the only thing they wanted to do was get back to their families.

On April 24, the *Sultana* made her regular stop in Vicksburg, Mississippi, to take on more passengers. Captain Mason docked

**A soda can can hold 90 pounds per square inch of pressure—3 times as much as a car tire.**

the ship to find thousands of soldiers waiting there. Under normal circumstances, the ship would have made a brief stop, allowed the prescribed number of passengers to board, and then departed. But one of the ship's three main steam boilers had sprung a leak and needed to be repaired.

First of all, Captain Mason made the decision to have a piece of metal welded over the leak to reinforce it (which took less than a day) instead of having the boiler replaced (which would have taken three days). While the boiler was being repaired, the waiting soldiers did everything they could to muscle their way onto the ship. Bribes were paid, and more and more men packed on. When the repairs were completed, Mason was eager to get underway, so he broke another rule. He let all of the passengers get onboard before their names were logged in. Result: The ship was overloaded and no one on shore had a complete or accurate copy of the passenger list.

When an Army officer raised his concerns, Mason assured him that the *Sultana* was a competent vessel that could more than carry the load. "Take good care of those men," the officer told him. "They are deserving of it."

## THE MIGHTY MISS

Four years of war had been hard on the series of levees and dikes that control the flow of the Mississippi River. The spring of 1865 saw heavy rains, which, combined with winter snowmelt, caused the river to rise to flood stage. By April it was several miles wide and the icy current was much stronger than usual.

But the *Sultana* was solid and Captain Mason an able river man. As the ship trudged slowly upriver, she made a few more scheduled stops, picking up even more men at each one. The huddled passengers filled every bit of space on the 260-foot-long vessel—the bottom hull, the lower decks, the cabins, the pilothouse, and the hurricane deck on top. Yet even though the soldiers were tired and packed in like sardines, their spirits were high. They sang songs, told war stories, and shared their plans for when they finally got home... unaware of the disaster to come.

On the cool night of April 26, 1865, the *Sultana* disembarked from Memphis around midnight, carrying an estimated 2,300 people—six times its capacity. There were only two lifeboats and 76 life preservers onboard.

## HELL AND HIGH WATER

At around 2 a.m., the overloaded *Sultana* had made it nine miles north of Memphis when her weakened boiler could take no more. It exploded. The other two boilers went in quick succession.

The tremendous blast split the ship in two. Burning-hot coals shot out like bullets. The horrified passengers were jarred awake, some sent hurtling through the air into the icy water, others scalded by the tremendous blast of steam. Still others were trapped on the lower decks to either suffocate, burn, or drown. The men on the top decks had a choice—albeit a dismal one: stay and face the spreading flames or try to swim to shore, more than a mile away in either direction.

One survivor remembered, "The men who were afraid to take to the water could be seen clinging to the sides of the bow of the boat until they were singed off like flies." Others who had waited too long on the hurricane deck were crushed when the two large smokestacks collapsed on them. Others slid down into the hottest part of the fire when the burning deck gave way.

Shrieks and screams pierced the night, as did the crackling of flames and the booms of small explosions. But loudest of all was the hissing sound as sections of the flaming steamboat sank into the water. Another survivor described it like this:

> The whole heavens seemed to be lighted up by the conflagration. Hundreds of my comrades were fastened down by the timbers of the decks and had to burn while the water seemed to be one solid mass of human beings struggling with the waves.

What was left of the *Sultana* drifted downstream until finally banking on a small island in the middle of the Mississippi River. The ship's broken, burning body then slowly disappeared into the dark water.

## DAWN OF THE DEAD

As first light rose on the river, the devastation was overwhelming. Hundreds upon hundreds of bodies were floating down the Mississippi. Dotted between the corpses were dazed survivors floating on makeshift rafts of driftwood and ship parts. Some sang marching songs to keep their spirits up. Others just floated silently among the carnage.

All the way to Memphis, men—alive and dead—were washing

up onshore. Barges and other steamships were dispatched for search and rescue. At least 500 men were treated at Memphis hospitals; 200 of them died there. Because the passenger list went down with the ship, no one knows for sure how many lives were lost that night, but most estimates put the number around 1,700—including Captain Mason.

## INTO THE DUSTBIN OF HISTORY

So why is the *Sultana* disaster such an unknown part of U.S. history? Mostly because of timing. After the bloodiest war in U.S. history, the nation was largely desensitized to death. What was another 1,700 in the wake of hundreds of thousands of casualties? The newspapers were full of articles about the end of the war, a new presidency, and a nation rebuilding. On the day before the disaster, the last Confederate army had surrendered and John Wilkes Booth had been captured. The story of the sinking of the *Sultana* was relegated to the back pages.

Another reason for the minimal coverage was that it was an embarrassing story. A lot of people—from the ship's captain to the army officers in charge of boarding—had failed miserably at their jobs. The Army was not anxious to publicize such a horrible dereliction of duty.

But the fact remains that the explosion and sinking of the *Sultana* was—and still is—the worst maritime disaster in U.S. history. Her bow is still lying on the muddy bottom of the Mississippi River as a sad memorial to the men who never made it home.

* * *

## REAL-LIFE COURT TRANSQUIPS

**Q:** So, you were unconscious, and they pulled you from the bucket. What happened then?

**A:** Mr. Stewart gave me artificial insemination, you know, mouth-to-mouth.

**Plaintiff's Attorney:** Why do you think your home developed cracks in the walls?

**Defendant's Attorney:** Objection! The witness has no expertise in this area, there is an obvious lack of foundation.

**"I had a lazy eye as a kid and it gradually spread to my whole body." —Tom Cotter**

# NOW THEY TELL US

*The "experts" told us one thing... and then a new set of experts comes along.*

## USDA FOOD PYRAMID

**They Used to Say:** A healthy diet includes lots of bread and cereal, plenty of dairy products, red meat, and very little fat. That's what the USDA—with the grateful support of the farming industry—had recommended since the 1950s, packaging it into a triangle-shaped "Food Guide Pyramid" in 1992.

**Now They Tell Us:** The Food Pyramid is unhealthy, will make you fat, and puts you at greater risk for heart disease. Leading nutritionists slammed the guidelines in 2001. "The food pyramid is tremendously flawed," said Dr. Walter C. Willett of Harvard. "It says all fats are bad; all complex carbohydrates are good; all protein sources offer the same nutrition, and dairy should be eaten in high amounts. None of this is accurate." A new guide is scheduled to be released in 2005.

## BRAIN CELLS

**They Used to Say:** You can't grow new brain cells.

**Now They Tell Us:** Oh yes you can. Researchers at Princeton University did an extensive study and proved in 1999 that many areas of the brain do indeed grow new brain cells, or neurons, throughout an adult's life. "The assumption has been for over a hundred years that there are no new neurons added," said psychologist Charles G. Gross, a co-leader of the study. "We have shown they are added, and to the regions of the brain involved in the highest cognitive function."

## SIPPY CUPS

**They Used to Say:** The sippy cup is a healthy way to wean a child from a bottle. Doctors have been recommending them for 50 years.

**Now They Tell Us:** According to childhood development experts, sippy cups make it harder for kids to learn the complicated action of drinking from a glass. That, in turn, slows the development of articulate speech. And because children often sip milk, juice, or other sugary drinks over several hours, sippy cups can promote tooth decay.

**Subject:** Daily sleep requirements

**They Used to Say:** You need at least eight hours of sleep a day.

**Now They Tell Us:** Sleeping eight hours a day might be fatal. The University of California did a six-year study in which they monitored such factors as the lifestyle, health, and sleep patterns of 1.1 million people. They found that subjects who slept eight hours a day were 12% more likely to have died during that six-year period than people who slept seven hours a day. People who slept nine hours were 23% more likely.

**Subject:** Iron

**They Used to Say:** Iron-rich foods are good for you.

**Now They Tell Us:** Drop that can of spinach, Popeye! One study at the University of Washington in 2003 suggested that people with a diet high in iron were 1.7 times more likely to get Parkinson's disease than those with a low-iron diet. Sources of iron: red meat and poultry. And, if it's combined with manganese, the risk goes up to 1.9 times more likely. Sources of iron and manganese: spinach, beans, nuts, and grains. But you'd have to eat an awful lot of these to overdo it. The researchers said that more study was needed before they could recommend any dietary changes.

**Subject:** Planets

**They Used to Say:** There are nine planets in our solar system.

**Now They Tell Us:** You're spaced out—there's only eight. Seventy years after it was first classified, the Hayden Planetarium in New York City, one of the nation's leading astronomical centers, removed Pluto from its list of planets in 2001. They said it's far too small—smaller than our moon—and is probably just a big lump of ice. The announcement drew much criticism from traditional astronomers, but officials at the center say they're just being defensive. "There is no scientific insight to be gained by counting planets," said Neil de Grasse Tyson, director of the planetarium. "Eight or nine, the numbers don't matter."

**In 2002 the average driver spent 62 hours stopped in traffic. L.A. drivers spent 136.**

# SO LONG, NEIGHBOR

*One thing that nearly all Americans born after 1965 have in common is that they grew up watching Mr. Rogers. He was one of the true pioneers of children's television. We haven't written much about him before, and when he passed away in 2003 we decided it was time we did.*

## HOME FOR THE HOLIDAYS

In 1951 a college senior named Fred McFeely Rogers finished school in Florida and went home to stay with his parents in Latrobe, Pennsylvania. He wasn't exactly sure what he wanted to do with his life. For a while he wanted to be a diplomat; then he decided to become a Presbyterian minister. He'd already made plans to enroll in a seminary after college, but as soon as he arrived home he changed his mind again.

Why? Because while he was away at school, his parents had bought their first TV set. Television was still very new in the early 1950s, and not many people had them yet. When Rogers got home he watched it for the very first time. He was fascinated by the new medium but also disturbed by some of the things he saw. One thing in particular offended him very deeply. It was "horrible," as he put it, so horrible that it altered the course of his life.

What was it that bothered him so much? "I saw people throwing pies in each other's faces," Rogers remembered. "Such demeaning behavior."

## KID STUFF

You (and Uncle John) may like it when clowns throw pies and slap each other in the face, but Fred Rogers was appalled. He thought TV could have a lot more to offer than pie fights and other silliness, if only someone would try. "I thought, 'I'd really like to try my hand at that, and see what I could do,'" Rogers recalled. So he moved to New York and got a job at NBC, working first as an associate producer and later as a director.

Then in 1953, he learned about a new experimental TV station being created in Pittsburgh. Called WQED, it was the country's first community-sponsored "public television" station. WQED wasn't even on the air yet, and there was no guarantee that an educational TV station that depended on donations from viewers to pay for programming would ever succeed. No matter—Rogers quit his secure job at NBC, moved to Pittsburgh with his wife, Joanne, and joined the station.

"I thought, 'What a wonderful institution to nourish people,'" Rogers recalled. "My friends thought I was nuts."

## LOW-INCOME NEIGHBORHOOD

When Rogers arrived at WQED in 1953, the station had just four employees and only two of them, Rogers and a secretary named Josie Carey, were interested in children's programming. The two created their own hour-long show called *The Children's Corner* and paid for all of the staging, props, and scenery (mostly pictures painted on paper backdrops), out of their own meager $75-a-week salaries.

Because *The Children's Corner* had to be done on the cheap, Rogers and Carey decided that much of the show would have to revolve around showing educational films that they obtained for free. Rogers was in charge of hustling up the free films and playing the organ off camera during the broadcast; Carey would host the show, sing, and introduce the films.

## LUCKY BREAK

That was how *The Children's Corner* was *supposed* to work, but the plan fell apart about two minutes into their very first broadcast. The problem wasn't that Rogers couldn't scrounge up any free films, it was that the films he *did* manage to get were so old and brittle that they were prone to breaking when played. Sure enough, on the first day of the show, on WQED's first day on the air, the first film broke.

Remember, this was before the invention of videotape, when television shows were broadcast live—so when the film broke, the entire show came to a screeching halt. *On the air.* In the broadcast industry this is known as "dead air"—the TV cameras are still on, and the folks at home are still watching, but there's nothing happening onscreen. Nothing at all.

## PAPER TIGER

At that moment Rogers happened to be standing behind a paper

**Nice doggie: British mail carriers report fewer dog bites than those in any other country.**

backdrop that had been painted to look like a clock. He quickly looked around and spotted "Daniel," a striped tiger puppet that the station's general manager, Dorothy Daniel, had given him the night before as a party favor at the station's launch party.

"When the first film broke, I just poked the puppet through the paper," Rogers remembered years later, "and it happened to be a clock where I poked him through. And he just said, 'It's 5:02 and Columbus discovered America in 1492.' And that was the first thing I ever said on the air. Necessity was the mother of that invention, because it hadn't been planned."

The puppet worked and the old films didn't, so *The Children's Corner* became an educational puppet show. Daniel Striped Tiger, who lives in a clock, remained a fixture on Rogers's shows for the rest of his broadcast career. Numerous other characters, including King Friday XIII, Lady Elaine Fairchilde, and X the Owl all made their debut on *The Children's Corner*.

## NEIGHBORHOOD WATCH

*The Children's Corner* stayed on the air for seven years; then in 1963 Rogers accepted an offer from the Canadian Broadcasting Corporation to host a 15-minute show called *Misterogers*, the first show in which he actually appeared on camera. (That year he also became an ordained Presbyterian minister.)

By 1965 *Misterogers* was airing in Canada and in the eastern United States, but it had the same problem that *The Children's Corner* had—not enough money. *Misterogers* ran out of funds and was slated for cancellation... until parents found out: when they learned the show was going off the air, they raised such a stink that the Sears Roebuck Foundation and National Educational Television (now known as the Public Broadcasting Service, or PBS), kicked in $150,000 apiece to keep the show on the air.

Lengthened to a full half hour and renamed *Mister Rogers' Neighborhood*, the show was first broadcast nationwide on February 19, 1968.

## INNER CHILD

Very early in his broadcasting career, Rogers drew up a list of things he wanted to encourage in the children who watched his show. Some of the items on that list: self-esteem, self-control,

**And it floats! When filled, the oil tanker *Jahre Viking* weighs 1.13 billion pounds.**

imagination, creativity, curiosity, appreciation of diversity, cooperation, tolerance for waiting, and persistence. *How* Rogers encouraged these things in his young viewers was heavily influenced by his own childhood experiences:

• **His grandfather.** Many of the most memorable things Rogers said to children were inspired by things his own grandfather, Fred Brooks McFeely, said to him. "I think it was when I was leaving one time to go home after our time together that my grandfather said to me, 'You know, you made this day a really special day. Just by being yourself. There's only one person in the world like you. And I happen to like you just the way you are,' " Rogers remembered. "That just went right into my heart. And it never budged." (Rogers named Mr. McFeely, the show's Speedy Delivery messenger character, after his grandfather.)

• **The neighborhood of make-believe.** Fred Rogers was a sickly kid who came down with just about every childhood disease imaginable from chicken pox to scarlet fever. He spent a lot of time in bed, quarantined on doctors' orders. To amuse himself, he played with puppets and invented imaginary worlds for them to live in. "I'm sure that was the beginning of a much later neighborhood of make-believe," Rogers said.

• **Explanations.** Like most children, when Rogers was very little, he was frightened by unfamiliar things—being alone, starting school, getting a haircut, visiting a doctor's office, etc. "I liked to be told about things before I had to do them," he remembered, so explaining new and unfamiliar things became a central part of the show. (On one episode he even brought on actress Margaret Hamilton, who played the Wicked Witch of the West in *The Wizard of Oz,* to explain that she was just pretending and that kids didn't need to be afraid.)

• **Sweaters.** Rogers got most of his sweaters from his mother, who knitted him a new one every year for Christmas. He wore them all on his show.

• **Sneakers.** Those date back to his days on *The Children's Corner*—"I had to run across the studio floor to get from the puppet set to the organ," Rogers explained. "I didn't want to make a lot of noise by running around in ordinary shoes."

**Do you know how long it takes Earth to go around the sun? 46% of Americans don't.**

## GOODBYE, NEIGHBOR

Rogers taped nearly 900 episodes of *Mr. Rogers' Neighborhood* over its more than 30 years on the air. They're still broadcast by more than 300 public television stations around the United States as well as in Canada, the Philippines, Guam, and other countries around the world. Videotapes of the show are used to teach English to non-native speakers (singer Ricky Martin credits Mr. Rogers with teaching him to speak English).

Rogers retired from producing new episodes of the show in December 2000, and the last new episode aired in August 2001. He came out of retirement briefly in 2002 to record public service announcements advising parents on how to help children deal with the anniversary of the September 11 attacks. He made his last public appearance on January 1, 2003, when he served as Grand Marshal of the Tournament of Roses Parade and tossed the coin for the Rose Bowl Game. Mr. Rogers passed away from stomach cancer two months later.

## THOUGHTS FROM MR. ROGERS

- "The world is not always a kind place. That's something children learn for themselves, whether we want them to or not, but it's something they really need our help to understand."
- "Anything we can do to help foster the intellect and spirit and emotional growth of our fellow human beings, that is our job. Those of us who have this particular vision must continue against all odds."
- "People don't come up to me to talk about the weather. I've even had a child come up to me and not even say hello, but instead say right out, 'Mr. Rogers, my grandmother's in the hospital.'"
- "So many people have grown up with the 'Neighborhood,' I'm just their dad coming along. You know, it's really fun to go through life with this face."

***One of the most common things people who met Mr. Rogers say about him is that he was the very same person off camera that he was on camera. And yet to the cynical, that seemed hard to believe. Was Fred Rogers really the person he appeared to be on TV...or was he too good to be true? Turn the page to find out.***

# NEIGHBORHOOD GOSSIP

*Like a lot of celebrities, Mr. Rogers was the subject of some preposterous rumors over the years. Here are three of the strangest.*

**MYSTERY:** Why did Mr. Rogers always cover his arms?
**URBAN LEGEND:** He was a sniper in Vietnam. He wore long-sleeved shirts, sweaters, and jackets to cover up the many tattoos he got while serving in the military.
**THE TRUTH:** Rogers never served in Vietnam or any other war; he began his career in television right after he graduated from college in the early 1950s. So why did he always wear long sleeves? Dressing somewhat formally was a technique he used to establish himself as an authority figure to the children who watched the show.

**MYSTERY:** *Mr. Rogers' Neighborhood* is a kids' show. So how come kids almost never appeared on the show?
**URBAN LEGEND:** Rogers was once convicted of abusing children and instead of jail, was sentenced to community service. Appearing on the show for more than three decades was how he served out his sentence. As a convicted child abuser, Rogers wasn't allowed to be alone with kids—even on the TV show.
**THE TRUTH:** Rogers got his start in broadcasting in the early 1950s, before the invention of videotape. Shows had to be broadcast live, which is why kids seldom appeared on *any* kids' shows back then—they are too unpredictable for live TV.

**MYSTERY:** How did Mr. Rogers really feel about kids?
**URBAN LEGEND:** After more than three decades of hosting a children's show, Mr. Rogers showed how he *really* felt about children on his very last show: he gave kids the finger on TV.
**THE TRUTH:** There is such a picture floating around on the Internet, but it's a fake—somebody doctored a real picture to make it look like Rogers was flipping the bird. It never happened. Anyway, by the end of his career new episodes were taped months in advance of broadcast, and such an image would never have been allowed to air.

**Number of holes in a Ritz cracker: 7—six in a hexagon shape, and one in the center.**

# WORD ORIGINS

*Ever wonder where certain words came from? Here are the interesting stories behind some of them.*

**MONEY**

**Meaning:** Currency; a medium of exchange in the form of coins and banknotes

**Origin:** "Hera, queen of the Greek gods, kept her name out of the vulgate [common speech] until she moved to Rome and became Juno. As Juno Moneta (Juno the Monitress), she presided over a Roman temple where gold was coined. Moneta became the eponym of money, and Moneta's temple a mint." (From *Thou Improper, Thou Uncommon Noun*, by Willard Espy)

**PADDY WAGON**

**Meaning:** A police van

**Origin:** "A carryover from the days when Irish immigrants were low men on the social totem pole and hence fair game when a roundup of miscreants was needed to create favorable publicity for the law enforcers. Paddy was a common nickname for Irishmen." (From *Dictionary of Word Origins*, by William and Mary Morris)

**EROTIC**

**Meaning:** Relating to sexual desire or excitement

**Origin:** "*Eros* was the god of love, and the fairest of the gods in the Greek pantheon. But he was vain and spoiled and for sport shot his love-poisoned arrows into the hearts of men and gods. At his festival, the *erotia*, married couples of the day were supposed to patch up their differences and end all quarrels. From the Greek name *Eros* comes the word *erotic*, meaning 'full of sexual desire,' or 'morbidly amorous.'" (From *Word Origins*, by Wilfred Funk)

**JUGGERNAUT**

**Meaning:** An overwhelming force that crushes anything in its path

**Origin:** "The word comes from Hindi; its origin lies in *Jagganath*, a Hindu god, the Lord of the World. The city of Puri in eastern India is the site of an annual festival in his honor at which the image of the god is carried on a gigantic wheeled vehicle 45 feet high, drawn through the streets by pilgrims. It was said (mostly inaccurately) that fanatical followers would throw themselves under the wheels." (From *Merriam-Webster's Dictionary of Allusions*, by Elizabeth Webber and Mike Feinsilber)

## COCKTAIL

**Meaning:** An alcoholic drink consisting of spirits mixed with other ingredients

**Origin:** "One idea is that it came from cockfighting. A cock's courage was fired up by slipping him a mixture of stale beer, gin, herbs, and flour, which was called *cock-ale*. More likely, the term was coined by Antoine Peychaud, a New Orleans restaurateur. During the 1800s, Antoine made drinks mixed from a number of different liquors. He served the wicked brew in little egg cups called *coquetier* in French. Wanting to give his drinks a special name, he simply Americanized the French word by changing it to cocktail." (From *Straight from the Horse's Mouth*, by Teri Degler)

## PHONY

**Meaning:** A fraudulent person or thing

**Origin:** "Newspaperman H. L. Mencken suggested that a maker of fake jewelry named Forney is the origin of this word, but few experts agree with him. The majority opinion is that *phony* is an alteration of *fawney*, British slang for a worthless ring. The word probably comes from the *fawney rig*, a con game in which a worthless ring is planted, and when someone 'finds' it he is persuaded by a 'bystander' that he should pay the bystander for his share in the find." (From *Word and Phrase Origins*, by Robert Hendrickson)

## POOPED

**Meaning:** Exhausted

**Origin:** "Englishmen headed for the New World found that violent waves did the most damage when they crashed against the stern (rear end), or *poop* of a vessel. Any ship that came out of a long bout with nature was said to be badly 'pooped.' Sailors who described the splintered stern of a ship often confessed that they felt as pooped as their vessel looked. Landsmen borrowed the sea-going expression and put it to use." (From *Why You Say It*, by Webb Garrison)

**Pound for pound, a hummingbird consumes the caloric equivalent 228 milkshakes per day.**

# EXILE ON EASY STREET

*It's a perennial news story: some dictator somewhere is oppressing his people, plundering his country's treasury, and defying international law. Then suddenly he's out of power. You assume he's in jail, but he's probably living in the lap of luxury.*

**DICTATOR:** Augusto Pinochet, Chile

**REIGN OF TERROR:** Pinochet came to power in a CIA-assisted coup in 1973. During his rule, tens of thousands of Chileans were tortured, killed, or "disappeared." Pinochet relinquished power amid growing opposition in 1990 but remained the commander-in-chief until 1998, when he became "senator-for-life."

**WHERE'D HE GO?** While visiting England in 1998, Pinochet was arrested by British authorities on charges of torture and genocide. During his house-arrest, he lived at Wentworth, an exclusive estate outside of London. Estimated cost: $10,000 a month. After a long legal battle, a British court ruled that he was too sick to stand trial.

Pinochet went back to Chile, where he was arrested again, with more than 200 charges against him. In 2002 the Chilean Supreme Court ruled him unfit for trial and all charges were dropped. During his house-arrest in Chile, he got the same royal treatment he had in England: he lived on a baronial estate overlooking the Pacific Ocean.

**DICTATOR:** Alfredo Stroessner, Paraguay

**REIGN OF TERROR:** He took over Paraguay in a military coup in 1954 and ruled for more than 35 years. (He was "reelected" eight times.) Stroessner was a participant in Operation Condor, a police action that tortured, disappeared, or executed hundreds of thousands of people in South America. And he helped turn Paraguay into a haven for Nazi war criminals.

**WHERE'D HE GO?** Stroessner was overthrown in 1989 and fled to neighboring Brazil, where he still lives a quiet, comfortable life.

**DICTATORS:** Ferdinand and Imelda Marcos, Philippines

**REIGN OF TERROR:** Ferdinand Marcos was elected President of the Philippines in 1966. Under the Philippine constitution, he would have had to leave office in 1973—so he declared martial law and scrapped the constitution. Having taken absolute control of the country, Marcos ordered numerous tortures and executions. And he stole more than $5 billion. When he was overthrown in 1986, the 1,220 pairs of shoes found in wife Imelda's closet infuriated the poverty-stricken nation and became an international symbol of greed.

**WHERE'D THEY GO?** To Hawaii. Ferdinand died in 1989, but with billions hidden in Swiss banks, Imelda has continued to live in luxury. (She was reported to have over 3,000 new pairs of shoes by the mid-1990s.) The Philippine government recovered $2 billion of the stolen funds, but Mrs. Marcos is still doing alright—in February 2003, she was seen shopping for diamonds in Italy.

**DICTATOR:** Mengistu Haile Mariam, Ethiopia

**REIGN OF TERROR:** Mengistu overthrew Emperor Haile Selassie in 1974 and turned to the Soviets for help in starting a Marxist regime. During the two-year campaign dubbed "the Red Terror," tens of thousands of "enemies of the revolution" were murdered. When families came to claim the bodies, they had to pay for the bullets that killed their loved ones before they could take them. After the fall of the Soviet Union in 1989, Mengistu lost support and was finally overthrown in 1991.

**WHERE'D HE GO?** He fled to Zimbabwe as a "guest" of President Robert Mugabe, where he still lives in a heavily guarded, luxurious mansion. Though he's formally charged with "crimes against humanity" in Ethiopia, Zimbabwe refuses to extradite him.

**DICTATOR:** Jean-Claude "Baby Doc" Duvalier, Haiti

**REIGN OF TERROR:** At the age of 19, he succeeded his father, "Papa Doc," as president-for-life. During his 15-year reign, tens of thousands of Haitians were tortured and killed. As Haiti turned into one of the world's poorest nations, Baby Doc stole an estimated $500 million.

**WHERE'D HE GO?** Although never officially granted asylum, Duvalier moved to France in 1986, taking the stolen money with him. He lived in a villa in the hills above Cannes, drove a Ferrari, and owned two apartments in Paris and a chateau.

**PARTIAL PAYBACK:** According to news reports, Duvalier went broke. How? He lost everything in his divorce from his wife, Michelle Duvalier, in the mid-1990s.

**Two out of three adults in the U.S. will need glasses at some point in their life.**

# THE LADY OF THE LINES

*If you've ever heard of the Nazca lines, you have this woman to thank for preserving them for posterity. And if you've ever doubted that one person can make a difference, think again...*

## HELP WANTED

In 1932 a 29-year-old German woman named Maria Reiche answered a newspaper ad and landed a job in Peru, tutoring the sons of the German consul. After that, she bounced from job to job and eventually found work translating documents for an archaeologist named Julio Tello.

One day she happened to overhear a conversation between Tello and another archaeologist, Toribio Mejia. Mejia described some mysterious lines he'd seen in a patch of desert about 250 miles south of the capital city of Lima, near the small town of Nazca. He tried to interest Tello in the lines, but Tello dismissed them as unimportant. Reiche wasn't so sure. She decided to go to Nazca and have a look for herself.

## MYSTERIOUS LINES

Gazing out across the desert floor, Reiche was amazed by what she saw: More than 1,000 lines crisscrossing 200 square miles of desert, some as narrow as footpaths, others more than 15 feet wide. Many ran almost perfectly straight for miles across the desert, deviating as little as four yards in a mile.

The lines were made by early Nazca people, etched into the desert floor between 200 B.C. and 700 A.D. They had created the lines by removing darkened surface fragments (known as "desert varnish") to reveal the much lighter stone underneath.

But why?

## WAITING FOR SUNDOWN

An American archaeologist and historian named Paul Kosok had a theory. At first he thought the lines might be irrigation ditches, but they weren't large enough or deep enough to transport water. Then he started to wonder if they might have some kind of astronomical significance. So, on June 21, 1941, the southern hemisphere's winter solstice, he went out into the desert and waited for the sun to set.

Sure enough, when the sun set, it did so at a point on the horizon that was intersected by one of the Nazca lines. The line seemed to serve as an astronomical marker, telling the Nazca people that the first day of winter had arrived.

## BIG BIRD

Kosok had also observed that while most of the Nazca lines were straight, some were curvy. But it wasn't until he plotted one on a piece of paper, then looked down to see that he'd drawn the outline of a giant bird, that he realized that some of the lines were *drawings*. The drawings were so large that they could not be made out by anyone looking at them from the ground.

With the discovery of the solstice line and the giant bird, Kosok became convinced that the Nazca lines were an enormous astronomical calendar, or, as he put it, "the world's largest astronomy book," with each line carefully laid out to correspond to something in the heavens above. Maybe, he speculated, the giant bird represented a constellation in the night sky. He offered Reiche a job helping him survey the lines so that he could prove his theory.

## LIFELONG PASSION

She took the job, and after a few months of tramping across the desert each day with little more than a canteen of water and a pencil and paper to record her observations, she found what she was looking for: a line that intersected with the sun on the southern hemisphere's summer solstice, December 21. That was all it took—Reiche was convinced that Kosok's theory was correct. And she would spend the rest of her life trying to prove it.

At first Reiche could afford to visit the Nazca lines only occasionally, and because she was German she was not allowed to work at the site at all during World War II. By 1946, however, she was living in Peru year-round and spending nearly all of her waking hours in the desert trying to unlock the secret of the lines. When Kosok left Peru in 1948, she continued without him.

Studying the lines wasn't as simple as it sounds. In those days, many of them were so obscured by dirt, sand, and centuries of new desert varnish that it was barely possible to find them. That they were distinguishable at all was thanks only to the fact that they were etched a few inches into the desert floor.

## CLEAN SWEEP

Reiche decided to "clean" the lines so that they could be more easily seen. First she tried using a rake. When that didn't work, she switched to a broom. It's estimated that over the next 50 years, she swept out as many as 1,000 of the lines by herself, carefully mapping the location of each one as she went along, and returning to the same lines at different times of day and in all lights to be certain that she was following their true courses.

In the process Reiche discovered—and *un*covered—as many as 30 drawings similar to the giant bird that Kosok had found, including numerous birds, two lizards, four fish, a monkey, a whale, a pair of human hands, and a man with an owl-like head. The scope of her work is astonishing: When you look at an aerial photograph of the Nazca lines—any photograph of any of the lines or ground drawings—there's a good chance that Reiche swept those lines herself. Mile after mile after mile of them, using only one tool—an ordinary household broom.

## LOST IN SPACE

Just as Reiche was almost single-handedly responsible for restoring the Nazca lines, she was also the first to bring them to public attention. Her 1949 book *Mystery on the Desert* helped to generate worldwide interest in the lines.

But what really put them on the map was a 1968 book written by a Swiss hotelier named Erich Von Daniken. His book *Chariots of the Gods* proposed that some of the lines were landing strips for alien spacecraft. According to Von Daniken's theory, aliens created the human race by breeding with primates, then returned to outer space. The early humans then etched the drawings into the desert floor, hoping to attract the aliens back to Earth.

**Since 1950, more than 600 people have been killed by avalanches in the U.S.**

## JOIN THE CROWD

*Chariots of the Gods* was an international bestseller, and its success prompted other people to write books of their own with more theories about the origin of the lines. One speculated the lines were ancient jogging tracks; another claimed they were launch sites for Nazcan hot-air balloonists. These books turned the Nazca lines into a New Age pop culture phenomenon, helping to attract tens of thousands of tourists to the site each year.

As a result, the Nazca lines began to suffer from overexposure—more and more tourists went out into the desert on foot, on dirt bikes, and in dune buggies, doing untold damage to the lines in the process.

Reiche did what she could to protect them. For years she lived in a small house out in the desert so that she could watch over the lines herself, and she used the profits from her writing and lecturing to pay security guards to patrol the desert. By the end of her life she was crippled by Parkinson's disease, but she continued to study the lines and was known to chase intruders away in her wheelchair. By the time of her death in 1998 at the age of 95, she was nearly deaf and almost completely blind. Not that it really mattered to her—"I can see every line," she said, "every drawing, in my mind."

## FINAL IRONY

Though Reiche devoted most of her life to proving that the Nazca lines are a giant astronomical calendar, that theory has been largely discarded. Researchers now believe that while a few of the lines may indeed point to astronomical phenomena such as the summer and winter solstices (with more than 1,000 lines running across the desert floor in all directions, even *that* may be a coincidence), most of the lines are processional footpaths linking various sacred sites in the desert. The ground drawings, they believe, are artwork the Nazcans made for their gods.

# MORE SIMPLE SOLUTIONS

*On page 585 we told you about some simple inventions that are changing the world. Here are a few more.*

## HIPPO WATER ROLLER

**Problem:** In South Africa, more than 15 million people have to carry water from wells or rivers to their homes—sometimes as far as six miles away. It's traditionally carried by balancing five-gallon buckets on top of the head, requiring many trips and often leading to neck and back injuries. How can people get water from one place to another without breaking their backs doing it?

**Simple Solution:** A big plastic drum with handles

**Explanation:** It looks like a lawn roller. Fill the large, barrel-shaped drum with water, screw on the lid, lay it on its side, attach the handles, and then just push or pull it home—the barrel becomes a wheel. It holds 20 gallons of water, which weighs 200 pounds. But the design makes the weight feel like 22 pounds, so even kids and the elderly can handle it. And it's made of UV-stabilized polyethylene, durable enough to ride over roots, rocks, and even broken glass. Cost: about $60. (The manufacturer, Imvubu Projects of Johannesburg, has donated thousands of the rollers to water-needy communities.)

## XTRABIKE

**Problem:** Bicycles are an extremely popular mode of transportation in developing nations—often it's the only mode. But carrying a lot of weight on a bicycle can be difficult, if not impossible, and dangerous. How can people carry goods and other large loads on their bikes?

**Simple Solution:** The Xtrabike, a heavy-duty bike rack

**Explanation:** Working in Nicaragua and Kenya, a company from Berkeley, California, called XAccess designed a steel-frame extension for the back wheels of a bicycle, with fold-down racks that turn it into a hauler of water, kids, or any other cargo. The design carries the weight low to the ground, so it still rides and turns normally, and an average person can comfortably haul as much as a

**Hot air: Iceland has so much geothermal power that it plans to end fossil fuel use by 2030.**

200-pound load. (Try doing that on a bike rack.) It costs about $50, which is a lot for many people, but XAccess has a solution for that, too. "Can't afford an Xtrabike?" they ask on their website. "We'll teach you how to make one."

## BAYGEN FREEPLAY RADIO

**Problem:** Many Africans can't get vital information about healthcare because they lack basic communication devices such as TVs and radios. In many areas there's no electricity, and the cost of one set of batteries could be an entire month's salary. How can people get the information they need?

**Simple Solution:** A wind-up radio

**Explanation:** Englishman Trevor Baylis learned about the problem in 1993 while watching a documentary on the spread of AIDS in Africa. Working with Andy Davis, who helped design the first Sony Walkman, by 1995 he had invented the BayGen Freeplay, a spring-driven radio. By 1997 tens of thousands had been sold—cheaply—in developing countries all over the planet. Wind the crank, and a specially designed coil spring powers a small generator, which in turn powers the receiver. How well does it work? Turn the crank for 30 seconds and you can listen to AM, FM, or shortwave stations for more than 30 minutes. And the spring can take 10,000 windings before it wears out. The BayGen has won endorsements from Prince Charles, Nelson Mandela, and the International Red Cross.

## FOLDABLE FAMILY PANEL COOK KIT

**Problem:** In many developing countries it is increasingly difficult to obtain fuel—mostly wood or coal—for cooking. How can people cook without fuel?

**Simple Solution:** A solar-powered oven

**Explanation:** Roger Bernard and Barbara Kerr of Solar Cookers International (SCI) developed such an oven, and the best part is that anybody can make one. For decades they have been doing workshops for families in impoverished villages, providing the materials and know-how to make solar ovens. The materials: some cardboard, aluminum foil, glue, and a plastic bag (an oven cooking bag works best). The oven really works, too. Even on partly sunny days, it will reach 300°F. Meat, beans, rice, vegetables, breads, and other

**First pilot ever to fly a loop-the-loop: Lincoln Beachy, on Nov. 18, 1913 (San Diego).**

foods can be cooked without using any fuel. It takes longer than conventional ovens (although for many dishes and on sunny days it doesn't), but the benefits outweigh this drawback. Another plus: Put the food in the solar oven, go about your day, and come back later—the solar cooker won't burn your food, it will just keep it hot.

## ADAPTIVE EYECARE

**Problem:** In 2002 the World Health Organization estimated that one billion people around the world who needed eyeglasses could not get them. In the African nation of Ghana alone, there were only 50 opticians for a population of 20 million. Poor eyesight means difficulties in reading, education, and employment. Without enough doctors, how can people get the glasses they need?

**Simple Solution:** Universal, adjustable eyeglasses

**Explanation:** In 1996 Oxford professor Dr. Joshua Silver started Adaptive Eyecare. After years of research, he had invented glasses with lenses that were filled with a clear silicon oil. A small pump on the frame changes the amount of oil in the lenses, thus altering their curvature. (The pump is removed after the adjustment.) That means that as a person's sight deteriorates over time, they don't have to go find an optician—they simply turn a knob until their vision is in focus, and voilà! A new pair of glasses! And each lens can be adjusted separately. The glasses are universal, since anyone can adjust them to their own eyes, which keeps manufacturing costs down. The glasses are sold to nonprofit groups and governments around the world, keeping with Dr. Silver's goal of improving the vision of the world's poorest people.

* * *

## WEIRD TALES OF THE STAGE

*The Bluebird* is a classic play about two children who go searching for the Bluebird of Happiness. A designer at a midwestern theater thought it would be a great idea to have *real* bluebirds fly around the theater at the end of the play. So he sprayed pigeons with blue paint and put them in little cages hanging above the audience. Apparently no one ever considered what the paint, combined with the heat from the lights, might do to the birds. On opening night, the cages were opened at the end of the show...showering a horrified audience with hundreds of dead "bluebirds."

**The Chinese were the first to use a decimal system, in the sixth century B.C.**

# FOUNDING (*hic!*) FATHERS

*Before they were (hic) alcoholic beverages, (hic) they were people (hic) who made alcoholic beverages (hic).*

## JOHN WALKER

**Background:** In 1820, at age 15, Walker started working in his father's grocery, wine, and spirit store in Kilmarnock, Scotland. Unhappy with the inconsistencies in the barrels of whiskey, he set out to refine the process. Walker soon became known throughout Scotland for his technique of blending single malt whiskies.

**Famous Name:** Walker's son Alexander joined him in 1856 and began marketing Walker's Kilmarnock Whisky in England and Australia, and later in the United States. In 1908 the company name was changed as a tribute to its founder, Johnnie Walker.

## DON FACUNDO BACARDI MASSÓ

**Background:** Born in Spain, Don Facundo emigrated to Cuba around 1830. There he discovered rum—a harsh "firewater" popular among pirates. A cultured man, Don Facundo made it his goal to create a smoother version that could be served in fine restaurants.

**Famous Name:** It took more than 30 years of experimenting with every step of the manufacturing process, but in 1862, Don Facundo perfected it and introduced Bacardi Rum. The family still runs the business today using the same secret technique created by Don Facundo 140 years ago.

## JASPER NEWTON DANIEL

**Background:** He was born in Tennessee in 1850, the youngest of 13 children, and ran away when he was only six years old. Little Jasper ended up living with a neighbor named Dan Call and earned his keep by helping him make moonshine whiskey. In 1863 Call sold his still to Jasper, who was then only 13.

**Famous Name:** Known as Jack, Jasper Daniel had a knack for making—and selling—whiskey, and distributed it to both sides during the Civil War. He used his war profits to build a real distillery.

A slight man at 5'2" and 120 pounds, Daniel relied on his personality as much as the quality of his whiskey to make sales. He

**Percent of the cost of a 12-ounce bottle of beer that goes to federal and state taxes: 43.**

always wore a mustache and goatee, a planter's hat, and a knee-length frock coat. He never appeared in public without his "costume." When postwar liquor laws changed, Daniel was the first man to register a distillery in the United States, which he called Jack Daniel Distillery No. 1.

### JOSÉ ANTONIO DE CUERVO

**Background:** Sent by the king of Spain, in 1758 José de Cuervo traveled to a small town in central Mexico. There he began cultivating the agave plant, which for thousands of years had been fermented by the indigenous peoples into a beverage known as *mezcal*. De Cuervo produced a more refined version of the liquor, which took on the name of the town in which it was made...Tequila.

**Famous Name:** His descendants have been producing it ever since, and have become one of Mexico's richest and most respected families. But it wasn't until the turn of the 20th century that Cuervo-produced tequila began to carry the name José Cuervo.

### PETER SMIRNOFF

**Background:** Peter Smirnoff's first batch of vodka came out of his still in 1864. Over the next 15 years, he became famous throughout Russia and in 1886 was named the royal distiller of Czar Alexander III. By 1900 Smirnoff was producing a million bottles of vodka per day.

**Famous Name:** One of Smirnoff's suppliers, Rudolph Kunett, fled Russia when the czar was overthrown and purchased the rights to sell Smirnoff vodka in the United States. The only problem: no one bought it—the vodka had a reputation as a harsh liquor that led to a bad hangover. Kunett finally gave up and sold his Connecticut distillery to G. F Hublein and Company in 1939. Part of the deal included the last 2,000 bottles of vodka. But they had no vodka corks left, so company president John Martin decided to put whiskey corks on them instead. That changed everything. In the South, a salesman sampled it, loved it, and came up with a new slogan: "Smirnoff's White Whiskey. No Taste. No Smell." It sold out. Why? Fewer people were drinking straight liquor in those days—they wanted something that could be mixed. So Martin resumed the vodka production, advertising it as a mixer. Today it's the bestselling liquor in the United States.

**The ocean sunfish produces up to 30 million eggs at a single spawning.**

# THE CAT'S MEOW

*We've done a lot of quote pages about dogs in past* Bathroom Readers. *Now, it's time for cats to have their day.*

"After scolding one's cat, one looks into its face and is seized by the ugly suspicion that it understood every word. And has filed it for reference."

**—Charlotte Gray**

"If a cat spoke, it would say things like, 'Hey, I don't see the problem here.'"

**—Roy Blount, Jr.**

"If cats could talk, they wouldn't."

**—Nan Porter**

"I have studied many philosophers and many cats. The wisdom of cats is infinitely superior."

**—Hippolyte Taine**

"Dogs come when they're called. Cats take a message and get back to you later."

**—Mary Bly**

"Cats keep their cool, no matter what. Even when they do things like fall or lose their balance, they'll walk away with an attitude that seems to say, 'I meant to do that.'"

**—Michael Jordan**

"Whether they be the musician cats in my band or the real cats of the world, they all got style."

**—Ray Charles**

"If cats seem distant and aloof it is because this is not their native planet—they are here just to visit and dominate."

**—Hank Roll**

"To bathe a cat takes brute force, perseverance, courage of conviction—and a cat. The last ingredient is usually the hardest to come by."

**—Stephen Baker**

"In order to keep a true perspective of one's importance, everyone should have a dog that will worship him and a cat that will ignore him."

**—Dereke Bruce**

"You may own a cat, but cannot govern one."

**—Kate Sanborn**

"The smallest feline is a masterpiece."

**—Leonardo da Vinci**

**Scaredy cat? Charles Lindbergh carried a Felix the Cat doll with him on his famous flight.**

# BRAINTEASERS

*Uncle John emerged from "the brainroom" giving these puzzles three thumbs up—one thumb for being fun, one thumb for being challenging, and one thumb for "I just learned something." (We still can't figure out where he got the extra thumb.)* *Answers on page 748.*

**1.** You're sitting on a bus. The kid next to you has a helium-filled balloon. She lets go of the balloon and it ends up against the ceiling, just about in the center of the bus. The driver suddenly hits the gas pedal and the bus lurches forward, throwing you back into your seat. What does the balloon do?

**a)** It moves backward. **b)** It moves forward.
**c)** It stays where it is.

**2.** How can you make the following equation correct without changing it:

8 + 8 = 91

**3.** You place an empty glass on one side of a balance scale and a one-pound weight on the other side. Then you fill the glass with water until the two sides are perfectly balanced. Now you put your finger down into the water without touching the glass. It makes the water level in the glass rise, but it doesn't overflow. What happens to the scale?

**a)** The glass side goes up. **b)** The glass side goes down.
**c)** It holds still.

**4.** You're sitting in a boat in a swimming pool. You have a large anchor in the boat. You drop the anchor into the water, and, of course, it sinks immediately. What happens to the water level in the pool?

**a)** It goes up. **b)** It goes down. **c)** It stays the same.

**5.** Try to solve this in your head: Take 1,000 and add 40 to it. Now add another 1,000. Now add 30. And another 1,000. Now add 20. Now add another 1,000. Now add 10. What's the total?

**Ask Virginia Woolf: Three percent of all English surnames are derived from animal names.**

# THE BIGGER THEY ARE...

*Sometimes making big business decisions means making big blunders, as these folks found out.*

## BAD APPLE

In 1988 Apple Computers hired a small computer company from Virginia called Quantum Computer Services to develop an online service for their customers. It was to be called AppleLink Personal Edition and was set to come out in 1989. But before Quantum could launch the service, Apple changed their minds and terminated their contract. Bad idea. Quantum had negotiated in their contract that if Apple let them go, they got to keep the technology. They launched the service themselves in late 1989, with a new name... America Online.

## STAR WARS: THE PUBLISHER'S MENACE

British book publisher Dorling Kindersley saw sales of its *Star Wars* books rise dramatically after the release of the movie *The Phantom Menace* in 1999. Elated company execs quickly ordered a huge printing for the Christmas sales season—and sold a whopping 3 million copies. The only problem—they had printed 13 million copies. Loss: $22.4 million. In January 2000, the already debt-plagued company admitted the mistake and CEO James Middlehurst resigned. In March, the once-prosperous worldwide publisher was sold to media giant Pearson. (*Note*: Ten million books would make a stack more than 150 miles high.)

## A TOBACCO COMPANY TELLS THE TRUTH!

In 2001 tobacco giant Philip Morris did a study of the effects of cigarette smoking for the leaders of the Czech Republic. The report they issued touted the "positive effects" that smoking has for government. It shortens people's lives, they said, which means lower costs for pensions, housing, and health care for the elderly. The details of the report were supposed to be private, but somehow the press got hold of them and made them public. Result: A major public relations blow to a company that had just spent $100 million to boost its image. Philip Morris issued an apology to the Czech people and then canceled plans to make similar reports in four other nations.

**On average, babies born in May are 7 ounces heavier than those born in other months.**

## A FINE ROMANCE (OR TWO)

In 1991 Random House editor Joni Evans thought she could cash in on the fame of TV's *Dynasty* star Joan Collins and offered her a $4 million contract—with a $1.3 million advance—to write two romance novels. (Collins's sister, Jackie, is a bestselling novelist.) Collins turned in manuscripts for *The Ruling Passion* and *Hell Hath No Fury*, but Evans thought they were terrible and wouldn't publish them. Random House sued Collins but couldn't get the advance money back. As if giving a huge advance to an unproven writer wasn't a big enough blunder, Evans missed a clause put in the contract stipulating that Collins would be paid whether or not her manuscripts were published. Result: Collins ended up with $2.6 million of Random House's cash for two books that never went to press.

## IT'S NOT OK

Before she joined Random House (see item above), Evans was a senior editor at the publishing house William Morrow, where she committed another blunder in an otherwise successful career. When Morrow was approached about the paperback rights of a certain new author, she advised her boss against it, sure that the book would never sell. The price for the rights at the time was $10,000...three months later, the rights went for $675,000. The book was the groundbreaking self-help title *I'm OK, You're OK*. It went to #4 on the *New York Times* Best Seller list in 1970 and has sold over 15 million copies since...most of them paperbacks.

## LISTEN CAREFULLY

In November 2001, the privately owned Japanese company Dentsu, the world's fourth largest advertising agency, decided to go public. They had the Wall Street firm UBS Warburg handle their initial public offering, and instructed the brokers to sell 16 shares at 610,000 yen ($4,925) each. But the brokers mistakenly listed 610,000 shares at 16 yen (about 13¢) each. Before they discovered the error, 65,000 of the shares had been sold. Warburg had to buy them all back on the open market. The exact amount of Warburg's loss was undisclosed, but it was estimated to be as high as $100 million.

**Q: What do you call the dent in the bottom of a champagne bottle? A: A *kick* (or a *punt*).**

# WINGING IT

*Anyone who's ever boarded an airplane has probably wondered how a 400-ton hunk of metal could possibly cruise through the air. Is it magic? No, it's physics! Here's a simplified explanation for all you porcelain pilots.*

## HOW ABOUT A LIFT?

The force that makes it possible for airplanes to fly is called *lift*. Lift is provided by the wings of an airplane. But how do the wings generate lift? There are two characteristics that help them get the plane off the ground:

### 1. The "Angle of Attack"

• If you've ever stuck your hand out of the window of a moving car, you already understand how the "angle of attack" works. If you tilt your hand so that the front edge of your hand is pointing upward, the air strikes the bottom surface of your hand and pushes it higher in the air.

• Changing the tilt of your hand so that the front edge is pointing downward has the opposite effect: the air strikes the top of your hand and pushes it down. By tilting the front edge your hand up and down, you can "fly" your hand up and down however you want. If this is difficult to understand, try it the next time you're in a car.

• If you look closely at the wings on an airplane, you'll notice that they're tilted. The front edge—known as the *leading edge*—is slightly higher than the *trailing edge*. Aircraft manufacturers do this so that when the airplane is moving through the air, more air strikes the bottom surface of the wing than the top, pushing the wing upward and helping the plane to fly.

### 2. The Shape

If you were to look at a cross-section of an airplane wing, it would look something like this:

The wing is shaped this way in order to take advantage of something called *Bernoulli's principle*. Understanding the "angle of attack" is pretty easy, but Bernoulli's principle is a little trickier:

• In 1738 Daniel Bernoulli, a Swiss mathematician, observed that when the velocity of a fluid increases, the pressure of that fluid decreases.

• You may not think of air as a fluid, but technically it is. So when air speed increases, air pressure decreases.

• Wings are shaped in such a way that the air that passes over the top surface of the wing moves faster than the air that passes underneath the bottom surface.

• That means that the air pressure underneath the wing is higher than the air pressure above it. This difference in pressure causes the air underneath the wing to literally *press* the wing upward in the air.

• Lift is measured the same way that weight is. If your airplane weighs 1,000 pounds, that means the wings have to generate more than 1,000 pounds of lift for the plane to leave the ground.

## STRAIGHT TALK

So how does the shape of a wing make the air passing over it move faster than the air moving underneath it? Well, as we all know, the shortest distance between two points is a straight line. And that's the secret:

• The bottom surface of the wing is relatively flat and straight, but the top is curved. An air molecule passing underneath the wing travels a fairly straight path, which means it travels a shorter distance than an air molecule that passes over the top of the wing. But since it does it in the same amount of time, it's actually moving at a slower rate than the molecule above the wing.

• This is where Bernoulli's principle comes in: since the air passing over the top of the wing is traveling faster than the air traveling underneath the wing, the air pressure above the wing is lower than the air pressure underneath the wing. This difference in air pressure causes the wing to rise in the air, and the plane to be able to fly.

**U.S. organization with the most members: AAA—the American Auto Association. (46 million.)**

# FREE WITH PURCHASE

*These days almost every retailer has some kind of loyalty program—frequent flyer miles, grocery store club cards, even low-tech cardboard punchcards at the local sandwich shop. But 100 years ago it all started... with trading stamps.*

## A REDEEMING IDEA

Back in 1896, a silverware salesman named Thomas Sperry was making his regular rounds of the stores in Milwaukee when he noticed that one store was having success with a unique program. They were rewarding purchases with coupons, redeemable for store goods. That gave Sperry an idea: why not give out coupons that weren't tied to merchandise from a particular store, but were redeemable anywhere in the country?

With backing from local businessman Shelly Hutchinson, he started the Sperry and Hutchinson Company, and began selling trading stamps. Here's how it worked:

• S&H sold stamps (they looked like small postage stamps, each with a red S&H insignia on a green background) to retailers.

• Retailers gave them to customers as a bonus for purchases, 10 stamps for each dollar spent.

• Customers collected the stamps in special S&H books until they had enough to trade back to Sperry and Hutchinson in exchange for merchandise like tea sets or cookware.

• Retailers who participated in the program hoped that customers would feel like they were getting something for free, which would entice them to continue to shop loyally at their stores.

• At first only a few stores across the country offered the stamps, but over the next 50 years, through economic recessions, the Roaring Twenties, the Great Depression, and two world wars, S&H's popularity grew steadily.

## POSTWAR FAD

Interest in trading stamps peaked in the 1950s. Why? More people lived in urban areas with more grocery stores to choose from. Bread, milk, and corn flakes are the same in every supermarket, so rival

**Call a cab: According to statistics, yellow cars and bright blue cars are the safest to drive.**

stores started looking for a way to set themselves apart from the competition. One way was by offering trading stamps.

Collecting trading stamps seemed like a fun way to get great stuff without raiding the household budget. So, with their books full of stamps, postwar consumers got televisions, blenders, transistor radios, and the most popular item, toasters.

Trading stamps became so popular that gas stations, drugstores, and dry cleaners got in on the act, too. By 1964 S&H was printing three times as many stamps as the U.S. Post Office. At the industry's peak in 1969, more than 80% of U.S. households were collecting stamps, and more than 100,000 stores were offering the most popular kind, Green Stamps. The S&H redemption catalog had the largest print run of any publication in the United States.

## A WORLD OF STAMPS

Green Stamps were the best known, but there were many other brands of trading stamps in the 1960s. If you shopped at Piggly Wiggly's, for instance, you'd get Greenbax, at A&P you'd get Plaid Stamps, at Kroger you'd get Top Value Stamps, and so on.

Stamps came in a rainbow of colors, too: Orange, Yellow, Red, Pink, Blue Chip, K&S Red, Triple-S Blue, Plaid, Gold Bond, Merchant Green, and World Green, to name a few. And they appeared under a dizzying variety of names: Top Value, Mor-Valu, Shur-Valu, King Korn, Regal, Big Bonus, Double Thrift, Buckeye, Buccaneer, Two Guys, Eagle, Gift House, Double "M", Frontier, Quality, Big "W," and many more.

The stamps had an actual cash value—if you brought in 1,000 stamps, S&H would cheerfully hand you $1.67. But no one cared about the stamps' cash value when catalogs offered tempting merchandise like clock radios and Corningware. What else could you get for your stamps? Fur coats, purebred pets, European vacations, even life insurance policies. King Korn got a lot of publicity in 1969 by offering a work by classic 20th-century American painter Thomas Hart Benton for 1,975 books.

In fact, publicity-hungry trading-stamp companies—always looking for a way to get a leg up over their many competitors—were willing to negotiate with collectors to provide just about anything equal to the cash value of the collected stamps. Some of the more unusual items:

• An eight-passenger Cessna airplane (paid for with Gold Bond stamps by a church congregation)

• A pair of gorillas (paid for with 5.4 million Green Stamps by an Erie, Pennsylvania, school who wanted to supply their local zoo)

• A donkey for an overseas church missionary

• An elephant (also intended for a local zoo)

• School buses, ambulances, and fire trucks

## TAKING A LICKING

Eventually, trading stamps became victims of their own popularity. So many stores were giving them away that there was no longer any reason to shop loyally at one store.

The rampant inflation of the 1970s didn't help, either. Businesses that gave trading stamps were perceived as charging higher prices. The 1973 oil embargo and gas shortage killed the program at gas stations, too, since consumers would shop at the gas station with the lowest price, not the station that gave Green Stamps.

But trading stamps didn't die out completely. S&H had $1 billion in annual revenue in 1981 when the company was sold and continued limping along for the next 18 years. By 1999 fewer than 100 stores offered Green Stamps. That's when Walter Beinecke, the great-grandson of founder Thomas Sperry, bought back S&H.

## IF YOU CAN'T LICK 'EM...

Under Beinecke's influence, S&H Green Stamps have been recast for the digital age—they're now Greenpoints, with bar-coded cards customers swipe at the registers of participating stores. (Don't worry, the company still redeems the old gummed stickers.)

Greenpoints offers 10 points for every dollar spent, just like it did in the 1960s. But goods are now valued accordingly. The leather wallet that cost one book of Green Stamps (1,200) now costs 9,600 Greenpoints. Four towels that could be bought with 1,200 Green Stamps cost 14,400 Greenpoints today. Camcorders go for 200,000.

The prizes consumers want have changed, too. People no longer want to redeem their points for towels or hair dryers—they're more interested in digital cameras, movie tickets, gift certificates (for Burger King, Blockbuster, and Pizza Hut), and Greenpoints' most popular redemption item, the George Foreman Grill (40,800). And if you have 13,800 Greenpoints, you can still get a toaster.

**How does this make you feel? There are 10 inkblots on the standard Rorschach test.**

# KING OF CANADA

*If politicians were awarded points for weirdness, there'd be plenty of competition... but this guy would win.*

## BLAND MASTER

William Lyon Mackenzie King was Canada's longest-serving prime minister, leading Canada through most of the Great Depression and all of World War II.

Born in 1874 in Kitchener, Ontario, King studied law and economics at the University of Toronto and Chicago University. Inspired to go into government service by his mother's tales of his grandfather, the rebel William Lyon Mackenzie, King became an astute politician and leader who made many lasting contributions to Canadian history.

In public he was an average-looking man who favored black suits with starched white collars. According to *Canada: A People's History*, King was "dull, reliable and largely friendless." When talking to the press or in Parliament, King was deliberately vague and opaque.

"It was hard to pin him down, to use his own words against him...because his speeches were masterpieces of ambiguity," writes Canadian historian Pierre Berton. To the public he was a master politician and a symbol of stability.

But the public didn't know about his private life.

## BEHIND CLOSED DOORS

In those days, a politician's private life really was private. Good thing for King, because behind his neutral facade, he was a first-class eccentric.

King never married, and in fact, seemed terrified of all women—except his mother. No woman, notes Berton, "could hope to compare for beauty, compassion, selflessness, purity of soul with his mother, who haunted his dreams... guiding his destinies, consoling him in his darker moments and leaving precious little time or space for a rival."

Isabel King continued to control her son even after her death. Long after she passed away, King held séances and regularly chatted with his mother's "spirit" about matters of state.

He liked to speak with other deceased figures as well. "He spent a lot of time communicating with departed relatives and the famous dead," states *Canada: A People's History*. "In 1934, he returned from Europe, having made friends with Leonardo da Vinci, a member of the de'Medici family, Louis Pasteur, and Philip the Apostle." He also contacted Prime Minister Wilfrid Laurier, British prime minister William Gladstone, Saint Luke, Saint John, Robert Louis Stevenson, and his grandfather.

## BAD RAP

King owned a crystal ball, but that's not how he contacted the spirit world. He had a special séance table through which spirits "spoke" to him by rapping out messages that he alone could decipher. Unfortunately, the messages weren't always accurate.

On September 2, 1939—one day after Nazi Germany invaded Poland to start World War II—King held a séance in which his dead father told him Hitler had been assassinated. The prime minister was greatly disappointed when he discovered this wasn't true.

King vastly underestimated the dangers posed by fascist leaders such as Hitler and Mussolini. After visiting Nazi Germany in the 1930s, King decided that Hitler was okay because he allegedly shared certain personality traits with the Canadian P.M. "I am convinced Hitler is a spiritualist," King wrote. "His devotion to his mother—that Mother's spirit is, I am certain, his guide."

King also dabbled in numerology and the reading of tea leaves, and held lengthy policy chats with his dog, an Irish terrier named Pat, to whom he liked to outline issues of national importance. (It's unclear what advice, if any, Pat offered in return.) He reportedly made decisions on national issues based on the position of the hands of the clock, as a vote was being taken in Parliament.

## CAN'T KEEP A SECRET

How do we know so much about King's private life today? He kept extensive diaries. He left explicit instructions that after his death for his butler to burn the diaries. But instead of burning them, the butler read them. Now they reside in Canada's National Archives.

# CHAN THE MAN

*As a kid, Uncle John spent many Saturday afternoons glued to the tube watching corny old B-movies featuring the white-suited Chinese detective, Charlie Chan. Though considered politically incorrect today, they're still on TV...and they're still corny.*

## THE MAN BEHIND CHAN

Charlie Chan has cast a portly shadow across the world of detective fiction since his creation in 1925. The wise and charming Oriental sleuth was the brainchild of a novelist and playwright from Warren, Ohio, named Earl Derr Biggers. Biggers got the idea for the character while on a visit to Honolulu in 1919, where he happened to read an article about real-life Chinese detective Chang Apana.

Charlie Chan debuted as a minor character in Bigger's novel *House Without a Key*, which was serialized for the *Saturday Evening Post* magazine and then turned into a silent movie in 1926. Readers loved Chan, so Biggers immediately wrote another story, this one with the Chinese detective in the lead. Then, for the next five years, Biggers wrote a new Charlie Chan novel every year.

## CAN UNDERSTAND CHAN GRAND PLAN

Biggers died in 1933, but his character lived on. Forty-five Charlie Chan films were produced by Twentieth Century Fox and then Monogram Studios during the 1930s and 1940s. The plots all followed the same formula: Charlie Chan, the world famous detective, would stumble upon a murder case in some exotic place like Paris, Cairo, or Monte Carlo. One or two of his sons—identified in chronological order as "Number One Son" and "Number Two Son"—would offer "Pop" their help. For the rest of the movie, these young detective wannabes would get in the way until Chan solved the case in spite of them. And along the way, he would offer numerous pearls of pithy Chinese wisdom.

## ONE CHAN, MANY MAN

Six different actors played the Chinese detective on-screen, but amazingly, none of them were Chinese. Warner Oland, probably the best-known and most popular, was Swedish. But Oland's heritage included some Mongolian blood, which is possibly what allowed him to pass for Asian on the screen when he added a moustache and goatee. In real life, Oland often spoke in stilted speech and referred to himself as "Humble Father," which gave some people the impression that he actually thought he *was* Charlie Chan.

After making 16 Chan films, Warner Oland died in 1938, but once again, Chan was too popular (and valuable) to die. Sidney Toler took his place, doing 22 more movies.

When Toler died in 1947, Roland Winters became Chan. Of all the Chans, Winters was the worst cast—he had a large nose and blonde hair. He tried to look Chinese by squinting and always insisted on being shot from the front so audiences wouldn't see his Caucasian profile. If he needed to speak to anyone at his side, he simply moved his eyes to the right or left. Winters made the last Chan film in the series, *The Sky Dragon*, in 1949.

## MORE CHAN, MANY FAN

The franchise extended to radio, too. Walter Connolly and Ed Begley, both Caucasians, played Charlie Chan on a show sponsored by Esso. The radio show ran from 1932 until 1948.

On television, *The New Adventures of Charlie Chan* premiered in 1957 and lasted less than a year. In the lead role was J. Carroll Naish, another Caucasian. In 1971 a made-for-TV movie, *Happiness Is a Warm Clue*, starred Ross Martin (he was Caucasian, too).

The last Charlie Chan movie, a parody called *The Curse of the Dragon Queen*, was made in 1981. It starred (non-Asian) Peter Ustinov as the detective. While in production, Chinese-American groups protested the film and several Asian-American extras were added to the cast.

## EPILOGUE

More than 75 years after his first appearance, Charlie Chan lives on. Biggers's novels have never gone out of print, and more than 40 of his movies regularly play on cable television. As Chan says, "Impossible to miss someone who will always be in heart."

**There are more varieties of orchid than of any other flower (30,000 at last count).**

# THE GLASS ARMONICA

*Benjamin Franklin invented bifocals, the lightning rod, an odometer, the Franklin stove, swim fins, and street lights. He also invented the glass armonica. (Doesn't everybody know that?)*

## SINGING WINEGLASSES

It's a classic party trick: Wet your finger and rub it around the rim of a wineglass. What you'll hear is a very pure musical note. Add some wine, and the pitch gets lower; remove some, and the pitch gets higher.

The singing wineglass trick has been around for hundreds of years. It's mentioned in Persian documents from the 1300s. There's a European reference to tuned water glasses dating from 1492. And Galileo wrote about the phenomenon in his book *Two New Sciences*, published in 1638. But it was Benjamin Franklin in the 1700s who turned the trick into a musical instrument.

Between the years 1757 and 1766, Franklin spent most of his time in Europe as an agent for the American colonies and often attended musical concerts. One evening in 1761, while listening to virtuoso Richard Puckridge perform on the "singing glasses," Franklin was struck with the beauty of the sound. He immediately set about inventing his own glass musical instrument.

## BEN INVENTS IT

Franklin worked with London glassblower Charles James to create a special set of glass bowls that did not need to be filled with water to make different musical notes because each was tuned to its own pitch. Painted different colors to represent each note of the scale, the bowls were nested inside each other and looked like a stack of goblets lying on their sides. An iron rod ran through them to a wheel, which was turned by a foot pedal. To create musical sounds, the player would touch the spinning glasses with moistened fingers. By the end of the year, Franklin had completed his invention and using the Italian word for harmony, he named it the *armonica*. He wrote,

> The advantages of this instrument are that its tones are incomparably sweet beyond those of any other; that they may be swelled and softened by stronger or weaker pressures of the fin-

> ger, and continued at any length; and that the instrument, being once well tuned, never again wants tuning.

## PLEASANT UNDER GLASS

The armonica was an overnight success. Franklin received orders for the instrument from customers in Paris, Versailles, Prague, and Turin. Marie Antoinette took lessons on it. The world's greatest composers, including Mozart, Beethoven, Donizetti, Richard Strauss, and Saint-Saëns, wrote music for it. Thomas Jefferson called it "the greatest present offered to the musical world in this century."

Because of its angelic tones, many people believed the glass armonica had healing powers. Franklin agreed: he used it to heal the "melancholia" of Princess Izabela Czartoryska of Poland in 1772. Dr. Franz Mesmer, the father of hypnotism, used the armonica to calm his patients during his magnetic séances. By 1790 more than 5,000 armonicas had been sold, making it the most celebrated musical instrument of the 18th century.

Then, just as quickly as it began, the musical fad ended.

## SHATTERED

Disturbing tales began to circulate about the harmful effects of the glass armonica. Virtuoso player Marion Davies had become extremely ill. Her health and nerves were said to have been ruined by her armonica playing. Other performers were beginning to complain of nervousness, numbness in their hands, muscle spasms, and dizziness. Even some listeners became ill.

In 1798 the German musicologist Friedrich Rochlitz wrote in the *Allgemeine Musikalische Zeitung*,

> The armonica excessively stimulates the nerves, plunges the player into a nagging depression and hence into a dark and melancholy mood that it is an apt method for slow self-annihilation. If you are suffering from any nervous disorder, you should not play it; if you are not yet ill you should not play it; if you are feeling melancholy you should not play it.

Then in 1808, Marianne Kirchgessner, a blind concert artist who had inspired Mozart to write for the armonica, died at the age of 39. Her death was said to be a result of "deterioration of her nerves caused by the vibrations of the armonica."

**...Because people kept telling him he had spinach in his teeth.**

Many believed the strange nerve disorders were caused by lead poisoning coming from the lead in the glass and in the paint. Others believed that the high-pitched harmonies, having mystical powers, invoked the spirits of the dead and drove listeners insane.

Nothing was ever proven against the glass armonica, but it didn't matter—people became so frightened of the instrument that few people would play one and few would even listen to one being played. By 1820 the armonica was all but forgotten.

## THE GLASS IS BACK

The glass armonica made a comeback in 1984, thanks to the efforts of master glassblower and musician Gerhard Finkenbeiner of Boston. The German-born Finkenbeiner first thought of making a glass instrument in 1956. After many years of experimenting, he finally re-created Franklin's armonica, using only lead-free quartz crystal for the glass. Some of the rims have gold baked into them to identify the pitches. (The ones with the gold bands are like the "black keys" on a piano. The "white keys" are clear. The gold bands—and they're real gold—are on the inside of the cups, so the player doesn't actually touch them.) Today, G. Finkenbeiner Inc. in Waltham, Massachusetts, continues to produce the beautiful singing glass armonica.

### WARNING

*(posted in J. C. Muller's armonica manual of 1788)*

If you have been upset by harmful novels, false friends, or perhaps a deceiving girl, then abstain from playing the armonica—it will only upset you even more. There are people of this kind—of both sexes—who must be advised not to study the instrument, in order that their state of mind should not be aggravated.

* * *

## MUSICAL IRONY

The song "When Irish Eyes Are Smiling" was written by a German named George Graff...who never went to Ireland in his life.

# THE RISE AND FALL OF THE WHIGS

*Andrew Jackson was one of the founders of the modern Democratic party (see page 470). But in a sense, he is the founder of two political parties: the Democrats, who loved him, and the Whigs, who hated him.*

## JACKSON IN OFFICE

Andrew Jackson, a.k.a. "Old Hickory," was probably the most popular man in the United States when he won the presidency in 1828. And when he left office in 1836, he was still considered the champion of the common man—if for no other reason than he angered (and impoverished) a lot of wealthy and powerful people during his two terms.

For starters, Jackson instituted a policy of filling federal government jobs by firing supporters of former president John Quincy Adams and replacing them with his own. And although he ran on an anti-corruption platform, his appointees were, as Jackson biographer Robert Remini puts it, "generally wretched." One of the worst was Samuel Swartwout, a Jackson crony who was appointed to the job of collector of customs in New York. In this position, Swartwout oversaw the collection of more cash than any other government official, about $15 million a year. Swartwout absconded to Europe with more than $1.2 million of it, "more money than all the felons in the Adams administration put together," Remini writes. Adjusting for inflation, Swartwout is *still* the worst embezzler in the history of the federal government.

Jackson also managed to alienate many of his fellow Southerners. In 1832 South Carolina passed a law banning exorbitant federal tariffs, and even considered seceding from the union. That prompted Jackson to threaten to personally lead an army into the state, put down the rebellion and hang the ringleaders himself. The crisis was eventually resolved when Congress lowered the tariffs, but by then Jackson had lost a lot of support in the South.

## THE BANK WAR

But what galvanized Old Hickory's opposition more than anything else was what he did to the American banking system.

**Charles Dickens's original phrase for Scrooge was "Bah Christmas," not "Bah Humbug."**

Like Thomas Jefferson before him, Jackson hated banks, believing them to be corrupt institutions that enriched the wealthy and well-connected. He especially hated the Second Bank of the United States. He hated it all the more when the bank and its director, Nicholas Biddle, sided with presidential candidate Henry Clay in the election of 1832 and even offered to lend money to pro-Clay newspapers to attack Jackson.

Big mistake—Jackson was furious that the bank would try to influence the outcome of the election. "The bank is trying to kill me," he complained, "but I will kill *it*."

## FROM SECOND TO NONE

When Jackson won reelection against Clay in a landslide in 1832, he set out to make good on his word. He ordered the Secretary of the Treasury to pay government expenditures out of the Treasury's Second Bank accounts, while making any deposits to state banks. (Critics called them Jackson's "pet" banks.) In less than three months, the federal government's deposits to the Second Bank dwindled to almost nothing.

Biddle was determined to save his bank and believed that the best way to do it was by *maximizing* the economic damage from Jackson's measures. He drastically cut back on lending, prompting banks all across the country to follow suit; the financial panic that resulted sent the country into a recession.

Businesses in every major American city failed, throwing thousands out of work. Yet somehow, the plan backfired—Jackson's popularity actually increased, and his image grew as the protector of the common person against the greed of aristocrats and bankers. In the end, Jackson got what he wanted: the Second Bank finally collapsed in 1841.

## BACKLASH

But the Bank War crystallized the political opposition to Jackson. Robert Remini writes in *The Life of Andrew Jackson*:

> The pressures of the Bank War and Jackson's imperial presidency finally brought a new party into being.... National Republicans, bank men, nullifiers, high-tariff advocates, friends of internal improvements, states' righters, and—most particularly—all those who abominated Jackson or his reforms slowly converged into a new political

**Because of the rotation of Earth, an object can be thrown farther if it's thrown west.**

coalition that quite appropriately assumed the name "Whig."

The word *whig*, a Scottish-Gaelic term that was first applied to horse thieves, later became the name for anti-royalists in the American Revolution. Now it would be used by the opponents of the executive tyranny of the man some called King Andrew I.

## WHAT GOES UP...

Had Jackson limited his economic meddling, perhaps the Panic of 1833–34 would have run its course without the Whigs emerging as a major political force. But he didn't.

By January 1835, he had managed to pay down the entire U.S. national debt ($60 million), and the federal government was collecting more revenues than it was spending. Jackson returned some of the surplus to the states, most of whom promptly spent it. Then, anticipating similar federal windfalls in the years to come, many states began borrowing against these future funds and spending that, too. In addition, Jackson's "pet" banks were now bulging with federal deposits, which allowed them to print and issue paper currency backed by federal monies. (In the 1830s, banks printed their own currency.) The country was soon awash with cash. Result: disaster.

The influx of so much capital into the economy led to huge inflation and soaring real-estate prices, creating a speculative economic bubble that burst in 1836 after bad weather led to crop failures in many parts of the country.

## ...MUST COME DOWN

As the U.S. economy began to teeter, foreign creditors started demanding payment in gold and silver out of a fear that American paper currency was losing its value. Jackson decided it would be good for the federal government to return to "sound money," too. On July 11, 1836, he ordered that all future payments for the sale of public lands (a major source of government income in the 1830s) be made in precious metals. Bank notes were no longer acceptable for these transactions, so they began to lose their value.

More bad news: A financial crisis rocked England, then the world's financial capital and a major buyer of American cotton, the country's largest export. The slump in the U.S. cotton market in turn caused the failure of hundreds of other related businesses.

"By the time Jackson finally retired in 1837, America was in the early stages of its biggest financial crisis to date," Paul Johnson writes in *A History of the American People*. "Far from getting back to 'sound money,' Jackson had paralyzed the system completely."

Jackson's heir apparent, Martin Van Buren, managed to squeak into office in the 1836 election, partly because the economic crisis was just beginning and nobody knew how bad it would be. But the 1840 election would be another story.

The recession deepened into a full-blown depression that dragged on for five long years, wiping out more than 600 banks and shuttering most of the factories in the East. Thousands of people lost their jobs, and food riots broke out in cities all over the nation.

Van Buren never had the popularity that Jackson enjoyed, and the depression ruined his chances for reelection.

## WHIGS TRIUMPHANT

In 1840 the Whigs borrowed heavily from the Jackson-Van Buren formula for victory. They put a war hero at the top of the ticket: General William Henry Harrison, who had defeated the Shawnee Indians at the Battle of Tippecanoe 30 years earlier. They staged "monster" rallies all over the country. And when a Democratic writer made the mistake of claiming that Harrison would just as soon "spend the rest of his days in a log cabin with a barrel of cider," he gave the Whigs a perfect campaign theme that they could use to distinguish their man from a sharp-dressing New York dandy like President Van Buren. Harrison rallies became "Log Cabin and Hard Cyder" rallies: supporters built log cabins at every campaign event and served copious amounts of hard cider to the crowds.

Van Buren, vilified by the Whigs as an effete elitist who drank wine from "coolers of silver," seemed a sissy by comparison. On election day, he carried only 7 states to Harrison's 19, and lost in the electoral college, 60 votes to Harrison's 234.

The Whigs also won their first majorities in both houses of Congress, and in 1840 there were Whig governors in 20 of the 26 United States—not bad for a party that was barely seven years old.

## WINNING THE BATTLE

The Whigs seemed to be on the brink of becoming permanently

**Pretty goofy: Disney's Goofy was once married...to an unnamed mystery woman.**

established as the second major party alongside the Democrats. But then their luck ran out.

• Sixty-seven-year-old Harrison delivered his inaugural address outdoors in the snow without wearing a hat, gloves, or overcoat. He spoke for more than an hour and a half (the longest inaugural speech in American history), contracted pneumonia, and died a month after taking office (the shortest presidency in American history).

• Vice President John Tyler, a former Democrat who joined the Whigs after falling out with Andrew Jackson, became president. But he was still a Democrat at heart, and he vetoed a number of pieces of Whig legislation, prompting all but one member of his cabinet to resign and splitting the Whig party in two. The Whig congressional caucus wrote Tyler out of the party.

• In 1844 the Whigs, still bitterly divided, lost the White House to Democrat James Knox Polk. In 1848 the Whigs repeated their 1840 strategy by putting a war hero at the top of the ticket—General Zachary Taylor, hero of the Mexican War—and won the White House. But on July 4, 1850, history repeated itself when President Taylor consumed large quantities of raw fruit, cabbages, and cucumbers, washed it all down with iced water…and then died from acute gastroenteritis five days later, a little more than a year into his first term as president.

## WHIGGING OUT

The Whig party was also divided over the issue of slavery. President Taylor himself had contributed to the split: as a plantation owner with more than 300 slaves, he so alienated anti-slavery Whigs in the north that many of them split off to form the Free Soil Party.

When Taylor died, Vice President Millard Fillmore (also a Whig) became president. He added to the controversy by signing the Fugitive Slave Law of 1850, which required the government to assist in the capture and return of runaway slaves to their owners, even in the anti-slavery states of the North. (Though Fillmore was personally opposed to slavery, he feared that ending it would lead to civil war, so he signed the law to cool the secessionist passions of the South.)

Historians generally credit such actions with postponing the

**At last count, 1,013 U.S. buildings have a sign that reads, "George Washington slept here."**

Civil War for 10 years, but they doomed Fillmore's chances for reelection and contributed to the destruction of the Whig Party. By 1848 Fillmore's hedging on slavery had cost the party support in the North; at the same time, the presence of anti-slavery politicians at the top of the party killed its support in the South. "Cotton Whigs," as the party's pro-slavery Southern faction was called, defected to the states-rights appeal of the Democratic Party. And by 1854, most anti-slavery "Conscience Whigs" had defected to a new party founded for the purpose of opposing slavery: the Republicans.

***To read about the rise of the Republican Party, turn to page 732.***

*   *   *

## AN "OBSCURE" TALE

One morning, a valgus hobberdehoy was cornobbled by a very old leptorrhinian calcographer. "You twiddlepoopy liripoop!" faffled the hobberdehoy, "You've given me a wem that smells of bodewash!"

"So sorry," belched the saprostomous calcographer. "I was unaware that my jumentous mundungus was cornobbling you."

"Whatever, you spodogenous whipjack! Now I must go to my xystus and run my balbriggan galligaskin through my chirogymnasts to get this wem out!"

The calcographer felt like a dasypygal pismire. "I have lost my toxophily," he said sadly.

"Wait a second," faffled the hobberdehoy. "Did you say toxiphily? You remind me of my toxophillic atmatertera. You have the same anisognathous mouth as she."

"Does she go by the name Esmerelda?" asked the calcographer.

"Why yes, yes she does. She was brideloped by a calcographer many moons ago."

And then they looked at each other.

"Bob?"

"Jim?"

And then Bob and his great great great grandfather Jim went happily to Bob's xystus to de-wem his ballbriggan galligaskin.

***(What are we saying? Turn to page 552 to find out.)***

# WHO KILLED JIMI HENDRIX?

*Jimi Hendrix had an astounding influence on pop culture. Yet few people of the 1960s were truly shocked when the musician died in 1970—he had a reputation for living hard and fast. Most people assumed he just burned out like a shooting star. But did he? Or was there more to it?*

## DEATH, DRUGS, AND ROCK 'N' ROLL

Hours before Jimi Hendrix died, he was working on a song entitled "The Story of Life." The last lines:

*The story of life is quicker than the wink of an eye.*
*The story of love is hello and goodbye,*
*Until we meet again.*

Perhaps no rock musician is more emblematic of the psychedelic 1960s than Hendrix. The flamboyant guitarist became famous not only for such onstage antics as lighting his guitar on fire, but also for the blistering performances that earned him recognition as a musical genius. Although only five albums were released during his lifetime, he was—and is—considered one of the greatest rock guitarists ever.

## OVER-EXPERIENCED

James Marshall Hendrix died in the squalid flat of a German girlfriend in London on September 18, 1970, after a long night of drinking and partying. After indulging in a smorgasbord of drugs and alcohol, he and his girlfriend returned to her apartment in the early hours of the morning where, according to the girlfriend, they both took some barbiturate pills to help them sleep.

A normal dose of the downers would have been just half a pill. The girlfriend claimed she took one pill. After Hendrix's death, an autopsy showed he had swallowed nine—18 times the recommended dosage. The autopsy also revealed "massive" quantities of red wine not only in his stomach, but also in his lungs. The quantity and combination of substances might well have been fatal if he hadn't first suffocated on the wine and his own vomit.

There is little mystery as to *what* killed Jimi Hendrix. The question is: *How* did it happen? Was it suicide, an accident…or murder? Ever since Hendrix's death, there have been those who believe there may have been more to the story than just another rock star done in by wretched excess. For some, things don't quite add up.

## FATAL MISTAKE OR FOUL PLAY?

Friends of Hendrix rule out suicide. According to them, Hendrix believed the soul of a person who committed suicide would never rest. In spite of his many personal and professional problems, he would never take his own life.

Was it an accident? Hendrix was known for being able to take greater quantities of drugs than anyone else in his circle. He may have mistaken the potent barbiturates for regular sleeping pills and grabbed his usual handful. On the other hand, as experienced a drug-taker as Hendrix was, he was unlikely to make that kind of mistake. Besides, it was common knowledge that drinking alcohol with downers is asking for serious trouble.

But the quantity of wine found inside him, and around him on the bed where he died, raises an intriguing question: Did he drink that much or was it poured down his throat by someone else? How did so much get into his lungs? Oddly, the autopsy showed a relatively low blood-alcohol level in his body, leading some to speculate that Hendrix drowned in the wine before much of it was absorbed into his system.

But who would want Jimi Hendrix dead? It may be impossible to know now, more than 30 years after his death, but here are some compelling possibilities:

4 **The Girlfriend.** According to the girlfriend, Monika Dannemann, she woke up the morning of the 18th, saw that Hendrix was sleeping normally, and went out for cigarettes. When she returned she saw that Hendrix had been sick and was having trouble breathing. She tried to wake him, and when she couldn't she began to panic and called musician Eric Burdon, with whom they had partied the night before. After first hanging up on her, Burdon called back and insisted Dannemann call an ambulance. Dannemann later told the press that Hendrix was alive when the ambulance arrived a few minutes later, about 11:30 a.m., and that she rode with him to the hospital. According to Dannemann, Hendrix was propped

upright on the trip and suffocated on the way.

The ambulance attendants tell a different story. According to author James Rotondi, the two men arrived at the apartment to find it empty...except for Hendrix lying in a mess on the bed, already dead. They say they went through the motions of trying to revive Hendrix because that was standard procedure, but to no avail. They wrapped up the body, carried it to the ambulance, and drove to the hospital; Hendrix was pronounced dead on arrival. The autopsy cautiously concludes that the exact cause and time of death are unknown, but evidence points to a time of death much earlier—possibly several hours before the ambulance arrived.

Was Monika Dannemann trying to cover up something? If so, what and why? The world may never know—she committed suicide in 1996.

4 **The Government.** Rock music has long been associated with rebellion, revolution, and social change, ideas that appeal to youthful fans but are a cause for concern for "the Establishment." It is well known that during the J. Edgar Hoover era, and perhaps even more recently, the FBI kept dossiers not only on political activists, but on actors, authors, and a wide variety of other potential "threats" as well. It is not surprising that influential musicians such as Jimi Hendrix would draw the interest of the U.S. government—but there may be more to it than that.

In his book *The Covert War Against Rock*, author Alex Constantine says Hendrix's FBI file, released in 1979 to a student newspaper in Santa Barbara, reveals that Hendrix was on a list of "subversives" to be placed in detainment camps in the event of national emergency. Hendrix was an icon of not only rock 'n' roll rebellion, but the Black Power and antiwar movements of the 1960s. Did U.S. intelligence agencies consider Hendrix not only subversive, but dangerous?

There are some conspiracy theorists who believe that Hendrix and other musicians, including Jim Morrison of The Doors, ex-Beatle John Lennon, and more recently, rappers Tupac Shakur and The Notorious B.I.G.—all of whom died under suspicious circumstances—may have been eliminated by the government. It would be remarkably easy to make the deaths look like accidents or murders committed by crazy fans—these musicians lived life close to the edge, anyway. Paranoid fantasy? Or could there be some truth to these fears?

4 **The Mob.** Government agents may not have been the only ones with an eye on Hendrix. Organized crime figures were involved with the music industry long before Hendrix was. To the Mob, the industry wasn't about music—it was about money and drugs. And there was plenty of both around Hendrix.

According to Constantine, Hendrix was muscled by the Mob after declining an invitation to play at the Salvation, a New York night club controlled by the Gambino crime family. Hendrix had been a regular at the club, but after the proprietor was murdered following an attempt to break free of Mob control, Hendrix evidently felt uncomfortable playing there. Shortly thereafter, Constantine says, a stranger approached Hendrix on the street and, while chatting, pulled out a .38 pistol and casually hit a target 25 feet away. Hendrix got the message and decided to play the club after all.

Another time, Hendrix was kidnapped from the Salvation by some thugs claiming to be part of the Mafia, Constantine claims. They took him to a Manhattan apartment and told him to call his manager, Michael Jeffery, and relay a demand to transfer his contract to the Mob…or else. Hendrix was rescued from the thugs by men sent by Jeffery, but later told people he thought Jeffery had arranged the whole thing.

So Hendrix may have had good reason not to trust his manager…

4 **The Manager.** Those seeking to tie together the loose ends of government agencies, the Mob, and enormous amounts of money need look no further than Michael Jeffery. Jeffery served in British Intelligence in the 1950s and years later boasted of underworld connections. As Hendrix's manager, Jeffery had control of millions of dollars earned by Hendrix, much of which was diverted by Jeffery to offshore bank accounts.

Hendrix became increasingly aware that Jeffery was cheating him, and just before his death made arrangements to cancel his management contract. The manager understandably could have been upset at the prospect of losing such a lucrative client—but why kill Hendrix? The answer could lie in the rumor that Jeffery had taken out a million-dollar life insurance policy on the star. Additionally, Jeffery could have made much more from the dozens of Hendrix albums released after the musician's death. (There were many hours of unreleased music.)

**Makes sense: A group of peacocks is called an *ostentation*.**

Whatever involvement the former intelligence agent may have had in Hendrix's death would have had to have been indirect; he was vacationing in Spain when Hendrix died. To some, Jeffery was further implicated when he himself died under unusual circumstances less than three years later, in a plane crash.

### FLY ON

A number of times in the weeks before his death the 27-year-old Hendrix asked friends, "Do you think I will live to be 28?" Did he have a premonition of what was coming? Friends say he was becoming increasingly paranoid…and perhaps with good reason. We may never know the truth about the death of Jimi Hendrix, but we do know that his life, as he wrote in his final song, was indeed "quicker than the wink of an eye."

* * *

## A TALE OF TWO CHORDS

In July 2003, hard-rock band Metallica announced that they were suing the Canadian band Unfaith over their use of the guitar chords E and F. "We're not saying we own those two chords individually, that would be ridiculous," Metallica's Lars Ulrich was reported to have said. "We're just saying that in that specific order, people have grown to associate E and F with our music."

Unfaith's lead singer, Erik Ashley, responded, "I thought it was a prank at first. Now I'm not sure what to think." Actually, he knew exactly what to think. Why? Because he created the prank.

But that didn't stop the media from running with the story without contacting the parties involved. ABC talk show host Jimmy Kimmel reported it, as did MSNBC's Jeannette Walls.

So why did Ashley do it? "To gauge just how willing America was to buy a story as extraordinary—as outlandish—as Metallica claiming ownership of a two-chord progression." He added, "If this week was any indication, America is all too willing to believe it."

But after all of Metallica's well-publicized attempts to sue online music downloaders, was it really that hard to believe? Said one anonymous chat room attendant: "I'm not sure what's worse—that the story is a fake, or that it was actually conceivable that Metallica would do that."

**At its peak, the Persian empire was roughly 2/3 the size of the United States.**

# THIS OLD (OUT)HOUSE

*In all our years writing* Bathroom Readers, *this is one of the strangest hobbies we've ever heard of. We're never going to look at a bottle collection the same way again.*

## TALKING TRASH

Try to imagine a world with no garbage collection—no garbage man to come and empty your trash cans, and no city or county dump to haul your old stuff to. What would you do with everything you have to throw away?

It wasn't so long ago that nearly everyone in America was faced with this problem. In the 19th century, few if any communities had trash collection, and not many had dumps, either. People were on their own. If trash was edible, they might feed it to animals or compost it for use in the garden. If it was flammable, they burned it. If they didn't know what else to do with it, they threw it in the backyard. "People had really messy yards," says archaeologist Liz Abel. "What they couldn't burn in the cookstove, they threw out back."

But if the item was small enough, oftentimes they went out to the outhouse and dropped it down the hole.

## THE FINAL FRONTIER

The people who tossed things into their privies probably assumed that what they disposed of would never see the light of day again. They were wrong. A growing number of antique collectors and amateur history buffs have made it their hobby to dig this stuff up. In the process they've uncovered clues about the daily lives led by people in the 19th century.

"It's amazing what you can tell about someone who lived more than a hundred years ago by what they threw in their outhouse," says Jeff Kantoff, a New York lumber salesman who digs up Brooklyn outhouses in his spare time. "You can tell how many people were in the family, did they have kids, were the kids boys or girls, did they have money, what were their ailments."

Such outhouse excavators—or "privy diggers," as they prefer to be called—insist that as disgusting as it may sound to the uniniti-

**World's biggest desert: Sahara, at 3.5 million sq. miles. The Gobi is #2, at 500,000.**

ated, outhouse digging is really not that bad. Decades of organic activity have converted all that old poop into compost indistinguishable from ordinary dirt. "There is no stink whatsoever," says John Ozoga, a Michigan geologist and privy-digging enthusiast.

## THE HOLE TRUTH

Privy digging dates back to the late 1950s, when antique bottle collecting began to take off as a hobby. Bottles are one of the most common items found in outhouses, not necessarily because people liked to drink soda, mineral water, or beer while they answered nature's call, but probably because tossing bottles down the privy was safer than having glass strewn all over the backyard.

And there's much more to find than just bottles. Privy diggers have found coins, clay pipes, pottery, silverware, ice skates, toys, shoes, pistols, billiard balls, false teeth, squirrel bones (people used to eat squirrels), and even Model T parts. In coastal areas it's also common to find oyster shells—*lots* of oyster shells—and not just because people liked to eat oysters. "Oyster shells were an early form of toilet paper," says Kantoff. "I don't know how they were used. I don't want to know."

Thanks to low oxygen levels, many items found in privies are in surprisingly good shape. Apples more than 150 years old still retain their color, and leather goods like shoes and saddlebags (yes, saddle bags) look like they were thrown away yesterday.

## LOCATION, LOCATION, LOCATION

The hardest thing about excavating an old outhouse is knowing where to dig. The outhouses themselves have long since been torn down, and the holes, or "vaults," underneath them have been covered over with dirt and forgotten, with few visible clues indicating where they are.

One way of finding likely places to dig is by consulting old fire insurance maps to see if they show outhouse locations. Another trick is to put yourself in the shoes of the home owner—if you had to place an outhouse on your property, where would you put it? They were usually far enough away from the main house to control odors, but not so far as to be inconvenient. In areas with harsh winters, the outhouse is likely to have been closer to the main house, so that people didn't have to trudge through snow to use the facilities. On city lots, the outhouse is likely to be right up against the back property line, frequently in a corner.

## PROBING QUESTIONS

Once privy diggers have identified likely areas to dig, they probe these locations, poking a seven-foot-long steel rod into the ground to see if they can detect the presence of a privy vault. What are they searching for? Any area that feels noticeably different from the surrounding ground. A "crunchy" layer could be glass bottles, fireplace ash (commonly dumped into outhouses), or household garbage, indicating the presence of a privy vault. In undisturbed dirt it's difficult to push the probe more than two or three feet into the ground, so if there's a spot in the yard that probes deeper than that, it may well be "the vault."

## PRIVY DIGGING DOS AND DON'TS

**1. Pick an outhouse that's on private property.** Privies on public land may be protected by historical preservation laws, so don't go digging up the backyard of the governor's mansion. When Tim Clements dug up a privy on the grounds of the University of Nebraska in 2001, he was arrested and charged with trespassing and theft. Private property is usually exempt from preservation laws.

**2. Ask before you dig.** Getting permission to dig in someone's backyard may be easier than you think—just offer to share the artifacts you find. "A lot of homeowners will agree so that they can have something that came from their house," says Illinois privy digger David Beeler.

**3. Keep digging.** When a privy vault became full, it was common to seal it up by filling the last few feet of the hole with dirt and garbage. There may well be plenty of interesting stuff in this "garbage layer," but most of the artifacts are likely to have sunk all the way to the bottom. So keep going.

**4. Check the sides and corners.** When an outhouse is in use, material "mounds up in the center," just below where people sat, says privy digger Peter Bleed. "Things tend to roll off to the sides."

**5. But wait, there's more!** When one privy vault filled up, a new one was dug—frequently right next to the old one. So if you find one privy vault, don't stop! Look for more nearby.

**The top-selling spice in the world? Pepper. Mustard is #2.**

# THE OUTHOUSE DETECTIVES

*It's amazing what you can learn about people who lived more than a century ago just by studying the junk they disposed of in their outhouses. Still don't believe us? Read on to find out what these privies reveal.*

**MAGNUM P.U.**

As we told you in the previous article (page 712), "privy diggers" are hobbyists who dig up old outhouses to collect the bottles and other objects that people tossed down there more than 100 years ago. These objects may be interesting in their own right, but they also shed light on the daily lives of the people who dropped them there. Some outhouse clues are subtler than others. See if you can figure out what these outhouse discoveries may reveal about their original owners.

**DISCOVERY:** A child's doll, recovered completely intact

**MYSTERY:** Most items that are disposed of in an outhouse have clearly been thrown away—they were garbage. It's unlikely that a 19th-century family would have thrown away even an unbroken doll. And yet it's not unusual to find perfectly intact dolls at the bottom of an outhouse. What are they doing down there?

**THEORY:** They ended up there by accident. "Lots of times, I think, little girls went to the bathroom and accidentally dropped their doll down there," says Michigan privy digger John Ozoga. "Dad wouldn't go get it."

**DISCOVERY:** A wide variety of items recovered from a "two-holer" (an outhouse with two holes to sit on instead of just one)

**MYSTERY:** Underneath one of the holes were perfume bottles, pieces of china, and containers of Ruby Foam tooth powder. Underneath the other hole: "I just found beer bottles piled up," Ozoga says. Why the difference?

**THEORY:** Two-holers, like modern public restrooms, were segregated according to sex. One side—in this case the side with the perfume bottles, china, and tooth powder—was for females; and the side with all the beer bottles was for males. Such a find may also provide insight into the family's attitude toward alcohol consumption: the outhouse was the only place where the men could enjoy a beer in peace.

**DISCOVERY:** Three bottles of Wilkerson's Teething Syrup, recovered from an outhouse in St. Charles, Missouri. (Teething syrup was used to help relieve a baby's teething pain.)

**MYSTERY:** What's remarkable about these bottles, privy diggers say, is that they are *never* found alone. "If you see one bottle in a privy hole, you'll see a lot of them," says privy digger David Beeler. Why?

**THEORY:** The syrup's active ingredient is opium, which is highly addictive. Babies who were given the syrup soon got hooked on the stuff, which meant that "parents had to keep on buying it to keep them from crying," Beeler explains.

**DISCOVERY:** Bottles, tin cans, and other brand-name items recovered from a 19th-century outhouse on Franklin Street in downtown Annapolis, Maryland. In the 19th century, that area was part of the African-American community.

**MYSTERY:** A surprisingly high percentage of the items recovered were national brands instead of local products. These findings correspond to other excavations of outhouses in the area, which suggests that African Americans used more national brands and fewer local brands than did white communities. Why?

**THEORY:** Anthropology professor Mark P. Leone, who directed the excavation, speculates that African Americans preferred national brands because the prices were set at the national level instead of by neighborhood grocers. By purchasing these brands, "they could avoid racism at the local grocery store, where shopkeepers might inflate prices or sell them substandard goods," he explains.

**DISCOVERY:** A "multitude" of Lydia Pinkham brand patent-medicine bottles, plus an entire set of gold-trimmed china dishes

**MYSTERY:** These items were recovered from an outhouse behind the 19th-century home of a wealthy Michigan family that was excavated by John Ozoga in the 1990s. The bottles were clustered in a single layer, and the china dishes were found right on top of them. Why?

**THEORY:** The wife had fallen ill at a young age and died. Ozoga speculates that she was treated with the patent medicine. When she died, the family emptied the house of her belongings—including the entire set of china, which they threw down the hole in the outhouse—to avoid catching whatever it was that killed her.

*　　*　　*

## WORDPLAY

*How confusing is English to learn? Try on these sentences for size.*

1. We have to **polish** the **Polish** furniture.
2. How can he **lead** if he can't get the **lead** out?
3. A skilled farmer sure can **produce** a lot of **produce**.
4. The dump was so full it had to **refuse refuse**.
5. The soldier decided to **desert** his **dessert** in the **desert**.
6. No time like the **present** to **present** the **present**.
7. A small-mouthed **bass** was painted on the big **bass** drum.
8. The white **dove dove** down into Dover.
9. I spent all of last **evening evening** out the pile.
10. That poor **invalid**, his insurance is **invalid**.
11. The bandage was **wound** around the **wound**.
12. They were much too **close** to the door to **close** it.
13. That buck sure **does** some odd things around the **does**.
14. The absent-minded **sewer** fell down into the **sewer**.
15. You **sow**! You'll reap what you **sow**!
16. The **wind** was way too strong to **wind** the sail.
17. After a **number** of injections, my jaw finally got **number**.
18. If you don't **object** to the **object**, I would like to **subject** the **subject** to a series of subjective objectives.

**Worldwide, Christmas has been celebrated on 135 different days of the year.**

# INTREPID: MASTER SPY

*Ever heard of William Stephenson? He was an inventor, industrialist, and the father of modern espionage. And if it hadn't been for him, the Germans might have won World War II. Here's the story of one of the most important—and least-known—men of the 20th century.*

## INTERNATIONAL MAN OF MYSTERY

Although he's not a household name, historians call William Stephenson the "single most important man in the war to defeat Hitler's Third Reich."

But he was reclusive. Never one to seek the public eye, Stephenson preferred to remain behind the scenes and let others take the glory. For this reason, many of the details of his life remain shrouded, and history books tend to contradict each other about his role. The following are factual (probably), agreed-upon (mostly) accounts of his life and work.

**Early years.** On January 11, 1896, William Samuel Clouston Stanger (changed to Stephenson a few years later) was born in the bleak prairie town of Winnipeg, Manitoba. From an early age, it was apparent to all around him that he was no ordinary child. He taught himself Morse code, commercial cryptography (the system of sending coded telegrams), and demonstrated a photographic memory. Stephenson's school principal described him as a boy with a "strong sense of duty and high powers of concentration."

## THE FIRST WORLD WAR

In August 1914, following the outbreak of World War I, that sense of duty prompted him to enlist with the Royal Canadian Engineers, who shipped him off to France. There, Stephenson was injured in a gas attack, and sent to England as an invalid labeled "disabled for life." But within a year he recovered and, although unfit to return to the trenches, he was equally unwilling to settle for a desk job.

So Stephenson joined the Royal Flying Corps, returned to France, and became one of World War I's most decorated fighter pilots, shooting down 26 enemy planes.

In 1918 Sergeant Stephenson's luck seemingly ran out when he was accidentally shot down by his own side in hostile territory. He was captured and sent to Holzminden Camp in Germany. But instead of letting imprisonment break him, the opportunistic young man turned it into a business venture: he stole items from the guards and traded them to other POWs in return for favors.

One of the items Stephenson lifted was a hand-held can opener. After determining that it had only been patented in Germany, Austria, and Turkey, he escaped from the prison camp—with the can opener. By 1919 he was back home in Winnipeg, where he patented the clamp-style can opener, calling it Kleen Kut. It's still in use today.

In 1922 he invented a device that improved the way photographs were sent over telephone lines (this device would later lead to the invention of television). Stephenson patented the wireless photography process and became a millionaire before he was 30.

## THE MAKING OF A SPY

Although he never planned to work in military intelligence, all of Stephenson's experiences pushed him in that direction. While teaching math and science at the University of Manitoba in the early 1920s, he was approached by a top-ranking British officer and invited to head up a team of cryptanalysts—people who analyze codes. Stephenson immediately left for England.

During his 19-year stay, he became friends with many powerful and influential people, including the authors George Bernard Shaw and H. G. Wells, the nabob of Bhopal, the Aga Khan, and actress Greta Garbo. But Stephenson's most important friendship was with Winston Churchill, a Conservative member of Parliament who was not in the good graces of the ruling Labour Party. Churchill and Stephenson shared an interest in technology and espionage; and both feared the rise of Nazi Germany.

## CHATTING WITH THE ENEMY

Stephenson's first dealings with the Nazis came in 1934 when an aircraft built by a company in which Stephenson was an investor, General Aircraft, won the King's Cup air race, the premier flying event of the 1930s. The plane caught the attention of some German military officials, who started a dialogue with Stephenson. To the Germans, Stephenson was nothing more than a rich private

**Montpelier, Vermont, is the only state capital without a McDonald's.**

citizen (he owned a cement company, a steel manufacturing plant, a movie studio, and real estate). But Stephenson took the opportunity to listen in on the Nazis.

What he learned terrified him: the Germans, with Chancellor Adolf Hitler in charge, were building military aircraft at an alarming rate—positioning themselves for something big... really big. Stephenson reported his findings to Churchill, who in turn reported them to British prime minister Neville Chamberlain. The warnings were ignored at first, but when Stephenson's claims were later verified, England began to prepare for war. Those reports also put Churchill back in the favor of Parliament, paving the way for his historic reign as prime minister.

And always forward-thinking, Stephenson made a bold recommendation, one that would have changed history but was rejected by the British foreign secretary, Lord Halifax. He proposed that British agents assassinate Hitler while they still had the chance. Halifax didn't see what Stephenson saw—he preferred to take a diplomatic approach.

## THE SECOND WORLD WAR

As predicted, Germany invaded Poland in 1939. Churchill was elected prime minister the following year, and one of his first acts was to appoint Stephenson station chief for the British Secret Service (SIS) in New York City. Why New York? Because in 1940, that's where Stephenson saw the greatest need. Britain's ambassador had reported that 9 out of every 10 Americans were determined to keep the United States out of the war. The Britons needed the Americans, so Stephenson used covert tactics to change their minds.

• He furnished the media with news bulletins and prepared scripts that spoke of Hitler's brutality.

• He worked to break up the American isolationist groups that had been growing in numbers since the first world war. One such group, led by Senator Gerald Nye, held a rally in Boston in September 1941. Thousands of pamphlets created by Stephenson's organization were handed out, accusing Nye of being a German sympathizer.

• After a speech by another isolationist, Congressman Hamilton Fish, Fish received a card that said, "Der Führer thanks you for your loyalty," and was secretly photographed while holding it. The photographs were then handed out to his supporters.

• An isolationist rally was to be held at Madison Square Garden, but Stephenson printed up hundreds of phony tickets with the wrong date to ensure a low turnout.

## INTREPID AND CAMP X

If all that didn't change the Americans' minds, the invasion of Pearl Harbor in December 1941 surely did. With war declared, both Churchill and President Franklin Roosevelt knew that solid intelligence would be key to winning the war. To that end, they assigned Stephenson the job that he had unknowingly been preparing for his entire life: spy trainer.

Under the code name "Intrepid" and the cover "Passport Control Officer," Stephenson ran Camp X, a secret facility somewhere near Toronto, Ontario. Camp X was a top-secret training ground where operatives were taught unconventional warfare techniques: how to kill with their bare hands; make lethal weapons out of household items; and blow up industrial installations. Others were trained in lock picking, safe blowing, infiltration, explosives, listening devices, and Stephenson's favorite, codes and ciphers.

Once their training was complete, agents were flown into occupied Europe on "moon planes" (plywood aircraft painted dull black to be nearly invisible at night), to conduct sabotage and spy operations. It was a perilous assignment—many agents did not return alive. But they were able to perform some of the war's most crucial covert missions, including the murder of Reinhard Heydrich, the brutal German commander who ruled Czechoslovakia.

## ENIGMA

But nothing Stephenson did was more important to the Allied war effort than his assistance in cracking the "Enigma" code, Germany's primary method of transmitting secret messages. An Enigma machine looked like an ordinary typewriter; an operator would type a message, then an internal set of rotors would translate the message into code. This code would be transmitted to another operator, who would use a corresponding Enigma machine to decipher it. Because the Nazis believed that Enigma was impossible to crack, they made widespread use of it, and Stephenson saw this reliance as their greatest weakness. Crack Enigma and the Germans would be helpless. When Polish agents stole an Enigma machine from a German convoy, they sent it straight to Intrepid at Camp X.

## ENTER CYNTHIA

Stephenson teamed up with Elizabeth Thorpe, a beautiful agent who went by the code name "Cynthia." To crack Enigma, they needed to intercept a coded message and then see that same message after it came out of an Enigma machine. So Stephenson instructed Thorpe to seduce some high-ranking diplomats who had received messages. Through a combination of guile and feminine prowess, Thorpe acquired a set of codebooks from her unsuspecting lovers. These codebooks unlocked the secrets of Enigma and helped turn the war against Germany in favor of the Allies.

Stephenson and his agents had many other covert successes during the war, including rescuing Niels Bohr, a leading atomic researcher in German-occupied Denmark. Had the Germans gotten to Bohr, they may have had the A-bomb first. But thanks to the rescue, Bohr was able to work on the Manhattan Project and help the United States build the weapon that would end the war.

## INTREPID'S LEGACY

For his efforts, Stephenson received a knighthood from the British and the Presidential Medal of Merit from the Americans (the first non-American to be given one). Ironically, he did not receive recognition from his native Canada until Prime Minister Joe Clark presented him with the Companion of the Order of Canada in 1980. Sir William died in Bermuda in 1989 at 93 years old, outside of the public eye, just the way he liked it.

But Intrepid's legacy goes even deeper. An aide to the chief of British Naval Intelligence during World War II, a young man named Ian Fleming, had the opportunity to observe Intrepid in action and was very taken with him. After the war, they became friends. While both were living in Jamaica, Stephenson would recount spy tales to his friend. That's when Fleming started writing a book about a spy called James Bond. Many of Agent 007's characteristics—his suaveness, brilliance, and slight cockiness—were lifted straight from Stephenson. In fact, Fleming described his secret agent as a "highly romanticized version of the true spy—and Bill Stephenson was the real thing."

**According to criminal law: Only 3 people are necessary for a disturbance to be called a riot.**

# BIRTH OF THE HELICOPTER

*It can fly almost anywhere in almost any kind of weather. It can hover like a bee or speed as fast as a falcon. But it took more than 2,000 years to figure out how to make it work.*

## A MARVELOUS TOY

The desire to fly has inspired inventors for thousands of years. Most of them designed winged aircraft that imitated the flight of birds. But a few put their energies into creating a vertical flying machine, known today as the helicopter.

The Chinese invented one around 400 B.C. It was just a stick with feathers tied to one end like a bouquet, but when the stick was spun quickly between the hands and let go, it flew up in the air. This ancient toy is the first known example of a vertical flying machine.

So where did the Chinese get the idea for their toy? Most likely from watching seeds of the maple tree flutter to the ground. The maple seed has a single leaf attached to it, which acts as a rotating wing. When the seed drops off the tree, the wind spins the leaf like a propeller, thus carrying the seed far from the tree.

## INTO THE AIR, JUNIOR BIRD MEN

About 2,000 years later, in 1754, Mikhail Lomonosov of Russia launched a large, spring-powered model resembling the Chinese toy. It was reported to have "flown freely and to a high altitude." More importantly, it proved that vertical flight was truly possible. All that was needed was the right engine.

Englishman Horatio Phillips thought the steam engine might be the solution. In 1840 he built the first vertical flight machine to be powered by an engine. His model aircraft weighed in at 10 kilograms (22 pounds) but it was still a toy. He discovered that the steam engine was much too heavy to be used in a full-scale machine.

Ponton d'Amecourt of France also made some steam-powered models in the 1860s but he's remembered more for the name he gave his machines than the machines themselves. He combined the Greek word *heliko* (spiral) with *pteron* (wing) to create the word *hélicoptère*.

## GENTLEMEN, START YOUR ENGINES

When the combustion engine hit the scene in the late 1800s, piloted vertical flight became possible. The breakthrough year was 1907. In Douai, France, brothers Charles and Louis Breguet built the first helicopter to lift a person up in the air. They only got a few inches off the ground, but they were flying!

That same year another Frenchman, Paul Cornu, flew his version of the helicopter to a height of almost six feet. His double-rotored craft looked like a pair of room fans mounted horizontally at each end of a giant bicycle, with a lawnmower-sized engine behind the seat. The craft was so unstable that it had to be tethered with sticks, held by men on the ground.

## SPIN DOCTORS

**Torque.** They had the right engine, but there were new obstacles. One was the problem of *torque*. That's the tendency of the spinning rotor to make the body of the aircraft turn in the opposite direction. Early choppers would spin up and around like insane tops. But a Russian engineer named Boris Yuriev came up with the solution in 1911. He suggested adding a vertical tail rotor off the rear of the fuselage to counter the unwanted spinning. He built one in 1912, and it worked, sort of: it didn't spin—but it didn't fly either—it lacked a powerful enough engine. Though it would need refining, Yuriev had solved the problem of torque.

**Dissymetrical lift.** When a helicopter is moving forward, one side of the rotating blades is advancing into the wind, and the other side is going backwards, away from the wind. The advancing side creates more lift, which caused the early helicopters to flip over during forward flight.

Spaniard Juan de la Cierva solved this problem. He was working on a helicopter-airplane hybrid called an autogyro when he came up with the concept of the "articulated blade." This blade was attached to the rotor with a flexible hinge. Called "flapping," this allowed the advancing blade to lift slightly, decreasing lift on one side, thus balancing the opposing forces. And it worked. He made his first successful flight in 1923. Ironically, the technology would be used for helicopters, and the autogyro never "took off."

At the same time great advances were being made on the *swashplate*, another very important piece of the puzzle. The swashplate was a system of adjustable rods and plates that allowed the pilot to control the angle of the blades—both simultaneously and individually. Simultaneous adjustment, called *collective control*, makes the chopper go up or down. Individual adjustment, called *cyclic control*, makes the helicopter go forward, backward, right or left. Now to put all the pieces together.

## GOING THE DISTANCE

Using all the up-to-date technology, in 1924 Etienne Oehmichen became the first man to fly a helicopter and actually control it. The Frenchman flew his homemade helicopter just over half a mile. It took 7 minutes, 40 seconds to make the flight. Average speed: 4.9 mph.

Corradino d'Ascanio of Italy set helicopter world records for altitude and flight duration in 1930. He got his chopper up to 57 feet and stayed aloft for 8 minutes, 45 seconds. Six years later, a German Focke-Wulf Fw-61 was flown to an altitude of 11,243 feet and a distance of 143 miles at a speed of 76 mph, making it the world's first fully practical helicopter.

But it was visionary aircraft designer Igor Sikorsky who was most responsible for getting the helicopter accepted as a full-fledged aircraft. He perfected the design of the helicopter that we know today, with its main rotor and single–tail rotor configuration. He called it the R4, and in 1941 it became the first helicopter to be put into mass production. Later models saw heavy service in the Pacific during WWII. By war's end, the helicopter had won over all skeptics and taken its legitimate place in the aviation community.

## MOST VERSATILE FLYING MACHINE

Today there are more than 40,000 helicopters in use around the world. No modern military is without them—they do everything from minesweeping to troop transport to antitank missions. Civilian applications of the helicopter are even broader. They are used for police surveillance and traffic news, and work as super taxis for the wealthy. Choppers rescue sailors from sinking ships, pluck lost hikers from the wilderness, and put out forest fires. It's estimated that since their widespread introduction in the 1940s, helicopters have helped save more than a million lives.

**A female black bear can weigh 300 pounds...but her babies weigh only half a pound at birth.**

## CHOPPER FACTOIDS

• Three things a helicopter can do that a plane can't:

1. Fly backward
2. Rotate as it moves through the air
3. Hover motionless

• It takes both hands and both feet to fly a helicopter, which makes it much more complex than flying a plane.

• The helicopter pilot has to think in three dimensions. In addition to cyclic control (forward, backward, left, and right), and collective control (up and down, and engine speed), there is rotational control (spinning in either direction on the axis).

• In 1956 Bell Aircraft Corporation introduced the HU-1. The "Huey" became the best-known symbol of the U.S. military during the Vietnam War.

• The first U.S. president to fly in a helicopter: Dwight D. Eisenhower, in 1957.

• In 1969 the Russian Mi-12 became the largest helicopter ever flown. It could lift a payload of 105,000 kilograms (231,485 pounds).

• In 1982 a Bell 206 completed the first solo crossing of the Atlantic by a helicopter.

• In 1483 Leonardo da Vinci made drawings of a fanciful craft he called a *helical air screw,* but it never got off the drawing board. His concept of "compressing" the air was similar to that used by today's helicopters. However, when a prototype was built recently at the Science Museum of London, it didn't work.

* * *

## REAL-LIFE COURT TRANSQUIP

**Prosecutor:** Did he pick the dog up by the ears?

**Witness:** No.

**Prosecutor:** What was he doing with the dog's ears?

**Witness:** Picking them up in the air.

**Prosecutor:** Where was the dog at this time?

**Witness:** Attached to the ears.

**South Florida is the only place on Earth where crocodiles and alligators coexist in the wild.**

# THE FRENCH FOREIGN LEGION

*Generations of kids—including Uncle John—dreamed of running away to join the Foreign Legion. In its day, it was probably the second most popular runaway destination (after the circus). It's been the subject of countless books, films, and TV shows, too. Here's a look at its history.*

## ATTRACTING FREE RADICALS

In July 1830, revolution broke out in France and after just three days of unrest the unpopular King Charles X was overthrown and the new "Citizen King," Louis Philippe, was installed in his place. The historic event inspired revolutionaries all over Europe—free thinkers and libertarians who felt stifled by their own monarchical governments. And these admirers began to pour into France by the tens of thousands.

However flattered Louis Philippe may have been by the attention, he wasn't happy with the idea of so many foreign radicals coming into the country. The revolution of 1830 was France's second in just 41 years, and Louis Philippe didn't feel like trying for a third.

The situation in France was made even more unstable by the fact that much of the French military was in North Africa. For more than 200 years, pirates operating out of the port city of Algiers had been disrupting shipping in the Mediterranean. In 1830 the French army captured the city, which ended the piracy. But France intended to colonize the entire region, so the army was staying... indefinitely.

## A CREATIVE SOLUTION

Louis Philippe devised a plan: In 1831 he created the Foreign Legion, hoping to solve both problems with one stroke. By drafting foreign-born males between the ages of 18 and 40 and sending them off to fight in North Africa, the king would clear France of foreigners and strengthen his forces in North Africa at the same time. And there was a bonus: The plan reduced the political cost of the colonial wars, because the Legion's casualties would be foreigners, not French.

"So what if 100,000 rifles fire in Africa?" Louis Philippe is reported to have said. "Europe does not hear them."

## NOM DE GUERRE

What would become one of the most famous features of serving in the Foreign Legion—*anonymat*, or serving under a false identity—came about because French officials cared more about getting the rabble out of the country than it did about confirming their identities. Even if they had wanted to verify the names people gave upon enlistment, there was no real means of doing so. So the Legion just enlisted people under whatever names they gave—even when people gave their true names, they were assumed to be false.

Over time the practice of enlisting under a false name became institutionalized, not to mention one of the Foreign Legion's strongest selling points: people with shady pasts could join up and begin their lives anew.

## NOBODY'S PERFECT

Getting foreign "undesirables" into the military and out of France turned out to be relatively easy. Shaping them into an effective fighting force was another matter.

More than thirty legionnaires deserted on the very first day in Algeria; the next day, the soldiers of one unit got drunk and attacked their commanding officers. Some legionnaires sold their pants and other parts of their uniform to buy alcohol, then returned to their units half naked and drunk. General René Savary, commander of the French forces in Algeria, insisted that the Legion be split into small groups and stationed in separate locations, fearing that "it would take only one drunken binge to touch off an insurrection."

Part of the problem was that officials back in France were so eager to clear the streets of foreigners that they sent *all* of them off to Algeria, even the sick and the insane. But the larger problem was that the French army did not take the Legion seriously as a fighting force. Legionnaires were given the worst and most dangerous jobs, such as draining mosquito-infested marshes, so that French casualties would be kept to a minimum.

Result: between 1831 and 1835, more than 3,200 legionnaires in

Algeria—about one out of every four—were killed or incapacitated by dysentery, typhoid, pneumonia, malaria, cholera, and other terrible diseases. That's in addition to those who died in battle.

## GONE TO SPAIN

Then in 1835, Spain asked for French help in putting down a military rebellion of their own. Louis Philippe didn't really want to help, but as an ally of Spain he was obliged to do something. His thoughts soon turned to the legionnaires—he could send *them*. This led to another crafty plan: rather than *lend* the Foreign Legion to Spain (which meant that he might one day have to take it back), he *gave* it to Spain, severing all of its ties to the French army in the process.

Now the Legion was the property of Spain, which meant that if the legionnaires were defeated, Spain, not France, would lose face. Plus, France wouldn't have to go to the trouble and expense of withdrawing the troops when the battle was over. The Legion was now Spain's problem, and it treated the legionnaires even worse than France had. Worn down by hunger, neglect, disease, desertion, and a string of military defeats (plus the fact that when legionnaires finished their term of service, they were free to go home), over the next several years the Foreign Legion dwindled away to almost nothing.

## THE FOREIGN LEGION, PART DEUX

That might well have been the end the Foreign Legion experiment, were it not for two factors: 1) Foreigners were still streaming into France, and 2) Louis Philippe still wanted to get rid of them. So on December 16, 1835, even as the original Foreign Legion was still limping along in Spain, the Citizen King created a *nouvelle légion* and started all over again. "The experiment," military historian Douglas Porch writes in *The Foreign Legion*, "gained a new lease on life almost as soon as it was abandoned."

The first waves of new recruits were handed over to Spain to reinforce the old Legion; then in late 1836, Louis Philippe started diverting them back to Algeria, which France had formally annexed two years earlier and was still trying to pacify.

This Legion was as unruly and unreliable as the first. In 1842 the governor-general of Algeria, General Thomas Bugeaud, complained to the minister of war, Marshal Nicolas Soult:

> ...the Foreign Legion will never offer a force upon which we can count....They fight badly; they march badly, they desert often. They try whenever the opportunity presents itself to sell the enemy their arms, their munitions, and their uniforms, and equipment....There is not one general officer who does not prefer to march with two of our good battalions than with five of the Foreign Legion....I seriously believe that we should cease to have such soldiers in Africa.

And yet somehow the Foreign Legion not only survived, but over the next few decades evolved into one of the most respected and feared fighting forces in Europe. How did that happen?

## TURNING LEMONS INTO LEMONADE

As it turns out, the fact that the soldiers in the Foreign Legion were considered expendable by the folks back home in France proved to be instrumental in turning the Legion's fortunes around.

These "disposable" soldiers were frequently the first men sent into battle and the last withdrawn; in the process, the survivors gained more fighting experience and skill than soldiers in other French military units. They also earned a reputation for incredible toughness.

Because the Foreign Legion saw so much action, it became a magnet for the most ambitious officers in the French army. These officers wanted adventure and also hoped that by leading units in combat while other officers sat at home, they would rise more quickly through the ranks.

## MOMENT OF TRUTH

Just how much the Foreign Legion changed over the years became evident during fighting in Mexico on April 30, 1863, when three officers and 62 legionnaires near the village of Camerón found themselves surrounded by more than 2,000 enemy soldiers.

The Legion had been sent to Mexico by French Emperor Napoleon III (Napoleon Bonaparte's nephew) with the ambition of setting up Archduke Maximilian of Austria as Emperor and turning the country into a French colony. (Napoleon III failed at both: Maximilian was overthrown and shot in 1867, and Mexico never did become a French colony.)

Cameron was the Foreign Legion's finest hour. Outnumbered by

**Wal-Mart is the world's largest private employer. (They had over 1.2 million employees in 2002.)**

more than 30 to 1, did the Legionnaires desert? Did they sell their pants and spend the money on booze? No—the 65 men took shelter in a hacienda and held off the Mexican army for nearly twelve hours, fighting until only five Legionnaires were left standing, each with only one bullet left to shoot.

Did they surrender then? No—after each man fired his last bullet, they charged the enemy with their bayonets. The fight didn't end until only three of the men were still alive, and then only when the Mexican commander agreed to let them keep their weapons and to provide medical treatment for a wounded lieutenant. More than 500 Mexican soldiers are believed to have died in the battle.

"Is this all that is left?" an astonished Mexican colonel asked when the last three were led from the hacienda. "These are not men. They are demons."

## THE FOREIGN LEGION TODAY

Since its founding, the Legion has been sent all over the world, fighting in every war that involved France. They've been sent to fight in a lot of losing causes, too, yet in spite of this—or maybe *because* of it—the Legion has retained its reputation as one of the toughest fighting forces in the world.

As the number of French possessions around the globe has dwindled in modern times, so has the size of the Foreign Legion, down from more than 36,000 troops in the 1960s to around 8,000 today. What do legionnaires do? France still has a few overseas possessions here and there, including French Guiana in South America and French Polynesia in the South Pacific, and it still has military ties to some former colonies that are now independent. The Legion is sent to these areas when needed, or to hot spots around the world—Bosnia, Somalia, Rwanda, and even Iraq during the first Gulf War—whenever France participates in United Nations peacekeeping efforts.

The Legion has proven very effective in this role. The United Nations has even debated creating a similar force of rapid-reaction troops, so that it doesn't have to rely on member nations to contribute their troops when needed. Who knows? Maybe someday soon if you decide you need a fresh start in life, you'll have *two* legions to run to instead of just one.

**Every year in the U.S., 7 tons of gold are used to make class rings.**

# JOIN THE PARTY: THE REPUBLICANS

*We've already told you where the Democrats came from (see page 470). Now here's the background of the Republican Party. In a nutshell, its story is the story of the country's growing resistance to slavery, which culminated in the Civil War. (For the previous chapter on the Whigs, see page 701.)*

## THE GREAT DIVIDE

By the time that Zachary Taylor, a Whig, was elected president in 1848, the country was deeply divided on the issue of slavery. Slavery was the backbone of the Southern economy, and the South was convinced that the only way to preserve it was to extend it into new western territories as they were admitted to the Union. The North was just as determined to confine its evils to those states where it was already entrenched. Nobody knew how to abolish slavery entirely without starting a civil war.

## FROM BAD TO WORSE

President Taylor's election only served to make matters worse. For starters, he was a plantation owner with more than 300 slaves, so even though he'd kept a low profile on the issue of slavery during the election, it was clear where he stood.

The idea of having a pro-slavery Whig president was more than many anti-slavery Whigs could take. Rather than support Taylor in the election, these "Conscience Whigs," as they became known, split off from the party and joined with the "Barnburners," an anti-slavery faction of New York Democrats. Together, they then merged with a third abolitionist party called the "Liberty Party" to form the "Free Soil Party." The Free Soil candidate for president was former president Martin Van Buren.

Taylor managed to win, anyway, thanks in large part to slavery supporters who hoped his administration would be strongly pro-slavery.

They were wrong. When California applied for admission to the Union as a free state, Taylor agreed and asked Congress to admit it immediately. But that created a problem: admitting California as a free state would upset the even balance of free and slave states, putting the free states in the majority.

## DRAWING THE LINE

If California were admitted as a free state, it would also upset the tradition set by the Missouri Compromise of 1820, banning slavery in the new territories north of latitude 36°30', but permitting it below that line. (Missouri is above the line, but the compromise allowed it to enter the Union as a slave state.) Technically this rule only applied to territories that were part of the Louisiana Purchase, and California wasn't part of the Louisiana Purchase.

But Southerners wanted the line to apply anyway, which would have made slavery legal in southern California. They were furious when President Taylor supported the admission of the entire territory as a free state. When these so-called "diehard" Southerners threatened to secede because of it, Taylor, a retired Army general, responded by promising to personally lead the Army against any state that tried to secede.

## WAR POSTPONED

California's admission never led to civil war, of course, if for no other reason than that Taylor died from indigestion barely a year into his presidency. His successor, Vice President Millard Fillmore (also a Whig), was willing to compromise. With Fillmore's encouragement, Senator Henry Clay of Kentucky pushed through Congress the Compromise of 1850, consisting of five measures:

1. A new Fugitive Slave Law got the federal government more directly involved in the capture and return of slaves who escaped into free states.

2. Buying and selling slaves was abolished within the city limits of Washington, D.C. (People in D.C. could still *own* slaves, they just couldn't buy or sell them there.)

3. California was admitted as a free state, ending the equal balance of slave and free states in the Union.

4. The territory east of California was divided into the Utah and New Mexico territories, with their final status as free or slave territories intentionally left vague. It was

**...Kentucky, Massachusetts, Pennsylvania, and Virginia are commonwealths.**

still possible that either Utah or New Mexico or both might choose to become slave states, and meanwhile, both slaveholders and opponents of slavery were free to settle in these territories.

5. The border between Texas (a slave state) and Mexico was formalized.

## ONE STEP FORWARD, TWO STEPS BACK

The Compromise of 1850 was intended to cool passions between the North and the South, and it worked...for a while. But as time passed, two of the five provisions in the compromise made things even worse than they already were.

The Fugitive Slave Act compelled federal marshals to assist in capturing slaves even if they opposed slavery. The marshals faced fines of up to $1,000—a lot of money in the 1850s—if they failed to do so. If a slave escaped while in their custody, *they* were liable for the full value of the slave. And for the first time, anyone who assisted a slave trying to escape could be fined and even jailed for up to six months. Fugitive slaves were denied a trial by jury and were not allowed to testify on their own behalf.

The Fugitive Slave Act was supposed to help Southern slave owners, but what it really did was turn many Northerners even more vehemently against slavery.

## SQUATTER SOVEREIGNTY

But what really inflamed passions was the unresolved status of the Utah and New Mexico territories, and the admission of California as a free state on the grounds that that was what Californians wanted. Letting citizens of a territory organize themselves as they saw fit sounds reasonable enough, but "popular sovereignty," as its supporters called it (opponents called it "squatter sovereignty"), proved to be very problematic.

Popular sovereignty undermined an important premise of the Missouri Compromise, which was that *Congress*, not the people, had the power to ban slavery in the territories. If California, New Mexico, and Utah could decide for themselves, didn't that mean that *all* new territories would have that right?

**In an average day, 3,000 Americans take up smoking. Most of them are kids under 18.**

## THE KANSAS-NEBRASKA ACT

Tensions escalated dramatically in 1854, when Senator Stephen A. Douglas of Illinois introduced legislation opening much of what was then known as "Indian Territory" to white settlement, which had previously been banned from the region.

Called the Kansas-Nebraska Act, the legislation carved two new territories—Kansas and Nebraska—from land previously used to relocate Native American tribes that had been forcibly moved from their ancestral lands east of the Mississippi River.

Both Kansas and Nebraska were part of the Louisiana Purchase. Both were entirely above the latitude 36°30' line, and according to the Missouri Compromise that meant that slavery was outlawed. But Douglas was determined to apply the principle of popular sovereignty to the new territories, giving settlers the right to decide the slavery question for themselves.

Douglas wasn't motivated by a desire to expand slavery—he wanted to get a northern transcontinental railroad built from Chicago (in his home state) to the Pacific. Running the tracks through Nebraska made the most sense, but to do that he needed to set up a new territory, and to do *that* he needed the support of the South. They weren't about to let another free territory evolve into another free state, so Douglas appeased them by applying the principle of popular sovereignty.

## THEM'S FIGHTIN' WORDS

Initially Douglas had only wanted to organize one territory—Nebraska. But Southerners had insisted on two, so Douglas proposed organizing both Nebraska and Kansas, applying the principle of popular sovereignty to both. Even that wasn't enough: Southerners in Congress wanted the language of the bill to specifically repeal the Missouri Compromise.

Douglas resisted at first, but then he and the Southerners, all Democrats, agreed to let President Franklin Pierce, also a Democrat, decide. Pierce sided with the South.

The Kansas-Nebraska Act infuriated Northerners, who for more than 30 years had viewed the 36°30' line as sacred. The act "took us by surprise," an Illinois Whig named Abraham Lincoln wrote later. "We were thunderstruck and stunned." But Douglas rammed the bill through both houses of Congress and in May 1854, Presi-

**Theodore Roosevelt was the most prolific presidential author, having written 40 books.**

dent Pierce signed it into law.

What followed in the Kansas Territory was four years of violent turmoil, as both sides of the slavery issue rushed settlers into Kansas to try to claim the territory for their side. On May 21, 1856, pro-slavery raiders sacked the town of Lawrence; three days later, a Connecticut abolitionist named John Brown retaliated and attacked some pro-slavery supporters at Pottawatomie Creek, killing five. By the end of the year more than 200 people had been killed in this mini civil war.

## THE PARTY'S OVER

There were several other casualties of the Kansas-Nebraska Act. President Pierce was one of them—he became so hated that the Democrats didn't even bother to nominate him for a second term. He just served out the rest of his first term and then went home.

The Whig Party was another casualty. Already damaged by the fight over the Compromise of 1850, it collapsed completely when anti-slavery Conscience Whigs bolted the party. By the end of 1854, the party—literally—was over.

So where did the Conscience Whigs go? Many of them joined with other anti-slavery elements to form a brand-new party that made its priority the opposition to slavery in new territories. Drawing its inspiration from the Jeffersonian Republicans, the party named itself the "Republican Party."

## THE ELECTION OF 1856

One other thing destroyed by the Kansas-Nebraska Act was Stephen A. Douglas's bid for the presidency in 1856. The struggle over his act had generated so much controversy that the Democrats passed on his candidacy and instead nominated former Secretary of State James Buchanan. What made Buchanan such an attractive candidate? According to historian David Herbert Donald, he "had the inestimable blessing of having been out of the country, as minister of Great Britain, during the controversy over the Kansas-Nebraska Act."

The Republicans nominated former California senator John C. Fremont as their candidate. Buchanan won, but Fremont made an impressive showing, winning 11 states.

## GREAT SCOTT

Just two days after Buchanan was inaugurated as president, the Supreme Court handed down its infamous Dred Scott decision. Years earlier, Scott, a slave, had been taken by his owner, a U.S. Army surgeon, to live in Illinois and the Wisconsin Territory, both of which outlawed slavery. Scott sued for his freedom, arguing that living where slavery was banned had made him a free man.

The Supreme Court disagreed, finding that as a Negro, Scott was not an American citizen to begin with and thus had no right to sue in federal court. And even if he did, the chief justice argued, *any* laws excluding slavery from U.S. territories were unconstitutional, because they violated the Fifth Amendment by depriving slave owners of their property without due process of law. "The right of property in a slave," he wrote, "is distinctly and expressly affirmed in the Constitution."

Suddenly, it seemed as if every state in the Union might become a slave state.

## THE FREEPORT FUMBLE

For many Americans the Dred Scott decision was the final straw. It seemed impossible that the North and the South could remain together as a country much longer. Even Abraham Lincoln observed (in a debate with Stephen A. Douglas the following year): "This government cannot endure permanently half slave and half free."

Lincoln was challenging Douglas for his seat in the U.S. Senate, and it was during the second of their seven debates that Douglas ruined his last chance to win the presidency. In Freeport, Illinois, on August 27, 1858, Lincoln challenged Douglas to reconcile popular sovereignty with the Dred Scott decision: If anti-slavery laws were unconstitutional, how were anti-slavery settlers supposed to ban slavery?

Douglas replied that if settlers refused to legislate a local "slave code" (local regulations that protected the rights of slave owners), slave owners would not bring their slaves into the territory because their property rights were not guaranteed.

Douglas's "Freeport Doctrine," as it became known, did little to appease Northerners and it cost him nearly all of his support in the South. He still managed to win the 1860 Democratic nomination for president, but Southern Democrats were so angry with

**First subject ever photographed by *National Geographic*: The city of Lhasa, Tibet, in 1905.**

him that, rather than support him, they split off from the party and nominated their own candidate, John C. Breckinridge.

## AND THE WINNER IS...

Abraham Lincoln, who'd just lost the race for Senate, became the Republican nominee for president. The Republican Party was barely six years old, but slavery was such a powerful issue—and Douglas's "Freeport Doctrine" such a huge blunder—that Douglas and Breckinridge split the Democratic vote...and Lincoln, a brand-new Republican, won.

But "it was ominous," David Herbert Donald writes, "that Lincoln had received *not a single vote* in 10 of the Southern states."

Lincoln was elected president on November 6, 1860; barely a month later, South Carolina seceded from the Union, and by the time Lincoln was sworn into office on March 4, 1861, Mississippi, Florida, Alabama, Georgia, Louisiana, and Texas had also seceded. The first shots of the Civil War were just five weeks away.

With the secession of the Southern states (and all of the Southern Democrats), the Republican Party was left in full control of the federal government. As the Civil War dragged on year after year, it seemed that Lincoln's reelection was doomed and that General George McClellan, a Northern Democrat running as a peace candidate, would defeat him. But the tide of the war eventually turned in the North's favor, and in 1864 Lincoln was reelected with 55% of the popular vote. The Civil War finally ended on April 9, 1865; Lincoln was assassinated five days later.

## THE RISE OF THE REPUBLICANS

Victory in the Civil War ushered in an era of Republican domination that lasted until the Great Depression of the early 1930s: of the 18 presidential elections held between 1860 and 1932, the Republicans won 14.

Born in an era of terrible crisis that threatened to destroy the Union, the Republican Party managed to save the Union and, in the process, established itself in very short order as one of the great political parties in American history.

***That's how America's major political parties, the Democratic and the Republican, began. A lot has changed in the last 100 years...but that's another story. Stay tuned.***

# SGT. PEPPERS LONELY HEARTS CLUB BAND

*"It was twenty years ago today" begins a record album that was released in 1967 and will still be celebrated many years from now. It wasn't actually the first pop concept record, its songs aren't necessarily the Beatles' best, and its supposed theme really isn't one…so why do people consider it one of the greatest albums ever made?*

## BACKGROUND

Fans may debate whether *Sgt. Peppers* is the best album the Beatles made, but no group, the Beatles included, ever made a more revolutionary one.

As great an achievement as *Sgt. Peppers* was, it wasn't produced in a vacuum. In the years leading up to its release, forces much broader than the Beatles themselves had been setting the stage for an industry-changing album to happen.

In fact, the artistic creativity released by the era's cultural and political turbulence was reaching boundary-busting proportions in 1966, the year that work on *Sgt. Peppers* began. Nowhere was that better reflected than in popular music. Bob Dylan's *Blonde on Blonde*, the Who's *A Quick One*, the Beach Boys' *Smile*, the Mothers of Invention's *Freak Out*, and the Rolling Stone's *Aftermath* all broke important new ground in pop music that year.

## WHATEVER YOU CAN DO, I CAN DO BETTER

These landmark releases—and others of similar quality—pushed the Beatles to even greater creative heights than they'd already achieved. No musician or band in that period could stay on top by mimicking earlier successes. With each new record, pop groups in both England and America sought to up the creative ante. It wasn't just a game—it was commercial survival.

In this competitive environment, the Beatles and the Beach Boys viewed each other as the primary challengers and tried to outdo the other with each new album. The Beach Boys released *Pet Sounds* in May 1966 as their answer to the Beatles' 1965 masterpiece *Rubber Soul* (itself spurred by the music of Bob Dylan). *Pet*

*Sounds*' clever songwriting and complex arrangements stunned the Beatles. Paul McCartney called it "the album of all time." But a new contender for that title was already in the can: the Beatles' *Revolver*. The new Beatles album had been completed a few weeks before *Pet Sounds*' release. It hit the record stores in August. And it was just the Beatles' opening shot across the Beach Boys' bow.

## BEATLE EVOLUTION

Although cultural forces laid the groundwork for *Sgt. Peppers*, tensions and changes within the band also played a major role. As they entered the studio in November 1966 to begin recording their new album, the four group members were conflicted: exhausted and bitter on the one hand, restless to reinvent themselves on the other.

Their exhaustion came from a brutal touring schedule arranged by their manager, Brian Epstein. They were also enraged at Epstein for not protecting them from rough treatment by police in the cities they were playing. And they were frustrated artistically—the new directions they'd taken on *Revolver* couldn't be reproduced live, which forced them to fulfill their touring contracts by playing in an earlier style that, in their minds, they'd moved beyond. But that didn't matter to their live audiences, especially their female fans, who screamed too loud to hear the music anyway.

Epstein was able (barely) to hold the Beatles together by promising to end the touring. The wild enthusiasm with which fans and critics greeted *Revolver* helped prepare them for the next phase of their careers. As producer George Martin said, the Beatles "all but owned the music business at that time." The size of their audience, their almost universal critical acclaim, and their unprecedented commercial success gave them the power to do whatever they wanted in the studio. They were ready to do something great.

## RECORDING THE ALBUM

Despite its legend as one of pop music's greatest "concept" albums, the making of *Sgt. Peppers* was hardly a carefully thought-out affair. Instead, the album came together in a serendipitous, almost haphazard fashion. Two of the best songs written for the new album never even appeared on it: "Strawberry Fields" and "Penny Lane."

The album had been intended to have an autobiographical

**Art History quiz: Q. What's the actual title of da Vinci's *Mona Lisa*? A. *La Gioconda*.**

theme that would reflect the band's early lives in Liverpool. Those plans had to be trashed when manager Epstein informed the group that they were overdue for a single. So they reluctantly decided, with producer Martin's pushing, to release "Strawberry Fields" and "Penny Lane" as a single with two "A" sides. It disqualified the songs from the new album, because in England songs appearing on the singles chart couldn't also appear on an album released in the same year. The change left only one finished track, Paul's "When I'm Sixty-Four," for the album project. Martin later called the decision to yank the songs "the biggest mistake of my professional life," but it cleared the way for the record that *Sgt. Peppers* would eventually become.

## THE SONGS

### *Side 1*

• **"Sgt. Peppers Lonely Hearts Club Band."** Not only was this theme not the original concept, but the title song wasn't even written until the album was half completed. Paul, who wrote the song, came up with the idea of basing the album on the notion that the Pepper band was real. He then suggested to Martin that he use studio effects to weave all the material together around that theme. (John didn't object to Paul taking control of the project. LSD had blurred the edges of his personality, leaving him content—and maybe grateful—to let someone else take charge.)

The Sgt. Pepper persona did something else for the band: it let them step outside themselves. "One of the problems of success was that people had begun to expect so much from them," writes Steve Turner in *A Hard Day's Write*. "As Beatles they had become self-conscious, but as the Lonely Hearts Club Band they had no expectations to live up to."

• **"With a Little Help from My Friends."** Paul and John "wanted to do a Ringo type of song," remembers journalist Hunter Davies, who witnessed them writing it. "That was what they thought was missing on the album so far." Keeping with the theme of the alternate band, Ringo sang under the guise of "Billy Shears." As with some of the other songs, "Little Help" has been accused of promoting drug use. But Paul maintains that the line "I get high with a little help from my friends" means "high" in the spiritual sense.

• **"Lucy in the Sky with Diamonds."** Despite rumors to the con-

**Top ticket price to the first Super Bowl in 1967: $12. Top price in 2003: $500.**

trary that persist to this day, it has nothing to do with LSD. The title, George Martin writes, refers to a drawing that John's then-young son Julian had brought home from school. It depicted a little girl hovering in a black sky, surrounded by stars. Julian explained, "It's Lucy, in the sky, with diamonds." (Lucy O'Donnel was his best friend in school at the time.) The song's imagery—tangerine trees, marmalade skies, and cellophane flowers—was mostly inspired by Lewis Carrol's *Through the Looking Glass*. "Surrealism to me is reality," said John. "Psychedelic vision is reality to me and always was."

• **"Getting Better."** On a 1964 tour, Ringo got sick and session drummer Jimmy Nichol subbed for five nights. After each concert, Paul and John would ask Nichol what he thought of his performance. Each time Nichol would reply, "It's getting better." They loved the phrase and laughed every time they thought of it. A real Lennon-McCartney song—Paul put down the optimistic foundation of the song: "It's getting better all the time." And John added his cynicism: "Can't get much worse."

• **"Fixing a Hole."** Yet another song believed to have been about drugs. (The "hole" was a heroin fix.) But Paul had just bought an old farmhouse, fixed it up, and penned a song about it. "If you're a junky sitting in a room and fixing a hole then that's what it will mean to you," he said. "But when I wrote it I meant if there's a crack, or the room is uncolourful, then I'll paint it."

• **"She's Leaving Home."** Paul read a news article about a 17-year-old girl named Melanie Coe who ran away from home and was inspired to write a song about her plight. McCartney was anxious to record the song soon after he finished it and called up George Martin to request an immediate orchestral score. Martin wasn't available that day because he was doing a session with another artist, Cilla Black. Impatient, McCartney went out and hired Mike Leander to do the job. He then brought in the score to record the next day. It was the only score that Martin didn't write for the Beatles in all his time working with them.

• **"Being for the Benefit of Mr. Kite."** The song is based on an 1843 circus poster that John owned. "I had all the words staring me straight in the face one day when I was looking for a song," he said. The swirling organ sounds that helped create the circus atmosphere weren't created by a professional organists but rather Martin and Lennon, who masked their inadequacies on the instru-

**How long was the Barenaked Ladies' song "One Week" #1 on the U.S. charts? One week.**

ment with studio tricks, including doubling the tape speed of certain parts and slowing down others. For some bits, Martin cut the master tape up, threw the pieces on the floor, and put them randomly back together.

***Side 2:***

• **"Within You Without You."** George's song about his newfound fascination with Indian mysticism, as well as one of his first songs performed on the sitar. None of the other Beatles were present when "WYWY" was recorded.

• **"When I'm Sixty-Four."** The tune is based on a pre-WWII-style pop melody written by Paul. In their first phase as an English club band, the Beatles used to play the melody as a timekiller when a club's PA system crashed during their set.

• **"Lovely Rita."** A real meter maid named Meta claimed she was the inspiration because she once booked one "P. McCartney" for 10 shillings. When Paul saw the ticket, he told her he liked her name and asked if he could write a song about it. True? Paul says he can't remember (but he admits it makes a nice story).

• **"Good Morning, Good Morning."** John wrote this as a poke at McCartney's irony-deficient song "Good Day Sunshine" on *Revolver*. The sly humor that fills the song turns darker on the fadeout sequence—in the series of farmyard sounds, each animal that appears is a predator of the one heard before it.

• **"A Day in the Life."** Although the album's finale is generally thought of as a John Lennon song, it was a true Lennon-McCartney collaboration, unlike many of the songs credited to both men. John had found inspiration reading the morning paper: "One story was about the Guinness heir who killed himself in a car. On the next page was a story about four thousand potholes in the streets of Blackburn, Lancashire, that needed to be filled." John wrote a dreamy melody around the stories, but he needed a middle section for the song and asked Paul if he had anything he could use. McCartney wrote the "Woke up, got out of bed..." portion, a song-within-a-song, that created an appropriately abrupt transition from the dreamy opening section. The two worked together over a period of a month with George Martin to record it.

After the two parts were recorded, they decided to fill the gap between them with a "dark, tumultuous orchestra crescendo." George Martin tells the story:

> At the beginning of the twenty-four bars, [I wrote] the lowest possible note for each of the 41 instruments in the orchestra. At the end of the twenty-four bars, I wrote the highest note. Then I put a squiggly line right through all twenty-four bars.

Other than that, how the orchestra got from low to high was up to them... provided they finished on the final E chord in unison.

## THE ALBUM COVER

Midway through the recording sessions, the Beatles knew they were making a landmark record, and they wanted a cover to match. But the most famous album jacket in the history of rock almost never happened.

Besides the Fab Four, the cover featured life-size portraits of cultural icons the Beatles admired, as well as—for a lark—many they didn't. The images ran the gamut from Bob Dylan to Frank Sinatra, Marlene Dietrich to Marilyn Monroe, W. C. Fields to Sonny Liston. John wanted to add Jesus and Hitler to the mix, but Jesus was scrapped because of the controversy John had created the year before when he compared the Beatles' popularity to Christianity. And Hitler was vetoed by the rest of the group.

The record company protested that the collage was a costly logistical nightmare, because permissions would have to be obtained from everyone pictured, and in the case of those who were dead, from their estates. But the band insisted—the Beatles knew they had created an unprecedented record and wanted a cover to match. A frustrated EMI handled the details, which involved sending hundreds of letters all over the world.

## IMMEDIATE IMPACT

*Sgt. Peppers Lonely Hearts Club Band* made its informal public debut from a window ledge outside the London flat of singer "Mama" Cass Elliot. The Beatles and assistant Neil Aspinall drove to Elliot's place at daybreak, dragged the speakers of her high-powered sound system out onto the ledge, put a tape of the album on, and cranked the volume all the way up. According to Aspinall, not one of the neighbors complained. In fact, several poked their heads out of their windows and smiled their approval. Everyone recog-

**Why don't they speak English? In England a cat is sometimes called a *moggy* (and noses are *conks*).**

nized whose music it was and were thrilled to be awakened by it.

For other musicians, though—especially ambitious ones—the music was a different kind of wake-up call. The Beach Boys' creative genius, Brian Wilson, was already showing signs of mental strain from trying to compete with *Revolver*. *Sgt. Peppers* may have added to Wilson's prodigious drug use, which just about finished him off—he soon entered a psychotic swoon that wouldn't end for decades. Another of the era's most admired songwriters, John Sebastian of the Lovin' Spoonful, recalls that *Sgt. Peppers* was "like throwing down a hat in the center of a ring... it seemed like an insurmountable task to come up with anything even in the same ballpark."

The group's nonmusician fans, of course, had no such reservations. The album was celebrated in Europe and America as if it signaled the dawning of world peace. All over the United States, rock and pop radio stations played nothing but *Sgt. Peppers* tracks for days—everything else seemed beside the point. It was endlessly written about in the press and dominated conversation, even among people not ordinarily fascinated with pop culture.

## WHY IT MATTERED

*Sgt. Peppers* is remembered by many as pop music's first concept album, but that is neither accurate nor the core of its greatness. According to many pop experts, the first true concept album in pop music was Frank Sinatra's *In the Wee Small Hours*, released in 1955. By the standard of the Sinatra album, in fact, *Sgt. Peppers* barely even qualifies as a concept record. Yes, the song "Sgt. Peppers Lonely Hearts Club Band" and its reprise sandwich the rest of the album (except for "A Day in the Life") between them. But the other songs barely relate to that theme.

Nor is *Sgt. Peppers* even the first significant concept album in rock. Music critics variously award that title to either 1966's *Freak Out* by the Mothers of Invention or The Who's *The Who Sell Out*, which preceded *Sgt. Peppers* in 1967.

Is it the quality of its songs, then, that makes *Sgt. Peppers* a landmark album? For sheer song-by-song excellence, many Beatle fans and music experts rate *Rubber Soul*, *Revolver*, *Let It Be*, *Abbey Road*, and *The White Album* higher.

**The audio book version of the King James Bible is 84 1/2 hours long.**

## TIMING IS EVERYTHING

So what was all the *Sgt. Peppers* fuss about? For one thing, no pop group before then had so perfectly expressed the tenor of its times. It all seemed to come together on that one album—from the era's spiritual quests to its social protests to its irreverent humor. Before then, no album had ever been more famous than the songs it employed. The year 1967 was also the zenith of 1960s optimism, and *Sgt. Peppers*, which was released in May, helped spread the word and inaugurate the "Summer of Love."

Just as importantly, no one had ever employed studio effects, electronic accents, and orchestral arrangements the way the Beatles did on this album. They revolutionized the way studio records would be made ever afterward. Many bands had access to the same recording equipment, but in the Beatles' and Martin's hands, the recording studio became its own musical instrument, and the studio album was transformed into a work of art utterly distinct from music that could be played onstage. If the Beatles and Martin could be turned loose in a studio today, they might well turn out something that would make even *Sgt. Peppers* pale in comparison. But nearly four decades have passed since the Lonely Hearts Club Band first hit the airwaves, and no other record has ever equalled its impact—or advanced popular music as far.

* * *

## DOUGH-BITUARY

Veteran Pillsbury spokesman, Pop N. Fresh, died yesterday of a severe yeast infection. He was 71. Fresh was buried in a lightly greased coffin. Many celebrities turned out to pay their respects, including Mrs. Butterworth, Hungry Jack, the California Raisins, Betty Crocker, and the Hostess Twinkies. The grave was piled high with flours, as long-time friend Aunt Jemima delivered the eulogy, describing Fresh as a man who never knew how much he was kneaded. Fresh rose quickly in show business though his later life was filled with turnovers. He was not considered a very smart cookie, wasting much of his dough on half-baked schemes. Even as a crusty old man, he was considered a roll model for millions. Fresh is survived by his wife. They have two children and one in the oven. He is also survived by his elderly father, Pop Tart. The funeral was held at 3:50 for about 20 minutes.

**Q: What was the true identity of Batman's nemesis, "The Penguin"? A: Oswald Cobblepot.**

# ANSWER PAGES

## BRI BRAINTEASERS

**(Answers from page 114)**

**1.** The third. Lions that haven't eaten in three years would already be dead.

**2.** Sure you can: yesterday, today, and tomorrow!

**3.** It's a wolf pack.

**4.** It's a game of Monopoly.

**5.** Freeze them first. Take the ice blocks out of the jugs and put them in the barrel. You will be able to tell which (frozen) water came from which jug.

**6.** The letter *e*, the most common letter in the English language, does not appear once in the entire paragraph.

**7.** They're the remains of a melted snowman.

**8.** The woman was a photographer. She shot a picture of her husband, developed it, and hung it up to dry.

**9.** Charcoal.

**10.** He is born in room number 1972 of a hospital and dies in room number 1952.

## SAM'S BRAINTEASERS

**(Answers for page 547)**

**1.** Mr. Red is wearing white, Mr. White is wearing blue, and Mr. Blue is wearing red.

**2.** By continuously removing one letter from either the beginning or the end of each word, you create new words, until you are left with a single letter.

*Sheath, heath, heat, eat, at, a*
*Pirate, irate, rate, ate, at, a*
*Ashamed, shamed, shame, sham, ham, am, a*
*Brandy, brand, bran, ran, an, a*

**3.** Twenty hours later, the faster clock was ahead by one hour. With every passing hour, the quicker clock gained three minutes on the slower one. (3 min. per hr. x 20 hrs. = 60 min., or 1 hr.)

**"Q" is the only letter of the alphabet that doesn't occur in the name of any state.**

**4.** Bozo asked the store manager for a box that was four feet by three feet, which has a diagonal measurement of…five feet.

**5.** *Stench* is the odd word out because all of the other words can be used as both nouns and verbs. Stench can only be used as a noun.

**6.** You or your brother.

**7.** When Sir Flushalot pulled a slip of paper from the bowl, he read it, exclaimed, "I've won!" and then quickly ate the paper. The remaining piece of paper said "The Snakes," and the queen's trickery was never revealed.

## BRAINTEASERS

**(Answers for page 686)**

**1. b)** It moves forward. When the van moves forward, the *heavier* air moves to the back of the van. The helium balloon is *lighter than air*, so it is pushed forward. Give it a try!

**2.** Turn it upside down. It becomes 16 = 8 + 8.

**3. b)** The glass side goes down. Just because you're not pushing down on the cup doesn't mean you're not pushing down. How much are you pushing down? An amount equal to the weight of the water that your finger displaces.

**4. b)** It goes down. When the anchor is in the boat, its weight is pulling the boat down causing an equivalent weight of water to be displaced in the pool. Example: If the anchor weighs 10 pounds, it displaces 10 pounds of water. But when you drop the anchor into the pool, it displaces only an equivalent *volume* of water, not an equivalent weight. If the anchor is one quart in volume, then it will only displace one quart of water, which is less than 10 pounds of water.

**5.** Did you say 5,000? Sorry, that is incorrect. The correct answer is 4,100. (Read the question again…slowly and carefully.)

## NAME THAT COUNTRY

**(Answers for page 409)**

**SAVED:** El Salvador
*El Salvador* is Spanish for "The Saviour." The Spanish conquered the Pipil, claimed the land, and gave it a new name in 1524.

**NOTHING TO IT:** Namibia

**THE NAMELESS NAME:** Australia

Pre-18th-century maps show a large land mass labeled *Terra Australis Incognita,* Latin for "The Unknown Southern Land." Geographers had never seen the land, but insisted that without it, the Earth would be lopsided.

**OVER THERE WHERE THE SUN COMES UP:** Japan

In China, *jih* means "sun," *pun* means "east," and since the sun rises in the east, *jih pun* means "sunrise." Referring to the islands east of China, it means "land of the rising sun." *Japan* derived from the Malaysian version of the Chinese name: *Japang.*

**GRECIAN FORMULA:** Great Britain

Pythaes sailed around this island around 300 B.C., naming it *Pretanic,* after the Pritani, or the Prits. *Pritani* is believed to be a Celtic word meaning "people with designs," because the Pritani were extensively tattooed. When the Anglo-Saxons attacked in the 400s, many Britons fled to the European continent and settled what became known as *Brittany.* To differentiate it from this "lesser" Britain, the island was thereafter called *Great Britain.*

**A BIT OBTUSE?:** England

After the Roman rule of Britain ended in 406 A.D., it became a battleground for many invaders. The most prominent were the Germanic tribes the Angles and the Saxons. The Angles came from a fishhook-shaped region in northern Germany called Angul (believed to be the origin of the word *angle*—to fish).

**WHY DON'T THEY SPEAK GERMAN?:** France

The Franks were a Germanic tribe that settled along the Rhine River in Germany during the third and fourth centuries. (Frankfurt is named after them.) They would go on to conquer nearly all of northern Europe, eventually settling in what is now France.

**OVERCOATIA:** Gabon

In the 15th century, Portuguese traders were the first Europeans to visit this land in Africa. They thought the Como River's estuary was shaped like a traditional hooded overcoat from their country called a *gabao,* so that's what they called it—which became *Gabon.*

**A typical *Playboy* centerfold weighs 15% less than a typical woman of the same age and height.**

# *UNCLE JOHN'S BATHROOM READER* CLASSIC SERIES

Find these and other great titles from the *Uncle John's Bathroom Reader* Classic Series online at **www.bathroomreader.com**.

Bathroom Readers' Institute
P.O. Box 1117
Ashland, OR 97520

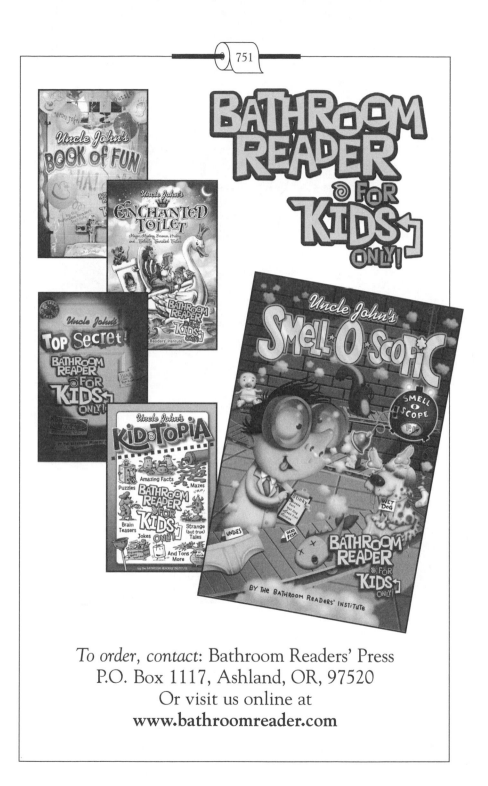

*To order, contact*: Bathroom Readers' Press
P.O. Box 1117, Ashland, OR, 97520
Or visit us online at
**www.bathroomreader.com**

# THE LAST PAGE

**FELLOW BATHROOM READERS:**

The fight for good bathroom reading should never be taken loosely—we must do our duty and sit firmly for what we believe in, even while the rest of the world is taking potshots at us.

We'll be brief. Now that we've proven we're not simply a flush-in-the-pan, we invite you to take the plunge: Sit Down and Be Counted! Log on to *www.bathroomreader.com* and earn a permanent spot on the BRI honor roll!

If you like reading our books...

VISIT THE BRI'S WEBSITE!

***www.bathroomreader.com***

- Visit "The Throne Room"—a great place to read!
- Receive our irregular newsletters via e-mail
- Order additional *Bathroom Readers*
- Face us on Facebook
- Tweet us on Twitter
- Blog us on our blog

*Go with the Flow…*

Well, we're out of space, and when you've gotta go, you've gotta go. Tanks for all your support. Hope to hear from you soon. Meanwhile, remember…

*Keep on flushin'!*